Lecture Notes in Computer Science 2762

Edited by G. Goos, J. Hartmanis, and J. van Leeuwen

Springer
*Berlin*
*Heidelberg*
*New York*
*Hong Kong*
*London*
*Milan*
*Paris*
*Tokyo*

Guozhu Dong Changjie Tang
Wei Wang (Eds.)

# Advances in Web-Age Information Management

4th International Conference, WAIM 2003
Chengdu, China, August 17-19, 2003
Proceedings

Series Editors

Gerhard Goos, Karlsruhe University, Germany
Juris Hartmanis, Cornell University, NY, USA
Jan van Leeuwen, Utrecht University, The Netherlands

Volume Editors

Guozhu Dong
Wright State University
Department of Computer Science and Engineering
Dayton, OH 45435, USA
E-mail: gdong@cs.wright.edu

Changjie Tang
Sichuan University
Department of Computer Science
Chengdu, 610064, China
E-mail: chjtang2002@sohu.com

Wei Wang
University of North Carolina at Chapel Hill
Department of Computer Science
Chapel Hill, NC 27599-3175, USA
E-mail: weiwang@cs.unc.edu



Cataloging-in-Publication Data applied for

A catalog record for this book is available from the Library of Congress.

Bibliographic information published by Die Deutsche Bibliothek
Die Deutsche Bibliothek lists this publication in the Deutsche Nationalbibliografie; detailed bibliographic data is available in the Internet at <http://dnb.ddb.de>.

CR Subject Classification (1998): H.2, H.3, H.4, I.2, H.5, C.2, J.1

ISSN 0302-9743
ISBN 3-540-40715-4 Springer-Verlag Berlin Heidelberg New York



Springer-Verlag Berlin Heidelberg New York
a member of BertelsmannSpringer Science+Business Media GmbH

http://www.springer.de



Typesetting: Camera-ready by author, data conversion by PTP-Berlin GmbH
Printed on acid-free paper SPIN: 10930823 06/3142 5 4 3 2 1 0

# Preface

With advances in the Internet and technologies around the World-Wide Web, research on design, implementation, and management of Internet- and Web-based information systems has become increasingly important. As more and more information of diverse type becomes available on the Internet and Web, query and retrieval as well as the management of information over the Internet become more complex and extremely difficult. Novel approaches to develop and manage Internet and Web information systems are in high demand. Following the successful conferences in 2000, 2001 and 2002, WAIM 2003 continued to provide a forum for researchers, professionals, and industrial practitioners from around the world to share their rapidly evolving knowledge and to report on new advances in Web-based information systems.

WAIM 2003 received an overwhelming 258 submissions from Australia, Canada, China, Denmark, France, Germany, Greece, Hong Kong, Japan, South Korea, Pakistan, Singapore, Sweden, Switzerland, Taiwan, Thailand, UK, USA, and Vietnam. Through careful review by the program committee, 30 papers were selected as regular papers, and 16 papers as short papers. As indicated by these numbers, WAIM 2003 is extremely selective: 11 and 17 areas, respectively, including text management, data mining, information filtering, moving objects, views, bioinformatics, Web and XML, multimedia, peer-to-peer systems, service networks, time-series streams, and ontologies. Two invited talks by Sushil Jajodia (George Mason University, USA) and Beng Chin Ooi (National University of Singapore) were on access control models and peer-to-peer systems. Two tutorials by Rakesh Agrawal (IBM, USA) and Weiyi Meng (State University of New York, USA) were on "privacy aware data management and analytics" and "metasearch engines." In addition, several systems were selected for demonstration at the conference. Regular and short papers, one invited talk, and brief summaries of demos are included in these proceedings.

We are grateful to the program committee members who helped tremendously in reviewing the large number of submissions. We appreciate the work by Jinze Liu and Wei Wang in setting up and managing the paper submission/review system, and by members of the WAIM 2003 organization committees. Finally, we would like to thank Sichuan University and Southwest Jiaotong University for organizing the conference.

August 2003

Guozhu Dong and Changjie Tang
Program Co-chairs
WAIM 2003

# Organization

WAIM 2003 was co-organized by Sichuan University and Southwest Jiaotong University in cooperation with the Database Society of CCF ACM SIGMOD. It was sponsored by the National Natural Science Foundation of China.

## Steering Committee

| | |
|---|---|
| Guozhu Dong | Wright State University, USA |
| Masaru Kitsuregawa | University of Tokyo, Japan |
| Jianzhong Li | Harbin Institute of Technology, China |
| Hongjun Lu (Chair) | Hong Kong University of Science and Technology |
| Xiaofeng Meng | Renmin University, China |
| Baile Shi | Fudan University, China |
| Jianwen Su | University of California (Santa Barbara), USA |
| Shan Wang | Renmin University, China |
| X. Sean Wang | George Mason University, USA |
| Ge Yu | Northeastern University, China |
| Aoying Zhou | Fudan University, China |

## Program Committee

| | |
|---|---|
| James Bailey | University of Melbourne, Australia |
| Edward Chang | University of California (Santa Barbara), USA |
| Gillian Dobbie | University of Auckland, New Zealand |
| Ming Fan | Zhengzhou University, China |
| Wenfei Fan | Bell Labs and Temple University, USA |
| Jianhua Feng | Tsinghua University, China |
| Jiawei Han | University of Illinois at Urbana-Champaign, USA |
| Shangteng Huang | Shanghai Jiaotong University, China |
| Yan Jia | National University of Defence Technology, China |
| Chen Li | University of California (Irvine), USA |
| Jianzhong Li | Harbin Institute of Technology, China |
| Jinyan Li | Institute of Inforcomm Research, Singapore |
| Qing Li | City University of Hong Kong, China |
| Li Zhanhuai | Northwestern Polytechnic University, China |
| Xuemin Lin | University of New South Wales, Australia |
| Huan Liu | Arizona State University, USA |
| Weiyi Liu | YunNan University, China |
| Wei-Ying Ma | Microsoft Research Asia |
| Weiyi Meng | State University of New York at Binghamton, USA |
| Xiaofeng Meng | Renmin University of China, China |
| Mukesh Mohania | IBM India Research Lab, India |
| Peng Ning | North Carolina State University, USA |
| Beng Chin Ooi | National University of Singapore, Singapore |
| Chaoyi Pang | CSIRO, Australia |
| Jian Pei | State University of New York at Buffalo, USA |
| Arnaud Sahuguet | Bell Laboratories, USA |
| Junyi Shen | Xi'an Jiaotong University, China |
| Baile Shi | Fudan University, China |
| Kyuseok Shim | Seoul National University, Korea |
| Wei Sun | Florida International University, USA |
| David Toman | University of Waterloo, Canada |
| Riccardo Torlone | Università Roma Tre, Italy |
| Guoren Wang | Northeastern University, China |
| Ke Wang | Simon Fraser University, Canada |
| Min Wang | IBM T.J. Watson Research Center, USA |
| Tengjiao Wang | Peking University, China |
| Wei Wang | University of North Carolina at Chapel Hill, USA |
| Xiong Wang | California State University at Fullerton, USA |
| Jiepan Xu | Nanjing University, China |
| Dongqing Yang | Beijing University, China |
| Jian Yang | Tilburg University, The Netherlands |
| Masatoshi Yoshikawa | Nagoya University, Japan |
| Ge Yu | Northeastern University, China |
| Jeffrey Yu | Chinese University of Hong Kong, China |
| Lihua Yue | University of Science and Technology, China |
| Xiuzhen Jenny Zhang | Royal Melbourne Institute of Technology, Australia |
| Aoying Zhou | Fudan University, China |
| Lizhu Zhou | Tsinghua University, China |
| Longxiang Zhou | Academy of Sciences, China |

## Referees

Kirach Altintas
Bart Amagasa
Amit Bhide
Anping Chen
Armando Cheng
Bin Chiu
Bo Choi
Byron Delgado
Carmem Edmund
Chang Feng
Chang-Ning Feng
Chao-Hui Sara Gopalkrishnan
Ching-Yung Guojie
Dawit Yimam Hara
Deepak Hatano
Deng He
Dickson Hidaka
Donggang Huang
Haixun Huang
Helen Jammalamadaka
Hiroyuki Jin
Hongbin Jin
Hongen Joshi
Huajun Kato
Jaekeol Kim
Jia Kolippakkam
Jialie Lee
Jian Li
Jigar Li
Jirong Li
Jun Li
Kai Li
Kemal Lim
Kenji Lin
Kerry Liu
Kirack Liu
Lei Liu
Liang Liu
Limin Liu
Linhao Liu
Lipyeow Liu
Liyu Lu
Mak Hon Chung Luo
Manish Mandvikar
Maurizio Mi
Michael Ming
Mike Missier
Min Mody
Ming Muhlberger
Mukul Orriens
Paolo Ortega
Qing Ortega
Qing Patrignani
Qing Prasher
Qing Qi
Qingfeng Seid
Ralf Shen
Ravi Chandra Shi
Raymond Sohn
Sham Sohn
Shihui Taylor
Soichiro Venkatesan
Song Wan
Srihari Suthan Wang
Tiantian Wang
Toshiyuki Wen
Vivekanand Wong
Wei Wu
Wei Xie
Weiwen Xiong
WenChang Xu
Wenxin Xu
Wenyin Xu
Wonyoung Yang
Xiaochun Yang
Xing Yang
Xuan Yang
Xue Ye
Yangdong Yu
Yi Yu
Yidong Yuan
Young-koo Zeng
Yuanyong Zhang
Yunfeng Zhang
Zhang Zheng
Zheng Zhihong
Zi Zhong
Zhong Zou

# Table of Contents

## WAIM 2003

## Invited Talks

Recent Advances in Access Control Models .......................... 1
*Sushil Jajodia*

Managing Trust in Peer-to-Peer Systems Using Reputation-Based Techniques .......................... 2
*Beng Chin Ooi, Chu Yee Liau, Kian-Lee Tan*

## Web

Advertising and Matching Agent Services on the World Wide Web ...... 13
*Hongen Lu*

Efficient Reduction of Web Latency through Predictive Prefetching on a WAN .......................... 25
*Christos Bouras, Agisilaos Konidaris, Dionysios Kostoulas*

Compact Encoding of the Web Graph Exploiting Various Power Laws (Statistical Reason Behind Link Database) .......................... 37
*Yasuhito Asano, Tsuyoshi Ito, Hiroshi Imai, Masashi Toyoda, Masaru Kitsuregawa*

Improving the Web Site's Effectiveness by Considering Each Page's Temporal Information .......................... 47
*Zhigang Li, Ming-Tan Sun, Margaret H. Dunham, Yongqiao Xiao*

## XML

Redundancy Free Mappings from Relations to XML .......................... 55
*Millist W. Vincent, Jixue Liu, Chengfei Liu*

UD($k,l$)-Index: An Efficient Approximate Index for XML Data .......... 68
*Hongwei Wu, Qing Wang, Jeffrey Xu Yu, Aoying Zhou, Shuigeng Zhou*

Logical Foundation for Updating XML .......................... 80
*Guoren Wang, Mengchi Liu*

XML Database Schema Integration Using XDD .......................... 92
*Doan Dai Duong, Vilas Wuwongse*

Xaggregation: Flexible Aggregation of XML Data .................... 104
*Hongzhi Wang, Jianzhong Li, Zhenying He, Hong Gao*

Efficient Evaluation of XML Path Queries with Automata .............. 116
*Bing Sun, Jianhua Lv, Guoren Wang, Ge Yu, Bo Zhou*

Managing XML by the Nested Relational Sequence Database System .... 128
*Ho-Lam Lau, Wilfred Ng*

Normalizing XML Element Trees as Well-Designed Document Structures for Data Integration ...................................... 140
*Wenbing Zhao, Shaohua Tan, Dongqing Yang, Shiwei Tang*

## Text Management

Classifying High-Speed Text Streams ................................ 148
*Gabriel Pui Cheong Fung, Jeffrey Xu Yu, Hongjun Lu*

Partition Based Hierarchical Index for Text Retrieval ................. 161
*Yan Yang, Baoliang Liu, Zhaogong Zhang*

A Genetic Semi-supervised Fuzzy Clustering Approach to Text Classification .......................................................... 173
*Hong Liu, Shang-teng Huang*

Partition for the Rough Set-Based Text Classification ................. 181
*Yongguang Bao, Daisuke Asai, Xiaoyong Du, Naohiro Ishii*

## Data Mining

Efficiently Mining Interesting Emerging Patterns ...................... 189
*Hongjian Fan, Kotagiri Ramamohanarao*

DENCLUE-M: Boosting DENCLUE Algorithm by Mean Approximation on Grids ............................................................. 202
*Cunhua Li, Zhihui Sun, Yuqing Song*

A New Fast Clustering Algorithm Based on Reference and Density ...... 214
*Shuai Ma, TengJiao Wang, ShiWei Tang, DongQing Yang, Jun Gao*

Classification Using Constrained Emerging Patterns ................... 226
*James Bailey, Thomas Manoukian, Kotagiri Ramamohanarao*

A New Multivariate Decision Tree Construction Algorithm Based on Variable Precision Rough Set ......................................... 238
*Liang Zhang, Yun-Ming Ye, Shui Yu, Fan-Yuan Ma*

A New Heuristic Reduct Algorithm Base on Rough Sets Theory ........ 247
*Jing Zhang, Jianmin Wang, Deyi Li, Huacan He, Jiaguang Sun*

## Bioinformatics

Using Rules to Analyse Bio-medical Data: A Comparison between C4.5 and PCL ... 254
*Jinyan Li, Limsoon Wong*

A Protein Secondary Structure Prediction Framework Based on the Support Vector Machine ... 266
*Xiaochun Yang, Bin Wang, Yiu-Kai Ng, Ge Yu, Guoren Wang*

## Peer-to-Peer System

Efficient Semantic Search in Peer-to-Peer Systems ... 278
*Aoying Zhou, Bo Ling, Zhiguo Lu, Weesiong Ng, Yanfeng Shu, Kian-Lee Tan*

Enacting Business Processes in a Decentralised Environment with p2p-Based Workflow Support ... 290
*Jun Yan, Yun Yang, Gitesh K. Raikundalia*

Peer-Serv: A Framework of Web Services in Peer-to-Peer Environment ... 298
*Qing Wang, Yang Yuan, Junmei Zhou, Aoying Zhou*

Dynamic Clustering-Based Query Answering in Peer-to-Peer Systems ... 306
*Weining Qian, Shuigeng Zhou, Yi Ren, Aoying Zhou, Beng Chin Ooi, Kian-Lee Tan*

## Service Networks

The RBAC Based Privilege Management for Authorization of Wireless Networks ... 314
*Dong-Gue Park, You-Ri Lee*

Data Securing through Rule-Driven Mobile Agents and IPsec ... 327
*Kun Yang, Xin Guo, Shaochun Zhong, Dongdai Zhou, Wenyong Wang*

Site-Role Based GreedyDual-Size Replacement Algorithm ... 335
*Xingjun Zhang, Depei Qian, Dajun Wu, Yi Liu, Tao Liu*

A Study on the Two Window-Based Marking Algorithm in Differentiated Services Network ... 344
*Sungkeun Lee, Byeongkyu Cho*

A Mobility-Aware Location Update Protocol to Track Mobile Users in Location-Based Services ... 352
*MoonBae Song, JeHyok Ryu, Chong-Sun Hwang*

An Optimized Topology Control Algorithm for Mobile Ad Hoc Networks ..... 360
*Daohua Yuan, Zhishu Li*

## Time Series, Similarity, and Ontologies

Efficient Evaluation of Composite Correlations for Streaming Time Series ..... 369
*Min Wang, X. Sean Wang*

An Efficient Computational Method for Measuring Similarity between Two Conceptual Entities ..... 381
*Miyoung Cho, Junho Choi, Pankoo Kim*

Ontology-Based Access to Distributed Statistical Databases ..... 389
*Yaxin Bi, David Bell, Joanne Lamb, Kieran Greer*

## Information Filtering

A Filter Index for Complex Queries on Semi-structured Data ..... 397
*Wang Lian, Nikos Mamoulis, David W. Cheung*

An Improved Framework for Online Adaptive Information Filtering ..... 409
*Liang Ma, Qunxiu Chen, Lianhong Cai*

An Image Retrieval Method Based on Information Filtering of User Relevance Feedback Records ..... 421
*Xiangdong Zhou, Qi Zhang, Li Liu, Ailin Deng, Liang Zhang, Baile Shi*

## Queries and Optimization

A New Similar Trajectory Retrieval Scheme Using k-Warping Distance Algorithm for Moving Objects ..... 433
*Choon-Bo Shim, Jae-Woo Chang*

TupleRank and Implicit Relationship Discovery in Relational Databases ..... 445
*Xiao (Andy) Huang, Qiang Xue, Jun Yang*

Top-*N* Query: Query Language, Distance Function, and Processing Strategies ..... 458
*Yuxi Chen, Weiyi Meng*

## Multimedia and Views

Scalable Query Reformulation Using Views in the Presence of Functional Dependencies ... 471
*Qingyuan Bai, Jun Hong, Michael F. McTear*

Multimedia Tampering Localization Based on the Perturbation in Reverse Processing ... 483
*Xianfeng Zhao, Weinong Wang, Kefei Chen*

Discovering Image Semantics from Web Pages Using a Text Mining Approach ... 495
*Hsin-Chang Yang, Chung-Hong Lee*

## Demos

Creating Customized Metasearch Engines on Demand Using SE-LEGO .. 503
*Zonghuan Wu, Vijay Raghavan, Weiyi Meng, Hai He, Clement Yu, Chun Du*

SQL-Relay: An Event-Driven Rule-Based Database Gateway ... 506
*Qingsong Yao, Aijun An*

CyberETL: Towards Visual Debugging Transformations in Data Integration ... 508
*Youlin Fang, DongQing Yang, ShiWei Tang, Yunhai Tong, Weihua Zhang, Libo Yu, Qiang Fu*

**Author Index** ... 511

# Recent Advances in Access Control Models

Sushil Jajodia

Center for Secure Information Systems, George Mason University, Fairfax, VA 22030-4444, USA

**Abstract.** Past generations of access control models, when faced with an access request, have issued a simple "yes" or "no" answer to the access request resulting in access being granted or denied. Recent advances in application areas have introduced new dimensions to access control needs, and for many applications such as business-to-business (B2B) applications and auctions "yes/no" responses are just not enough.

This talk will discuss several access control models that have been recently proposed to address these emerging needs including models that provide policy-neutral flexible access control and their efficient implementations; models that incorporate richer semantics for access control, such as adding provisions and obligations. We will also discuss the recent work on policy algebras for combining independent authorization specifications.

G. Dong et al. (Eds.): WAIM 2003, LNCS 2762, p. 1, 2003.

# Managing Trust in Peer-to-Peer Systems Using Reputation-Based Techniques

Beng Chin Ooi, Chu Yee Liau, and Kian-Lee Tan

Department of Computer Science
National University of Singapore
3 Scinece Drive 2, Singapore 117543

**Abstract.** In this paper, we examine the issue of managing trust in peer-to-peer systems. In particular, we focus on reputation-based schemes. We look at some design considerations in implementing distributed reputation-based systems, namely storage, integrity, metrics and changing of identity. We provide a survey of related work on the storage and integrity issues, and present our solution to address these issues.

## 1 Introduction

The social impact of reputation on an individual or group is long known. Research has shown that reputation plays a vital role in the decision of initiating an interaction and the pricing of services. For example, [1] has shown that the rating in eBay's [2] feedback system does encourage transactions and in some occasions making the item sold by a highly rated seller to be higher in price.

In electronic marketplaces, the reputation that a user has is the result of aggregating all the impressions of the other users that interacted with the user in the past. A reputation system is an effective way to facilitate the trust in a P2P system. It collects and aggregates the feedback of participants' past behaviors, which is known as reputation, and publishes the reputations so that everyone can view it freely. The reputation informs the participant about other's ability and disposition, and helps the participant to decide who to trust. Furthermore, reputation system also encourages participant to be more trustworthy and discourages those who are not from participating.

Existing reputation systems are those implemented in online store and auction site, such as eBay [2] and Amazon [3]. In eBay, after buying a collectible in an auction, the buyer can go back to the site and rate the seller for prompt shipping and whether the physical item actually matched the description in the auction. The rating given by the buyer is recorded into the seller's reputation by the website. When the subsequent buyer wishes to make a purchase from the seller, he can refer to seller's reputation before he makes any decision. If the reputation shows that the previous buyers were mostly well treated, then the seller is honest and worth dealing with. With reputation schemes in place sellers are highly motivated to offer the best possible service to every single buyer.

Existing work on peer-to-peer applications focuses on routing and discovery [4,5], data exchange [6] and caching [7]. Trust has gained lesser attention despite

G. Dong et al. (Eds.): WAIM 2003, LNCS 2762, pp. 2–12, 2003.

its importance. In this paper, we will examine the issue of managing trust in peer-to-peer systems that are based on reputation. We will look at some design considerations in implementing distributed reputation-based systems, namely storage, integrity, metrics and changing of identity. We provide a survey of related work on the storage and integrity issues, and present our initial effort to address these issues.

The rest of this paper is organized as follows. In the next section, we discuss the design considerations for distributed reputation-based systems. Section 3 surveys existing reputation-based systems in terms of their storage and integrity issues. In Section 4, we present our solution to these two issues. Finally, we conclude in Section 5.

## 2 Design Considerations

Although peer-to-peer systems have been extensively studied in the past few years, the research on peer-to-peer reputation has been relatively small in number. Here, we provides an overview on the study of various peer-to-peer reputation systems. To begin with, we start with discussion of the design considerations of reputation system for peer-to-peer.

1. Storage of the reputation information. The reputation has to be stored in a distributed manner, but with high availability, especially in P2P systems where peers can appear offline from time to time. Additionally, the reputation should be retrieved efficiently since it is used frequently.
2. Integrity of the reputation information. The integrity of the reputation information will dictate the usefulness of a reputation system. While in a centralized design, the integrity issue can be easily addressed, it is much more challenging in a decentralized environment.
3. Reputation metrics. Reputation metrics provide the representation of a user's reputation. The complexity of the calculation of reputation metric will undermine the performance of the whole system.
4. Changing of identity. In a peer-to-peer system, due to its decentralized nature, changing of identity is extremely easy and usually zero-cost. This is slightly different as compared to real-world where shifting of identity is usually more complicated, which often involve government or authority. A good reputation system should prevent any incentive of changing identity.

## 3 Survey of Existing Peer-to-Peer Repuation-Based Systems

This section briefly reviews some of the existing P2P reputation systems, focusing particularly on the storage and integrity issues. We start by giving an overview of the reputation systems.

### 3.1 Overview

Kevin A. Burton designed the OpenPrivacy Distributed Reputation System [8] on P2P, which is derived from the distributed trust model. It proposed the concept of reputation network, which is composed by identities (representing nodes) and evaluation certificates (representing edges). Therefore, the trustworthiness of the identities can be estimated from a visible sub-graph of the reputation network.

P2PREP [9] is a reputation sharing protocol proposed for *Gnutella*, where each peer keeps track and shares with others the reputation of their peers. Reputation sharing is based on a distributed polling protocol. Service requesters can assess the reliability by polling peers.

Karl Aberer and Zoran Despotovic [10] proposed a trust managing system on the P2P system P-Grid [11] (Managing trust). It integrates the trust management and data management schemes to build a full-fledged P2P architecture for information systems. The reputations in this system are expressed as complaints; the more complaints a peer gets, the less trustworthy it could be. This system assumes peers in the network to be honest normally. After each transaction, and only if there is dissatisfaction, a peer will file a complaint about the unhappy experience. To evaluate the reputation of a peer involves searching for complaints about the peer.

Dietrich Fahrenholtz and Winfried Lamersdof [12] introduced a distributed reputation management system (RMS). In RMS, reputation information is kept by its owner, and public key cryptography is used to solve the integrity and non-repudiation issues. During each transaction, a portal acts as a trusted third party to resolve the possible disputation during the reputation update.

Kamvar et. al [13] proposed a reputation management system, EigenRep, for P2P file sharing systems such as Gnutella to combat the spread of inauthentic file. In their system, each peer is given a global reputation that reflects the experiences of other peers with it.

### 3.2 Storage of Reputation Information

**OpenPrivacy.** In OpenPrivacy, the reputation information is stored in a certificate. The system is similar in concept to *web of trust* [14]. A peer certifies another peer through the use of certificate. Every certificate stores the value of the target's reputation and the confidence of the certificate creator. To prevent tampering, each certificate is digitally signed with the private key of the certificate creator. These certificates are stored at the certificate creator as well as the certification target.

**P2PRep.** In P2PRep, every peer in the system stores their interaction experience with other peers (based on pseudonym). This reputation records are being updated every time an interaction takes place. These reputation records can be used by other peers to make decision when initializing an interaction. In this case, before a peer consumes a service, the peer polls other peers about their knowledge of the service provider. At the end of the interaction, the service consumer updates the reputation of the provider and at the same time updates the credibility of the peers that addressed opinion on the provider.

**Managing Trust.** Managing Trust stores the complaints about a peers in the P-Grid [11]. The underlying idea of the P-Grid approach is to create a virtual binary search structure with replication that is distributed over the peers and supports efficient search. The construction and the search/update operations can be performed without any central control or global knowledge.

**RMS.** RMS also stores the reputation information in a certificate. However, RMS is different from OpenPrivacy in the implementation of the reputation certificate. In RMS, there exists a trusted third party to record the transaction history for the subscribers. The transaction history that the trusted party stored is used by others to check the correctness of the certificate presented by a peer.

**EigenRep.** In EigenRep, two types of value, local and global, are being stored in the systems. The local value is stored in every peer and the global value, which is derived from multiple local values, are being handled by random peers in a distributed hash table (DHT) such as CAN [15] or Chord [4].

**Discussion.** All of the aforementioned reputation systems use decentralized storage for storing the reputation information. This is very important as centralized storage for reputation information will limit the scalability of the P2P reputation system in the long term and affect the performance for retrieving the reputation information.

Efficient retrieval of reputation information minimizes the communication overhead. For instance, to retrieve reputation for a peer in *RMS* or *OpenPrivacy*, we need to issue only a query message to the peer since the certificate stores all the reputation information of the peer. In *EigenRep* and *Managing Trust*, the cost of retrieving reputation information is proportional to retrieving information from DHT system and P-Grid respectively. However, the cost for *P2PRep* to retrieve reputation information is proportional to the O(N) for the network with N peers.

### 3.3 Integrity of Reputation Information

**OpenPrivacy.** Integrity of the reputation information stored in *OpenPrivacy* is preserved through the use of cryptography means. Every certificate is digitally signed by the private key of the certificate creator. A peer needs the public key of the certificate creator in order to verify the validity of the certificate and the information stored within. If the content of the certificate is tampered, the verification of the certificate will fail.

**P2PRep.** The integrity of the reputation information is also being protected with cryptography means. Unlike *OpenPrivacy*, the reputation is only being encrypted and signed for the purpose of transmission. Since the reputation information is being stored at the rating peer and not the target peer, there is very minimal risk that the target peer is able to change the reputation information. However, the risk do exist when the reputation information traveled from the sender to the requestor. Therefore the protocol defined in P2PRep provides integrity (and confidentiality when needed). Before the reputation information is transferred, it is being signed with the private key of the sender so that the information will be intact while being transmitted.

**Managing Trust.** In *Managing Trust*, the integrity of the complaints depend on the behavior of peers in the network. In order to overcome this problem, the system assumes the probability of the peers in the P-Grid storage system that are malicious is $\pi$. This value cannot be greater than a certain maximum, $\pi_{max}$. Its storage infrastructure is configured in such a way that $r$ replicas must satisfy the condition $\pi^r_{max} < \varepsilon$ , where $\pi^r_{max}$ is the average probability of $r$ replicas and $\varepsilon$ the acceptable tolerance.

**RMS.** In *RMS*, the integrity is preserved through the signature of the trusted third party. The trusted third party could be implemented as a centralized server or multiple servers. If it is implemented across multiple servers, there must be trust between the servers.

**EigenRep.** The integrity of the reputation information in *EigenRep* also depends on the trustworthiness of the peers that calculate and store the global reputation value. However, the system reduces the possibility of malicious acts through random selection of peers that calculate the global values and redundancy in global value.

**Discussion.** It seems that one of the most challenging issues of decentralized reputation management system is the integrity of the reputation information. On one hand, cryptography techniques that preserved the integrity of the reputation information seems effective, it suffers from the overhead of verification. The number of public keys needed to verify the reputation depend on the number of certificates to be verified and for a large number of certificates, the cost of retrieving the public keys can be very high. On the other hand, the integrity of information on systems such as *Managing Trust* and *EigenRep* depends on the storage infrastructure.

## 4 Our Solution

We propose a P2P reputation scheme that aims at providing efficient retrieval of reputation information and providing integrity of the information. In our scheme, the reputation is maintained by the owner. This greatly simplifies the problem of storing reputation information. In addition, the retrieval of the reputation information can be done efficiently without any additional communication cost. By having the owner to store the reputation information, there is the risk of information integrity. To protect the integrity of the reputation, we have introduced the notion of reputation certificate we termed *RCert*. At the same time we have proposed protocols to facilitate the update of the reputation information.

### 4.1 Components

**Public Key Infrastructure (PKI).** PKI [16] is employed to provide security properties which include confidentiality, integrity, authentication and non-repudiation. All these are achieved through the use of symmetric and asymmetric cryptography as well as digital signatures. We have omitted the confidentiality requirement in our proposed scheme as our goal is not to provide communication secrecy among peers.

**Entities.** There are two entities in the system. A peer that provides services (service provider) and a peer that consumes services (service consumer). In P2P system, a peer can act as a service provider as well as service consumer. This is because in P2P there is no true distinction between server and client. Entities in the network has a pair of public and private keys that represent its identity. At the same time, the pair of keys is used in the digital signature process. We assume there exists a mechanism that allows a peer to be located and contacted given its identity. This can be achieved through the use of P2P systems such as [4], that provide efficient lookup mechanisms.

**Roles.** There are two different roles a peer plays. After a peer has finished consuming a service provided by a peer, it takes up the role of a *rater*. The peer that provides the services will be termed *ratee*. The *rater* is responsible for evaluating the *ratee* based on the experience of the interaction with *ratee*. We shall defer the protocol used in the rating process to section 4.2.

**Reputation Certificates (*RCert*).** *RCert* consists of two components: header and *RCertUnit*. The information is updated by the service consumer each time after a transaction has taken place. Every update is appended to the end of *RCert* and is digitally signed by the *ratee* to prevent the owner from changing the information. Figure 1 depicts the format of *RCert*.

*RCert* header gives information about its owner, such as owner's identity and owner's public key. This information binds the *RCert* to its owner. Besides, the header also includes information about *RCert* such as *RCert*'s current ID and previous ID if this certificate is not the first created by the owner. With the ID information, this allows the owner to create a new *RCert* but still provides a pointer to previous *RCert* owned by the owner. When an *RCert* grows too

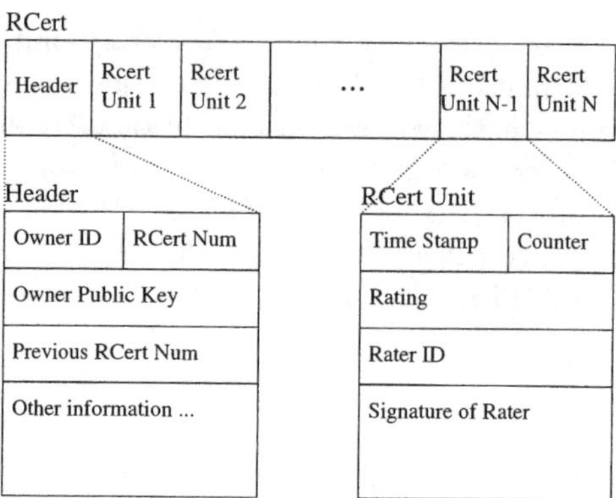


**Fig. 1.** Format of the *RCert*

big, the owner can create a new *RCert* and provides the reference to the old *RCert* in the header. The old *RCert* can be stored locally in the system and will only be sent to service requester which requested it. *RCertUnit* contains the following entries:

- *TimeStamp* - issued by the owner right before a transaction is started. It is digitally signed by the issuer and is used as a proof of transaction.
- *Rating* - this is the comment given by a peer that had the transaction with the owner. It records the transaction experience of the *rater* with the owner.
- *RaterID* - this is the identity of the peer that created this rating (*RCertUnit*).
- *Signature* - the signature is created by the *rater*, using its private key, on the entire *RCert* including the header for the integrity of the *RCert*.

### 4.2 The Protocol – *RCertPX*

The *RCertPX* protocol involves ten steps and is shown in figure 2. Assuming a peer needs certain service from other peers. It first uses resource discovery mechanism such as those mentioned in [17,18] to locate service provider (step 1). All the peers that have the resources needed by the requesting peer send their replies together with their Reputation certificates (*RCert*) (step 2). Upon receiving the *RCert*, the requester needs to verify the validity of the *RCert* (step 3). This is done by checking the last *RCert Unit* in the *RCert* by contacting the *rater*. If the *rater* returns a *Last-TimeStamp* that has not been revoked, the *RCert* is valid (step 4). A *Last-TimeStamp* consists of three elements:

- *TimeStamp* issued by service provider
- Status of the *TimeStamp* (valid/revoked)
- *RevokedPeer* - identity of the party authorized the revoked

The *Last-TimeStamp* provides the validity of the *RCert* currently used by an *RCert* owner. In the event where the last *rater* is not available (eg. offline),

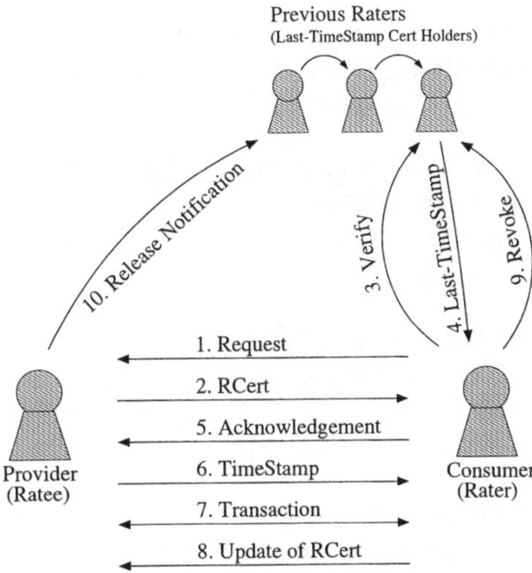


**Fig. 2.** *RCertP* Protocol

the requester can try to contact the preceding *raters* until there is one that is available. In this case, the verification is done by checking on the *Last-TimeStamp* in the following way. The *TimeStamp* information in the *Last-TimeStamp* should match those on the *RCertUnit* created by the *rater* and since the *Last-TimeStamp* has been revoked, the *RevokedPeer* in the *Last-TimeStamp* must match the next *rater* specified in the *RCert*. This verification mechanism provides more information about the transaction history of the *RCert*'s owner and refrains a peer from using any of its old *RCert*.

After evaluating all the *RCert*, the requesting peer makes decision on which peer to choose as service provider and sends an acknowledgement to the provider (step 5). The acknowledgment is digitally signed with the requester's private key and it shall be used as a proof of transaction request.

This is followed by the sending of TimeStamp from the provider to the requester (step 6). The TimeStamp is signed by the provider and in this protocol it contains the time value on the provider machine and the transaction counter. The requester will then verify the time and signature on the timestamp by using the public key of provider. We do not assume there exists a synchronized time between requester and provider. However, there should be a way for the requester to check the correctness of the time (e.g., the time should not be too different from the time in requester system). The counter incorporated reflects the latest information about the transaction sequence. For instance, if there have been 20 transaction so far, the counter information in the *TimeStamp* should reflect 21 as its value.

Peers then start the transaction (step 7). Upon completion of the transaction, the service requester starts to rate its service provider. The *rater* (service requester) updates the *RCert* sent to it in step 2 by adding the timestamp from step 6, followed by the rating based on the transaction experience. The *rater* also added its ID. The *rater* completes the updates by hashing the content of the certificate and digitally signs the hash with its private key. In addition, the *rater* will perform two extra steps.

1. The *rater* needs to create and store the $Last - TimeStamp$ and make it available to others when needed.
2. If the *rater* is not the first one to rate the service provider, it needs to contact the previous *rater* to 'revoke' the piece of $Last - TimeStamp$ store.

Next, the *rater* sends the updated certificate to the *ratee* (step 8). The *rater* then issues a request to the preceding *rater* to revoke the timestamp stored there by sending the latest timestamp sent to it by the *ratee.* To verify the request, the preceding *rater* checks the timestamp.

- The time in timestamp must be more current than the one currently stored.
- The counter in the timestamp must be the next number to the one currently stored.
- The timestamp must indeed sign by the *ratee.*

Once the preceding *rater* is convinced that the timestamp sends to it is correct, it revokes the timestamp information stored locally by creating a status 'revoke' and place a digital signature on the revoked timestamp (step 9). Upon receiving the acknowledgement that the preceding *rater* has revoked the timestamp on its side, the current *rater* sends the updated reputation certificate to the *ratee.* The *ratee* should use the updated certificate for its next transaction. Finally, the provider notifies the previous *rater* that it can remove its Last-TimeStamp Certificate.

### 4.3 Analysis and Discussion

*RCertPX* provides the assurance that if an *RCert* is presented and the signature is verified to be valid, it means that the content in the *RCert* has not been changed by the owner. This is achieved through the use of digital signature on the entire *RCert.* In addition, *Last-TimeStamp* used in the protocol provides information about the validity of *RCert.* With the *Last-TimeStamp,* a requester can verify the validity of the *RCert* by contacting previous *rater.* If the *Last-TimeStamp* has not been revoked, it indicates that the *RCert* is up to date; otherwise, the *RCert* is an old one, and might not be valid. This prevents the provider from discarding the unsatisfied rating by reusing its old *RCert.*

Three parties are evolved in this protocol. They are the *ratee*, the current *rater* and one of the the previous *raters.* In the following discussion, we show that if anyone of them is malicious, the correctness of the *RCert* will not get tampered.

In the case where *ratee* turns malicious, it will be able to send a blank *RCert* to the user. Therefore, a blank *RCert* should be regarded as having very low correctness. A malicious *ratee* will not be able to reuse its old *RCert.* This is because the *Last-TimeStamp* introduced provides the mechanism to prevent this from happening. When a *ratee* is using back the old *RCert*, during verification of the *RCert*, its act will be exposed.

On the other hand, if the current *rater* acts maliciously, it can either refuse to give a rating or give an invalid signature on the *RCert*. However, this will not cause any problem at all. When the *rater* refuse to give any rating, the *ratee* can present the acknowledgement sent by the *rater* during transaction confirmed (step 5 of *RCertPX*) that the *rater* has indeed requested for the transaction. In the event where *rater* purposefully gives an invalid signature on the *RCert*, the *ratee* can present the acknowledgement to the previous *rater* to request arbitration. Then the previous *rater* can require the current *rater* to present his update again. If the current *rater* refuse to give the update, or present an invalid one, the previous *rater* can cancel the revocation on its *Last-TimeStamp*. If the current *rater* present a valid update, the previous rater will send it to the *ratee*.

When the previous *rater* acts maliciously, it can:

1. refuse to present the *Last-TimeStamp*
2. give a revoked *Last-TimeStamp* even if it has not been revoked

For case 1, if the current *rater* cannot get the *Last-TimeStamp*, it cannot verify the validity of *RCert*. The same thing happens when the previous *rater* is off-line for the moment. This is very common in the P2P networks. Our amendment to this problem is to use a group of previous *raters* rather a single previous *rater*. Each previous *rater* keeps a count number on the *Last-TimeStamp*, whose initial value is the total number of previous *raters*. In each revocation of *Last-TimeStamp*, the count number is reduced by 1. When the count number reaches 0, the *Last-TimeStamp* is revoked completely, and the *rater* leaves the previous *rater* group automatically. Therefore, if the number of previous *raters* is $N$, the last $N$ raters are all capable of verifying the validity of *RCert*. When the last previous *rater* refuses to present the *Last-TimeStamp*, the current *rater* can refer to the second last previous *rater*. If there are enough previous raters, there is always a previous rater that can do the verification.

For case 2, to prevent the previous *rater* from giving a forged revoked *Last-TimeStamp*, we require it to present a certificate by the revoker as well. If it cannot show any evidence of the revocation, the current rater can regard the *Last-TimeStamp* as a fresh one.

## 5 Conclusion

In this paper, we have look at how trust can be managed using reputation-based systems. Besides looking at existing solution, we have also presented our solutions to address the storage and integrity issues. In particular, we have proposed the notion of *RCert* and the RCertPX protocol. Although *RCertPX* can prevent tampering of the *RCert*, it cannot prevent malicious participants collude to distort the reputation information. For example, if the *ratee* and current *rater* collude, they might succeed to discard the latest ratings of the *RCert*. However, with our mechanism, it is harder for the *rater* to achieve this as it will need to collude with $N$ previous *ratees* at the same time. We are currently looking at how to address this collusion issue.

## References


1. P. Resnick, R. Zeckhauser, E. Friedman, and K. Kuwabara. Reputation systems. In *Communications of the ACM*, 2000.
2. eBay. ebay home page. http://www.ebay.com.
3. Amazon. Amazon home page. http://www.amazon.com.
4. I. Stoica, R. Morris, D. Karger, F. Kaashoek, and H. Balakrishnan. Chord: A scalable Peer-To-Peer lookup service for internet applications. In *Proceedings of the 2001 ACM SIGCOMM Conference*, pages 149–160, 2001.
5. A. Crespo and H. Garcia-Molina. Routing indices for peer-to-peer systems. In *Proceedings of the 22nd International Conference on Distributed Computing Systems*, pages 23–30, VIenna, Austria, July 2002.
6. W. S. Ng, B. C. Ooi, K. L. Tan, and A. Zhou. PeerDB: A p2p-based system for distributed data sharing. In *Proceedings of the 19th International Conference on Data Engineering*, Bangalore, India, March 2003.
7. P. Kalnis, W.S. Ng, B.C. Ooi, D. Papadias, and K.L. Tan. An adaptive peer-to-peer network for distributed caching of olap results. In *ACM SIGMOD 2002*, 2002.
8. K. A. Burton. Design of the openprivacy distributed reputation system. http://www.peerfear.org/papers/openprivacy-reputation.pdf, May 2002.
9. F. Cornelli, E. Damiani, S. D. C. di Vimercati, S. Paraboschi, and P. Samarati. Choosing reputable servents in a p2p network. In *Proceedings of the eleventh international conference on World Wide Web*, 2002.
10. K. Aberer and Z. Despotovic. Managing trust in a peer-2-peer information system. In *Proceedings of the tenth international conference on Information and knowledge management*, 2002.
11. K. Aberer. P-grid: A self-organizing access structure for p2p information systems. In *Proc. of COOPIS*, 2001.
12. D. Fahrenholtz and W. Lamersdorf. Transactional security for a distributed reputation management system. 2002.
13. S. D. Kamvar, M. T. Schlosser, and H. Garcia-Molina. Eigenrep: Repuation management in p2p networks. In *Proceedings of the twelfth international conference on World Wide Web*, May 2003.
14. P. Zimmermann. Pretty good privacy user's guide, volume i and ii. Distributed with the PGP software, 1993.
15. S. Ratnasamy, P. Francis, M. Handley, R. Karp, and S. Shenker. A scalable content addressable network. In *Proceedings of the 2001 ACM SIGCOMM Conference*, 2001.
16. PKI. Public-key infrastructure. http://www.ietf.org/html.charters/pkix-charter.html.
17. Gnutella. The gnutella protocol specification v0.4, june 2001. http://www.clip2.com/GnutellaProtocol04.pdf.
18. I. Clarke, O. Sandberg, B. Wiley, and T. Hong. Freenet: A distributed anonymous information storage and retrieval system. In *Proc. of the ICSI Workshop on Design Issues in Anonymity and Unobservability*, 2000.

# Advertising and Matching Agent Services on the World Wide Web

Hongen Lu

School of Information Technology
Deakin University
221 Burwood Highway, Burwood
VIC 3125, AUSTRALIA
helu@deakin.edu.au

**Abstract.** The World Wide Web is evolving from its early stage, solely a collection of online text and images, into a huge marketplace for service providers and consumers. This market is still growing at an accelerate speed far more beyond anyone or any central server's control. How to locate information providers, and how to integrate information agents in such an open dynamic environment are new challenges. In this paper, I propose a language for agent services description. This language allows developers to plug in an independent suitable language to specify the constraints. Multiple matching strategies based on agent service ontology are given to help agents locating appropriate service providers. The series of strategies consider various features of service providers, the nature of requirements, and more importantly the relationships among services.

## 1 Introduction

The World Wide Web is evolving from its early stage, solely a collection of online text and images, into a huge marketplace for service providers and consumers. Information service providers, such as Ahoy [9], ShopBot [5], and SportsFinder [8], are programs that assist people to find specific information from the Web. They are capable to provide the services such as locating a person's homepage, finding the cheapest available prices for music CDs, or finding sports results of a team or a player. More and more people nowadays are rely on the Web to pay their bills, to do their banking, to book tickets, just name a few. Online services are a essential part of our daily life. This is also the main drive force for the successes of online business sites, for example, eBay. This market is still growing at an accelerate speed far more beyond anyone or any central server's control. How to locate information providers, and how to integrate information agents in such an open dynamic environment are new challenges; since in such a dynamic domain, applications are developed geographically dispersed over the Internet, and they become available or disappear unexpectedly. This is one of the basic problems facing designers of open, multi-agent systems for the Internet, the connection problem — finding the other agents who might have the information or other capabilities that you need [3].

G. Dong et al. (Eds.): WAIM 2003, LNCS 2762, pp. 13–24, 2003.

In [6], two basic approaches to this connection problem are distinguished: *direct communication*, in which agents handle their own coordination and *assisted coordination*, in which agents rely on special system programs to achieve coordination. However in the Web application domain, only the latter approach promises the adaptability required to cope with the dynamic changes in this environment. In this paper, I present a mediator based architecture for agents advertising and locating services, a agent capability description language and multiple matchmaking strategies are given. The next section is about the mediator architecture, followed by agent service ontology, service description language, multiple matching strategies and some examples.

## 2 Mediator Based Architecture

In [4], they have recently described a solution space to the connection problem based on assisted coordination. The special system programs for coordination are called middle agents. I introduce a special kind of middle agent, mediator. A mediator is a software module that exploits encoded knowledge about some sets or subsets of data to create information for a higher layer of applications [11]. In [2], a mediator is an information producing or serving entity in a large-scale internetworked environment. I present a mediator based middle agent architecture for agent services advertising and requesting. The architecture is given in Figure 1.

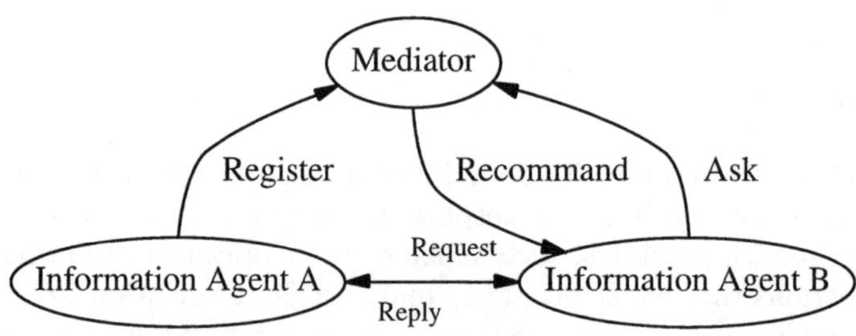


**Fig. 1.** Mediator Based Architecture

In my design, a mediator stores the services offered by different agents in the existing environment, and when a new agent is introduced into the environment it can register its capability to the mediator, using an agent service description language, if this agent wants its service to be used by others. Information agents can also unregister their services to the mediator when they want to quit the cooperation or exit. Also when an information agent receives a query or a subtask within a query that can not be solved by itself, it can request the mediator to find out other agents that have the capability or a set of agents who can work cooperatively to provide that service.

## 3 Agent Services Ontology

Since each information agent is developed individually over the Internet, their capabilities are different from each other. SportsFinder [8] can find the sports results of golf, cycling, football and basketball etc. for users; while Ahoy [9] is good at locating people's homepages. However considering in a given application domain, for instance sports, there exists a hierarchy relationship among these information agents. For example, information agent $\mathcal{A}$ can find all the results for Australian football teams, while agent $\mathcal{B}$ can only find the results of AFL (Australian Football League), in this case the service agent $\mathcal{B}$ can provide is a subset of agent $\mathcal{A}$, i.e. Service($\mathcal{B}$) $\subset$ Service($\mathcal{A}$).

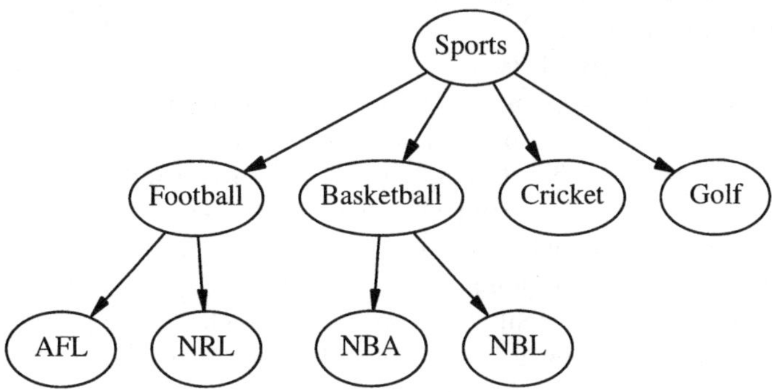


**Fig. 2.** A Fragment of Sports Service Ontology

In this section, I characterise agent service relations. Let $S_i$ denotes the service of information agent $\mathcal{IA}_i$, and a set of sports names and/or competitions names to express what the service is about. For the above example, we have Service($\mathcal{B}$)=$\{$AFL$\}$.

- **Identical Service:** In this relationship the two services can provide the same function in spite of the fact that they may have different service names. As we know, information agents are being built over the Web using different programming languages and architectures. It is no surprised to have two agents running on different hosts that can offer the same service. Obviously, two identical services can substitute each other.
- **Subservice:** This relationship characterises two services offered by agents, in which one service's function is only a part of another. For instance, in the case of a Carlton Soccer Club information agent, which can just extract the scores for Carlton Soccer Club, its service is a subservice of a NSL (National Soccer League) agent, which can find the results for all the teams in the National Soccer League. Of course the service which is a subservice of another can be alternated by its "*parent*" service.

- **Substitute Service:** Identical services and subservices are two special cases of substitute service relationship. But the difference is that identical services can substitute each other, while the subservice can only be alternated by its "*parent*" service, not vice versa.
- **Partial Substitute Service:** This relationship describes two services that have some common subservices. For instance, an agent that can get the tennis scores for the US Open tournament and another one for the Australia Open tournament may have a common subservice for Pete Sampras's performance in these two Grand Slams, which is the service of an information agent to follow the results of famous tennis stars. In some circumstances, partial substitute services can be alternated with each other, such as where the service agent is offering, just by chance, the common subservice with its partial substitute service, that is, the agent is not offering its full service to others at the moment.
- **Reciprocal Service:** If two services are reciprocal, that means they have no subservices in common, but they can work together to offer a "*bigger*" service. From this definition we know that in case there is no current agent available to provide the "*bigger*" service, these two reciprocal services can cooperate as a single agent for this task. In the real world there is the case where, for a soccer fan who is eagerly following English football, there are two already existing information agents – one for the English Primer League and one for the English Football Association Cup - which may perfectly satisfies his needs. This gives us a message that by combining the current agents in a different manner, we can tailor the system to meet new requirements.

To find the service relationship between two information agents, the middle agent should keep the knowledge of the domain service. The knowledge the middle agent would need to match the services of information agents is effectively an ontology of services. The agent service ontology contains all the services of information agents as well as their relationships. Agent service ontology is an key element to perform meaningful services description and matching.

## 4 Agent Capability Description Language

In order to achieve the agent behaviour described in Fig 1, it is necessary to explicitly represent and communicate the capabilities of various information agents that developed distributively over the Internet using different architecture and languages. For this purpose, an agent capability description language is provided.

The language begins with the word `capability` followed by a set of keyword-value pairs as in KQML. The syntax of ACDL in Figure 3 allows the plug in of an independent *constraint language*, that is the syntax of the ACDL is open at this point. This is described in the **constraint-language** field, which tells which language is used to present the constraints that should be hold on input, output and input-output. Also the **cap-id** field allows the specification of a name for this capability. The name for the capability is used to enable the middle agent

```
<acdl> ::= ( capability
               :cap-id <name>
               :constraint-language <name>
               :input ( <param-spec>+ )
               :output ( <param-spec>+ )
               :input-constraints ( <constraint>+ )
               :output-constraints ( <constraint>+ )
               :io-constraints ( <constraint>+ )
               |:cap-ontology <name>
               |:isa <name>
               |:privacy <name>
               |:quality <name> )

<param-spec> ::= ( <name> <term> )
<term>       ::= <constant> | <variable> |
                   ( <constant> <term>+ )
<constant>   ::= <name>
<variable>   ::= ?<name>
<name>       ::= <Identifier>

<constraint> ::= << expression in constraint-language >>
```

**Fig. 3.** A draft syntax for ACDL in BNF

to build a service ontology, and allows the **isa** field to naming a capability from which this capability will inherit the description. These two fields make it easier and simple to write a service description based on the already existed service ontologies, which is given as the value of **cap-ontology** field. The **privacy** and **quality** fields describe to what degree can other agents access this service and what the quality of this service is respectively.

However, it is necessary to define at least one constraint language that can be used to represent the constraints in the description. I think first-order predicate logic (FOPL) is a promising option to specify constraints. It resembles a subset of KIF. Here I adopt a definition of FOPL from [10] in Figure 4.

## 5 Multiple Matching Strategies

One function of a mediator is to provide the information, such as agent name, port, and capability to query agent, so that the query agent knows which agents to cooperate with to solve its problem. This process is called "*matching*". To suit the different requirements of agent service consumers, multiple matching strategies are given considering various features of service providers and consumers.

```
<formula>    ::= ( <quant> <c-form> ) | <c-form>

<quant>      ::= ( <quantifier> <variable>+ )
<quantifier> ::= forall | exists

<c-form>     ::= <literal> | ( not <formula> ) |
                 ( and <formula> <formula>+ ) |
                 ( or <formula> <formula> ) |
                 ( implies <formula> <formula> ) |
                 ( iff <formula> <formula> ) |
                 ( xor <formula> <formula> )

<literal>    ::= <constant> | ( = <term> <term> ) |
                 ( <constant> <term>+ )
```

**Fig. 4.** Syntax of FOPL in BNF

### 5.1 Type Matching

In the following definition, if type $t_1$ is a subtype of type $t_2$, it is denoted as $t_1 \preceq_{st} t_2$.

**Definition 1. Type Match** *Let $\mathcal{C}$ be a service description in our ACDL containing: an input specification $I^{\mathcal{C}}$ containing the variables $v_1, \ldots, v_n$, and output specification $I^{\mathcal{O}}$ . Let $\mathcal{T}$ be a service request in ACDL with input specification $I^{\mathcal{T}}$ containing variables $u_1, \ldots, u_m$, and output specification $O^{\mathcal{T}}$. $\mathcal{C}$ is type matched with $\mathcal{T}$ , if*

$$I^{\mathcal{T}} \preceq_{st} I^{\mathcal{C}} \text{ and}$$
$$O^{\mathcal{C}} \preceq_{st} O^{\mathcal{T}}$$

*where $I^{\mathcal{T}} \preceq_{st} I^{\mathcal{C}}$ means $\forall v_i \in I^{\mathcal{C}}\ \exists u_j \in I^{\mathcal{T}}$ that $u_j \preceq_{st} v_i$ and for $i \neq k$, $u_j \preceq_{st} v_i$, and $u_l \preceq_{st} v_k$, we have $j \neq l$.*

This is the simplest strategy that only matches the types in the input and output fields of service advertisements against the correspondent field in requirements. It makes sure that a provider can take the inputs of requester, and its outputs are compatible with the requester's.

### 5.2 Constraint Matching

Constraint matching considers the constraint parts in agent service descriptions.

**Definition 2. Constraint Match** *Let $\mathcal{C}$ be a capability description in ACDL with input constraints $C_I^{\mathcal{C}} = \{\ C_{I_1}^{\mathcal{C}}, \ldots, C_{I_{k_{\mathcal{C}}}}^{\mathcal{C}}\ \}$ and output constraints $C_O^{\mathcal{C}} = \{\ C_{O_1}^{\mathcal{C}}, \ldots, C_{O_{l_{\mathcal{C}}}}^{\mathcal{C}}\ \}$. Let $C_I^{\mathcal{T}} = \{\ C_{I_1}^{\mathcal{T}}, \ldots, C_{I_{k_{\mathcal{T}}}}^{\mathcal{T}}\ \}$ and $C_O^{\mathcal{T}} = \{\ C_{O_1}^{\mathcal{T}}, \ldots, C_{O_{k_{\mathcal{T}}}}^{\mathcal{T}}\ \}$ be the input and output constraints respectively of service $\mathcal{T}$. $\mathcal{T}$ is constraint matched with $\mathcal{C}$ if*

$$C_I^{\mathcal{T}} \preceq_\theta C_I^{\mathcal{C}} \text{ and}$$
$$C_O^{\mathcal{C}} \preceq_\theta C_O^{\mathcal{T}}$$

*where* $\preceq_\theta$ *denotes the* $\theta$*-subsumption relation between constraints. For* $C_I^{\mathcal{T}} \preceq_\theta C_I^{\mathcal{C}}$ *means* $\forall C_{I_i}^{\mathcal{T}} \in C_I^{\mathcal{T}}\ \exists C_{I_j}^{\mathcal{C}} \in C_I^{\mathcal{C}}$ *that* $C_{I_i}^{\mathcal{T}} \preceq_\theta C_{I_j}^{\mathcal{C}}$ *and for* $i \neq k$, $C_{I_i}^{\mathcal{T}} \preceq_\theta C_{I_j}^{\mathcal{C}}$, *and* $C_{I_k}^{\mathcal{T}} \preceq_\theta C_{I_l}^{\mathcal{C}}$, *we have* $j \neq l$.

Since all the constraints are given in `constraint-language`, the details of $\theta$-subsumption depends on the constraint-language. In first order predicate logic, which is the constraint-language in examples, constraints are a set of clauses. The definition of clause $\theta$- subsumption is given below.

**Definition 3. Clause $\theta$-subsumption** *A clause* $C$ *is* $\theta$*-subsumed by another clause* $D$*, denoted as* $C \preceq_\theta D$*, if there exists a substitution* $\theta$ *such that* $C \subseteq \theta(D)$.

From the above two definitions, it is straightforward to design an algorithm to check all the relevant constrains.

### 5.3 Exact Matching

Exact match is most strict matching. It requires both the types and constraint fields are well matched. This strategy deals with the services that have the same functions but with different variable and type names. Considering the huge amount of Web-based applications which implemented over times and locations, there are many cases that developers may select different naming space.

### 5.4 Partial Matching

Partial match is a combination of type match and constraint match, but both loose a little bit. This strategy aims at services that are not completely matched, but have some functions in common. It is defined as follow:

**Definition 4. Partial Match** *Let* $\mathcal{C}$ *be a service description in our ACDL containing: an input specification* $I^{\mathcal{C}}$ *containing variables* $V_{I_1}^{\mathcal{C}}, \ldots, V_{I_{n_\mathcal{C}}}^{\mathcal{C}}$*, and output specification* $O^{\mathcal{C}}$ *with variables* $V_{O_1}^{\mathcal{C}}, \ldots, V_{O_{m_\mathcal{C}}}^{\mathcal{C}}$*, and* $\mathcal{C}$*'s input constraints* $C_I^{\mathcal{C}} = \{\ C_{I_1}^{\mathcal{C}}, \ \ldots,\ C_{I_{k_\mathcal{C}}}^{\mathcal{C}}\ \}$ *and output constraints* $C_O^{\mathcal{C}} = \{\ C_{O_1}^{\mathcal{C}}, \ \ldots,\ C_{O_{l_\mathcal{C}}}^{\mathcal{C}}\ \}$*. Let* $\mathcal{T}$ *be another agent service with the correspondent description parts as: input* $I^{\mathcal{T}}$ *containing variables* $V_{I_1}^{\mathcal{T}}, \ldots, V_{I_{n_\mathcal{T}}}^{\mathcal{C}}$*, and output specification* $O^{\mathcal{T}}$ *with variables* $V_{O_1}^{\mathcal{T}}, \ldots, V_{O_{m_\mathcal{T}}}^{\mathcal{T}}$*, and* $\mathcal{T}$*'s input constraints* $C_I^{\mathcal{T}} = \{\ C_{I_1}^{\mathcal{T}}, \ \ldots,\ C_{I_{k_\mathcal{T}}}^{\mathcal{T}}\ \}$ *and output constraints* $C_O^{\mathcal{T}} = \{\ C_{O_1}^{\mathcal{T}}, \ \ldots,\ C_{O_{l_\mathcal{T}}}^{\mathcal{T}}\ \}$*. We define* $\mathcal{T}$ *is partial matched with* $\mathcal{C}$ *if*

$$\exists V_{I_i}^{\mathcal{T}} \in I^{\mathcal{T}}, \exists V_{I_j}^{\mathcal{C}} \in I^{\mathcal{C}} \text{ that } V_{I_i}^{\mathcal{T}} \preceq_{st} V_{I_j}^{\mathcal{C}}$$
$$\exists V_{O_j}^{\mathcal{C}} \in O^{\mathcal{C}}, \exists V_{O_i}^{\mathcal{T}} \in O^{\mathcal{T}} \text{ that } V_{O_j}^{\mathcal{C}} \preceq_{st} V_{O_i}^{\mathcal{T}}$$
$$\exists C_{I_i}^{\mathcal{T}} \in C_I^{\mathcal{T}}, \exists C_{I_j}^{\mathcal{C}} \in C_I^{\mathcal{C}} \text{ that } C_{I_i}^{\mathcal{T}} \preceq_\theta C_{I_j}^{\mathcal{C}}$$
$$\exists C_{O_j}^{\mathcal{C}} \in C_O^{\mathcal{C}}, \exists C_{O_i}^{\mathcal{T}} \in C_O^{\mathcal{T}}, \text{ that } C_{O_j}^{\mathcal{C}} \preceq_\theta C_{O_i}^{\mathcal{T}}$$

The above definition means for two capability descriptions, if some of their input, output variables have subtype relations, and there are constraint clauses in their input and output constraint specifications that are $\theta$- subsumption, these two services are partial matched. Semantically, in some circumstances, i.e. the unmatched variables and constraints are irrelevant; the partial matched service is applicable.

### 5.5 Privacy Matching

Due to a service provider agent's privacy restriction, the matching result actually is sent to the service provider instead to the service requester. In other words, the provider agent wants to control the communication with consumers, it does not want to expose itself before knowing who are requesting its service. The process of privacy matching has the following steps:

- The service provider agent specifies its privacy value as `high`, which indicates its privacy should be protected, in the advertisement it sent to the mediator;
- The mediator finds out some service requesters who might be looking for such a service. In this step the mediator can use any matching strategies suitable for the circumstances at the moment except privacy matching, which is actually being carried out;
- The mediator forwards the contact details of service requester agents to the provider instead of giving the identity of the provider to the requester;
- The service provider agent will decide which requesters it would like to offer its service to, and then it will contact them to make a deal.

### 5.6 Cooperative Matching

Matching is a process based on a cooperative partnership between information providers and consumers. In our SportsAgents [7] system, a mediator is introduced to solve the connection problem. SportsAgents is an open multi-agent system to answer a user's query about sports, for instance "which is the best sports city in Australia?". In SportsAgents three types of agents, mediator, information agents and interface agents, are implemented. To find the best sports city may require the cooperation of different sports information agents. The mediator finds the current available information agents who have the capability that the query agent (information consumer) is asking for. In case no available agent can fulfill the query service itself, the mediator will infer the available services to find a set of available information agents that can cooperate in some way to provide the requested service. This algorithm requires an arbitrary amount of deduction and knowledge to match any given service and request. It exploits service ontology, knowledge on the application domain, to discover the hidden relationships among currently available services. The algorithm for cooperative service matching is given in Algorithm 1.

**Algorithm 1** matching($S$: Service, *head*: Hierarchy)

Given $S$, the service an information agent requests, agent table *AgentTable*, which contains the contact information of currently available information agents, and the service ontology *Head*. Each node in the service ontology has the following structure:

```
public class Service extends Vector
{
      String name;
      Service up;
      Service down;
      Service next;
          ⋮
}
```

this algorithm returns the agents contact information and their relationships.

```
find = false; head = Head;
Agent-found =null; relation = null;
if AgentTable.index(S) = true then {
        while (AgentTable.query(S) != null) {
              Agent-found = Agent-found
                  ADD AgentTable.query(S);
         }
         relation = find-relation(S, head);
         find = true;
    }
else {
    if head.name ≃ S.name then {
        service = head.down;
        while (service != null AND !find) {
              matching(S, service);
              service = service.next;
        }
    }
    else {
        matching(S, head.down);
        matching(S, head.next);
    }
}
return Agent-found, relation. □
```

**Fig. 5.** Cooperative Matching Algorithm

## 6 Agent Services Matching in SportsAgents

SportsAgents [7] is an open multi-agent system to answer sports questions, it exploits a mediator based architecture. Following let us look at some examples in SportsAgents illustrating the above definitions and the matching strategies.

### 6.1 Example 1: Type Matching

Considering the following agent capability description of SportsFinder [8]:

```
(capability
    :cap-id SportsFinder
    :constraint-language fopl
    :input ( (Team ?team) )
    :input-constraint (
         (elt ?team TeamName)
         (CompeteIn ?team Sports) )
    :output (
         (TeamScore ?score) )
    :output-constraint ( (Has Score ?team ?score) ) )
```

The above description shows that SportsFinder can find out the scores of a sports team. Suppose the mediator has already received the above service advertisement. Then some information agent sends the following service request to the mediator:

```
(capability
    :cap-id SoccerResult
    :constraint-language fopl
    :input ( (SoccerTeam ?soccer_team) )
    :input-constraint (
           (elt ?soccer_team TeamName)
           (CompeteIn ?soccer_team Soccer) )
    :output ( (Score ?result) )
    :output-constraint ( Has Score ?soccer_team ?result) ) )
```

When applying the type matching algorithm on these two service descriptions, we have input variable `soccer_team` as a subtype of `team` and output type `TeamScore` as a subtype of `Score`, thus `SoccerResult` is signature matched against `SportsFinder`. That means the service of `SportsFinder` can take the variables of the request as input, and its output is compatible with the variables' types of request. From this example it is easy to understand that type match relation is not commutative. For the above two descriptions, service `SportsFinder` is not type matched with `SoccerResult`, although vice versa.

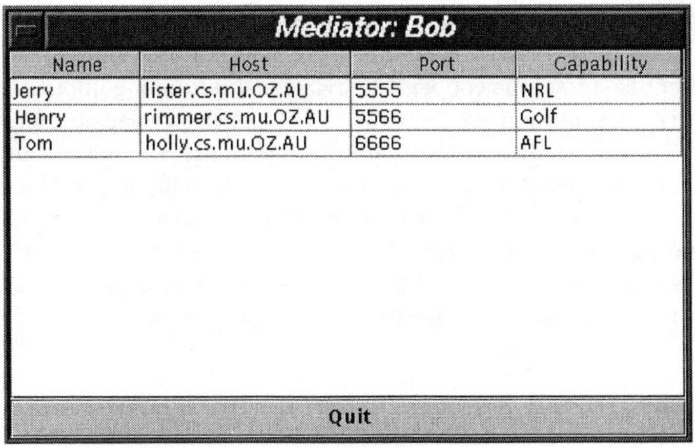

Mediator: Bob

| Name | Host | Port | Capability |
|---|---|---|---|
| Jerry | lister.cs.mu.OZ.AU | 5555 | NRL |
| Henry | rimmer.cs.mu.OZ.AU | 5566 | Golf |
| Tom | holly.cs.mu.OZ.AU | 6666 | AFL |

Quit

**Fig. 6.** Mediator

### 6.2 Example 2: Cooperative Matching

Consider the scenario in Figure 6. Currently there are three agents available in sports domain. Information agents Tom and Jerry can provide the service of getting the results of AFL and NRL (National Rugby League) respectively. However to answer a user's query "which is the best sports city in Australia?", agent must know the result of one of the most popular sports, Football, of Australia. Unfortunately, none of the current available information agents has that capability. Using cooperative matching algorithm, it can be inferred that Tom and Jerry can work cooperatively to get the information. So the mediator will reply the request information agent with Tom and Jerry's contact information as well as their cooperative relationship. This can not be achieved in IMPACT [1] platform. I believe inference and some reasoning abilities are necessary for mediators to provide intelligent matchmaking. Domain specific mediators can be built to help discover other information agents in a specific domain. To select a suitable matching strategy, an agent should consider the features of a service request, the attributes of service advertisements,the current load of mediator, and other environmental attributes. Different developers can utilise various decision models to select a matching strategy or a combination of above strategies to satisfy their requirements.

## 7 Conclusion

Agent services advertising and matching is one of the fundamental problems in building open Web-based applications. Mediator-based architecture is a step towards for this goal. In this architecture, new information agents can be easily incorporated into an existing multi-agent application. This makes the system open to new applications and flexible to organize agent cooperation. The mediator in this architecture serves as middle agent that not only solves the connection problem, but also infers the cooperation relationships among information agents, this will direct information agents to forge a cooperation to answer a user's query. In such a way, information agents can improve their capabilities, and information gathering from the Web becomes more scalable. The proposed agent service description language gives a flexible method for developers to plug in a suitable independent constraint language; it is more expressive for service quality and the privacy of service providers. Multiple matching strategies provide more flexible methods for agent service consumers to locate providers.

## References


1. Khaled Arisha, Sarit Kraus, V. S. Subrahmanian, and etal. IMPACT: Interactive maryland platform for agents collaborating together. *IEEE Intelligent Systems*, 14(2) :64–72, March–April 1999.
2. Son Dao and Brad Perry. Information mediation in Cyberspace: Scalable methods for declarative information networks. *Journal of Intelligent Information Systems*, 6(2/3):131–150, May 1996.
3. Keith Decker, Katia Sycara, and Mike Williamson. Matchmaking and brokering. In *Proceedings of the Second International Conference on Multi-Agent Systems (ICMAS-96)*, December 1996.
4. Keith Decker, Katia Sycara, and Mike Williamson. Middle-Agents for the Internet. In *Proceedings of Fifteenth International Joint Conference on Artificial Intelligence (IJGAI-97)*, pages 578–583, Nagoya, Japan, August 1997.
5. Robert B. Doorenbos, Oren Etzioni, and Daniel S. Weld. A scalable comparison-shopping agent for the World Wide Web. In *Proceedings of the First International Conference on Autonomous Agents*, 1997.
6. Michael R. Genesereth and Steven P. Ketchpel. Software agents. *Communications of the AGM*, 37(7):48–53, July 1994.
7. Hongen Lu and Leon Sterling. Sportsagents: A mediator-based multi-agent System for cooperative information gathering from the world wide web. In *Proceedings of the Fifth International Conference on the Practical Application of Intelligent Agents and Multi-Agent Technology (PAAM 2000)*, pages 331–334, Manchester, UK, April 2000.
8. Hongen Lu, Leon Sterling, and Alex Wyatt. Knowledge discovery in SportsFinder: An agent to extract sports results from the Web. In *Methodologies for Knowledge Discovery and Data Mining, Third Pacific-Asia Conference (PAKDD-99) Proceedings*, pages 469–473. Springer, 1999.
9. Jonathan Shakes, Marc Langheinrich, and Oren Etzioni. Dynamic reference sifting: A case study in the homepage domain. In *Proceedings of the Sixth International World Wide Web Conference*, pages 189–200, 1997.
10. Gerhard Jürgen Wickler. *Using Expressive und Flexible Action Representations to Reason about Capabilities for Intelligent Agent Cooperation.* PhD thesis, University of Edinburgh, Edinburgh, Scotland, April 1999.
11. Gio Wiederhold. Mediators in the architecture of future information systems. *IEEE Computer*, 25(3), March 1992.

# Efficient Reduction of Web Latency through Predictive Prefetching on a WAN

Christos Bouras[1, 2], Agisilaos Konidaris[1, 2], and Dionysios Kostoulas[2]

[1] Research Academic Computer Technology Institute – CTI, Riga Feraiou 61, GR-26221, Patras, Greece
{bouras, konidari}@cti.gr

[2] Computer Engineering and Informatics Department, University of Patras, GR-26500, Patras, Greece
kostoula@ceid.upatras.gr

**Abstract.** This paper studies Predictive Prefetching on a Web system that provides two levels of caching before information reaches the clients. We analyze prefetching on a Wide Area Network with the above mentioned characteristics. First, we provide a structured overview of predictive prefetching and show its wide applicability to various computer systems. The WAN that we refer to is the GRNET academic network in Greece. We rely on log files collected at the network's Transparent cache (primary caching point), located at GRNET's edge connection to the Internet. We present the parameters that are most important for prefetching on GRNET's architecture and provide preliminary results of an experimental study, quantifying the benefits of prefetching on the WAN.

## 1 Introduction

Prefetching is a technique used to enhance several computer system functions [3, 4, 5, 6, 9, 11, 13]. It has been used to enhance operating systems, file systems and of course Web based systems. It is always useful to be able to foresee a request in such systems, in order to be able to service it before it is actually placed, since this would boost system performance. Prefetching systems always run the risk of misusing or even abusing system resources in order to execute their functions.

The ultimate goal of Web prefetching is to reduce what is called User Perceived Latency(UPL) on the Web [1, 2, 7, 8, 12]. UPL is the delay that an end user (client) actually experiences when requesting a Web resource. The reduction of UPL does not imply the reduction of actual network latency or the reduction of network traffic. On the contrary in most cases even when UPL is reduced, network traffic increases. The basic effect of prefetching on a Web system is to "separate" the time when a resource is actually requested by a client from the time that the client (user in general) chooses to see the resource.

G. Dong et al. (Eds.): WAIM 2003, LNCS 2762, pp. 25–36, 2003.

## 2 Caching in the Wide Area

Local Area Networks (LANs) usually include several clients configured to use a single Proxy/cache server, which in turn is connected and provides access to the Internet. In this work we look at the case of several LANs inter-connected with the use of a broadband backbone that provides access to the Internet through one main access point. This is the case of the Greek Research Network, GRNET [10]. In the case of the GRNET WAN we find 3 levels of caching. The first is the simple client browser caching mechanism, the second is the LAN Proxy server caching mechanism and the third is a Transparent caching mechanism implemented at the Athens edge router node, where the WAN is connected to the Internet. The simplified Prefetching architecture (without network equipment such as switches, routers etc) that we will study in this paper is presented in Figure 1. The Transparent cache initiates demand requests to Web servers represented by normal directed lines but also prefetching requests represented by the dotted directed lines between the Transparent cache and the Internet.

## 3 The n Most Popular Approach

In the following sections we present the two approaches that we followed for prefetching at the Transparent cache. First, we present the "Most popular" document approach and then the Prediction by Partial Matching (PPM) approach.

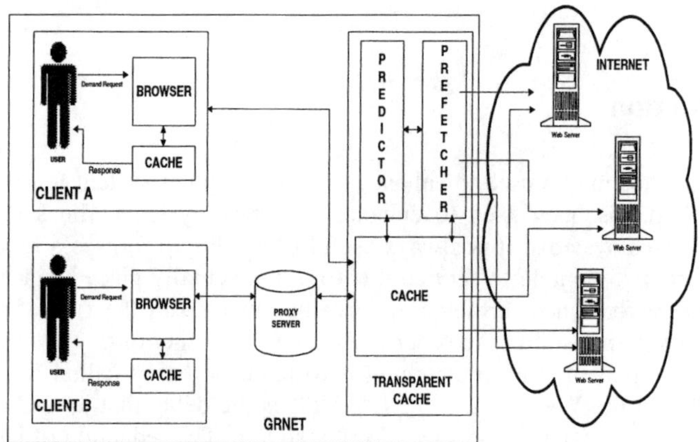


**Fig. 1.** The Prefetching architecture used in this paper

### 3.1 Popularity Ranking

Page popularity ranking is a process of log data analysis used to determine pages that are likely to be requested next. This process is applied for each user separately (in case predictions are based on user log data only) and overall (in case predictions are based on log data by all users). As mentioned in previous sections, user log data is separated into session files. Therefore, page popularity ranking is first carried out at a session level. For any page in a user's session, all instances of it in that session are found and a popularity list is created, on the top of which exists the page that has been requested most by the user in the current session. Adding up page popularity data from all user sessions, we create a new popularity list that represents user's navigation habits in general (user-based page popularity ranking). In the same way, another page ranking is performed, which takes data from all users into account (overall page popularity ranking).

However, the basic process of log data analysis is that of finding for every web page those requested more frequently after it. We look for pages that were accessed within $n$ accesses after a specified page. The parameter $n$ is called lookahead window size. We choose the lookahead window size to be equal to 5. Any page requested within $n$ accesses after a specified page was requested is considered to be a n-next page of it. For every page in the log data we find the frequency of visits within the lookahead window size, of all other pages found to be a n-next page to it.

**Algorithm 1.** Building the prediction model for the user-based "most popular" approach

**Input:** Prediction model constructed so far, user's training log data
**Output:** Updated prediction model

*For every request in user's training log data:*
    *Set user's current request as active*
        *For each user's request within n requests after active:*
            *If request not in active request's n-next popularity list:*
                *Insert request in active request's n-next popularity list*
                *Request popularity = 1*
            *If request in active request's n-next popularity list:*
                *Request popularity++*
*Sort active request's n-next popularity list by popularity*

### 3.2 Decision Algorithm

In a simple form of the decision algorithm, prefetching is decided for any page suggested by the prediction algorithm. We characterize this decision policy as an aggressive prefetching policy. However, when available bandwidth is limited we need to restrict our model and perform prefetching only for those predicted pages that appear to have a high chance of being requested. Those are the pages with high dependency to the currently displayed page or pages whose content does not seem to change frequently. This decision policy is called strict prefetching policy. The whole prediction process for the case of the user-based prediction is shown in Algorithm 2.

**Algorithm 2.** Predicting a user's next request given the prediction model, the current (last) request, the dependency threshold and the frequency of change threshold

**Input:** Prediction model, user's current request, dependency threshold, frequency of change threshold
**Output:** A set of predicted pages

*For every request in user's simulation data:*
*Set user's current request as active*
*For each of m most popular requests in active request's n-next popularity list:*
*Check request as prefetching candidate*
*If policy == aggressive:*
*Add request in set of predicted pages*
*If (policy == strict) && (size > average size):*
*If (dependency > dependency threshold) && (frequency of change < frequency of change threshold):*
*Add request in set of predicted pages*

## 4 The Prediction by Partial Matching Approach

Prediction by Partial Matching (PPM) is a context modeling algorithm which keeps track of the occurrence of events and their sequence. It then provides (and always keeps track of) a probability for the occurrence of the next event based on previous event occurrence and sequence. In our case an event is a request to a URL. We keep track of the URLs being requested by users (through traces) and build an m context trie, representing their occurrence and their sequence. Next, we describe all algorithms used to evaluate prefetching at the Transparent cache with the use of PPM as the prefetcher. It is not in the scope of this work to elaborate on PPM due to space limitations. The procedure we follow can be found in [14].

The algorithms used to evaluate PPM at the Transparent cache are presented next.

**Algorithm 3.** Building prediction model from users' access patterns (training process)

**Input:** Structure representing prediction model of order m constructed so far, user's training log data
**Output:** Updated prediction model

*Current context [0] = root node of structure*
*For every request in user's training log data:*
*For length m down to 0:*
*If request not appearing as child node of current context [length] in structure:*
*Add child node for request to current context [length]*
*request occurrence = 1*
*current context [length+1] = node of request*
*if request appearing as child node of current context [length] in structure:*
*request occurrence ++*
*current context [length+1] = node of request*
*current context [0] = root node of structure*

**Algorithm 4.** Prediction Process (predicting user's next request given the prediction model, the previous requests and the confidence threshold for each order of model)

**Input:** Structure representing prediction model of order m, previous k requests, confidence threshold for each order of prediction model
**Output:** A set of predicted pages

*For length 1 to k:*
*Current context [length] = node representing access sequence of previous length requests*
*For length k down to 1:*
*For each child node of current context [length]:*
*If (request occurrence for child node / request occurrence for parent) >= confidence threshold for order length:*
*Add request of child node in set of predicted pages*
*Remove duplicates from set of predicted pages*

## 5 Experimental Study

In order to evaluate the performance benefits of the two prefetching schemes introduced in the previous paragraphs, we use trace-driven simulation. As mentioned access logs of GRNET Transparent cache are used to drive the simulations. The results presented in this paper are based on logs of web page requests recorded over a 7-day period. In each execution, simulation is driven on requests of a different group of users. In all experiments, 80% of the log data is used for training (training data) and 20% for testing (testing data) to evaluate predictions. Furthermore, all traces are preprocessed, following the five filtering steps described in a previous section.

The basic performance metrics used in our experimental study are *Prefetching Hit Ratio, Usefulness of Predictions* and *Network Traffic Increase.*

The three evaluation metrics mentioned above are used for both the "Most popular" approach and the PPM approach. However, two additional metrics are used to evaluate the performance of the "Most popular" prefetching model. These are *Average Rank* and *"Most popular" prefetch effectiveness.*

### 5.1 Most Popular Approach Evaluation

If user-based prediction is performed and all pages suggested by the prediction algorithm are prefetched, the prefetching hit ratio appears to be equal to 48%, for prefetching window size equal to 5. Usability of predictions is equal to 27,5% and traffic increase per request is found to be 6%. Moreover, the average rank of successfully prefetched documents is 2 and the prefetch effectiveness equals 52%. If we use n-next popularity data obtained from the general population in our predictions, instead of user log data, prefetch effectiveness is a bit higher (54%). However, this requires an 18% traffic increase. This is expected, since in the case of overall prediction there is greater availability of n-next popularity data. Therefore, prefetching is performed for more requests and more documents are prefetched. As a result, the cost in bandwidth is greater, but prefetch effectiveness is higher. If traffic increase is limited to 8%, then prefetch effectiveness will be equal to 50%. It is clear that for the same traffic increase the performance results of user-based prediction are better than those of overall prediction since user data implies more accurately the user's future web behavior.

It is obvious that a small value of the prefetching window size provides better accuracy of predictions. Actually, the less documents a client is allowed to prefetch, the higher its prefetching hit ratio will be, as only highly probable objects are going to be prefetched. Practicing simulation for a prefetching window size equal to 3 and user-based prediction, we experience a significant increase of hit ratio (58%) compared to the case of a prefetching window size equal to 5 (48%). In addition, less bandwidth is required to apply the prefetching method (4% traffic increase). However, usability of predictions is lower (25%) compared to the case of a prefetching window size equal to 5 (27,5%), as less prefetching actions are performed. The results of overall prediction for m equal to 3 are similar to those taken for m equal to 5.

Generally, results of applying prefetching are good when: (i) a lot of prefetching is being done and (ii) prefetching is successful. In the first case, substantial traffic increase is required. Therefore, if we want to keep bandwidth cost low, we need to improve the prediction ability of our prefetching model. This can be done either by improving the prediction algorithm, so as to increase its accuracy of predictions, or by applying prefetching only for those cases that predictions seem to be secure. Since no prediction process can ensure success, we try prefetching those documents that appear as prefetching candidates and have good chances of being requested. A web page has a greater chance of being requested next, if its dependency to the currently displayed page is high. Furthermore, we need to avoid prefetching for pages that change regularly. Therefore, security thresholds are used. In our experiments, if a document has a greater size than the average, it is prefetched only if its dependency is greater than 0.5 and its frequency of change is not greater than 0.5. In this case, the prefetching window size refers to the maximum number of prefetched pages.

For user-based prediction and a prefetching window size equal to 5, the prefetch effectiveness of a strict policy is almost as high as that of the aggressive policy (51%), while traffic increase is limited to 4%. It is clear that by using such a policy we manage high performance with lower cost in bandwidth, as the number of prefetched objects is limited. Actually, comparing these results (m = 5) to those of the aggressive policy (m = 5 and m = 3), we see that we experience prefetch effectiveness almost equal to that of the aggressive algorithm for m = 5, but with traffic increase equal to that of the m = 3 case. Moreover, hit ratio is higher (51%) for the same prefetching window size, with little cost in usefulness of predictions. Table 1 shows results taken for all three cases of user-based prediction. Figure 5 compares performance results of user-based and overall prefetching.

**Table 1.** Performance results for user-based "most popular" prediction

| | **Hit Ratio** | **Usefulness of predictions** | **Prefetch Effec-tiveness** | **Network Traffic Increase** | **Average Rank** |
|---|---|---|---|---|---|
| Aggressive policy, m = 5 | 48% | 27,5% | 52% | 6% | 2 |
| Aggressive policy, m = 3 | 58% | 25% | 42% | 4% | 1 |
| Strict policy, m =5 | 51% | 27% | 51% | 4% | 2 |

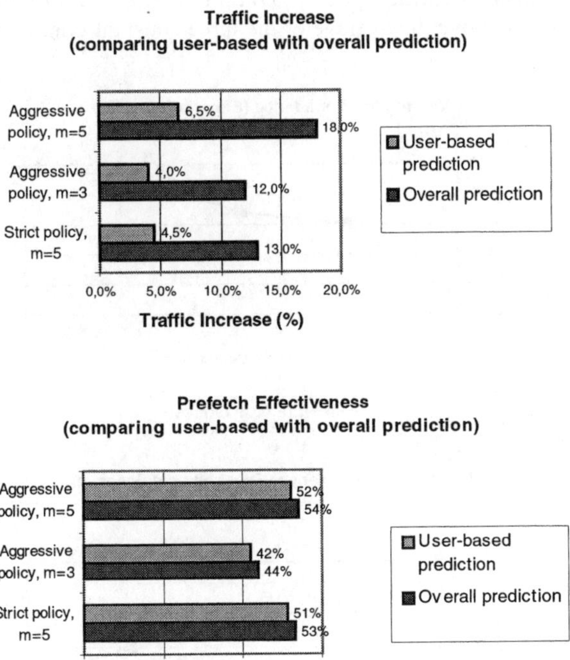


**Fig. 2.** Comparison of user-based and overall prediction scenarios for all policies (graphs should be read in pairs of bar charts)

## 5.2 Prediction by Partial Matching Approach Evaluation

Large values of confidence cause fewer predictions to be made, thus, reducing the network traffic. Additionally, the accuracy of predictions increases since only the highly probable pages are prefetched. However, the usefulness of predictions decreases due to the limited number of prefetched pages.

Figure 6 shows that for values of confidence between 0 and 0.3 any slight increase in the confidence's value results in significant increase of the hit ratio with less significant cost in the usefulness of predictions. Additionally, values greater than 0.7 have the opposite effect on performance parameters. Therefore, values of confidence between 0.3 and 0.7 are preferable as they provide better performance results.

If higher order contexts are trusted more than low order contexts and are assigned a smaller confidence, we have the case of weighted confidence. Figure 7 compares the cases of constant and weighted confidence. The horizontal lines represent the performance of the algorithm with weighted confidence which takes the values of 0.8 to 0.6 (reducing in steps of 0.1) for orders 1 to 3. This algorithm is compared with three others that use constant confidence from 0.6 up to 0.8. Diagrams show that weighted confidence performs above the average of the three constant-confidence algorithms.

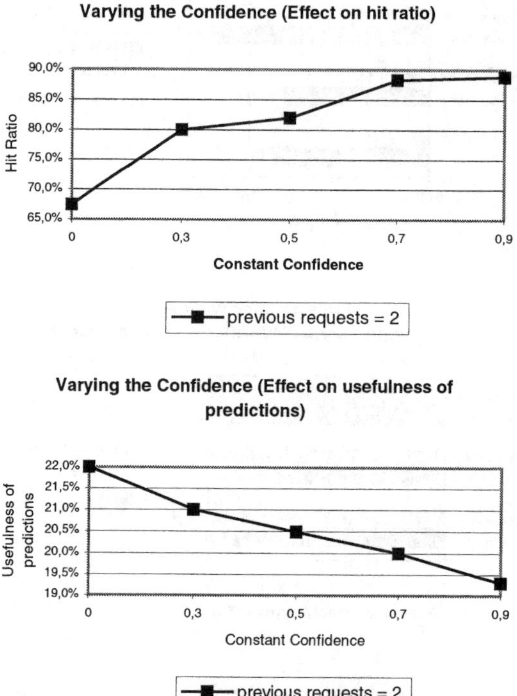


**Fig. 3.** Varying confidence. Effect on performance of PPM approach

### 5.3 Comparing "Most Popular" and PPM Performance

Figure 9 shows that in any case the PPM approach has significantly better accuracy of predictions and less traffic increase than the "Most popular" approach. On the other hand, the "Most popular" algorithm has higher usefulness of predictions. It is necessary to mention here that the complexity of the "most popular" case is much less than that of the PPM case, since a simple algorithm, with no special operational or storage requirements, is used for the construction of the "n-next most popular" prediction model.

It is obvious that the performance of the Prediction by Partial Matching approach on any of the specified metrics varies depending on the values of the parameters. If an aggressive policy that allows many pages to be predicted is used, usefulness of predictions will be high, causing, however, high network overhead and low hit ratio. On the other hand, a strict policy will result in accurate predictions and reduced traffic increase but its coverage will be limited. Two such cases are shown in Table 2. The

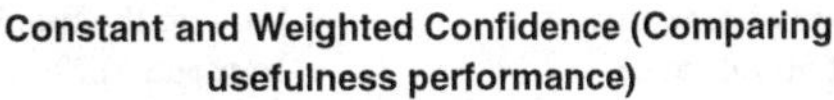


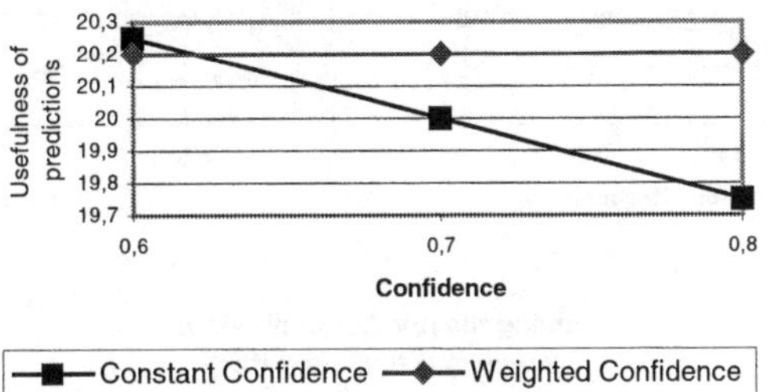


Constant and Weighted Confidence (Comparing hit ratio performance)

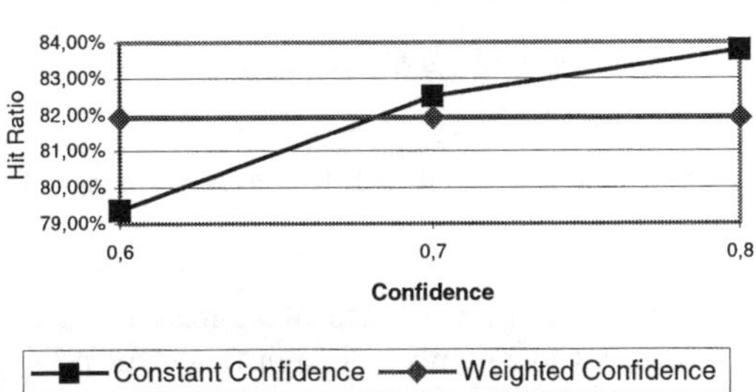


**Fig. 4.** Comparing constant and weighted confidence

first predicts almost a quarter of the total number of requests with hit ratio equal to 73%. The second one has higher accuracy (85%) but usefulness shrinks to 18,25%.

To have a clearer picture of performance differences of the two prefetching approaches we try to find proportional cases of them. For the case of the "Most popular" aggressive policy with prefetching window size equal to 5 we choose the case of PPM with previous requests equal to 1 and confidence equal to 0. We choose these values for the PPM parameters as the "Most popular" case uses also one previous request in predictions (the last request) and has no confidence limitations applied. For the case of the "Most popular" strict policy with a prefetching window size equal to 5, we choose the case of PPM with previous requests equal to 1 and confidence equal to 0.5. These values of PPM parameters are selected since the strict "Most popular" case uses only the last request in predictions and the threshold of the decision algorithm is also equal to 0.5. Figure 10 shows results taken for comparing these proportional cases.

All results studied in the above paragraphs clearly show that the application of prefetching in the Wide Area can be quite beneficial. Even with the use of a simple prediction algorithm, as the "n-next most popular" algorithm proposed in this paper, the

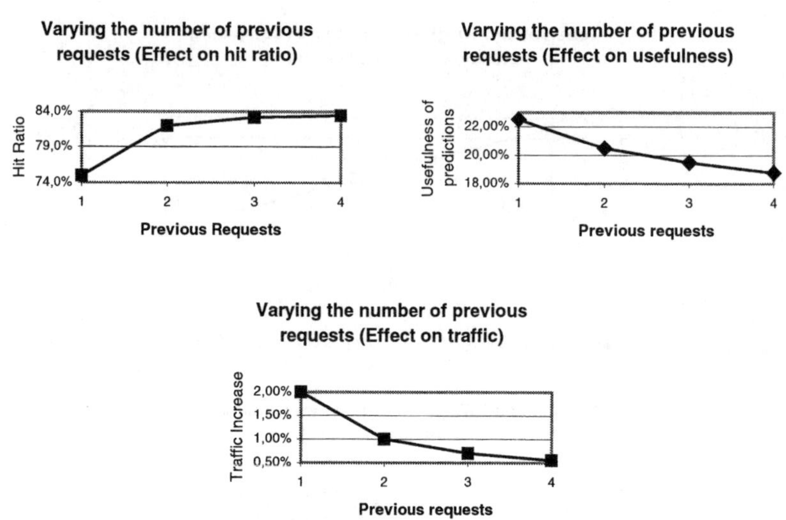


**Fig. 5.** Varying previous requests number. Effect on performance of PPM approach

accuracy of predictions can reach 58% (case of aggressive, user-based policy with prefetching window size equal to 3) with an insignificant for a WAN increase of network traffic equal to 4%. If a more complex algorithm is used, which is a variation ofthe Prediction by Partial Matching algorithm in this paper, we show that a high fraction of user requests (18,25%–23%) can be predicted with an accuracy of 73%–85%, while bandwidth overhead added is not higher than 2%. In fact, performance results are better, if we take into account that many of the prefetched requests will be used by more than a single end user, as prefetching in that case is performed for ICP requests made by Proxy servers.

**Table 2.** Efficiency of PPM approach

| | Hit Ratio | Usefulness of predictions | Network Traffic Increase |
|---|---|---|---|
| Aggressive policy, previous requests = 1, confidence = 0,2-0,3 | 73% | 23% | 2% |
| Strict policy, previous requests = 4, confidence = 0,7-0,9 | 85% | 18,25% | < 0,5% |

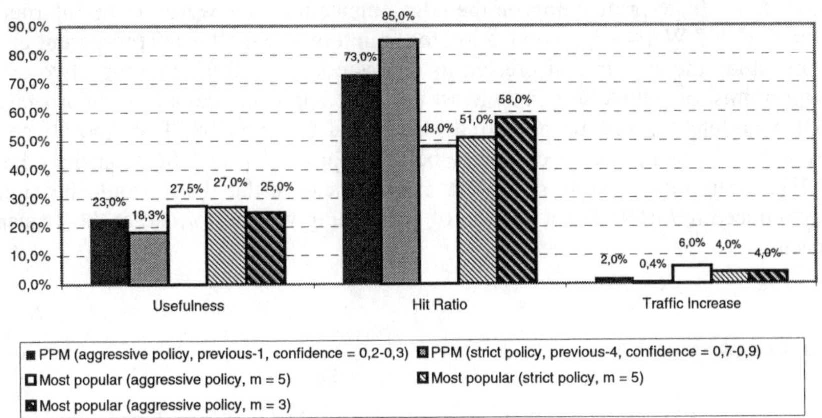


**Fig. 6.** "Most popular" and PPM performance for strict and aggressive prefetching policy

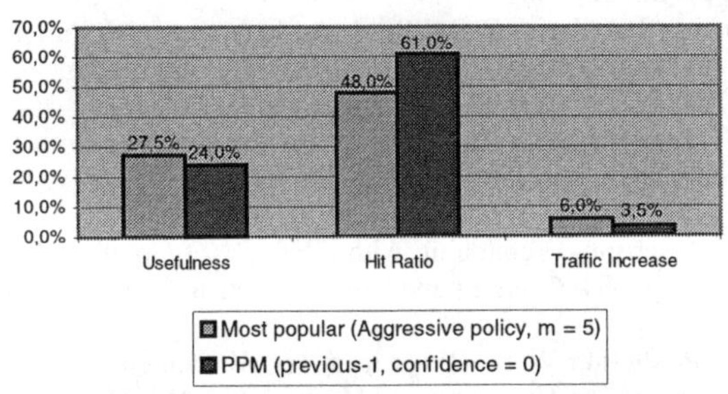


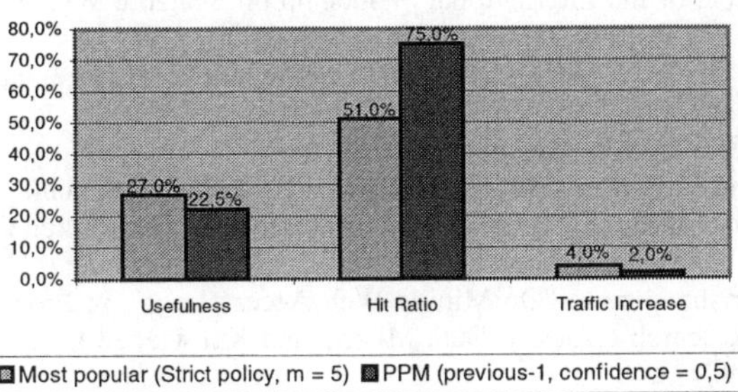


**Fig. 7.** Comparing "Most popular" and PPM performance (using proportional cases)

## 6 Future Work and Conclusions

In order to evaluate prefetching on the edge connection of a WAN to the Internet we use the GRNET WAN edge connection to the Internet, which is a Transparent cache. We first study the system and present its characteristics. After employing two different algorithms for prefetching, a "n Most Popular" approach and a PPM approach, we find that prefetching can be potentially beneficial to the GRNET WAN. Of course many further issues must be explored, before deploying prefetching on the edge of GRNET. Preliminary results provide a clear indication that UPL would be significantly reduced in GRNET if a version of prefetching was performed at the Transparent cache.

## References


1. M. Arlitt, "Characterizing Web User Sessions", ACM SIGMETRICS Performance Evaluation Review, Volume 28, Issue 2 pp.50–63, 2000.
2. B. Brewington and G. Cybenko, "Keeping up with the changing Web", IEEE Computer, 33(5) pp. 52–58, 2000.
3. X. Chen and X. Zhang, "Coordinated data prefetching by utilizing reference information at both proxy and Web servers", ACM SIGMETRICS Performance Evaluation Review, Volume 29, Issue 2 pp. 32–38, 2001.
4. X. Chen, X. Zhang, "Popularity-Based PPM: An Effective Web Prefetching Technique for High Accuracy and Low Storage", in Proc. of the 2002 International Conference on Parallel Processing (ICPP'02), Vancouver, B.C., Canada, 2002, pp. 296–304.
5. E. Cohen and H. Kaplan, "Prefetching the means for document transfer: A new approach for reducing Web latency", in Proc. of IEEE INFOCOM, Tel Aviv, Israel, 2000, pp. 854–863.
6. B. D. Davison, "Assertion: Prefetching with GET is Not Good" in Proc. of The Sixth International Workshop Web Caching and Content Distribution, Elsevier, Boston, 2001, pp. 203–215.
7. B. D. Davison, "Predicting Web actions from HTML content" in Proc. of the The Thirteenth ACM Conference on Hypertext and Hypermedia (HT'02), College Park, MD, 2002, pp. 159–168.
8. D. Foygel and D. Strelow, "Reducing Web Latency with Hierarchical Cache based Prefetching", in Proc. of the International Workshop on Scalable Web Services, (in conjunction with ICPP'00), Toronto, Ontario, Canada , 2000, pp. 103.
9. E. Gelenbe and Qi Zhu, "Adaptive control of pre-fetching", Performance Evaluation 46 pp. 177–192, Elsevier, 2001.
10. GRNET, Web Site: http://www.grnet.gr/.
11. T. I. Ibrahim and C. Z. Xu, "Neural Nets based Predictive Prefetching to Tolerate WWW Latency", in Proc. of the 20th International Conference on Distributed Computing Systems, Taipei, Taiwan, 2000, pp. 636–643.
12. Joshi and R. Krishnapuram, "On Mining Web Access Logs", in Proc. of ACM SIGMOD Workshop on Research Issues in Data Mining and Knowledge Discovery, Dallas, Texas, 2000, p.p. 63–69.
13. J. I. Khan and Q. Tao, "Partial Prefetch for Faster Surfing in Composite Hypermedia", in Proc. of USITS 2001, San Francisco, California, USA, 2001.
14. T. Palpanas and A. Mendelzon, "Web Prefetching Using Partial Match Prediction". in Proc. of the Web Caching Workshop, San Diego, CA, USA, 1999.

# Compact Encoding of the Web Graph Exploiting Various Power Laws

## Statistical Reason Behind Link Database

Yasuhito Asano[1], Tsuyoshi Ito[2], Hiroshi Imai[2], Masashi Toyoda[3], and Masaru Kitsuregawa[3]

[1] Department of System Information Sciences, Tohoku University, 05 Aoba, Aramaki, Aoba-ku, Sendai, 980-8579 Japan

[2] Department of Computer Science, The University of Tokyo, 7-3-1 Hongo, Bunkyo-ku, Tokyo, 113-0033 Japan

[3] Institute of Industrial Science, The University of Tokyo, 4-6-1 Komaba, Meguro-ku, Tokyo, 153-8505 Japan

**Abstract.** Compact encodings of the web graph are required in order to keep the graph on main memory and to perform operations on the graph efficiently. Link2, the second version of the Link Database by Randall et al., which is part of the Connectivity Server, represented the adjacency list of each vertex by the variable-length nybble codes of delta values. In this paper, the fact is shown that certain variables related to the web graph have power distributions, and the reason is explained why using variable-length nybble codes in Link2 led to a compact representation of the graph from the statistical viewpoint on the basis of the relationship between power distributions and generalization of the variable-length nybble code. Besides, another encoding of the web graph based on these fact and relationship is proposed, and it is compared with Link2 and the encoding proposed by Guillaume et al. in 2002. Though our encoding is slower than Link2, it is 10% more compact than Link2. And our encoding is 20% more compact than the encoding proposed by Guillaume et al. and is comparable to it in terms of extraction time.

## 1 Introduction

The world wide web has evolved at a surprisingly high speed both in its size and in the variety of its content. The analyses of the structure of the web have become more and more important for the information retrieval from the web.

While the text and markups in each page contain vast amount of information, the structure of the hyperlinks among pages is often used extensively, both by itself [3,4] and in combination with the content of pages [5]. One of the reasons the link structure is useful for the information retrieval is that the meaning of links is usually independent of language: a link from a page $u$ to a page $v$ means the author of $u$ thinks $v$ has relevant or valuable information to $u$.

The abstraction of how pages are linked together is the web graph. The web graph is a directed graph whose vertices represent web pages and whose edges

G. Dong et al. (Eds.): WAIM 2003, LNCS 2762, pp. 37–46, 2003.

hyperlinks among them. Among the studies on the structure of the web graph are [1, 3, 4, 5]. The strong component decomposition is one method to describe the structure of the graph, and it requires the depth-first search of the graph. Other methods also require the operations on the graph.

When designing an algorithm to treat a large data like the web graph, one must be careful not only with its time complexity but also its space consumption. Once it requires more than the amount of the main memory available on the system, it usually requires much more time than when all the necessary data is on the main memory, sometimes to the extent that the algorithm itself becomes useless.

It is a good idea to encode the web graph in a compact format to keep it on the main memory. Though general compression algorithms such as bzip2 or gzip gives high compression ratio, they have one significant drawback: the extraction of small fragments of the data is slow. Usually many small fragments of the graph are needed for the operation on the graph such as the depth-first search. It is better to use the encoding methods which support the extraction of fragments as needed.

The web graph has several properties which distinguish itself from other graphs. One of them is "power law" about the distribution of the out-degrees and the in-degrees of vertices. By using these properties appropriately, a compact encoding method is obtained.

Let us review two previous studies on efficient encodings of the web graph: Link2 described in the citation [6] and the encoding proposed by Guillaume et al. [2]. They had a common point that pages were numbered sequencially in the lexicographical order of their URLs, and that the graph was represented by the list of the adjacency lists of all the vertices. They were different in the representation of the adjacency list of a vertex.

Now their difference will be described.

The Link Database [6] is part of the Connectivity Server which provides access to a large web graph, and Link2 is the second version of the Link Database. In Link2, each adjacency list was sorted in ascending order and represented by the list of the delta values of its elements. The delta value of the first element of the list is its difference from the source of the link, and the delta value of each of the other elements is the difference between its previous element and itself. They observed that the delta values tended to be close to zero, resulting from a kind of locality of the web graph that the destinations of the links originating at the same page are often near from each other. According to this observation, they used variable-length nybble codes to represent the delta values in their encoding of the web graph. By combining this representation with other techniques, Link2 encoded a graph in 11.03 bits per edge on average. The latest version Link3 used some other techniques to compress the whole graph to achieve less than 6 bits per edge. However, the compression techniques used in Link3 took longer time to decompress.

Guillaume et al. [2] proposed another compact encoding of the web graph. In their encoding, each element of an adjacency list was stored as a signed integers representing the length of the link, which is defined as the difference between the indices of the source and the destination pages of the link. The locality utilized here is that many links are short, which is more restricted than that utilized in Link2. They observed the length of a link had a power distribution. However, in their encoding, the length of a link was represented in either a Huffman code, 16-bit integer or 32-bit integer according to its absolute value, and the property of the power distribution was not utilized very much.

Our encoding utilizes the locality which is the same as that utilized by Link2, and the exact relationship between the distribution of the delta values of the adjacency lists and the optimal encoding of them.

The rest of this paper is organized as follows. Section 2 explains the fact that integers which have a power distribution are encoded most efficiently in a generalization of the variable-length nybble code. In section 3, the characteristics of web graph are described which were obtained from observation of an actual web graph, and the reason Link2 is efficient is explained. Section 4 proposes another encoding of the web graph according to our observation in the previous section. Sections 5 gives the details about and the results of the experiments to show the usefulness of the proposed encoding. Section 6 concludes this study.

## 2 Power Distribution and Variable-Length Block Codes

Let $\alpha > 1$. A random variable which takes positive integer values is said to have the power distribution of the exponent $-\alpha$ when its probability function $f(n)$ satisfies

$$f(n) = \frac{1}{cn^\alpha} \quad (n \geq 1) \quad \text{where } c = \sum_{n=1}^{\infty} \frac{1}{n^\alpha}.$$

Integers which have a power distribution are encoded efficiently in a generalization of the variable-length nybble code, which we call a *variable-length block code*. In the variable-length block code with $k$-bit blocks, a positive integer $n$ is first represented in the base $2^k$. Each digit in this base $2^k$ number is represented in $k$ bits. This $k$-bit sequence is called a *block*. A bit 1 is appended for each block except for the last block, for which a bit 0 is appended.

For example, an integer 92 is represented as 1011100 in binary, and it is represented as $01\underline{1}01\underline{1}11\underline{1}00\underline{0}$ in the variable-length block code with 2-bit blocks.

The variable-length block code with 3-bit blocks is called the *variable-length nybble code*. A "nybble" means a 4-bit-long sequence. The name of the variable-length nybble code comes from the fact that each block including the appended bit is four bits long.

A positive integer $n$ is represented in asymptotically $\big((k+1)/k\big) \log n$ bits long in the variable-length block code with $k$-bit blocks.

The following fact is obtained from Kraft's inequality about instantaneous codes: when a random variable $X$ has a probability function $f(X)$, the instantaneous code which gives the minimum average codeword length when used to represent $X$ is the code in which the codeword for $n$ is $-\log_2 f(n)$ bit long. Therefore, if $X$ has the power distribution of the exponent $-\alpha$, the most efficient instantaneous code in terms of average codeword length is the variable-length block code with $1/(\alpha - 1)$-bit blocks.

Note that Huffman encoding is the shortest instantaneous code only when we do not count the space needed to store the code table.

## 3 Observation of Actual Web Graph and Reason Behind Link2

We explained how delta values were used to encode the adjacency list of a vertex in Link2. Note that there are two different kinds of delta values. The delta value of the first element in a list is the difference between the source and the destination of the link, and the delta values of the rest are the differences between their previous elements and themselves. We call the delta value of the first element *initial distance*, and the delta values of the rest *increments*. Because initial distance and increment are different things, they may well have different distributions, hence different optimal representations.

To observe how the initial distances and increments in our encoding are distributed when used to represent an actual web graph, we analyzed Toyoda and Kitsuregawa's web graph [7] of pages in .jp domain collected in 2002, after removing pages whose URLs do not look like HTML files. This graph consists of 60,336,969 pages of 297,949 servers.

We extracted the subgraph representing each server from this graph, and analyzed the distributions of the absolute value of initial distance and of the value of increment independently. These subgraphs have 221,085,322 edges in total.

Figure 1 shows that the absolute value of initial distance has the power distribution with the exponent of about $-7/6$, and the increment has the power distribution with the exponent of about $-4/3$.

These facts mean initial distances and increments will be represented efficiently in the variable-length block codes with 6-bit and 3-bit blocks, respectively.

Because most delta values are actually increments, it is a good approximation to represent delta values altogether in the variable-length block codes with 3-bit blocks, a.k.a. the variable-length nybble codes. This is why the encoding used by Link2 is compact.

## 4 Proposed Encoding

As we saw in the previous section, the two kinds of delta values, namely initial distances and increments, have the power distributions of different exponents. By utilizing this fact and the distributions of other variables related to the web graph, a new encoding of the web graph is obtained.

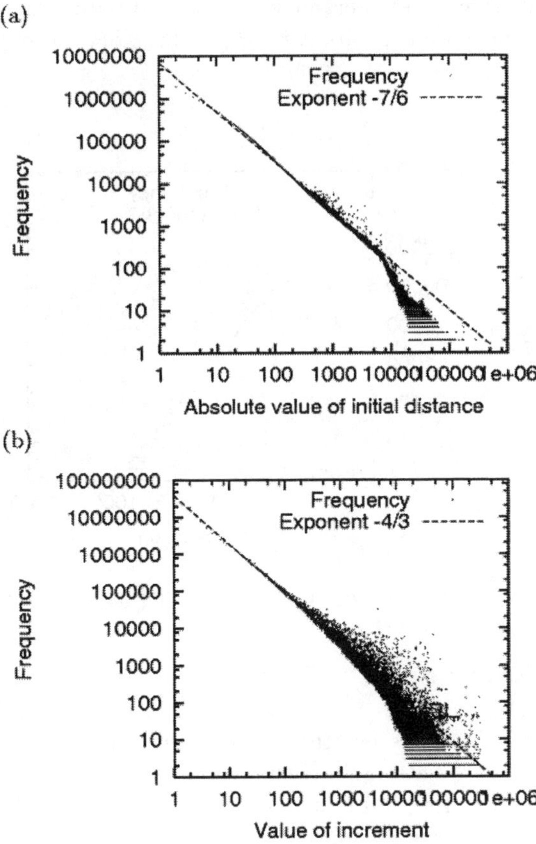


**Fig. 1.** The distributions of (a) initial distances and (b) increments. Both axes are in logarithmic scale.

A high-level description of our encoding is the same as that of Link2: pages are represented by sequence numbers in the lexicographical order of URLs, and the graph is represented by the list of the adjacency lists of all the vertices, where each adjacency list is sorted in ascending order and each element of an adjacency list is represented by its delta value. The difference lies in the way each delta value is represented.

According to the observation in the previous section, we propose the following encoding of the web graph.

*Encoding adjacency list of one vertex.* Suppose a vertex $v$ has out-degree $d$. Then the adjacency list of $v$ has one initial distance and the list of $(d-1)$ increments. Consecutive 1s in the list of increments are compressed using the run-length encoding.

We treat 1s in the list of increments specially because the increments of 1 appear frequently because they appear when a directory index page has links to all the files in that directory.

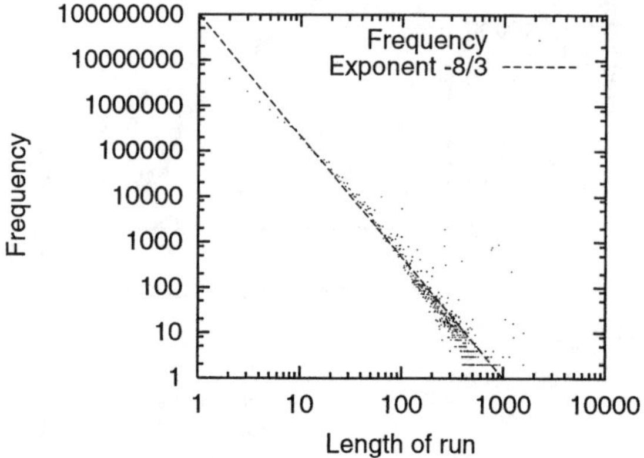


**Fig. 2.** The distributions of the length of the runs consisting of the increments of 1. Both axes are in logarithmic scale.

From the actual data, the lengths of these runs have the power distribution with the exponent of about $-8/3$ as shown in Figure 2. Because we now stick to instantaneous codes for simple and fast decoding, the best we can do is to represent them in the variable-length block code with 1-bit blocks.

As a result, this adjacency list is represented by its initial distance, followed by mixture of actual increments and run-lengths of increments of 1, followed by the end-of-list mark. The initial distance, the increments and the run-length are represented in the variable-length block codes with 6-bit, 3-bit and 1-bit blocks, respectively.

*Encoding a whole graph.* The number of vertices is represented in the variable-length block code with 3-bit blocks, and the adjacency lists of the vertices are represented using the encoding described above.

To make random access possible, a balanced binary tree $T$ with each leaf representing one adjacency list is used. Each subtree $T'$ of this binary tree is represented by the concatenation of the encodings of the left child tree of $T'$ and of the right child tree of $T'$, preceded by the length of the first part represented in the variable-length block code with 2-bit blocks. The whole graph is represented by the representation of $T$. This way, the adjacency list of a given vertex can be located in $O(\log n)$ time where $n$ is the number of the vertices of the graph.

Note that our encoding have four parameters: the lengths of blocks to represent initial distances, increments, run-lengths of the increments of 1, and the lengths of the representations of left-children of inner nodes of the binary tree

$T$. If another, slightly different graph has to be encoded, one can tune these parameters according to the actual graph.

## 5 Experiments, Results and Discussions

Experiments were performed to see how compact the proposed encoding method is and how efficient its decoding is.

The graphs used in them are Toyoda and Kitsuregawa's web graph divided into each server, as described in section 3.

### 5.1 Compression Ratio

The proposed encoding algorithm was implemented and the web graphs were encoded. Guillaume et al.'s encoding with Huffman codes was also implemented and the results were compared.

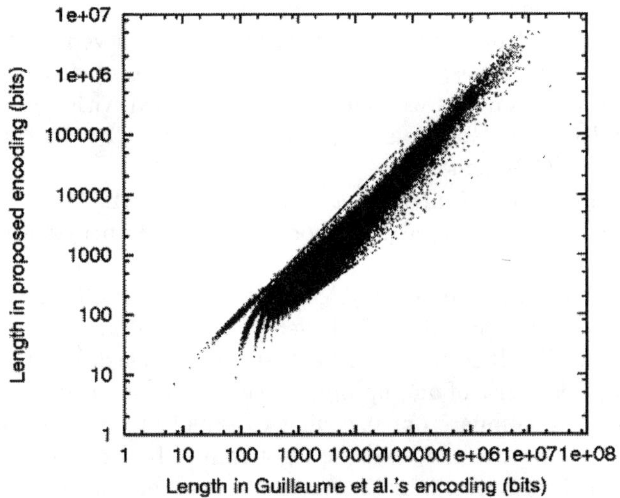


**Fig. 3.** The comparison of the compactness of Guillaume et al.'s encoding with Huffman codes and that of the proposed encoding. Both axes are in logarithmic scale.

Figure 3 shows the result of the comparison. Our encoding produced 9.7 bits per edge on average while Guillaume et al.'s produced 27.0 bits per edge. These numbers have to be treated with care. In our method, the length of blocks of variable-length block codes of integers were adjusted to produce the best result for our dataset, while Guillaume et al.'s was used as it was with Huffman code table adjusted to be optimal.

It may be fair to compare the number of bits our method produced per edge for our dataset with the number of bits their method produced per edge for their dataset. In the citation [2], their encoding with Huffman codes produced 12.3 bits per edge. Compared to this figure, our method gives 20% less number of bits per edge than Guillaume et al.'s.

According to the citation [6], Link2 produced 11.03 bits per edge on average when used to encode their dataset with 61 million vertices and 1 billion edges. Compared to this, our encoding produces 10% shorter encoding.

From these observation, the proposed encoding successfully utilized a wide range of locality the web graph has and the distributions of various variables related to the web graph including initial distances and increments, and these facts resulted in a better compression ratio than Guillaume et al.'s method and Link2.

### 5.2 Extraction Time

A corresponding decoding algorithm for the proposed encoding method was implemented and the time taken by the depth-first search on the encoded web graphs was measured. The comparison with the case using Guillaume et al.'s encoding with Huffman codes was also performed.

For each graph, depth-first search starting from each vertex was performed to visit every vertex at least once and follow every edge exactly once.

Benchmark program was written in C++, compiled with GNU C++ Compiler 3.0.1 and executed on Solaris 2.6 on Sun Ultra 60 with UltraSPARC-II 360Hz CPU and 1GB memory.

Figure 4 shows that Guillaume et al.'s and our method are comparable in extraction time. Guillaume et al.'s method took 5.1 $\mu$sec. per edge and ours took 3.5 $\mu$sec. per edge.

This means that the use of variable-length block codes did not impact time needed to decode adjacency lists of the vertices of the graph compared to Guillaume et al.'s method. It seems this is because most of the decoding time is taken to find the adjacency list of an appropriate vertex in the balanced binary tree.

It is difficult to compare our encoding to Link2 in terms of the extraction time because we have not executed the algorithm of Link2 on our environment. However, at our best guess, Link2 is faster than our encoding because Link2 is fixed for the variable-length nybble code. The variable-length nybble code can be decoded faster than general variable-length block codes because in the variable-length nybble code, it is sufficient to simply split one byte into two nybbles to extract blocks, while in general variable-length block codes, operations on bit by bit are needed.

## 6 Conclusion

It was clarified that the compact encoding by Link2 came from the fact that the delta values of the adjacency lists had the power distribution with the exponent of about $-4/3$ by observing the actual data. Furthermore, it was found that the initial distances and the increments had the power distributions of the different

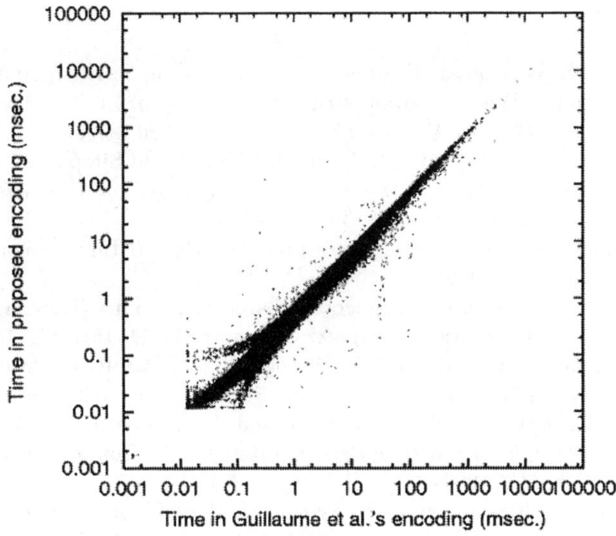


**Fig. 4.** The comparison of the time taken by the depth-first search of the graphs encoded in Guillaume et al.'s method with Huffman codes and that in the proposed method. Both axes are in logarithmic scale.

exponents. By using the distributions of initial distances, increments and other variables, we obtained another compact encoding of the web graph. Especially, the connection between power distributions and variable encodings has turned to be useful to encode the web graph efficiently.

The qualitative comparison of our method with Link2 and Link3 in terms of compression ratio and extraction time is yet to be performed.

Widely-known "power law" about the distribution of the out-degrees and the in-degrees of vertices is not used in our method. Using it and the distribution of other variables may lead to more efficient encoding method.

Our method has several parameters and it has hopefully application to other kinds of graphs than the web graphs. The optimal parameters of the variable encodings used in the method may be different for different kinds of graphs. Currently, to adopt our method to other kinds of graphs, it is required to tune the parameters by observing the distributions of initial distances and increments of the actual graph. However, our method have few parameters and the tuning will be easier than encodings with more parameters. The general discussion for usefulness and optimal parameters of our method to other kinds of graphs needs more experiments using different graphs.

## References

1. A. Z. Broder, S. R. Kumar, F. Maghoul, P. Raghavan, S. Rajagopalan, R. Stata, A. Tomkins and J. Wiener. Graph structure in the web. In *Proceedings of the 9th International World Wide Web Conference*, pp. 309–320, 2000.
2. J.-L. Guillaume, M. Latapy and L. Viennot. Efficient and Simple Encodings for the Web Graph. In *Proc. the 3rd International Conference on Web-Age Information Management, LNCS 2419*, pp. 328–337, 2002.
3. J. M. Kleinberg. Authoritative Sources in a Hyperlinked Environment. *Journal of ACM*, **46**(5):604–632, 1999.
4. S. R. Kumar, P. Raghavan, S. Rajagopalan and A. Tomkins. Trawling the Web for Emerging Cybercommunities. *Computer Networks*, **31**(11–16):1481–1493, 1999.
5. L. Page, S. Brin, R. Motwani and T. Winograd. The PageRank Citation Ranking: Bring Order to the Web. Technical Report, Stanford University, 1998.
6. K. Randall, R. Stata, R. Wickremesinghe and J. L. Wiener. The Link Database: Fast Access to Graphs of the Web. Research Report 175, Compaq Systems Research Center, Palo Alto, CA, 2001.
7. M. Toyoda and M. Kitsuregawa. Observing evolution of Web communities. In *Poster Proceedings of the 11th International World Wide Web Conference (WWW2002)*, 2002.

# Improving the Web Site's Effectiveness by Considering Each Page's Temporal Information*

Zhigang Li[1], Ming-Tan Sun[1], Margaret H. Dunham[1], and Yongqiao Xiao[2]

[1] Dept. of Computer Science and Engineering, Southern Methodist University Dallas, TX 75275-0122, USA
{zgli,msun,mhd}@engr.smu.edu

[2] Dept. of Math and Computer Science, Georgia College & State University Milledgeville, GA 31061, USA
{yxiao}@gcsu.edu

**Abstract.** Improving the effectiveness of a web site is always one of its owner's top concerns. By focusing on analyzing web users' visiting behavior, web mining researchers have developed a variety of helpful methods, based upon association rules, clustering, prediction and so on. However, we have found little attention has been spent in studying the temporal property associated with each page at a given web site, which, under our investigation, in fact has stored valuable information that could disclose extra useful user behaving knowledge. In this paper we study and propose a new web mining technique – temporal web log mining – by taking frequently-overlooked temporal information regarding each page of a given web site into account and integrating it with human heuristics. The discovered temporal web patterns then could be used to improve the web site's effectiveness.

## 1 Introduction

Nowadays explosive emergence of web sites inevitably poses a serious, if not the most, challenge to their owners. That is, how they can design their web sites more effectively so as to attract more users. Depending on different situations, the term "effective" could have a variety of meanings. For example, an effective commercial web site, compared to its competitors, should be good at attracting more people to hang around, making them stay longer and turning more of them into profitable customers. While for a research institute, its web site is supposed to possess a friendly and comfortable browsing structure where a web user can easily find the desired information at pages he/she has expected.

Data mining researchers have been making their contribution by conducting comprehensive studies mining the web, such as web log mining [7,9], collaborative filtering [5], association rules [6], clustering [4], prediction [8] and so on. We also originally stepped into this field by proposing an efficient algorithm [10] to mine web traversal patterns.

* This work is supported by NSF under Grant No. IIS-9820841 and IIS-0208741.

G. Dong et al. (Eds.): WAIM 2003, LNCS 2762, pp. 47–54, 2003.

Although all the above work has proven very useful, recently we have begun to notice in web logs there is still some extra information that is often overlooked and deserves further investigation. For example, our survey indicates that people normally pay no attention to the temporal information associated with each page. They don't care about how long a web user may stay at each page in his/her traversal path and most of time this kind of staying-time information is simply discarded in the log cleansing stage. However, staying-time in our eyes could be taken as another effective way to measure the user's subjective preference to each page he/she has visited, which is due to the following intuitive thought – *normally a user tends to stay longer at those pages that interest him/her during the browsing period* (of course we need to exclude the chance that the user is idling before the computer).

Based upon this intuitive thought we propose a new web log mining technique by taking temporal information of each web page, called "staying-time", into account and further discover extra useful knowledge hidden in web logs. We will first quickly go back over some of the related work in Section 2, then formalize the problem and the algorithm in Section 3, and then present some experiment results in Section 4 before finally conclude the paper in Section 5.

## 2 Related Work

While working on recommender system Mobasher et al. proposed a scalable framework [6] making use of association rules mined from web logs. They viewed each transaction as a set of pageviews $s_t = \{p_i^t | 1 \leq i \leq l \text{ and } w(p_i^t) = 1\}$ where $p_i^t$ stands for a page of the web site while $w(p_i^t)$ is a binary value meaning there was a certain kind of action (1) or not (0). In other words, they only cared about the page where there was an event happening, such as purchasing a product or accessing a document, while were pretty nonchalant to other pages, disregarding that maybe quite a few users had stayed at these pages for a sufficiently long time.

Similar to Mobasher's work, Yun and Chen extended the normal web pattern mining by considering all items purchased along the access path [11]. They defined a transaction pattern as $< s_1 s_2 ... s_y : n_1\{i_1\}, n_2\{i_2\}, ..., n_x\{i_x\} >$ where $i_1, ..., i_x$ are items purchased and $\{n_1, n_2, ..., n_x\} \subseteq \{s_1, s_2, ..., s_y\} \subseteq$ {all pages at the web site}. Their defect is the same – only focusing on user traversal path with items already purchased and missing those from potential customers.

So far the best work we have found showing the appropriate respect to the time spent at each page was presented in [3]. While working on search engine page ranking algorithm, Ding et al. noticed that the page relevance could not be judged appropriately by counting its selection frequency. They argued and demonstrated that the relevance could be better measured by considering the time duration at each page and linkage structure analysis. Their approach once again confirms our thought – the staying-time at each page is very helpful in disclosing users' traversal behavior and could be used to contribute to mining more knowledge from web logs.

## 3 Mining Log with Temporal Information

In this section we are going to present the detailed problem and mining algorithm. Since the staying-time is one of our focuses, how to retrieve it accurately becomes the first problem. But, as mentioned in the literature, there have been other tricky concerns, like efficiency, securiy and privacy, due to the existence of web proxies, cookies, etc. For the space and time limitation, we will not dwell on these issues and just follow the common practice discussed in [2,8]. For example, we assume page accessing from the same IP address is looked as from the same user and a session is automatically terminated provided the next access from the same user is more than 1800 seconds later. For staying-time, intuitively we take it as the difference between two accesses from the same user in the current session. For the last page accessed in a given session, its staying-time has to be estimated – it is assumed uniformly distributed based upon the staying-time of its immediately preceding page. The advantage of taking this estimation is that we thus will not confront some eccentrically long staying-time that may last more than 1800 seconds.

### 3.1 Problem Formulation

With appropriately cleansed and identified web sessions in hand, we are ready to define temporal web log mining as follows. Suppose $\mathcal{P} = \{p_1, p_2, ..., p_n\}$ is the set of all pages at the web site where $p_i (i = 1, 2, ..., n) \in \mathbf{Z}^+$. Also $\mathcal{S} = \{s_1, s_2, ..., s_m\}$ is the set of all identified sessions where $s_i$ is composed of a sequence of pairs $< p_i, t >_s$, which are interpreted as "in the $s_{th}$ session a user has stayed at page $p_i$ for $t$ seconds". Since all sessions are treated equally and the relative order doesn't matter at all, the subscript session number $s$ is normally neglected and we will use $< p_i, t >_s$ and $< p_i, t >$ interchangeably in the following context when no ambiguity arises.

**Definition 1.** *A* ***temporal web pattern*** *is defined as* $\{< p_{i_1}, t_{i_1} >, < p_{i_2}, t_{i_2} >, ..., < p_{i_l}, t_{i_l} >\}$ *where* $p_{i_j} \in \mathcal{P}$ *and* $0 \leq t_{i_j} \leq 1800$ $(j = 1, 2, ..., l)$. *Based on that, a* ***frequent temporal web pattern*** *is a temporal web pattern where* $\sum_{w=1}^{l} t_{i_w} \geq t_{minimal}$ *and* $|\widetilde{S}| \geq support_{overall} \times |\mathcal{S}|$. *Here* $\widetilde{S} \subseteq \mathcal{S}$ *and is composed of all* $s_j (\in \mathcal{S})$ *for which* $\{p_{i_1}, p_{i_2}, ..., p_{i_l}\} \subseteq \{p_{j_1}, p_{j_2}, ..., p_{j_{|s_j|}}\}$ *and* $\sum_{w=1}^{l} t_{i_w} \geq support_{local} \times \sum_{w=1}^{|s_j|} t_{j_w}$. $support_{overall}$, $support_{local}$ *and* $t_{minimal}$ *are three given threshold parameters. Then a* ***maximal temporal web pattern*** *is a frequent temporal web pattern that is not contained in any other frequent temporal web pattern found in S. In other words, suppose* $\{< p_{i_1}, t_{i_1} >, < p_{i_2}, t_{i_2} >, ..., < p_{i_u}, t_{i_u} >\}$ *is a maximal temporal web pattern, then there cannot be another frequent temporal web pattern* $\{< p_{j_1}, t_{j_1} >, < p_{j_2}, t_{j_2} >, ..., < p_{j_v}, t_{j_v} >\}$ *such that* $\{p_{i_1}, p_{i_2}, ..., p_{i_u}\} \subset \{p_{j_1}, p_{j_2}, ..., p_{j_v}\}$.

Please notice that, although the temporal web pattern $\{< p_{i_1}, t_{i_1} >, < p_{i_2}, t_{i_2} >, ..., < p_{i_l}, t_{i_l} >\}$ looks somehow similar to the web transaction defined in [6], they are two totally different definitions. [6] only cared about the page where there was a pre-defined event happening, such as purchasing a product, by throwing out any others; and all kept pages are considered indiscriminatingly. But in our definition we keep every page and its associated temporal information in hand, which enables us to treat each page individually and pay more attention to those more interesting. The same analysis can be easily applied to tell the difference between Yun and Chen's [11] and ours.

**Definition 2.** *For given threshold parameters,* ***temporal web log mining*** *is to find all maximal temporal web pattern* $\{< p_{i_1}, t_{i_1} >, < p_{i_2}, t_{i_2} >, ..., < p_{i_l}, t_{i_l} >\}$ *from* $\mathcal{S}$. *Multiple maximal temporal web patterns with the identical page access sequence and similar staying-time could be merged to make pattern obvious.*

By the way, in our experience, human heuristics is also very important in making the whole mining process more effective. For instance, the web site owner is usually a domain expert for the site content and knows better if a user is really interested in a certain page, based upon evaluating his/her action, like typing in some feedback, clicking on a related link, accessing a designated document, etc. It is therefore beneficial to take these heuristics into the temporal web log mining, as shown in the following definition.

**Definition 3.** *A* ***user event*** *is a pre-defined action happening at a page, such as purchasing a product, downloading a software, accessing a document, etc., which further demonstrates the user's interest in this page. Temporal web log mining will also find the maximal temporal web pattern* $\{< p_{i_1}, t_{i_1} >, < p_{i_2}, t_{i_2} >, ..., < p_{i_l}, t_{i_l} >\}$, *provided 1)* $\exists\, p_{i_x} (x = 1, 2, ..., l)$ *and the user event has happened at* $p_{i_x}$, *and 2)* $|\overline{\mathcal{S}}| \geq support_{overall} \times |\mathcal{S}|$, *where* $\overline{\mathcal{S}} \subseteq \mathcal{S}$ *and is composed of all* $s_j (\in \mathcal{S})$ *for which* $\{p_{i_1}, p_{i_2}, ..., p_{i_l}\} \subseteq \{p_{j_1}, p_{j_2}, ..., p_{j_{|s_j|}}\}$.

### 3.2 Mining Algorithm

In this section we sketch the algorithm for temporal web log mining, followed by an illustrative example showing how it works. In the algorithm we will employ a suffix-tree based OAT$_{temporal}$ algorithm, which actually is an extension of the efficient online and adaptive algorithm suggested in our previous work [10] and extended here by taking extra staying-time of each page into account.

**Algorithm** (Temporal Web Log Mining)
**Input:**
  $\mathcal{S}$; // all cleansed sessions
  $support_{overall}, support_{local}, t_{minimal}$; // threshold parameters
  $user\_event$; // human heuristics
**Output:**
  $PS$; // set of all found maximal temporal web patterns;
**Begin:**
  // find maximal web patterns in $\mathcal{S}$ by temporarily focusing only on
  // web pages themselves and disregarding associated temporal information

```
OAT_temporal(S, support_overall);
// consider both staying-time and user event, and scan all maximal
// frequent sequences once to find maximal temporal web patterns
PS = 0; // initialization
For each found maximal frequent sequence {<p_{i1}, t_{i1}>, ..., <p_{il}, t_{il}>}
   If user_event ≠ 0 and has happened at one of the pages
      Generate S̄; // as defined in Definition 3
      If |S̄| > support_overall × |S|
         // record the maximal temporal web pattern
         PS+ = {<p_{i1}, t_{i1}>, <p_{i2}, t_{i2}>, ..., <p_{il}, t_{il}>};
   Else
      sum = Σ_{w=1}^{l} t_{iw}; // t_{iw} is the associated staying-time with p_{il}
      Generate S̃; // as defined in Definition 1
      // check if temporal requirement is satisfied
      If sum > t_minimal and |S̃| > support_overall × |S|
         PS+ = {<p_{i1}, t_{i1}>, <p_{i2}, t_{i2}>, ..., <p_{il}, t_{il}>};
   Output PS;
End.
```

Let's look at the following example scenario to see how this algorithm works. Suppose for a mini web site containing only 10 pages there are 5 identified sessions, as shown in Table 1. Also suppose $support_{overall} = 40\%$, $support_{local} = 20\%$ and $t_{minimal} = 400s$.

**Table 1.** Sample user sessions

| Session No. | Page Access Info |
|---|---|
| $s_1$ | $\{< p_1, 80 >, < p_3, 100 >, < p_4, 80 >, < p_5, 100 >, < p_6, 200 >, < p_7, 300 >\}$ |
| $s_2$ | $\{< p_1, 10 >, < p_2, 50 >, < p_3, 50 >, < p_4, 40 >, < p_6, 100 >, < p_8, 100 >\}$ |
| $s_3$ | $\{< p_1, 30 >, < p_8, 300 >, < p_9, 600 >, < p_{10}, 200 >, < p_9, 900 >\}$ |
| $s_4$ | $\{< p_6, 500 >, < p_7, 350 >, < p_1, 50 >, < p_3, 30 >\}$ |
| $s_5$ | $\{< p_5, 200 >, < p_7, 150 >, < p_8, 60 >, < p_9, 30 >, < p_2, 1600 >\}$ |

By applying OAT$_{temporal}$ algorithm first, we can find the following maximal web patterns, including $\{< p_1, 80 >, < p_3, 100 >, < p_4, 80 >, < p_6, 200 >\}_1$, $\{< p_1, 10 >, < p_3, 50 >, < p_4, 40 >, < p_6, 100 >\}_2$, $\{< p_6, 200 >, < p_7, 300 >\}_1$, $\{< p_6, 500 >, < p_7, 350 >\}_4$, $\{< p_8, 300 >, < p_9, 600 >\}_3$ and $\{< p_8, 60 >, < p_9, 30 >\}_5$. Considering $support_{local}$ and $t_{minimal}$, scanning all discovered maximal frequent sequences and generating the corresponding $\widetilde{\mathcal{S}}$ or $\overline{\mathcal{S}}$, we can obtain $\mathcal{PS} = \{\{< p_1, 80 >, < p_3, 100 >, < p_4, 80 >, < p_6, 200 >\}_1, \{< p_6, 200 >, < p_7, 300 >\}_1, \{< p_6, 500 >, < p_7, 350 >\}_4, \{< p_8, 300 >, < p_9, 600 >\}_3\}$.

Then useful knowledge could be derived as follows. For example, combining the second pattern $\{< p_6, 200 >, < p_7, 300 >\}_1$ and the third one $\{< p_6, 500 >, < p_7, 350 >\}_4$ tells us after hanging around at page $p_6$ for a while a user might still show strong interests in page $p_7$. Then the web site owner could insert another page between them to somehow force the user to stop by the new one before reaching $p_7$, which can reasonably convey more information to the user and make him/her stay longer at this site without much confusion or distraction. If it is further learnt there were quite a lot user events, like product-purchasing and document-downloading, happening at page $p_6$ but only few at page $p_7$, in spite of the fact that page $p_7$ also looks very interesting and many similar events are supposed to happen there, we might infer there was something abnormal with page $p_7$, possibly due to the poor design, wrong links, and so on, which could trigger further investigation and correction if needed.

## 4 Some Initial Experiments

We have conducted some experiments based upon the web logs garnered from the web server of School of Engineering in our university, which spanned 28 months, from August 1999 to December 2001. The web logs were approximately 7.4 GB in its raw format and 230 MB after cleansing. The session identification was then processed by following the discussion in previous log preparation section, which generated 2,814,234 sessions that included 9,081,128 page accesses totally. By the way, it's also concluded there were 953,289 users from different sources visiting 48,973 different pages at this web server.

After log preparation, the staying-time distribution in all sessions was plotted in Figure 1. But, we first filtered out the staying-time from those short sessions, which contain only one or two pages. The reason was simple, we either could not estimate the staying-time (for the one-page session) or the uniformly distributed estimation would take up to half of the whole temporal information and be too dominant in our eyes (for the two-page session). All other longer sessions were kept and the whole time scope (between 0 sec and 30 min) was divided unevenly into 10 consecutive spans, which we believed could better characterize users' behavior.

This plot disclosed a lot to us. The somewhat high percentage of short staying-time (less than 5 seconds) could be rationally explained by considering that most people just stayed briefly at hub pages with high access frequency (like homepages of each department, research lab, faculty, student or some other indexing pages), whose major function is to guide users to go ahead and find other pages in which they are interested. Moreover, if we could combine the four time spans in the middle (from 1 to 20 minute(s)), that would generate a time span that covered a page's staying-time with more-than-half probability (52%) with the least number of consecutive time spans (4). Such heuristic information could be used to help us decide if staying-at-a-page was from an interested user (who didn't leave quickly or idled for a relative long time), set reasonable initial value to threshold parameter like $t_{minimal}$, or merge similar maximal temporal web patterns.

With varying threshold parameters we mined the web logs after sessions had all been identified. For example, in line with the staying-time distribution

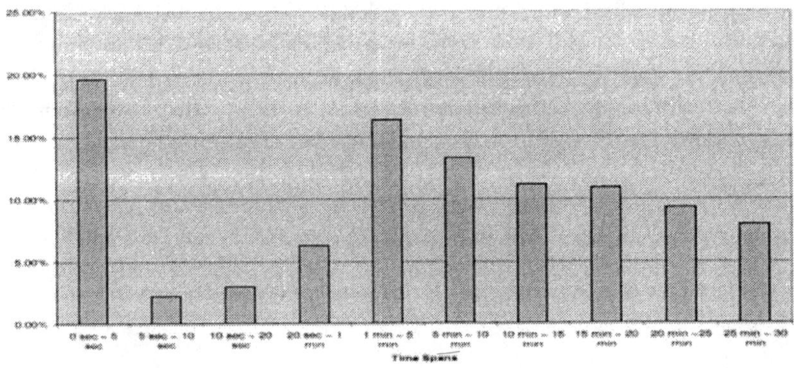

**Fig. 1.** Page access staying-time distribution in all sessions

(in Figure 1) we normally required that a page could not be regarded as effective unless its staying-time was longer than 2 minutes. In addition, considering it's getting harder and harder to interpret the meaning of discovered maximal temporal web patterns as the number of effective pages in them increases, we limited our attention to those patterns with at most 5 effective pages. Therefore $t_{minimal}$ was assumed between 2 and 10 minutes while $support_{overall}$ and $support_{local}$ were normally varied from 5% and 30%, or a little bit higher.

The results were quite encouraging and some interesting web patterns and concerned knowledge stood out with staying-time taken into account. For example, there was a maximal temporal web pattern that contained the department course introduction page, the concerned faculty's homepage, and the old courses (including syllabus and homework) he/she offered previously. Staying-time of the first and the third pages was quite long, normally lasting for several minutes, while the faculty's homepage's staying-time was pretty short. Then we concluded if the faculty wanted to enroll more students to his/her new course, he/she should highlight it somehow at his/her homepage in case students missed it since normally they went to old courses very quickly. By the way, another observation astonishing to us in this pattern was that, although students normally jumped from course introduction page to faculty's homepage, there was no link between them. Thus a favorable modification should be to connect the course introduction with its designated teaching faculty, whenever possible, to facilitate browsing. Such an improvement discovery further verifies our approach's advantage as discussed in the previous section.

## 5 Conclusion

In this paper we have proposed a new web log mining technique – temporal web log mining – which takes the staying-time of each page into account. By introducing this temporal information we could further extend the common web patten mining and find more useful knowledge hidden in web logs. The importance of staying-time was also well argued and supported in previous related work [3,1].

The introduction of temporal information is only a promising trial of our ongoing web mining research projects. We are also planning to apply it to some running commercial web sites, which we believe should be the best proof to this new approach. Our future work will focus on integrating other techniques, like session generalization [4], web page size consideration, to make this new approach more flexible and comprehensive. A more efficient on-the-fly mining algorithm is well under investigation.

## References


1. B. Berendt, B. Mobasher, M. Spiliopoulou, and M. Nakagawa. The impact of site structure and user environment on session reconstruction in web usage analysis. In *Proceedings of the 4th WebKDD Workshop*, 2002.
2. R. Cooley, B. Mobasher, and J. Srivastava. Data preparation for mining world wide web browsing patterns. *Journal of Knowledge and Informatino*, 1999.
3. C. Ding, C. H. Chi, and T. Luo. An improved usage-based ranking. In *Proceedings of 2002 Web-Age Information Management Conference (WAIM)*, 2002.
4. Y. Fu, K. Sandhu, and M. Y. Shih. Fast clustering of web users based on navigation patterns. In *Proceedings of 1999 World Multiconference on Systemics, Cybernetics and Informatics (SCI/ISAS)*, 1999.
5. J. Herlocker, J. Konstan, and J. Riedl. Explaining collaborative filtering recommendations. In *Proceedings of 2000 ACM Conference on Computer Supported Cooperative Work*, 2000.
6. B. Mobasher, H. Dai, T. Luo, and M. Nakagawa. Effective personalization based on association rule discovery from web usage data. In *Proceedings of 2001 ACM Workshop on Web Information and Data Management (WIDM)*, 2001.
7. J. Pei, J. Han, B. Mortazavi-Asl, and H. Zhu. Mining access patterns efficiently from web logs. In *Proceedings of 2000 Pacific-Asia Conference on Knowledge Discovery and Data Mining (PAKDD)*, 2000.
8. S. Schechter, M. Krishnan, and M. Smith. Using path profiles to predict http request. In *Proceedings of 1998 International World Wide Web Conference*, 1998.
9. R. Srikant and Y. Yang. Mining web logs to improve website organization. In *Proceedings of 2001 International World Wide Web Conference (WWW)*, 2001.
10. Y. Xiao and M. H. Dunham. Efficient mining of traversal patterns. *Data & Knowledge Engineering*, 39(2):191–214, 2001.
11. C. H. Yun and M. S. Chen. Mining web transaction patterns in an electronic commerce environment. In *Proceedings of 2000 Pacific-Asia Conference on Knowledge Discovery and Data Mining (PAKDD)*, 2000.

# Redundancy Free Mappings from Relations to XML

Millist W. Vincent, Jixue Liu, and Chengfei Liu

School of Computer and Information Science
University of South Australia
{millist.vincent, jixue.liu, chengfei.liu }@unisa.edu.au

**Abstract.** Given the fact that relational and object-relational databases are the most widely used technology for storing data and that XML is the standard format used in electronic data interchange, the process of converting relational data to XML documents is one that occurs frequently. The problem that we address in this paper is an important one related to this process. If we convert a relation to an XML document, under what circumstances is the XML document redundancy free? Drawing on some previous work by the authors that formally defined functional dependencies and redundancy in XML documents, we show that for a very general class of mappings from a relation to an XML document, the XML document is always redundancy free if and only if the relation is in Boyce-Codd normal form (BCNF).

## 1 Introduction

The eXtensible Markup Language (XML) [5] has recently emerged as a standard for data representation and interchange on the Internet [14,1]. As a result of this and the fact that relational and object-relational databases are the standard technology in commercial applications, the issue of converting relational data to XML data is one that frequently occurs. In this conversion process of relational data to XML data, there many different ways that relational data can be mapped to XML data, especially considering the flexible nesting structures that XML allows. This gives rise to the following important problem. Are some mappings 'better' than others? Firstly, one has to make precise what is meant by 'better'. In this paper we extend the classical approach used in relational database design and regard a good design as one which eliminates redundancy. The relationship between normal forms and redundancy elimination has been investigated, both for the relational case [11,8,10] and the nested relational case [2], and in particular it has been shown that *Boyce-Codd normal form* (BCNF) [7] is a necessary and sufficient condition for the elimination of redundancy in relations when the only constraints are *functional dependencies* (FDs). However, this approach to determining good database designs depends on having FDs defined in relations. In some recent work [12,13], we showed how to extend the definition of FDs in relations to FDs in XML (*called XFDs*). Since this current

G. Dong et al. (Eds.): WAIM 2003, LNCS 2762, pp. 55–67, 2003.

paper depends heavily on this work, we first outline the contributions of this previous work.

The definition of an XFD was proposed in [12,13] and justified formally by showing that for a very general class of mappings from a relation to an XML document, a relation satisfies a unary FD (only one attribute on the l.h.s. of the FD) if and only if the corresponding XML document satisfies the corresponding XFD. Thus there is a natural correspondence between FDs in relations and XFDs in XML documents. The other contributions of [12] were firstly to define a set of axioms for reasoning about the implication of XFDs and to show that the axioms are sound for arbitrary XFDs. The final contribution was to define a normal form, based on a modification of the one proposed in [3], and prove that it is a necessary and sufficient condition for the elimination of redundancy in an XML document.

In this paper we address the following problem. Suppose we are given a single relation and wish to map it to an XML document. There are many such mappings and in particular a deeply nested structure, rather than a flat structure, may be chosen because it better represents the semantics of the data. We then want to determine what mappings result in the XML document being redundancy free. Knowing this is important for systems designers because they would obviously wish to avoid mappings which result in the introduction of redundancy to the XML document. The class of mappings that we consider is a very general class of mappings from a relation into an XML document first proposed in [12,13]. The class takes a relation, first converts it into a nested relation by allowing an *arbitrary* sequence of nest operations and then converts the nested relation into an XML document. This is a very general class of mappings and we believe that it covers all the types of mappings that are likely to occur in practice. The main result of the paper then shows that, for the case where all FDs in the relation are unary, any mapping from the general class of mappings from a relation to an XML document will always be redundancy free if and only if the relation is in BCNF. This result is of reassurance to system designers because it allows them a great degree of flexibility in determining how to map a relation into an XML document, and thus they can make their mapping decision on other criteria apart from eliminating redundancy. We also note, importantly, that if the relation is not in BCNF, then some mappings in the general class considered produce redundancy free XML documents, whereas others produce XML documents with redundancy.

## 2 Preliminary Definitions

In this section we present some preliminary definitions that we need before defining XFDs. We model an XML document as a tree as follows.

**Definition 1.** *Assume a countably infinite set* $\mathbf{E}$ *of element labels (tags), a countable infinite set* $\mathbf{A}$ *of attribute names and a symbol* $S$ *indicating text. An* XML tree *is defined to be* $T = (V, lab, ele, att, val, v_r)$ *where* $V$ *is a* finite *set of nodes in* $T$*;* $lab$ *is a function from* $V$ *to* $\mathbf{E} \cup \mathbf{A} \cup \{S\}$*;* $ele$ *is a partial function* *from $V$ to a sequence of $V$ nodes such that for any $v \in V$, if $ele(v)$ is defined then $lab(v) \in \mathbf{E}$; att is a partial function from $V \times \mathbf{A}$ to $V$ such that for any $v \in V$ and $l \in \mathbf{A}$, if $att(v,l) = v_1$ then $lab(v) \in \mathbf{E}$ and $lab(v_1) = l$; val is a function such that for any node in $v \in V, val(v) = v$ if $lab(v) \in \mathbf{E}$ and $val(v)$ is a string if either $lab(v) = S$ or $lab(v) \in \mathbf{A}$; $v_r$ is a distinguished node in $V$ called the root of $T$ and we define $lab(v_r) = root$. Since node identifiers are unique, a consequence of the definition of val is that if $v_1 \in \mathbf{E}$ and $v_2 \in \mathbf{E}$ and $v_1 \neq v_2$ then $val(v_1) \neq val(v_2)$. We also extend the definition of val to sets of nodes and if $V_1 \subseteq V$, then $val(V_1)$ is the set defined by $val(V_1) = \{val(v) | v \in V_1\}$.*

*For any $v \in V$, if $ele(v)$ is defined then the nodes in $ele(v)$ are called* subelements *of $v$. For any $l \in \mathbf{A}$, if $att(v,l) = v_1$ then $v_1$ is called an* attribute *of $v$. Note that an XML tree $T$ must be a tree. Since $T$ is a tree the set of ancestors of a node $v$, is denoted by $Ancestor(v)$. The children of a node $v$ are also defined as in Definition 1 and we denote the parent of a node $v$ by $Parent(v)$.*

We note that our definition of *val* differs slightly from that in [6] since we have extended the definition of the *val* function so that it is also defined on element nodes. The reason for this is that we want to include in our definition paths that do not end at leaf nodes, and when we do this we want to compare element nodes by node identity, i.e. node equality, but when we compare attribute or text nodes we want to compare them by their contents, i.e. value equality. This point will become clearer in the examples and definitions that follow.

We now give some preliminary definitions related to paths.

**Definition 2.** *A* path *is an expression of the form $l_1.\cdots.l_n$, $n \geq 1$, where $l_i \in \mathbf{E} \cup \mathbf{A} \cup \{S\}$ for all $i, 1 \leq i \leq n$ and $l_1 = root$. If $p$ is the path $l_1.\cdots.l_n$ then $Last(p) = l_n$.*

For instance, if $\mathbf{E}$ = {`root, Division, Employee`} and $\mathbf{A}$ = {`D#, Emp#`} then `root, root.Division, root.Division.D#,` `root.Division.Employee.Emp#.S` are all paths.

**Definition 3.** *Let $p$ denote the path $l_1.\cdots.l_n$. The function $Parnt(p)$ is the path $l_1.\cdots.l_{n-1}$. Let $p$ denote the path $l_1.\cdots.l_n$ and let $q$ denote the path $q_1.\cdots.q_m$. The path $p$ is said to be a* prefix *of the path $q$, denoted by $p \subseteq q$, if $n \leq m$ and $l_1 = q_1, \ldots, l_n = q_n$. Two paths $p$ and $q$ are equal, denoted by $p = q$, if $p$ is a prefix of $q$ and $q$ is a prefix of $p$. The path $p$ is said to be a* strict prefix *of $q$, denoted by $p \subset q$, if $p$ is a prefix of $q$ and $p \neq q$. We also define the intersection of two paths $p_1$ and $p_2$, denoted but $p_1 \cap p_2$, to be the maximal common prefix of both paths. It is clear that the intersection of two paths is also a path.*

For example, if $\mathbf{E}$ = {`root, Division, Employee`} and $\mathbf{A}$ = {`D#, Emp#`} then `root.Division` is a strict prefix of `root.Division.Employee` and `root.Division.D#` $\cap$ `root.Division.Employee.Emp#.S` = `root.Division`.

**Definition 4.** *A* path instance *in an XML tree $T$ is a sequence $\bar{v}_1.\cdots.\bar{v}_n$ such that $\bar{v}_1 = v_r$ and for all $\bar{v}_i, 1 < i \leq n, v_i \in V$ and $\bar{v}_i$ is a child of $\bar{v}_{i-1}$. A* *path instance* $\bar{v}_1.\cdots.\bar{v}_n$ *is said to be* defined over the path $l_1.\cdots.l_n$ *if for all* $\bar{v}_i, 1 \leq i \leq n$, $lab(\bar{v}_i) = l_i$. *Two path instances* $\bar{v}_1.\cdots.\bar{v}_n$ *and* $\bar{v}'_1.\cdots.\bar{v}'_n$ *are said to be* distinct *if* $v_i \neq v'_i$ *for some* $i$, $1 \leq i \leq n$. *The path instance* $\bar{v}_1.\cdots.\bar{v}_n$ *is said to be a* prefix *of* $\bar{v}'_1.\cdots.\bar{v}'_m$ *if* $n \leq m$ *and* $\bar{v}_i = \bar{v}'_i$ *for all* $i, 1 \leq i \leq n$. *The path instance* $\bar{v}_1.\cdots.\bar{v}_n$ *is said to be a* strict prefix *of* $\bar{v}'_1.\cdots.\bar{v}'_m$ *if* $n < m$ *and* $\bar{v}_i = \bar{v}'_i$ *for all* $i, 1 \leq i \leq n$. *The set of path instances over a path* $p$ *in a tree* $T$ *is denoted by* $Paths(p)$

For example, in Figure 1, $v_r.v_1.v_3$ is a path instance defined over the path `root.Division.Section` and $v_r.v_1.v_3$ is a strict prefix of $v_r.v_1.v_3.v_4$

We now assume the existence of a set of legal paths $P$ for an XML application. Essentially, $P$ defines the semantics of an XML application in the same way that a set of relational schema define the semantics of a relational application. $P$ may be derived from the DTD, if one exists, or $P$ be derived from some other source which understands the semantics of the application if no DTD exists. The advantage of assuming the existence of a set of paths, rather than a DTD, is that it allows for a greater degree of generality since having an XML tree conforming to a set of paths is much less restrictive than having it conform to a DTD. Firstly we place the following restriction on the set of paths.

**Definition 5.** *A set* $P$ *of paths is* consistent *if for any path* $p \in P$, *if* $p_1 \subset p$ *then* $p_1 \in P$.

This is natural restriction on the set of paths and any set of paths that is generated from a DTD will be consistent.

We now define the notion of an XML tree conforming to a set of paths $P$.

**Definition 6.** *Let* $P$ *be a consistent set of paths and let* $T$ *be an XML tree. Then* $T$ *is said to* conform *to* $P$ *if every path instance in* $T$ *is a path instance over a path in* $P$.

The next issue that arises in developing the machinery to define XFDs is the issue is that of missing information. This is addressed in [12] but in this paper, because of space limitations, we take the simplifying assumption that there is no missing information in XML trees. More formally, we have the following definition.

**Definition 7.** *Let* $P$ *be a consistent set of paths, let* $T$ *be an XML that conforms to* $P$. *Then* $T$ *is defined to be* complete *if whenever there exist paths* $p_1$ *and* $p_2$ *in* $P$ *such that* $p_1 \subset p_2$ *and there exists a path instance* $\bar{v}_1.\cdots.\bar{v}_n$ *defined over* $p_1$, *in* $T$, *then there exists a path instance* $\bar{v}'_1.\cdots.\bar{v}'_m$ *defined over* $p_2$ *in* $T$ *such that* $\bar{v}_1.\cdots.\bar{v}_n$ *is a prefix of the instance* $\bar{v}'_1.\cdots.\bar{v}'_m$.

For example, if we take $P$ to be {`root`, `root.Dept`, `root.Dept.Section`, `root.Dept.Section.Emp`, `root.Dept.Section.Project`} then the tree in Figure 1 conforms to $P$ and is complete.

The next function returns all the final nodes of the path instances of a path $p$ in $T$.

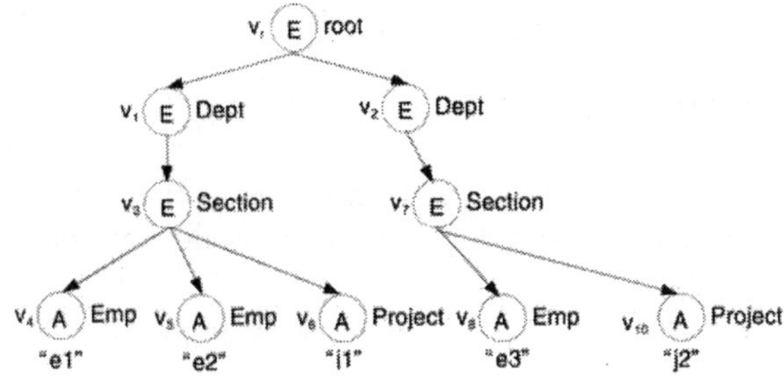


**Fig. 1.** A complete XML tree.

**Definition 8.** *Let $P$ be a consistent set of paths, let $T$ be an XML tree that conforms to $P$ . The function $N(p)$, where $p \in P$, is the set of nodes defined by $N(p) = \{\bar{v} | \bar{v}_1. \cdots .\bar{v}_n \in Paths(p) \wedge \bar{v} = \bar{v}_n\}$.*

For example, in Figure 1, $N(\texttt{root.Dept}) = \{v_1, v_2\}$.
We now need to define a function that returns a node and its ancestors.

**Definition 9.** *Let $P$ be a consistent set of paths, let $T$ be an XML tree that conforms to $P$. The function $AAncestor(v)$, where $v \in V \cup \mathbf{N}$, is the set of nodes in $T$ defined by $AAncestor(v) = v \cup Ancestor(v)$.*

For example in Figure 1, $AAncestor(v_3) = \{v_r, v_1, v_3\}$. The next function returns all nodes that are the final nodes of path instances of $p$ and are descendants of $v$.

**Definition 10.** *Let $P$ be a consistent set of paths, let $T$ be an XML tree that conforms to $P$. The function $Nodes(v, p)$, where $v \in V \cup \mathbf{N}$ and $p \in P$, is the set of nodes in $T$ defined by $Nodes(v, p) = \{x | x \in N(p) \wedge v \in AAncestor(x)\}$*

For example, in Figure 1, $Nodes(v_1, \texttt{root.Dept.Section.Emp}) = \{v_4, v_5\}$. We also define a partial ordering on the set of nodes as follows.

**Definition 11.** *The partial ordering $>$ on the set of nodes $V$ in an XML tree $T$ is defined by $v_1 > v_2$ iff $v_2 \in Ancestor(v_1)$.*

## 3 Strong Functional Dependencies in XML

We recall the definition of an XFD from [12]. For simplicity, we consider the case where there is only one path on the l.h.s.

**Definition 12.** *Let $P$ be a set of consistent paths and let $T$ be an XML tree that conforms to $P$ and is complete. An XML* functional dependency (XFD) *is a statement of the form: $p \rightarrow q$ where $p \in P$ and $q \in P$. $T$* strongly satisfies *the XFD if $p = q$ or for any two distinct path intances $\bar{v}_1. \cdots .\bar{v}_n$ and $\bar{v}'_1. \cdots .\bar{v}'_n$ in*

*Paths(q) in T,* $val(\bar{v}_n) \neq val(\bar{v}'_n)) \Rightarrow val(Nodes(x_1,p)) \cap val(Nodes(y_1,p)) = \emptyset$), *where* $x_1 = \max\{v|v \in \{\bar{v}_1,\cdots,\bar{v}_n\} \wedge v \in N(p \cap q)\}$ *and* $y_1 = \max\{v|v \in \{\bar{v}'_1,\cdots,\bar{v}'_n\} \wedge v \in N(p \cap q)\}$.

We note that since the path $p_i \cap q$ is a prefix of $q$, there exists only one node in $\bar{v}_1.\cdots.\bar{v}_n$ that is also in $N(p_i \cap q)$ and so $x_i$ is always defined and unique. Similarly for $y_i$.

We now illustrate the definition by some an example.

*Example 1.* Consider the XML tree shown in Figure 2 and the XFD `root.Department.Lecturer.Lname` $\rightarrow$ `root.Department.Lecturer.Subject.SubjName.S`. Then $v_r.v_1.v_5.v_{13}.v_{17}.v_{22}$ and $v_r.v_2.v_9.v_{15}.v_{21}.v_{24}$ are two distinct path instances in *Paths*(`root.Department.Lecturer.Subject.SubjName.S`) and $val(v_{22}) =$ `"n1"` and $val(v_{24}) =$ `"n2"`. So $N$(`root.Department.Lecturer.Lname`$\cap$ `root.Department.Lecturer.Subject.SubjName.S`) $= \{v_5, v_6, v_9\}$ and so $x_1 = v_5$ and $y_1 = v_9$. Thus $val(Nodes(x_1,$ `root.Department.Lecturer.Lname`$))$ $= \{$`"l1"`$\}$ and $val(Nodes(y_1,$ `root.Department.Lecturer.Lname`$))=\{$`"l1"`$\}$ and so the XFD is violated. We note that if we change *val* of node $v_{10}$ in Figure 2 to `"l3"` then the XFD is satisfied.

Consider next the XFD `root.Department.Head` $\rightarrow$ `root.Department`. Then $v_r.v_1$ and $v_r.v_2$ are two distinct paths instances in *Paths*(`root.Department`) and $val(v_1) = v_1$ and $val(v_2) = v_2$. Also $N$(`root.Department.Head` $\cap$ `root.Department`) $= \{v_1, v_2\}$ and so $x_1 = v_1$ and $y_1 = v_2$. Thus $val(Nodes(x_1,$ `root.Department.Head`$)) = \{$`"h1"`$\}$ and $Val(Nodes(y_1,$ `root.Department.Head`$)) = \{$`"h2"`$\}$ and so the XFD is satisfied. We note that if we change *val* of node $v_8$ in Figure 2 to `"h1"` then the XFD is violated.

## 4 Mapping from Relations to XML

As our technique for mapping relations to XML Trees is done via nested relations, we firstly present the definitions for nested relations.

Let $U$ be a fixed countable set of atomic attribute names. Associated with each attribute name $A \in U$ is a countably infinite set of values denoted by $DOM(A)$ and the set **DOM** is defined by **DOM** $= \cup DOM(A_i)$ for all $A_i \in U$. We assume that $DOM(A_i) \cap DOM(A_j) = \emptyset$ if $i \neq j$. A *scheme tree* is a tree containing at least one node and whose nodes are labelled with nonempty sets of attributes that form a partition of a finite subset of $U$. If $n$ denotes a node in a scheme tree $S$ then:

- $ATT(n)$ is the set of attributes associated with $n$;
- $A(n)$ is the union of $ATT(n_1)$ for all $n_1 \in Ancestor(n)$.

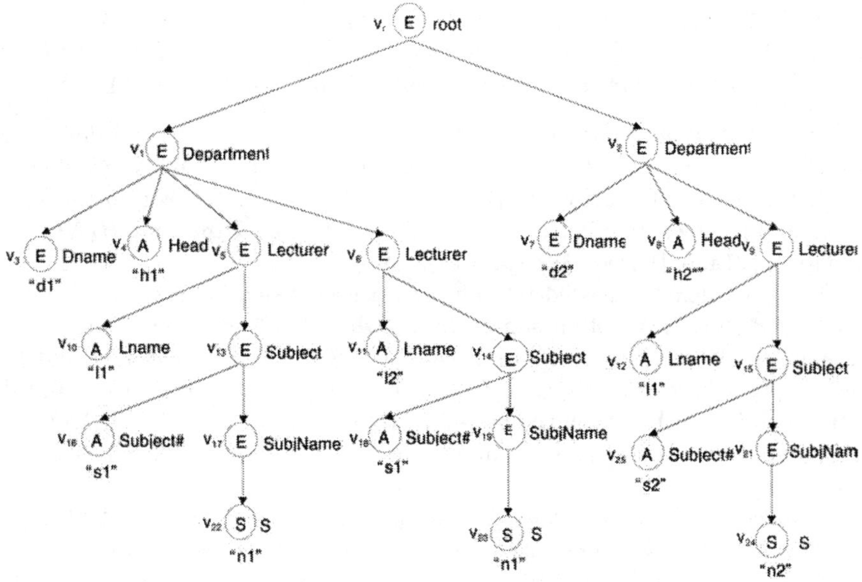


**Fig. 2.** An XML tree illustrating the definition of an XFD

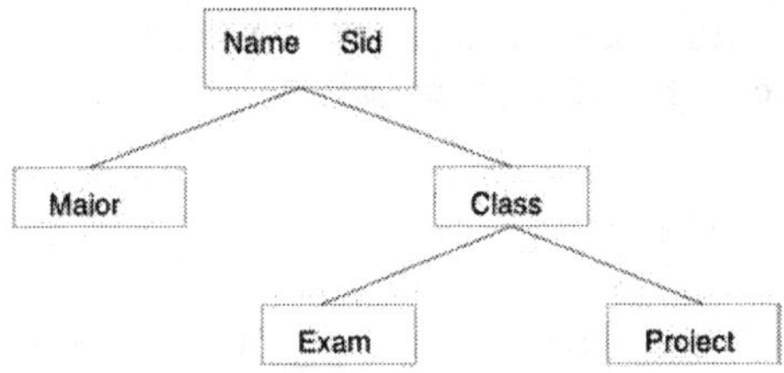


**Fig. 3.** A scheme tree

Figure 3 illustrates an example scheme tree defined over the set of attributes {`Name, Sid, Major, Class, Exam, Project`}.

**Definition 13.** *A* nested relation scheme *(NRS) for a scheme tree $S$, denoted by $N(S)$, is the set defined recursively by:*

*(i) If $S$ consists of a single node $n$ then $N(S) = ATT(n)$;*

*(ii) If $A = ATT(ROOT(S))$ and $S_1, \cdots, S_k, k \geq 1$, are the principal subtrees of $S$ then $N(S) = A \cup \{N(S_1)\} \cdots \{N(S_k)\}$.*

For example, for the scheme tree $S$ shown in Figure 3, $N(S) =$ {`Name, Sid`, {`Major`}, {`Class`, {`Exam`}, {`Project`}}}. We now recursively define the domain of a scheme tree $S$, denoted by $DOM(N(S))$.

**Definition 14.** *(i) If $S$ consists of a single node $n$ with $ATT(n) = \{A_1, \cdots, A_n\}$ then $DOM(N(S)) = DOM(A_1) \times \cdots \times DOM(A_n)$;*

*(ii) If $A = ATT(ROOT(S))$ and $S_1, \cdots, S_k$ are the principal subtrees of $S$, then $DOM(N(S)) = DOM(A) \times P(DOM(N(S_1))) \times \cdots \times P(DOM(N(S_k)))$ where $P(Y)$ denotes the set of all nonempty, finite subsets of a set $Y$.*

The set of *atomic attributes* in $N(S)$, denoted by $Z(N(S))$, is defined by $Z(N(S)) = N(S) \cap U$. The set of higher order attributes in $N(S)$, denoted by $H(N(S))$, is defined by $H(N(S)) = N(S) - Z(N(S))$. For instance, for the example shown in Figure 3, $Z(N(S)) =$ {`Name, Sid`} and $H(N(S)) =$ {{`Major`}, {`Class`, {`Exam`}, {`Project`}}}.

Finally we define a nested relation over a nested relation scheme $N(S)$, denoted by $r^*(N(S))$, or often simply by $r^*$ when $N(S)$ is understood, to be a finite nonempty set of elements from $DOM(N(S))$. If $t$ is a tuple in $r^*$ and $Y$ is a nonempty subset of $N(S)$, then $t[Y]$ denotes the restriction of $t$ to $Y$ and the restriction of $r^*$ to $Y$ is then the nested relation defined by $r^*[Y] = \{t[Y] | t \in r\}$. An example of a nested relation over the scheme tree of Figure 3 is shown in Figure 4.

A tuple $t_1$ is said to be a *subtuple* of a tuple $t$ in $r^*$ if there exists $Y \in H(N(S))$ such that $t_1 \in t[Y]$ or there exists a tuple $t_2$, defined over some NRS $N_1$, such that $t_2$ is a subtuple of $t$ and there exists $Y_1 \in H(N_1)$ such that $t_1 \in t_2[Y_1]$. For example in the relation shown in Figure 4 the tuples

< `CS100`, {`mid-year, final`}, {`Project A, Project B, Project C`} > and < `Project A` > are both subtuples of

< `Anna`, `Sid1`, {`Maths, Computing`}, {`CS100`, {`mid-year, final`}, {`Project A, Project B,Project C`}} >.

| **Name** | **Sid** | **{Major}** | **{Class** | **{Exam}** | **{Project}}** |
|---|---|---|---|---|---|
| Anna | Sid1 | Maths | CS100 | Mid-year | Project A |
| | | Computing | | Final | Project B |
| | | | | | Project C |
| Bill | Sid2 | Physics | P100 | Final | Prac 1 |
| | | | | | Prac 2 |
| | | Chemistry | CH200 | Test A | Experiment 1 |
| | | | | Test B | Experiment 2 1 |

**Fig. 4.** A nested relation.

We assume that the reader is familiar with the definition of the nest operator, $\nu_Y(r^*)$, and the unnest operator, $\mu_{\{Y\}}(r^*)$, for nested relations as defined in [9, 4].

The translation of a relation into an XML tree consists of two phases. In the first we map the relation to a nested relation whose nesting structure is arbitrary and then we map the nested relation to an XML tree.

In the first step we let the nested relation $r^*$ be defined by $r_i = \nu_{Y_{i-1}}(r_{i-1}), r_0 = r, r^* = r_n, 1 \leq i \leq n$ where $r$ represents the initial (flat) relation and $r^*$ represents the final nested relation. The $Y_i$ are allowed to be arbitrary, apart from the obvious restriction that $Y_i$ is an element of the NRS for $r_i$.

In the second step of the mapping procedure we take the nested relation and convert it to an XML tree as follows. We start with an initially empty tree. For each tuple $t$ in $r^*$ we first create an element node of type `Id` and then for each $A \in Z(N(r^*))$ we insert a single attribute node with a value $t[A]$. We then repeat recursively the procedure for each subtuple of $t$. The final step in the procedure is to compress the tree by removing all the nodes containing nulls from the tree. We now illustrate these steps by an example.

*Example 2.* Consider the flat relation shown in Figure 5.

| Name | Sid | Major | Class | Exam | Project |
|---|---|---|---|---|---|
| Anna | Sid1 | Maths | CS100 | Mid-year | Project A |
| Anna | Sid1 | Maths | CS100 | Mid-year | Project B |
| Anna | Sid1 | Maths | CS100 | Final | Project A |
| Anna | Sid1 | Maths | CS100 | Final | Project B |

**Fig. 5.** A flat relation.

If we then transform the relation $r$ in Figure 5 by the sequence of nestings $r_1 = \nu_{PROJECT}(r)$, $r_2 = \nu_{EXAM}(r_1)$, $r_3 = \nu_{CLASS,\{EXAM\},\{PROJECT\}}(r_2)$, $r^* = \nu_{MAJOR}(r_3)$ then the relation $r^*$ is shown in Figure 6. We then transform the nested relation in Figure 6 to the XML tree shown in Figure 7

| Name | Sid | {Major} | {Class | {Exam} | {Project}} |
|---|---|---|---|---|---|
| Anna | Sid1 | Maths | CS100 | Mid-year | Project A |
| | | | | Final | Project B |

**Fig. 6.** A nested relation derived from a flat relation.

We now recall the result from [12] which establishes the correspondence between satisfaction of FDs in relations and satisfaction of XFDs in XML. We denote by $T_{r^*}$ the XML tree derived from $r^*$.

**Theorem 1.** *Let $r$ be a flat relation and let $A \to B$ be a FD defined over $r$. Then $r$ strongly satisfies $A \to B$ iff $T_{r^*}$ strongly satisfies $p_A \to q_B$ where $p_A$ denotes the path in $T_{r^*}$ to reach $A$ and $q_B$ denotes the path to reach $B$.*

## 5 Redundancy Free Mappings from Relations to XML

We now give our definition of redundancy taken from [12]. Firstly, let us denote by $P_\Sigma$ the set of paths that appear on the l.h.s. or r.h.s. of any XFD in $\Sigma$, the set of XFDs for the application.

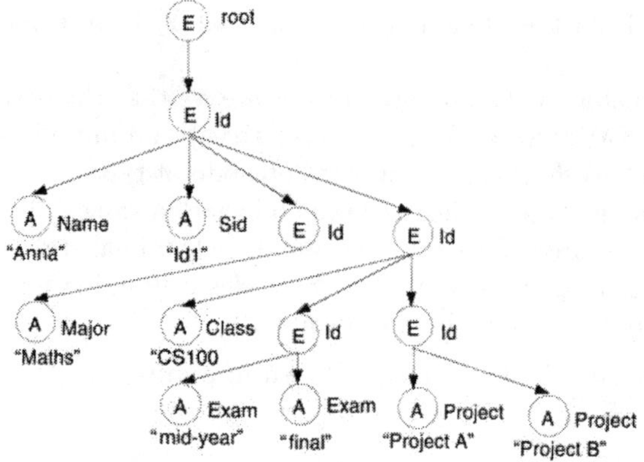


**Fig. 7.** An XML tree derived from a nested relation

**Definition 15.** *Let $T$ be an XML tree and let $v$ be a node in $T$. Then the change from $v$ to $v'$, resulting in a new tree $T'$, is said to be a* valid change *if $v \neq v'$ and $val(v) \neq val(v')$.*

We note that the second condition in the definition, $val(v) \neq val(v')$, is automatically satisfied if the first condition is satisfied when $lab(v) \in \mathbf{E}$.

**Definition 16.** *Let $P$ be a consistent set of paths and let $\Sigma$ be a set of XFDs such that $P_\Sigma \subseteq P$ and let $T$ be an XML tree that conforms to $P$ and satisfies $\Sigma$. Then $T$ is defined to* contain redundancy *if there exists a node $v$ in $T$ such that* every *valid change from $v$ to $v'$, resulting in a new XML tree $T'$, causes $\Sigma$ to be violated.*

We now illustrate this definition by an example.

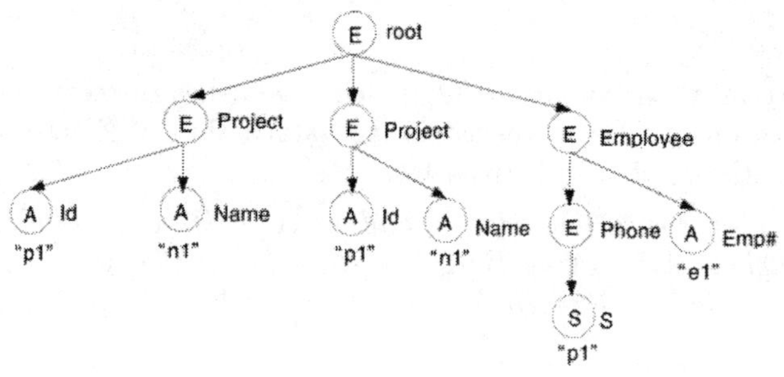


**Fig. 8.** XML tree illustrating redundancy.

*Example 3.* Let $P$ be the set of paths
{`root`, `root.Project`, `root.project.Id`,
`root.Project.Name`, `root.Employee`, `root.Employee.Phone`,
`root.Employee.Emp#`, `root.Employee.Phone.S`}. Consider the set of $\Sigma$ of XFDs {`root.Project.Id` $\rightarrow$ `root.Project.Name`} and the XML tree $T$ shown in Figure 8. Then $T$ contains redundancy because $T$ is consistent with $P$ and satisfies $\Sigma$ yet every valid change to either of the `Name` nodes results in `root.Project.Id` $\rightarrow$ `root.Project.Name` being violated.

One important benefit of an XML tree being redundancy free, as we shall now show, is that it eliminates certain update problems in a similar fashion to the way that eliminating redundancy in relations eliminates update problems [11].

**Definition 17.** *Let $P$ be a consistent set of paths and let $\Sigma$ be a set of XFDs such that $P_\Sigma \subseteq P$ and let $T$ be an XML tree that conforms to $P$ and satisfies $\Sigma$. Then $T$ is defined to have a* modification anomaly *if there exists a node $v$ in $T$ such that there exists some valid change to $v$ that results in $\Sigma$ being violated.*

For instance, the tree in Figure 8 has a modification anomaly since the change of the *val* of either of the `Name` nodes to `''n2''` results in $\Sigma$ being violated. We then have the following important result.

**Theorem 2.** *Let $P$ be a consistent set of paths and let $\Sigma$ be a set of XFDs such that $P_\Sigma \subseteq P$ and let $T$ be an XML tree that conforms to $P$ and satisfies $\Sigma$. Then $T$ has no redundancy iff $T$ has no modification anomaly.*

**Proof.**
*If:* The contrapositive, that if $T$ contains redundancy then it has a modification anomaly follows directly from the definitions.

*Only If:* We shall show the contrapositive that if $T$ has a modification anomaly then it contains redundancy. It follows directly from the definition of an XFD is that if one valid change to $v$ results in the violation of $\Sigma$ then all valid changes to $v$ result in the violation of $\Sigma$. Thus if $T$ has a modification anomaly then it will also contain redundancy. □

Next, we have the main result of the paper which shows that all mappings from a relation to an XML tree are redundancy free provided that the relation scheme is in BCNF.

**Theorem 3.** *Let $\Omega$ denote the set of all mappings from relations to XML trees as defined in Section 4. Let $R(A_1, \ldots, A_n)$ denote a relation scheme, let $\Sigma_R$ denote a set of unary FDs defined over $R$ and let $rel(R)$ denote the set of all relations defined over $R$ which satisfy $\Sigma_R$. Let $T_\Omega$ be the set defined $T_\Omega = \{T | \exists r \in rel(R) \exists \omega \in \Omega (T = \omega(r))\}$. Then every tree in $T_\Omega$ is redundancy free iff $R$ is in BCNF.*

We note that in the case of the relational scheme not being in BCNF, then some mappings result in redundancy whereas others are redundancy free. This is shown in the following example.

*Example 4.* Consider the relation scheme $R(A, B, C)$, the set $\Sigma$ of FDs $\{A \to B\}$ and the relation $r$ defined over $R$ shown in Figure 9. Suppose we then map $r$ to an XML document in two ways. In the first, we use the mapping $\omega_1$ which does no nesting. The resulting tree is shown in Figure 10 (a). This tree contains redundancy since any valid change to either of the $B$ nodes results in the violation of the XFD `root.Id.A` $\to$ `root.Id.B`. In the second mapping, $\omega_2$, we first nest on $C$ and then on $B$ then convert to a tree. The resulting tree is shown in Figure 10 (b). This tree contains no redundancy since every valid change to the $B$ node results in the XFD `root.Id.A` $\to$ `root.Id.Id..B` still being satisfied.

| A | B | C |
|---|---|---|
| $a_1$ | $b_1$ | $c_1$ |
| $a_1$ | $b_1$ | $c_2$ |

**Fig. 9.** A flat relation.

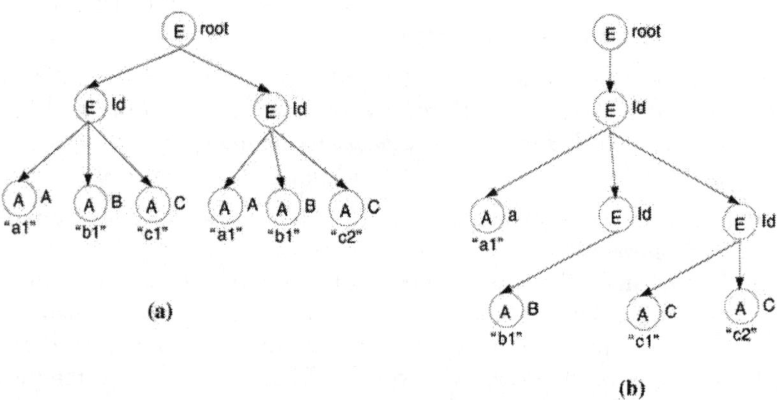


**Fig. 10.** XML trees from different mappings.

## 6 Conclusions

The problem that we have addressed in this paper is one related to this process of exporting relational data in XML format. The problem is that if one converts a relation to an XML document, under what circumstances is the XML document redundancy free? Being redundancy free is an important property of an XML document since, as we show, it guarantees the absence of certain types of update anomalies in the same fashion that redundancy elimination and BCNF ensures the elimination of update anomalies in relational databases [11].

Drawing on some previous work by the authors [13,12] that formally defined functional dependencies and redundancy in XML documents, we show that for a very general class of mappings from a relation to an XML document, the XML document is always redundancy free if and only if the relation is in Boyce-Codd normal form (BCNF). This result gives systems designers a great degree of flexibility in deciding how to map relations to XML without introducing redundancy. We also show that if the relation is not in BCNF then some mappings produce XML documents with redundancy whereas other mappings produce redundancy free XML documents.

## References


1. S. Abiteboul, P. Buneman, and D. Suciu. *Data on the Web.* Morgan Kaufmann, 2000.
2. W.Y. Mok anmd Y.K. Ng and D. Embley. A normal form for precisely characterizing redundancy in nested relations. *ACM Transactions on Database Systems*, 21(1):77–106, 1996.
3. M. Arenas and L. Libkin. A normal form for xml documents. In *Proc. ACM PODS Conference*, pages 85–96, 2002.
4. P. Atzeni and V. DeAntonellis. *Foundations of databases.* Benjamin Cummings, 1993.
5. T. Bray, J. Paoli, and C.M. Sperberg-McQueen. Extensible markup language (xml) 1.0. Technical report, http://www.w3.org/Tr/1998/REC-xml-19980819, 1998.
6. P. Buneman, S. Davidson, W. Fan, and C. Hara. Reasoning about keys for xml. In *International Workshop on Database Programming Languages*, 2001.
7. E.F. Codd. Recent investigations in relational database systems. In *IFIP Conference*, pages 1017–1021, 1974.
8. M. Levene and M. W. Vincent. Justification for inclusion dependency normal form. *IEEE Transactions on Knowledge and Data Engineering*, 12:281–291, 2000.
9. S.J. Thomas and P.C. Fischer. Nested relational structures. In P. Kanellakis, editor, *The theory of databases*, pages 269–307. JAI Press, 1986.
10. M. W. Vincent. A new redundancy free normal form for relational database design. In B. Thalheim and L. Libkin, editors, *Database Semantics*, pages 247 –264. Springer Verlag, 1998.
11. M. W. Vincent. Semantic foundations of 4nf in relational database design. *Acta Informatica*, 36:1–41, 1999.
12. M.W. Vincent and J. Liu. Strong functional dependencies and a redundancy free normal form for xml. Submitted for publication, 2002.
13. M.W. Vincent and J. Liu. Functional dependencies for xml. In *Fifth Asian Pacific Web Conference*, 2003.
14. J. Widom. Data management for xml - research directions. *IEEE data Engineering Bulletin*, 22(3):44–52, 1999.

# UD($k,l$)-Index: An Efficient Approximate Index for XML Data*

Hongwei Wu[1], Qing Wang[1], Jeffrey Xu Yu[2], Aoying Zhou[1], and Shuigeng Zhou[1]

[1] Department of Computer Science and Engineering
Fudan University, 220 Handan Rd, Shanghai, China
{hwwu,qingwang,ayzhou,sgzhou}@fudan.edu.cn
[2] Department of Systems Engineering and Engineering Management
The Chinese University of Hong Kong, Shatin, NT, Hong Kong, China
yu@se.cuhk.edu.hk

**Abstract.** XML has become the main standard of data presentation and exchange on the Internet. Processing path expressions plays a key role in XML queries evaluation. Path indices can speed up path expressions evaluation on XML data by restricting search only to the relevant portion. However, to answer all path expressions accurately, traditional path indices group data nodes according to the paths from the root of the data graph to the nodes in question, regardless of the paths fanning out from these nodes. This leads to large indices size and low efficiency of branching path expressions evaluation. In this paper, we present UD($k,l$)-indices, a family of efficient approximate index structures in which data nodes are grouped according to their incoming paths of length up to $k$ and outgoing paths of length up to $l$. UD($k,l$)-indices fully exploit local similarity of XML data nodes on their upward and downward paths, so can be used for efficiently evaluating path expressions, especially branching path expressions. For small values of $k$ and l, UD($k,l$)-index is approximate, we use validation-based approach to find exact answers to the path expressions. Experiments show that with proper values of $k$ and $l$, UD($k,l$)-index can improve the performance of path expressions evaluation significantly with low space overhead.

## 1 Introduction

With the rapidly increasing popularity of XML for data representation, there is a lot of interest in query processing on XML data. Various query languages [1,2,3,4,7] have been proposed recently. Processing path expressions plays a key role in XML queries evaluation. Naive evaluation of path expressions requires exhaustive search through the whole XML document, which is obviously inefficient. Path indices (structural summaries) are introduced to speed up path expressions evaluation by restricting the search only to the relevant portion of

* This work is supported by the National Natural Science Foundation of China under Grant No. 60228006.

G. Dong et al. (Eds.): WAIM 2003, LNCS 2762, pp. 68–79, 2003.

queried XML data. Thus the extraction of path index structures from semi-structured data has received a lot of attention recently [8,9,14,10,15]. Examples of such index structure include DataGuide [9], 1-index [13], the Index Fabric [5] and A($k$)-index [11]. The need to create path index structures for semi-structure data was clearly identified in the Lore project [12], and DataGuide was proposed in response [9,15]. The approach taken by DataGuide and followed by other work is to create a structural summary in the form of a labelled, directed graph. The idea is to preserve all paths of the data graph in the summary graph, while keeping as few nodes and edges as possible. As proposed in [9,13], it is possible to associate an extent with each node in the summary to produce an index graph. However, these kinds of indices are so large that they may be several times the size of original data. That is because they are precise summaries: all paths starting from the root in XML data are recorded although long paths may be seldom used, and each data node can appear more than once in DataGuide. A($k$)-index considers local similarity of the data nodes to reduce index size, so can effectively support plain (non-branching) path queries. But it pays attention only to the upward similarity of the nodes, while neglects their downward similarity. Consequently this index is inefficient in handling branching path queries.

In this paper, we propose a new approximate index structure, namely UD($k,l$)-index, for efficient evaluation of path expressions, especially branching path expressions. The index is a little larger than A($k$)-index in size, but it is substantially faster than A($k$)-index and 1-index in branching path expressions evaluation.

The rest of the paper is organized as follows. Section 2 describes the fundamental concepts and models used in the paper. Section 3 presents the UD($k,l$)-index and the algorithm for its construction, introduces the evaluation techniques of path expressions on our index graph and explains how to incrementally maintain a UD($k,l$)-index. Section 4 reports the experiment result. And finally, Section 5 concludes the paper.

## 2 Preliminaries

In this section we will introduce some concepts and definitions that will be useful throughout the paper. We model XML as a directed labelled graph, G = ($V_G$, $E_G$, $\sum_G$, lab, oid, val, root), called an *XML data graph*. Here, $V_G$ is a set of nodes. $E_G$ is a set of edges where each edge indicates a parent-child element or element-value relationship. $\sum_G$ is the set of all tags (labels) in the XML document. Three mapping functions are given, lab, oid and val: lab is a function which associates a node in $V_G$ with a label in $\sum_G$, oid is a function which maps a node in $V_G$ to a unique identifier, and val is a function that is used to associate a value with a leaf element, which has no outgoing edges. Finally, the root is the unique root node in $V_G$ with a tag ROOT.

Fig. 1 shows a segment of information about the top soccer league (the premiership) in England, represented as an XML data graph. In Fig. 1, the numeric identifiers inside nodes represent oids. The solid lines indicate the parent-child

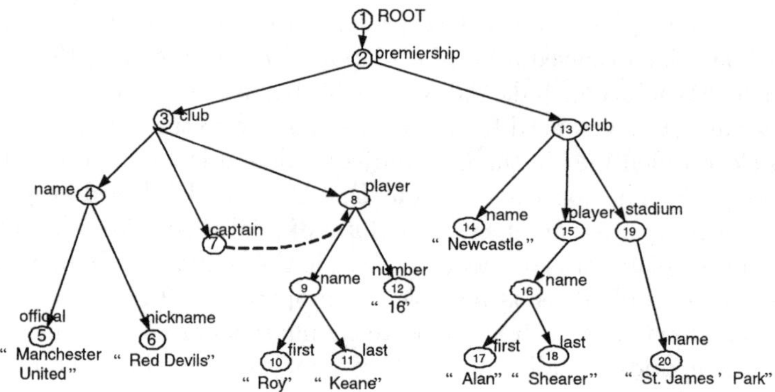


**Fig. 1.** The premiership XML data graph

relationships between elements. The leaf elements in the XML graph have values. Edges drawn by dashed lines show the general references between elements, which can be implemented with the ID/IDREF mechanism or XLink [6] syntax.

A *label-path* is a sequence of labels $l_1 \ldots l_p$ (p≥1), separated by separators (/). A *data-path* in G is a sequence of nodes, $n_1 \ldots n_p$ (p≥1), separated by /, and for $1 \leq i \leq p$, where $n_i$ is the parent of $n_{i+1.}$We define a *basic regular path* expression, $R$, in terms of sequencing (/), alteration (|), repetition (*) and optional expression (?) as shown below.

$R ::= \varepsilon \mid \_ \mid l \mid R/R \mid R|R \mid (R) \mid R? \mid R^*$

Here, $l \in \sum_G$ , and the symbol '_' is a special symbol that matches any $l_i \in \sum_G$. Furthermore, a *branching path* expression is defined as:

$BR := R[R] \mid R/BR \mid BR/BR \mid BR/R$

Here $R$ is a basic regular path expression. For a branching path expression $R_1[R_2]$, the path expression branches at the last label appearing in $R_1$. We call the label a *branching point.* A branching path expression consists of two kinds of paths, namely, a primary path and several condition paths. The *primary path* is the path by removing all parts between brackets '[' and ']' (including the brackets themselves), whereas a *condition path* is the path between brackets '[' and ']'. A path expression without any branching point is called a *plain path* expression.

Primary path expressions begin with the root element of an XML data graph, and the initial ROOT label is implied if omitted. Given a branching path expression, R, we say that R matches a node in an XML data graph, if the label-path of the node in question matches R. The result of evaluating R is the set of nodes in $V_G$, which match R. For example in Fig. 1, the plain path expression, *ROOT/premiership/club/player*, has two nodes in its result, {8, 15}, because the label-path for the two data-paths 1/2/3/8 and 1/2/13/15, matches the path expression. Two additional examples are given below for the premiership XML data graph: the plain path expression, *ROOT/_*/name*, will return {4, 9, 14, 16, 20}, and the branching path expression, *ROOT/premiership/club [name/nickname]*, retrieves all the clubs with a nickname, and has only node 3 in its result set.

# 3 The UD($k,l$)-Index

The 1-index and the DataGuide precisely encode all paths in the XML data graph, including both long and complex paths. Hence, even though two nodes are similar, they may be stored in different extents due to a long or complex path. However, such long and complex paths are rare and tend to contribute disproportionately to the complexity of an accurate structural summary [10]. Based on this observation, we attempt to build index graphs that take advantage of local similarity, in order to reduce the size of the index graphs. It is important to know that we support downward similarity as well as upward similarity, while 1-index and A($k$)-index do not support downward similarity. Supporting downward similarity can significantly reduce cost when processing branching path expressions. For example, in Fig. 1, 1-index or A($k$)-index will group node 3, 13 together, but branching path expression *ROOT/premiership/club[name/nickname]* will only return node 3. In other words, such indexing will include some nodes when handling branching path expressions. In this paper, we distinguish these nodes, for example node 3 and 13, based on the subgraphs rooted at them, using UD($k,l$)-index.

In the following, we will define up-bisimulation and down-bisimulation, and discuss their properties and how to construct/query/maintain an index based on up/down-bisimulation.

A symmetric, binary relation $\approx^u$ on $V_G$ is called an up-bisimulation, if for any two data nodes u and v with u $\approx^u$ v, we have that: a) u and v have the same label; and b) for any parent u' of u, there is a parent v' of v such that u' $\approx^u$ v' and vice-versa.

Two nodes u and v in G are said to be up-bisimilar, if there is some up-bisimulation $\approx^u$ such that u $\approx^u$ v.

A symmetric, binary relation $\approx_d$ on $V_G$ is called a down-bisimulation, if for any two data nodes u and v with u $\approx_d$ v, we have that: a) u and v have the same label; and b) for any parent u' of u, there is a child v' of v such that u' $\approx_d$ v' and vice-versa.

Two nodes u and v in G are said to be down-bisimilar, if there is some down-bisimulation $\approx_d$ such that u $\approx_d$ v.

A ud-bisimulation $\approx_d^u$ is a symmetric and binary relation which is an up-bisimulation and also down-bisimulation. Two nodes u and v in G are said to be ud-bisimilar if they are up-bisimilar and also down-bisimilar.

For example, in Fig. 1, object 8 and 15 are up-bisimilar, but not down-bisimilar, since 8 has a child labeled by tag 'number' while 15 not. Object 14 and 20 are down-bisimilar but not up-bisimilar, since 14 has a parent labeled by tag 'club' while 20 not.

## 3.1 The UD($k,l$)-Index

We propose the UD($k,l$)-index which classifies data graph nodes according to their incoming paths of length up to $k$ and outgoing paths of length up to $l$,

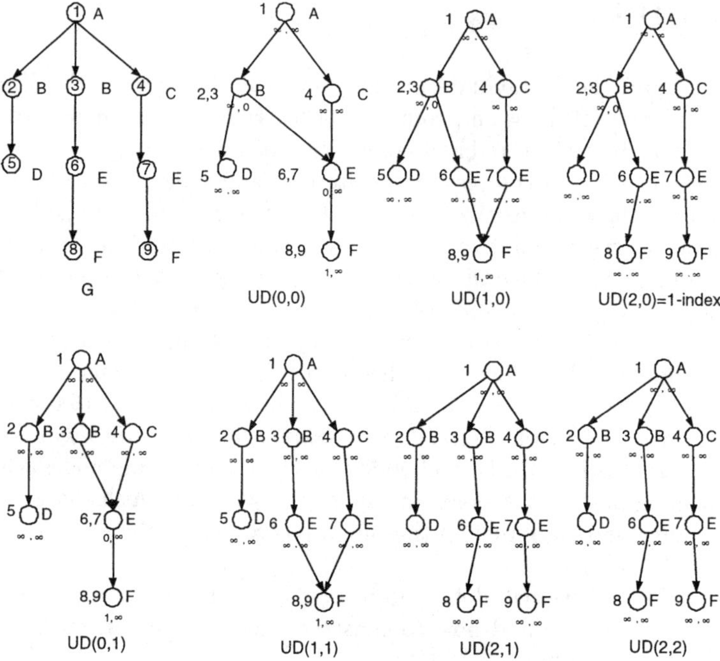


**Fig. 2.** A sequence of UD$(k, l)$-indices

using a notion of $k$-$l$-bisimilarity defined below. If node u and v satisfy u $\approx_l^k$ v, we say that u and v have an up-bisimilarity of $k$ and a down-bisimilarity of $l$.

$\approx_l^k$ *(k-l-bisimilarity)* is defined with three conditions: a) for any two nodes, u and v, u $\approx_0^0$ v iff u and v have the same label; b) node u $\approx_l^k$ v iff u $\approx_l^0$ v and for each parent u' of u, there is a parent v' of v such that u' $\approx_l^{k-1}$ v', and vice versa; and c) node u $\approx_l^k$ v iff u $\approx_0^k$ v and for each child u' of u, there is a child v' of v such that u' $\approx_{l-1}^k$ v', and vice versa.

Note that $k$-$l$-bisimilarity defines an equivalence relation on the nodes of the data graph. We call this $k$-$l$-bisimulation. An index graph can be constructed based on the $k$-$l$-bisimulation by creating an index node for each equivalence class, associating the data nodes in the class to the extent of the node (referred as ext [X], if the index node is X), and adding an edge from index node A to index node B if there is an edge in G from a data node in ext [A] to a data node in ext [B]. We call this the UD$(k, l)$-index. Increasing $k$ or $l$ refines the partition induced by this equivalence relation by splitting certain equivalence classes. If $l$=0, the UD$(k, l)$-index degenerates to the A$(k)$-index. By increasing $k$ continuously, it will reach a fixed-point at which we get 1-index. When increasing $l$, the partition will be refined sequentially until another fix-point is reached. This process is illustrated in Fig. 2 in which the numbers near index nodes enumerate the oids of the data nodes in their extents and the symbols under index nodes indicate the up-bisimilarity and down-bisimilarity of the data nodes in their extents.

Two bisimilarities of a node-set are defined below, down-bisimilarity and up-bisimilarity. Givne a set of nodes, $\sum$. The *down-bisimilarity* of $\sum$ is defined as: a) if there is only one data node in $\sum$, the down-bisimilarity of the node-set is $\infty$; and b) if there are more than one data nodes in $\sum$, the bisimilarity is the minimum down-bisimilarity of u and v in $\sum$. Analogously, we can define the *up-bisimilarity of* $\sum$.

For simplicity, we refer to the up-bisimilarity and the down-bisimilarity of the extent of an index node as the up-bisimilarity and down-bisimilarity of the index node respectively. For example, in UD(0,0) of Fig. 2, the index node labeled by tag 'F' has a down-bisimilarity of $\infty$ and an up-bisimilarity of 1.

In A($k$)-index, $k$ is used to indicate the bisimilarity of each index node, regardless of the fact that in A($k$)-index, some index nodes can have a bisimilarity larger than $k$. For example, in UD(0,0)-index (is also A(0)-index) graph of Fig. 2, the index node labeled by string 'F' has an up-bisimilarity of 1, which is larger than 0. So if $k$ is used as its bisimilarity, we will validate more data nodes in may-be data set. In UD($k,l$)-index, each index node is associated with an up-bisimilarity $ub$ and a down-bisimilarity $db$, which are called *individual bisimilarities.* By this mechanism, we can reduce the time for constructing index remarkably and reduce the number of nodes that need to be validated (or increase the number of nodes guaranteed to be true). We now describe some properties of these index graphs.

**Property 1**. For two data nodes u and v, if u $\approx_l^k$ v, then the sets of label-paths of length $m$ ($m \leq k+1$) into them are the same, and the sets of label-paths of length $n$ ($n \leq l$) from them are also the same.

**Property 2**. The UD($k,l$)-index is precise for any plain path expression of length $m$ ($m \leq k+1$), is precise for any condition path of length $n$ ($n \leq l$).

**Property 3**. The UD($k,l$)-index is approximate for plain path expressions of length $m$ ($m > k+1$) or condition paths of length $n$ ($n > l$), i.e. its result set only is a may-be result set, not a must-be result set. We need validate some data nodes against the data graph.

**Property 4**. The UD($k,l$)-index is safe, i.e. its result for any path expression always contains the data graph result for that query. There may be "false-positive", but will never be "false-negative".

**Property 5**. The UD($k$+1,$l$)-index is either equal to or a refinement of the UD($k,l$)-index. The UD($k,l$+1)-index is also either equal to or a refinement of the UD($k,l$)-index.

Property 1-4 are the foundations of our branching path queries evaluation technique. By Property 4, we can guarantee that the result for any query on our index is a superset of final result set, and there will be no danger of skipping over any right data node. By property 2, we can guarantee that our index is precise for any frequent shorter path expression, so there will be no need to validate the may-be result set against the data graph and the may-be result set is a must-be result set. By property 3, for longer primary paths or condition paths, we must validate the may-be result sets. The properties will be embodied by the process of the branching path queries evaluation in Section 3.3.

By property 5, the UD($k$+1,$l$)-index or UD($k$,$l$+1)-index can be obtained from UD($k, l$)-index by splitting some index nodes, and this is the foundation of the following UD($k, l$)-index construction algorithm.

### 3.2 The Construction of UD($k, l$)-Index

The index graph is created in two steps. First, we classify all the data nodes according to their labels, so we get a list of node-sets, each of which has a unique label. Then we compute the up-bisimilarity for each set. Then we repeatedly split the node set with smallest *ub* until the smallest *ub* is not less than the given parameter $k$. Then we compute the down-bisimilarity for each set and then split downwards until the smallest *db* is not less than $l$. The second step is to create create index nodes and create edges between the index nodes. We first create a index for each node-set. For any edge from data node u to data node v in G, if there is no edge from index node A (the index node u belongs to) to index node B (the index node v belongs to), we add an edge from A to B.

The UD($k, l$)-index degenerates to A($k$)-index when we take $l$ as 0 except that each node-set has a *ub* as up-bisimilarity and a *db* as down-bisimilarity. Thus in each iteration we know the node-sets with smallest *ub*/*db* are to be divided , then we split these node-sets directly while in A($k$)-index construction we need to check every node-set to see if it can be divided. So the UD($k, l$)-index construction time is much shorter then A($k$)-index. This will be shown in the experiments.

### 3.3 Branching Path Queries Evaluation

In this subsection we present our strategies for query processing on UD($k, l$)-index graph. The strategies are based on validation.

As is known, a regular path expression can be converted to a DFA. We can take the XML data as the DFA input, and run the DFA to find which nodes can drive the DFA to a final state. That is to say, the nodes match the regular path expression. A branching path expression can be converted into several DFAs, thus we can process the branching path expression by running the corresponding DFAs on the data graph. If the index graph exists, we can run them on index graph instead of data graph in order to reduce the evaluation cost. Evaluation of branching path queries on an index graph proceeds as follows:

1. Create a DFA A according to the primary path of the branching path and create a DFA $A_i$ for each condition path.
2. Run the DFA A on the index graph, i.e. the index graph is traversed depth-first, while making corresponding state transitions in the automation for matching.
3. Create tables for branching points to record their middle-results.
4. When the DFA A reaches a branching point, we suspend the running of A and start up the DFA $\mathrm{A}_i$ corresponding to the condition path. When $\mathrm{A}_i$ reaches a final state, we stop $\mathrm{A}_i$ and validate data nodes in the index

node reached by A and record the validate true data nodes in the middle result table. Then we resume the DFA A. If $A_i$ can't reach a final state, the DFA A won't continue matching forward, instead, it will run backward to its previous state, then continue running.

5. Create a table to avoid repeatedly visiting an index node in the graph in the same state of the automata, i.e. if we look up the table and find we have traversed the node in this state, we skip the node to traverse next node, thus we can avoid infinite loops from cycles.
6. When a node in the index graph is reached while the DFA A reaches an final state, the validated true or guaranteed true data nodes in that index node will be added to the final result.

From the properties of UD($k,l$)-index, we know that the middle result at a branching point or the "final" result is only may-be result set, so for longer queries we need to validate some nodes in the result set on the data graph.

$$\underbrace{A_1/\cdots/A_{i_1}}_{n_1}[\underbrace{B_1/\cdots/B_{j_1}}_{m_1}]/\underbrace{A_{i_1+1}/\cdots/A_{i_2}}_{n_2}[\underbrace{B_{j_1+1}/\cdots/B_{j_2}}_{m_2}]/\cdots/\underbrace{A_{i_x+1}/\cdots/A_{i_{x+1}}}_{n_{x+1}}$$

The branching path expression is separated into several sections at the branching points. For an index node N in the middle result at branching point $A_{i_1}$, the data node in ext [N] only may be a middle result. So we need to validate it upwards and downwards. If N.db$\geq m_{i_1}$, by property 2 we needn't validate downwards. If N.ub+1$\geq n_{i_1}$ and this is the first section, we needn't validate upwards. Otherwise, we need to validate against the data graph. In A($k$)-index, the condition is that $k+1 \geq n_{i_1}$. Because N.ub$\geq k$ as can be seen from Section 3.1, the condition N.ub+1$\geq n_{i_1}$ is weaker than the condition $k+1 \geq n_{i_1}$, thus we only need validate less data nodes upwards than in A($k$)-index.

The upward validation is handled by a reverse execution of the DFA on the data graph beginning with each node in ext [N] and ending with the nodes in the previous middle result set. The downward validation is analogous. The validation cost is expensive, but we can use the shared path optimization technique introduced by [11] to cut down the validation cost greatly.

### 3.4 Incremental Maintenance

If UD($k,l$)-index is to be useful for query evaluation, we must keep it consistent when the source data change. Since re-creating index is a time-cost work, it is necessary to build an incremental update algorithm.

UD($k,l$)-index considers the $k$-up-bisimilarity and $l$-down-bisimilarity of the data nodes, so the effect on the index of any update in the data graph is limited locally to a "neighborhood" of upward distance $l$ and downward distance $k$. So the index graph can be incrementally maintained as follows when an update comes about:

- If the update is inserting a subtree T at node v, we parse T in depth-first fashion and insert each node. When inserting a node $\delta$ at node $\theta$, we first split and recombine the index nodes of upward distance $l$ from $\theta$. Then we

```
Procedure insertSubTree(T,v)
begin
  θ:=the root node of subtree T;
  insertANode(θ,v);
  foreach child δ of θ do
    insertANode(δ, θ);
  φ:=v;
  while φ is not the root data node do
    ρ:=the index node containing φ;
    update the ub of ρ;
    φ:=the parent of φ;
end
Procedure insertANode(δ, θ)
begin
  ω := θ;
  for i:=1 to l do
    ρ:=the index node containing ω;
    remove ω from ρ;
    if ρ contains no data node then
      delete ρ;
    insert ω into the right index node ζ;
    update the ub of ζ and ρ;
    update the db of ζ;
    ω:=the parent of ω;
  insert δ into the right index node η;
end
```

```
Procedure deleteSubTree(T,v)
begin
  foreach data node in subtree T do
    remove θ from corresponding index node;
  ω:=v;
  for i:=1 to l do
    ρ:=the index node containing ω;
    remove ω from ρ;
    if ρ contains no data node then
      delete ρ;
    insert ω into the right index node ζ;
    update the ub of ζ and ρ;
    update the db of ζ;
    ω:=the parent of ω
  φ:=v;
  while φ is not the root data node do
    ρ:=the index node containing φ;
    update the ub of ρ;
    φ:=the parent of φ;
end
```

**Fig. 3.** UD$(k, l)$-index update algorithm

insert the node $\delta$ into appropriate index node. The algorithm is described in Fig. 3 where the right index node $\zeta$ indicates the index node having the same $k$-length upward path and $l$-length downward path as $\omega$ and the right index node $\eta$ indicates the index node having the same $k$-length upward path as $\delta$ and without outgoing edges.

– If the update is deleting a subtree T at node v, we first remove all the data nodes in subtree T from the corresponding index nodes which they belong to. Then we split and recombine the index nodes of upward distance $l$ from v. The algorithm is described in Fig. 3.

## 4 Experiment

In this section we explore the performance of the UD $(k, l)$-index. The experiments were performed on a machine with 1.7GHZ CPU and 256M RAM. Our experiments are over 10MB XMark XML benchmark [16] data set. The XMark data model an auction site. The queries are generated randomly according to the DTD of the XMark data.

The *cost of evaluation*: In the absence of a standard storage scheme for graph-structured data, we use the numbers of nodes accessed, including index nodes and data nodes, as the cost of evaluation.

### 4.1 The Size of the Index Graph

Fig. 4 shows the index graph size with different values of parameters $k$, $l$. From previous sections we know the difference between UD$(k, 0)$ and A$(k)$ is only the

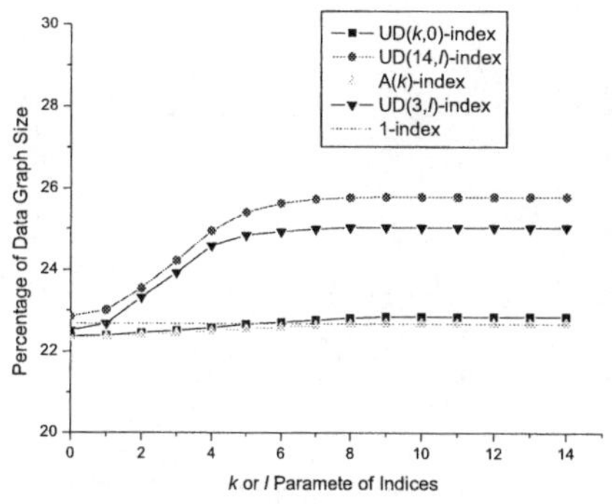


**Fig. 4.** UD($k,l$)-index size

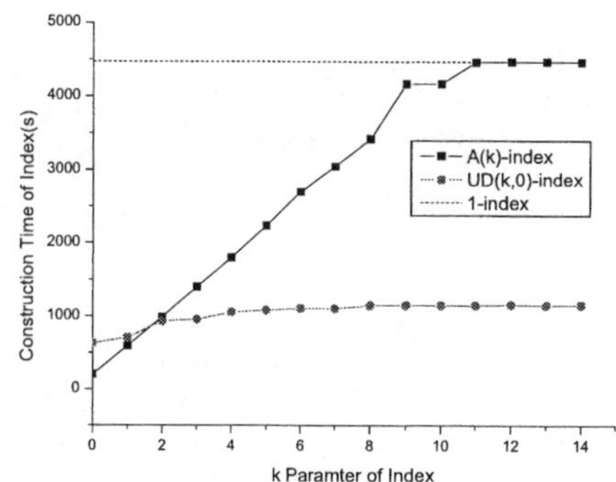


**Fig. 5.** UD($k,l$)-index construction time

*ub* and *db* associated with each index node. So the UD($k$, 0)-index size is a little larger than that of A($k$)-index. The value 3 is preferred k parameter an the value 2 is preferred l parameter as will shown in Section 4.3 and Section 4.4. The UD(3,2)-index size is 23% of the data graph size and this is close to the percentage of UD(3,0) or A(3) index size. The UD(14, $l$)-index curve shows that the index size is at most 26% of the data graph size.

### 4.2 The Construction Time of UD($k,l$)-Index

Fig. 5 shows the construction time of UD($k$, 0)-index and A($k$)-index with different parameter $k$. Because in UD($k$,0)-index each index node is associated with an upward similarity *ub* and a downward similarity *db*, when $k$=0, the construction time of UD(0,0)-index is longer than that of A(0)-index due to extra computation of *ub* and *db* for each index node. But when $k$ >1, the time of UD($k$, 0)-index is much shorter than that of A($k$)-index because in UD($k$,0)-index in each iteration we know which index nodes (i.e. the index nodes with the smallest *ub*) can be split in this iteration while in A($k$)-index we need complex computation to determine the nodes to be split. From the figure we can see that the time of UD($k$,0)-index increases slower with the increase of parameter $k$, while the time of A($k$)-index increases much faster.

### 4.3 Performance for Plain Path Expressions

Fig. 6 shows the evaluation cost of UD($k$,$l$)-index with different $k$. The execute cost is averaged over 15 plain path expressions and normalized to the execution cost on the data graph. From the figure, we can see that the plain path expressions cost on UD($k,l$)-index is only a little lower than on A($k$)-index. That is because the downward bisimilarity of UD($k,l$)-index has no use for the plain path expressions evaluation and the individual upward bisimilarity (the *ub* of each index node) is the contributing factor of the little improvement. With $k$=3, the evaluation cost on UD($k,l$)-index has the lowest value, and with value of $k$

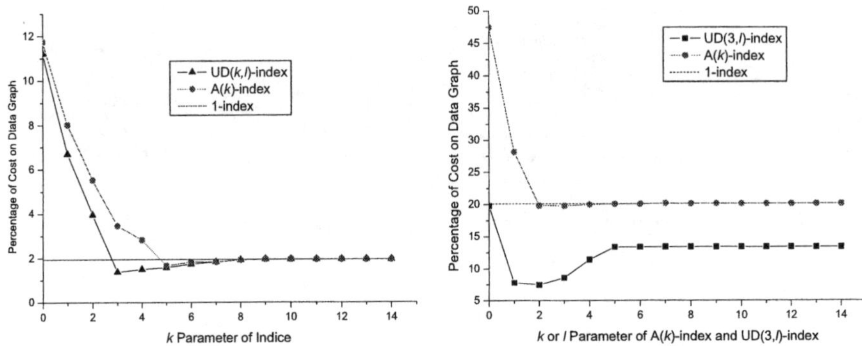


**Fig. 6.** Plain path queries costs

**Fig. 7.** Branching path queries costs

increasing, the cost becomes higher until it equals to the cost on 1-index. The reason is that with larger value of $k$, evaluation on UD$(k, l)$-index may access less data nodes for validation but more index nodes due to excessive splitting of the index nodes.

### 4.4 Performance for Branching Path Expressions

Section 4.3 shows that with $k$=3, UD$(k, 0)$-index performs best for plain path queries. So in this subsection, we discuss the impact of $l$ parameter for UD$(3, l)$-index. Fig. 7 shows the evaluation cost of UD(3,$l$)-index with different $l$. The execute cost is averaged over 15 branching path expressions and normalized to the execution cost on the data graph. From the figure, we can see that UD(3,$l$)-index has lower cost than A($k$)-index and 1-index. The reason is that UD(3,$l$)-index makes moderate split both upwards and downwards, so it can efficiently handle the branching path queries and the size is close to others. At the point where $l$=2, UD$(3, l)$-index has the least evaluation cost. The preferred $l$ parameter value (i.e. 2) is smaller than the preferred $k$ parameter value (i.e. 3) because the length of condition path is always not as long as that of the primary path.

## 5 Conclusion

In this paper, we have presented the UD$(k, l)$-index, an efficient approximate index structure for evaluation of path expressions. The UD$(k, l)$-index fully exploits local similarity of XML data nodes on their upward and downward paths, so it can efficiently evaluate the path expressions, especially branching path expressions. It is a generalization of the A($k$)-index that neglects the downward bisimilarity of the nodes. With $l$=0, UD$(k, l)$-index degenerates to A($k$)-index except the individual bisimilarity, but it still has less construction time and better performance than A($k$)-index. With $l$ >0, UD$(k, l)$-index is substantially faster than 1-index and A($k$)-index in processing the branching path expressions. By varying $k$ and $l$, this family of indices offers a smooth tradeoff between index graph size and accuracy.

The proposed techniques may be expanded to handle more complex path conditions such as selection and predication. This is a part of our future work. Investigating techniques to choose proper $k$ and $l$ parameters for given source data and specific query workload is another interesting issue.

## References


1. S. Abiteboul. Quering semi-structured data. In *Proc. of Int'l Conf. on Database Theory (ICDT)*, pages 1–18, 1997.
2. P. Buneman, R. Kaushik, and D. Suciu. A query language and algebra for semistructured data based on structural recursion. *Proc. of Int'l Conf. on Very Large Databases (VLDB)*, 9(1):76–110, 2000.
3. D. Chamberlin et al. XQuery 1.0: An XML Query Language. W3C Working Draft, June 2001. `http://www.w3.org/TR/xquery`.
4. J. Clark and S. DeRose. XML Path Language (XPath). W3C Working Draft, Nov. 1999. `http://www.w3.org/TR/xpath`.
5. B. Cooper, N. Sample, M. J. Franklin, G. R. Hjaltason, and M. Shadmon. A fast index for semistructured data. In *Proc. of Int'l Conf. on Very Large Databases (VLDB)*, pages 341–350, 2001.
6. S. DeRose, E. Maler, and D. Orchard. The xlink standard, June 2001. `http://www.w3.org/TR/xlink`.
7. A. Deutsch, M. Fernandez, D. Florescu, A. Levy, and D. Suciu. A query language for XML. In *Proc. of Int'l World Wide Web Conf. (WWW)*, 1999.
8. A. Gionis, M. Garofalakis, R. Rastogi, S. Seshadri, and K. Shim. XTRACT: A system for extracting for document type descriptors from XML documents. In *Proc. of ACM SIGMOD Conf. on Management of Data*, pages 165–176, 2000.
9. R. Goldman and J. Widom. Dataguides: Enabling query formulation and optimization in semistructured databases. In *Proc. of Int'l Conf. on Very Large Databases (VLDB)*, pages 436–445, 1997.
10. R. Goldman and J. Widom. Approximate dataguides. In *the WorkShop on Query Processing for Semistructured Data and Non-Standared Data Formats, Jerusalem, Israel*, 1999.
11. R. Kaushik, P. Shenoy, P. Bohannon, and E. Gudes. Exploiting local similarity for efficient indexing of paths in graph structured data. In *Proc. of IEEE Int'l Conf. on Data Engineering (ICDE)*, 2002.
12. J. McHugh, S. Abiteboul, R. Goldman, D. Quass, and J. Widom. Lore: A database management system for semistructured data. *SIGMOD Record*, 26(3), 1997.
13. D. Milo and D. Suciu. Index structure for path expression. In *Proc. of Int'l Conf. on Database Theory (ICDT)*, pages 277–295, 1999.
14. S. Nestorov, S. Abiteboul, and R. Motwani. Extracting schema from semistructured data. *SIGMOD Record*, 27(2):295–305, jun 1998.
15. S. Nestorov, J. Ullman, J. Weiner, and S. Chawathe. Representative objects: Concise representations of semistructured, hierarchical data. In *Proc. of IEEE Int'l Conf. on Data Engineering (ICDE)*, pages 79–90, 1999.
16. XMark. The XML benchmark project. `http://monetb.cwi.nl/xml/index.html`.

# Logical Foundation for Updating XML

Guoren Wang and Mengchi Liu

School of Computer Science, Carleton University
Ottawa, Ontario, Canada K1S 5B6
{wanggr, mengchi}@scs.carleton.ca

**Abstract.** With the extensive use of XML in applications over the Web, how to update XML data is becoming an important issue because the role of XML has been expanded beyond traditional applications in which XML is used for data representation and exchange over the Web. Several languages have been proposed for updating XML data, but they have two main drawbacks. One is these updating languages are based on low-level graph-based or tree-based data models so that update requests are thus expressed in a nonintuitive and unnatural way and update statements are too complicated to comprehend. The other is there is still no consensus about the logical foundation for XML updates. This paper presents a declarative language for updating XML data based on a high-level data model and systemically describes its semantics.

## 1 Introduction

With the extensive use of XML in applications over the Web, how to update XML data is becoming an important issue because the role of XML has been expanded beyond traditional applications in which XML is used for data representation and exchange over the Web. So far, several languages for extracting and querying XML data have been proposed, such as *XPath* [4], *Quilt* [6], *XML-QL* [7], *XQuery* [8], *XML-RL* [11] and *XQL* [15]. These languages do not support the manipulation operations on XML data. On the other hand, several languages have been proposed to support both querying and manipulating XML data, such as *Lorel* [2], *CXQuery* [5] and *XPathLog* [13]. All these XML query and manipulation languages except for *XML-RL* adopt low-level graph-based or tree-based data models, which are too difficult for users to comprehend. Therefore, a novel data model for XML is proposed in [10], in which XML data is modeled in a way similar to complex object models [1,14]. Based on this high-level data model, a rule-based declarative XML query language, XML-RL, is presented in [11].

The Lore system [2] has a simple declarative update language with the functions of creating and deleting database names, creating a new atomic or complex object, modifying the value of an existing atomic or complex object. In addition, bulk loading a database is supported by the update language. However, it does not support update requests on ordered data. XPathLog [13] is a rule-based data manipulation language. It only supports creation and modification of elements. CXQuery [5] is also a rule-based data manipulation language and its update

G. Dong et al. (Eds.): WAIM 2003, LNCS 2762, pp. 80–91, 2003.

language is similar to XPathLog, but simpler. XUpdate [12] is an XML update language and is a working draft of W3C. It allows users to create, insert, update and remove selected elements and attributes, and uses the expression language defined by XPath to locate elements or attributes to be updated. Update requests on ordered or unordered data are considered in XUpdate. The unique feature of XUpdate is that its syntax complies with the XML specification. Tatarinov et al. [16] extends *XQuery* with update, including *deletion*, *insertion*, *replacement* and *rename* of component elements or attributes. Update requests on ordered or unordered data are also considered and complex updates at multiple levels within a hierarchy are supported and specified using nested update operations. All the existing update languages do not support updates of complex objects or expressed them with a more complicated and unnatural way due to the use of lower level data models.

The paper [17] extends the XML-RL query language with the functionality of data manipulation including *insertion*, *deletion* and *replacement*.

The XML-RL update language has the following advantages over other XML update languages.

(1) It is the only update language supporting the high level data model. Therefore, it can represent update requests in a simple, natural, and powerful way.
(2) It is designed to deal with ordered and unordered data.
(3) It can express complex multiple level update requests in a hierarchy in a simple and flat way. Some existing languages have to use nested updates to express such complex requests, which are too complicated and non-intuitive to comprehend.
(4) Most of existing languages use *rename* to modify tag names in a far different from updating values. Our language modifies tag names, values and objects in a unified syntax by using three kinds of logical binding variables: *object variables*, *value variables*, and *name variables*.
(5) It directly supports the functionality of updating complex objects while all other update language do not support these operations.

In this paper, we formally define the syntax and semantics of the XML-RL update language based on logic programming. The remainder of this paper is organized as follows. Section 2 gives the formal syntax of schema, database, the XML-RL update language. Section 3 formally presents the semantics of the XML-RL update language, including *well-formed* schemas, *well-formed* databases and the semantics of various update operations. Finally, Section 4 concludes this paper. Due to the limitation of space, the proofs of theorems are omitted in this paper.

## 2 Syntax

In this section, we define the formal syntax of schema, database and update language.

### 2.1 Schema Syntax

We assume the existence of the following sets:

(1) a set $\mathcal{C}$ of constants;
(2) a set $\mathcal{V}$ of variables. A variable name begins with \$ followed by a constant, for example $\$salary$;
(3) a set of basic types $\mathcal{T} = \{\#PCDATA, CDATA, ID, IDREF, IDREFS\}$;

**Definition 1.** An *attribute rule* is of the form $@H_E \leftarrow t$, where $H \in \mathcal{C}$ is an attribute name, $E \in \mathcal{C}$ is the element name to which the attribute belongs, and $t \in (\mathcal{T} - \{\#PCDATA\})$ is the data type of the attribute.

**Definition 2.** An *element rule* is of the form $H \leftarrow \mathcal{B}$, where $H \in \mathcal{C}$ is an element name and $\mathcal{B}$ is one of the following forms:

(1) $\#PCDATA$. Such a rule is called an *atomic* element rule;
(2) $B?$, where $B \in \mathcal{C}$ is an element name. Such a rule is called an *optional* rule;
(3) $B*$, where $B \in \mathcal{C}$ is an element name. Such a rule is called a *duplicate* rule;
(4) $B_1|...|B_n$ with $n > 0$, where for each $B_i (1 \leq i \leq n)$, $B_i \in \mathcal{C}$ is an element name. Such a rule is called a *choice* rule;
(5) $@A_{1H}, ..., @A_{mH}, B_1, ..., B_n$ with $m \geq 0$ and $n \geq 0$, where $@A_{iH} \in \mathcal{C} (1 \leq i \leq n)$ is an attribute name of the element H to be described by the rule and $B_i \in \mathcal{C} (1 \leq i \leq n)$ is an element name. Such a rule is called a *tuple* rule;
(6) Forms composed by (1), (2), (3), (4), and (5) in a usual way. This is called a *composite* rule.

The following are examples of various rules.

Attribute rules : $@id_{course} \leftarrow ID$, $@takes_{students} \leftarrow IDREFS$
Atomic element rules: $name \leftarrow \#PDCATA$, $title \leftarrow \#PCDATA$
Optional rules : $A \leftarrow B?$, $C \leftarrow D?$
Duplicate rules : $teachers \leftarrow teacher*$, $students \leftarrow student*$
Choice rules : $person \leftarrow faculty|staff|student$,
$publication \leftarrow book|journal|conference|techReport$
Tuple rules : $faculty \leftarrow @id_{faculty}, name, address, teaches$,
$student \leftarrow @id_{student}, name, address, takes$
Composite rules : $department \leftarrow (faculty|student|course)*$,
$university \leftarrow (@id_{university}, department*)$

**Definition 3.** Let $p = A \leftarrow B$ be either an *element rule* or an *attribute rule*. Then $A$ is the head of the rule, denoted by $head(p)$, and $B$ the body of the rule, denoted by $body(p)$.

**Definition 4.** A schema $S$ consists of two parts: a root element $R$ and a set of rules $P$, denoted by the ordered pair $(R, P)$. $root(S)$ is used to refer to $R$ and $rules(S)$ is used to refer to $P$.

## 2.2 Database Syntax

In the following, we first give the formal syntax of objects, then give the formal syntax of database.

**Definition 5.** The notion of *objects* is defined inductively as follows:

(1) Let $c \in \mathcal{C}$ be a constant. Then $c$ is a *lexical object.*
(2) Let $o_1,...,o_n$ be objects with $n \geq 0$. Then $<o_1,...,o_n>$ is a *list* object. In particular, if each $o_i (1 \leq i \leq n)$ is a lexical object, then $<o_1,...,o_n>$ is called a *lexical list* object.
(3) Let $a \in \mathcal{C}$ be a constant and $o$ be either a constant or a list of lexical objects. Then $@a{:}o$ is an *attribute* object and $a$ is the *name* of the object and $o$ is the *value* of the object.
(4) Let $e \in \mathcal{C}$ be a constant and $o$ be either a *lexical* object or a *tuple* object. Then $e{:}o$ is an *element* object and $o$ is the *value* of the element $e$.
(5) Let $@a_1,...,@a_m$ be attribute objects and $e_1,...,e_n$ be element objects with $m \geq 0$ and $n \geq 0$. Then $(@a_1, ..., @a_m, e_1, ..., e_n)$ is a *tuple* object. In particular, it represents an *empty* object in the case of $m{=}0$ and $n{=}0$.

The following are examples of various objects:
Lexical objects: *Computer Science*, *Ottawa*
List objects: $<CS100,CS200>$, $<2000,3000>$
Attribute objects: $@id{:}E200$, $@supervisee{:}<S100,S200>$
Tuple objects: ($street$:56 *Broson*, $city$:*Ottawa*, $state$:*Ontario*, $zip$:$K2B$ $6M8$)
Element objects: $course$:($@cid{:}CS300$, $cname{:}DBMS$,
$desc{:}Implementation\ Techniques$,
$takenBy$:($@students$:3000), $taughtBy$:($@teachers$:2000))

**Definition 6.** Let $o_1$ and $o_2$ be two objects. Then $o_1 \in o_2$ if $o_1$ is a nested object of $o_2$.

**Definition 7.** Let $o$ be an object. Then $o$ is *regular* if $o$ is not an element object with a value of list object and $\not\exists o' \in o$($o'$ is an element object and $o'$ has a value of list object). If an object is *regular* , we call it has a *regular* form.

**Definition 8.** Attribute objects and element objects are called *named* objects while lexical objects, list objects and tuple objects are called *anonymous* objects.

The following are some examples of named objects and anonymous objects.
Named objects: @id:S100, salary:$40,000
Anonymous objects: *Ontario*,<CS100,CS200>,(@courses:$<CS100, CS200>$)

**Definition 9.** Let $o$ be an object. Then $name(o)$ is defined as a function to get the name part of $o$. In particular, it returns *null* if $o$ is an *anonymous* object. Similarly, $value(o)$ is defined as a function to get the value part of $o$.

**Definition 10.** Let $o$ be an object. Then $o$ is *normalized* if $\not\exists o' \in o$($o'$ is a named object with a value of tuple $(o'_1,...,o'_n)$ and for any two adjoining objects $o_i$ and $o_{i+1} (1 \leq i < n)$ $(name(o_i){=}name(o_{i+1}))$). If an object is *normalized*, then we call it has a *normalized* form.

In the paper, the *regular* form of XML documents is used for the data model because it is the most natural and straightforward way for representing XML objects as in the complex object model. Therefore, the extensional database representing XML documents is defined as follows.

**Definition 11.** An *database* $\mathcal{DB}$ of a schema $S$ is defined as the ordered pair $(S, o)$, where $o$ is a named element object with the *regular* form.

### 2.3 Syntax of XML-RL Update Language

In this section, we present the formal syntax of the XML-RL update language.

**Definition 12.** The notion of *terms* are defined inductively as follows:

(1) Let $c \in \mathcal{C}$ be a constant. Then $c$ is a *lexical* term.
(2) Let $v \in \mathcal{V}$ be a variable. Then $v$ is a *variable* term.
(3) Let $t_1,...,t_n$ be lexical or variable terms with $n \geq 0$. Then $<t_1,...,t_n>$ is a *list* term.
(4) Let $a$ be a constant or variable and $t$ be either a lexical, variable or a list of lexical terms. Then $@a \Rightarrow t$ is an *attribute* term and $t$ is the *value* of attribute $a$.
(5) Let $e$ be a constant or variable and $t$ be an term. Then $e \Rightarrow t$ is an *element* term and $t$ is the *value* of element $e$.
(6) Let $@a_1,...,@a_m$ be attribute terms and $e_1,...,e_n$ be element terms with $m \geq 0$ and $n \geq 0$. Then $(@a_1, ..., @a_m, e_1, ..., e_n)$ is a *tuple* term. In particular, it represents an empty term in the case of $m$=*0* and $n$=*0*.

The following are examples of various terms.

Lexical terms : *2314343*, *440 Albert*
Variable terms : $price, $salary
List terms : <*CS100*, *CS200*, *CS300*>, <*2000*, *3000*>
Attribute terms: *@id*⇒$id,*@courses*⇒<*CS300*>
Element terms : *$name*⇒*Jones Gillmann*, *desc* ⇒ *Basic concepts*
Tuple terms : (*@students*⇒*3000*),
(*street*⇒*56 Broson*, *city*⇒*Ottawa*, *state*⇒*Ontario*)

**Definition 13.** A term is *ground* if it contains no variables.

**Definition 14.** The notion of expressions are defined inductively as follows:

(1) *Arithmetic*, *logical*, and *string* expressions are defined using terms in the usual way.
(2) Let $L$ be a list term and $A$ be an arithmetic expression. Then L[A] is a *list selection* expression.
(3) Let $T$ be a tuple term and $E$ be a logical expression. Then T[E] is a *tuple selection* expression.
(4) Let v be a variable term and E be a term. Then v(E) is a *variable selection* expression. A variable term is the simplest form of variable selection expression.
(5) Let $E_1$ and $E_2$ each be either an element term, a variable selection expression or a *tuple selection* expression. Then $E_1/E_2$ and $E_1//E_2$ are *path selection* expressions.

(6) Let $U$ be a url and P be an element term, a variable selection expression or path selection expression. Then $P$, $(U)/P$, and $(U)//P$ are *query* expressions.

The following are examples of expressions.

List selection expressions : $@courses[3]$, $@student[0]$

Tuple selection expressions : $student[@sid \Rightarrow S100]$,
$course[taughtBy[@faculty \Rightarrow F100]]$

Variable selection expressions : \$faculty(faculty⇒[firstname⇒Smith])
\$student(student⇒\$studentValue)

Path selection expressions : $/department/faculty[@id \Rightarrow F200]$,
$//student[name \Rightarrow JounesGillmannandtakes/@courses[2] \Rightarrow CS200]$

Query expressions : $(www.scs.carleton.ca)//course/cname$,
$(www.scs.carleton.ca)/department/faculty[name \Rightarrow AlleyStrivastava]/title$

**Definition 15.** An expression is *ground* if it contains no variables.

**Definition 16.** Let $E$ be either a *list* term or a *tuple selection* expression and $\$v$ be a variable term. Then *insert E Into $\$v$*, *insert E before* $\$v$ and *insert E after* $\$v$ are *insert-into*, *insert-before* and *insert-after* declarations, respectively.

**Definition 17.** Let $E$ be either an *element* term, a *list* term, or a *tuple selection* and $\$v$ be a variable term. Then *replace* $\$v$ *with E* is a *replacement* declaration.

**Definition 18.** Let $\$v$ be a variable term. Then *delete* $\$v$ is a *deletion* declaration.

**Definition 19.** Let $e_1, ..., e_n$ be query expressions and $u_1, ..., u_m$ be update declarations. Then *Querying* $e_1, ..., e_n$ $u_1, ..., u_m$ is an update query.

**Example 1.** The following update statement inserts a new faculty *Charis Adson* after *Bob Smith.*

**Querying** (URL)/department/\$f(faculty⇒[name⇒
[firstname⇒Bob, lastname⇒Smith ]])
**Insert** faculty⇒[@id⇒F300, name⇒[firstname⇒Charis, lastname⇒Adson],
title⇒Professor, salary⇒\$70,000]
**After** \$f

where the variable *\$f* holds a *faculty* element for *Bob Smith.* After the update operation, a new *faculty* element is added after *Bob Smith.*

**Example 2.** The following update statement adds some new data for faculty objects whose value is *null.*

**Querying** (URL)/department/\$f(faculty⇒null)
**Replace** \$f **With** faculty⇒[@id⇒0278,
name⇒[firstname⇒Nency, lastname⇒White],
title⇒instructor, salary⇒\$35,000]

where the variable *\$f* holds faculty objects with *null* value, and the value of all *null* faculty objects is replaced with the complex value specified by the *with* clause.

**Example 3.** The following update statement deletes the value of salary for a faculty whose *id* is *F200.*

**Querying** (URL)/department/faculty⇒[@id⇒F200, salary⇒$s]
**Delete** $s
where $s holds the value of *salary* objects of the *faculty* object whose *id* is *F200*. So deleting $s means the values of the selected *salary* objects are set to *null*.

## 3 Semantics

In this section, we define the semantics of schema, database and the update language. We first discuss *well-formed* schema and *well-formed* objects, then define *well-formed* database based on well-formed schema and *well-formed* objects. Finally we define the formal semantics of the update language.

### 3.1 Semantics of Schema

We first define *non-terminating* rules, and *reachable* and *unreachable* symbols, then define a class of *well-formed* schema.

**Definition 20.** Let $P$ be a set of rules. Then a rule $p$ is *non-terminating* with respect to $P$ if and only if p is not an atomic element rule or an attribute rule and $\exists B \in body(p)$ such that

(1) there does not exist $q \in (P - \{p\})$, $head(q) = B$, or
(2) for $\forall q \in (P - \{p\})(head(q) = B$ and $q$ is non-terminating with respect to $P - \{p\})$.

**Example 4.** For the set of rules
$P = \{A \leftarrow B, C, D,\ \ B \leftarrow E, F,\ \ C \leftarrow \#PCDATA,\ \ D \leftarrow H, G,\ \ E \leftarrow \#PCDATA,$ $F \leftarrow \#PCDATA,\ \ G \leftarrow \#PCDATA\}$, the following are examples of *non-terminating* and *terminating* rules.
Non-terminating: $A \leftarrow B, C, D,\ \ D \leftarrow H, G$
Terminating : $B \leftarrow E, F,\ \ C \leftarrow \#PCDATA,\ \ E \leftarrow \#PCDATA,$
$F \leftarrow \#PCDATA,\ \ G \leftarrow \#PCDATA$

**Definition 21.** Let $C \in \mathcal{C}$ be a constant, $p$ a rule, and $P$ the set of rules. Then $C$ is *unreachable* from $p$ with respect to $P$ if and only if $C \neq head(p)$ and there does not exist a sequence of rules $q_1, q_2 ..., q_n$ with $n \geq 1$ such that $(head(p) \in body(q_n)) \wedge (head(q_n) \in body(q_{n-1})) \wedge ... \wedge (head(q_i) \in body(q_{i-1})) \wedge ... \wedge (head(q_2) \in body(q_1)) \wedge (head(q_1) = C)$. Similar, we can define $C$ is *reachable* from $p$ with respect to $P$.

**Example 5.** For the set of rules $P = \{A \leftarrow B, C,\ B \leftarrow D, E,\ D \leftarrow F, G,\ H \leftarrow I, J,$ $I \leftarrow K, L,\ \ K \leftarrow M, N\}$, $A$ is *reachable* from rules $B \leftarrow D, E$ and $D \leftarrow F, G$, and $H$ is *reachable* from rules $I \leftarrow K, L$ and $K \leftarrow M, N$, while $A$ is *unreachable* from rules $I \leftarrow K, L$ and $K \leftarrow M, N$ and $H$ is *unreachable* from rules $B \leftarrow D, E$ and $D \leftarrow F, G$.

**Definition 22.** A *well-formed* schema $S$ is defined as follows:

(1) for $\forall p_1 \in rules(S) \forall p_2 \in rules(S)(head(p_1) \neq head(p_2))$;
(2) for $\forall p \in rules(S)(p$ is not *non-terminating* with respect to *rules(S)*);
(3) for $\forall p \in rules(S)(root(S)$ is *reachable* from $p$ with respect to *rules(S)*).

**Definition 23.** Let $E \in C$ be a constant and $P$ be a set of rules. Then the projection of $S$ on $E$, $\Pi_E P$, is defined as the set of rules $\Pi_E P = \{p | p \in P$ and $E$ is reachable from $p$ with respect to $P\}$.

For Example 4, $\Pi_B P = \{B \leftarrow E, F,\ E \leftarrow \#PCDATA,\ F \leftarrow \#PCDATA\}$, $\Pi_D P = \{D \leftarrow H, G,\ G \leftarrow \#PCDATA\}$. For Example 5, $\Pi_A P = \{A \leftarrow B, C,\ B \leftarrow D, E,\ D \leftarrow F, G\}$ and $\Pi_H P = \{H \leftarrow I, J,\ I \leftarrow K, L,\ K \leftarrow M, N\}$.

**Definition 24.** Let $E \in C$ be a constant and $S$ be a schema. Then the ordered pair ($E$, $\Pi_E rules(S)$) is defined as the subschema of $S$ with respect to $E$.

It is obvious that $\Pi_E rules(S) \subseteq rules(S)$ according to Definition 23.

**Theorem 1.** All subschemas of a *well-formed* schema are also *well-formed.*

### 3.2 Semantics of Database

In this section, we first define *well-formed* objects and satisfaction of a *well-formed* object with respect to a *well-formed* schema. Then we define a class of *well-formed* database.

**Definition 25.** A *well-formed* object is defined inductively as follows:

(1) A lexical object is always *well-formed.*
(2) A list object $<o_1, ..., o_n>$ is *well-formed* if each $o_i (1 \le i \le n)$ is a lexical object.
(3) Let $@a{:}o$ is an attribute object. Then it is *well-formed* if the following hold:
  (a) $a$ is a lexical object.
  (a) $o$ is either a lexical object or a well-formed list object.
(4) Let $e{:}o$ be an element object. Then it is *well-formed* if the following hold:
  (a) $e$ is a lexical object.
  (b) $o$ is either a lexical object or a *well-formed* tuple object.
(5) A tuple object $(@a_1, ..., @a_m, e_1, ..., e_n)$ with $m \ge 0$ and $n \ge 0$. Then it is *well-formed* if the following hold:
  (a) Each $@a_i (1 \le i \le m)$ is a *well-formed* attribute object.
  (b) Each $e_i (1 \le i \le n)$ is a *well-formed* element object.

**Theorem 2.** Let $o$ be a *well-formed* object. Then $\forall o' \in o$ is also *well-formed.*

**Definition 26.** Let $S$ be a *well-formed* schema and $o$ be a *well-formed* named object. Then the satisfaction of $o$ with respect to $S$ is defined recursively as follows:

(1) if $o$ is a simple attribute object $@A \Rightarrow C$ and $root(S) = @A$, then $o$ is *satisfiable* for $S$;
(2) if $o$ is a lexical list attribute object $@A \Rightarrow <C_1, C_2, ..., C_n>$ with $n \ge 1$, $root(S) = @A$, and for $\forall p \in rules(S)(head(p) = A \wedge body(p) = IDREFS)$, then $o$ is *satisfiable* for $S$;
(3) if $o$ is a simple element object $E \Rightarrow C$, $root(S) = E$, and $\exists p \in rules(S)$ $(head(p) = root(S))$, one of the following holds for rule $p$, then $o$ is *satisfiable* for $S$;
  (a) $p$ is an *atomic* rule;
  (b) $p$ is an *optional* rule $E \leftarrow B?$, and $o$ is *satisfiable* for subschema ($name(B)$, $\Pi_{name(B)} S$)

(c) $p$ is a *duplicate* rule $E \leftarrow B*$, and $o$ is *satisfiable* for subschema $(name(B), \Pi_{name(B)}S)$
(d) $p$ is a *choice* rule $E \leftarrow (E_1|...,|E_n)$ with $n \geq 1$, $\exists E_i \in \{E_1, ..., E_n\}$ $E_i$ is #PC-DATA or $o$ is *satisfiable* for subschema $(name(E_i), \Pi_{name(E_i)}S)$.
(e) $p$ is a tuple rule $E \leftarrow (E_1,...,E_n)$ with $n \geq 1$, $\exists E_i \in \{E_1, ..., E_n\}(E_i$ is #PC-DATA or $o$ is *satisfiable* for subschema $(name(E_i), \Pi_{name(E_i)}S))$, and for each other $E_j \in \{E_1, ..., E_n\}$ is either *#PCDATA*, $E_j?$, or $E_j*$.

(4) if $o$ is an element object with a value of tuple $(E \Rightarrow (@a_1, ..., @a_m, e_1, ..., e_n))$ with $m \geq 0$ and $n \geq 0$, $root(S)=E$, and $\exists p \in rules(S)(head(p) = root(S))$, one of the following holds for rule $p$, then $o$ is satisfiable for S;
(a) $m=0$ and $n=0$, that is $o$ is an empty object with element type $E$;
(b) $p$ is an *atomic* rule, $m=0$ and $n=1$, and $e_1$ *satisfiable* for subschema $(name(e_1), \Pi_{name(e_1)}(S)$;
(c) $p$ is an *optional* rule $E \leftarrow B?$, $m=0$ and $n=1$, $name(e_1)=B$, and $e_1$ is *satisfiable* for subschema $(name(e_1), \Pi_{name(e_1)}(S))$;
(d) $p$ is a *duplicate* rule $E \leftarrow B*$, $m=0$, $name(e_i)=B(1 \leq i \leq n)$, and $e_i$ is *satisfiable* for subschema $(name(e_i), \Pi_B(S))$;
(e) $p$ is a *choice* rule $E \leftarrow (B_1|...|B_s)$, $m=0$ and $n=1$, and $e_1$ is *satisfiable* for subschema $(name(e_1), \Pi_B(S))$;
(f) $p$ is a *tuple* rule $E \leftarrow (@A_1, ..., @A_t, B_1, ..., B_s)$, $m=t$ and $n \leq s$, and
(i) $a_i(q \leq i \leq m)$ is *satisfiable* for $\Pi_{name(a_i)_E}(S)$;
(ii) there are a sequence $B_{i1}, ...B_{in}$, for each $e_j(1 \leq j \leq n)$ $name(e_j)=B_{ij}$, for each $B_k(B_k \notin \{B_{i1}, ...B_{in}\} \wedge B_k \in \{B_1, ..., B_s\} \wedge B_k$ is of the form either $B_k?$ or $B_k*)$ and $e_i$ is *satisfiable* for $\Pi_{name(e_i)}(S)$;

**Theorem 3.** Let S be a well-formed schema and o is satisfiable for S. Then for $\forall o' \in o$, $o'$ is satisfiable for $\Pi_{name(o')}S$.

**Definition 27.** A database $\mathcal{DB}=(S, o)$ is *well-formed* if the following hold:

(1) $S$ is a *well-formed* schema;
(2) $o$ is a *well-formed* element object;
(3) $o$ is *satisfiable* for schema $S$.

**Definition 28.** Let $C \in \mathcal{C}$ be a constant and $\mathcal{DB} = (S, o)$ be a database. Then a sub-database of $\mathcal{DB}$ with respect to $C$, denoted by $\Pi_C\mathcal{DB}$, is defined as the ordered pair $(\Pi_C S, \{o_1, ..., o_n\})$ such that $o_1 \in o,...,o_n \in o$, $name(o_1)=...=name(o_n)=C$.

**Theorem 4.** Given a *well-formed* database $\mathcal{DB} = (S, o)$ and its subdatabase $\Pi_C\mathcal{DB}=(\Pi_C S, \{o_1, ..., o_n\})$. Then $\forall o_i(1 \leq i \leq n)$ is *satisfiable* for $\Pi_C S$.

### 3.3 Semantics of Update Language

In the above sections, we define the formal semantics of schema and database. In this section we first define the formal semantics of expressions. Then we define the formal semantics of the update language described in Section 2.3.

**Definition 29.** Let $\mathcal{DB} = (S, o)$ be a database. Then the *level* of a nested object $o' \in o$, denoted by $level(o')$, is defined as the depth of $o'$ nested in $o$.

In particular, the level of the root object in the database is defined as *0*, i.e. $level(o)=0$.

**Definition 30.** Let $\mathcal{DB} = (S, o)$ be a *well-formed* database. Then the semantics of expressions on $\mathcal{DB}$ is defined inductively as follows.

(1) The semantics of *arithmetic*, *logical* and *string* expressions are defined in the usual way.
(2) Let $L[A]$ be a list selection expression and $L$:$<o_1, ..., o_n>$ be the target object. Then the result of the expression is $o_A$ in the case of $1 \leq A \leq n$. Otherwise the result is *null*.
(3) Let $T[E]$ be a tuple selection. Then the result of the expression is defined as $\delta_E(\Pi_T \mathcal{DB}) = (\Pi_T S, \{o' | o' \in o$ and $name(o') = T$ and $E(o')$ is $true\})$.
(4) Let $E_1/E_2$ be a path selection expression. Suppose that the result of $E_1$ is $(\Pi_A S, \{o_{11}, ..., o_{1m}\})$ and the result of $E_2$ is $(\Pi_B S, \{o_{21}, ..., o_{2n}\})$. Then the result of the expression is defined as $(\Pi_B S, \{o' | o' \in \{o_{21}, ..., o_{2n}\}$ *and* $\exists o''$ $(o'' \in \{o_{11}, ..., o_{1m}\} \wedge o' \in o'' \wedge level(o'') - level(o') = 1)\})$. We can define the semantics of path selection expression $E_1//E_2$ in a similar way.
(5) Let $P$, $(U)/P$ and $(U)//P$ be query expressions. We can define the semantics for query expressions $(U)/P$ and $(U)//P$ similar to item (4) except that the result of expression $(U)$ is $(S, o)$. Here, consider the query expression $P$. If $P$ is a path expression, then its semantics is defined by item (4). If it is an element term, then its result is defined as the sub-database $(\Pi_P S, \{o' | o' \in o$ and $name(o') = P\})$.

**Definition 31.** Let $o$ and $s$ be objects, and $o' \in o$ a nested object of $o$. Then the *substitution* of object $s$ for $o'$ in $o$, $o(o'/s)$, is defined as: object $o'$ within object $o$ is replaced by object $s$.

**Theorem 5.** Let $\mathcal{DB}$=(S,o) be a well-formed database and $t$ be an object satisfiable for $\Pi_{name(t)} S$. For $\forall s \in o$, if name($s$)=name($t$), then $o' = o(s/t)$ is satisfiable for S.

**Theorem 6.** Let $\mathcal{DB} = (S, o)$ be well-formed, $o' = o(s/t)$ a substitution of object $t$ for $s$ in o, level(s)-level($o''$)=1(i.e. $o''$ is the parent object of s), and $o''' = o''(s/t)$. If $o'''$ is satisfiable for $\Pi_{name(o''')}(S)$, then $o'$ is satisfiable for S.

**Definition 32.** Let $\mathcal{DB} = (S, o)$ be a *well-formed* database and *querying* $Q_1$,...,$Q_n$ $U$ be an updating query on the database. Then the semantics of the updating query, $\mathcal{DB}' = (S, o')$, is defined as follows:

(1) *insert* $E$ into \$v.
  (a) \$v is an element object with a value of tuple $s = name(s)$: $(@a_1, ..., @a_m, e_1, ..., e_m)$. Then $o' = o(s/s')$ is defined as: if $E$ is an attribute object, then $s' = name(s)$:$(@a_1, ..., @a_m, E, e_1, ..., e_n)$; if $E$ is an element object, then $s' = name(s)$: $(@a_1, ..., @a_m, e_1, ..., e_n, E)$. In light of Theorem 6, if $s'$ is not satisfiable for $\Pi_{name(s)} S$, then the insert-into operation is not allowed.
  (b) \$v is an object with a value of list object $s$=$<ID_1$,...,$ID_n>$. Then $o' = o(s/s')$ and $s'$=$<ID_1$,...,$ID_n$,$E>$.
  (c) Otherwise, the insert-into operation is not allowed.

(2) *insert E before* \$v. Assume the parent object of \$v is s.
   (a) s is an element object with a value of tuple $s$ = $name(s)$: ($@a_1, ..., @a_m,\ e_1, ..., e_m$). Then $o'=o(s/s')$ is defined as: if \$v is an attribute object and $@a_i$=\$v, then $s'=name(s)$:($@a_1$,...,$@a_{i-1}$,$E$, $@a_i$,...,$@a_m$,$e_1$, ..., $e_n$); if \$v is an element object and $e_i$=\$v, then $s'=name(s)$:($@a_1$,...,$@a_m$,$e_1$,...,$e_{i-1}$, $E$,$e_i$,...,$e_n$); According to Theorem 6, if $s'$ is not satisfiable for $\Pi_{name(s)}S$, then the insert-before operation is not allowed.
   (b) s is an object with a value of list object $s=<ID_1,...,ID_n>$ and \$v=$ID_i$. Then $o'=o(s/s')$ and $s'=<ID_1,...,ID_{i-1},E,ID_i,...,ID_n>$.
   (c) Otherwise, the insert-before operation is not allowed.

(3) *insert E after* \$v. We can define the semantics of the insert after operation in a similar way to the insert before operation.

(4) *delete* \$v.
   (a) If \$v is the value of object s, then $o'=o(s/s')$ and $s'$ is name(s)⇒*null*. According to Theorem 6, if $s'$ is not satisfiable for $\Pi_{name(s)}S$, then the deletion operation is not allowed.
   (b) If the parent object of \$v is an element object with a value of tuple $s=name(s)$:($@a_1$, ...,$@a_m$,$e_1$,...,$e_n$), then if \$v=$@a_i$ then $s'=name(s)$: ($@a_1$,...,$@a_{i-1}$,$@a_{i+1}$,...,$@a_m$, $e_1$,...,$e_n$); if \$v=$e_i$, then $s'=name(s)$: ($@a_1$,...,$@a_m$, $e_1$,...,$e_{i-1}$,$e_{i+1}$,$e_n$); According to Theorem 6, if $s'$ is not satisfiable for $\Pi_{name(s)}S$, then the deletion operation is not allowed.
   (c) Otherwise, the deletion operation is not allowed.

(5) *replace* \$v *with E*.
   (a) Assume \$v is a value of object s. Then a new object $s'$ is constructed with name(s):E and $o'=o(s/s')$. According to Theorem 5, if $s'$ is not satisfiable for $\Pi_{name(s)}S$, then the replacement operation is not allowed.
   (b) Assume \$v is the name of object s. Then a new object $s'$ is constructed with E:value(s) and $o'=o(s/s')$. Assume that t is the parent of s, according to Theorem 6, if $t'=t(s/s')$ is not satisfiable for $\Pi_{name(t)}S$, then the replacement operation is not allowed.
   (c) Assume \$v is an object and t is the parent object of \$v with a value of tuple t=$name$(t):($@a_1$,...,$@a_m$,$e_1$,...,$e_n$). If E=$@a_i$ then a new object $t'$ is constructed with name(t):($@a_1$,...,$@a_{i-1}$,E,$@a_{i+1}$,...,$@a_m$,$e_1$,...,$e_n$) and $o'=o(t/t')$. Similarly, if E=$e_i$, the a new object $t'$ is constructed with name(t):($@a_1$,...,$@a_m$,$e_1$,...,$e_{i-1}$,E, $e_{i+1}$,...,$e_n$) and $o'=o(t/t')$. According to Theorem 5, if $t'$ is not satisfiable for $\Pi_{name(t)}S$, then the replacement operation is not allowed.
   (d) Otherwise, the replacement operation is not allowed.

## 4 Conclusions

We have described a declarative XML update language which is based on the XML-RL data model and query language, and systematically defined the syntax and semantics of schema, database, and the XML-RL update language including insertion, deletion and replacement. We are implementing the XML-RL system that supports XML-RL queries and updates at Carleton University.

**Acknowledgement.** Guoren Wang's research is partially supported by the Teaching and Research Award Programme for Outstanding Young Teachers in Post-Secondary Institutions by the Ministry of Education, China (TRAPOYT) and National Natural Science Foundation of China under grant No. 60273079. Mengchi Liu's research is partially supported by National Science and Engineering Research Council of Canada.

## References

1. S. Abiteboul, R. Hull, et al. Foundation of Databases. Addison Wesley, 1995.
2. S. Abiteboul, D. Quass, J. McHugh, J. Widom, J. Wiener. The Lorel Query Language for Semistructured Data. Int. J. on Digital Libraries 1997, 1(1): 68–88.
3. A. Bonifati and S. Ceri. Comparative Analysis of Five XML Query Languages. SIGMOD Record 29(1): 68–79 (2000).
4. J. Cark and S. DeRose. XML Path Language (XPath), ver. 1.0. Tech. Report REC-xpath-19991116, W3C, Nov. 1999.
5. Y. Chen and P. Revesz. CXQuery: A Nodel XML Query Language. This is available at `http://citeseer.nj.nec.com/539624.html`.
6. D. Chamberlin, J. Robie, D. Florescu. Quilt: An XML Query Language for Heterogeneous Data Sources. Proc. of 3rd Int'l Workshop WebDB, Dallas, 2000, 1–25.
7. A. Deutsch, M.F. Fernandez, et al. A Query Language for XML. Proceedings of the 8th International World Wide Web Conference, Toronto, Canada, 1999.
8. P. Fankhauser. XQuery Formal Semantics: State and Challenges. SIGMOD Record 30(3), 2001: 14–19.
9. M. Fernandez, A. Malhotra, J. Marsh, M. Nagy, N. Walsh. XQuery 1.0 and XPath 2.0 Data Model. W3C Working Draft 15 November 2002. This is available at `http://www.w3.org/TR/2002/WD-query-datamodel-20021115/`.
10. M. Liu. A logical foundation for XML. In Proc. of the 14th Int'l Conf. on Advanced Information Systems Engineering(CAiSE'02), Toronto, Canada, 2002, 568–583.
11. M. Liu and T.W. Ling. Towards declarative XML querying. In Proc. of The 3rd Int'l Conf. on Web Information Systems Engineering(WISE'02), Singapore, 2002.
12. A. Laux, L. Martin. XUpdate - XML Update Language. W3c Working Draft, 2000. It is available at `http://www.xmldb.org/xupdate/xupdate-wd.html`.
13. W. May. XPathLog: A Declarative, Native XML Data Manipulation Language. Proc. of IDEAS'01, Grenoble, France, 2001, 123–128.
14. T. Rühl and H. E. Bal. The nested object model. In Proceedings of 6th ACM SIGOPS European Workshop on Matching Operating Systems to Application Needs, September 1994, Dagstuhl Castle, Germany, 134–137.
15. H. Ishikawa, K. Kubota, Y. Kanemasa. XQL: A Query Language for XML Data. W3C Workshop on Query Language, Boston, Massachussets, USA, 1998.
16. I. Tatarinov, Z.G. Ives, A.Y. Halevy, D.S. Weld. Updating XML. In Proceedings of 2001 SIGMOD, Santa Barbara, CA, 2001.
17. G. Wang, M. Liu, L. Lu. Extending XML-RL with update. In Proceedings of International Database Engineering and Applications Symposium (IDEAS03), Hong Kong. July 16–18, 2003.

# XML Database Schema Integration Using XDD

Doan Dai Duong[1] and Vilas Wuwongse[2]

[1] Informatics Department, Hue University, 32 Le Loi, Hue, Vietnam
ddduong.sp@hueuni.edu.vn
[2] Computer Science & Information Management Program,
Asian Institute of Technology, Pathumthani 12120, Thailand
vw@cs.ait.ac.th

**Abstract.** XML database schema integration has lately received increasing attention. It helps to obtain unified representation of all participating databases of an organization, facilitating their information access and utilization. The presented XML database schema integration framework follows *one short strategy* [3]. The system is capable of integrating simultaneously *n* schemas. Possible conflicts between XML schemas are detected and their resolutions proposed. A *normal form of XML schema* is also given; it provides a unique declaration of an XML schema and avoids ambiguous schema representation. XML Declarative Description (XDD) [16] is used as the framework's underlying model.

## 1 Introduction

The Web could be viewed to be a very large, loosely-coupled set of heterogeneous databases each of which is a Web site. Although their data normally have an individual structure, Web databases do not typically conform to any well-known rigid structure, such as a relational or object schema. In order to make the data in a Web database understandable to humans, the names of attributes could be included within the data fields yielding self-describing data. The language most likely to be accepted as standard representation for such data is XML[1], leading to a new class of databases, i.e., XML databases. These XML databases can be newly built or obtained by conversion of existing databases into XML format. Since XML databases are normally distributed on the Web, their integration demands important and interesting research. One main problem of the integration of databases, both XML and conventional ones, is their schema integration, which combines the schemas of participating databases into a unified one. This unified schema will enable users to access with a single global view a set of distributed, but related data.

Most of the previously developed integration systems, such as Tukwila [12], HERA [14], DIXSE [7] and LoPix [10], aim to handle XML databases. Even though these systems have achieved certain results, they still have limitations. In DIXSE, authors tried to integrate Document Type Definitions (DTDs) into a common conceptual schema. For this purpose, a meta-modeling language named Telos is used

---

1 http://www.w3.org/TR/REC-XML

G. Dong et al. (Eds.): WAIM 2003, LNCS 2762, pp. 92–103, 2003.

to present the data model and the derived conceptual schemas. Besides, the system used DIXml, a declarative language for specifying a DTD mapping onto a conceptual schema. By using DIXml, the system is more efficient in metadata processing. However, due to DTD's limited capability to describe complex data types and contents, details of participating schemas and information required for their integration might not be expressible, obstructing accurate and efficient integration. Moreover, while even Telos is strong in representing metadata modeling, it does not follow XML syntax, whence it cannot be integrated with XML data in a uniform environment to be processed. In the Tukwila integration system, the authors deal with integration of extracted data from sources. Every data source is mapped to the mediated schema via its own schema. Whenever users pose a query, Minicon algorithms [12] are applied to optimize it. X-scan operator [12] works as a recursive function to extract data from sources. Because the system does not integrate individual data source schemas before processing queries, extracted data with overlap and conflicts between them are unpredictable. These data are too crude for users, who expect a human friendly result. In LoPix, people manipulate and restructure databases with several XML trees. By linking sub-trees, fusing elements and defining synonyms, data can be restructured and integrated into a result tree [10]. For this purpose, the author uses a logic-based language XPathLog [10] to integrate XML documents. However, its author has only referred to simple cases of schema conflicts. It must be pointed out that there are many other conflicts between schemas which need to be resolved such as those due to structure, data type, constraints, etc., in addition to synonym ones. Even though the LoPix system can resolve synonymous conflicts in the simplest case, where the conflicts are caused by different namespaces, the building of a framework which can cover all possible conflicts between schemas remains a great challenge.

In view of the existing problems, a new framework for integrating XML database schemas is proposed. It is one among the few systems that follow *one short strategy* [3], i.e., it is capable of integrating $n$ schemas simultaneously. Moreover, this framework can resolve all of the major schema conflicts in a unified manner. This achievement is due to the capability of the framework's modeling language - XDD [16], an XML-based information representation scheme. Unlike Telos and XPathLog, it allows one to model all components of XML databases, i.e., extensional and intensional databases as well as constraints and queries [15]. In addition, it can also express rules, ontologies and axioms, whence it enables schema integration mechanisms and conflict resolution guidelines to cooperate harmoniously. When compared with [11], the newly proposed conflict resolution guidelines help resolve conflicts among the schemas of XML databases as well as those among the schemas of relational and object-oriented databases.

Section 2 gives a brief overview of XDD, Section 3 explains integration strategies, Section 4 describes the proposed integration framework architecture and its components, Section 5 presents the schema integration steps in detail, analyzes schema conflicts and develops their resolutions; finally, Section 6 concludes the paper.

## 2 XML Declarative Description

*XML Declarative Description (XDD)* [16] is an XML-based information representation, which extends ordinary, well-formed XML elements by incorporation of variables for an enhancement of expressive power and representation of implicit information into so called XML expressions. Ordinary XML elements - XML expressions without variable - are called *ground XML expressions.* Every component of an XML expression can contain variables, e.g., its expression or a sequence of sub-expressions *(E-variables),* tag names or attribute names *(N-variables),* strings or literal contents *(S-variables),* pairs of attributes and values *(P-variables)* and some partial structures *(I-variables).* Every variable is prefixed by *'$T:'*, where *T* denotes its type; for example, $S:value and $E:expression are *S-* and *E-variables,* which can be specialized into a string or a sequence of XML expressions, respectively.

An *XDD description* is a set of *XML clauses* of the form:

$$H \leftarrow B_1, \ldots, B_m, \beta_1, \ldots, \beta_n,$$

where $m, n \geq 0$, $H$ and the $B_i$ are XML expressions and each of the $\beta_i$ is a predefined XML *constraint*—useful for defining a restriction on XML expressions or their components. The XML expression $H$ is called the *head*, the set $\{B_1, \ldots, B_m, \beta_1, \ldots, \beta_n\}$ the *body* of the clause. When the body is empty, such a clause is referred to as an *XML unit clause*, otherwise it is a *non-unit clause*, i.e., it has head as well as body. A unit clause $(H\leftarrow.)$ is often denoted simply by $H$ and referred to as a *fact*. Moreover, an XML element or document can be mapped directly onto a *ground XML unit clause.* The elements of the body of a clause can represent constraints, whence XML clauses (both unit and non-unit ones) can express facts, taxonomies, implicit and conditional relationships, constraints, axioms as well as ontology – set of taxonomies together with their axioms. Given an XDD description $D$, its meaning is the set of all XML elements which are directly described by and are derivable its unit and non-unit clauses, respectively.

## 3 Integration Strategies

Paper [3] classifies the integration strategies into: *binary* and *n-ary strategies*:

The first allows integration of two schemas at a time and can be subdivided into *ladder* and *balanced strategies*, depending on the order of the schemas to be integrated. The second allows integration of *n* schema at a time ($n > 2$). An *n-ary* strategy is *one shot*, when *n* schemas are integrated in a single step; it is *iterative* otherwise.

Most existing systems follow binary strategies [6,10], where the sequence of pair-wise schemas to be integrated must be decided carefully. This requires in-depth understanding and an analysis of participating schemas. Moreover, since only two schemas are integrated at a time, the number of integration and conflict resolution operations is relatively large.

Although the disadvantages of binary strategies are obvious and well-known to database designers, there has been no framework flexible and powerful enough to support n-ary integration strategies. The greatest difficulty of n-ary integration strategies is the analysis and merging of participating schemas while still separating and keeping track of the changes to each of their elements, so that mappings between participating and integrated schemas can be established later. With XDD, the framework treats every participating schema as a large XML expression. Therefore, one may process *n* schemas at one time by treating them as a single schema consisting of *n* large XML expressions. With this strategy, a considerable amount of semantic analysis can be performed before merging and the maintenance of a large amount of track-keeping temporary data is avoided. This integration process is simpler and the processing steps required are less when compared with those employing binary strategies.

# 4 Integration System Architecture

This part considers the components of the proposed integration system. The internal structure and function of each component will be explained in detail.

## 4.1 System Overview

The inputs of the system are the schemas of source or local XML databases. Attached with these schemas is a common ontology, which contains their metadata and is expressed in terms of RDF[2] or DAML+OIL[3]. Information from the ontology is used to resolve conflicts among local schemas. The system's output is the integrated schema and the mapping between individual local schemas and the global schema.

## 4.2 System Architecture

A framework which simultaneously integrates heterogeneous XML databases is proposed. It is subdivided into three layers: *Data sources, schema cleaning and union, mediating layers*, discussed in the following sections.

### 4.2.1 Data Source Layer

This layer contains the input into the system, i.e., XML databases (XDB) [2, 15], their schemas and their common ontology. The schemas are assumed to be expressed in terms of XML Schema[4] which is much more expressive than DTD. In addition to XML databases, data sources could actually be in the form of relational database, object-oriented database, HTML or text file. However, their schemas must be transformed into XML format and expressed in XML Schema, which is normally possible due to the expressive power of XML.

The common ontology serves as the system's metadata and is basically represented in terms of RDF or DAML+OIL. However, RDF and DAML+OIL are not sufficiently

---

[2] http://www.w3.org/TR/REC-rdf-syntax/

[3] http://www.w3.org/TR/daml+oil-walkthru/

[4] http://www.w3.org/TR/xmlschema-0/

powerful to represent all the needed information. They are just capable of expressing simple relationships between classes and objects, but not complex relationships, axioms and constraints. The expressive power of RDF and DAML+OIL is enhanced by their embedment into XDD, resulting in RDF and DAML+OIL being able to express implicit information, rules, axioms and constraints, whence, most of the metadata information required by integration processes can be represented. XDD-based RDF or DAML+OIL contain XML expressions the tag names of which follow those specified in RDF and DAML+OIL.

### 4.2.2 Schema Cleaning and Union Layer

The main task of this layer is to remove namespaces and combine participating schemas. There are two sub-components in this layer.

*Namespace elimination* and *Schema combination.* The first of these components removes from all participating schemas their namespaces which might make similar or even the same tag names look different. The schemas, the namespaces of which have been removed, will be combined into a single XML document by the second component and then sent to the upper - mediating layer.

### 4.2.3 Mediating Layer

The mediator is the central component of the architecture. It consists of a set of rules that correspond to the axioms of and constraints on classes and their properties. Application of rules to a set of facts allows one to infer new facts. Rules can be applied recursively, i.e., the result of a rule can be input to other rules. The rules can be expressed in XET [1], an XDD-based rule language.

The mediator's main task is to resolve conflicts and integrate different schemas into a common schema for all participating databases. It contains the three sub components: *Normal form conversion, conflict handler and schema integration.*

*Normal form conversion* transforms all elements in participating schemas into a common format. With the normal form, all conflicts can easily be resolved in the next component without worrying about interleaving each other. After transforming all elements into the normal form, the *conflict handler* is used to solve conflicts between elements. All kinds of conflicts are examined and the sequence of the rules to be used is also considered carefully.

The *schema integration* component removes data redundancy and merges elements, yielding the final result – the integrated global schema.

## 5 Detailed Steps of Schema Integration

The integration of schemas is divided into the five steps: *Schema cleaning and union, normal form conversion, conflict resolution, schema merging and reconstruction.* Due to the limited space available, only some concrete (XDD) rules are presented.

### 5.1 Schema Cleaning and Union

The main task of this step is the preparation of all work for the other integration processes in two sub-steps. Firstly, the *namespaces* of all participating schemas are removed, because these namespaces will lead to misinterpretation of terms. Moreover, XDD cannot be employed to solve schema conflicts while namespaces remain. For example, in XDD, *xsd:string* and *ms:string* are considered to differ completely, although they represent the same data type string. Hence, the removal of namespaces is necessary.

Secondly, after their namespaces have been removed, input schemas are combined into a single XML schema document so that all of them can later be integrated simultaneously. XDD will treat each input schema just as an XML expression, and hence can deal simultaneously with their integration.

### 5.2 Normal Form Conversion

The main task here is the conversion of all elements into a combined schema in a common form. In order to gain an understanding for the reason why all schemas have to be converted into a common form, the problem will be analyzed next:

Fig. 1a and Fig. 1b display two typical schemas that describe the same set of XML documents. Obviously, the two schemas are *semantically equivalent*, but they have different structures due to the difference in their declaration. This situation occurs often when schemas are specified by different designers. This difference leads to the system treating them totally differently and sometimes a lot of effort is required to integrate them even though they are the same. It will be much better to detect these syntactic differences in the input schemas and eliminate them before the start of the integration process and reduce the time and complexity of the processes.

After examining many cases of this problem, it has been found that its major causes are: *The declaration of data types and arbitrary references of XML elements.* A solution to this problem is to convert all participating schemas into a common *normal form*.

***Definition***
*Schema S is in normal form if and only if:*
*For any elements E, A, B of S,*

- *if A is the data type of E, then A is defined immediately after the definition of E,*
- *if B is referenced by E, then E is replaced by B.*

Schema 1 in Fig. 1a is not, Schema 2 in Fig. 1b is in the normal form.

Normal form conversion transforms an XML schema into a complete nested structure. Instead of storing temporary variables for reference elements and referred data types, an XML processor can now process a normal form schema straightaway, because it contains neither reference elements nor referred data types. Besides, a schema in normal form readily yields information about the paths between elements, which is useful for resolving many structural conflicts.

```
<schema>
<element name="Bookstore">
      <complexType>
            <element name="Book" type="books">
            <element ref ="Magazine"/>
      <complexType>
  <element>
  <complexType name="books">
      <element name="Title" type="string"/>
      <element name="ISBN" type="string"/>
      < element name="Author" type="string"/>
  </complexType>
  <element name="Magazine">
    <complexType>
      <element name="Title" type="string"/>
      <element name="Date" type="date"/>
      <element name="Publisher" type="string"/>
    </complexType>
  </element>
</schema>
```

**a.** XML schema 1

```
<schema>
<element name="Bookstore">
 <complexType>
   <element name="Book">
   <complexType>
     <element name="Title" type="string"/>
     <element name="ISBN" type="string"/>
     < element name="Author" type="string"/>
   </complexType>
   </element>
   <element name="Magazine">
   <complexType>
     <element name="Title" type="string"/>
     <element name="Date" type="date"/>
     <element name="Publisher" type="string"/>
   </complexType>
   </element>
 </complexType>
</element>
</schema>
```

**b.** XML schema 2

**Fig. 1.** The two equivalent schemas

### 5.3 Conflict Resolution

Here conflicts between schemas are detected and resolved by using the information from the ontology. XDD rules are used to represent the resolution.

**Running Example**

Fig. 2 illustrates an example of solving conflicts between schemas. There are three XML schemas coming from three sources. Rectangular nodes represent elements, and circular nodes attributes. Consider the *School* element in the three schemas: Schema 1 (Fig. 2a) has *Dormitory* and *Student_Library*, Schema 2 (Fig. 2b) *Professor* and *School_Library*, Schema 3 (Fig. 2c) *Employee* as sub-elements. This running example is used in the rest of this section.

#### 5.3.1 Conflicts and Their Classification

There has been a lot of research attempting to resolve schema conflicts. Reference [11] introduces various conflicts between XML schemas, but fails to resolve all of them. The present work inherits results from the above research, but introduces some new resolutions.

Classify conflicts into four main types: *Name*, *Structural*, *Constraint* and *Data* type.

*5.3.1.1 Name conflicts*

There are two sources of name conflicts: *Homonyms* and *synonyms*.

**Homonyms:** When terms refer to different real world objects or concepts, they are known as homonyms. In Fig. 2b the term *name* is the *name of Borrower*, while in Fig. 2c, it is the *name of Professor*. Of course, the meaning of these two terms is completely different. It cannot be the same. One solution to this problem is to add a prefix to each element.

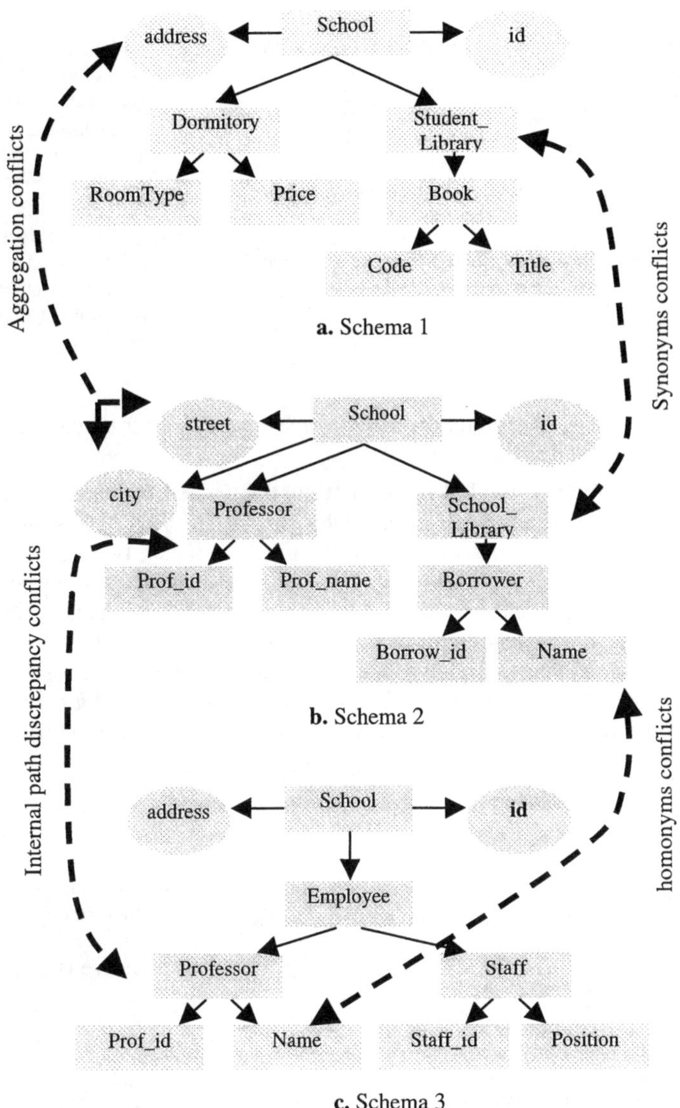


**Fig. 2.** The running example

**Synonyms:** When two different terms refer to the same real world object or concept, they are also known as synonyms. In Fig. 2, the two element names *Student_library* (Fig. 2.a) and *School_Library* (Fig. 2.b) represent the same element *Library*. In this case, the ontology is used to discover the similarity between terms. These synonyms of terms must be detected and reconciled when integrating heterogeneous data sources. The XDD rule for solving synonyms follows:

```
<xsd:element name=$S:common_name $P:att source="A">      % This rule specifies that
  $E:exp                                                 % if there are two similar
</xsd:element>                                           % elements $S:name1 and
<xsd:element name=$S:common_name $P:att source="B">      % $S:name2 in schemas A
  $E:exp                                                 % and B, and $S:name1
</xsd:element>                                           % and $S:name2 are
  ← <xsd:element name=$S:name1 $P:att source="A">       % synonyms. Then they
      $E:exp1                                            % are replaced by the
    </xsd:element>                                       % $S:common_name and
    <xsd:element name=$S:name2 $P:att source="B">        % the content of each
      $E:exp2                                            % element is the union of
    </xsd:element>                                       % all elemnts.
    [synonyms($S:common_name,$S:name1, $S:name2),
    $E:exp=Union($E:exp1, $E:exp2)]
```

*5.3.1.2 Structural conflicts*

There are four sources of structural conflict: Missing-item, internal path discrepancy, aggregation, generalization/specialization.

**Missing-item conflict:** This kind of conflict happens when the same elements have different numbers of sub-elements or attributes. In Fig. 2a, *School* has only two sub-elements: *Dormitory* and *Student_Library*. In Fig. 2b, it has two sub-elements are *Professor* and *School_Library*. In Fig. 2c, it has one sub-element: *Employee*.

Missing-item conflicts can be detected by comparing sub-elements or attributes of a particular element. The resolution of this problem is to unite all sub-elements and attributes of the same elements. In the running example, sub-elements of *School* in the integrated schema are the union of all the elements *Dormitory*, *Library (converted from Student_Library and School_Library)*, *Professor* and *Employee*. The XDD rule for solving missing-item conflict (*union rule*) is:

```
<xsd:element name=$S:name $P:att source= "Integrated">   % This rule specifies that
  <xsd:complexType>                                      % if there are two similar
    $E:exp3                                              % elements $S:name in
  </xsd:complexType>                                     % two schemas A and B,
</xsd:element>                                           % then their contents are
  ← <xsd:element name=$S:name $P:att source="A">        % the union of all sub
      <xsd:complexType>                                  % elements
        $E:exp1
      </xsd:complexType>
    </xsd:element>
    <xsd:element name=$S:name $P:att  source="B">
      <xsd:complexType>
        $E:exp2
      </xsd:complexType>
    </xsd:element>
    [$E:exp3=Union($E:exp1,$E:exp2)]
```

**Internal path discrepancy conflict:** Internal path discrepancies arise when two paths to the same element only match partially or not at all. In Fig. 2b, the element *Professor* is the immediate child node of the element *School*, while in Fig. 2c, *Professor* is the child node of *Employee*, not the immediate child node of *School*.

In order to resolve internal path discrepancy conflicts, first, one has to resolve missing-item conflicts, and then to remove redundant elements. The elements to be removed are decided based on the information from the ontology, which is given to support integration processes. For instance, the information from the ontology tells:

*Professor is subClass of Employee*, whence, in this case, the element *Professor* - the child of *School* - need be removed.

**Aggregation conflicts:** Aggregation conflicts happen when elements or attributes in one schema are the result of aggregation of some elements or attributes in another schema. In Fig. 2a and Fig. 2b, the attribute *address* is the result of aggregation of the *street* and *city* attributes. This problem's resolution is based on information from the ontology and defines a new data type from existing elements or attributes. In order to resolve aggregation conflicts, first the union rule is applied which yields the result of Fig. 3a, where only some important elements are shown.

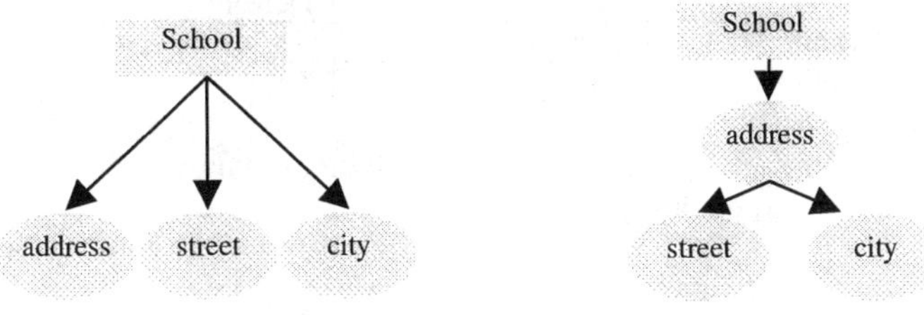


a. Union of two schemas b. Creation of new data type

**Fig. 3.** Resolution of aggregation conflicts

Then a new data type is created by combination of elements. For instance, based on the information from the ontology, it is known that *street and city are subClasses of address*. Hence the XDD rule is applied to create a new data type (see Fig. 3b), which is established like existing XDD rules.

**Generalization/specialization:** This kind of conflict happens when an element in one schema is more specific (general) than an element in another schema [11]. Fig. 4 shows an example of generalization/specialization.

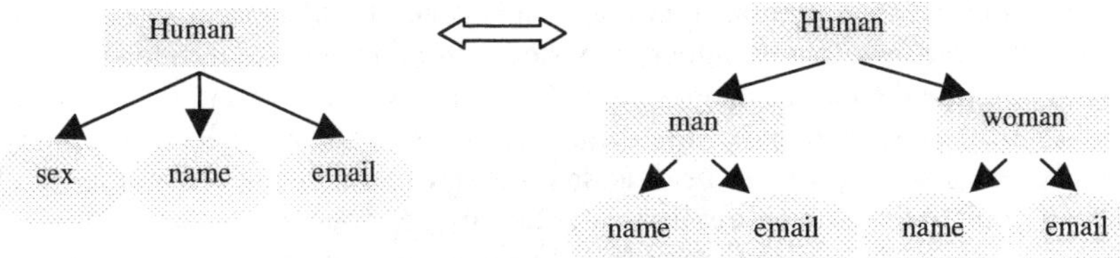


**Fig. 4.** Generalization/specification conflicts

Theoretically speaking, the solution of this problem is to consult the ontology for a decision. However, it is interesting that a generalization/specialization conflict can be automatically resolved by sequential application of the union rule and elimination rule. In this case, by using information from the ontology, one finds $human \cap sex="male" \Rightarrow man$ and $human \cap sex="female" \Rightarrow woman$. So the attribute *sex* is no longer necessary for the schema and can be removed.

*5.3.1.3 Constraint conflicts*

During schema integration, constraint conflicts between elements often occur. The guideline for solving constraint conflicts is to weaken the constraints. For example, Table 1 shows the possible constraints of attributes from different schemas and the resolution in an integrated schema.

**Table 1.** The resolution for fixed and default value

| Schema1 | Schema2 | Target Schema |
|---|---|---|
| Require | Optional | Optional |
| Optional | Fixed | Optional |
| Fixed | Default | Default |
| Default | Prohibited | – |
| Prohibited | Require | * |

The symbol "–" means no constraint value, whereas symbol "*" means the target value must be consulted by designers.

### 5.4 Reconstruction of the Integrated Schema

After resolution of conflicts, schemas are ready to be merged. First, unnecessary tags are removed. Then, the contents of participating schemas are combined into one integrated schema file. This file may contain many redundant elements which should be removed. A guideline for the elimination of redundant elements is to remove sub-trees in order to retain the more general structure.

## 6 Conclusions

The proposed system is one of the few frameworks which can simultaneously integrate *n* heterogeneous XML schemas. It employs XDD as its underlying model for the representation of common ontology and general rules, and for resolution guidelines required by various integration steps. In addition, the system uses XML Schema to describe database schemas. With this approach, the system is more flexible when it comes to resolving conflicts and merging schemas. All major possible conflicts between schemas have been addressed and their resolutions proposed. The problem of equivalent schema conflicts, defined by the concept of normal form, has been addressed and it has been demonstrated how to convert a schema into its normal form. As a result, XML schemas can be declared uniformly and ambiguities avoided, which are caused by arbitrary schema declaration. With the expressive power of XML Schema, the proposed approach can also integrate the schemas of other types of databases, e.g., relational and object-oriented databases, if the schemas can be translated into or represented by XML Schema. Moreover, as Web application metadata could be described in terms of XML Schema, the proposed approach can readily be extended to deal with the integration of such metadata. A prototype system [13] has been implemented in order to verify the effectiveness of the approach.

## References


1. Anutariya, C., Wuwongse, V., and Wattanapailin, V. An Equivalent-Transformation-Based XML Rule Language. Proc. of the International Workshop on Rule Markup Languages for Business Rules in the Semantic Web, Sardinia, Italy (2002)
2. Anutariya, C., Wuwongse, V., Nantajeewarawat, E., and Akama, K. Towards a Foundation for XML Document Databases. Proc. of 1st International Conference on Electronic Commerce and Web Technologies (EC-Web 2000), London, UK. Lecture Notes in Computer Science, Springer Verlag, Vol. 1875, (2000) 324–333
3. Batini, C., Lenzerini, M., and Navathe, S. B. A Comparative Analysis of Methodologies for Database Schema Integration. ACM Computing Surveys. Vol. 18, No. 4, (1986) 323–364.
4. Bertino, E., Ferrari, E. XML and Data Integration. IEEE Internet Computing. Vol. 5, No.6, (2001) 75–76
5. Bouguettaya, R. K., and Parazoglou, M. On Building a Hyperdistributed Database. Journal of Information Systems. Vol. 20, No.7, (1995) 557–577
6. Elmasri, R., Larson, J., and Navathe, S. Integration algorithms for federated databases and logical database design. Tech Rep. Honeywell Corporate Research Center (1987)
7. Gianolli, P., Mylopoulos, J. A semantic approach to XML based data integration. Proc. of the 20th. International Conference on Conceptual Modelling (ER), Yokohama, Japan (2001)
8. Jakobovits, R. Integrating Heterogeneous Autonomous Information Sources. Univ of Washington Technical Report, UW-CSE-971205, (1997)
9. Levy, A. Y., Rajaraman, A., and Ordille, J. J. Querying Heterogeneous Information Sources Using Source Descriptions. Proc. of the 22nd VLDB Conference, Bombay, India, (1996) 251–262
10. May, W. A Framework for Generic Integration of XML Data Sources. International Workshop on Knowledge Representation meets Databases (KRDB 2001), Roma, Italy (2001)
11. Pluempitiwiriyawej, C., Hammer, J. A Classification Scheme for Semantic and Schematic Heterogeneities in XML Data Sources. Technical report TR00-004. University of Florida. (2000)
12. Pottinger, R., and Levy, A. A scalable algorithm for answering queries using views. Proc. of 26th VLDB Conference, Cairo, Egypt, (2000) 484–495
13. The XSIS system. Available online http://www.cs.ait.ac.th/~b02238/XSIS/
14. Vdovjak, R., Houben, G. RDF based Architecture for Semantic Integration of Heterogeneous Information Source. http://wwwis.win.tue.nl/~houben/respub/wiiw01.pdf
15. Wuwongse, V., Akama, K., Anutariya, C., and Nantajeewarawat, E. A Data Model for XML Databases. Journal of Intelligent Information Systems, Vol. 20, No. 1, (2003) 63–80.
16. Wuwongse, V., Anutariya, C., Akama, K., and Nantajeewarawat, E. XML Declarative Description (XDD): A Language for the Semantic Web. IEEE Intelligent Systems, Vol. 16, No. 3, (2001) 54–65

# Xaggregation: Flexible Aggregation of XML Data[1]

Hongzhi Wang, Jianzhong Li, Zhenying He, and Hong Gao

Department of Computer Science and Technology, Harbin Institute of Technology
whongzhi@0451.com, lijz@banner.hl.cninfo.net
hzy_hit_cn@sina.com, gaohong@mail.banner.com.cn

**Abstract.** XML is an important format of information exchange and representation. One of its features is that it has tag representing semantics. Based on this feature, an extensive aggregation of operation of XML data, Xaggregation, is represented in this paper. Xaggregation permits XPath expression decorating dimension property and measure property. With Xaggregation, statistics of XML data becomes more flexible with function of aggregating heterogeneous data and hierarchy data along some path of XML. Xaggregation could be embedded in query language of XML such as XQuery. In this paper, the definition of Xaggregation is presented, as well as the semantics and application of it. Implementation of Xaggregation based on native XML database with XML as tree structure is also designed.

## 1 Introduction

XML is an important information representation format. On one hand, because of its extendability, it is used widely as information exchange format. On the other hand, model of XML could be considered as semi-structured [1], information representation ability of which is stronger than that of tradition relational database. Therefore, XML database has its special meaning. XML warehouse is often used as cache of information integration system based on XML is an. XML database is also used as web database.

Today, one usage of database especial massive database is for decision support. Aggregation is a basic operation of decision support.

There are many aggregations definition and implementation methods of relational database. But in XML database, the work of aggregation is quite little. [6, 7, 8] is a serious of work of a kind of aggregation related to XML. It uses XML data as decoration of dimension properties. In [12], an operation to implementation aggregation of XML stream is presented. This operation is to aggregate a series of XML documents into one based on their same parts, and do not touch the real statistics of the information contained in XML document.

[1] Supported by the National Natural Science Foundation of China under Grant No.60273082; the Defence Pre-Research Project of the 'Tenth Five-Year-Plan' of China no.41315.2.3

G. Dong et al. (Eds.): WAIM 2003, LNCS 2762, pp. 104–115, 2003.

Aggregation of data in XML format should be different from that of relational database in semantics. With stronger representation ability of tag representing semantics, aggregation of XML should be extended. Possible extensions of aggregation of XML data are:

- The aggregation of the same property should permit a special set of paths, such as a path set defined with XPath[2]. That is to say, the dimension property and measure could be a set of object in XML document. The object in various positions of XML document with various paths could be aggregated together.
- The structure of XML document should be considered, representing the complex way of aggregation. This process is quite like roll-up operation in common aggregation with the difference of multiple roll-up paths that make up of a complex structure.

With above extensions, the aggregation of information in XML format becomes flexible.

In aggregation on relational database, the property to be aggregated up is measure property and the property the aggregation based on is dimension property. This paper continues to use these definitions to describe new aggregation. In this paper, *path* of a node n in XML tree refers to the path from root of the tree to n. Node a nearer to root than node b is defined as a is higher than b.

In this paper, a special aggregation operation based on XML, Xaggregation, is presented. This operation permits XPath decorating dimension properties and measure properties. We believe this paper to be the first to consider this instance of aggregation in XML data.

However, the implementation of this kind of aggregation is more complex, because of not only complex process of aggregation, but also various logic and storage structures of XML data.

XML database has several storage structures. Mainly, four kind storage of XML databases are used, common file system, OO database, relational database and native XML database[11]. Native XML database is used more and more because its implementation is optimized specially for XML data. Relational database [9, 10] is also widely used to store and process query of XML data. But because of the core idea of storing XML data in relational database depends on decomposing of schema of XML data into tables. Xaggregation needs travel of path, as will bring out many join operations. The efficiency is affected. Therefore, the implementation of Xaggregation in this paper is based on native XML database with tree structure.

This paper focuses on the definition of aggregation on XML data as well as implementation of Xaggregation on native XML database. The contribution of this paper includes:

- Operation Xaggregation are defined. The usage of Xaggregation is presented by example.
- Implementation algorithm of Xaggregation is presented. The implementations are based on native XML database.

This paper is structured as follows. Section 2 presents the motivation of defining new aggregation operation. Xaggregations are defined in section 3. Implementation of

Xaggregation is presented in section4. Section 5 gives experiments of Xaggregation and related works are summarized in section 6. Section 7 draws the conclusion.

## 2 Motivation

In this section, we consider motivation for the present work. As mentioned in introduction, the Xaggregation satisfies requirements of aggregation on XML data. Xaggregation serves many purposes:

- **Complex document structure:** The object to be aggregated in the same XML document may in various positions of the XML document. For example, statistics of the salary level of a company, the organization of the company may be complex. Some parts may be vertical structure, and some another parts may be flat structure. The properties to statistics may in different path. With Xaggregation, this kind of statistic could be represented and implementation.
- **Data distribution:** Data in information integration system distributes in various autonomy data sources in internet. The data could be considered as one XML document [1]. Representation and implementation of aggregation on this kind of data need Xaggregation, because properties to be aggregated may be in various paths in autonomy data sources with respective schema.
- **Hierarchy information aggregation:** aggregation of XML data could be along different paths. E.g. statistics of the salary level of the company with complex structure on various organizations with different granularity needs aggregation along various paths because properties to aggregate may be in different structures.

## 3 Definition of XAggregation

Aggregation on XML data is distinguished to that of relational database mainly because of the tree structure of XML data. Therefore, aggregation of XML data, Xaggregation, focus on data with Xpath [2], a flexible path description . In this section, the definition XAggregation operation and its properties are introduced.

### 3.1 The Definition of XAggregation

Xaggregation is aggregation on measure property b, decorating by an XPath pathb, grouping by dimension property k also decorating by an XPath pathk. The object the aggregation based on, just like a tuple of aggregation in relational database, is defined as aggregation object with the node identifying it called common root. The result of Xaggregation is the aggregation result of measure property in aggregation object grouping on dimension property satisfying XPath description in query.

In Xaggregation, both measure property and dimension property do not have a single property description as relational database but a set of descriptions. If an aggregation object has more than one measure property, the aggregation of these objects could be considered as its measure value. In the aggregation of relational database, the measure in tuples with the same dimension value could be aggregated together. While in Xaggregation on XML document, under the same common root there may be more than one dimension properties with the same tag but different value or Xpath. Semantics of one aggregation expression may have different meanings. Therefore restriction is to be added to Xaggregation. We have chosen the following because we believe they can all be useful in different instance.

ANY_VALUE: If one aggregation object contains more than one dimension properties, this aggregation object is considered as objects each with a single dimension property value and the aggregation result of measure property values. If there are multiple dimension properties in the same aggregation object with only one value, they are considered as one dimension property during aggregation.

ANY_PATH: If one aggregation object contains more than one dimension properties, this aggregation object in a single aggregation is considered as objects each with a single dimension property value and the aggregation result of measure property value. Only when the path and value of dimension properties are both same, they are considered same during aggregation.

COMPOUND_VALUE: If one aggregation object contains more than one dimension properties, this aggregation object is considered as an object with the combination of dimension property value and the aggregation result of measure property value. Judging rule of the aggregation objects to aggregate is that they have same dimension property, as means the combinations of dimension of them are same.

COMPOUND_PATH: If one aggregation object contains more than one dimension properties, this aggregation object is considered as object with the combination of dimension property value with path and the aggregation result of measure property values. Judging criterion of the aggregation objects to aggregate together is they have same dimension property, as means the combinations of dimension of them are same, both path and value of each element of the combination should be same.

### 3.2 Expression of XAggregation

A simple expression of Xaggregation could be described as:

*fun*([$path_a$]/a/[$path_b$]/b) group by [*feature*][$path_a$]/a/[$path_k$]/k

In the description, $path_a$, $path_b$ and $path_k$ represent the paths of element a, b and k respectively. *fun* is aggregation function, which may be avg, sum, count, min, max and so on. The semantics of the expression is to aggregate all the value of bs in object a satisfying $path_b$ with a unique value of k under the same object with root tag a satisfying $path_k$ and assemble the aggregate value and k value in result. Feature is one of ANY_VALUE, ANY_PATH, COMPOUND_VALUE and COMPOUND_PATH. Default value of feature is ANY_VALUE.

The representation could be embedded into XQuery[3] easily with format:

for $pn in distinct-values(document(*document_name*)//[$path_a$]/a/[$path_k$]/k)
let $i := document(*document_name*)//[$path_a$]/a
group by $pn

```
return
<result>
<dimension>$pn</dimension>
<aggvalue> {fun($i/[path_b]/b)} </aggvalue>
</result>
```

### 3.3 Explanation of Xaggregation

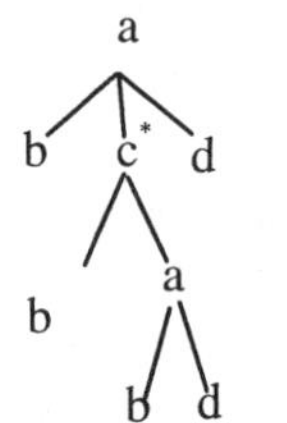


**Fig. 1.** Sample branch

It is different from data in XML format and relation is that object under XML tag may be both single value and combine object while that of relational is just a value. Hence the condition of valid aggregation is:

With aggregation function sum, avg, measure property, b, should be a simple value. With aggregation function min and max, measure property should have predefined order relation. With aggregation function count, measure property could be both simple value and combine object.

Dimension property could be both simple value and combine object. When executing aggregation, aggregation objects with the dimension properties same in both value and structure are considered to be aggregated.

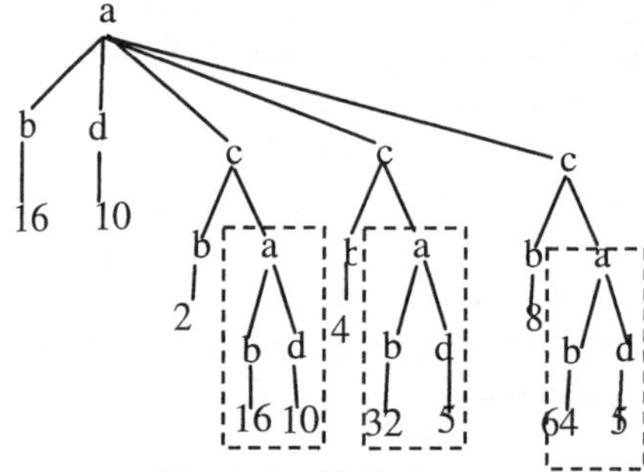


**Fig. 2.** An XML fragment

Because of recursion node of schema of XML document, there may be more than one common root in a path. E.g. when aggregation is sum (a/*/b) group by a/*/d, if there are branch as a/c/a/c/b in schema, there are several instances satisfying the aggregation schema. The aggregation of this structure is computed in the following rules:

If there is more than one common root in a path, aggregation is executed along the path from lower level to higher level. Only aggregation objects under a common root could be aggregated. Aggregation objects without any common root upper to them are aggregated.

The semantics of the aggregation along with path is that aggregate all the values of a measure property decorated by a special dimension property.

### 3.4 An Example of Xaggregation

Fig.2 is a XML document fragment with the schema in fig.1. In this XML document fragment, the fragment in gashed bound is treated as a group of aggregation object. Nowhere in what model, aggregation results of these elements in this level are (10, 16) and (5, 96). In the bracket, the former number represents the value of dimension property and the latter number represents the result of aggregation. For the tag a in the root of the fragment, the results of the aggregation in four models are shown as following:

ANY_VALUE: (5, 142), (10,142)

ANY_PATH: (a/d, 10, 142), (a/c/a/d, 5, 142), (a/c/a/d, 10, 142)

COMPOUND_VALUE: ((10, 5), 142)

COMPOUND_PATH: (((a/d, 10), (a/c/a/d, 5), (a/c/a/d, 10)), 142)

Aggregation results of them are same because all of measure properties under root node a are considered as to be aggregated. In the four models, result representations are different. If there are upper aggregation objects of root a, in different model, different values of this level are used for aggregation

# 4 Implementation of Extended Aggregation

In this section, implementation algorithm of XAggregation is presented. All the implementation is based on native XML database, in which XML documents are stored in tree mode. An XML document is processed as an ordered label tree, defined as XML tree. But our algorithm doesn't depend on special storage structure.

The idea of XAggregation implementation is to compute aggregation result during traversing XML tree. Main data structure of the algorithm is stack_list representing aggregation nodes in the path, contains three parts: aggregation result, dimension list, dimension-result list. Aggregation result is the aggregation result of this node, which is computed during traversing children of this aggregation node. Dimension list records values of dimension properties under this aggregation node. Dimension-result list records aggregation results and dimension values of children of this aggregation object.

XAggregation algorithm is a recursive process. When a common root is met, a new node n is pushed into a stack_list l. The value of aggregation result and dimension property is stored in n. If a measure property is met, the value of it is aggregated to all nodes in l the path to whom satisfies path condition. When a dimension property is met, the value of it is connected to the dimension-result list of all nodes in l satisfying path condition. When the computation of an aggregation is finished, the aggregation result of top in l is aggregated to the node under it and the dimension list and dimension-result list is merged into the node under it. Distinguish of the four kinds of aggregation model is that the dimension information stored in dimension list and dimension-result list is different.

Description of the algorithm is shown as follows. In order to simply the description of algorithm, the algorithm described here could only process queries with just one dimension property and one measure property. Access of the tree is considered as an interface of native XML database. Extension of the algorithm is easy.

**Algorithm1 Xaggregation algorithm:**

void Xagg(c, $p_d$, $p_m$, $p_c$, $path_d$, $path_m$, $path_c$, $path_r$, $path_t$, $stack_b$, func, l)

**Input**: r: the root of current XML sub-tree;

$p_d$: the name of dimension property;

$p_m$: the name of measure property;
$p_c$: the name of common root of $p_m$ and $p_c$;
$path_d$: the path of dimension property in query;
$path_m$: the path of measure property;
$path_c$: the path of common root in query;
$path_r$: the path of *root* in entire XML document;
$path_t$: the path from current node to its nearest ancestor with label $p_c$;
$stack_b$: a lstack_list to store the value of measure properties and dimension properties along the aggregation path;
func: aggregation function

**Method Description**

```
path_r'=path_r+c; path_t'=path_t+c; t=label_of(root);
if (p_d= =t && path_t= =path_d){// if a dimension property is met
        connect the value of this node to dimension list in the top of stack_b
        for(each node n in stack_b except top){
                if (path_r-n.path ==p_d){
                        connect the value of this node to dimension list in the top of
stack_b
                }
        }
        return;
}
else if(p_m= =t&&path_t= =path_m){// a measure property is met
        aggregate the value of measure to result in the top of stack_b
        for(each node n in stack_b except top){
                if (path_r-n.path ==p_m){
                        add the value of measure to sum in n
                }
        }
        return;
}
else if (p_c= =t and path_r= =path_c){//a common root is met
        path_t'=NULL;
        push a new list node n into l;
}
for (each of the child of root c){
        plain_agg(c, p_d, p_m, p_c, path_d, path_m, path_c, path_r', path_t', stack_b, func);
}
if (p_c= =t and path_r= =path_c){//a common root is to be pop up from stack_b
        stack_list_node l_n=the top of stack_b;
        output(the aggreagation value of l_n)
        pop stack_b;
        merge(top of stack_b, l_n);
}
return
```

**Note of Algorithm1:**

- symbol '+' is overloaded for path as connect two path and symbol '-' is also overloaded. $Path_a$-$path_b$ means cutting $path_b$ as the prefix of $path_a$, if $path_b$ is not the prefix of $path_a$, NULL is returned.
- Function merge is to aggregate the aggregation results in two lists with same dimension property value. For different model, the judging condition of "same" is different.
- Function output is determined by the requirement of result's schema. The result could be outputted as a series of tuples with position information. With the information, tuples could be assembled to result with special schema.
- If func is avg, both the result of aggregation sum and count should be recorded.

# 5 Experiments

In this section, we present an experimental evaluation of our Xaggregation implementation algorithm using real and synthetic data sets. We execute our algorithm directly on original XML documents. We traverse XML document as a tree but only contain a single branch in memory.

## 5.1 Experimental Setup

### 5.1.1 Hardware and Software Environment

Our algorithm is implemented in Microsoft Visual C++ on a PIII running at 850MHZ with 128M memory RAM.

### 5.1.2 Data Sets

In order to test the algorithm comprehensively, both real data set and synthetic data set are used.

Real data set we used is Shakes. The set contains 36 XML documents with size 7.31M, 327461 nodes and 179871 elements. In order to execute the aggregation, we connect all the documents into one, shakes.xml , with an additional root.

The query on Shakes is

```
for $pn in distinct-values(document("shakes.xml")//*/SPEECH/*/SPEAKER)
let $i := document("shakes.xml")//*/SPEECH
group by $i//*/$pn
return
<result>
<dimension>$pn</dimension>
<aggvalue> {count($i//*/LINE)} </aggvalue>
</result>
```

```
< !ELEMENT root (a*, f*)>
<!ELEMENT f (a*, b*, c*)>
<!ELEMENT d(a, f*, c)>
<!ELEMENT a (#PCDATA)>
<!ELEMENT b (#PCDATA)>
<!ELEMENT a (#PCDATA)>
```

a.DTD of Set B

```
< !ELEMENT root (a*, f*)>
<!ELEMENT f (a*, b, d, c*)>
<!ELEMENT d(a, b, f*, c)>
<!ELEMENT a (#PCDATA)>
<!ELEMENT b (#PCDATA)>
<!ELEMENT a (#PCDATA)>
```

b. DTD of Set C

**Fig. 3.** Schema of Test Data Sets

This query has special semantics as "statistics how many line each speaker has said in all Shakes plays".

The schema of real data is simple and the number of measure properties and dimension properties is small. In order to further test our algorithm, synthetic data sets are designed with fixed schema using XMLgenerator[13]. Two data sets, named Set B and Set C, are generated with different schema as are presented in fig.3. XML documents with various size and structure are generated. The core task of Set B is to test the relationship between file size, number of nodes and process efficiency. The core task of Set C is to test the relation ship between the structure and process efficiency, especially when the recursive common root exists.

For compare, the query on the two synthetic is the same:

```
for $pn in distinct-values(document("b.xml")//*/f/*/c)
let $i := document("b.xml")//*/f
group by $i//*/$pn
return
<result>
<dimension>$pn</dimension>
<aggvalue> {sum($i//*/a)} </aggvalue>
</result>
```

## 5.2 Experimental Results

Results of experiment on Shakes and Set B are presented in table 1.

From Table 1, it is noted that in Set B, the growth rate of speed of data process is faster along with the file size. Although the comparison of string is slower than that of number, the process speed of Shakes is faster than Set B, because there are more nodes with no relation with aggregation in Shakes than those of XML documents in Set B. Our algorithm is related to not only document size but also number of nodes of common root, measure properties and dimension properties. Results of experiment on Set C is in Table 2.

**Table 1.** Comparison of Experiment Result of Shakes and Set B

| Data set | File size | Number of nodes | Number of Elements | Process time(s) |
|---|---|---|---|---|
| Shakes | 7.31M | 327461 | 179871 | 9.713 |
| Set B | 64.1K | 6862 | 3501 | 0.16 |
| Set B | 628K | 66262 | 33201 | 15.321 |
| Set B | 1.63 M | 174442 | 87381 | 87.355 |
| Set B | 17.7M | 1863252 | 933191 | 1700.354 |

**Table 2.** Comparison of Experiment Result of Set C

| Group id | File size | Number of nodes | Number of Elements | Maximum Number of level | Process time(s) |
|---|---|---|---|---|---|
| 1 | 11.3k | 1181 | 748 | 8 | 0.110 |
| 2 | 646K | 65549 | 41518 | 15 | 9.063 |
| 3 | 658K | 67235 | 42277 | 8 | 6.178 |
| 4 | 2.39M | 234785 | 203977 | 8 | 16.924 |
| 5 | 2.81M | 284250 | 199277 | 11 | 104.74 |
| 6 | 17.4M | 1771441 | 1121918 | 21 | 2087.501 |

In Table 2, the file size and number of elements of group 2 and group 3, group 4 and group 5 is similar but the query process efficiency is quite different. It is because in our algorithm, the deeper a measure property is, the more add operation should be executed. The query process speed gap between group 4 and group 5 is larger than that between group 2 and group3, because the structure of these XML documents becomes different when adjusting parameters to obtain fit document size. It could be concluded that our algorithm is sensitivity to the structures of XML documents, even when they have same schema.

Comparing Table 1 with Table 2, query process efficiency of Set C is higher than that of Set B, when XML tree is not too high. The reason is that the number of measure properties and dimension properties in the documents of Set C in less than that of Set B, but the number of common roots is contrast. That is to say, the affect of number of measure properties and dimension properties is more than that of number of common root and level. But the height of XML tree has large affect on the efficiency of query process.

## 6 Related Work

As an important part of query, expression of group and aggregation are defined in some of query languages. In XML query languages, LORLE and XML-GL aggregate functions are fully implemented, XSL and XQL implementation aggregation partly, XML-QL does not support aggregation[5]. XQuery[3] considers group and aggregation. In query language with aggregation, the properties are permitted to be decorated by path information. But none of them considers the complex instance when path of property is described using complex path expression such as XPath, although XQuery uses XPath as its path description standard.

Some algebra for XML also defines group and aggregation [14, 15, 16]. But none of the aggregation definitions could represent the instance of recursion.

Process query with XPath is hot in research of XML[17, 18, 19, 20]. Most of them focus on selection and projection of XPath. These works could be used for effective implementation of Xaggregation on special storage structure. However, none of them relates to aggregation directly.

## 7 Conclusion and Future Work

In this paper, Xaggregation, an operation of aggregation on XML data is presented. It is flexible for aggregation of objects in XML document decorating with XPath. It could be used in statistics of XML documents with complex structure, such as recursion properties or distributed in various autonomy sites in internet. Xaggregation could be embedded into Xquery. Implementation algorithm is presented in this paper.

Our algorithm is based on native XML database stored as a tree but not on special storage. Efficiency of our algorithm is not high. It is necessary to design special algorithms of special storage. In distribution environment, information transmission time should be considered. These problems are left for further work..

## References


1. S. Abiteboul, P. Buneman, D. Suciu: Data on the Web: From Relations to Semistructured Data and XML. Morgan Kaufmann Publishers, (2000).
2. World Wide Web Consortium: XML Path Language (XPath) 2.0. http://www.w3.org/TR/xpath20/
3. World Wide Web consortium: XQuery 1.0: An XML Query Language. http://www.w3.org/TR/xquery/.
4. J. Gray, A. Bosworth, A. Layman and H. Piramish: Data Cube: A Relational Aggregation Operator Generalizing Group-By, Cross-Tab, and Sub-Totals. In Proc. of ICDE, (1996).
5. A. Bonifati, S.Ceri: Comparative Analysis of Five XML Query Languages. ACM SIGMOD Record 29(1) (2000).
6. D. Pedersen, K. Riis, T. B. Pedersen: XML-Extended OLAP Querying. In Proc of 14th International Conference on Scientific and Statistical Database Management (2002).
7. D. Pedersen, K. Riis, and T. B. Pedersen: Cost Modeling and Estimation for OLAP-XML Federations. In Proc. of DaWaK, (2002) 245–254.
8. D. Pedersen, K. Riis, and T. B. Pedersen: Query optimization for OLAP-XML federations. In Proc. Of the fifth ACM international workshop on Data Warehousing and OLAP, (2002).

9. A. Deutsch, M. F. Fernandez, D. Suciu: Storing Semi-structured Data with STORED. In Proc of SIGMOD Conference (1999).
10. J. Shanmugasundaram, K. Tufte, C. Zhang, G. He, D. J. DeWitt, J. F. Naughton: Relational Databases for Querying XML Documents: Limitations and Opportunities. In Proc of VLDB Conference (1999).
11. F. Tian, David J. DeWitt, J. Chen, C. Zhang: The Design and Performance Evaluation of Alternative XML Storage Strategies. SIGMOD Record special issue on "Data Management Issues in E-commerce", (2002).
12. K. Tufte and D. Mater: Aggregation and Accumulation of XML Data. IEEE Data Engineering Bulletin, 24(2) (2001) 34–39.
13. http://www.alphaworks.ibm.com/tech/xmlgenerator. August 20, 2001
14. D. Beech, A. Malhotra, and M. Rys: A formal data model and algebra for xml. Communication to the W3C (1999)
15. P. Fankhauser, M. Fernandez,A.Malhotra,M.Rys,J.Simeon, and P. Wadler: The XML Query Algebra. http://www.w3.org/TR/2001/WD-Query-algebra-20010215.
16. L. Galanis, E. Viglas, D.J. DeWitt, J.F. Naughton and D. Maier: Following the Paths of XML Data: An Algebraic Framework for XML Query Evaluation. Available at http://www.cs.wisc.edu/niagara/papers/algebra.pdf (2001)
17. K. Shim, C. Chung, J. Min: APEX: An Adaptive Path Index for XML data. In Proc. of ACM SIGMOD (2002).
18. T. Grust: Accelerating XPath location steps. In Proc. of ACM SIGMOD (2002).
19. G. Gottlob, C. Koch, and R. Pichler: Efficient algorithms for processing XPath queries. In Proc of 28th VLDB Conference (2002).
20. S. Chien, Z. Vagena, D. Zhang, V. J. Tsotras: Efficient Structural Joins on Indexed XML Documents. In Proc of 28th VLDB Conference (2002).

# Efficient Evaluation of XML Path Queries with Automata

Bing Sun, Jianhua Lv, Guoren Wang, Ge Yu, and Bo Zhou

Northeastern University, Shenyang, China
{sunb,dbgroup,wanggr,yuge}@mail.neu.edu.cn

**Abstract.** Path query is one of the most frequently used components by the various XML query languages. Most of the proposed methods compute path queries in instance space, i.e. directly facing the XML instances, such as XML tree traversal and containment join ways. As a query method based on automata technique, automata match (AM) can evaluate path expression queries in schema space so that it allows efficient computation of complex queries on vast amount of data. This paper introduces how to construct query automata in order to compute all regular expression queries including those with wildcards. Furthermore, a data structure named schema automata is proposed to evaluate containment queries that are very difficult from the conventional automata point of view. To improve the efficiency of schema automata, methods to reduce and persistent them are proposed. Finally, performance study of the proposed methods are given.

## 1 Introduction

Most XML query languages [2,3,6,5,12] use path queries as their core components. The input of path queries are path expressions (*PEs*). *PEs* can be divided into steps connected by path operators. Different operators have different properties, and the main target of path query systems is to compute these operators correctly and efficiently.

XML tree traversal is a basic and simple way [11]. It tests all XML tree nodes one by one in certain order to see if they are instances of the given *PE*. This way is effective but not efficient. There are some improved methods upon tree traversal. They can reduce the searching space of traversal and improve performance. However, since all nodes on pathes leading to candidate results must be accessed at least once, it is not expected to be an efficient way. Another popular method is containment join (*CJ*) [4,8]. It gives each XML node a code as its id. Codes of instances corresponding to *PE* steps are gotten from indices, and they are joined up to compute the path operators between them. *CJ* is well designed to evaluate containment queries, which are queries containing ancestor-descendant operator ("//"). *CJ* is an efficient method and it can be easily implemented in relational database systems. However, it does not support closure operators ("*", "+").

Methods discussed above are facing XML instances. Tree traversal ways access instances to acquire their children, siblings or attributes; *CJ* ways join up

G. Dong et al. (Eds.): WAIM 2003, LNCS 2762, pp. 116–127, 2003.

two instance sets and form a new one. These methods are regarded as executing in instance space. Speed of these methods is highly relevant to the amount of instances they process. Therefore, if they run on large scale XML documents, the efficiency will extremely decrease. The structure of an XML document is usually defined by DTD or XML schema, and their structures are much more stable than that of XML documents. Thus, if there is a method that runs in schema space, it will performs well much better on large documents. Automata match (*AM*) is such a method. It builds a path schema tree (*PST*) as index, and converts *PEs* to query automata. Then, the nodes on *PST* are matched with the status of query automata. Finally, the results are gotten on the nodes that matches the accepting status. *AM* does not deal with XML instances directly except results retrieval. Experimental results prove that it is efficient on large documents. *AM* approach has been proposed first in [7], but it does not describe how to evaluate ancestor-descendant operator. This question are fully resolved in this paper.

Most path query system allows *PEs* being arbitrary complex by nested structure. Moreover, some special path operators are very time-consuming in common ways, so the complexity of the *PEs* can extraordinarily affect the efficiency of query processing. These operators need to be studied carefully. Closure operators defined in regular expressions are useful and important for querying nested structured XML data. They are very difficult to evaluate by ordinary methods for most systems including RDBMS do not support them. Rewriting them into repeated joins is a feasible but time-consuming way. Since there always exists an equivalence automata for each regular expression, closure operators can be convert to automata components naturally. Therefore, *AM* can easily deal with closure operators.

Altmel and Franklin proposed an algorithm to perform efficient filtering of XML document in the selective information dissemination environments [1]. Automata were used to denotes user profiles and a SAX interfaced parser was used to activate the automata when parsing documents in there approach. They were facing XML documents directly while *AM* is facing schemas of XML documents for better performance.

Ancestor-descendant operator "//" is another operator widely used in path expressions, which is a non-regular operator. This operator is used to find all descendant XML nodes of the context nodes. It can also be considered as a "wildcard" of any path expressions that may occur there. Several ways has been proposed to compute it. Rewriting this operator into path expressions is a usual and universal way. However, if the document structure is very complex, the expressions generated will be extremely complicated or even it is impossible to generate equivalent expressions. *CJ* stands for a series of algorithms designed to compute "//". Ancestor nodes and descendant nodes are retrieved into two lists respectively, and the two lists are joined using certain algorithms. *CJ* is effective, and it is suitable to compute queries like "a//b" with the support of indices. However, its speed depends on the amount of data being joined. Therefore, if there are wildcards in *PEs*, like "a//*", the speed will be extremely lower. *AM* cannot handle "//" directly like "*" and "+" since it is not a regular operator. In this paper a data structure named schema automata (*SA*) is proposed to compute "//". *SA* is built either from XML documents, DTD, XML Schema or *PST*. It can be built dynamically while evaluating queries, or stored in database as an index. In addition, it can be optimized to get higher performance.

The remainder of this paper is organized as follows. Section 2 introduces some basic concepts relevant to *AM* method and puts forward *AM* algorithm. Section 3 illustrates the construction of query automata. Section 4 gives the definition and manipulation of *SA*. Section 5 shows how to optimize *SA*. Section 6 studies the performance of *AM* and *SA*. Finally, Section 7 concludes the paper.

## 2 Basic Concepts and Automata Match Algorithm

In this section, some concepts and *AM* algorithm are introduced. *AM* is a method that matches path schema with automata status, so the concepts of path schema and automata are proposed first. Let $D$ be an XML document, and $PST_D$ is an index named path schema tree of $D$. Let $Q$ be path expression of a query. $Q$ is converted into an query automata in *AM*, and the automata is denoted by $FSA_Q$.

Each XML node has a **node schema**, which describes the type of the node. For example, an XML element node tagged *book* and a node tagged *name* are considered have different types, so they have different schemas. Node schema is also called **schema** for short. Different categories of XML nodes have different definitions and representations of their schemas.

Each XML document is regarded as having a distinct schema identified by its URI. More often than not, only one XML document is involved in our discussion, so a string "/" is used to denote schema of the document in this situation. In additional, all text nodes have a same schema, denoted by a constant string *text*(). For element nodes, two have same schema if and only if they have same element names. It is similar for attribute nodes. For an XML document $D$, all schemas in it composes a set, denoted by $\Sigma_D$. This paper uses Latin letters like $a$ and $b$ to represent schemas. A function $Inst(a)$ stands for the set of instances whose schemas are $a$.

XML data are structured as a tree, and each XML node is associate with a path from root to it. The schemas of the nodes on the path formulate a sequence. This sequence is called **path schema**. The set of path schemas in an XML document $D$ is denoted by $\Psi_D$. Obviously, $\Psi_D \subset \Sigma_D^*$. Path schemas are denoted by Greek letters like $\alpha$ and $\beta$. Each XML node has a path schema, and each path schema corresponds to a set of nodes. This set is called **instance set** of the path schema. For a path schema $\alpha \in \Psi_D$, $Inst(\alpha)$ denotes the instance set of $\alpha$. An index named path instance tree ($PIT_D$) are built in *AM* system. Instance set of a schema can be get easily on $PIT_D$. Given a schema $\alpha \in \Psi_D, |\alpha| > 1$, the **parent path schema** of $\alpha$ is defined as $parent(\alpha) = left(\alpha, |\alpha|)$. $|\alpha|$ denotes the length of sequence $\alpha$, and $left(\alpha, n)$ means getting $n$ schemas from path schema $\alpha$ from left. There has a similar definition for $right$, which will be used later.

It can be easily proved that if two XML nodes have parent-child relationship, the parent node's path schema is the parent path schema of the child node's. Another index $PST_D$ is used to store and management path schemas. Figure 1 gives the logical structure of a sample $PST$. Each node on the tree denotes a path schema gotten along the path from root to it. It can be get from the graph that $PST_D$ node "15" denotes path schema $ade$ and "10" denotes $abcfgkcf$.

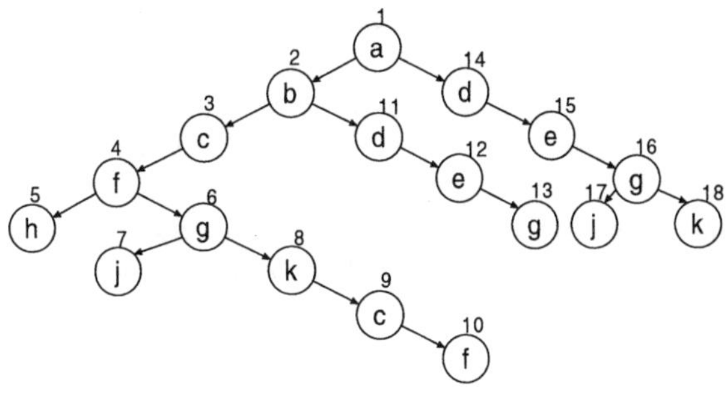


**Fig. 1.** Sample path schema tree

Many XML query languages use **path expressions** to represent query requirements. A typical kind of path expression is regular path expression, which has concatenation, alternation and closure operations. Ancestor-descendant operator is a non-regular operator. To support all these queries, path expression used in this paper is defined in fig.2. One closure operator, one-or-more closure, does not occur in Fig.2, because it can simply overwrite using rule $E^+ \Leftrightarrow EE^* \Leftrightarrow E^*E$. A single step of path expression may contain predicates, and ways to dealing with predicates are discussed in other paper[7].

```
PathExpr ::= PathExpr '/' PathExpr
           | PathExpr '//' PathExpr
           | PathExpr '|' PathExpr
           | PathExpr'*'
           | '('PathExpr')'
           | SchemaName
```

**Fig. 2.** BNF of path expression

Since AM algorithm computes queries represented by automata, conversion from path expressions to automata is the first step of the query processing. These automata are called query automata. A query automata $FSA_Q$ is a finite states automata, having the form $FSA_Q$ $A = (K_A, \Sigma_A, \delta_A, s_A, F_A)$. $\Sigma_A$ is alphabet of the automata. $FSA_Q$ is used to represent query instead of path expression, so $\Sigma_A$ should be a set of schemas. There can be some other symbols in $\Sigma_A$ besides schemas. To do the transformation and normalizing on $FSA_Q$, a symbol denoting empty schema is necessary. Greek letter $\varepsilon$ is used. Before "//" being rewritten, it is represented in $FSA_Q$ using a wildcard symbol $\xi$. Path expressions having the form of "$E_1//E_2$" is rewritten to "$E_1/\xi/E_2$". $\xi$ is a symbol that denotes any schema or arbitrary combination of schemas. With these expansion, we have $\Sigma_A \subseteq \Sigma_D \cup \{\varepsilon, \xi\}$. $K_A$ is status set, $s_A$ is start status and $F_A$ is set of accepting status. $s_A \in K_A$ and $F_A \subseteq K_A$. Finally, $\delta : K_A \times \Sigma_A \rightarrow K_A$ is transition function.

Path schemas can be regarded as sentences of schemas. If a path schema $\alpha$ can be accepted by a query automata $FSA_Q$, all XML nodes in $Inst(\alpha)$ are results of the query. To find all path schemas that can be accepted by $FSA_Q$ efficiently instead of testing them one by one, a relation on path schema set and status set of automata called **match relation** is propose. Match relation $R \subseteq \Psi_D \times \Sigma_A$ is defined inductively as follows.

1. $("/", s_A) \in R$;
2. for $\alpha, \beta \in \Psi_D$, $p, q \in K_A$, if $(\alpha, p) \in R \wedge \alpha = parent(\beta) \wedge \delta(p, \beta) = q$, then $(\beta, q) \in R$.

Using match relation $R$, an algorithm of automata match can be get in algorithm 1. Step 2-4 are discussed in detailed in other papers, and this paper focus on step 1. Section 3 shows how to convert path expressions containing closure operators into query automata, and Sect.4 introduce how to deal with ancestor-descendant operator.

**Algorithm 1** AM algorithm

AUTOMATAMATCH($D$, $Q$)
**input:** XML document $D$, path expression $Q$
**output:** Query results

1: Convert *PE* $Q$ into query automata $FSA_Q$;
2: Compute match relation $R$;
3: Find all path schemas that can be accepted by $FSA_Q$ from R;
4: Get all result XML nodes on PIT.

## 3 Construction of Query Automata

In *AM* algorithm, *PEs* are transformed into query automata for evaluation. First, *PEs* are converted to expression trees by parser. On expression trees, ancestor-descendant operator is treated as an operator node, and it is substituted by a branch containing $\xi$ using equation $// = /\xi/$. If the path expressions contain other operators like one-or-more closure operator "+" and optional operator

"?", some other rules like $E^+ \Leftrightarrow EE^* \Leftrightarrow E^*E$ and $E? \Leftrightarrow E|\varepsilon$ can be used to substitute them with basic operators. After substitution, only three operators "/", "|" and "*" can appears on expression trees.

A expression tree is a binary tree, and a query automata can be built by traversing it. Each leaf node can be transformed to an automata chip, which itself is a query automata. Furthermore, each branch node combines its both children's automata to form a new one. A procedure $\text{ConAut}(n)$ denotes the automata chip transformed from branch $n$. Obviously, for path expression query $Q$, $FSA_Q = \text{ConAut}(Q)$. The remains of this section conforms to the calculation of procedure ConAut. $\Sigma_Q \subseteq \Sigma_D \cup \{\varepsilon, \xi\}$ denotes the set of expression tree's leaf nodes, and $\Psi_Q$ denotes the set of all path expressions. Procedure New (q) creates a new automata status, assigns it to q and returns it.

For simple node $a \in \Sigma_D$, obviously, $\text{ConAut}(a) = (\{\text{New}(q_0), \text{New}(q_1)\}, \{a\}, \{q_0, a, q_1\}, q_0, \{q_1\})$. Moreover, $\text{ConAut}(\varepsilon) = (\text{New}(q), \emptyset, \emptyset, q, \{q\})$. The disscussion of how to compute $\text{ConAut}(\xi)$ is left to Sect. 4.

Before coming to the branch nodes, a new notion is introduced as following. **$\varepsilon$-connection transition function** of two automata $M_1$ and $M_2$, $\hat{\delta}_{M_1}^{M_2} : F_{M_1} \times \{\varepsilon\} \to \{s_{M_2}\}$ is a set of transitions from all accepting status of $M_1$ to the start status of $M_2$. With the help of concept of $\hat{\delta}$, the transformation of branch node can be defined.

Let $Q_1$, $Q_2$ be two *PEs*. If $M_1 = \text{ConAut}(Q_1)$, $M_2 = \text{ConAut}(Q_2)$ then $\text{ConAut}(Q_1/Q_2) = (K_{M_1} \cup K_{M_2}, \Sigma_{M_1} \cup \Sigma_{M_2}, \delta_{M_1} \cup \delta_{M_2} \cup \hat{\delta}_{M_1}^{M_2}, s_{M_1}, F_{M_2})$. To calculate '|', two single-status automata are created. Let $I_1 = \text{ConAut}(\varepsilon)$, $I_2 = \text{ConAut}(\varepsilon)$. Notice that $I_1$ is not same as $I_2$ because they are different on status. $\text{ConAut}(Q_1|Q_2) = (K_{M_1} \cup K_{M_2} \cup K_{I_1} \cup K_{I_2}, \Sigma_{M_1} \cup \Sigma_{M_2}, \delta_{M_1} \cup \delta_{M_2} \cup \hat{\delta}_{I_1}^{M_1} \cup \hat{\delta}_{I_1}^{M_2} \cup \hat{\delta}_{M_1}^{I_2} \cup \hat{\delta}_{M_2}^{I_2}, s_{I_1}, F_{I_2})$. Finally for closure operator, $\text{ConAut}(Q_1^*) = (K_{M_1} \cup K_{I_1} \cup K_{I_2}, \Sigma_{M_1}, \delta_{M_1} \cup \hat{\delta}_{M_1}^{M_1} \cup \hat{\delta}_{I_1}^{M_1} \cup \hat{\delta}_{M_1}^{I_2} \cup \hat{\delta}_{I_1}^{I_2}, s_{I_1}, F_{I_2})$.

The automata generated by $\text{ConAut}(Q)$ are finite but not deterministic. It should be normalized and simplified. Figure 3 gives a sample query automata converted from $a/(b|d)//g^*$, where $\xi$ is remaining as a label.

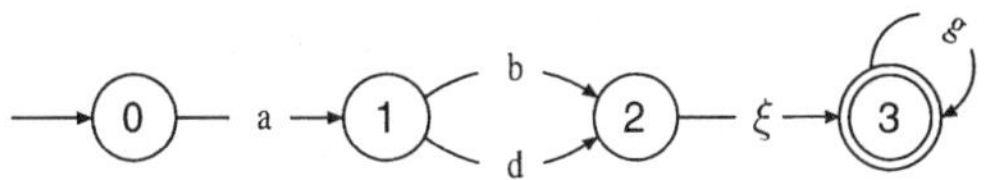


**Fig. 3.** Sample query automata

## 4 Schema Automata

As seen in Sect. 3, all expression tree nodes except $\xi$ can be transformed to automata, for they are all parts of regular expression. $\xi$ is no means a regular symbol or operator, and it is rewritten with schema automata in *AM*, a data structure constructed according to XML documents.

For a document $D$, its schema automata $SA_D$ is a automata that accepts all sub-sequence of path schemas of $D$. Obviously, if $CA_D$ has been built, it can be directly used to rewrite $\xi$, i.e. ConAut($\xi$) = $CA_D$. Definition 1 defines schema automata inductively, and Prop.1 shows the correctness of the replacement. It can be easily proved.

**Definition 1.** *For an arbitrary XML document $D$, let $L(FSA)$ denote language accepted by $FSA$, an automata $SA_D = (K_S, \Sigma_S, \delta_S, s_S, F_S)$ is a schema automata if and only if*

1. $\Sigma_S \subseteq \Sigma_D$;
2. $\varepsilon \in L(SA_D)$, *i.e.* $s_S \in F_S$;
3. $\Psi_D \subseteq L(SA_D)$;
4. *for* $\forall \alpha \in \Psi_D$ *and* $|\alpha| > 1$, *if* $\alpha \in L(SA_D)$ *then* $left(\alpha, |\alpha| - 1) \in L(SA_D)$ *and* $right(\alpha, |\alpha| - 1) \in L(SA_D)$.

**Proposition 1.** *Substitution* ConAut($\xi$) = $SA_D$ *holds correctness.*

Schema automata can be built from XML document, DTD or XML Schema. Algorithm 2 shows how to construct schema automata from an XML document. Structure automata is an automata that accepts all path schemas of a document, and it is equivalence with schema graph given by Fig.1. With schema automata ConAut($\xi$) is replace by $SA_D$ and "//" is efficiently computed.

**Algorithm 2** Construct Schema Automata

ConstructSchemaAutomata($D$)
**input:** XML document $D$
**output:** schema automata $SA_D$

Construct a structure automata $TA_D = (K_T, \Sigma_T, \delta_T, s_T, F_T)$ from $D$;
New($s_S$), New($f_S$);
$\delta_S \leftarrow \delta_T$;
**for all** $q \in K_T$ **do**
  $\delta_S \leftarrow \delta_S \cup \{(s_S, \varepsilon, q), (q, \varepsilon, f_S)\}$;
**end for**
Construct $SA_D = (K_T \cup \{s_S, f_S\}, \Sigma_T \cup \{\varepsilon\}, \delta_S, s_S, \{f_S\})$;
Normalize and simplify $SA_D$;
**return** $SA_D$.

For an XML document with schema structure like Fig.1, its schema automata is shown by Fig.4. It is complex even for simple structured documents, and extremely complicate for more complex ones.

## 5 Optimizations for Schema Automata

Schema automata can be used to rewrite ancestor-descendant operator and compute query correctly. However, it is relatively large and complex, and it needs to

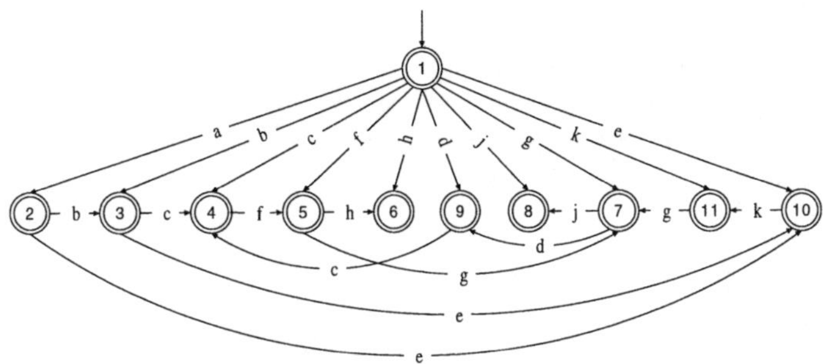

**Fig. 4.** Sample schema automata

be simplified for higher performance. Schema automata are built according to the structure of XML documents regardless what the path expressions are. With analysis of path expressions' structures, schema automata can be reduced. This paper proposes a method, reducing with preceding and following sets (RWS), to enhance performance.

Given a path expression query $Q$, for each symbol $\omega$ of $Q$, preceding set of $\omega$, $PS_Q(\omega) \subseteq \Sigma_D$ is the set of all schemas that can occur just before $\omega$ in generation procedures of path schemas, while following set of $\omega$, $FS_Q(\omega) \subseteq \Sigma_D$ is defined to the set of schemas occurring after $\omega$. For example, in *PE* $a/(b|d)^*/\xi/g$, $PS_Q(\xi) = a, b, d$ and $FS_Q(\xi) = g$. For a input *PE* $Q$, $PS_Q(Q) = FS_Q(Q) = \xi$.

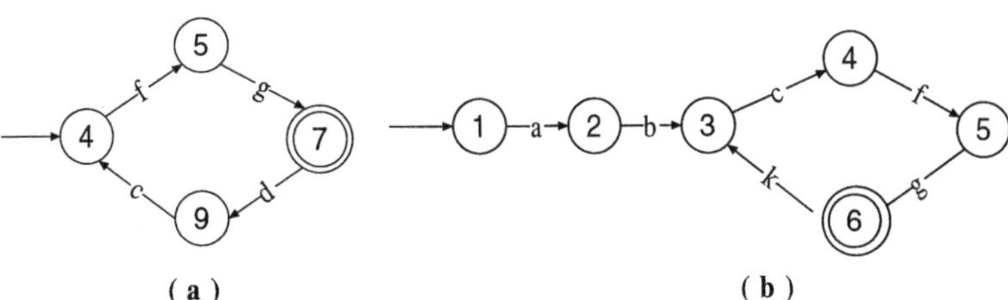

**Fig. 5.** Reduced schema automata

Consider a $\xi$ in *PE* $Q$, it is not an arbitrary wildcard. It follows some schemas in $PS_Q(\xi)$ and leads schemas in $FS_Q(\xi)$. Therefore, if it is rewritten with schema automata $SA_D$, the components that are not following or leading these schemas can be discarded. The reduction is effective, which can be seen through study of an example. Figure 5(a) gives the reduced version of schema automata of Fig.4 for *PE* $a/b/c//g$, and Fig.5(b) is the query automata after normalization and simplification. The algorithm of reduction is given by Algor.3. The algorithm traverse the status of $SA_D$ twice. For the first time it finds all possible status reached from schemas in $ps$, and the second time it finds status can reach schemas in $fs$.

**Algorithm 3** Reduce schema automata

```
ReduceSchemaAutomata(SA_D, ps, fs)
input: schema automata SA_D, schema sets ps and fs
output: reduced schema automata RSA_D
if ξ ∈ ps then
   waitset ← K_S;
else
   waitset ← {};
   for all schema a ∈ ps do
      waitset ← waitset ∪ {δ_S(s_S, a)};
   end for
end if
S_S ← waitset, visitedset ← {}, reducedset ← {};
while waitset not empty do
   p = pop(waitset), visitedset ← visitedset ∪ {p};
   for all b that δ_S(p, b) = q exists do
      if b ∈ fs then
         reducedset ← reducedset ∪ {p};
      end if
      if q ∉ visitedset then
         waitset ← waitset ∪ {q};
      end if
   end for
end while
F_R ← reducedset, visitedset ← {};
while reducedset not empty do
   r = pop(reducedset), visitedset ← visitedset ∪ {r};
   for all c that δ_S(w, c) = r exists do
      if w ∉ visitedset then
         reducedset ← reducedset ∪ {w};
      end if
   end for
end while
K_R ← visitedset, I ← ConAut(ε);
RSA_D ← (K_R ∪ K_I, Σ_S, δ_S ∩ (K_R × Σ_S × K_R) ∪ ({(s_I, ε)} × S_S), s_I, F_R);
return RSA_D;
```

Schema automata can be built dynamically when queries are processing. However, for a better performance, it should be stored on the disk. A schema automata on the disk is called persistent schema automata (*PSA*). The most frequent operation on *PSA* is looking up transition function. Thus the transition function is design to have B+ tree-like structure. Each element of the function is a entry on the node, and a node will spilt when full.

In our approach, *AM* is implemented on a native XML database system. However, *AM* can also implemented on other platforms such as RDBMS. In RDBMS, *PSA* is represented by a transition function table with 3 fields: (From, Schema, To). The function value can be easily gotten using *SELECT* statement.

## 6 Performance Evaluation

In this section, performance of *AM* is studies though experiments. An *AM* query system has been implemented on a native XML database system XBase [10,14]. Furthermore, a typical containment join method, stack tree join (*STJ*) algorithm [8], is implemented on the same platform for comparison. There is two optimization strategy proposed in Sect.5, *RWS* and *PSA*. Four *AM* approaches are proposed to evaluate performance of optimization methods. They are original *AM*, *AM+RWS*, *AM+PSA* and *AM+RWS+PSA*. These four methods are compared to *STJ* in experiments.

The parameters of benchmark platform are PIII933 CPU, 128M SDRAM, and 20GB HD and MS Win2k OS. The programs are written and run on MS VC6. Two data sets are used in experiments. One is XMark [13], a standard data set used to study the performance of different length of path queries, and the other is designed by ourself, denotes by CMark, to fully exploit how *AM* performs on containment queries. There is 20 queries totally in XMark, for the convenience of study, we select 4 queries out of 20, each represents one type of query. The path expressions are listed in Tab.1, $Q_4 - Q_7$. We used a 100M XML document in the benchmark (factor 1.0 of XMark). XML documents conforms to Fig.1 are used as CMark, and we use different scales of document size from 20M to 100M. XML documents are generated by XML Generator developed by IBM. $Q_1$, $Q_2$ and $Q_3$ in Tab.1 are containment queries designed and used in the bench mark.

**Table 1.** XMark and CMark query expressions

| | |
|---|---|
| $Q_1$: $a/b/c//g$ | $Q_5$: $/site/regions/australia/item/description$ |
| $Q_2$: $a//e//j$ | $Q_6$: $/site/closed\_auctions/closed\_auction/annotation/description$ |
| $Q_3$: $a/(b\|d)/(g\|h)$ | $/text/site/closed\_auctions/closed\_auction/annotation$ |
| $Q_4$: $/site/people$ $/person$ | $Q_7$: $/description/parlist/listitem/parlist/listitem/text/emph$ $/keyword$ |

Figure 6 gives the performance of *STJ* and *AM* on XMark. Because there is no "//" operators in the queries, there is no differences between four *AM* methods. The performance of schema automata are studied later in this section. Figure 6 shows that, *AM* has no obvious predominance comparing to *STJ* when querying short pathes. However, for long pathes, *AM* absolutely defeats *STJ*. The response time of *STJ* on $Q_4$ are almost 10 times of *AM*'s. Conclusion can be drawn from these results that *AM* is an efficient methods to process path queries, especially for long pathes.

Figure 6 gives the performance of these methods on containment queries. It can be seen clearly from the figure that fully optimized *AM* (*AM+RWS+PSA*) always performs much better than *STJ*. *RWS* and *PSA* are effective optimization on *AM*. Further more, in most cases, these two methods are performs rival. *AM*

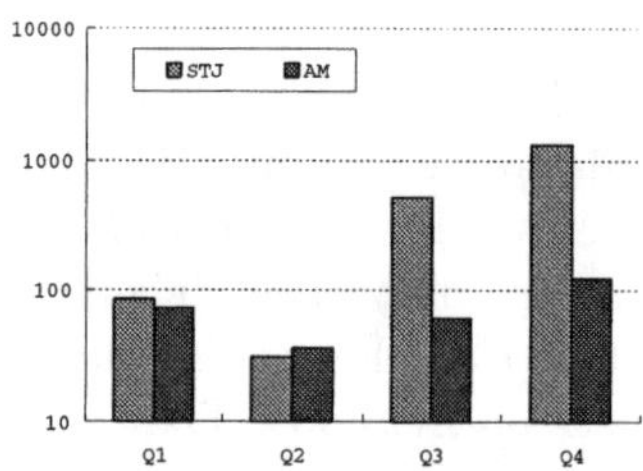


Fig. 6. Performance of XMark (100M)

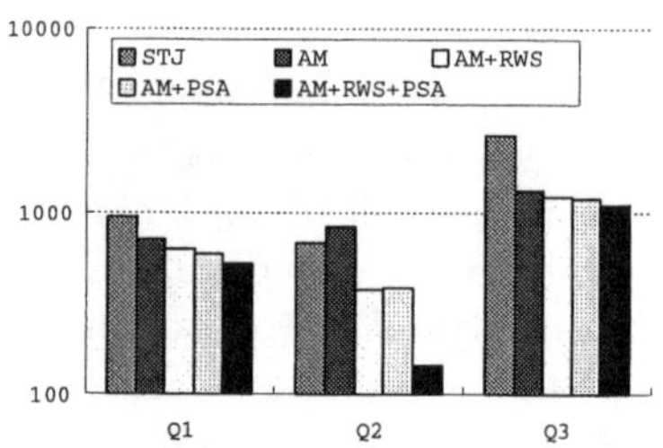


Fig. 7. Performance of CMark (100M)

without any optimization performs better than *STJ* on $Q_5$ and $Q_7$, but it is less efficient on $Q_6$. This is because there is two "//" operators in $Q_6$, and in our implementation, two schema automata are constructed during the query processing, and the query automata becomes very complex. This problem can be solved using any of the two optimization strategies.

## 7 Conclusion

In this paper, we proposed a novel method *AM* to evaluate path queries on XML data. A data structure *SA* and two optimize strategy *RWS* and *PSA* for better performance are proposed to compute containment queries with *AM* effectively. *AM* is a very efficient method to evaluate path queries, it is running in schema space, and it performs extraordinary well on long-path queries. *SA* extends the query abilities of *AM* on containment queries, and optimize strategies *RWS* and *PSA* can quicken the procedure. It can be seen from experimental results that *AM* method has low increasing speed of response time when data size scales up. Thus, *AM* performs better on large size data than other methods. In future work, we intend to improve *AM* method to query XML data in all directions other than just along a path. Moreover, a more complete performance study will be done to reveals the properties of schema-space query methods.

**Acknowledgement.** This project is partially supported by the Teaching and Research Award Programme for Outstanding Young Teachers in Post-Secondary Institutions by the Ministry of Education, China (TRAPOYT) and National Natural Science Foundation of China under grant No. 60273079 and 60173051.

## References

1. M. Altmel and M. Franklin. Efficient filtering of XML documents for selective dissemination of information. Proc. of the 26th VLDB Conf. Cario, Egypt, 53–63, 2000.

2. S. Abiteboul, D. Quass, J. McHugh, J. Widom, J. Wiener. The Lorel Query Language for Semistructured Data. Int. J. on Digital Libraries 1997, 1(1): 68–88.
3. A. Berglund, S. Baog, D. Chamberlin, et al. XML Path Languages (XPath), ver 2.0. W3C Working Draft 20 December 2001, Tech. Report WD-xpath20-20011220, W3C, 2001. http://www.w3.org/TR/WD-xpath20-20011220.
4. S.-Y. Chien, Z. Vagena, D. Zhang, V. J. Tsotras and C. Zaniolo. Efficient Structual Joins on Indexed XML Documents. Proc. of VLDB Conf., Hong Kong, China, 2002.
5. A. Deutsch, M. Fernandez, D. Florescu, A. Levy, D. Suciu. XML-QL: A Query Language for XML. http://www.w3.org/ TR/NOTE-xml-ql/. 1999.
6. P. Fankhauser. XQuery Formal Semantics: State and Challenges. SIGMOD Record 30(3), 2001: 14–19.
7. J. Lv, G. Wang, J. X. Yu, G. Yu, Hongjun Lu and Bing Sun. A New Path Expression Computing Approach for XML Data. VLDB Workshop on Efficiency and Effectiveness of XML Tools, and Techniques, Hong Kong, China, 2002.
8. S. Al-Khalifa, H. V. Jagadish, N. Koudas, J. M. Patel, D. Srivastava and Y. Wu, Structural Joins: A Primitive for Efficient XML Query Pattern Matching. Proc. of ICDE, 2002.
9. J. Lv, G. Wang, G. Yu. Storage, Indexing and Query optimization in A High Performance XML Database System. Proc. of the 2002 PYIWIT Conf. 2002. Japan.
10. H. Lu, G. Wang, G. Yu, Y. Bao, J. Lv and Y. Yu. Xbase: Making your gigabyte disk queriable. Proc. of the 2002 ACM SIGMOD Conf. 2002.
11. J. McHugh and J. Widom. Query optimization for XML. Proc. of the 25th VLDB Conf., Edinburgh, Scotland, 315–326, 1999.
12. D. Chamberlin, J. Robie, D. Florescu. Quilt: An XML Query Language for Heterogeneous Data Sources. In Proc. of Third Int'l Workshop WebDB, Dallas, USA, May 2000.
13. A.R. Schmidt, F. Waas, M.L. Kersten, D. Florescu, I. Manolescu, M.J. Carey, and R. Busse. The XML Benchmark Project. Tech. Report, CWI, Amsterdam, Netherlands, 2001.
14. G. Wang, H. Lu, G. Yu, Y. Bao. Managing Very Large Document Collections Using Semantics. Journal of Computer Science and Technology. May 2003, 18(3): 403–406.
15. G. Yu, G. Wang, A. Makinouchi. A Distributed and Parallel Object Database Server System for Windows NT, Proc. of Conf. on Software: Theory and Practice, Beijing, Aug. 2000.

# Managing XML by the Nested Relational Sequence Database System

Ho-Lam Lau and Wilfred Ng

Department of Computer Science,
The Hong Kong University of Science and Technology
{lauhl, wilfred}@cs.ust.hk

**Abstract.** We have established the Nested Relational Sequence Model (NRSM), which is an extension of the Nested Relational Data Model in order to handle XML data. The NRSM incorporates the *value order*, the *sibling order* and the *ancestor order*. In this paper, we demonstrate NRS operations by examples and illustrate how XML queries can be formulated. We discuss the work related to implementing the NRSD System and present our preliminary results concerning the use of the system. We confirm the benefits of reducing the data size in NRSD.

## 1 Introduction

XML is becoming a standard format for representing and exchanging data on the World-Wide-Web. With the growth of electronic commerce, the quantity of XML documents on the Web has rapidly increased. To cope with the large amount of XML documents, we need a DBMS that is efficient enough to handle the storage, management and retrieval of XML documents. This depends on establishing an effective data model in a formal manner. A data model also serves as a foundation for future XML DBMSs development.

There are some inadequacies in the existing approaches for mapping XML documents into common DBMSs. First, the hierarchical structure of XML does not easily fit into the relational data model. Second, the complex nested tags and multi-value features of XML documents cause the normalization problem. This requires extra storage space and may even introduce errors when updating the data. Third, in some existing approaches like [1, 2], information about a complex object is often scattered over many relations, leading to a non-trivial correspondence between a real-world object and its database representation. Fourth, handling orders in RDBMSs may lead to many additional columns for each relation, thus, increasing the storage cost. Therefore, we have proposed the Nested Relational Sequence Model (NRSM), which is an extension of the Nested Relational Data Model (NRDM) [4, 8] in order to cater for the nesting structure and node ordering of XML documents.

Like the NRDM, the NRSM supports composite and multi-valued attributes, which are essential for representing hierarchically structured information such as XML data. In the NRSM, XML data are stored in the NRS relations. The NRS

G. Dong et al. (Eds.): WAIM 2003, LNCS 2762, pp. 128–139, 2003.

relations are similar to the Nested Tables (NTs) of the NRDM, they contain multiple rows and columns. The NRS relations inherit the desirable features of the NTs, such as minimizing data redundancy and having more expressive power; they are also extended to support ordering of XML data by using sequences. Since ordering is an important feature of XML, nested tuple sequences are allowed in NRS relations.

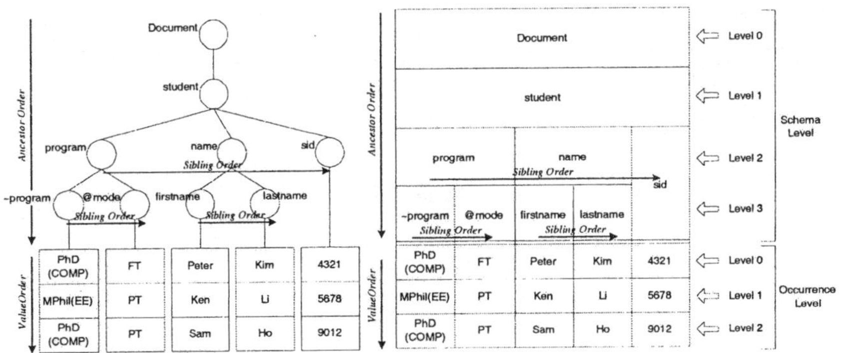


**Fig. 1.** The Merged Data Tree and NRS relation showing three types of orders

The NRSM incorporates three types of ordering as follows: (1) *value order*, the order on data values; (2) *sibling order*, the order of tags which share the same parent; and (3) *ancestor order*, the hierarchical order between parent and child tags. Figure 1 portrays the three types of orders in a MDT: *tuple 1* for *Peter Kim* has the value order prior to *tuple 2* for *Ken Li*, which in turn, has the value order prior to *tuple 3* for *Sam Ho*. In the schema level, the ancestor order is from the top to the bottom, *Document* has the ancestor order prior to *student* and *student* has the ancestor order prior to *name* and so on. On level 2 of the schema level, it shows the three children of *student*. The sibling order is *<program, name, sid>*. Note that the sibling order only applies to the attributes which share the same parent. On level 3, the attribute *~program* has the sibling order over *@mode*, but it does not have the sibling order over the attributes *firstname* or *lastname*, since they have different parents.

An important feature in our model is that any XML data sharing the same path expression can be collapsed into the same node and be regarded as a sequence of data elements. This shows the benefit of using nested data, which eliminates a substantial amount of redundancy in XML documents.

The NRSM preserves the original structure of XML documents, in general, they can be retrieved from NRS relations without loss of information. Descriptive information such as *comments* and *processing instructions* can also be stored in an NRS relation and are regarded as data nodes. The proposed method for mapping between XML documents and NRS relations is straightforward enough to implement on top of many practical DBMSs such as Oracle. If an XML document is not associated with a DTD, then we extract an approximated DTD from the XML data to provide a basis for constructing the corresponding NRS schema. A benefit resulting from this approach is that if several XML documents of similar structures are combined into a single NRS relation, we are able to generate an optimized DTD for them.

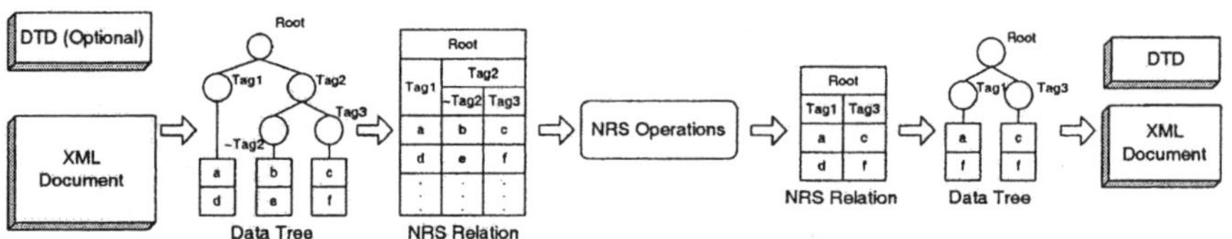


**Fig. 2.** Mapping an XML document to an NRS relation and retrieving under NRS operations

Figure 2 demonstrates the mapping between an XML document and an NRS relation. We represent the document as a *merged data tree* (MDT), where leaf nodes are sequences of data values, called the *data nodes*, and non-leaf nodes are the labels of the XML tags and attributes, called the *label nodes*.

XML documents are not necessarily associated with DTDs, therefore, two simple and efficient algorithms to map XML documents into MDTs are proposed. After we have mapped XML documents into a MDT, we can generate an NRS relation. An NRS relation allows nesting of data and maintains the order of the values. The XML semantics and the order of the document structure are preserved in both MDTs and NRS relations. The mapping between MDTs and NRS relations is reversible. After an XML document is transformed into its corresponding NRS relation, we can apply a sequence of NRS operations on the relation to formulate useful queries.

We introduce a set of operations called the NRS operations by examples. The NRS operations are combinations of the refinements of existing relation algebra together with some newly defined operations, such as the *swap* and *rearrange* operations, to allow users to manipulate the structure and contents of the NRS relations. An important feature of our query language is that it preserves the nesting and ordering of original XML data in the output answer. The output of NRS operations is always an order-preserving NRS relation, which can be converted back to XML with our proposed retrieval algorithm. The details of the NRS operations can be found in [5, 6]. Herein, our discussion is to focus on the issue of how to implement a database system based on the NRSM. It is a middleware which acts between the user and the DBMSs based on the NRSM as the data model in order to help the user perform queries on the XML data.

The rest of the chapter is organized as follows: Section 2 discusses the storage and retrieval of XML data in the NRSM. Section 3 highlights the main features of NRS operations with examples. Section 4 describes the architecture of the implementation of the NRS database system (NRSD System) and presents the preliminary experimental results. Finally, we give our conclusions in Section 5.

## 2 Storing and Retrieving XML Data in NRSM

Throughout this section, the XML document and DTD shown in Figure 3 are used to illustrate some concepts developed in the NRSM. This XML document contains information about the professors in a university. Each professor (*prof*) comprises information about his department (*dept*), name (*name*) and student (*stud*). Each student is given a student id (*sid*) for identification and they can take any number of courses (*course*) during their studies.

```
<!ELEMENT people(prof+)>
<!ELEMENT prof(dept, pname), stud*>
<!ELEMENT dept(#PCDATA)>
<!ELEMENT pname(#PCDATA)>
<!ELEMENT stud(#PCDATA, course*)>
<!ATTLIST stud sid CDATA #REQUIRED>
<!ELEMENT course(#PCDATA)>

<people>
  <prof>
    <dept>CS</dept>
    <pname>Kim</pname>
    <stud sid="588">Jerry
      <course>c670</course>
    </stud>
    <stud sid="142">Lam
      <course>c334</course>
      <course>c670</course>
    </stud>
  </prof>
  <prof>
    <dept>EE</dept>
    <pname>Sun</pname>
    <stud sid="298">Au</stud>
    <stud sid="915">Lou
      <course>c670</course>
    </stud>
    <stud sid="611">Ray
      <course>c630</course>
      <course>c334</course>
    </stud>
  </prof>
</people>
```

**Fig. 3.** The sample DTD (sample.dtd) and XML (sample.xml)

We now give the definition of a merged data tree, which is essentially a tree representation of an XML document in the NRSM.

**Definition 1 Merged Data Tree** *A merged data tree (MDT), $T$ is defined as $T =< r, D, L >$, where $r$ is the root, $D$ is a set of data nodes and $L$ is a set of label nodes.*

By representing XML documents as MDTs, XML data that share the same path expression can be merged together and stored under the same label node, and thus, eliminating a substantial amount of redundancy. It also preserves the value, sibling and ancestor orders of XML data. Figures 4(a) shows a MDT, $T$, which corresponds to the DTD and the XML document shown in Figure 3. The root node of $T$ is the node *people* at Level 0, the level value of nodes increments from the top to the bottom as shown in Figure 4(a). Circles are used to represent label nodes, while rectangles are used to represent data nodes. From now on we simplify "$< a >$" (a sequence having one atomic value) as "$a$".

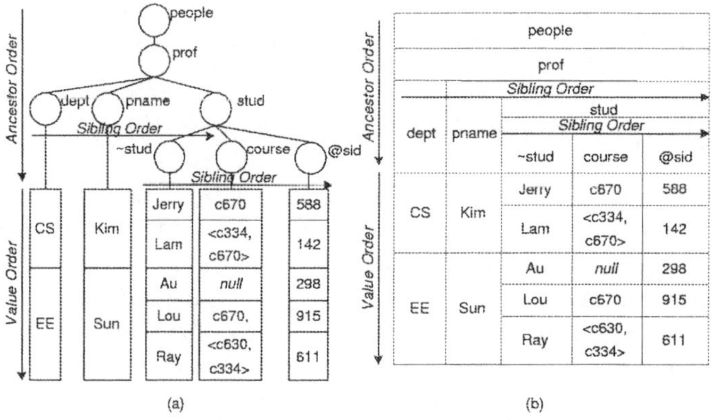


**Fig. 4.** The (a) MDT and (b) NRS relation for sample.xml and sample.dtd

**Definition 2 (Nested Relational Sequence Relation)** *An Nested Relational Sequence Relation (an NRS Relation), R, is defined by* $R =< N, S, O >$*, where* $N$*,* $S$ *and* $O$ *denotes the name, the schema and the occurrence of* $R$ *respectively.* $S = \{a_1, a_2, ..., a_i\}$ *is equal to a set of attributes,* $a_i$*.* $O = \{t_1, t_2, ..., t_i\}$ *is equal to a sequence of tuples,* $t_i$ *over* $S$*. We use the notation* $O[a_i] = \{t_1[a_i], t_2[a_i], ..., t_i[a_i]\}$ *to represent a sequence of atomic value in* $O$ *which is corresponding to the attribute* $a_i$*.*

Figure 4(b) shows the table which represents an NRS relation, which is corresponding to the DTD and the XML document in Figure 3. The name $N$ for this NRS relation is *people*, it is the same as the top-level element of the sample XML document. The upper part of the table is the *schema* $S$ and the lower part of the table is the *occurrences* $O$. Compared with an XML document, the schema can be viewed as a sequence of labels of XML elements and attributes, while the occurrences can be viewed as a sequence of data values.

In the NRSM, three kinds of orderings are maintained; they are the *value*, *sibling* and *ancestor orders*. The value order is the order of tuples in the occurrence level. It follows the sequence of data in the original XML document from top to bottom. For example in Figure 4(b), we can check that $t_1$ *Kim* has a value order prior to $t_2$ *Sun*".

Both the sibling order and the ancestor order are the orders of attributes at the schema level. The sibling order is the order of attributes under the same parent from left to right. In XML documents, the sibling order is equivalent to the order of tags at the same nesting level with the same parent. If tag $A$ appears before tag $B$ in an XML document, $A$ comes before $B$ in the sibling order. In Figure 4(b), under the attribute $prof+$, the attribute $^\wedge$(*dept*, *pname*) has the sibling order prior to the attribute *stud*∗. For the child attribute of *stud*∗, their sibling order is < ∼*stud*, *course*∗, @*sid* >.

The ancestor order is the hierarchical order between the parent and child attributes at the schema level. The parent attribute are prior to their child attributes in terms of the ancestor order. Ancestor order represents the hierarchical order of the nested tags in XML documents. This order is essential to XML data, especially for locating a tag using path expression. For example, in Figure 4(b), we have to write the path expression "*/people/prof+/stud*/course**" to locate the tag *course* but not the path expression "*/people/stud * /prof + /course**".

In XML documents, tags are organized in a hierarchical manner and they are allowed to be nested to any level. The nesting tags represent the parent-child relationships. Since tags are allowed to share the same label, these multi-valued data are represented as a sequence of data under the same column of the NRS relation. In the NRSM, nesting of data is allowed within another sequence, each item in the sequence can be another sequence of data. For example, in the sample XML document in Figure 3, each *prof* may supervise several *stud* and each *stud* may take several *course*. In other words, a *prof* may have a sequence of *stud*, in which, another sequences of *course* are contained. In Figure 4(b), the *course* taken by the *stud* of *prof* "*Kim*" is represented as the sequence <c670, <c334, c670>>. This sequence contains another sequence <c334, c670>, because the *stud* "*Lam*" has taken two courses.

Within the NRSM, we are able to transform a MDT into an NRS relation and vice versa [5, 6]. The XML semantics and the order of the document structure are preserved in both MDTs and NRS relations, and the mapping between MDTs and NRS relations is reversible. After an XML document is transformed into its corresponding NRS relation, we can then apply a sequence of NRS operations, such as *nest* and *unnest* operations on the relations to manipulate the XML data. Figure 4(b) shows the NRS relations corresponding to the MDTs in Figure 4(a). For details of the mapping, the reader can refer to [5, 6].

## 3 NRS Operations and Running Examples

We define a set of algebraic operations on NRSM [5, 6], which is employed to formulate a query over an NRS relation. These operations enable users to retrieve XML information from NRS relations. The output result of these operations is an NRS relation, taking one or more NRS relations as input. These operations are introduced in [5, 6]. We now use some examples to show how to perform queries using NRS operations. In this section, the example queries are operating on the sample NRS relation as shown in Figure 4(b). It is the NRS relation corresponding to the XML document and its DTD as shown in Figures 3.

**($Q_1$) List the names of the students who are taking the course "c670".** This query can be expressed in XQuery as follows:

```
FOR $s IN document("sample.xml")//people/prof/stud
WHERE $s/course = "c670"
RETURN $s/text().
```

We first transform the XML document "*sample.xml*" and its DTD into the corresponding NRS relation, R, which has been shown in Figure 4(b). Then we perform the following sequence of operations:

1. $S \leftarrow \pi_{/people/prof/stud}(R)$
2. $T \leftarrow \sigma_{/stud/course=\text{“c670”}}(S)$
3. $R_{result} \leftarrow \pi_{/stud/\sim stud}(T)$

For the sake of clarity, we use the temporary NRS relations, $S$ and $T$, for storing the results at each step. In the first step, we perform a projection on "*people/prof/stud*" over $R$. Then we perform the selection according to the condition "$/stud/course$ = "c670"" over $S$. Finally, we perform a projection on "*/stud/ stud*" over $T$, which generates the required results $R_{result}$. The temporary NRS relations $S$ and $T$ for this query are shown in Figure 5.

S:

| sutd* | | |
|---|---|---|
| ~stud | course* | @sid |
| Jerry | c670 | 588 |
| Lam | c334<br>c670 | 142 |
| Au | - | 298 |
| Lou | c670 | 915 |
| Ray | c630<br>c334 | 611 |

T:

| sutd* | | |
|---|---|---|
| ~stud | course* | @sid |
| Jerry | c670 | 588 |
| Lam | c334<br>c670 | 142 |
| Lou | c670 | 915 |

$R_{result}$:

| sutd* |
|---|
| ~stud |
| Jerry |
| Lam |
| Lou |

**Fig. 5.** Generated NRS relations for answering the query $Q_1$

We then transform the resulting NRS relation by using its corresponding DTD. The conformed XML document can be represented as follows:

```
<!ELEMENT stud(#PCDATA)>
<stud>Jerry</stud>
<stud>Lam</stud>
<stud>Lou</stud>
```

**($Q_2$) Create a new XML document with the format given below, where $X$ is the number of professors, $Y$ is the number of students in the department and $Z$ the name of the department:**

```
<university>
   <dept numProf="X" numStud="Y">Z</dept>
</university>
```

First, we create a new NRS relation named *university* with the given schema *university (dept (~dept, @numProf, @numStud))* using the operation $New(\uplus)$. Then we insert the value of *dept* corresponding to the *dept* of $R$. Each *dept* has two attributes, *numeProf* and *numStud.* Thus, we use the aggregate function "$Count(\varsigma)$" to find out the number of professors and students in the *dept.* The operations are shown below and the corresponding NRS relations are shown in Figure 6.

1. $S \leftarrow \uplus_{(university(dept(\sim dept,@numProf,@numStud)))}$;
2. $S' \leftarrow \oplus_{(university/dept/\sim dept=R/people/prof/dept)}(S)$;
   For each data value under "$university/dept/$" :

3. $R_{result} \leftarrow \oplus_{(university/dept/@numProf=\varsigma(/people/prof/pname)(T)),\ university/dept/@numStud=\varsigma(/people/prof/stud/\sim stud)(T))}(S'),$
$where\ T = \sigma_{(R/people/prof/dept=university/dept)}(R).$

S:

| university | | |
|---|---|---|
| dept | | |
| ~dept | @numProf | @numStud |
| | | |
| | | |

S?

| university | | |
|---|---|---|
| dept | | |
| ~dept | @numProf | @numStud |
| CS | | |
| EE | | |

$R_{result}$:

| university | | |
|---|---|---|
| dept | | |
| ~dept | @numProf | @numStud |
| CS | 1 | 2 |
| EE | 1 | 3 |

**Fig. 6.** Generated NRS relations for the query $Q_2$.

The resulting NRS relation and its corresponding DTD and XML document can be represented as follows:

```
<university>
   <dept numProf="1" numStud="2">CS</dept>
   <dept numProf="1" numStud="3">EE</dept>
</university>
```

# 4 Implementation of the NRSD System

In this section, we discuss the architecture, the interface design and other implementational details of the NRSD System and then we give some experimental results to illustrate that the system is desirable.

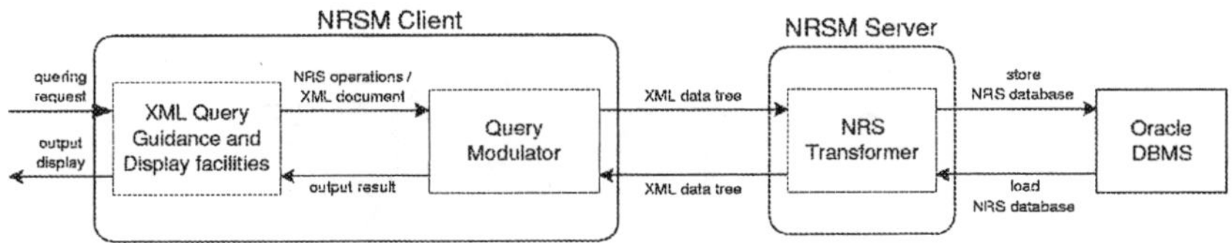


**Fig. 7.** The architecture of the NRSD System.

The NRSM model is deployed by adopting the usual client-server strategy. Figure 7 shows the architecture of the NRSD System. The system acts as a middleware between the users and the DBMS. The server is responsible for translating MDTs into NRS relations, which are managed by the underlying Oracle DBMS [14]. The client is responsible for (1) translating the output results of NRS operations into XML documents in order to answer querying from users and (2) dealing with the requests of different XML display formats and providing guidance for users when imposing queries. There are three main components in the NRSD System: (1) the *Query Guidance and Display Facilities* (QGDF), (2) the *Query Modulator* (QM), and (3) the *NRS Transformer* (NT).

The QGDF is responsible for handling the interaction and display facilities of the NRSD System. It provides a simple and user-friendly interface to help users perform queries on the XML data. The QM translates the queries and controls the mapping between XML documents and MDTs. The NT unit performs the mapping between MDTs into the NRS relations. The main function of the NT is to map an NRS relation into its corresponding set of relations in the underlying Oracle DBMS. The flow of a query follows the steps listed below:

1. Before starting a query, the relational tables stored in Oracle DBMS are transformed into a MDT by the NT and send to the QM.
2. The QM passes the MDT to the QGDF. The QGDF constructs the content of the interface and displays the MDT to the user.
3. The system is ready for users to initiate a query.
4. For each NRS operation that the user performs, the QGDF collects the required parameters from the user interface and sends them to the QM.
5. The QM updates the MDT and communicates with the NT about the updated data. Finally, the QM returns the querying result to the QGDF for display.
6. Step 4 is repeated if the user requests to perform another NRS operation.

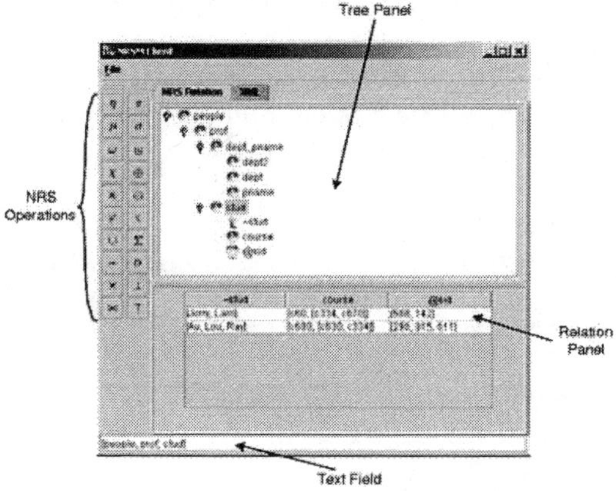


**Fig. 8.** The interface of the NRSD System.

We have implemented the NRSM client interface by using *Java*$^{TM}$ 2 *Platform Standard Edition v1.4.0* [11] and *Simple API for XML* (SAX) [3] to help users initiate XML queries. The SAX parser provides an event-driven and serial-access mechanism for accessing XML documents. We choose SAX as an XML parser in the NRSD System because of its high speed and less memory-intensive mechanism when parsing an XML document. We depict the user interface of the Query Guidance in Figure 8. The interface consists of three main components: (1) a list of NRS operations on the left, (2) a *main panel* in the middle, and (3) a *text field* at the bottom. In the main panel, there are two tabs which allow users to change between the view of the NRS relation and the corresponding XML document. The main panel is divided into two halves: the upper half is the *tree panel*, which is an area displaying the nesting structure of the NRS relation; the lower half is the *relation panel*, which is an area showing the data of each column. In the tree panel, different symbols are used to represent different types of tags. For example, the symbol "*e*" denotes an element, the symbol "@" denotes an attribute and the symbol "*t*" denotes text data. Aided by the interface given by Figure 8, we are able to initiate a query described by the following steps.

1. Select the *NRS Relation* tag from the main panel.
2. Identify the schema of the column from the tree panel. Then the relation panel displays the corresponding part of the NRS relation.
3. Select the attribute in the relation panel. The path of the selected sub-schema is displayed in the text field on the bottom of the interface.
4. Finally, click on a NRS operation button in the list in order to perform the query.

DBMS supports object data types such as a *collections of objects* and *nested tables* [10]. These object data types are useful for deploying an NRS relation, since they can support ordered collections of structured objects from the implementation point of view. The object types provided by *Oracle8i* are similar to the class mechanism supported by *Java* and *C++*. The following example shows how an object type is specified in order to implement the *prof+* object in our sample NRS relation:

```
1. CREATE TYPE DeptPname AS OBJECT
(
dept   VARCHAR(10),
pname  VARCHAR(20)
);
2. CREATE TYPE Courses AS VARRAY(99) OF VARCHAR(4);
3. CREATE TYPE Student AS OBJECT
(
stud   VARCHAR(20),
course Courses,
sid    VARCHAR(3)
);
4 CREATE TYPE Prof AS OBJECT
(
dp     DeptPname
stud   Student,
);
5. CREATE TYPE Prof_Table AS TABLE OF Prof;
6. CREATE TABLE people
(
   professor Prof_Tables
) NESTED TABLE professor STORE AS professor_table;
```

In the statements 1–4, a new type *courses* is created instead of just using *VARCHAR*, since *course** in the NRS relation may be an empty sequence. In the statements 5 - 6, we create a storage table *professor_table*, which is associated with the nested table column *professor*. The column serves as the storage for all the corresponding nested data.

We have been running some experiments using real life data on the NRSD System in order to show the effectiveness of the system. All queries are conducted on a *Pentium III 550MHz* computer with 256Mb RAM and 30Gb hard disk. For the input source, we borrow parts of the XML document from the *Digital Bibliography & Library Project* (DBLP) [9]. The DBLP maintains a server that provides bibliographic information on major computer science journals and proceedings. In the DBLP XML document, the maximum number of child tags per element is twelve and the deepest nesting level is four. In the experiment, we test the NRSD System by loading XML documents of different size. Table 1 shows the results of our experiment. We can see that the table spaces required for storing the XML documents is approximately 85% of the original size of the documents. With the growth of size, the number of tables and size of schema become steady. It is due to the fact that NRSM collapses data of the same tags label into the same data nodes, resulting in very minimal redundancy.

**Table 1.** Experimental results of the NRSD System with different XML document sizes.

| Size of NRS schemas (bytes) | Number of all tables in Oracle DBMS | Table space including schema and table overheads (kilobytes) | Input XML file size (kilobytes) | Percentage of table space required |
|---|---|---|---|---|
| 414 | 23 | 1,987 | 2,404 | 82.65% |
| 1368 | 61 | 8,159 | 9,318 | 87.56% |
| 1380 | 63 | 12,399 | 14,251 | 87.00% |
| 1404 | 66 | 16,722 | 18,817 | 88.87% |
| 1425 | 67 | 24,076 | 28.791 | 83.62% |

The result of size reduction is obtained without performing any compression on the database, this can serve as a starting point for further XML data compression. Note that one fundamental difference between using NRS relations and imposing usual XML compression is that we are able to query in NRSM based on a set of algebraic operations, which is difficult to perform in a compressed domain. We are improving the grouping algorithm and trying to further decrease the table space for storing XML data of NRS relations in the NRSD System. The benefit of data size reduction is useful for exporting the XML data from one database system to another.

## 5 Conclusions

We introduced the NRSM and demonstrated with examples how to formulate XML queries in terms of NRS operations. We have discussed the implementational issues of the NRSD System which uses Java and SAX API on top of the *Oracle8i*. We also presented the design of an interface using Java Swing Classes to guide the user to initiate queries. The NRSD System is a middleware system between the users and the underlying relational DBMS, it allows users to perform queries and operate on the structure of the XML data. The preliminary results shows that the table space required for storing XML data with the NRSD System is significantly less than the size of the original XML documents, which is mainly due to the fact that NRSM eliminates the redundant data from the XML documents.

We are further improving the NRSM in several areas. First, as the results of our experiments are obtained without any compression on data, we believe that a compression algorithm can be applied to the NRSM such that the storage size can be further reduced but we still preserve the querying facilities. Second, we are improving the grouping algorithm on data nodes which have the same labels. Third, we are working on the translation of XQuery into NRS operations. Finally, we are still carrying out experiments concerning querying over the NRS databases, we then will be more clear about the performance of the NRS operations in the NRSD System.

## References


1. D. Beech, A. Malhotra and M. Rys. *A Formal Data Model and Algebra for XML.* Communication to the W3C, (1999).
2. D. Florescu and D. Kossman. *A Performance Evaluation of Alternative Mapping Schemes for Storing XML Data in a Relational Database.* In: Proc. of VLDB99, (1999).
3. D. Megginson. *Simple API for XML.* In: http://www.saxproject.org/, (2002).
4. H. Kitagawa and T. L. Kunii. *The Unnormalized Relational Data Model. For Office Form Processor Design.* Springer-Verlag, (1989).
5. H. L. Lau and W. Ng, *Querying XML Data Based on Nested Relational Sequence Model.* In: Proc. of Poster Track of WWW, (2002).
6. H. L. Lau and W. Ng, *The Development of Nested Relational Sequence Model to Support XML Databases.* In: Proc. of IKE'02, pp. 374–380, (2002).
7. M. A. Weiss, *Data Structures and Algorithm Analysis in C++.* 2nd edition, Addison-Wesley, (1999).
8. M. Levene. *The Nested University Relation Database Model.* Springer-Verlag, vol 595, (1992).
9. M. Ley. *Digital Bibliography & Library Project.* In: http://dblp.uni-trier.de/, (2002).
10. Oracle Corporation. *Oracle9i.* In: http://www.oracle.com/, (2003).
11. Sun Microsystems, Inc. *Java 2 Platform, Standard Edition.* In: http://java.sun.com/j2se/, (2003).
12. W. Ng. *Maintaining Consistency of Integrated XML Trees.* International Conference on Web-Age Information Management WAIM'2002. Lecture Notes in Computer Science Vol. 2419, Beijing, China, pages 145–157, (2002).

# Normalizing XML Element Trees as Well-Designed Document Structures for Data Integration[1]

Wenbing Zhao, Shaohua Tan, Dongqing Yang, and Shiwei Tang

Center for Information Science, Peking University, Beijing 100871, China
{zhaowb, tan}@cis.pku.edu.cn, {dqyang, tsw}@pku.edu.cn

**Abstract.** Normalizing the design of XML Schemas is important in the data integration with predefined integrated content. As the essential of XML schemas, XML element tree are introduced to represent all the possible data structure of the same type XML documents. The strategy of declaring elements is proposed. It is depicted that a general picture of XML element tree consistent with Keys to identify any part of such a tree.

## 1 Introduction

As the standard data exchange format on the Web, XML is often used in data integration recent years. Data integrations mainly have two typical scenarios. One is with dazzling free-evolved web sites as the data sources and tries to categorize and integrate the information. The other is with the relatively stable data sources, such as the databases or authoritative Web sites, and tries to integrate the distributed information in a certain domain. As the document structures, XML schemas are required in both cases. They are extracted from the sources in the former and usually provided a priori in the later. Some researches have been carried out on extracting and aggregating XML schemas from the sources [1][2]. Meanwhile, as suggested in [3] the need for database-like functionality to efficiently provide and access data through the Web, it is in great demand to focus on normalizing the XML schemas consistent with the identity constraints during the design of data integration in the second scenario. Because the identity constraints are indispensable when assembling the data from different sources belonging to one object, and checking the consistency of the schemas and constraints is an expensive task [4]. As far as we know, there is little work done on this topic.

There are several proposals for XML schema, such as DTD [5], XML Schema [6], UCM [7], etc. But after all, an XML schema is a node-labeled tree. In order to concentrate on the tree-structure and leave behind the implementation details, we use XML Element Tree to describe XML schema. It is easy to be transformed into other schema languages. Here we emphasize the relation between XML element tree and XML Schema.

[1] This work is supported by the Natural Key Fundamental Research and Development Plan (973) of China under grant G1999032705.

G. Dong et al. (Eds.): WAIM 2003, LNCS 2762, pp. 140–147, 2003.

A well-designed XML element tree of electronic medical record shows in Fig.1, which is used to integrate the medical records of persons involved in health insurance from certain hospitals. It can be declared valid Keys on any part of the tree. These constraints are especially useful when assembling the records from different hospital for an individual. We discuss the normalization of XML element tree below.

The rest of this paper is organized as follows. Section 2 defines the grammar of XML element tree. Section 3 proposes the strategies of declaring elements. With Key as the example of the identity constraints in [6], Section 4 discusses a general picture of XML element tree consistent with Keys to identify any part of it.

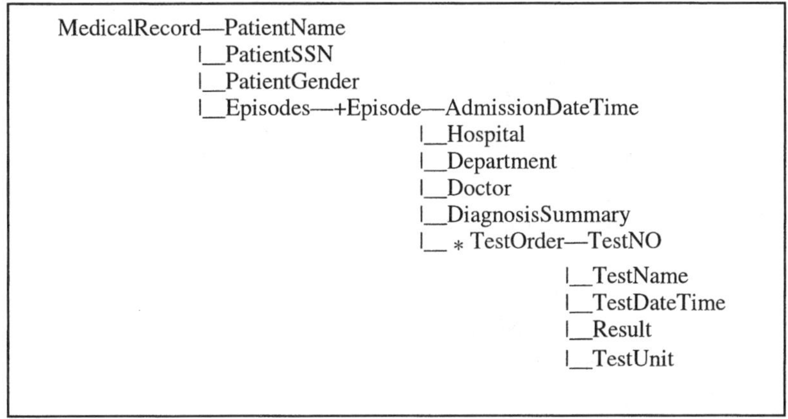


**Fig. 1.** An Example of XML Element Tree

## 2 The Grammar of XML Element Tree

Derived from XML graph model in [8], an **XML Element Tree** is a node-labeled rooted tree to represent the data structure of the same type XML documents. It is denoted as $T=(V, E)$, in which $V$ is a set of nodes for the elements and $E$ is a set of edges denoting parent-child or sibling relationships between the elements. An XML element tree must matches the following production for *Logic_Tree* in Fig.2. The counterpart of grammar graph is shown in Fig.3 and an example in Fig.1. Compared with the tree model in XPath [9], it consists only of element nodes except other types that help little to the document structure. Attribute node is a special one that will be discussed in section 3.1. The root of an XML element tree is not abstract but a real node standing for the XML document element. It can be treated in the same way with other nodes. Data type is not defined in XML element tree.

Three kinds of constructors, *sequence*, *choice* and *all*, are defined in [6]. Let $S$ denote a set of element candidates. **Exclusive choice of** $S$ means that there is one and only one member of $S$ that can be instantiated in an XML document. **Common choice of** $S$ means that every member of $S$ may occur no more than once in any order in an

XML document. In XML Schema, *choice* does the exclusive choice and *all* does the common choice. In XML element tree, the concatenations and frequency marks accomplish the same restriction. *Sibling_Concatenation* is a natural expression for *sequence*. Frequency mark '?' and *Sibling_Concatenation* do common choice. No exclusive choice can be expressed. Thus, when translating an XML element tree into XML Schema, more rigorous instructions for constructing need to be declared.

```
Logic_Tree :: = Root { Sub_Tree }                                          (1)
Sub_Tree :: = Child_Concatenation Element_With_Frequency
                { Sibling_Concatenation Element_With_Frequency }
                { Sub_Tree }                                               (2)
Element_With_Frequency :: = [ Frequency_Mark ] Element                     (3)
Frequency_Mark :: = '?' | '*' | '+'                                        (4)
Child_ Concatenation :: = '—'                                              (5)
Sibling_Concatenation :: = '|__'                                           (6)
Root :: = '<' Name '>'                                                     (7)
Element :: ='<' Name '>' | '<' '&' Name '>'                                (8)
Note:
1. '? ' notes 0 or 1, '*' 0 or more and '+' 1 or more.
2. The production for Name is the same as that in [1], so it is omitted here.
```

**Fig. 2.** The Productions for XML Element Tree

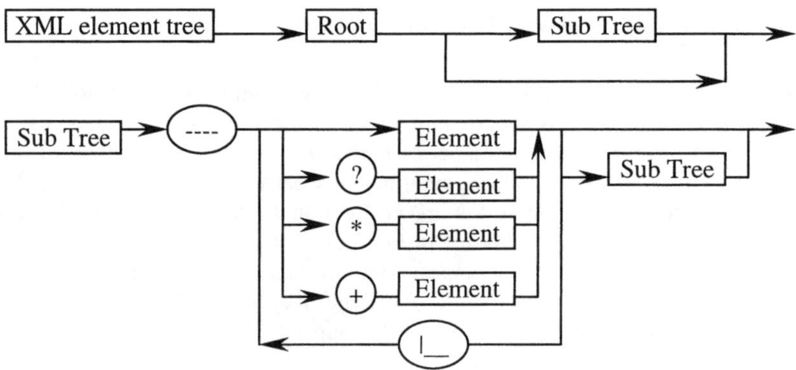


**Fig. 3.** The Grammar Graph of XML Element Tree

## 3 Declaring Element Appropriately

XML is favorable for data exchange because it is can express the profuse semantics. It is nearly free to define element except for a few reserved words. Here are some strategies for declaring elements in a well-designed XML element tree.

### 3.1 Element vs. Attribute

XML allows an element to have attributes. From the technical view, element can accomplish all the functions of attribute, while attribute looks more compact and neat [10] compared with sub-element. So, if a data item may be involved in a query about the integrated data, it should be declared as an element in XML element tree. If it is never required as integrated data, it needn't be represented in XML element tree for it is used in the implementation.

### 3.2 Element Type

There are two kinds of element type in [5]. In an XML element tree, a non-reference leaf element has special mixed content that is a character data block and has no sub-elements. The type of reference leaf element is described in the original declaration. In common mixed content, the sequence of the character data blocks and sub-elements interspersed among them is crucial and meaningful. None of the separated data block can be selected directly through path expression [9]. Therefore, an internal node must have element content. So that, each character data block in the integration can be referred to by the name of the tag surrounded it.

### 3.3 Leaf Element

Because of the internal nodes in XML element tree having element contents, leaf elements are the minimal units to filter and contain data. The name and content of a leaf element makes up a pair that denotes a 1:1 mapping from semantics to structure. Let $X$ denote the name and $Y$ the content, the mapping is $is(X) \Leftrightarrow Y$.

If a data item has **atomic semantics**, it may be taken as the minimal query target on which no sub-query can be constructed. This definition is expressed in a practical way to avoid describing what is 'semantics' in the abstract. **Atomic value** is the minimal structural granularity of a data item, which is borrowed from First Normal Form in relational database theory [11].

A leaf element has atomic value. But this cannot guarantee it has the atomic semantics. The data block of leaf content may be divided into several sub-strings. Each can be taken as a smaller query target under a new name other than the leaf element name. In such a case there is a n:1 mapping from semantics to structure between the names of the possible query targets and the content of the leaf element. Let $X_i$ denote the name of a query target based on such a sub-string, that is $is(X) \leftrightarrow Y \Rightarrow \exists X_i$ , $is(X_i) \leftrightarrow substring_{X_i}(Y)$. Predication $substring_{X_i}()$ stands for the dividing mode to produce the sub-string named $X_i$. The semantic granularity of the leaf element is thought to be too coarse to grasp the precise meanings of the content. So leaf elements should be refined to have both atomic value and atomic semantics at the same time. That is $is(X) \leftrightarrow Y \Rightarrow \neg(\exists X_i, is(X_i) \leftrightarrow substring_{X_i}(Y))$.

# 4 Keys and XML Element Tree

The identity constraints are indispensable to the integrated data. It is with the identifiers that the data from heterogeneous sources can be assembled precisely into the integrated objects for the users to query about. XML Schema has three types of identity constraints. We take Key as example to discuss the well-designed XML element tree content with the identity constraints.

## 4.1 The Characteristic of the Nodes in a Key

A Key comprises the key node set and target node set in [6]. According to the validation rules for Keys in [6], the characteristic of the nodes in a Key are discussed in an XML element tree. This is expected to help normalize a well-designed XML element tree content with the identity constraints.

Let $T$ denote an XML element tree. $T=(V, E)$. $T$ can be also looked as a poset, on the understanding that every edge in $E$ stands for a parent-child relationship between two nodes in $V$. For a Key defined in [6], let a node set $V^{key}$ denote the key node set and $V^{target}$ the target node set.

**Theorem 1.** For a Key, each node in $V^{key}$ must be leaves in $T$. Let $v$ denote a node in $T$, $f_v$ the appearance frequency of $v$. $\forall v(v \in V^{key} \Rightarrow f_v = 1)$.

Let a node $v^p$ denote the least upper bound of $V^{key}$ and $V^{target}$. According to XPath [9], when the nodes in $V^{key}$ are evaluated with a related target node in $V^{target}$ as the content node, the involved part of $T$ is the subtree $T_{sub}^{v^p}$ of $T$ with $v^p$ as the root. The branches of $T_{sub}^{v^p}$ are those ones that each has at least one node either belonging to $V^{key}$ or $V^{target}$ in the path from $v^p$ down to a leaf. Taken that the nodes in $V^{key}$ and $V^{target}$ are non-reference element nodes and every level relative Key [12] in a Key is unary, we get Theorem 2.

**Theorem 2.** Let a node $v^{key} \in V^{key}$ and $v^{target} \in V^{target}$. Let $\lfloor v^{target}, v^p)$ denote the node set whose members are the nodes in the path from $v^{target}$ to $v^p$. If $v^{target}$ and $v^p$ are not the same node, $v^{target} \in \lfloor v^{target}, v^p)$ and $v^p \notin \lfloor v^{target}, v^p)$; or else $\lfloor v^{target}, v^p)$ is empty. Define $\lfloor v^{key}, v^p)$ ditto. A Key is valid, when all the followings are true:

(1) $\forall v^{key}(\forall v'(v' \in \lfloor v^{key}, v^p) \rightarrow f_{v'} = 1))$.

(2) For every $v^{target}$ in $V^{target}$, if $\lfloor v^{target}, v^{p})\neq\Phi$, then $\forall v''(v''\in\lfloor v^{target}, v^{p})\rightarrow f_{v''}\leq 1)$, or else $v^{target}=v^{p}$, there is no restriction on $f_{v^{target}}$.

**Proof:** Because $v^{p}=LUB(V^{key}\bigcup V^{target})$, $T_{sub}^{v^{p}}$ is the minimal subtree that includes all the target nodes and key nodes.

(1) Giving a proof by contradiction. Assume that in a valid Key, for a $v^{key}$, $\exists v^{\alpha}\in\lfloor v^{key}, v^{p})(f_{v^{\alpha}}=0)\vee(f_{v^{\alpha}}>1)$. In case that $f_{v^{\alpha}}=0$, a subtree $T_{sub}^{v^{\alpha}}$ with $v^{\alpha}$ as the root, may be null in a certain instance of $T_{sub}^{v^{p}}$. Then $v^{key}$ may not be evaluated and the complete key-sequence cannot be produced. In case that $f_{v^{\alpha}}>1$, $T_{sub}^{v^{\alpha}}$ may have multiple instances in a certain instance of $T_{sub}^{v^{p}}$ and each has an instance of $v^{key}$. $v^{key}$ may have multiple values in such an instance of $T_{sub}^{v^{p}}$. It is illegal to make a key-sequence. The assumption is false.

(2) Giving a proof by contradiction in case that $\lfloor v^{target}, v^{p})\neq\Phi$. Assume that in a valid Key, for a $v^{target}$, $\exists v^{\beta}\in\lfloor v^{target}, v^{p})(f_{v^{\beta}}>1)$. A subtree $T_{sub}^{v^{\beta}}$ with $v^{\beta}$ as the root may have multiple instances in a certain $T_{sub}^{v^{p}}$ instance that has a key-sequence. Each $T_{sub}^{v^{\beta}}$ instance includes at least one instance of $v^{target}$. Thus the multiple $v^{target}$ instances in the $T_{sub}^{v^{p}}$ instance have to share one key-sequence. The assumption is false.

In case that $\lfloor v^{target}, v^{p})=\Phi, v^{target}=v^{p}$. The subtree including $v^{target}$ degenerates into a node $v^{target}$ and then $T_{sub}^{v^{p}}$ comprises all the paths from $v^{key}$ to $v^{p}$. Thus there is no restriction on $f_{v^{target}}$. □

## 4.2 An XML Element Tree Consistent with Keys

An XML element tree consistent with Keys is such a tree on which valid Keys can be declared to identify any part of it.

**Theorem 3.** Let $v_{*}$ denote an internal node in $T$, $f_{v_{*}}=0$ or $f_{v_{*}}>1$. If $v_{*}$ is a target node in a valid Key, there is a complete fixed subtree, in which the appearance frequency of each node is 1 except the root, in $T$ with $v_{*}$ as the root.

**Proof:** Let $T_{v_{*}}^{sub}$ denote the maximum subtree in $T$ with $v_{*}$ as the root and $V_{v_{*}}^{key}$ the key nodes set of the Key with $v_{*}$ as the target node. Let

$v^p = LUB(\{v_*\} \bigcup V_{v_*}^{key})$. According to Theorem 2, $v^p$ and $v_*$ are the same node and all the nodes in $V_{v_*}^{key}$ are in $T_{v_*}^{sub}$. Let $v_{v_*}^{key}$ denote a node in $V_{v_*}^{key}$. Assume that for the target node $v_*$ in a valid key, there does not exist such a complete fixed subtree $T_{v_*}^{fixed}$ in $T$, $T_{v_*}^{fixed} \subseteq T_{v_*}^{sub}$. Then there must exist a path from $v_{v_*}^{key}$ to $v^p$ in $T_{v_*}^{sub}$, which includes at least one node $v'''$, $f_{v'''} = 0$ or $f_{v'''} = 1$. In both case, $v_*$ cannot be a target node in a valid Key. So there must exist $T_{v_*}^{fixed} \subseteq T_{v_*}^{sub}$ and all the members of $V_{v_*}^{key}$ are leaves of $T_{v_*}^{fixed}$. □

For $Key_i$ in $T$, if its key nodes set $V_i^{key}$ is given and the corresponding target nodes set $V_i^{target}$ includes all of the possible target nodes that can be constrained by $V_i^{key}$, $V_i^{target}$ is the **full target nodes set** $V_i^{full-target}$ constrained by $V_i^{key}$ of $Key_i$.

Let node $v_i = LUB(V_i^{key} \bigcup V_i^{full-target})$. $v_i \in (V_i^{key} \bigcup V_i^{full-target})$. For a given $V_i^{key}$, there is at most one node with the appearance frequency greater than 1 in the $V_i^{full-target}$. If the node exists, it is $v_i$. Construct a subtree $T_{v_i}^{Key}$ with all of the nodes in $V_i^{key} \bigcup V_i^{full-target}$. Let $T_{v_i}^{sub}$ denote the maximum subtree in $T$ with $v_i$ as the root. $T_{v_i}^{Key} \subseteq T_{v_i}^{sub} \subseteq T$. $Key_i$ is just effective in $T_{v_i}^{Key}$, because it is a relative Key [12]. Namely, $Key_i$ can only identify the instances of the nodes in $V_i^{full-target}$ in a given instance of the parent of $v_i$. If there is a node $v_{i+1}$ in $T_{v_i}^{sub}$, $f_{v_{i+1}} > 1$ and $v_{i+1}$ is other than $v_i$, it should declare $Key_{i+1}$ on the maximum subtree $T_{v_{i+1}}^{sub}$ with $v_{i+1}$ as the root, to identify $v_{i+1}$ instances in a given $T_{v_i}^{sub}$ instance. If several XML documents based on the same XML element tree $T$ are involved in one data integrating process, each document should be identified respectively. Therefore, even if the root of $T$ is designed to appear only once, $T$ need have a complete fixed subtree that includes a key node set to identify the instances of $T$. Due to the relativity of Key, each element instance in an XML document based on $T$ is identified externally by the combination of the Keys encountered in the path from the root of $T$ to the node itself.

As a result, for a well-designed XML element tree, the root and every internal node with appearance frequency great than 1 should have a complete fixed subtree that has some leaves comprising a potential key node set. So that, it is capable to declare Keys for the root and every internal node in XML Schema in order to absolutely identify any part of an XML document based on the XML element tree.

## 5 Conclusion

For the data integration using XML with predefined integrated content and relatively stable data sources, normalizing the design of XML schemas is important, which leads to well-designed schemas facilitating the implementation and execution of the application. XML element tree are introduced to represent all the possible data structures of the same type XML documents in data integration. As the essential of XML document schema, they can be easily transformed into schemas using any XML schema proposal. Our work is focus on normalizing the design of XML element tree. The strategy of declaring elements is proposed. The identity constraints are indispensable in data integration. We depict a general picture of XML element tree consistent with Keys to identify any part of it.

The normalized design of XML element tree have helped us successfully developed several prototypes and applications, such as XYS and TSI. They needs further design principles if considering the query processing and optimizing. These topics are for the future work with the development of XML query languages.

**Acknowledgement.** Dr. Yang Lianghuai gave valuable comments on this paper.

## References

[1] Chidlovskii, B.: Schema extraction from XML collections, Proc. of the second ACM/IEEE-CS joint conference on Digital libraries, 2002.
[2] Chan, C.-Y., Fan, W., Felbery, P., Garofalakis, M., Rastogi, R.: Tree pattern aggregation for scalable XML data dissemination, Proc. of the 28th VLDB Conference, 2002.
[3] Vianu, V.: A Web Odyssey: from Codd to XML, Proc. of the 12th ACM SIGMOD-SIGACT-SIGART symposium on principles of database systems, 2001.
[4] Arenas, M., Fan, W., Libkin, L.: What's Hard about XML Schema Constraints?, Proc.of the 13th international conference on database and expert systems applications, 2002.
[5] Extensible Markup Language (XML), http://www.w3.org.
[6] XML Schema Part 1: Structures, http://www.w3.org.
[7] Fan, W., Gabriel M. Kuper, G., Simeon, J.: A unified constraint model for XML, Proc. of the tenth international conference on WWW, 2001.
[8] Abiteboul, S., Buneman, P., Suciu, D.: Data on the Web, Morgan Kaufmann, 2000.
[9] XML Path Language (XPath), http://www.w3.org.
[10] Laurent, S., Cerami, E.: Building XML Applications, McGraw-Hill, 1999.
[11] Codd, E.: A relational model of data for large shared data banks, Communications of the ACM, 13(6): 377–387, 1970.
[12] Buneman, P., Davidson, S., Fan, W., Hara, C., Tan, W.-C.: Keys for XML, Computer Networks, 39(5): 473–487, 2002.

# Classifying High-Speed Text Streams

Gabriel Pui Cheong Fung[1], Jeffrey Xu Yu[1], and Hongjun Lu[2]

[1] Dept. of Systems Engineering & Engineering Management
The Chinese University of Hong Kong
Hong Kong, China
{pcfung, yu}@se.cuhk.edu.hk

[2] Dept. of Computer Science
The Hong Kong University of Science and Technology
Hong Kong, China
hjlu@cs.ust.edu.hk

**Abstract.** Recently, a new class of data-intensive application becomes widely recognized where data is modeled best as transient open-end streams rather than persistent tables on disk. It leads to a new surge of research interest called data streams. However, most of the reported works are concentrated on structural data, such as bit-sequences, and seldom focus on unstructural data, such as textual documents. In this paper, we propose an efficient classification approach for classifying high-speed text streams. The proposed approach is based on sketches such that it is able to classify the streams efficiently by scanning them only once, meanwhile consuming a small bounded of memory in both model maintenance and operation. Extensive experiments using benchmarks and a real-life news article collection are conducted. The encouraging results indicated that our proposed approach is highly feasible.

## 1 Introduction

In the rapid growth of Web-technology, information becomes ever more pervasive and important. A new class of data-intensive application becomes widely recognized where data is modeled best as transient open-end streams rather than persistent tables on disk. As a result, it leads to a new surge of research interest called data streams. As data streams are open-end in nature and are huge in volume, it is impossible to: 1) hold the entire data streams in memory for analysis; and 2) store on disk as fast processing is desired. A feasible solution is to reduce the number of data scans down to one with bounded memory space.

In this paper, we focus on text streams classification. We propose a novel text stream classification, called MC (Match-and-Classify), by extending our previous work on text classification[5]. This approach is based on maintaining two kinds of sketches: 1) class sketch; and 2) document sketch. The text streams classification is a multi-label classification that assigns a document to multiple classes, whereas our previous work deals with only single-label text classification.

Extensive experiments are conducted using two benchmarks and a real-life news article collection. The quality (accuracy) and efficiency (CPU/memory)

G. Dong et al. (Eds.): WAIM 2003, LNCS 2762, pp. 148–160, 2003.

**Table 1.** Symbols and their meanings

| Symbol | Meaning |
|---|---|
| $f_i$ | Feature $i$ |
| $f_{i,x}$ | Feature $i$ in $x$, $x \in \{d, k\}$ |
| $l_d$ | The number of features in $x$, $x \in \{d, k\}$ |
| $N_k$ | The number of documents in $k$ |
| $N$ | The total number of classes |
| $nf_{i,d}$ | Frequency of $f_i$ in $d$ |
| $df_{i,k}$ | The number of documents containing $f_i$ in $k$ |
| $C_i$ | The set of classes containing feature $f_i$ |
| $\omega_{i,x}$ | The relative importance of $f_i$ in $x$, $x \in \{d, k\}$ |
| $w_{i,y}$ | The weight of $f_i$ in $y$, $y \in \{\tilde{d}, \tilde{k}\}$ |

of MC are compared with some of the existing text classification approaches. It shows that MC achieves high accuracy and exhibits low CPU cost and low memory consumption. The order sensitivity, model updating, as well as the significant of document sketches and class sketches are also studies.

## 2 Text Streams Classification

Text streams classification is a kind of text classification but with some unique characteristics added:

1. The documents queued in a stream is infinite.
2. It requires continuously model maintenance. As the concepts of the documents in the streams may change from time to time, model updating is necessary for maintaining a high quality classifier.
3. Only limited memory space is provided to rebuild the classifier and operate the system. For space efficiency, the number of scan on the documents must be few. For time efficiency, both updating and operation must be conducted very fast.

Note that the first issue causes the last two. However, the last two issues are conflict. In traditional text classification, rebuilding a classifier requires feature selection and/or feature weighting, which implies a large number of data scans over the documents archived (high computational cost and large memory).

## 3 Similarity-Based Text Streams Classification

Defining two kinds of sketches: class sketch and document sketch. A class (document) sketch is an approximator for the class (incoming document). Let $d$ and $k$ be a document and a class, respectively; $\tilde{d}$ and $\tilde{k}$ be the corresponding document sketch and class sketch, respectively. A high similarity between $\tilde{k}_j$ and $\tilde{d}_i$ indicates that $d_i$ should belongs to $k_j$. Hence, the quality and efficiency of MC relies on how the sketches approximate the distinctive features. For fast performance, the information in a sketch should be minimized. In MC, the information in a sketch only includes the features appearing in the documents archived.

### 3.1 Sketches and Text Streams Classification

Table 1 shows a list of symbols and their meanings. The class sketch and document sketch are:

$$\tilde{d} = \langle (f_{1,d}, w_{1,d}), (f_{2,d}, w_{2,d}), \cdots, (f_{l_d,d}, w_{l_d,d}) \rangle$$
$$\tilde{k} = \langle (f_{1,k}, W_{1,k}), (f_{2,k}, W_{2,k}), \cdots, (f_{l_k,k}, W_{l_k,k}) \rangle$$

Given $\tilde{d}$ and $\tilde{k}$, their similarity are measured by Jaccard coefficient:

$$S(\tilde{d}, \tilde{k}) = \frac{\sum_{i \in \tilde{d}} (w_{i,d} \cdot W_{i,k})}{\sum_{i \in \tilde{d}} w_{i,d}^2 + \sum_{i \in \tilde{d}} W_{i,k}^2 - \sum_{i \in \tilde{d}} (w_{i,d} \cdot W_{i,k})} \quad (1)$$

Jaccard coefficient is chosen because it expresses the degree of overlapping between $\tilde{d}$ and $\tilde{k}$ as the proportion of overlapping between them. It provides both intuitive and practical fitness to our model.

Given $N$ predefined classes, $k_1, k_2, \cdots, k_N$, MC first computes $\tilde{d}$ on $d$. By following Equation (1), MC sorts all class sketches such that $S(\tilde{d}, \tilde{k}_i) \geq S(\tilde{d}, \tilde{k}_j)$ for $i < j$. Finally, MC determines the top class sketches, $\tilde{k}_1, \tilde{k}_2, \cdots, \tilde{k}_K$, such that $E(\tilde{k}_i) \leq E(\tilde{k}_{i+1})$ for $i < K$ and $E(\tilde{k}_K) > E(\tilde{k}_{K+1})$, where

$$E(\tilde{k}_i) = \frac{1}{2}(S(\tilde{d}, \tilde{k}_i)^2 - S(\tilde{d}, \tilde{k}_{i+1})^2) \quad (2)$$

and classifies $d$ into $k_1, k_2, \cdots, k_K$.

### 3.2 Class Sketch Generation

The weight $W_{i,k}$ for $f_i$ in $k$ is computed as follows:

$$W_{i,k} = AI_{i,k} \cdot \left( \sqrt{2} \cdot \frac{WC_{i,k}^2 \cdot CC_i^2}{\sqrt{WC_{i,k}^2 + CC_i^2}} \right) \quad (3)$$

Here, $\sqrt{2}$ is used for normalization such that $0 \leq W_{i,k} \leq 1$. $WC_{i,k}$, the Within-Class Coefficient, is used to measure the relative importance of $f_i$ within $k$:

$$WC_{i,k} = \frac{\log_2(df_{i,k} + 1)}{\log_2(N_k + 1)} \quad (4)$$

$WC_{i,k}$ reflects the fact that features appearing frequently within a class is critical in term of classification. In Equation (4), both numerator and denominator are logarithmic, as the frequency of a feature appearing over many documents is rare. Similar finding is also reported in[7].

$CC_i$, the Cross-Class Coefficient, is used to measure the relative importance of $f_i$ among all classes:

$$CC_i = \frac{1}{\log N} \cdot \log \frac{N}{\alpha} \quad (5)$$

where $\alpha = (\sum_{k=1}^{N} WC_{i,k})/(\max_{k \in C_i}\{WC_{i,k}\})$. $1/\log(N)$ is used for normalization such that $0 \leq CC_i \leq 1$.

Note that $\alpha$ gives a ratio between $\sum WC_{i,k}$ for all classes $k$ that contain $f_i$ and the maximum of $WC_{i,k}$. Hence, $\sum$ is used to gather the total importance of a feature across all classes, and the maximum is used to average the summation value. If a feature is regarded as important in many classes, then this feature is obviously not important for classification.

$CC_i$ gives a global view across classes. Suppose that there are two features, $f_i$ and $f_j$, where $f_i$ appears in $m$ classes and $f_j$ appears in $n$ classes. There are two cases:

- **Case-1** ($m \gg n$): Obviously, $f_j$ provides far more precious information for text classification than $f_i$. In other words, a feature is more valuable if its occurrence is skewed.
- **Case-2** ($m = n$): In this case, we argue that it is not realistic to weight the importance of a feature, $f_i$, by simply counting the number of classes that $f_i$ appears, as in[17]. We assign a higher weight to the feature in which more documents in a class contains it.

$AI_i$, the Average-Importance Coefficient, is used to measure the average importance of $f_{i,d}$ over all individual documents in $k$:

$$AI_{i,k} = \left(\frac{\omega_{i,k}}{df_{i,k}}\right)^{\beta_{i,k}} \tag{6}$$

$$\omega_{i,k} = \sum_{d \in k} \omega_{i,d} \tag{7}$$

$$\omega_{i,d} = \frac{\log_2(nf_{i,d} + 1)}{\log_2(l_d + 1)} \tag{8}$$

Note that a feature appears $n$ times does not imply that it is $n$ times more important[4,6,13], we therefore take a logarithmic relationship rather than a linear relationship. The term within the bracket is to average the weights of $f_i$ among all documents in $k$. The average estimator, $\beta_{i,k}$, is used to determine the suitability of this average:

$$\beta_{i,k} = \frac{1}{1 + WC_{i,k}} \tag{9}$$

For instance, given two features: $f_i$ and $f_j$, such that $f_i$ appears in most documents but $f_j$ appears in a few documents. It is more confident to declare that the average of $f_i$ is more likely to reflect the true status of it than that of $f_j$.

Unlike $WC_{i,k}$ and $CC_i$ which are designed at class level, $AI_{i,k}$ handles the importance of a feature within an individual document. It is introduced to reduce the discrepancy among weights, and increase the recall and precision of the model.

As for memory consumption, MC only needs to keep $df_{i,k}$ and $\omega_{i,k}$ in memory. Also, we can easily maintain the model to reflect the new features in the text stream.

### 3.3 Document Sketch Generation

When handling text streams, we need to figure out the feature importance. This is usually done by considering the features' distribution within the incoming document. In practice, we may need to deal with a text stream in a document basis (one document at a time). Thus, the sample size is insufficient. Document sketch is proposed to estimate the true significance of features in an incoming document:

$$\overline{AI}_i = \left( \frac{\sum_{k=1}^{N} \omega_{i,k}}{\sum_{k=1}^{N} df_{i,k}} \right)^{\overline{\beta}_i} \tag{10}$$

$\overline{AI}_i$ is the average weights of $f_i$ over all classes, which is similar to Equation (9):

$$\overline{\beta}_i = \frac{1}{1 + \overline{WC}_i} \tag{11}$$

$$\overline{WC_i} = \frac{\log_2(\sum_{k=1}^{N} df_{i,k} + 1)}{\log_2(\sum_{k=1}^{N} N_k + 1)} \tag{12}$$

However, only the above is insufficient. We cannot assume that every incoming document that contains $f_i$ shares the same distribution. In other words, there are some risks in using Equation (10). Thus, a geometric distribution is formulated:

$$R_i = \left( \frac{1}{1 + \overline{nf}_i} \right) \times \left( \frac{\overline{nf}_i}{1 + \overline{nf}_i} \right)^{nf_{i,d}} \tag{13}$$

$$\overline{nf}_i = \overline{AI}_i \times nf_{i,d} \tag{14}$$

Finally, $w_{i,d}$ in $\tilde{d}$ is computed by combining Equation (10) to (14):

$$w_{i,d} = \omega_{i,d}^{1-R_i} \times \overline{AI}_i^{R_i} \tag{15}$$

## 4 Related Work

In this section, we re-examine two well-known text classification approaches: Naive Bayes (NB) and Support Vectors Machine (SVM).

NB is a probabilistic-base algorithm that computes the posterior probability of an unseen document given a particular class[9,10]. The merit of it lies on little consumption of computational resources. Its building cost is linear with the size of the training set[3,12], and its operation cost is also low. Based on the independent assumption of words, it only stores the probabilities of the features appearing in each class[14]. Consequently, it is possible to update the model continuously and incrementally. However, NB requires significant text preprocessing, such as feature selection[11], or else its quality will be poor. Note that feature selection needs to scan all of the features in each document from scratch during model updating.

SVM is based on statistical learning theory for solving two-class pattern recognition problem[16]. It attempts to generate a decision hyperplane that maximizes the margin between the positive and the negative examples in a training set using quadratic programming approach[2]. Based on our knowledge, SVM is the best algorithm in terms of accuracy[1,8,19]. However, the building cost is quadratic with the size of the training set[2]. Also, SVM requires feature weighting or else it performance degrades[8]. These make SVM not much appropriate for text stream classification.

### 4.1 Memory Consumption

Let $n$ be the number of documents; $m$ be the average number of features in a document; $c$ be the total number of classes. Furthermore, all features are digitalized.

For NB, each class needs to store the document frequency and the total term frequency for each feature. The memory consumption for a feature in a class is 12 bytes (4 for feature, 4 for document frequency, and 4 for term frequency). Recall that a feature may appear in multiple classes. The total memory for NB is about double of $12 \times m \times c$.

For SVM, each feature is associated with a weight. A corpus requires $8 \times m \times n$ byte to be stored. For building a classifier, a matrix is needed that requires additional $4 \times n^2$ byte. Hence, it requires $c \times (8 \times m \times n + 4 \times n^2)$ bytes.

For MC, only a small bounded memory is needed. For each feature, it stores a weight and the document frequency (total 8 bytes). Thus, about $12 \times m \times c$ bytes is needed, which is about half of NB in the worst case scenario. Note that MC is not a binary classifier, such that the space would reduced significantly.

## 5 Experimental Evaluations

All of the experiments were conducted on a Sun Blade-1000 workstation with 512MB physical memory and a 750MHz Ultra-SPARC-III CPU running Solaris 2.8. All features are stemmed, in which punctuation marks, stop-words, numbers, web page addresses and email addresses are ignored.

For measuring the quality of classification, recall, precision and F1-measure are used[18]. In the following, we use M-X and m-X to denote macro-values and micro-values respectively, where X belongs to recall, precision or F1.

### 5.1 Data Sets

Two benchmarks and a news collection received from Reuters (News-Collection) are used for testing. Table 2 summarized them.

- **Reuters-21578**: We take the ModApte-split and select the classes that have at least one document for training and testing. There are 9,128 documents assigned to one class and 1,660 documents assigned to multiple classes. This corpus is highly skewed. Figure 1 summarized its distribution.

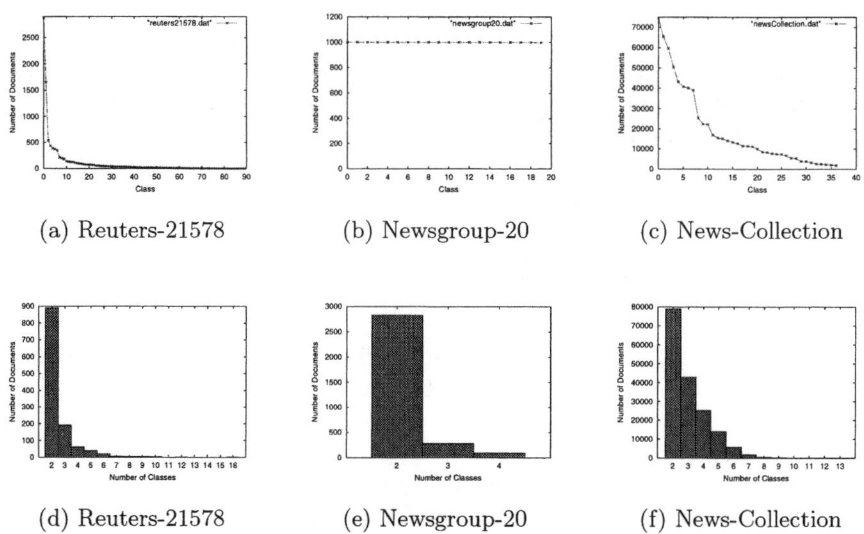


(a) Reuters-21578 (b) Newsgroup-20 (c) News-Collection

(d) Reuters-21578 (e) Newsgroup-20 (f) News-Collection

**Fig. 1.** Document distribution. (a) Highly skewed. (b) Evenly distributed. (c) Slightly skewed. (d)-(f) Number of documents in multiple classes

**Table 2.** A summary of the corpora used.

| **Dataset** | **Training** | **Testing** | **Classes** | **Features** |
|---|---|---|---|---|
| Reuters-21578 | 7,769 | 3,019 | 90 | 13,270 |
| Newsgroup-20 | 14,694 | 1,633 | 20 | 25,245 |
| News-Collection | 280,000 | 70,000 | 38 | 206,897 |

- **Newsgroup-20**: There are 13,126 documents assigned to one class and 3,201 documents assigned to multiple classes. The documents are evenly distributed among different classes. Figure 1 summarized its distribution.
- **News-Collection**: A very large set of news articles archived through Reuters directly from October 2000 to October 2002. Our task is to assign the news articles to the Morgan Stanley Capital International (MSCI) code. Note that Reuters has already classified these articles into the corresponding classes. Figure 1 summarized its distribution.

## 5.2 Implementations

For NB, the Multinomial Mixture model is used[11,19]. Features are selected using information gain (IG) and are chosen based on $m{-}F1$. Recall that classifier updating requires re-selecting the features by calculating IG again, which takes most of the computational cost.

For SVM, we use the package SVM$^{light}$(`http://svmlight.joachims.org`). The weight of each feature is calculated by $tf \cdot idf$ scheme and are normalized to unit length[13]. The classifier is updated base on the newly received documents

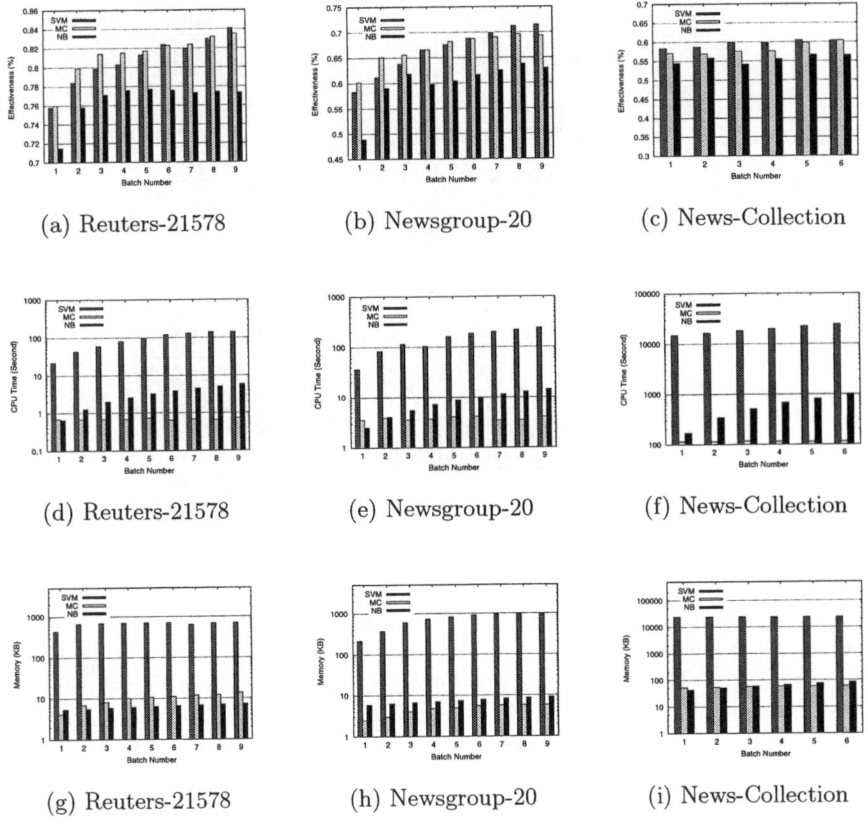


(a) Reuters-21578 (b) Newsgroup-20 (c) News-Collection

(d) Reuters-21578 (e) Newsgroup-20 (f) News-Collection

(g) Reuters-21578 (h) Newsgroup-20 (i) News-Collection

**Fig. 2.** Classification efficiency. (a), (b) and (c) show the accuracy in terms of m-F1; (d), (e) and (f) show the CPU time; (g), (h) and (i) show the memory consumption.

and the previously learned support vectors[15]. The classifier updating requires re-calculating the feature weights, which leads to a significant overhead.

MC is implemented using Java (300 lines implementation). Neither feature selection nor weighing is necessary. Thus, no other extra operations are necessary in classifier updating.

### 5.3 Text Stream Classification Quality

Documents are divided into $n$ equal-sized batches. Classifiers are built using the first batch, and evaluate using the second batch. Then, we update the classifier using the second batches, and evaluate it using the third batch, and so on so forth.

Table 3 shows the average accuracy for each of the three algorithms where $n = 10$. The accuracy of MC is similar to that of SVM, and is superior to that of NB. In particular, MC performs significantly well in terms of recall (M-R and m-R). Although MC does not outperform SVM in terms of accuracy, its low CPU

**Table 3.** Results of text stream classification

| | Method | m-P | m-R | m-F1 | M-P | M-R | M-F1 |
|---|---|---|---|---|---|---|---|
| Reuters-21578 | SVM | 0.840 | 0.789 | 0.824 | 0.543 | 0.609 | 0.569 |
| | MC | 0.800 | 0.831 | 0.815 | 0.557 | 0.721 | 0.628 |
| | NB | 0.741 | 0.799 | 0.767 | 0.336 | 0.524 | 0.406 |
| Newsgroup-28 | SVM | 0.722 | 0.625 | 0.685 | 0.694 | 0.619 | 0.667 |
| | MC | 0.693 | 0.643 | 0.667 | 0.694 | 0.609 | 0.678 |
| | NB | 0.632 | 0.585 | 0.597 | 0.633 | 0.623 | 0.620 |
| News-Collection | SVM | 0.633 | 0.582 | 0.604 | 0.526 | 0.478 | 0.502 |
| | MC | 0.539 | 0.668 | 0.587 | 0.485 | 0.502 | 0.497 |
| | NB | 0.603 | 0.489 | 0.556 | 0.493 | 0.367 | 0.378 |

**Table 4.** Result of large batch testing

| | Method | m-P | m-R | m-F1 | M-P | M-R | M-F1 |
|---|---|---|---|---|---|---|---|
| Reuters-21578 | SVM | 0.912 | 0.802 | 0.857 | 0.533 | 0.479 | 0.505 |
| | MC | 0.807 | 0.851 | 0.828 | 0.498 | 0.650 | 0.564 |
| | NB | 0.776 | 0.751 | 0.763 | 0.401 | 0.378 | 0.381 |
| Newsgroup-20 | SVM | 0.882 | 0.617 | 0.726 | 0.873 | 0.618 | 0.724 |
| | MC | 0.721 | 0.669 | 0.694 | 0.722 | 0.686 | 0.703 |
| | NB | 0.671 | 0.608 | 0.638 | 0.670 | 0.639 | 0.655 |
| News-Collection | SVM | 0.658 | 0.632 | 0.643 | 0.518 | 0.495 | 0.503 |
| | MC | 0.540 | 0.671 | 0.591 | 0.406 | 0.579 | 0.487 |
| | NB | 0.603 | 0.489 | 0.536 | 0.583 | 0.335 | 0.425 |

cost in both the classifier updating and operation makes it highly recommended for text stream classification.

Figure 2 (a), (b) and (c) show the m-F1 of the three algorithms whenever a new batch arrives. For all of the algorithms, m-F1 increases from the first batch and become saturated after 4-5 batches. This is because the classifiers obtain a relatively sufficient samples from the corpus. In all cases, NB always performs inferior to the other two. The accuracy of MC and SVM are similar. M-F1 shows the similar behaviors, but are omitted due to the limit of space. Figure 2 (d), (e) and (f) show the CPU cost (including both classifier rebuilding and preprocessing costs) using the three data sets. Note that MC outperforms both NB and SVM, significantly. Figure 2 (g), (h) and (i) show the estimated memory consumption using the estimation given in previous section.

### 5.4 Large Batch Testing

In this section, we take the whole dataset as a single large batch. In other words, we assume a large number of documents come together in a very small time window. Table 4 and Figure 3 summarized the results. Note that CPU cost includes preprocessing cost and maintenance cost.

### 5.5 MC Analysis

Four detailed analysis are conducted: a) the accuracy of different components in class sketches; b) the significant of the average estimator in document sketch; c) the classifier rebuilding necessity; d) the sensitivity to documents arrival order.

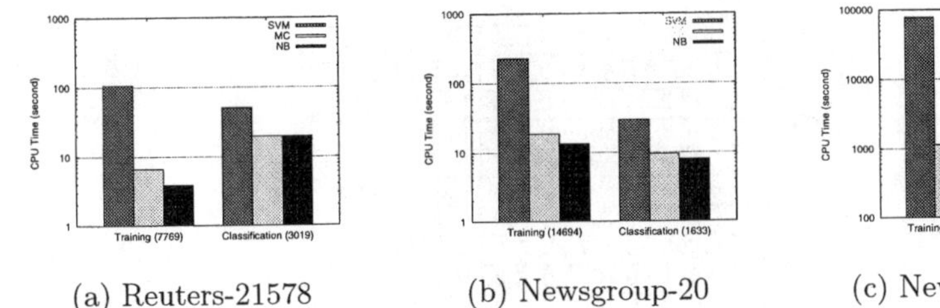

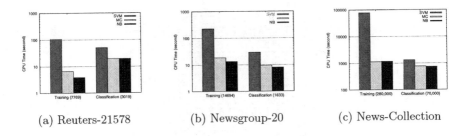

(a) Reuters-21578 (b) Newsgroup-20 (c) News-Collection

**Fig. 3.** Efficiency (text classification)

**Table 5.** Experiment setup.

| Exp. No. | use $WC_{i,k}$ | use $CC_i$ | use $AI_{i,k}$ |
|---|---|---|---|
| 1 | √ | × | × |
| 2 | × | √ | × |
| 3 | √ | √ | × |
| 4 | √ | √ | + |
| 5 | × | × | √ |
| 6 | × | × | + |
| 7 | √ | × | √ |
| 8 | × | √ | √ |
| 9 | √ | √ | √ |

**Table 6.** Results of the testing.

| Exp. No. | Reuters-21578 | | Newsgroup-20 | |
|---|---|---|---|---|
| | m-F1 | M-F1 | m-F1 | M-F1 |
| 1 | 0.007 | 0.391 | 0.005 | 0.234 |
| 2 | 0.028 | 0.200 | 0.018 | 0.125 |
| 3 | 0.745 | 0.350 | 0.514 | 0.459 |
| 4 | 0.815 | 0.515 | 0.604 | 0.640 |
| 5 | 0.780 | 0.375 | 0.584 | 0.578 |
| 6 | 0.699 | 0.318 | 0.510 | 0.513 |
| 7 | 0.775 | 0.374 | 0.531 | 0.578 |
| 8 | 0.686 | 0.350 | 0.482 | 0.508 |
| 9 | 0.828 | 0.564 | 0.694 | 0.703 |

**Class Sketch.** Nine experiments are conducted (Table 5) to examine the significance of $WC_{i,k}$, $CC_i$ and $AI_{i,k}$. + indicates that $AI_{i,k}$ is used without $\beta_{i,k}$.

Table 6 shows the results using Reuters-21578 and Newsgroup-20. Exp. 9, which includes all of the coefficients, performs the best. Using either $WC_{i,k}$ or $CC_i$ (Exp. 1 and Exp. 2 ) gives an unsatisfactory results. A combination of them yields a significant improvement (Exp. 3). Ignoring the average estimator (Exp.6) yields an inferior result.

**Table 7.** Document sketch testing

| Exp. | Reuters-21578 | | Newsgroup-20 | | News-Collection | |
|---|---|---|---|---|---|---|
| | m-F1 | M-F1 | m-F1 | M-F1 | m-F1 | M-F1 |
| with $\overline{\beta}_i$ | 0.828 | 0.564 | 0.694 | 0.703 | 0.591 | 0.487 |
| no $\overline{\beta}_i$ | 0.803 | 0.552 | 0.673 | 0.682 | 0.562 | 0.470 |

**Document Sketch.** In our model, a document sketch is influenced by the entire feature distribution. Table 7 shows the necessity of the influence. "with $\overline{\beta}_i$" denotes that $\overline{\beta}_i$ is used, whereas "no $\overline{\beta}_i$" denotes that $\overline{\beta}_i$ is set to 1. The results show that $\overline{\beta}_i$ plays an important role in text stream classification.

**Classifier Rebuilding.** Three different cases are tested:

**Table 8.** Order sensitivity testing

| No. | m-P | m-R | m-F1 | M-P | M-R | M-F1 |
|---|---|---|---|---|---|---|
| 1 | 0.716 | 0.667 | 0.691 | 0.713 | 0.681 | 0.696 |
| 2 | 0.719 | 0.662 | 0.689 | 0.724 | 0.687 | 0.705 |
| 3 | 0.714 | 0.673 | 0.693 | 0.710 | 0.685 | 0.697 |
| 4 | 0.718 | 0.668 | 0.692 | 0.717 | 0.683 | 0.700 |
| 5 | 0.719 | 0.663 | 0.690 | 0.719 | 0.678 | 0.698 |
| 6 | 0.740 | 0.675 | 0.706 | 0.740 | 0.697 | 0.718 |
| 7 | 0.710 | 0.665 | 0.687 | 0.713 | 0.683 | 0.698 |
| 8 | 0.731 | 0.677 | 0.703 | 0.736 | 0.693 | 0.714 |
| 9 | 0.732 | 0.678 | 0.704 | 0.729 | 0.694 | 0.711 |
| 10 | 0.712 | 0.657 | 0.684 | 0.715 | 0.675 | 0.694 |
| s.d. | 0.0100 | 0.0069 | 0.0078 | 0.0104 | 0.0070 | 0.0083 |

**Table 9.** The accuracy of classifier rebuilding

| Exp. | m-P | m-R | m-F1 | M-P | M-R | M-F1 |
|---|---|---|---|---|---|---|
| 1 | 0.725 | 0.672 | 0.698 | 0.722 | 0.687 | 0.704 |
| 2 | 0.700 | 0.634 | 0.666 | 0.702 | 0.652 | 0.676 |
| 3 | 0.693 | 0.643 | 0.667 | 0.694 | 0.589 | 0.678 |

- **Exp-1**: Rebuild the classifier whenever a document arrives. Note that neither NB nor SVM can handle it, as they have to perform expensive document preprocessing.
- **Exp-2**: MC is rebuilt in a random manner. The size of each batch varies. This experiment simulates the real-life situation such that the classifier needs to be rebuilt in a certain time interval.
- **Exp-3**: MC is rebuilt such that the number of documents in a batch is fixed.

Table 9 shows the results. The average accuracy of Exp-1 is the best. This suggests that continuously classifier rebuilding will increase the accuracy of a text stream classifier in a long term. The difference between Exp-2 and Exp-3, in terms of the average accuracy, is not significant.

**Order Sensitivity.** We test whether MC is sensitive to the order of document arrival using Newsgroup-20. We place all documents in a queue randomly and repeat the testing as described above. We repeat the whole process 10 times and report the average. Table 8 shows the results. Since the standard deviation is small, we concluded that MC may not be sensitive to the order of document arrival.

## 6 Conclusion and Future Work

In this paper, we proposed a novel text stream classification approach (MC). MC does not need to generate any sophisticated models. The main advantages of MC are: 1) it could achieve high accuracy; 2) model can be rebuilt efficiently regardless the size of the batches; 3) only a small bounded memory is required; 4) no advance document preprocessing is necessary in any circumstances.

As our future work, we will extend this research in several directions: 1) study the timing at which the model should be rebuilt; 2) methods to automatically remove unnecessary features; 3) the model resistance to noise; and 4) study the possibility of combing text stream and data stream.

**Acknowledgments.** The work described in this paper was partially supported by grants from the Research Grants Council of the Hong Kong Special Administrative Region, China (CUHK4229/01E, DAG01/02.EG14).

## References

1. S. Chakrabarti, S. Roy, and M. V. Soundalgekar. Fast and accurate text classification via multiple linear discriminant projections. In *Proceedings of the 28th Very Large Database Conference*, 2002.
2. N. Cristianini and J. Shaws-Taylor. *An Intorduction to Support Vector Machines and Other Kernel-Based learning Methods.* Cambridge University Press, 2000.
3. R. O. Duda, P. E. Hart, and D. G. Stork. *Pattern Classification.* Wiley Interscience, 2nd edition, 2001.
4. W. B. Frakes and R. Baeza-Yates. *Information Retrieval: Data Structures and Algorithms.* Prentice Hall PTR, 1992.
5. G. P. C. Fung, J. X. Yu, and W. Lam. Automatic stock trend prediction by real time news. In *Proceedings of 2002 Workshop in Data Mining and Modeling*, 2002.
6. W. R. Greiff. A theory of term weighting based on exploratory data analysis. In *Proceedings of SIGIR-98 21th ACM International Conference on Research and Development in Information Retrieval*, pages 11–19, 1998.
7. J. D. Holt and S. M. Chung. Efficient mining of association rules in text databases. In *Proceedings of 8th International Conference on Information and Knowledge Management*, pages 234–242, 1999.
8. T. Joachims. Text categorization with support vector machines: Learning with many relevant features. In *Proceedings of 13th European Conference on Machine Learning*, pages 137–142, 1998.
9. D. D. Lewis. An evaluation of phrasal and clustered representations on a text categorization task. In *Proceedings of SIGIR-92 15th ACM International Conference on Research and Development in Information Retrieval*, pages 37–50, 1992.
10. D. D. Lewis. Naive (bayes) at forty: The independence assumption in information retrieval. In *Proceedings of 13th European Conference on Machine Learning*, pages 4–15, 1998.
11. A. McCallum and K. Nigam. A comparison of event models for naive bayes text classification. In *AAAI 1998 Workshop on Learning for Text Categorization*, 1998.
12. D. Meretakis, D. Fragoudis, H. Lu, and S. Likothanassis. Scalable association-based text classification. In *Proceedings of 10th International Conference on Information and Knowledge Management*, pages 5–11, 2001.
13. G. Salton and C. Buckley. Term-weighting approaches in automatic text retrieval. *Information Processing and Management*, 24(5):513–523, 1988.
14. F. Sebastiani. Machine learning in automated text categorization. *ACM Computing Surveys*, 34(1):1–47, 2002.
15. N. A. Syed, H. Liu, and K. K. Sung. Incremental learning with support vector machines. In *Proceedings of SIGKDD-99, 5th International Conference on Knowledge Discovery and Data Mining*, pages 313–321, 1999.

16. V. Vapnik. *The Nature of Statistical Learning Theory.* Springer, 1995.
17. K. Yamamoto, S. Masuyama, and S. Naito. Automatic text classification method with simple class-weighting approach. In *Natural Language Processing Pacific Rim Symposium*, 1995.
18. Y. Yang. An evaluation of statistical approaches to text categorization. *Information Retrieval*, 1-2(1):69–90, 1999.
19. Y. Yang and X. Liu. A re-examination of text categorization methods. In *Proceedings of SIGIR-99 22th ACM International Conference on Research and Development in Information Retrieval*, pages 42–49, 1999.

# Partition Based Hierarchical Index for Text Retrieval

Yan Yang[1,2], Baoliang Liu[1], and Zhaogong Zhang[1,2]

[1] Harbin Institute of Technology, No.92, West Da-Zhi Street, Harbin, Heilongjiang, China
yangyan@mail.banner.com.cn
zhangzhaogong@0451.com
liubaoliang@db.hit.edu.cn

[2] Heilongjiang University, No.74, Xuefu street, Harbin, Heilongjiang, China

**Abstract.** Along with single word query, phrase query is frequently used in digital library. This paper proposes a new partition based hierarchical index structure for efficient phrase query and a parallel algorithm based on the index structure. In this scheme, a document is divided into several elements. The elements are distributed on several processors. In each processor, a hierarchical inverted index is built, by which single word and phrase queries can be answered efficiently. This index structure and the partition make the postings lists shorter. At the same time, integer compression technique is used more efficiently. Experiments and analysis show that query evaluation time is significantly reduced.

## 1 Introduction

Most queries in digital library consist of simple lists of words. In our research, we get the query logs from Excite. Statistical analysis on these query logs shows that there are 76 percent of the total 91189 queries include phrases. In phrase queries, 36 percent are two-word queries, 22 percent are three-word queries and 11 percent are four-word queries. The others are 31 percent. We can see from this analysis that phrase queries are frequently used in digital library. So phrase query evaluation is a key issue in digital library.

There are some indices for text retrieval that can support phrase queries. Justin Zobel gave a detailed comparison of inverted files and signature files and demonstrated that the former is superior to the later not only in query evaluation time but also in space [1]. Inverted index is a general method for text retrieval [2], but the postings list is very long. Some systems emit the stopping words, but makes a small number of queries cannot be evaluated, while many more evaluate incorrectly [3].

There are a lot of integer compression techniques can be used in the postings lists[4]. Elias gamma code is efficient for small integers but not suited to large integers. Elias delta codes are somewhat shorter than gamma codes for large integers, but not suitable for small integers. Text compression techniques are combined with block addressing [5]. Alistair Moffat etc. show that the CPU component of query response time can be similarly reduced, at little cost in terms of storage, by the inclusion of an

G. Dong et al. (Eds.): WAIM 2003, LNCS 2762, pp. 161–172, 2003.

internal index in each compressed inverted list [6]. Falk Scholer etc. revisit the compression of inverted lists of document postings, considering two approaches to improving retrieval efficiency: better implementation and better choice of integer compression schemes [7]. There are some distributed algorithms to build global inverted files for very large text collections [8]. But there are no suitable distributed algorithms to answer phrase queries in parallel computer.

Nextword index, which can index phrase directly, is proposed by Hugh E. Williams and Justin Zobel [9]. The nextword index can efficiently evaluate two-word phrase queries, but the size is large. Except that, nextword index can not efficiently support phrase queries that contain more than two words. An optimization algorithm is given for phrase querying with a nextword index [10]. It shows that careful consideration of which words are evaluated in a query plan and optimization of the order of evaluation of the plan can reduce query evaluation costs by more than a factor of five. But nextword index processing is still not particularly efficient, as the nextwords must be processed linearly and for rare firstwords the overhead of the additional layer of structure may outweigh the benefits. And the size of the nextword index is huge as usual. D.Bahle introduced new compaction techniques for nextword indexes, which allow full resolution of phrase queries without false match checking [11]. The novel techniques lead to significant savings in index size. But the drawback is that query optimization is difficult. Combination of inverted index and nextword index can reduce both the size of the index and the query evaluation time. Dirk Bahle combines the nextword index and the inverted index, which is a more efficient index structure to support phrase query [12]. But more than two words queries are still not efficiently supported.

This paper explores new techniques for efficient evaluation of phrase queries. This scheme supports not only single word queries, but also equal or more than two words phrase queries efficiently. A document is divided into several elements. The elements are distributed on several processors. In each processor, a hierarchical inverted index is built, by which 1 to 4-word phrase queries can be evaluated directly. This index structure and the partition make the postings lists shorter. At the same time, integer compression techniques can be used more efficiently. We explore the properties of single word queries and phrase queries. Experiments and analysis show that query evaluation time can be significantly reduced.

## 2 Preparations

### 2.1 Query Modes

In digital library, a query is a sequence of words. So how many words a query includes is very important for the index structure. Different index structure has different efficiency to answer queries in digital library.

Statistics in SPIRE2001 [11] shows that 64 percent of the total 33286 phrase queries are composed of two words. 24 percent are three words, 8 percent are four words and less than 4 percent are equal or more than 5 words. In this statistics, all the 33286 phrase queries are surrounded by quotation marks. Statistics in [12] gives the similar information.

[11] and [12] account for only phrase queries that enclosed in quotes. Actually a user gives a word list without quotes, but the user expects that the words are adjacent. So, we get the Excite logs freely from the web and analyze the total 91189 queries. Only 25 percent of the queries are one word queries. The other 75 percent of the queries contain at least two words, which we call phrase queries without quotes. In these queries, 27% are two-word queries, 16% are three-word queries and 8 % are four-word queries. The total number of more than four words queries is about 24%. We can see from this analysis that 1 to 4 words queries are often used in digital library. More than 4 words queries are frequently used too. So in digital library, inverted index and nextword index are not enough. Based on above statistics, a digital library should efficiently support at least 1 to 4 words queries. More than four words queries should be efficiently support too.

## 2.2 Introduction of Inverted Index and Nextword Index

Inverted index is a common method for text retrieval. It allows evaluation of single word and phrase queries. An inverted index is a two-level structure. The upper level is all the index words for the collection. The lower level is a set of postings lists, one per index word. Following the notation of Zobel and Moffat [13], each posting is a triple of the form: $<d, f_{d,t}, [o_1, \ldots, o_{fd,t}]>$ where $d$ is the identifier of a document containing word $t$, the frequency of $t$ in $d$ is $f_{d,t}$, and the $o$ values are the positions in $d$ at which $t$ is observed. An example of inverted index is shown in Figure 1.

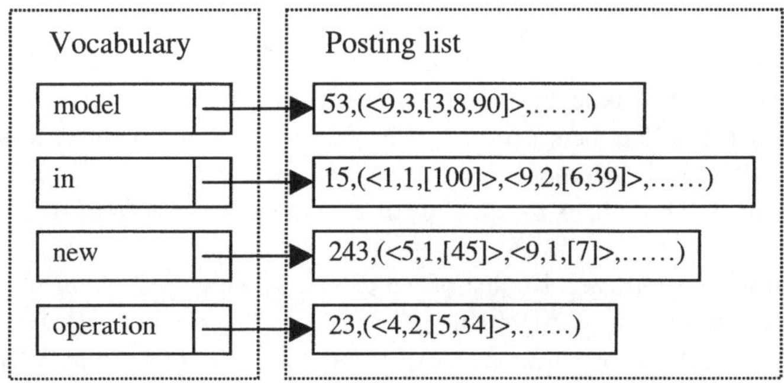


**Fig. 1.** An inverted index for a collection with a vocabulary of four words

The nextword index takes the middle ground by indexing pairs of words and, therefore, is particularly good at resolving phrase queries. A nextword index is a three-level structure. The highest level is of the distinct index words in the collection, which we call *firstwords*. At the middle level, for each firstword there is a data structure of *nextwords*, which are the words observed to follow that firstword in the indexed text. At the lowest level, for each nextword there is a postings list of the positions at which that firstword-nextword pair occurs. An example nextword index is shown in Figure 2. For phrase queries of more than two words, multiple postings lists must be fetched from the nextword index to resolve the query.

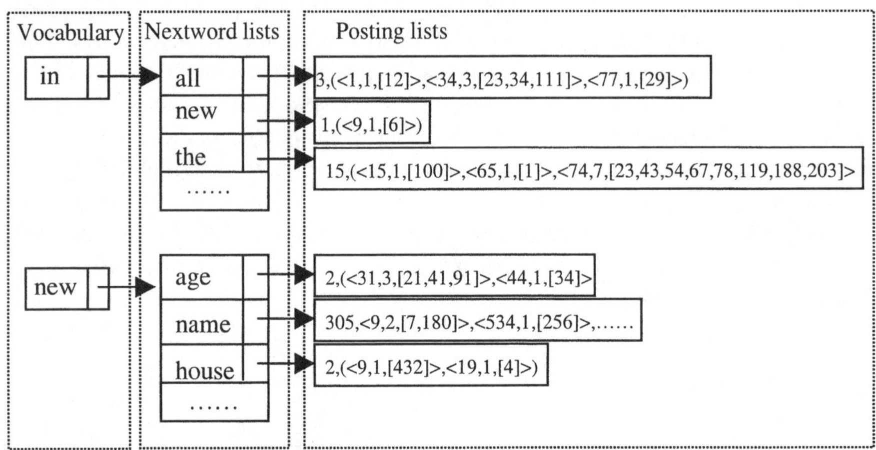


**Fig. 2.** A nextword index with two firstwords

### 2.3 Some Definitions

To explain the hierarchical index structure, the following definitions are given.

Definition 1. A *document d* is a sequence of words $w_1$...... $w_n$. A document can be divided into several *elements*. Each word $w_i$ is labeled with an *offset* $o_i$. Offsets are positive integers.

Definition 2. An *element* is a sequence of word $w_i$...... $w_j$. An *element* is an independent part of a document, such as a chapter of a book. We give each word in an element a partial offset begin from 1. The partial offset in an element is smaller than the global offset in a document.

Definition 3. The offsets $o_1$,......, $o_n$ in document *d* are *ordinal* if $o_i = i$ for $1 \leq i \leq n$.

Definition 4. A *phrase p* is a list of words $s_1 \ldots s_j$, which $j \geq 2$. A *term t* is a word or a phrase, that is *term t* is $s_1 \ldots s_j$, which $j \geq 1$.

Definition 5. A *query* is a sequence of terms $t_1$...... $t_m$, for $1 \leq i \leq m$, *m* is the *length* of the query, term $t_i$ is a list of words or phrases $s^i_1 \ldots s^i_j$. When $m=1$, the *answer* of the query is a set of documents $S_1$, where a document $w_1 \ldots\ldots w_n$ in $S_1$ satisfies that for some $k > 0$, $s^1_i = w_{k-1+i}$ for $1 \leq i \leq j$. When $m>1$, the *answer* of the query is a set of documents $S = S_1 \cap \ldots \cap S_m$, where $S_k$ is the answer of the one term query $t_k$ for $1 \leq k \leq m$.

Definition 6. A query, whose length is equal or more than 5, has to be divided into 3 and 4 words queries to process. An *optimized subquery* is the optimized division scheme to divide the more than 4 words phrase query to a sequence of 3 and 4-word phrases and give the optimized evaluation order of the subqueries.

Definition 7. A *hierarchical index* is a mapping from 1 to 4-word terms $f_1..f_t$, where the $1 \leq t \leq 4$, to postings lists. A *postings list* for 1-word or 2-word phrase is a set of documents (*d*) while a list for 3 or 4-word phrase is a set of (*d,B*) pairs, where *d* is a document identifier and *B* is a set of indicators. An *indicator b* describes an occurrence of the term $f_1 \ldots f_t$, in *d* at *position k*, that is, an occurrence of $f_i = w_{k+i-1}$, for some k where $1 \leq k \leq n$ *and* $1 \leq i \leq t$. An indicator *i* at position *k* in document *d* is *elementary* if $i = o_k$ is an integer.

Definition 8. In a *hierarchical index of elements,* the *position* is a pair of element number and partial offset in an element.

## 3 Hierarchical Inverted Index Structure

There are two problems in conventional index structure to efficiently support phrase queries. The first is that to support phrase queries in conventional inverted index, the position information must be stored, which makes the postings list very long. The second is that to answer a phrase query, the postings lists of each word in the phrase have to be merged, which takes a long time.

Statistical has shown that 1 and 2-word queries are most commonly proposed by users. 3 and 4-word phrases are frequently used also. To support 1 to 4-word phrase query efficiently, hierarchical index is proposed. In this index structure, position information need not be stored in the postings list of 1 to 2 word phrases. Thus the length of the postings list is dramatically reduced and the efficiency is improved. At the same time, the frequently used 1 to 4-word phrase queries can be answered directly without the merge operation, which reduces the query evaluation time also.

To answer more than 4 words queries there must be some positions stored. As we all known, a long phrase appears less time than a short phrase. In another words, the more words contained in a phrase, the shorter the postings list is. Statistics show that the length of the postings list of 3-word phrases with position information is 1.32 times of that without position information. For 4-word phrases, the factor is 1.1. So we store position information of 3 and 4 words phrase in the postings list. More than 4 words queries are answered by merging the 3 and 4 words lists.

The hierarchical index structure is shown in figure 3. The first level is a list of all the distinct words in the document set. Each word in the first level has a list of second words, which appears in the document set next to this word. The third level contains all the next words for each first-second words pair in the document set. The forth level contains all the next words for each 3-word phrase in the first three levels. We call the four-level index the *hierarchical index*. Any single word, two-word phrase, three-word phrase or four-word phrase in the document set can be found in the index structure.

Each word in the hierarchical index structure, except the words in the first level, corresponds to a phrase, which is the words list from the *root word* to it. We call the phrase *path phrase*. The *root word* is the word in the first level. For example, the word "set" in the third level corresponds to the path phrase "in all set". The word "in" is the root word.

Each word in the index has a pointer into a postings list. The postings lists of the words in the first level and the path phrases corresponding to the words in the second level store the file identifiers in which the word or phrase occurs and the in document frequency. For each path phrase corresponding to the words in the third level and the fourth level, the file identifiers, the in document frequency and the positions the path phrase appear in each document is stored in the postings list. As we have seen in figure 3, the pointer pointing to the postings list is interleaved with the pointer into the next words succeed the word or path phrase in first three levels.

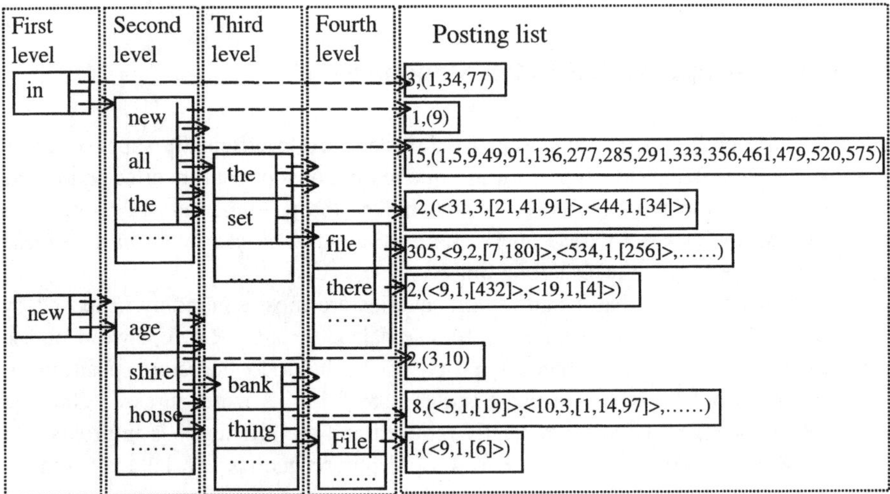


**Fig. 3.** Hierarchical inverted index structure

## 4 Document Partition and Distribution

There are still two problems of the hierarchical index. First, the index for 1to 4-word is built, which makes the vocabulary of the index larger than that of original index structure. Second, the longer the document is the larger the offset in the postings list is. More space is used to store large number. This is also shortcoming of traditional inverted index and nextword index. Two efficient ways on massive data processing is compression and parallel processing. We partition each document into several elements. Then distribute these elements to several processors. All the processors work parallel to answer a query. Distribution of the documents makes the vocabulary in each processor smaller than the whole vocabulary of the hierarchical index. At the same time, by partitioning the documents, the offsets in each element are smaller than the offsets in a document. Elias gamma codes can work well and the compression rate is improved.

As defined in the above definition, a document is expressed as follows:

*In next word indexes, the postings lists for phrases are typically short, because most*
*1 2 3 4 5 6 7 8 9 10 11 12 13 14*
*pairs only occur infrequently.*
*15 16 17 18*
*For example, the postings list for the firstword-nextword pair "the"."who" is orders*
*19 20 21 22 23 24 25 26 27 28 29 30 31 32*
*of magnitude smaller than the postings lists for these words in an inverted file. It follows*
*33 34 35 36 37 38 39 40 41 44 43 45 45 46 47 48*
*that phrase query evaluation can be extremely fast.*
*49 50 51 52 53 54 55 56*

In every two lines, the first line is the sequence of the words in a document. The second line is the absolute positions of the words in the document. We can see that the absolute position of the term is increasing sequentially. In a long document this position number will be very large.

Several compression techniques are often used in text retrieval. Elias codes and Golomb codes are two of the most often used methods of integer coding. Elias code includes Elias gamma code and Elias delta codes. Elias Gamma coding is efficient for small integers but is not suited to large integers. For large integers, parameterized Golomb codes or Elias delta code are more suitable. File partitioning divide one document into several parts, which reduces the absolute position numbers. When Elias Gamma codes are used, the rate of the compression is higher.

Element-based partition is used in this paper. Every document has its inherent structure. As defined above, we call an integrated part of a document an *element*, such as a chapter, a section, a paragraph etc. Element-based method divides a document into several elements. The element-based partition technique avoids the page-spanning problem. In this technique, a document is seen as the connection of several elements. Each element is given a sequential number. In each element we record the absolute position of each word within this element. Partial absolute position numbers in element instead of whole absolute position numbers in document makes the position number lesser. An example of the partial document is as follows. The above document is partitioned into two elements.

*In next word indexes, the postings lists for phrases are typically short, because most*
*1 2 3 4 5 6 7 8 9 10 11 12 13 14*
*pairs only occur infrequently.*
*15 16 17 18*
*For example, the postings list for the firstword-nextword pair "the"."who" is orders*
*1 2 3 4 5 6 7 8 9 10 11 12 13 14*
*of magnitude smaller than the postings lists for these words in an inverted file. It follows*
*15 16 17 18 19 20 21 22 23 24 25 26 27 28 29 30*
*that phrase query evaluation can be extremely fast.*
*31 32 33 34 35 36 37 38*

File partition can improve the compression rate of some integer coding. Element-based file partition technique can support content and structure based query processing, and do favor to define different rank to different elements. The definition of element shows that an element is an independent part of a document and the element-based document partition is based on the structure of the document. Another benefit is that if we distribute the elements to several processors, parallel processing becomes possible.

By using element-based document partition technique, there are no adjacent words in different elements. We use the round robin method to distribute the elements to several processors. File distribution has the following advantages. The first, the postings list of a word or a phrase in a processor is a subset of the whole postings list of the word or phrase. So the length of the postings list is lesser and the query efficiency is improved. The second, the absolute position number of a word or phrase in a document is converted into the partial position number in an element. The position number is smaller than original and the rate of the compression is improved. The third, the compression method is different from the method used in [11]. The optimization techniques can be used in this method. The fourth, the vocabulary in each processor is a subset of the whole vocabulary. That is the vocabulary in each processor is smaller. The times of I/O is less than original index structure and the quantity of the I/O data is less than the original index structure too.

In each processor there is a hierarchical index. In the postings lists of each word in each level, the partial in document frequency is stored.

## 5 Query Evaluation Algorithm

A query is expressed as a list of words and phrases. For single word query, the first level of the vocabulary in each processor is searched parallel to find the query word. If the word exists in the vocabulary, the postings list of the word is read from disk. All the document identifiers contains the word are stored in a temporary structure along with the partial in document frequency the word appears in the document. Then the temporary structure in each processor, which has answers, is merged. The result of the merge is sorted by in document frequency. The higher ones are returned to the user. 2 to 4-word phrase queries are answered similar with single word queries. Except that when the first word of the query phrase is found in the first level of the vocabulary, the next level of the hierarchical index must be continually searched to find if the query phrase exist in the vocabulary. If the query phrase is found, the postings list of the corresponding path phrase is read from disk and the document identifiers and the partial in document frequencies are got. Then partial postings list in each processor is merged to get the answer documents.

When the query contains more than 4-word phrase, the query phrase must be divided into optimized subqueries, which contains 3-word phrase or 4-word phrases. The division operation must take into account two rules. One is keeping the number of merge operation least. The other is length of the postings list of the query phrase be shortest. Each subquery is processed as 3 or 4-word phrase queries. These subqueries are submitted to all the processors. Each processor processes each optimized subquery sequentially to get the partial answers of the subquery. All the partial answers are connected to get the final answers of the more than 4-word phrase query. When all the processors finished the subqueries and the connection operation, the answers in each processor are joined, the false answers are deleted and the final answers of the query are got.

When the user query contains more then one term, we treat each term as an independent query. The intersection of the answer of each term query is the final answer of the user query. The execution of the term query is as above.

The formal description of the parallel query evaluation algorithm is defined as follows:

*Parallel Query evaluation algorithm*

```
Input: a hierarchical index and a query t1…tm,. Each ti
can be regarded as a sequence of optimized subqueries
si1…sil, for 1≤ i ≤ m, 1≤l≤4.
Output: a set of documents.

The result set R is set to Null;
For i=1 to m do
   The optimized subqueries si1…sil for term ti, is sent
to each processor;
   If l≤4
      Each processor do parallel:
         search the phrase in the hierarchical index in
this processor;
         if found, the postings list is read from disk
to get the file identifiers and the partial in document
frequencies as the partial result and the partial re-
sult is returned;
         if not found, NULL list is returned from the
processor.
   If l>4
      Each processor do parallel:
         for each optimized subquery sik in the
optimized order
            search the optimized subquery in the hier-
archical index in this processor;
            if found the postings list is read from
disk to get the partial results;
            if not found, NULL list is returned from
the processor;
         connect the partial results of the optimized
subqueries in each processor as the final partial
results;
         return the final partial result from the
processor;
   merge the partial results from each processor as the
answer of the term ti and add the partial frequencies;
   the answer of the term ti is intersect with set R to
get a new set R;
the set R is the final answer of the query t1…tm.
```

## 6 Experiments and Analysis

To analysis the cost of storage space, we define the following symbols.

$N_w$ : the number of words in a document set.

$N_f$ : the number of documents in the document set.

$S_w$ : the size of each word.

$S_p$ : the size of a pointer

$S_{id}$ : the size of each fid.

$S_{pos}$ : the size of each offset.

$L_i$ : the average length of inverted lists for *i*-word phrase with offsets, for any $i>j$, $L_i<L_j$.

$L_i$': the average length of inverted lists for *i*-word phrase without offsets, for any $i>j$, $L_i'<L_j'$.

$n_i$ : the number of next words of a *i*-word phrase, for any $i>j$, $n_i<n_j$.

In our experiment, the values are set as table 1.

**Table 1.** Values of the symbols in our experiment

| | | | | | |
|---|---|---|---|---|---|
| $N_w$ | 60000 | $n_1$ | 188 | $L_2'$ | 255 |
| $N_f$ | 4980 | $n_2$ | 60 | $L_3$ | 14.2 |
| $S_w$ | 20 | $n_3$ | 4 | $L_3'$ | 10.8 |
| $S_p$ | 4 | $L_1$ | 154698 | $L_4$ | 3.5 |
| $S_{id}$ | 4 | $L_1'$ | 2852 | $L_4'$ | 3.2 |
| $S_{pos}$ | 4 | $L_2$ | 822.3 | | |

**Table 2.** Size of first level and other levels in vocabulary

| | Size of the first level of the vocabulary | Size of other levels for one word in the first level in the vocabulary | The size of the postings list of a word or a phrase |
|---|---|---|---|
| Inverted | 1.44M | 0 | 619K |
| Nextword | 1.68M | 4.5K | 11.4K,3.3K |
| Hierarchical | 1.68M | 6K | 11.4K,1K,57byte,14byte |

In table2, we give the size of the first level, size of the other levels of a word in the first level and the size of the postings list of a word or phrase. In nextword or hierarchical index, to answer a query, the first level of the vocabulary is searched first, then next words of the corresponding word, then the next words of the corresponding phrase, etc. So we can store the other levels of the vocabulary except the first level in disk. It is read into memory when needed. The postings list is also stored in disk.

When we find a word or a phrase in the user query, the postings list of the word or phrase is read into memory.

We distribute the vocabulary and the postings list in $n_p$ processors. In each processor, the size of the vocabulary is less than the whole vocabulary, while the postings list is one of $n_p$ of the original size. To evaluate the cost of query, following symbols are used.

$T_{hash}$: the time for hash a word in a bucket;

$T_{I/O}$: the time for read a byte from disk;

$T_{search}$: the time used to read a byte in memory;

$T_{seek}$: the time used to find a block in disk.

For the time for disk I/O is much longer then the time for operation in memory, $T_{hash}$ and $T_{search}$ is omitted sometimes. The query evaluation time is shown in table 3.

**Table 3.** Query evaluation time of phrase queries

| | 1-word query | 2-word query | 3-word query | 4-word query | $n$-word query($n$>4) |
|---|---|---|---|---|---|
| Inverted | $T_{seek}$+ $L_1$*$T_{I/O}$ | 2*$T_{seek}$+ 2*$L_1$*$T_{I/O}$ | 3*($T_{seek}$+ $T_{I/O}$*$L_1$) | 4*($T_{seek}$+ $T_{I/O}$*$L_1$) | $n$*($T_{seek}$+ $T_{I/O}$*$L_1$) |
| Next-word | $T_{seek}$+ $L_1$'*$T_{I/O}$ | 2*$T_{seek}$+ ($L_2$+$n_1$)*$T_{I/O}$ | 4*$T_{seek}$+2* $T_{I/O}$*($n_1$+$L_2$) | 4*$T_{seek}$+2* $T_{I/O}$*($n_1$+$L_2$) | $n$*$T_{seek}$+ $\lceil n/2 \rceil$*$T_{I/O}$*($n_1$+$L_2$) |
| Hierarchical | $T_{seek}$+ $L_1$'*$T_{I/O}$ | 2*$T_{seek}$+($L_2$' +$n_1$)*$T_{I/O}$ | 3*$T_{seek}$+$T_{I/O}$*( $n_1$+$n_2$+$L_3$) | 4*$T_{seek}$+$T_{I/O}$*($n_1$ +$n_2$+$n_3$+$L_4$) | $n$*$T_{seek}$+$\lceil n/4 \rceil$*$T_{I/O}$*( $n_1$+$n_2$+$n_3$+$L_4$) |

This table shows that both single word query and phrase query, hierarchical index is better than the other two index structure. See 1-word query first. Experiments show that $L_1$>$L_1$', so hierarchical index structure has the same efficiency as nextword index structure, which is better than traditional inverted index. For $L_1>L_1'>L_2>L_2'>L_3>L_3'>L_4>L_4'$, $n_1>n_2>n_3$ and experiments show that $L_1>n_1+L_2$, $L_1>n_1+n_2+L_3$, $L_1>n_1+n_2+n_3+L_4$, for phrase queries, hierarchical index is better than traditional inverted index and the nextword index. When we partition the documents into elements and distribute the elements into several processors, the query efficiency is better.

## 7 Conclusion

This paper has shown that phrase query is frequently used in digital library. Efficiently query evaluation of phrase query is an important problem. We propose a new hierarchical index structure to efficiently evaluate phrase queries and a parallel algorithm based on document partition. Using this structure, 1 to 4 words phrase queries can be answered directly. For more than 4 word queries, the query evaluation time is shorter than original inverted index and nextword index.

We partition a document into several elements and distribute the elements into several processors. Thus parallelization and compression is used, which improve the query efficiency more. This partition based hierarchical index can be expanded to content and structure based query. The elements can be a title, abstract, a chapter, a section or other interested parts. So element-based query can be efficiently supported in this index structure.

## References


1. Zobel, J., Moffat A., and Ramamohanarao K. Inverted files versus signature files for text indexing. *ACM Transactions on Database Systems*. 1998.
2. D. Harman, E. Fox, R. Baeza-Yates, W. Lee. Inverted files. In W.Frakes and R.Baeza-Yates, Eds., *Information Retrieval: Data Structure and Algorithms,* Chapter 3, pp.28–43. Prentice-Hall. 1992.
3. G. W. Paynter, I. H. Witten, S. J. Cunningham, and G. Buchanan. Scalable browsing for large collections: A case study. *In Proc. of the 5th ACM International Conference on Digital Libraries*, pages 215–223, San Antonio, 2000.
4. Hugh E., Williams and Justin Zobel. Compressing Integers for Fast File Access. *The computer Journal*, Vol.42, No.3, 1999.
5. Gonzalo Navarro, Edleno Siilva de Moura, Marden Neubert, Nivio Ziviani, Ricardo Baeza-Yates. Adding Compression to Block Addressing Inverted Indexes. *Kluwer Academic publishs.* 2000.
6. Alistair Moffat, Justin Zobel. Self Indexing Inverted Files for Fast Text Retrieval. *ACM Transactions on Information Systems*, Vol. 14, No. 4, Pages 349–379, October 1996.
7. Falk Scholer, Hugh E. Williams, John Yiannis, Justin Zobel. Compression of Inverted Indexes for Fast Query Evaluation. *Annual ACM Conference on Research and Development in Information Retrieval.* 2002.
8. Berthier Ribeiro-Neto, Edleno S. Moura, Marden S. Neubert, Nivio Ziviani. Efficient Distributed Algorithms to Build Inverted Files. *Annual ACM Conference on Research and Development in Information Retrieval.* 1999.
9. Hugh E. Williams, Justin Zobel, Phil Anderson. What's Next? Index Structures for Efficient Phrase Querying. *Proceedings of the Tenth Australasian Database Conference,* 1999.
10. Dirk Bahle, Hugh E. Williams, Justin Zobel. Optimized Phrase Querying and Browsing of Large Text Databases. *In Proc. Of Australasian Computer Science Conference*, 2001.
11. D.Bahle, H.E.Williams, J.Zobel. Compaction Techniques for Nextword Indexes. In Proc. 8th *International Symposium on String Processing and Information Retrieval (SPIRE2001),* pages 33–45, San Rafael, Chile, 2001.
12. Dirk Bahle, Hugh E. Williams, Justin Zobel. Efficient Phrase Querying with an Auxiliary Index. *Annual ACM Conference on Research and Development in Information Retrieval.*2002.
13. J. Zobel and A. Moffat. Exploring the similarity space. *SIGIR Forum*, 32(1):18–34, 1998.

# A Genetic Semi-supervised Fuzzy Clustering Approach to Text Classification

Hong Liu and Shang-teng Huang

Dept. of Computer Science, Xinjian Building 2008, Shanghai Jiaotong University, Shanghai 200030,China
{liuhongshcn,royhuang}@hotmail.com

**Abstract.** A genetic semi-supervised fuzzy clustering algorithm is proposed, which can learn text classifier from labeled and unlabeled documents. Labeled documents are used to guide the evolution process of each chromosome, which is fuzzy partition on unlabeled documents. The fitness of each chromosome is evaluated with a combination of fuzzy within cluster variance of unlabeled documents and misclassification error of labeled documents. The structure of the clusters obtained can be used to classify future new documents. Experimental results show that the proposed approach can improve text classi-fication accuracy significantly, compared to text classifiers trained with a small number of labeled documents only. Also, this approach performs at least as well as the similar approach – EM with Naïve Bayes

## 1 Introduction

There is a great need to design efficient content-based retrieval, searching and filtering for the huge and unstructured online repositories on the internet. Automated Text Classification[1], which can automatically assign documents to pre-defined classes according to their text contents, has become a key technique to accomplish these tasks.

Various supervised learning methods have been applied to construct text classifiers from a priori *labeled* documents, e.g., Naïve Bayes [2]. However, for complex learning tasks, providing sufficiently large set of labeled training examples becomes prohibitive.

Compared to labeled documents, *unlabeled* documents are usually easier to obtain, with the help of some tools like Digital Library, Crawler Programs, and Searching Engine. Therefore, it is reasonable to learn text classifier from both labeled and unlabeled documents. This learning paradigm is usually referred as *semi-supervised* learning, and some previous approaches have been proposed to implement it, e.g., *co-training* [3], EM with Naïve Baye s[4] and *transductive* SVM [5].

While the approaches above attempt to feed unlabeled data to *supervised* learners, some other approaches consider incorporating labeled data into unsupervised learning, e.g., *partially supervised fuzzy clustering* [6].

G. Dong et al. (Eds.): WAIM 2003, LNCS 2762, pp. 173–180, 2003.

For learning text classifier from *labeled* and *unlabeled* documents, this paper proposes a semi-supervised fuzzy clustering algorithm based on GA [7]. By minimizing a combination of *fuzzy within cluster variance on unlabeled documents* and *misclassification error of labeled documents* using GA, it attempts to find an optimal fuzzy partition on unlabeled documents. The structure of the clusters obtained can be used to classify a future new document.

The remaining of the paper is organized as follows. Section 2 gives the problem definition. In section 3, major components of our algorithm are introduced, and the overall algorithm itself – Genetic Semi-Supervised Fuzzy Clustering (GSSFC) is described. Section 4 illustrates how to classify a new document with the aid of the results obtained by GSSFC. Experimental results and discussion are given in Section 5. Finally, section 6 concludes the paper.

## 2 Problem Definition

We are provided with a small number of labeled documents and a large number of unlabeled documents. Using Vector Space Model, all the labeled and unlabeled documents can be denoted in a matrix form:

$$\boldsymbol{X} = \left\{ \underbrace{\boldsymbol{x}_1^l, ..., \boldsymbol{x}_{n_l}^l}_{labeled} \mid \underbrace{\boldsymbol{x}_1^u, ..., \boldsymbol{x}_{n_u}^u}_{unlabeled} \right\} = \boldsymbol{X}^l \cup \boldsymbol{X}^u \tag{1}$$

Here, $l$ indicates the designation *labeled* documents, and$u$, as a superscript, indicates the designation *unlabeled* documents. (In other context, $u$ may indicate the name of a membership function or value appropriately, when it doesn't appear as a superscript.) Moreover, $n_l = |\boldsymbol{X}^l|$, $n_u = |\boldsymbol{X}^u|$, and $n = |\boldsymbol{X}| = n_l + n_u$.

A matrix representation of a fuzzy $c$-partition of $\boldsymbol{X}$ induced by equation (1) has the form:

$$\boldsymbol{U} = \left[ \overbrace{\begin{bmatrix} u_{11}^l & u_{12}^l & \cdots & u_{1n_l}^l \\ u_{21}^l & u_{22}^l & \cdots & u_{2n_l}^l \\ . & . & \cdots & . \\ . & . & \cdots & . \\ u_{c1}^l & u_{c2}^l & \cdots & u_{cn_l}^l \end{bmatrix}}^{\boldsymbol{U}^l} \overbrace{\begin{bmatrix} u_{11}^u & u_{12}^u & \cdots & u_{1n_u}^u \\ u_{21}^u & u_{22}^u & \cdots & u_{2n_u}^u \\ . & . & \cdots & . \\ . & . & \cdots & . \\ u_{c1}^u & u_{c2}^u & \cdots & u_{cn_u}^u \end{bmatrix}}^{\boldsymbol{U}^u} \right] \tag{2}$$

Here, the fuzzy values of the column vectors in $\boldsymbol{U}^l$ are assigned by domain experts after a careful investigation on $\boldsymbol{X}^l$. In general, for $1 \le i \le c$, $1 \le h \le n_l$, $1 \le j \le n_u$, equation (2) should satisfy the following conditions:

$$u_{ih}^l \in [0,1], \quad \sum\nolimits_{i=1}^{c} u_{ih}^l = 1, \quad u_{ij}^u \in [0,1], \quad \sum\nolimits_{i=1}^{c} u_{ij}^u = 1 \tag{3}$$

The goal of the problem is to construct, using $\boldsymbol{X}$, a text classifier. Our basic idea is to find a fuzzy $c$-partition on $\boldsymbol{X}^u$, which can minimize *fuzzy within cluster variance of unlabeled documents* and *misclassification error of labeled documents*, and then, use the structure of the clusters obtained to classify future new documents.

### Misclassification Error of Labeled Documents

In order to get good generalization performance, the text classifier to be constructed should minimize the misclassification error of labeled documents. We will use the variance of the fuzzy memberships of labeled documents to measure the misclassification error. In detail, given a fuzzy $c$-partition on $\boldsymbol{X}^u$, the $c$ cluster centers $\boldsymbol{v}_1, \boldsymbol{v}_2, \ldots, \boldsymbol{v}_c$ can be computed as follows:

$$\boldsymbol{v}_i = \frac{\sum_{k=1}^{n_l} \left(u_{ik}^l\right)^m \boldsymbol{x}_k^l + \sum_{k=1}^{n_u} \left(u_{ik}^u\right)^m \boldsymbol{x}_k^u}{\sum_{k=1}^{n_l} \left(u_{ik}^l\right)^m + \sum_{k=1}^{n_u} \left(u_{ik}^u\right)^m}, \quad 1 \le i \le c \tag{4}$$

For $i = 1, 2, \ldots, c$, and $j = 1, 2, \ldots, n_l$, the fuzzy memberships of labeled documents can be re-computed as follows:

$$u_{ij}^{l'} = \left[ \sum_{h=1}^{c} \left( \frac{\left\| \boldsymbol{x}_j^l - \boldsymbol{v}_i \right\|}{\left\| \boldsymbol{x}_j^l - \boldsymbol{v}_h \right\|} \right)^{2/(m-1)} \right]^{-1} \tag{5}$$

Accordingly, the *misclassification error of labeled documents*, denoted as $E$, can be measured as a weighted sum of variance between $u_{ij}^l$ and $u_{ij}^{l'}$, with weights equal to $\left\| \boldsymbol{x}_j^l - \boldsymbol{v}_i \right\|^2$, that is,

$$E = \sum_{j=1}^{n_l} \sum_{i=1}^{c} \left( u_{ij}^{l'} - u_{ij}^l \right)^m \left\| \boldsymbol{x}_j^l - \boldsymbol{v}_i \right\|^2 \tag{6}$$

### Fuzzy Within Cluster Variance of Unlabeled Documents

Although minimizing misclassification error of labeled documents is necessary for the text classifier to get good generalization ability, it is not sufficient, as minimizing misclassification error of a small labeled documents only would very likely lead to the problem of so-called *over-fitting*.

*Fuzzy within cluster variance* is a well-known measurement of cluster quality in fuzzy clustering, which is defined as:

$$J_m(\boldsymbol{U}^u, \boldsymbol{V}) = \sum_{j=1}^{n_u} \sum_{i=1}^{c} \left(u_{ij}^u\right)^m \left\| \boldsymbol{x}_j^u - \boldsymbol{v}_i \right\|^2 \tag{7}$$

Here, $m$ is treated as the parameter controlling the fuzziness of the clusters, $m > 1$. We can see that minimizing fuzzy within cluster variance is equal to maximizing the similarity of documents within the same cluster. Thus, we argue that *fuzzy within cluster variance of unlabeled documents* can play the role of *capacity control*[8] in our problem.

Based on equation (7) and (6), we can clarify our objective function as follows:

$$f(\boldsymbol{U}^u, \boldsymbol{V}) = J_m + \alpha \cdot E \tag{8}$$

Here, $\alpha > 0$ is a positive regularization parameter, which maintains a balance between *fuzzy within cluster variance of unlabeled documents* and *misclassification error of labeled documents.* The choice of $\alpha$ depends very much on the number of labeled documents and unlabeled documents. To ensure that the impact of the labeled documents is not ignored, the value of $\alpha$ should produce approximately equal weighting of the two terms in equation (8). This suggests that $\alpha$ should be proportional to the rate $n_u / n_l$.

At this time, our problem has been converted to *minimization of the objective function in equation*(8). We should point out that this objective function is similar to the objective function appeared in [6]. Unfortunately, we found the optimization method used in [6] can be trapped by local extrema. However, GA uses population-wide search instead of a point-search, and the transition rules of it are stochastic instead of deterministic. So, the probability of reaching a false peak is much less than that in other conventional optimization methods. In this paper, we use GA to resolve this optimization problem. More specifically, we will use a procedure proposed in [9] but modified to suit to our problem.

## 3 Genetic Semi-supervised Fuzzy Clustering (GSSFC)

In this section, major components of GA overall algorithm itself are described.

### 3.1 Major Components of GA

- **Representation and Its Initialization**

In our algorithm, $\boldsymbol{U}^u$s, whose form are illustrated in equation (2), play the role of *chromosomes.* $\boldsymbol{U}^u$s are initialized randomly.

- **Fitness Function**

The fitness function being used is the objective function in equation (8).

- **Selection**

A *roulette wheel* selection method[7] is used for selecting population members to reproduce. Each member of the population gets a percentage of the roulette wheel based on its fitness.

- **Crossover**

Suppose $P_c$ is the probability of crossover, then $(P_c b)$ chromosomes will undergo the crossover operation in the following steps:

**Step 1.** Generate a random real number $r_c$, $r_c \in [0,1]$, for the given $k$th chromosome.

**Step 2.** Select the given $k$th chromosome for crossover if $r_c < P_c$.

**Step 3.** Repeat Steps 1 and 2 for$k = 1, \dots, b$, and produce $(P_c b)$ parents, averagely.

**Step 4.** For each pair of parents, for example, $\boldsymbol{U}^{u1}$ and $\boldsymbol{U}^{u2}$, the crossover operation on $\boldsymbol{U}^{u1}$and $\boldsymbol{U}^{u2}$will produce two children $\boldsymbol{U}^{u(b+1)}$and $\boldsymbol{U}^{u(b+2)}$as follows:

$$\boldsymbol{U}^{u(b+1)} = c^1 \boldsymbol{U}^{u1} + c^2 \boldsymbol{U}^{u2}, \boldsymbol{U}^{u(b+2)} = c^2 \boldsymbol{U}^{u2} + c^1 \boldsymbol{U}^{u1} \tag{9}$$

where $c_1 + c_2 = 1$ and $c_1 \in [0,1]$ is a random real number.

- **Mutation**

Mutation is usually defined as a change in a single bit in a solution vector. This would correspond to a change of one element $u^u_{ij}$of a chromosome $\boldsymbol{U}^u$ in our problem.

### 3.2 Overall Algorithm

The overall algorithm is given in Table 1.

**Table 1.** Genetic Semi-Supervised Fuzzy Clustering Algorithm

**Inputs**: $\boldsymbol{X}^l$, the set of labeled documents; $\boldsymbol{X}^u$, the set of unlabeled documents; $U^l$ a fuzzy $c$-partition on $\boldsymbol{X}^l$.
**Output**: $\boldsymbol{U}^u$ a fuzzy $c$-partition on $\boldsymbol{X}^u$ a fuzzy $c$-partition on $\boldsymbol{X}$ and $c$ cluster centers $\boldsymbol{v}_1, \boldsymbol{v}_2, \ldots, \boldsymbol{v}_c$.
**Choose parameters**: $m > 1$, the degree of fuzziness; $b$, the population size; *max_gen*, the number of generations; $Pc$, the probability of crossover; $Pm$, the probability of mutation; $\alpha$,the regularization parameter in fitness function.
**STEP 1 Initialize**
Initialize $\boldsymbol{U}^u$ randomly and set $gen = 0$.
**STEP2 Evaluation**
For $i = 1, 2, \ldots, c$, compute the current cluster center $\boldsymbol{v}_i$ using equation (4).
For $i = 1, 2, \ldots, c$, and $j = 1, 2, \ldots, nl$, compute the new fuzzy membership $u^{l'}_{ij}$ for labeled document $x^l_j$ with respect to cluster $i$, using equation (5).
For $k = 1, 2, \ldots, b$, compute fuzzy within cluster variance $J^k_m$ for $\boldsymbol{U}^{uk}$ using equation (7), compute misclassification error $E^k$ for $\boldsymbol{U}^{uk}$ using equation (6), and compute the fitness $f^k$ for $\boldsymbol{U}^{uk}$ using equation (8).
**STEP3 Selection**
For $k = 1, 2, \ldots, b$, generate a random real number $r_s \in[0,1]$, and if $f^{k-1} < r_s < f^k$, then select $\boldsymbol{U}^{uk}$.
**STEP4 Crossover**
For $k = 1, 2, \ldots, b/2$, generate a randome number $r_c \in[0,1]$, and if $r_c \leq P_c$, then perform the crossover on the $l$th and $m$th chromosomes, which are randomly selected.
**STEP5 Mutation**
For $k = 1, 2, \ldots, b$, and $j = 1, 2, \ldots, n_u$, generate a randome number $r_m \in[0,1]$, and if $r_m \leq P_m$, then generate new elements in the $j$th column of the $k$th chromosome;
**STEP6 Termination**
If $gen < max\_gen$, then let $gen = gen + 1$ and go to **STEP 2**. Otherwise, the algorithm stops.

## 4 Classification with the Aid of Results of GSSFC

The structure of the clusters learned above reflects the natural structure of the documents collection, so it can be used to classify future new documents.

In detail, given a new document $\boldsymbol{x}$, and the $c$ cluster centers $\boldsymbol{v}_1, \boldsymbol{v}_2, \ldots, \boldsymbol{v}_c$, obtained with GSSFC, the fuzzy membership of $\boldsymbol{x}$, with respect to class $i$, $u_i$can be computed in the similar way as in equation (5):

$$u_i = \left[ \sum_{h=1}^{c} \left( \frac{\|\boldsymbol{x} - \boldsymbol{v}_i\|}{\|\boldsymbol{x} - \boldsymbol{v}_h\|} \right)^{2/(m-1)} \right]^{-1} \tag{10}$$

Thus, $\boldsymbol{x}$ is assigned to $c$ classes, with corresponding fuzzy memberships $u_1$, $u_2$, $\ldots$, $u_c$ respectively.

In some applications, the need is to assign $\boldsymbol{x}$ to exactly one of $c$ classes. For this purpose, some defuzzify methods, for example, so-called Maximum Membership Rule (MMR) can be used. In detail, $\boldsymbol{x}$ can be assigned to class $i$, where $i = \underset{h=1,2,\ldots c}{\arg} \max(u_h)$.

## 5 Experimental Setup and Results

In out experiments, Naïve Bayes classifier (NBC)[2] is used as a basic classifier, which is trained using labeled documents only. Also, we will compare our method to the approach proposed by Nigam[4], namely EM with Naïve Bayes.

**Benchmark Documents Collection 1**

**20-Newsgroups** dataset consists of Usenet articles collected by K. Lang[10] from 20 different newsgroups. The task is to classify an article into the one newsgroup (of twenty) to which it was posted. From the original data set, three different data sets are created. The labeled set contains a total of 6000 documents (300 documents per class). We create a set of unlabeled set of 10000 documents (500 documents per class). The remaining 4000 documents (200 documents per class) form the subset of test documents. Different numbers of labeled documents are extracted from the labeled set with uniform distribution of documents over the 20 classes. The use of each size of labeled set comprises a new trial of the experiments below.

Each document is presented as a TFIDF weighted word frequency vector and then be normalized.

**Benchmark Documents Collection 2**

The second dataset WebKB[11] contains web pages gathered from computer science departments at four universities. The task is to classify a web page into the appropriate one of the four classes: **course**, **faculty**, **student** and **project**. Documents not in one of these classes are deleted. After removing documents which contain the relocation command for the browser, this leaves 4183 examples. We create four test sets, each containing all the documents from one of the four complete computer science departments. For each test set, an unlabeled set of 2500 pages is formed by randomly selecting from the remaining web pages. Labeled sets are formed by the same method as in 20-Newsgroups. Stemming and stop-word removal are not used. As with the 20-Newsgroups, each document is presented as a TFIDF weighted word frequency vector, and then normalized.

Parameters in GSSFC are selected as follows: The degree of fuzziness $m = 2$; the maximum generation $max\_gen = 2000$; population size $b = 50$; the probability of crossover $P_c = 0.7$; the probability of mutation $P_m = 0.1$.

Figure 1 shows the classification accuracy of NBC (no unlabeled documents), the classifier constructed through GSSFC and EM with NBC on **20-Newsgroups** and WebKB respectively. The vertical axis indicates average classification accuracy on test sets, and the horizontal axis indicates the amount of labeled documents on a log scale.

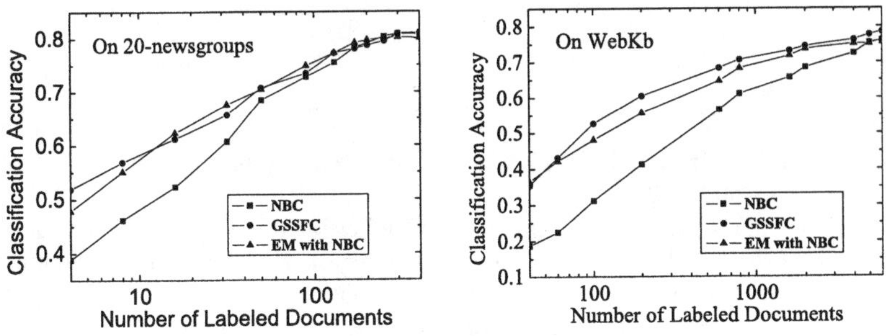


**Fig. 1.** Classification Accuracy

Naïve Bayes classifier provides an idea of the performance of a base classifier, *if no unlabeled documents are used.* The dot curve in Figure 1 shows that, by increasing the number of labeled documents from low to high, a significant improvement in accuracy is got. These results support the justice and necessity to find methods to learn classifier from unlabeled documents in addition to labeled documents, when labeled documents are sparse.

The classifier constructed through GSSFC performs significantly better than traditional Naïve Bayes classifier. For example, with 200 labeled documents (10 documents per class), the former reaches an accuracy of 41.3%, while the latter reaches 60.5%. This presents a 19.2% gain in classification accuracy.

Another way to view these results is to consider how unlabeled documents can reduce the need for labeled documents. For example, with 20-Newsgroups, for NBC to reach 70% classification accuracy, more than 2000 labeled documents are needed, while only less than 800 labeled documents for GSSFC. This indicates that incorporating a mall number of labeled documents into a large number of unlabeled documents can help constructing a better classifier than that constructed using a mall number of labeled documents alone. The essential reason is that, although unlabeled documents do not provide class label information, but they can provide much structural information of the feature space of the particular problem. It is this information that helps us attaining a better classifier, when labeled documents are sparse.

As for GSSFC and EM with Naïve Bayes, the fomer performs at least as well as the latter.

## 6 Conclusion

In summary, we have proposed a genetic semi-supervised fuzzy clustering algorithm, which can learn text classifier from both labeled and unlabeled documents. Experiments are carried out on two separated benchmark document collections. The results indicated that, by combining both labeled and unlabeled documents in the training process, the proposed algorithm can learn a better text classifier than traditional inductive text classifier learners, for instance Naïve Bayes, when labeled documents are sparse. Also, GSSFC performs at least as well as EM with Naïve Bayes. GSSFC is an effective way to construct text classifiers from labeled and unlabeled documents.

## References

1. Sebastiani, F.: Machine learning in automated text categorization. ACM Computing Surveys, 34(1). (2002) 1–47
2. Tzeras, K., Hartman, S.: Automatic indexing based on bayesian inference networks. In Proc 16th Ann Int ACM SIGIR Conference on Research and Development in Information Retrieval (SIGIR'93). (1993) 22–34.
3. Blum, A., Mitchell, T.: Combining Labeled and Unlabeled Data with Co-Training. Proceedings of the 11th Annual Conference on Computational Learning Theory. (1998) 92–100.
4. Nigam, K., McCallum, A., Thrun, S., Mitchell, T.: Text classification from labeled and unlabeled documents using EM. Machine Learning, 39(2/3). (2000) 103–134.
5. Joachims, T.: Transductive Inference for Text Classification using Support Vector Machines. Proceedings of the 16th International Conference on Machine Learning. (1999) 200–209.
6. Pedrycz, W., Waletzky, J.: Fuzzy clustering with partial supervision. IEEE Trans. on Systems, Man, and Cybernetics, 27(5). (1997) 787–795.
7. Michalewicz, Z.: Genetic Algorithm + Data Structures = Evolution Programs. Third ed., New York: Springer-Verlag. (1996).
8. Vapnik, V. N.: The Nature of Statistical Learning Theory. New York: Springer-Verlag. (1995).
9. Zhao, L., Tsujimura, Y., Gen, M.: Genetic algorithm for fuzzy clustering. Proceedings of the IEEE International Conference on Evolutionary Computation. (1996) 716–719.
10. Lang, K.: NewsWeeder: learning to filter Netnews. Proceedings of the 12th International Conference on Machine Learning. (1995) 331–339.
11. Craven, M., DiPasquo, D., Freitag, D., McCallum, A., Mitchel, T., Nigam, K., Slatteryet, S.: Learning to construct knowledge bases from the World Wide Web. Articial Intelligence,118(1-2). (2000) 69–113.

# Partition for the Rough Set-Based Text Classification

Yongguang Bao[1], Daisuke Asai[1], Xiaoyong Du[2], and Naohiro Ishii[1]

[1] Department of Intelligence and Computer Science, Nagoya Institute of Technology, Nagoya, 466-8555, Japan
{baoyg, ishii}@egg.ics.nitech.ac.jp
[2] School of Information, Renmin University of China, 100872, Beijing, China
Duyong@mail.ruc.edu.cn

**Abstract.** Text classification based on Rough Sets theory is an effective method for the automatic document classification problem. However, the computing multiple reducts is a problem in this method. When the number of training document is large, it takes much time and large memory for the computation. It is very hard to be applied in the real application system. In this paper, we propose an effective way of data partition, to solve the above problem. It reduces the computing time of generating reducts and maintains the classification accuracy. This paper describes our approach and experimental result.

## 1 Introduction

As the volume of information available on the Internet and corporative intranets continues to increase, there is a growing need for tools finding, filtering, and managing these resources. The purpose of text classification is to classify text documents into classes automatically based on their contents, and therefore plays an important role in many information management tasks. A number of statistical text learning algorithms and machine learning techniques have been applied to text classification. These text classification algorithms have been used to automatically catalog news articles [1] and web pages [2], learn the reading interests of users [3], and sort electronic mails [4].

However, a non-trivial obstacle in good text classification is the high dimensionality of the data. Rough Sets theory introduced by Pawlak [5] is a non-statistical methodology for data analysis. It can be used to alleviate this situation. In [9], we proposed the RSAR-M which is an effective text classification system based on Rough Sets theory. When classifying new documents according to this systems, a minimum set of keywords called reduct is used. However when the number of training documents increases, the number of dimensions of words processed increases. As a result, the large computing time and large memory are needed to generate multiple reducts. Moreover there is a case where it is impossible to compute because a required memory is insufficient. It is very hard to be applied in the real application system.

G. Dong et al. (Eds.): WAIM 2003, LNCS 2762, pp. 181–188, 2003.

In this paper, we propose an effective method which can reduce the computing time and decrease the amount of memory for generating reducts by data partition. Our new method can generate multiple reducts quickly and effectively when compared with the previous system. It was verified that the method can maintain the high classification accuracy.

The remainder of this paper is organized as follows: Section 2 introduces the basic concept of Rough Sets theory, and text classification based on Rough sets. Section 3 provides a description of the proposed system. Section 4 describes experimental results. A short conclusion is given in the final section.

## 2 Rough Sets and Text Classification

### 2.1 Rough Sets

**Information Systems.** An information system is composed of a 4-tuple as follows:

$$S =< U, Q, V, f >$$

where $U$ is the closed universe, a finite nonempty set of $N$ objects $(x_1, x_2, ..., x_N)$, $Q$ is a finite nonempty set of $n$ features $\{q_1, q_2, ..., q_n\}$, $V = \bigcup_{q \in Q} V_q$, where $V_q$ is a domain(value) of the feature $q$, and $f : U \times Q \rightarrow V$ is the total decision function called the information such that $f(x, q) \in V_q$, for every $q \in Q$, $x \in U$.

Any subset $P$ of $Q$ determines a binary relation on U, which will be called an indiscernibility relation denoted by $INP(P)$, and defined as follows: $xI_By$ if and only if $f(x, a) = f(y, a)$ for every $a \in P$. Obviously $INP(P)$ is an equivalence relation. The family of all equivalence classes of $INP(P)$ will be denoted by $U/INP(P)$ or simply $U/P$; an equivalence class of $INP(P)$ containing $x$ will be denoted by $P(x)$ or $[x]_p$.

**Reduct.** Reduct is a fundamental concept of rough sets. A reduct is the essential part of an information system that can discern all objects discernible by the original information system.

Let $q \in Q$. A feature $q$ is *dispensable* in $S$, if $IND(Q - q) = IND(Q)$; otherwise feature q is *indispensable* in $S$.

If $q$ is an indispensable feature, deleting it from $S$ will cause $S$ to be inconsistent. Otherwise, $q$ can be deleted from $S$.

The set $R \subseteq Q$ of feature will be called a *reduct* of $Q$, if $IND(R) = IND(Q)$ and all features of $R$ are indispensable in $S$. We denoted it as $RED(Q)$ or $RED(S)$.

Reduct is the minimal subset of condition features $Q$ with respect to decision features $D$, none of the features of any minimal subsets can be eliminated without affecting the essential information. These minimal subsets can discern decision classes with the same discriminating power as the entire condition features.

The set of all indispensable from the set $Q$ is called $CORE$ of $Q$ and denoted by $CORE(Q)$:

$$CORE(Q) = \cap RED(Q)$$

### 2.2 Text Classification Based on Rough Sets

A non-trivial obstacle in good text classification is the high dimensionality of the data. Rough Sets theory can be used to alleviate this situation [7]. A. Chouchoulas and Q. Shen proposed a Rough Set Attribute Reduction method (RSAR) for text classification that tests E-mail messages. Given corpora of documents and a set of examples of classified documents, the technique can quickly locate a minimal set of co-ordinate keywords to classify new documents. As a result, it dramatically reduces the dimensionality of the keyword space. The resulting set of keywords of rule is typically small enough to be understood by a human. This simplifies the creation of knowledge-based IF/IR sys-tems, speeds up their operation, and allows easy editing of the rule bases employed. But we can see that with the increasing number of categories, its accuracy becomes to be an unacceptable level, from the experimental results of RSAR in [7]. In [9], we proposed the RSAR-M which is an effective text classification based on Rough Sets, as shown in Figure 1.

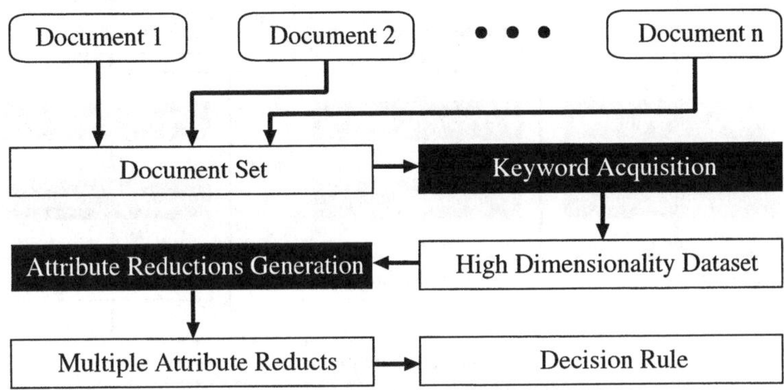


**Fig. 1.** Data flow through the system RSAR-M

## 3 Partition for Text Classification

RSAR-M in [9] is an very effective text classification system. It can get the high classification accuracy. However, here is one problem in this method, that is the computing of the multiple reducts. When the number of training documents increases, the number of dimensions of words processed increases. As a result, the large computing time and large memory are needed to generate multiple reducts. It is very difficult to use RSR-M to the real application system. In this section, we propose two effective methods to improve the performance of RSAR-M. Using the document partition or attribute partition, the new system can generate reducts quickly and effectively, and can maintain the high classification accuracy.

### 3.1 Document Partition for Text Classification

Figure 2 shows a data flow through the new system. We call this system Documents Partition RSAR-M System(DP-RSAR-M). The DP-RSAR-M generates multiple reducts as follows. First, the DP-RSAR-M divides a document set into several document subsets. Then, it uses each document subset to generate multiple reducts. In the stage of partition, to avoid the deviation in the number of classes in each subset, DP-RSAR-M uses the uniform partition for each class. In order to use the different knowledge as many as possible, DP-RSAR-M generates new reducts using the information on reducts already generated. By this means, the same attribute is not included in the different reducts in DP-RSAR-M.

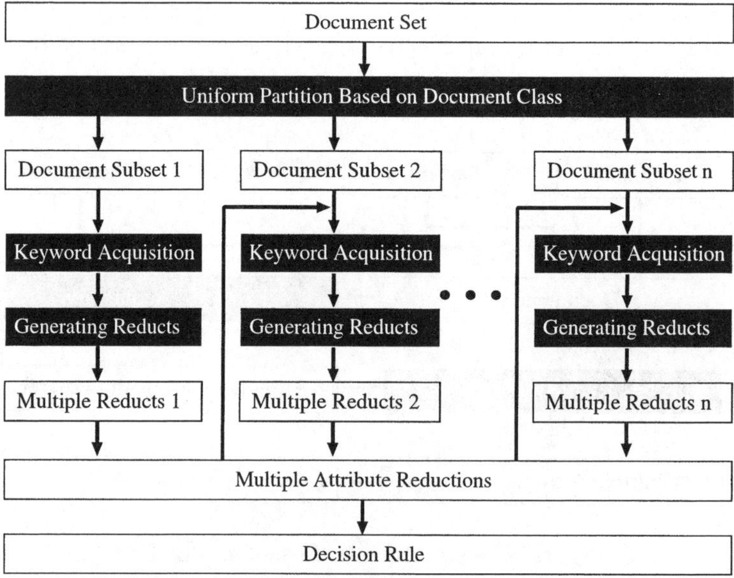


**Fig. 2.** Data flow through the system DP-RSAR-M

### 3.2 Attribute Partition for Text Classification

The high dimensionality of keywords is the reason of reducts computing problem. If we divide the high dimensionality keywords into some keywords subsets, and generate multiple reductions uslng the keywords subsets, then the compting time of generating reductions will be reduced. This section use the attribute partition to improve the performance of RSAR-M.

Figure 3 shows data flow through the new system. We call this system Attribute Partition RSAR-M System(AP-RSAR-M). The AP-RSAR-M generates

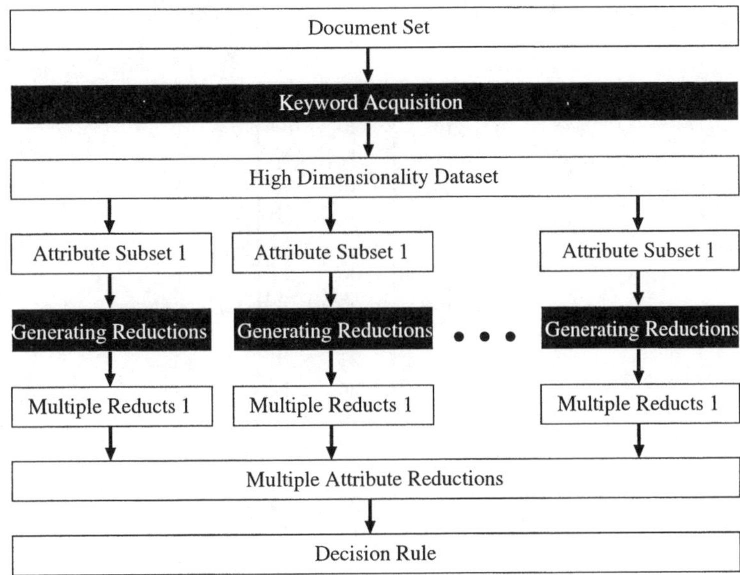


**Fig. 3.** Data flow through the system AP-RSAR-M

multiple reducts as follows. First, the AP-RSAR-M divides the high dimensionality keywords into several keywords subsets. Then, it generates multiple reducts using each keywords subset.

Compared with DP-RSAR-M, the reduction generated by DP-RSAR-M is not a real reduction of the original system, it is a real reduct of subset system, but just a candidate of reduct of the original system. In the case of AP-RSAR-M, the reduction is a real reduct of the original system.

## 4 Experiments and Results

For evaluating the efficiency of our new systems, we compared them with the RSAR-M in the multiple reducts computing time and classification accuracy. The Reuters collection is used in our experiment, which is publicly available at http://www.research. att.com/ lewis/reuters21578.html. Documents in the Reuters collection were collected from Reuters newswire in 1987. To divide the collection into a training and a test set, the modified Apte("ModApte") split has been most frequently used. It is also used in our experiment. 135 different classes have been assigned to the Reuters documents. Fifteen different classes of the Reuters collection are used in our experiment. Table 1 shows the number of training and test data which were used in our experiment.

Fig. 4 shows the experimental result of computing time. The "2-categories" shows the data includes gnp and cocoa, The "3-categories" shows the data includes gnp, cocoa and cpi, and so on. "RSAR-M(1)" means the RSAR-M

**Table 1.** The number of training and test documents

| class | training | test |
|---|---|---|
| gnp | 49 | 34 |
| cocoa | 41 | 15 |
| cpi | 45 | 26 |
| jobs | 32 | 18 |
| copper | 31 | 17 |
| reserves | 30 | 14 |
| grain | 38 | 134 |
| rubber | 29 | 12 |
| ipi | 27 | 10 |
| iron-steel | 26 | 12 |
| veg-oil | 19 | 37 |
| alum | 29 | 20 |
| tin | 17 | 12 |
| nat-gas | 22 | 29 |
| bop | 15 | 28 |

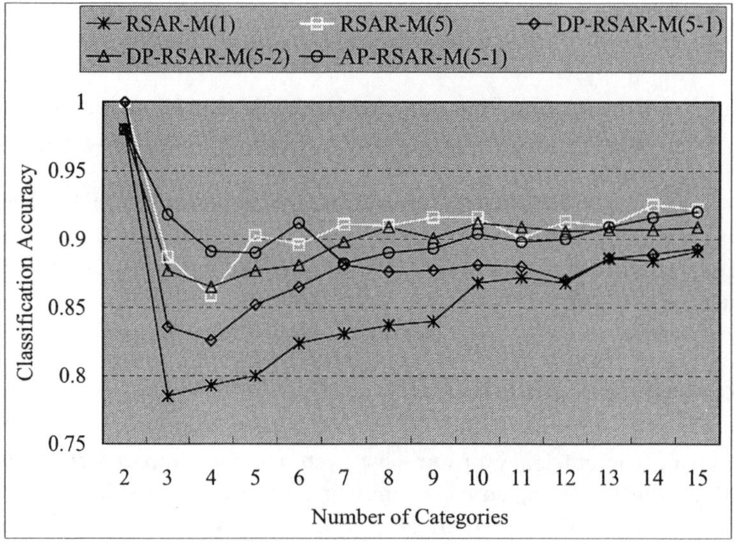


**Fig. 4.** Comparison of Reduct Computing Times(Sec.)

which generates one reduct without documents partition. "RSAR-M(5)" means the RSAR-M which generates five reducts without documents partition. "DP-RSAR-M(5-1)" means the DP-RSAR-M which divides a document set into five document subsets, and each document subset generates one reduct. That is, "DP-RSAR-M(5-1)" generates five reducts in total. "DP-RSAR-M(5-2)" means the DP-RSAR-M which divides a document set into five document subsets, and each document subset generates two reducts. That is, "DP-RSAR-M(5-2)" generates ten reducts in total. "AP-RSAR-M(5-1)" means the AP-RSAR-M which divides the high dimensionality keywords into five keywords subsets, and each keywords subset generates one reduct.

As can be see from Fig. 4, the computing times of "DP-RSAR-M(5-1)" , "DP-RSAR-M(5-2)" and "AP-RSAR-M(5-1)" is much shorter than "RSAR-M(5)". Especially, the computing times of "DP-RSAR-M(5-1)" and "DP-RSAR-M(5-2)" is shorter than "RSAR-M(1)".

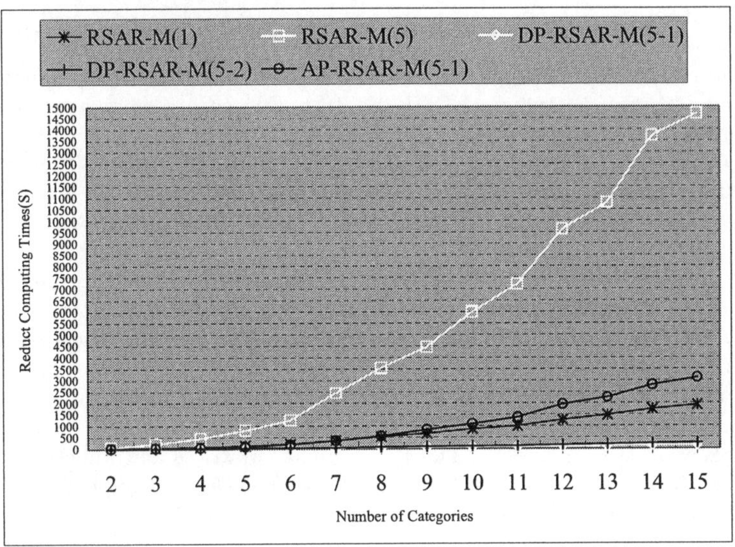


**Fig. 5.** Comparison of Classification Accuracy

Fig. 5 shows the experimental results of classification accuracy. As it can be seen, "DP-RSAR-M(5-2)" and "AP-RSAR-M(5-1)" achieves the high accuracy as "RSAR-M(5)". "DP-RSAR-M(5-1)" gets the higher accuracy than "RSAR-M(1)".

The above experiment results show that our new systems can reduce the computing time of reducts generation greatly and maintain the high classification accuracy. The data partition is an effective method to improve the performance of RSAR-M system.

## 5 Conclusion

This paper proposes an effective method to solve the above problem which improves the performance of RSAR-M. It uses data partition to reduce the modle. The first method is the document partition. In the Documents Partition RSAR-M System, it divides a document set into several document subsets firstly. Then, it uses each document subset to generates multiple reducts. The second way is the keywords partition. In the Attribute Partition RSAR-M sysytem, it divides the high dimensionality keywords into several keywords subsets firstly. Then, it uses each keywords subset to generate multiple reducts. The experimental results show that the data partition is an effective method to improve the performance of RSAR-M. The new system in this paper can get the multiple reducts quickly and maintain the high classification accuracy. As a result, it is efficient and robust text classifier, and can be used in the really application.

## References

1. T. Joachims, "Text Classification with Support Vector Machines: Learning with Many Relevant Features", ECML-98, 10th European Conference on Machine Learning, 1998, pp. 170–178.
2. M. Craven, D. Dipasquo, D. Freitag, A. McCallum, T. Mitchell, K. Nigam & S. Slattery, "Learning to Symbolic Knowledge from the World Wide Web", Proceeding of the 15th Na-tional Conference on Artificial Intelligence (AAAI-98), 1998, pp. 509–516.
3. K. Lang, "Newsweeder: Learning to Filter Netnews", Machine Learning: Proceeding of the Twelfth International (ICML95), 1995, pp. 331–339.
4. Y. Yang, "An Evaluation of Statistical Approaches to Text Classification", Journal of Infor-mation Retrieval, 1, 1999, pp. 69–90.
5. Z. Pawlak, Rough Sets–Theoretical Aspects of Reasoning about Data, Kluwer Academic Publishers, Dordrecht. (1991)
6. A. Skowron & C. Rauszer, "The Discernibility Matrices and Functions in Information Systems", in R. Slowinski (ed.) Intelligent Decision Support – Handbook of Application and Advances of Rough Sets Theory, Kluwer Academic Publishers, Dordrecht, 1992, pp. 331–362.
7. A. Chouchoulas & Q. Shen, "A Rough Set-Based Approach to Text Classification", In 7th International Workshop, RSFDGrC'99, Yamaguchi, Japan, 1999, pp. 118–129.
8. N. Ishii & Y. Bao, "A Simple Method of Computing Value Reduction", Proceedings of CSITeA02, pp. 76–80, 2002,Brazil.
9. Y. Bao, D. Asai, X. Du, K. Yamada & Naohiro Ishii, "An effective rough set-based method for text classification", 4th International Conference on Intelligent Data Eengineering and Automated Learning(LNCS-IDEAL03), March 21–23, 2003, Hong Kong, in printing.
10. C.J. van Rijsbergen, Information retrieval, Butterworths, United Kingdom, 1990.

# Efficiently Mining Interesting Emerging Patterns

Hongjian Fan and Kotagiri Ramamohanarao

Dept. of CSSE, The University of Melbourne, Parkville, Vic 3052, Australia
{hfan,rao}@cs.mu.oz.au

**Abstract.** Emerging patterns (EPs) are itemsets whose supports change significantly from one class to another. It has been shown that they are very powerful distinguishable features and they are very useful for constructing accurate classifiers. Previous EP mining approaches often produce a large number of EPs, which makes it very difficult to choose interesting ones manually. Usually, a post-processing filter step is applied for selecting interesting EPs based on some interestingness measures.

In this paper, we first generalize the interestingness measures for EPs, including the minimum support, the minimum growth rate, the subset relationship between EPs and the correlation based on common statistical measures such as chi-squared value. We then develop an efficient algorithm for mining only those interesting EPs, where the chi-squared test is used as heuristic to prune the search space. The experimental results show that our algorithm maintains efficiency even at low supports on data that is large, dense and has high dimensionality. They also show that the heuristic is admissible, because only unimportant EPs with low supports are ignored. Our work based on EPs for classification confirms that the discovered interesting EPs are excellent candidates for building accurate classifiers.

**Keywords:** Emerging patterns, measures of interestingness, classification, data mining

## 1 Introduction

Classification is an important data mining problem. Given a training database of records, each tagged with a class label, the goal of classification is to build a concise model that can be used to predict the class label of future, unlabelled records. Many classification models have been proposed in the literature [14]. Recently a new type of knowledge patterns, called emerging patterns (EPs), was proposed by Dong and Li [4] for discovering distinctions inherently present between different classes of data. EPs are defined as multivariate features (i.e., itemsets) whose supports (or frequencies) change *significantly* from one class to another. The concept of emerging patterns is very suitable for serving as a classification model. By aggregating the differentiating power of EPs, the constructed classification systems [5,10,11,6,7] are usually more accurate than other existing state-of-the-art classifiers. The idea of emerging patterns is also applied in

G. Dong et al. (Eds.): WAIM 2003, LNCS 2762, pp. 189–201, 2003.

bioinformatics successfully, from the discovery of gene structure features to the classification of gene expression profiles [12,9].

A major difficulty involved in the use of EP is how to efficiently mine those EPs which are useful for classification, because it has been recognised that an EP mining algorithm can generate a large number of EPs, most of which are actually of no interest for modelling or classification purpose. Being able to mine only useful EPs is important, since it can save mining of many unnecessary EPs and identifying interesting ones from a huge number of EPs.

What makes emerging patterns interesting? The measures of interestingness are divided into objective measures - those that depend only on the structure of a pattern and the underlying data used in the discovery process, and the subjective measures - those that also depend on the class of users who examine the pattern [15]. We define interestingness of an EP in objective terms. An EP is interesting, if it (1) has minimum support; (2) has minimum growth rate; (3) has larger growth rate than its subset; (4) highly correlated according to common statistical measures such as chi-square value. The first condition ensures an EP is not noise by imposing a minimum coverage on the training dataset; the second requires an EP has sharp discriminating power; the third regards those "minimal" EPs as interesting, because if any subset of an EP has larger growth rate, the EP itself is not so useful for classification; generally speaking, the last states that an EP is interesting, if the distribution (namely, the supports in two contrasting classes) of its subset is *significantly* different from that of the EP itself, where the difference is measured by the $\chi^2$-test [2]. Experiments show that the set of interesting EPs is orders of magnitude smaller than the set of general EPs. In the case that a user wants to use EPs for classification, the subjective measure of EPs can be defined as their usefulness. To evaluate objective interesting EPs against the subjective measure, we have built classifiers using those EPs. High accuracy on benchmark datasets from the UCI Machine Learning Repository [3] shows that mining EPs using our method can result in high quality EPs with the most differentiating power.

The task of mining EPs is very difficult for large, dense and high-dimensional datasets, because the number of patterns present in the datasets may be exponential in the worst case. What is worse, the Apriori anti-monotone property, which is very effective for pruning search space, does not apply to emerging pattern mining. It is because if a pattern with $k$ items is not an EP, its super-pattern with $(k+1)$ or more items may or may not be an EP.

Recently, the merits of a pattern growth method such as FP-growth [8], have been recognized in the frequent pattern mining. We can use FP-growth to mine EPs: we first find frequent itemsets in one data class for a given support threshold, and then check the support of these itemsets against the other class. Itemsets satisfying the four interestingness measures are interesting EPs. There are several difficulties with this approach: (1) a very large number of frequent patterns will be generated when the support is low; (2) a lot of frequent patterns in one class turn out not to be EPs since they are also frequent in the other class; (3) it selects interesting EPs as post-analysis.

To overcome these difficulties, we propose Interesting Emerging Pattern Miner (iEPMiner) for efficiently extracting only the interesting emerging patterns. iEPMiner uses a tree structure to store the raw data. It recursively partitions the database into sub-database according to the patterns found and search for local patterns to assemble longer global one. iEPMiner operates directly on the data contained in the tree, i.e., no new nodes are inserted into the original tree and no nodes are removed from it during the mining process. The major operations of mining are counting and link adjusting, which are usually inexpensive.

The problem of mining EPs can be seen as to search through the power set of the set of all items for itemsets that are EPs. With low minimum settings on support and growth rate, the candidate interesting EPs embedded in a high-dimensional database are often too numerous to check efficiently. We push the interestingness measures into the pattern growth to reduce the search space. We also use the $\chi^2$-test as heuristic to further prune the search space. The heuristic is admissible because (1) it greatly improves the efficiency of mining; (2) only EPs with the lowest supports are lost. Experiments show that iEPMiner achieves high efficiency on large high-dimensional database with low support and growth rate, and successfully mines the top 90% interesting EPs.

### 1.1 Related Work

Dong and Li [4] introduced the concept of emerging patterns and they also proposed the notion of borders as a means for concisely describing emerging patterns. They formalised the notion of set intervals, defined as collections $S$ of sets that are interval closed - if $X$ and $Z$ are in $S$ and Y is a set such that $X \subseteq Y \subseteq Z$, then $Y$ is in $S$. The collection of emerging patterns discovered from different classes of data, which is typically very large, can be represented by borders, defined as the pair of the sets of the minimal itemsets and of the maximal ones, which are usually much smaller. A suite of algorithms, which manipulates only borders of two collections, were proposed for mining emerging patterns. However, they depend on border finding algorithms such as Max-Miner [1]. In fact, the task of mining maximal frequent patterns is very difficult, especially when the minimum support is low (e.g. 5% or even 0.1%). For example, for the UCI Connect-4 dataset, the Max-Miner, one of the most efficient previously known algorithm for finding maximal frequent itemsets, needs more than three hours when minimum support is 10%. Furthermore, the process of extracting the embodied EPs with supports and growth rates from the borders and selecting the interesting one is very time-consuming. In contrast, our algorithm mine interesting EPs directly from the raw data.

ConsEPMiner [16] mines EPs satisfying several constraints including growth-rate improvement constraint. It follows an Apriori level-wise, candidate generation-and-test approach. It is still not efficient when the minimum support is low. For the UCI Connect-4 dataset, ConsEPMiner needs about 6 hours when support is 3%. In comparison, our algorithm can finish in less than 10 minutes, with little loss of interesting patterns.

Recent work in [13] proposed to use "shadow patterns" to measure the interestingness of minimal JEPs. Shadow patterns are those immediate subsets of a minimal JEP. If the growth rates of these shadow patterns are on average around small numbers like 1 or 2, compared with the infinite growth rate of the JEP, it is regarded as *adversely interesting*, because the JEP is "unexpected" and the conflict may reveal some new insights into the correlation of the features. Their interestingness measure is a specific case of our correlation measure, since the level of adversity can be detected by $\chi^2$-test. They do post-analysis of mined JEPs, while we push the interestingness measures into the mining process.

## 2 Interesting Measures of Emerging Patterns

Suppose a data object $obj = (a_1, a_2 \cdots a_n)$ follows the schema $(A_1, A_2 \cdots A_n)$, where $A_1, A_2 \cdots A_n$ are called attributes. Attributes can be categorical or continuous. For a categorical attributes, all the possible values are mapped to a set of consecutive positive integers. For a continuous attributes, its value range is discretized into intervals, and the intervals are also mapped to consecutive positive integers. By doing so, a raw set of data objects is encoded into the binary transaction database. We call each (attribute, integer-value) pair an *item*.

Let $I$ denote the set of all items in the encoding dataset $D$. A set $X$ of items is also called an itemset, which is defined as a subset of $I$. We say any instance $S$ contains an itemset $X$, if $X \subseteq S$. The support of an itemset $X$ in a dataset $D$, $supp_D(X)$, is $count_D(X)/|D|$, where $count_D(X)$ is the number of instances in $D$ containing $X$. Assume two data classes $D_1$ and $D_2$, the growth rate of an itemset $X$ in favour of $D_2$ is defined as $GrowthRate(X) = GR(X) = supp_{D_2}(X)/supp_{D_1}(X)$ (where $GR(X) = 0$, if $supp_{D_2}(X) = supp_{D_1}(X) = 0$; $GR(X) = \infty$, if $supp_{D_2}(X) > 0$ and $supp_{D_1}(X) = 0$). An Emerging Pattern $Y$ favouring $D_2$ is an itemset whose growth rate from $D_1$ to $D_2$ is at least $\rho (\rho > 1)$. The support of $Y$ in $D_2$, denoted as $supp(Y)$, is called the support of the EP.

### 2.1 Interesting Emerging Patterns

We formally define the objective interestingness of an EP. An EP, $X$, is interesting, if

1. $supp(X) \geq \xi$, where $\xi$ is a minimum support threshold;
2. $GR(X) \geq \rho$, where $\rho$ is a minimum growth rate threshold;
3. $\forall Y \subset X, GR(Y) < GR(X)$.
4. $|X| = 1$ or $|X| > 1 \wedge (\forall Y \subset X \wedge |Y| = |X| - 1 \wedge chi(X,Y) \geq \eta)$, where $\eta = 3.84$ is a minimum chi-value threshold and $chi(X,Y)$ is computed using the following contingency table [2].

| | $X$ | $Y$ | $\sum row$ |
|---|---|---|---|
| $D_1$ | $count_{D_1}(X)$ | $count_{D_1}(Y)$ | $count_{D_1}(X) + count_{D_1}(Y)$ |
| $D_2$ | $count_{D_2}(X)$ | $count_{D_2}(Y)$ | $count_{D_2}(X) + count_{D_2}(Y)$ |
| $\sum column$ | $count_{D_1+D_2}(X)$ | $count_{D_1+D_2}(Y)$ | $count_{D_1+D_2}(X) + count_{D_1+D_2}(Y)$ |

The first condition ensures an EP has minimum coverage on the training dataset; the second requires an EP has sharp discriminating power; the third explores the subset relationship of EPs, i.e., interesting EPs are not "subsumed" by their subsets; the last states that for any immediate subset of an interesting EP with length more than 1, its support distribution in both classes are *significantly* different from that of the EP itself. One can use other statistical measures such as the entropy gain, the gini index and the correlation coefficient in place of chi-square value. The bigger the value, the more confident we are to say that their distributions are different. We choose 3.84 as the minimum chi-value threshold, since it gives us 95% confidence, which is enough in many real life applications. If a length-$k$ EP's distribution is *significantly* different from that of any of its length-$(k-1)$ subsets, it shows that adding one item from length-$(k-1)$ subsets makes its behaviour on two classes quite different. It also means that those items which make up of the EP, are highly correlated.

We give an example to see how contingency tests are performed in the process of mining. Let $X = \{a, b, c\}, Y = \{a, b\}$. Suppose $|D_1| = |D_2| = 100$ and $count_{D_1}(Y) = 80$, $count_{D_2}(Y) = 60$, $count_{D_1}(X) = 60$, $count_{D_2}(X) = 35$, then we have the following observed contingency table (left). For each pair $(i, j) \in \{D_1, D_2\} \times \{X, Y\}$, we calculate the expectation under the assumption of independence:

$$E_{ij} = \frac{count_{D_1+D_2}(j) \times (count_i(X) + count_i(Y))}{count_{D_1+D_2}(X) + count_{D_1+D_2}(Y)}.$$

The results are shown in the following expected contingency table (right).

The observed contingency table

| | Y | X | $\sum row$ |
|---|---|---|---|
| $D_1$ | 80 | 60 | 140 |
| $D_2$ | 85 | 35 | 120 |
| $\sum column$ | 165 | 95 | 260 |

The expected contingency table

| | Y | X | $\sum row$ |
|---|---|---|---|
| $D_1$ | 89 | 51 | 140 |
| $D_2$ | 76 | 44 | 120 |
| $\sum column$ | 165 | 95 | 260 |

The chi-square value is the normalised deviation of observation from expectation; namely,

$$chi(X, Y) = \sum_{i \in \{D_1, D_2\}} \sum_{j \in \{X, Y\}} \frac{(O_{ij} - E_{ij})^2}{E_{ij}}.$$

From the above two tables, the computed $\chi^2$ value is 5.405. Since $\chi^2 \geq 5.02$ (at 97.5% significance level), we say that the distributions of $X$ and $Y$ are different with a confidence of 97.5%, which is higher than the minimum of 95%.

### 2.2 Chi-Squared Pruning Heuristic

Our tree based algorithm mines EPs in a pattern growth manner. How do we push the interestingness measures into mining? It is straightforward to push the measure 1 and 2 into the pattern growth (see next section for details). But it is hard to push the measure 3 and 4, because we may not have "seen" all the subsets of the current pattern. A heuristic is proposed to prune as early as possible the search space, i.e., those patterns which are very likely turn out not to satisfy condition 3 or 4. The heuristic is based on the following lemma.

**Lemma 1.** *Let $X, Y, Z$ be itemsets. $Y = X \cup \{i\}$, $Z = Y \cup \{j\}$, $S = X \cup \{j\}$, where $i$ and $j$ are items. If $chi(X, Y) < \eta$, $P(\{i\}|X)P(\{j\}|X) = P(\{i,j\}|X)$, and $\eta = 3.84$, then we have $chi(S, Z) < \eta$ with least 95% confidence.*

Proof. Since $\eta = 3.84$, $chi(X, Y) < \eta \Longleftrightarrow chi(X, X \cup \{i\}) < 3.84$. We say $i$ is independent from $X$ with at least 95% confidence. So we have $P(X \cup \{i\}) \approx P(X)P(\{i\})$. $P(\{i\}|X)P(\{j\}|X) = P(\{i,j\}|X) \Longleftrightarrow$

$$\frac{P(\{i\} \cup X)}{P(X)} * \frac{P(\{j\} \cup X)}{P(X)} = \frac{P(\{i,j\} \cup X)}{P(X)} \Longrightarrow P(\{i\}) * \frac{P(\{j\} \cup X)}{P(X)} \approx \frac{P(\{i,j\} \cup X)}{P(X)}.$$

So $P(X \cup \{i,j\}) \approx P(X \cup \{j\})P(\{i\})$, which means $i$ is independent from $X \cup \{j\}$. Thus, we have $chi(X \cup \{j\}, X \cup \{j, i\}) < 3.84$ with at least 95% confidence.

The lemma has an assumption: $P(\{i\}|X)P(\{j\}|X) = P(\{i,j\}|X)$. Although it is not true for all the cases in real datasets, experiments show that for most cases we have $P(\{i\}|X)P(\{j\}|X) \approx P(\{i,j\}|X)$, which is good enough for mining interesting EPs. When $chi(X, Y) < \eta = 3.84$, from the lemma, $Z$ definitely will not be interesting since it does not satisfy condition 4. Our mining method can stop growing $Y$ immediately to avoid searching and generating unnecessary candidate patterns.

The $\chi^2$-test (*chi*() function) can be used as an effective heuristic for pruning search space. By pruning long patterns as soon as possible, we usually obtain a relatively small set of EPs. One pass over the set of EPs can select the interesting EPs according to the four interestingness measures. In contrast, if iEPMiner does not use the heuristic, it needs to search a huge space, which produces a lot of uninteresting patterns first and discards them later. Experiments show that the $\chi^2$-test heuristic makes iEPMiner more efficient by an order of magnitude. We also investigate what patterns the heuristic search may lose. Detailed analysis over many datasets from the UCI Machine Learning Repository and high accuracy of the classifiers based on our mined interesting EPs confirm that it loses only unimportant EPs. So the $\chi^2$-test pruning heuristic is admissible, although it is non-monotone.

## 3 Mining Interesting Emerging Patterns

### 3.1 Pattern Tree

Without loss of generality, we use lexicographic order as a partial order on the set of all items, denoted as $\prec$.

**Definition 1.** *A Pattern Tree (P-tree) is a tree structure defined below.*

1. *It consists of one root, a set of item prefix subtrees as the children of the root, and a header table.*

2. *Each node in the item prefix subtrees consists of four fields: item-name, $count_{D_1}$, $count_{D_2}$ and node-link, where item-name registers which item this node represents, $count_{D_1}$ registers the number of transactions in $D_1$ represented by the portion of the path reaching this node, $count_{D_2}$ registers such number in $D_2$, and node-link links to the next node in the P-tree carrying the same item or null if there is none.*
3. *Each entry in the header table consists of three fields: (1) item-name; (2) head of node-link, which points to the first node in the P-tree carrying the item; (3) $total_{D_1}$,the sum of all $count_{D_1}$ in the item's corresponding node-link; (4) $total_{D_2}$,the sum of all $count_{D_2}$ in such node-link.*
4. *The tree is ordered: if a node $M$ is the parent of a node $N$, and item $i$ and $j$ appear in $M$ and $N$ respectively, then $i \prec j$.*

Note that nodes with the same item-name are linked in sequence via node-link, which facilitates tree traversal. Unlike the FP-tree [8], the P-tree is only traversable top-down (from root to leaves), i.e., there is no pointer from child to parent nodes. The construction of the P-tree can be found in [6]. The P-tree of the example dataset from Figure 1 is shown in Figure 2.

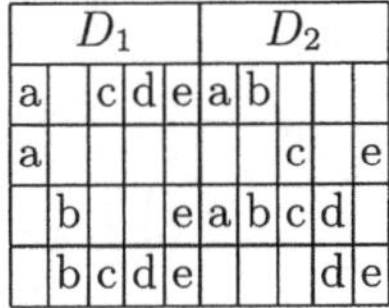

| $D_1$ | | | | | $D_2$ | | | | |
|---|---|---|---|---|---|---|---|---|---|
| a | | c | d | e | a | b | | | |
| a | | | | | | | c | | e |
| | b | | | e | a | b | c | d | |
| | b | c | d | e | | | | d | e |

**Fig. 1.** A dataset containing 2 classes as an example

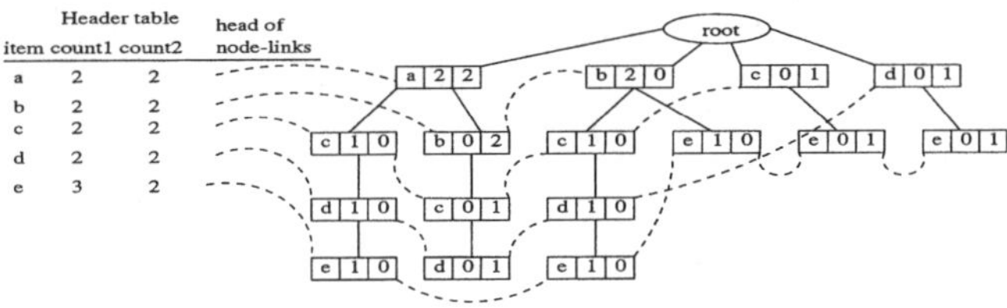


**Fig. 2.** The P-tree of the example dataset

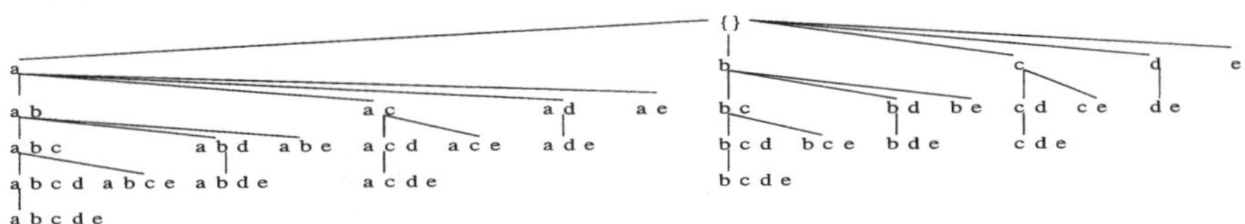


**Fig. 3.** A complete set enumeration tree over $I$, with items lexically ordered

## 3.2 Using P-Tree to Mine Interesting Emerging Patterns

We show the ideas of mining by using the tree shown in Figure 2. Let $\xi = 1$ be a minimum support threshold, and $\rho = 2$ a minimum growth rate threshold. Let us examine the mining process based on the constructed tree shown in Figure 2. Basically, we have to calculate the supports in both $D_1$ and $D_2$ for the power set of $I = \{a, b, c, d, e\}$ and then check each itemset against the four interestingness measures. We use the set enumeration tree shown in Figure 3 as the conceptual framework to explore the itemset space. The itemsets are "generated" in the specific order: first visit the node, then visit the right and left subtree. Namely, the itemsets are considered in the following order:

- $\{e\}$
- $\{d\}$, $\{d, e\}$
- $\{c\}$, $\{c, e\}$, $\{c, d\}$, $\{c, d, e\}$
- $\{b\}$, $\{b, e\}$, $\{b, d\}$, $\{b, d, e\}$, $\{b, c\}$, $\{b, c, e\}$, $\{b, c, d\}$, $\{b, c, d, e\}$
- $\{a\}$, $\{a, e\}$, $\{a, d\}$, $\{a, d, e\}$, $\{a, c\}$, $\{a, c, e\}$, $\{a, c, d\}$, $\{a, c, d, e\}$, $\{a, b\}$, $\{a, b, e\}$, $\{a, b, d\}$, $\{a, b, d, e\}$, $\{a, b, c\}$, $\{a, b, c, e\}$, $\{a, b, c, d\}$, $\{a, b, c, d, e\}$

For $e$, we get its counts in both classes from the head table, denoted as $[e{:}3; 2]$ (the two numbers after ":" indicate the supports in $D_1$ and $D_2$, respectively). {e} is not an EP since its growth rate $1.5 < \rho$.

For $d$, we have $[d{:}2; 2]$. {d} is not an EP. We try to grow {d} via concatenation of $e$ with it. $e$'s counts in both classes change from $[e{:}3; 2]$ to $[e{:}2; 1]$, when only those $e$ co-occurring with $d$ are counted. This can be done by going through $d$'s node-links and visit those $d$'s subtrees. We simply refer the process to recounting $e$ under {d}, which is frequently used in the following. Note that the other two $e$ are not counted since they are not in such subtrees. Then we get $[d{:}2; 2, e{:}2; 1]$, where $\{d, e\}$ is an EP of growth rate 2.

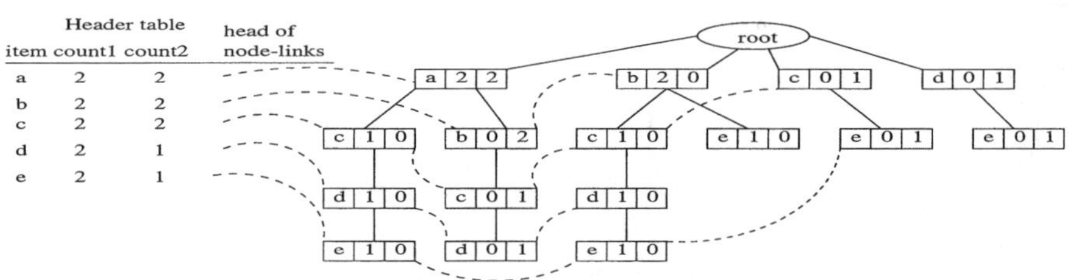


**Fig. 4.** The P-tree after adjusting the node-links and counts of $d$ and $e$ under $c$

For $c$, we have $[c{:}2; 2]$. $\{c\}$ is not an EP. Now we have $e$ and $d$ to concatenate with $c$. The P-tree after the node-links and counts of $e$ and $d$ are adjusted is shown in Figure 4. We try $e$ first. After recounting $e$ under $\{c\}$, we obtain $[c{:}2; 2, e{:}2; 1]$, where $\{c, e\}$ is an EP of growth rate 2. We then try $d$. After recounting $d$ under $\{c\}$, we obtain $[c4{:}2; 2, d{:}2; 1]$, where $\{c, d\}$ is an EP of growth rate 2. Because $\{c, d\}$ has supports in $D_1$ and $D_2$ quite different from $\{c\}$, it may produce interesting patterns to further grow $\{c, d\}$ by adding $e$. After recounting $e$ under {c,d}[1], we obtain $[c{:}2; 2, d{:}2; 1, e{:}2; 0]$, where $\{c, d, e\}$ is an EP of infinite

[1] Since only those $d$ under $c$ are linked by its node-links, it is easy to go through $d$'s node-links looking for $e$.

growth rate. Usually, an EP with infinite growth rate is called a JEP(Jumping EP).

For $b$, we have $[b{:}2;2]$. $\{b\}$ is not an EP. Now we have $e$, $d$ and $c$ to concatenate with $b$. We try $e$ first. After recounting $e$ under $\{b\}$, we obtain $[b{:}2;2, e{:}2;0]$, where $\{b,e\}$ is a JEP. We try $d$ next. After recounting $d$ under $\{b\}$, we obtain $[b{:}2;2, d{:}1;1]$. Because the support distributions of $\{b,d\}$ and $\{b\}$ are the same, it is very unlikely that we can get interesting EPs by further growing $\{b,d\}$. In fact, $\{b,d,e\}$ with support counts 1 and 0 in $D_1$ and $D_2$, is not interesting since its subset $\{b,e\}$ is also a JEP. It can be seen that our chi-squared heuristic effectively prunes a lot of uninteresting patterns from consideration. We then try $c$. After recounting $c$ under $\{b\}$, we obtain $[b{:}2;2, c{:}1;1]$. For the same reason, we do not further grow $\{b,c\}$.

For $a$, we have $[a{:}2;2]$. $\{a\}$ is not an EP. Now we have $e$, $d$, $c$ and $b$ to concatenate with $a$. We try $e$ first. After recounting $e$ under $\{a\}$, we obtain $[a{:}2;2, e{:}1;0]$, where $\{a,e\}$ is a JEP. We try $d$ next. After recounting $d$ under $\{a\}$, we obtain $[a{:}2;2, d{:}1;1]$. For the above reason, we do not further grow $\{a,d\}$. We then try $c$. After recounting $c$ under $\{a\}$, we obtain $[a{:}2;2, c{:}1;1]$. Again we do not further grow $\{a,c\}$. Lastly, we try $b$. After recounting $b$ under $\{a\}$, we obtain $[a{:}2;2, b{:}0;2]$, where $\{a,b\}$ is a JEP. We do not further grow a JEP, since supersets of a JEP is not interesting.

```
;; assume I = {1, ···, N}
;; and 1 ≺ ··· ≺ N
Procedure iEP-Miner(root) {
  for i = N downto 1 do {
    β = {i};
    if is-iEP(β), then output β;
    mine-subtree(β);
  }
  prune uninteresting EPs;
}

Procedure mine-subtree(β) {
  Let k be the last item of β;
  for all items which appear in k's subtrees,
    adjust their node-links and accumulate counts;
  for j = N downto k+1 do {
    γ = β ∪ j;
    if is-iEP(γ), then output it;
    if chi(γ, β) ≥ η, mine-subtree(γ);
  }
}
```

**Fig. 5.** iEP-Miner pseudo-code

### 3.3 iEP-Miner

The high-level description of iEP-Miner is given in Figure 5. The main procedure iEP-Miner takes the root of the P-tree as input and performs the mining solely in the P-tree. The procedure mine-subtree() is called recursively. It always tries to grow the current pattern $\beta$ by adding a new item. The function is-iEP() checks whether an itemset satisfies the interestingness measure 1, 2 and 4. The chi-squared pruning heuristic, the test "$chi(\gamma,\beta) \geq \eta$", is used to prune a huge number of patterns which are definitely uninteresting. The set of the generated candidate interesting EPs is relatively small, and one pass over the set can filter out those which does not satisfies the interestingness measure 3. The final set is our defined interesting EPs.

## 4 Performance Study

We now report a performance evaluation of iEP-Miner. We carried out experiments on many datasets from the UCI Machine Learning Repository, and all of them exhibited significant improvement in performance. For lack of space, we only present the results on the following large, high-dimensional datasets.

| Dataset | Records | Avg. Record Width | No. of Binary items |
|---|---|---|---|
| adult | 45,225 | 15 | 154 |
| connect-4[2] | 61,108 | 43 | 128 |
| mushroom | 8124 | 23 | 121 |

All experiments were conducted on a Dell PowerEdge 2500 (Dual P3 1GHz CPU, 2G RAM) running Solaris 8/x86, shared by many users of the University of Melbourne.

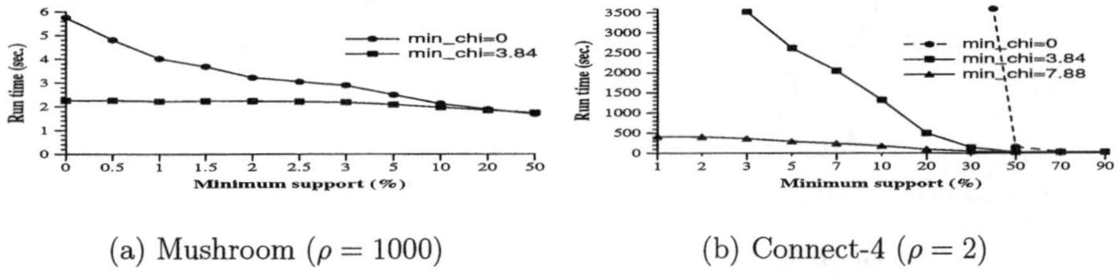


(a) Mushroom ($\rho = 1000$) (b) Connect-4 ($\rho = 2$)

**Fig. 6.** Scalability with support threshold

The interestingness of emerging patterns is determined by three parameters, where $\xi$ is a minimum support threshold, $\rho$ is a minimum growth rate threshold and $\eta$ is a minimum chi-square value threshold. The scalability of iEP-Miner with support threshold is shown in Figure 6.

**Table 1.** The effectiveness of the chi-squared pruning heuristic

| # of EP searched | adult | connect4 | mushroom |
|---|---|---|---|
| without heuristic | 6,977,123 | 16,525,078 | 4,373,265 |
| with heuristic | 191,765 | 369,443 | 89,624 |
| Ratio | 36.4 | 44.7 | 48.8 |

To show the effectiveness of the chi-squared pruning heuristic, we investigate how many candidate EPs we need to "look at" before interesting EPs are generated. The results are shown in Table 1. It can be seen that a huge amount of search space is pruned because our heuristic stops early growing many unpromising branches.

**Table 2.** Comparison between general EPs and interesting EPs

ADULT ($\xi = 0\%, \rho = 10000$, maximum length = 11)

| | 0-1% | 1-2% | 2-3% | 3-4% | 4-5% | 5-6% | 6-8% | 8-100% | 0-100% |
|---|---|---|---|---|---|---|---|---|---|
| all EPs | 10,490,845 | 4,366 | 963 | 255 | 126 | 51 | 16 | 0 | 10,496,622 |
| all iEPs | 10,072 | 92 | 20 | 9 | 6 | 3 | 4 | 0 | 10,206 |
| mined iEPs | 9,239 | 83 | 19 | 9 | 6 | 3 | 4 | 0 | 9,363 |
| Ratio | 1,041.6 | 47.5 | 48.2 | 28.3 | 21 | 17 | 4 | 1 | 1,028.5 |
| missing iEPs | 8.3% | 9.8% | 5% | 0 | 0 | 0 | 0 | 0 | 8.3% |

CONNECT-4 ($\xi = 1\%, \rho = 2$, maximum length = 10)

| | 1-2% | 2-4% | 4-6% | 6-10% | 10-40% | 40-100% | 0-100% |
|---|---|---|---|---|---|---|---|
| all EPs | 13,837,899 | 5,938,079 | 1,372,383 | 729,788 | 242,461 | 0 | 22,120,610 |
| all iEPs | 2,064 | 2,130 | 747 | 487 | 407 | 0 | 5,835 |
| mined iEPs | 1,940 | 1,993 | 712 | 487 | 407 | 0 | 5,539 |
| Ratio | 6704.4 | 2787.8 | 1837.2 | 1498.5 | 595.7 | 1 | 3791 |
| missing iEPs | 6% | 6.4% | 4.7% | 0 | 0 | 0 | 5.1% |

MUSHROOM ($\xi = 0\%, \rho = 10000$, maximum length = 6)

| | 0-2% | 2-4% | 4-7% | 7-10% | 10-30% | 30-70% | 70-100% | 0-100% |
|---|---|---|---|---|---|---|---|---|
| all EPs | 8,113,592 | 312,120 | 123,256 | 18,861 | 44,480 | 2,015 | 0 | 8,614,333 |
| all iEPs | 1,032 | 546 | 360 | 175 | 416 | 72 | 0 | 2,606 |
| mined iEPs | 1,002 | 536 | 360 | 175 | 416 | 72 | 0 | 2,526 |
| Ratio | 7862 | 571.6 | 342.4 | 107.8 | 106.9 | 30 | 1 | 3312 |
| missing iEPs | 2.9% | 1.8% | 0 | 0 | 0 | 0 | 0 | 3.1% |

In order to have some ideas of what proportion of EPs are interesting, we compare the set of "all EPs"(satisfying the support and growth rate threshold only, and their maximum length is no more than the maximum length of all interesting EPs), "all iEPs"(satisfying the four interestingness measures) and "mined iEPs"(satisfying the four interestingness measures, but not complete due to the heuristic) in terms of their distributions in support intervals. The results are shown in Table 2. The ratio is the number of "all EPs" in the specified interval divided by that of "all iEPs". The last row gives the percent of missing iEPs over "all iEPs" due to heuristic searching. We highlight some interesting points:

- The set of all interesting EPs is 1000-3000 times smaller than the set of all general EPs.
- The ratios decreases from left to right, which means that our interestingness measures eliminate a large number of EPs with low supports, while tend to keep EPs with higher supports. This is desirable and reasonable, since EPs with higher supports are definitely more preferable for classification given the same growth rate. On the other hand, an EPs with high support does not necessarily mean that it is useful, since its subset may have higher support.
- We stress that the set of our mined interesting EPs is very close to the set of true interesting EPs: they are *exactly the same* at high support; only at

very low support, some interesting EPs are ignored. The chi-squared pruning heuristic is very effective since the top 90% interesting EPs are discovered by our algorithm.

## 5 Conclusions

In this paper, we have proposed four objective interestingness measures for EPs and developed an efficient algorithm, iEPMiner, for mining only the interesting EPs based on a tree data structure. The chi-squared pruning heuristic is used to mine EPs by growing only promising branches. This achieved considerable performance gains: the heuristic makes iEPMiner orders of magnitude faster. Although it gives up the completeness of interesting EPs, the heuristic always discovers the top 90% interesting EPs, which are sufficient to build high accurate classifiers in many real life applications.

## References

1. R.J. Bayardo. Efficiently mining long patterns from databases. In *Proc. ACM-SIGMOD'98*, pages 85–93, Seattle, WA, USA, June 1998.
2. Robert M. Bethea, Benjamin S. Duran, and Thomas L. Boullion. *Statistical methods for engineers and scientists.* New York : M. Dekker, 1995.
3. C.L. Blake and C.J. Merz. UCI repository of machine learning databases, 1998.
4. G. Dong and J. Li. Efficient mining of emerging patterns: Discovering trends and differences. In *Proc. ACM-SIGKDD'99*, pages 43–52, San Diego, CA, Aug 1999.
5. G. Dong, X. Zhang, L. Wong, and J. Li. Classification by aggregating emerging patterns. In *Proc. the 2nd Intl. Conf. on Discovery Science,* pages 30–42, Tokyo.
6. H. Fan and K. Ramamohanarao. An efficient single-scan algorithm for mining essential jumping emerging patterns for classification. In *Proc. 2002 Pacific-Asia Conf. Knowledge Discovery and Data Mining (PAKDD'02)*, Taipei, Taiwan.
7. H. Fan and K. Ramamohanarao. A bayesian approach to use emerging patterns for classification. In *Proc. 14th Australasian Database Conference (ADC2003).*
8. J. Han, J. Pei, and Y. Yin. Mining frequent patterns without candidate generation. In *Proc. ACM-SIGMOD'00*, pages 1–12, Dallas, TX, USA, May 2000.
9. L. Wong J. Li. Identifying good diagnostic genes or genes groups from gene expression data by using the concept of emerging patterns. *Bioinformatics*, 18(5):725–734, 2002.
10. J. Li, G. Dong, and K.Ramamohanarao. Making use of the most expressive jumping emerging patterns for classification. *Knowledge and Information Systems*, 3(2):131–145, 2001.
11. J. Li, G. Dong, K. Ramamohanarao, and L. Wong. DeEPs: A new instance-based discovery and classification system. *Machine Learning*, To appear.
12. J. Li, H. Liu, J. R. Downing, and L. Wong A. Yeoh. Simple rules underlying gene expression profiles of more than six subtypes of acute lymphoblastic leukemia (all) patients. *Bioinformatics*, 19(1):71–78, 2003.
13. J. Li and L. Wong. Geography of differences between two classes of data. In *Proc. 6th European Conf. on Principles of Data Mining and Knowledge Discovery*, pages 325–337, Helsinki, Finland, Aug 2002.

14. T. Lim, W. Loh, and Y. Shih. A comparison of prediction accuracy, complexity, and training time of thirty-three old and new classification algorithms. *Machine Learning*, 40:203–228, 2000.
15. A. Silberschatz and A. Tuzhilin. What makes patterns interesting in knowledge discovery systems. *IEEE Transactions on Knowledge and Data Engineering*, 8(6):970–974, 1996.
16. X. Zhang, G. Dong, and K.Ramamohanarao. Exploring constraints to efficiently mine emerging patterns from large high-dimensional datasets. In *Proc. ACM-SIGKDD'00*, pages 310–314, Boston, USA, Aug 2000.

# DENCLUE-M: Boosting DENCLUE Algorithm by Mean Approximation on Grids*

Cunhua Li[1,2], Zhihui Sun[1], and Yuqing Song[1]

[1] Department of Computer Science and Engineering,
Southeast University, Nanjing, P.R.China
[2] Department of Computer Science,
Huaihai Institute of Technology, Lianyungang, P.R.China
cli@hhit.edu.cn

**Abstract.** Many data mining applications require clustering of large amount of data. Most clustering algorithms, however, do not work and efficiently when facing such kind of dataset. This paper presents an approach to boost one of the most prominent density-based algorithms, called DENCLUE. We show analytically that the method of adjusted mean approximation on the grid is not only a powerful tool to relieve the burden of heavy computation and memory usage, but also a close proximity of the original algorithm. An adjusted mean approximation based clustering algorithm called DENCLUE-M is constructed which exploits more advantages from the grid partition mechanism. Results of experiments also demonstrate promising performance of this approach.

## 1 Introduction

With the fast progress of information technology, the amount of data stored in database has increased sharply. Although various clustering algorithms were constructed, few of them show preferable efficiency when dealing with large dataset with huge number of high dimensional data items. This common awareness has attracted researchers to find ways of scaling up the clustering methods to large datasets [1,2]. Ideally, an approach of boosting an algorithm should reduce the algorithm's memory usage and computation complexity remarkably while still keep desirable clustering accuracy. This is the standpoint of this article in dealing with the scaling problem.

### 1.1 Related Work

There are many clustering algorithms developed from different approaches, such as Hierarchical, Model- and Optimization-Based, Density-Based or Hybrid. Among them a spectrum of well-known algorithms are grid-based. Generally, the term grid-

* Supported by the National Natural Science Foundation of China under Grant No. 79970092; the Natural Science Foundation of the education board of Jiangsu Province under Grant No. 02KJB520012.

G. Dong et al. (Eds.): WAIM 2003, LNCS 2762, pp. 202–213, 2003.

based implies an algorithm uses a certain scheme to partition the data space into a set of hypercubes (we call them grids here after for convenient), such as equi-width, equi-depth, adaptive or optimal-grid partition of the data space [1],[2]. With the partitioning mechanism, an algorithm holds information of the data points scanned from databases into the grids, performs data retrieval, aggregates statistical values of the data on the grid level [3,4,5,6]. Grid-based approach also enables an algorithm to manage the dataset in an effective manner, such as storing the data points in $K^*$-tree or $X$-tree [3,7,9], which is very efficient for storage and fast retrieval. The most prominent representatives of the grid-based algorithms are GridClustering [3], Wavecluster [4], CLIQUE [5], STING [6] and DENCLUE [7].

DENCLUE is a highly commented algorithm that employs grid-partition mechanism for data object handling and retrieving. However, with a close look into the algorithm, we find that it is still improvable for even better achievement by taking into account of the mean value (we call it the "gravity center" here after) of the data points in the grids. By imbedding a grid-level mean approximation scheme, the revised algorithm can break the bottleneck of the core memory. In addition, the approximation scheme greatly relieves the burden of complicated pointwise computation with minor loss of clustering accuracy.

### 1.2 Our Contribution

We demonstrate why and how the gravity center of the points in a grid can play an important role in data clustering. We analyze the error introduced by mean approximation on the grids and study the behavior of the relative error on a statistical base. We show that mean approximation can be adjusted to close approximate the point-to-point computation of the density values. Based on this line of consideration, we construct a clustering algorithm and design several experiments to reveal the performance of the algorithm.

## 2 A Fast Overview of DENCLUE Algorithm

Firstly, we need a fast overview of the DENCLUE (DENsity-based CLUstEring) algorithm developed by Hinneburg *et al.* The definitions and ideas it introduced are essential for us to forward our results.

### 2.1 Definitions in DENCLUE

Let $A = \{A_1, A_2, ..., A_k\}$ be a set of domains under the Euclidean space, and $S = A_1 \times A_2 \times ... \times A_k$ be the minimum bounding hyper-rectangle of the data space. The input $D$ is a set of $k$-dimensional data objects in $S$ and $|D| = N$.

**Definition 1. (Influence Function)** *The influence function of a data object* $q \in D$ *is a function* $f_B^q : D \to R_0^+$, *such that* $\forall p \in D$, $f_B^q(p) = f_B(q, p)$.

The influence functions can be square wave function, Gauss function, etc. An influence function has the property: $f_B^q(p_1) \geq f_B^q(p_2)$ *iff* $dist(q,p_1) \leq dist(q,p_2)$ [8]. In this paper, we simply choose the Gaussian influence function $f_{gauss}^q(p) = e^{-\frac{d(p,q)^2}{2\sigma^2}}$ for all of our discussion.

**Definition 2. (Density Function)** *Given dataset* $D$, *the density function of the data space* $S$ *is defined as:* $f_{Gauss}^D(p) = \sum_{i=1}^{N} f_{Gauss}^{q_i}(p) = \sum_{i=1}^{N} e^{-\frac{d(p,q_i)^2}{2\sigma^2}}$, $\forall p \in S$.

**Definition 3. (Density Attractor)** *A point* $p^* \in S$ *is called a density attractor if and only if* $p^*$ *is a local maximum of the density function. A point* $p \in D$ *is said to be density-attracted to a density-attractor* $p^*$ *if there exist a series of points* $p = p^0,\ldots,p^s \in D$, $d(p^s,p^*) < \varepsilon$, *such that* $p^i = p^{i-1} + \delta \cdot \frac{\nabla f^D(x^{i-1})}{\| \nabla f^D(x^{i-1}) \|}$, $i = 1,\ldots,s$. *Where* $\nabla f^D(p) = \sum_{i=1}^{N}(p_i - p) f^{p_i}(p)$ *is the gradient of the density function at point* $p$.

**Definition 4.** *A center-defined cluster (wrt to* $\sigma,\xi$ *) for a density attractor* $p^*$ *is a subset* $C \subseteq D$, *with* $p \in C$ *being density attracted by* $p^*$ *and* $f^D(p^*) \geq \xi$. *Points* $p \in D$ *are called outliers if they are density-attracted by a local maximum* $p_0^*$ *with* $f^D(p_0^*) < \xi$. *An arbitrary-shape cluster (wrt to* $\sigma,\xi$ *) for the set of density attractors* $X$ *is a subset* $C \subseteq D$, *where*

*1.* $\forall p \in C, \exists p^* \in X : f^D(p^*) \geq \xi$, *p is density attracted to* $p^*$ *and*

2\. $\forall p_1^*, p_2^* \in C, \exists$ *a path* $P \subset F^k$ *from* $p_1^*$ *to* $p_2^*$ *with* $\forall p \in P : f^D(p) \leq \xi$.

The clusters and the members of a cluster can vary depending on the parameter $\sigma$ and $\xi$. A detailed discussion on how to choose proper parameters to achieve satisfactory clustering patterns of the dataset is given in [7].

## 2.2 Implementation Issues of DENCLUE

Based on the above ideas, DENCLUE employs the following strategies to fulfil its clustering algorithm.

Partition the data space $S$ into grids with equal width $2\sigma$ in each of the $k$ dimension and maps all the data points into proper grids. Further, the populated grids are mapped to a set of one-dimensional keys for fast allocation and retrieval.

Only grids that are highly populated are considered (with $N_c \geq \xi_c$ ). Those highly populated grids are connected depending on their neighboring contiguity to construct a grids map. The grids map with the points contained in it is the final dataset for the clustering, while the points in the sparse grids are ignored as outliers.

Practically, DENCLUE uses local density and gradient to approximate the global density and gradient by considering the influence of nearby points exactly whereas neglecting those laying farther then the distance threshold $\sigma_{near} = \lambda\sigma$. In the clustering procedure, a hill-climbing algorithm guided by the gradient is used to determine a point's density attractor and thus the cluster it belongs.

### 2.3 Comments

As addressed in section 1.1, DENCLUE inherits advantages both from grid partition and density consideration. It has a firm mathematical foundation and generalizes other clustering methods, such as DBSCAN, *k*-Means clusters. The algorithm is stable with respect to outliers and capable of finding arbitrarily shaped clusters. While no clustering algorithm could have less than $O(N)$ complexity, the runtime of DENCLUE scales sub-linearly with $O(N \log N)$.

However, the algorithm is still improvable for more efficiency or for larger datasets. Firstly, DENCLUE need to hold all of the original data to fulfil its clustering procedure. Thus, its behavior depends on the memory availability. For a large dataset that cannot fit into the main memory, swap in and swap out of the data objects can degrades its behavior sharply. Secondly, for each data object of the dataset, the algorithm has to compute its local density value by summing up all the influences of nearby objects with a point wise manner, whether those points are crowded together or distributed sparsely. It pays no attention to the statistical information of the grids around a data object. This negligence also complicates the algorithm markedly.

## 3 Mean Approximation and Error Adjustment

### 3.1 Key Ideas of Our Approach

The key idea of our paper is to take more advantages from the grid mechanism. We first take an overview of the basic considerations that inspired us to develop the adjusted mean approximation algorithm.

Because of the skewness of the dataset, the densities of the occupied grids are different. For a given threshold $\xi$ as in Definition 4, we can prove that all the objects in a "dense-enough " grid must belong to the same cluster. Thus, we can assign all points in such kind of "dense-enough" grids to certain clusters and free them from memory before the clustering procedure start. Instead, we keep a set of aggregate values about such kind of grid for the clustering phase.

The clustering procedure only handles the data objects not in "dense-enough" grids. But, dislike the method employed in DENCLUE which computes an object's density value by point-to-point summing up the influences from all of the data objects, our method computes an object's density function by a grid-to-point manner. For each data object, only one visit to each grid is enough to fulfill the approximated density computation, regardless how many points in the grid. Clearly, mean approximation can inevitably result in sacrifice of accuracy to the algorithm. However, we can prove that the error is well adjustable.

To fulfill our formal deduction, we need to assume that all the objects within a single grid distribute uniformly. We argue this local uniformity assumption is reasonable because, practically, the data space is always partitioned with a properly small edge-width.

### 3.2 Definitions and Main Results

**Definition 5. (Gravity Center of the Grid)** *Let* $C$ *be a grid occupied by* $N_C$ *data points* $p_i = (x_{i1},...,x_{ik})$, $i = 1,...,N_C$, *the gravity center* $G_C$ *of* $C$ *is defined by:*

$$G_C = (x_1^*,...,x_k^*) = (\frac{1}{N_C}\sum_{i=1}^{N_C} x_{i1},...,\frac{1}{N_C}\sum_{i=1}^{N_C} x_{ik}).$$

**Definition 6.** *Let* $C$ *be a grid with gravity center* $G_C$. $\forall q \in D$, *the influence and the mean influence of* $C$ *on to* $q$ *is defined by:*

$$f^C(q) = \sum_{i=1}^{N_C} f^{p_i}(q) = \sum_{i=1}^{N_C} e^{-\frac{d(q,p_i)^2}{2\sigma^2}}, \quad \tilde{f}^C(q) = N_C \cdot f^{G_C}(q) = N_c \cdot e^{-\frac{d(q,G_C)^2}{2\sigma^2}}.$$

**Theorem 1.** *Let* $\xi$ *be the threshold as defined in Definition 4 and* $\lambda\sigma$ *the edge-width of the grids. For a grid* $C$ *such that* $N_C \geq \xi\, e^{k\lambda^2/2}$, *then all the points in* $C$ *must belong to the same cluster.*

Proof. Since the length of the longest diagonal of a $\lambda\sigma$-width grid is $\sqrt{k}\lambda\sigma$ in a $k$-dimensional data space, thus, $\forall p,q \in C$, $d(p,q) \leq \sqrt{k}\lambda\sigma$. Therefore $\forall p \in C$, we have:

$$f^D(p) = \sum_{q\in D} f^q(p,q) \geq \sum_{q\in C} f^q(p) \geq N_C \cdot f(\sqrt{k}\lambda\sigma) \geq \xi\, e^{k\lambda^2/2} \cdot e^{-k\lambda^2/2} = \xi.$$

Let $p^*$ be the density attractor for $p$. Since $f^D(p^*)$ is the local maximum of the density function, therefore, $f^D(p^*) \geq f^D(p) \geq \xi$. Thus $p$ is a member point of the cluster attracted by $p^*$. Let $p' \in C$ and $p' \neq p$, $p'$ is attracted by attractor $p_1{}^*$. From Definition 3, $p'$, $p$ must belong to the same cluster because the density value at each point of $C$ is large than $\xi$.

The following theorems deal with error estimation of $\tilde{f}^C(q)$ with relate to $f^C(q)$ on a data point.

**Theorem 2.** *Let* $C = \{(x_1, x_2,...,x_k) \mid -\frac{1}{2}\lambda\sigma \leq x_j < \frac{1}{2}\lambda\sigma\}$ *be the* $k$*-dimensional grid centered at the origin of the data space* $S$, $P = \{p_1, p_2,..., p_n\}$ *be the partial set of dataset* $D$ *uniformly occupying* $C$ *and* $q = (y_1, y_2,..., y_k) \in S$ *be an arbitrary data point in* $S$. *We denote by* $Err(\lambda,n,k) \doteq \frac{\tilde{f}^C(q) - f^C(q)}{\tilde{f}^C(q)}$ *the relative error of* $\tilde{f}^C(q)$ *with relate to* $f^C(q)$. *Then* $Err(\lambda,k) = \lim_{n\to\infty} Err(\lambda,n,k) = 1 - (\frac{2\pi}{\lambda^2})^{\frac{k}{2}} \prod_{j=1}^{k} (F(\frac{\lambda}{2} - \frac{y_j}{\sigma}) - F(-\frac{\lambda}{2} - \frac{y_j}{\sigma}))\, e^{\frac{y_j^2}{2\sigma^2}}$.

Proof. With the pre-assumption that the data points distribute uniformly within grid $C$, the gravity center of the $n$ data objects must be the origin $o$. By the definition of $Err(\lambda,n,k)$, we have

$$\lim_{n\to\infty} Err(\lambda,n,k) = \lim_{n\to\infty} \frac{ne^{-d^2(0,q)/2\sigma^2} - \sum_{i=1}^{n} e^{-d^2(p_i,q)/2\sigma^2}}{ne^{-d^2(0,q)/2\sigma^2}}$$

$$= 1 - \lim_{n\to\infty} \frac{e^{d^2(0,q)/2\sigma^2}}{n} \sum_{i=1}^{n} e^{-d^2(p_i,q)/2\sigma^2}.$$

Again, with the property of uniformly distribution of the points in $C$, we can get

$$\lim_{n\to\infty}\frac{(\lambda\sigma)^k}{n}\cdot\sum_{i=1}^{n}e^{-d^2(p_i,q)/2\sigma^2}=\int\ldots\int_C e^{-d^2(p,q)/2\sigma^2}dX=\int\ldots\int_C e^{-\sum_{j=1}^{k}\frac{(x_j-y_j)^2}{2\sigma^2}}dx_1\ldots dx_k$$

$$=\prod_{j=1}^{k}\int_{-\frac{\lambda\sigma}{2}}^{\frac{\lambda\sigma}{2}}e^{\frac{(x_j-y_j)^2}{2\sigma^2}}dx_j\,.$$

Thus

$$\lim_{n\to\infty}\frac{1}{n}\sum_{i=1}^{n}e^{-\frac{d^2(q_i,q)}{2\sigma^2}}=(\frac{1}{\lambda\sigma})^k\prod_{j=1}^{k}\int_{-\frac{\lambda\sigma}{2}}^{\frac{\lambda\sigma}{2}}e^{-\frac{(x_j-y_j)^2}{2\sigma^2}}dx_j=(\frac{2\pi}{\lambda^2})^{\frac{k}{2}}\prod_{j=1}^{k}(F(\tfrac{\lambda}{2}-\tfrac{y_j}{\sigma})-F(-\tfrac{\lambda}{2}-\tfrac{y_j}{\sigma}))\,.$$

Therefore

$$Err(\lambda,k)=\lim_{n\to\infty}Err(\lambda,n,k)=1-(\frac{2\pi}{\lambda^2})^{\frac{k}{2}}\prod_{j=1}^{k}(F(\tfrac{\lambda}{2}-\tfrac{y_j}{\sigma})-F(-\tfrac{\lambda}{2}-\tfrac{y_j}{\sigma}))\,e^{\frac{y_j^2}{2\sigma^2}}$$

**Corollary 1.** *For any dimension k and any* $q\in S$, *we have* $\lim_{\lambda\to 0}Err(\lambda,k)=0$.

Proof. Since

$$\lim_{\lambda\to 0}\frac{\sqrt{2\pi}}{\lambda}(F(\tfrac{\lambda}{2}-\tfrac{y_j}{\sigma})-F(-\tfrac{\lambda}{2}-\tfrac{y_j}{\sigma}))\,e^{\frac{y_j^2}{2\sigma^2}}$$

$$=\lim_{\lambda\to 0}\frac{1}{\lambda}\int_{-\frac{\lambda}{2}-\frac{y_j}{\sigma}}^{\frac{\lambda}{2}-\frac{y_j}{\sigma}}e^{-\frac{x_j^2}{2}}dx_j\,e^{\frac{y_j^2}{2\sigma^2}}$$

$$=\lim_{\lambda\to 0}\frac{1}{2}(e^{-\frac{(\frac{\lambda}{2}-\frac{y_j}{\sigma})^2}{2}}+e^{-\frac{(\frac{\lambda}{2}+\frac{y_j}{\sigma})^2}{2}})\,e^{\frac{y_j^2}{2\sigma^2}}=1\,.$$

Therefore $\lim_{\lambda\to 0}Err(\lambda,k)=0$.

Clearly, for any fixed value of $\lambda$ and $k$, the values of both $\tilde{f}^C(q)$ and $f^C(q)$ decrease to 0 quickly as the point $q$ moving away from the cube $C$. On the other hand, if $q$ is at the gravity center of the data objects in grid $C$ (i.e., $q=0$), then we have the following important corollary.

**Corollary 2.** *Let* $q=0$ *and* $\lambda=\alpha k^{-\beta},\alpha,\beta>0$, *where k is the dimension of the dataset, then*

$$\lim_{k\to\infty}Err(\lambda,k)=\lim_{k\to\infty}Err(\alpha k^{-\beta},k)=\begin{cases}0, & \beta>\frac{1}{2}\\ 1-e^{-\alpha^2/24}, & \beta=\frac{1}{2}\\ 1, & \beta<\frac{1}{2}\end{cases}$$

Proof. Since $\lambda>0$, thus $2F(\frac{\lambda}{2})-1=\frac{2}{\sqrt{2\pi}}\int_{-\infty}^{\frac{\lambda}{2}}e^{-\frac{t^2}{2}}dt-1=\frac{2}{\sqrt{2\pi}}\int_{0}^{\frac{\lambda}{2}}e^{-\frac{t^2}{2}}dt$.

If $q=0,\lambda=\alpha k^{-\beta}$, then

$$Err(\alpha k^{-\beta},k)\;=1-\frac{(\sqrt{2\pi}(2F(\frac{\lambda}{2})-1))^k}{\lambda^k}=1-(\frac{2}{\alpha k^{-\beta}}\int_0^{\frac{\alpha k^{-\beta}}{2}}e^{-\frac{t^2}{2}}dt)^k=1-h(k)\,.$$

For the function $h(k)=(\frac{2}{\alpha k^{-\beta}}\int_0^{\frac{\alpha k^{-\beta}}{2}}e^{-\frac{t^2}{2}}dt)^k$, we have

$$Lim_{k\to\infty} \ln h(k) \overset{\gamma=k^{-1}}{=} Lim_{\gamma\to 0} \frac{-\beta\ln\gamma + \ln\int_0^{\frac{\alpha\gamma^\beta}{2}} e^{-\frac{t^2}{2}}dt}{\gamma}$$

$$= Lim_{\gamma\to 0} \frac{-4\alpha^2\beta(3\beta-1)\gamma^{2\beta-1} + \alpha^4\beta^2\gamma^{4\beta-1}}{16(1+\beta) - 4\alpha^2\beta\gamma^{2\beta}} = \begin{cases} 0, & \beta > 1/2 \\ -\alpha^2/24, & \beta = 1/2 \\ -\infty, & \beta < 1/2 \end{cases}$$

By now, it is easy to see that the theorem holds true with trivial deduction.

Corollary 2 depicts that if the width of the hypercube is chosen properly in relation with the dimension $k$, then the maximum of relative error $Err(\lambda,k)$ decreases steadily to zero ($\lambda=\alpha k^{-\beta}, \beta>1/2$) or asymptotically close to a constant value ($\lambda=\alpha k^{-\beta}$, $\beta=1/2$) as the dimension of the dataset getting higher. This property enables us to construct stable approximation of $f^C(q)$ by $\tilde{f}^C(q)$ regardless the dimension of the dataset.

Even though the results of theorem 2 and its corollaries only hold true under the "ideal" situation where the data points are uniformly distributed in grids, they are still valuable for us to approximate the value of $f^C(q)$ using $\tilde{f}^C(q)$ when the points in grids are arbitrarily distributed. Our experiment (see Section 6) validated the puniness of accuracy loss of the adjusted mean approximation. Below, we generalize the above results to any pair of hypercube $C$ and point $q$ as expressed in Theorem 3. We omit the proof for the reason of space limitation.

**Theorem 3.** *Let* $MBR_C = \{(x_1, x_2, ..., x_k) \mid x_j^{low} \le x_j < x_j^{upp}, x_j^{upp} - x_j^{low} \le \lambda\sigma\}$ *be the Minimum Bounding Rectangle (MBR) spanned by the partial data set* $P \subset D$ *in an arbitrary grid* $C$. *Let* $G_C = (x_1^*, ..., x_k^*)$ *be the gravity center of* $P$ *and* $q = (y_1, y_2, ..., y_k)$ *an arbitrary data point in data space* $S$. *Then*

$$\lim_{n\to\infty} Err(n,k) = 1 - (2\pi)^{\frac{k}{2}} \prod_{j=1}^{k} \frac{1}{x_j^{upp} - x_j^{low}} \left(F\left(\frac{x_j^{upp}-y_j}{\sigma}\right) - F\left(\frac{x_j^{low}-y_j}{\sigma}\right)\right) e^{\frac{(x_j^*-y_j)^2}{2\sigma^2}}$$

We call $\mu = (2\pi)^{\frac{k}{2}} \prod_{j=1}^{k} \frac{1}{x_j^{upp} - x_j^{low}} \left(F\left(\frac{x_j^{upp}-y_j}{\sigma}\right) - F\left(\frac{x_j^{low}-y_j}{\sigma}\right)\right) e^{\frac{(x_j^*-y_j)^2}{2\sigma^2}}$ ***the adjustment factor*** for the value of $\tilde{f}^C(q)$. Thus, the relation $\mu\tilde{f}^C(q) = f^C(q)$ holds true under the idealized situation where the data point is uniformly distributed in $MBR_C$ of $C$.

## 4 DENCLUE-M: An Algorithm Applying Mean Approximation on the Grids

### 4.1 Overview

Based on the results of section 3, we are ready to construct our mean approximated algorithm of DENCLUE. This section outlines the main steps of DENCLUE-M. Here the parameter $\lambda = k^{-1/2}$.

**Grid Partition:** In DENCLUE-M, the data space is partitioned with edge-width $\sigma / \sqrt{k}$ in each dimension, where $k$ is the dimension of the data space and $\sigma$ the parameter employed in the Gaussian influence function.
**Data Scanning:** In the data scanning phase, DENCLUE-M manages three groups of aggregate values for each of the grids: the counter $N_C$, the gravity-center $G_C$ and the $MBR_C$ (i.e., the lower and upper bound values of the partial dataset in $C$). DENCLUE-M drops all the points in a grid as soon as the value of $N_C$ exceeds the threshold addressed in Theorem 1 and links these points to a predefined cluster table.
**Data Clustering:** Similar mechanism as in DENCLUE is employed. The difference of DENCLUE-M is that all the computations are mean approximation based. That is, for each point $q \in D$ being clustered, we compute $\sum_C \mu_c \tilde{f}^C(q)$ instead of $\sum_{p \in D} f(q,p)$ for the density value and $\sum_C (X^* - q)\mu_c \tilde{f}^C(q)$ instead of $\sum_{p \in D} (p-q) f^p(q)$ for the gradient at point $q$.

## 4.2 The Algorithm of DENCLUE-M

**Input:** Dataset $D$, parameter $\sigma, \xi$
**Output:** Cluster pattern of dataset $D$
**Phase 1. Data Scanning and Information Gathering**

```
Procedure scanning_and_Information_Gathering
  {For each point q, do {
     Maps q to a proper grid C, updates Nc, Gc and MBRc;
     If Nc< ξ e^{1/2} then inserts q into the tree node
        corresponding to C;
     Else links q and all points in C to corresponding
  Cluster
        and frees all points in C, marks C as Dense; }}
```

**Phase 2. Clustering**

```
Procedure scanning_and_Information_Gathering
  {For each populated grid C not marked as Dense, do {
      For each point q in C, do {
         Computes the value of Σ_C μc f~^C(q) and
  Σ_C (X* - q)μc f~^C(q) at
           q and seeks its density attractor.
         If Σ_C μc f~^C(X*) < ξ , marks q and all the points on
  the
           way of seeking X' as outliers;
         Else links q and all the points on the way of
  seeking
           X' to the cluster attracted by X'. }}}
```

**Remarks:** (1) Localization of the algorithm can be implemented easily just as in DENCLUE. (2) For each of the grids marked as *Dense* in data scanning phase, merge all the contiguous grids and chooses the gravity center of the points in it as the density attractor. By doing so, the hill climbing procedure can be done seamlessly among all the populated grids.

## 5 The Complexity of DENCLUE-M

As discussed in [7], the clustering granularity of DENCLUE-M also depends on the two thresholds $\xi$ and $\sigma$. Generally, the larger the value of $\xi$, the more the points filtered out as outliers and the smaller the cluster patterns. On the other hand, for fixed value of $\xi$, the larger the value of $\sigma$, the bigger the influence of one point to the other. Accordingly, the more the points linked to the clusters and less the outliers found. We refer to [7] for detailed discussion on this aspect of the DENCLUE-M.

DENCLUE-M has an overall complexity of $O(N + MM_0\xi\sqrt{e})$, where $N = |D|$, $M$ is the total number of populated grids and $M_0$ the number of grids that have the population under $\xi\sqrt{e}$. In the scanning phase, handling all the $N$ data points has the complexity of $O(N)$. In the clustering phase, only the $M_0\xi\sqrt{e}$ points in $M_0$ grids need to be handled. This phase needs at most $M$ visit to all the populated grids to compute the density value and gradient for each of the point. Thus, it has the complexity of $O(MM_0\xi\sqrt{e})$ and the overall complexity of DENCLUE-M is $O(N + MM_0\xi\sqrt{e})$. The worst case happens when none grid has the population above $\xi\sqrt{e}$, such that $M_0\xi\sqrt{e} = N$ and the complexity of DENCLUE-M become $O((M+1)N)$.

On the other hand, DENCLUE-M's dynamical data releasing strategy enables the algorithm to treat much larger dataset. In fact, the maximum memory usage for DENCLUE-M to hold the data objects in "sparse" grids is $O(M_0\xi\sqrt{e})$, which is independent to the scale of the dataset.

However, DENCLUE-M still has shortcomings in that: (1) It's behavior still depends on the proper choice of the parameters $\xi$ and $\sigma$. (2) For an extraordinary high dimensional dataset that has hundreds of attributes, the partitioned data space may have too many sparsely occupied grids for DENCLUE-M to cluster the dataset effectively. However, High dimensionality challenges all the clustering algorithms that need far more research effort [3,5].

## 6 Performance Results

To investigate how the mean approximation affects the density function, we designed and ran three sets of experiments on synthetic and real world datasets.

The first experiment dealt with a 2-D dataset on the square $[0,20]\times[0,20]$, which contained 400 data objects jointly generated by normal, Poisson and random generators (See Figure 1(a)). The square was partitioned with $\sigma = 0.5$ on both dimensions.

Figure 1(b) and 1(c) indicate the Gaussian density function of the origin dataset and the mean approximated density function respectively. Doubtless, the right two figures are almost identical over the square. We further clustered the dataset with both DENCLUE and DENCLUE-M under same pairs of $\xi$ and $\sigma$, the output cluster patterns ware identical in all the runs. The results of this experiment prove the applicability of our mean approximation approach.

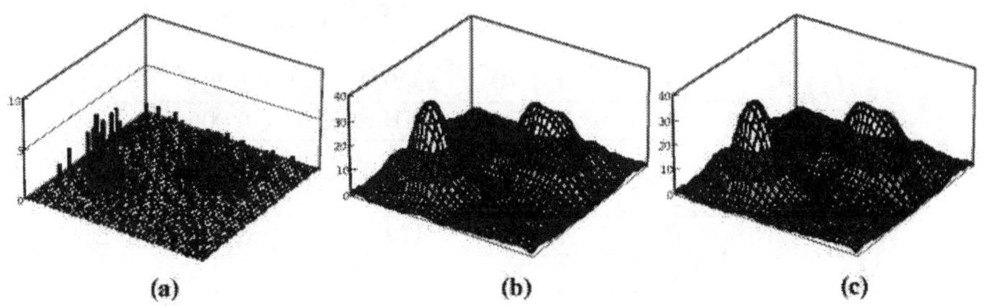

**Fig. 1.** Mean Approximation on 2-D dataset. (a) Distribution of the objects. (b) Density function of the original dataset (i.e. $\sum_{p\in D} f(q,p)$ ). (c) Mean approximated density function (i.e. $\sum_C \mu_c \tilde{f}^C(q)$ )

The second experiment evaluated the error introduced by mean approximation. A single grid of $Width = 0.5$ with varied dimensions ( $k = 2,10,50$ respectively ) occupied by different number of points ( $N_c$ ) along with a point from different distances $d(q,G_c)$ was used.

Table 1 listed the absolute error ( $a.e. = \mu_c \tilde{f}^C(q) - f^C(q)$ ) and the relative error ( $r.e. = (\mu_c \tilde{f}^C(q) - f^C(q)) / f^C(q)$ ) of the different runs. The results show that: (1) When $d(q,G_C)$ is small (here $d(q,G_C)$ =0), then the relative error is minor. For a point $q$ far away from the grid, the error is still ignorable since the minority of the absolute value. (2) The accuracy of the adjusted mean values on crowded grids ( $N_C$ =100,500) are better than that on the sparse grids. (3) The approximation accuracy is still acceptable even for the high dimensional data space ( $k = 50$ )

The third experiment tested time efficiency of DENCLUE-M contrast to DENCLUE. The data used was the Forest Cover Type Dataset from the UCI KDD achieve consisting of 581,012 rows of records with 55 attributes. The reconstructed dataset contains the first three normalized numerical attributes (elevation, aspect and slope) along with the attribute of tree cover type. The value of $\sigma$ was set to 0.002 for the Gaussian influence function. In each run, the same value of $\xi$ was chosen for both DENCLUE-M and DENCLUE such that they can produce the same cluster results. However, in DENCLUE-M, the data space had to be partitioned with edge-width = 0.01 in relation with the chosen value of $\sigma$.

**Table 1.** Absolute and relative error under different grid density and point-to-grid distance

| $k$ | $N_C$ | $d(q,G_C)$ | $\mu_c\tilde{f}^C(q)$ | $f^C(q)$ | $a.e.$ | $r.e.$ |
|---|---|---|---|---|---|---|
| 2 | 5 | 0 | 4.836 | 4.796 | 0.04 | 0.8 % |
| | | 2 | 0.0023 | 0.001 | 0.0004 | 21% |
| | 500 | 0 | 460.54 | 460.6 | -0.07 | -0.01% |
| | | 2 | 0.263 | 0.275 | -0.012 | -4.3 % |
| 10 | 10 | 0 | 3.837 | 3.632 | 0.205 | 5 % |
| | | 2 | ≈ 0 | ≈ 0 | - | - |
| | 500 | 0 | 331.70 | 329.9 | 1.709 | 0.5 % |
| | | 2 | 0.1896 | 0.196 | -0.006 | -3.3 % |
| 50 | 5 | 0 | 1.24 | 1.16 | 0.08 | 6.8 % |
| | | 2 | ≈ 0 | ≈ 0 | - | - |
| | 100 | 0 | 13.042 | 12.67 | 0.368 | 2.9 % |
| | | 2 | ≈ 0 | ≈ 0 | - | - |

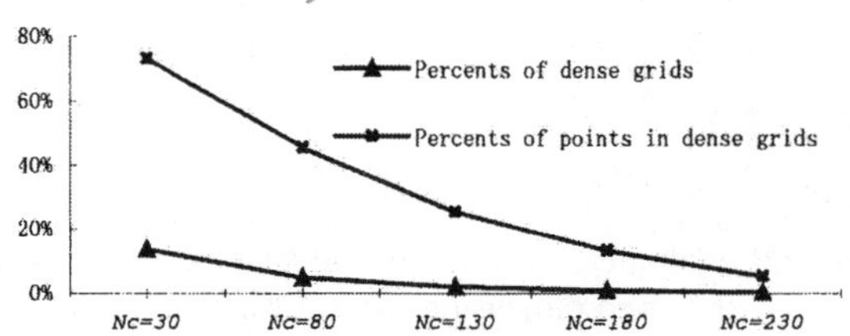


**Fig. 2.** Percents of dense grids and data objects occupied under different density thresholds.

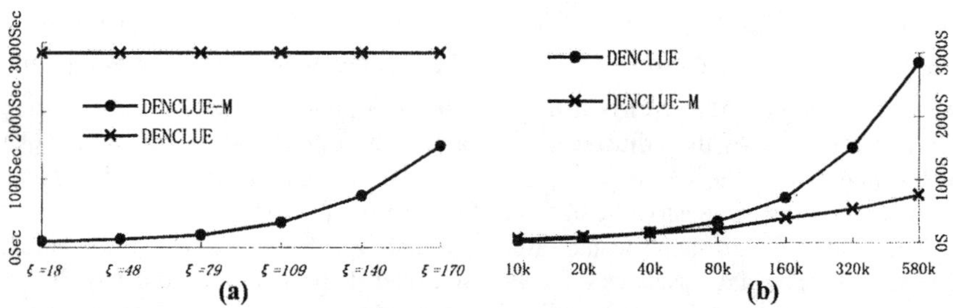


**Fig. 3.** (a) Time usage comparison between DENCLUE and DENCLUE-M on computation of the density values under different thresholds. (b) Comparison of time usage of the computation under different dataset size.

Figure 2 shows percents of dense grids and data objects occupied them under different density thresholds ( $N_C = \sqrt{e}\xi$ from 30 to 230). Figure 3(a) indicates the times used by DENCLUE and DENCLUE-M to process density function computation with locality = 0.08 under varied density threshold $\xi$ (i.e., time to compute $\sum_{d(p,q)<0.08} f^{p}(q)$ and $\sum_{d(X_C^*,q)<0.08} \mu_C \tilde{f}^{C}(q)$ respectively). Figure 3(b) shows the times used by both algorithms to process the same computation on partial dataset ($N=10000$ up to 581012, $\xi=100$). This experiment speaks well for DENCLUE-M's ability of mass object filtering and computation strength relieving.

## 7 Conclusion

Recently, the identification of clustering as a central task in Data Mining has attracted researchers to investigate the scaling of clustering methods to large datasets. The key concerns of scaling are memory usage reduction and time efficiency boosting. This paper focus on the effects of mean approximation to construct a density-based, grid-level-approximated clustering algorithms. We analyze the error introduced by this kind of proximity mathematically and present results of extensive experiments that show its properties of high capability, minor loss of accuracy. Due to the promising performance, we believe our approach is reasonable and applicable in dealing with the problem.

## References


1. Han, J., Kamber, M.: Data Mining: Concepts and Techniques. Morgan Kaufmann Publishers, 335–398 (2000)
2. Jain, A. K., Murty, M. N., Flynn, P. J.: Data Clustering: A Review. ACM Computing Surveys, 31(3), (1999) 264--323
3. Hinneburg, A., Keim, D.A.,: Optimal Gird-Clustering: Towards Breaking the Curse of Dimensionality in High-Dimensional Clustering, In Proc. Of the 25th VLDB Conf., Edinburgh, Scotland (1999)
4. Sheikholeslami, G., Chatterjee, S., Zhang, A.: Wave-Cluster: A Mlti-Resolution Clustering Approach for Very Large Spatial Databases. In Proc. 24th VLDB Conf., (1998) 428–439, New York
5. Aggrawal, R., Gehrke, J., Raghawan, D. P.: Automatic Subspace Clustering of High Dimensional Data for Data Mining Applications. In Proc. ACM SIGMOD Int. Conf. On Management of Data , Seattle, WA, (1998) 94–105
6. Wang, W., Yang, J., Muntz, R.: STING, A Statistical Information Grid Approach to Spatial Data Mining. In Proc. 23rd VLDB Conf., Athens, Greece, (1998) 186–195
7. Hinneburg, A., Keim, D.A.: An efficient approach to clustering in large multimedia databases with noise. In Proc. 1998 Int. Conf. Knowledge Discovery and Data Mining (KDD'98), New York, (1998) 58–65
8. Scott, D.: Multivariate Density Estimation. Wiley and Sons (1992)
9. Berchtold, S., Keim, D., Kriegel, H.P.: The X-tree: An Index Structure for High- Dimensional Data. In Proc. Int. Conf. on Very Large Databases, (1996) 28–39

# A New Fast Clustering Algorithm Based on Reference and Density*

Shuai Ma[1], TengJiao Wang[1], ShiWei Tang[1,2], DongQing Yang[1], and Jun Gao[1]

[1] Department of Computer Science, Peking University, Beijing 100871, China
{mashuai, tjwang, gaojun}@db.pku.edu.cn
http://www.pku.edu.cn

[2] National Laboratory on Machine Perception, Peking University, Beijing 100871, China
{tsw,dqyang}@pku.edu.cn

**Abstract.** Density-based clustering is a sort of clustering analysis methods, which can discover clusters with arbitrary shape and is insensitive to noise data. The efficiency of data mining algorithms is strongly needed with data becoming larger and larger. In this paper, we present a new fast clustering algorithm called CURD, which means Clustering Using References and Density. Its creativity is capturing the shape and extent of a cluster with references, and then it analyzes the data based on the references. CURD preserves the ability of density based clustering method's good advantages, and it is much efficient because of its nearly linear time complexity, so it can be used in mining very large databases. Both our theoretic analysis and experimental results confirm that CURD can discover clusters with arbitrary shape and is insensitive to noise data; In the meanwhile, its executing efficiency is much higher than R*-tree based DBSCAN algorithm.

## 1 Introduction and Related Work

Clustering analysis is the process of grouping a set of physical or abstract objects into clusters of similar objects. A cluster is a collection of data objects that are similar to one another within the same cluster and are dissimilar to the objects in other clusters [1]. Clustering analysis can be used as a stand-alone tool to get insight into data distribution or as a preprocessing step for other data mining algorithms. It is used in many diversified applications such as image compression, market segmentation, and spatial discovery. Clustering is also a challenging field of research where its potential applications pose their own special requirements. The following are typical requirements of clustering in data mining: scalability, ability to deal with different types of attributes, discovery of clusters with arbitrary shape, minimal requirement for domain knowledge

* Supported by the National High Technology Development 863 Program of China under Grant No. 2002AA4Z3440; the Foundation of the innovation research institute of PKU-IBM; the National Grand Fundamental Research 973 Program of China under Grant No. G1999032705.

G. Dong et al. (Eds.): WAIM 2003, LNCS 2762, pp. 214–225, 2003.

to determine input parameters, ability to deal with noisy data, insensitive to the order of input data, high dimensionality, constraint-based clustering, interpretability and usability [1]. A number of different algorithms have been proposed, such as K-MEANS, DBSCAN, BIRCH, CURE, CLIQUE, MAFIA, OPTIGRID, ROCK, CHAMELEON, AMOEBA and $C^2P$ [2-12]. All these algorithms attempt to overcome one or some requirements mentioned above through different approaches, but most of these algorithms cannot reach perfect results. Clustering large and high dimensional data is still an open problem.

K-MEANS is a partitioning clustering algorithm, which takes the input parameter, k, and partitions a set of n objects into k clusters so that the resulting intra-cluster similarity is high but the inter-cluster similarity is low. The algorithm attempts to determine k partitions that minimize a certain criterion function. Typically the square-error criterion is used. The time complexity of K-MEANS is $O(tkn)$, where n is the number of objects, k is the number of clusters, and t is the number of iterations. Normally k, t<<n, so it is scalable and efficient in processing large data sets. However K-MEANS have some disadvantages: the users need to specify k, the number of clusters, which is hard to decide in advance; the selection of k initial objects has great effect on the final clustering result and algorithm's efficiency; the partition based clustering algorithms could split large clusters to minimize the square-error [5].

CURE is a bottom-up hierarchical clustering algorithm, which starts by placing each object in its own cluster and then merges similar atomic clusters into larger and larger clusters, until the number of clusters is k. At each step, the pair of clusters merged are the ones between which the distance is the minimum. CURE points out that neither the centroid-based approach nor the all points approach works well for non-spherical or arbitrary shaped clusters, so CURE adopts a middle-ground between the centroid and the all points extremes. CURE chooses a constant number c of well-scattered points in a cluster, which capture the shape and extent of the clusters, thus the ability of processing arbitrary clusters is improved. The time complexity of CURE is $O(n^2)$ for low dimensional data, and $O(n^2 logn)$ for high dimensional data, so CURE adopts random sampling and partitioning technologies in order to process large data sets.

DBSCAN is a density based clustering algorithm, which grows regions with sufficiently high density into clusters and defines a cluster as a maximal set of density-connected points. DBSCAN discovers clusters with arbitrary shape with noise and is insensitive to the order of input data. The time complexity of DBSCAN is $O(n^2)$; with the support of spatial access methods such as R*-tree its time complexity reduces to $O(nlogn)$. We should point out that DBSCAN does not consider the time of establishing R*-tree, which often consumes a lot of time.

CLIQUE is a grid and density based clustering algorithm, which has the fastness of grid-based approaches and the ability to process high dimension data. CLIQUE considers little about the distribution of data when partitioning data into grid cells and uses the statistical information stored in the grid cells, so the clustering quality is lowered.

In this paper we propose a new fast clustering algorithm named CURD (Clustering Using Reference and Density). The remainder of the paper is organized as follows. In section 2, we present CURD algorithm. In section 3, we analyze the performance from different points of view. Discussion remarks and future work are made in section 4.

## 2 CURD Algorithm

CURD algorithm is first motivated by CURE algorithm, and it uses references to correctly represent the shape and extent of a cluster. References are not real input points, but virtual points, which are different from the represents of CURE. In addition, the number of references used to represent a cluster is not constant, which is more reasonable than using fixed number as CURE. CURD algorithm takes the density approach, similar to DBSCAN, to eliminate the effect of noise data. The time complexity of CURD is approximately equal to K-MEANS's, so its efficiency is very high. The references of CURD consider much about the spatial geometric feature of data, thus the clustering quality is higher than grid-based clustering algorithms. High dimensional data can be transformed into one single dimension space based on distance [13,14], so CURD can process high dimensional data from this point. The distance computation of high dimensional data is the same as 2 dimensional data, so we use Euclidean distance and 2 dimensional spaces to analyze CURD algorithm.

### 2.1 Definitions

Definition 1: (density of point) Given a point p and a distance dRadius, the number of points in the circular region, where p is the center and dRadius is the radius, is called the density of p based on distance dRadius, denoted by Density(p,dRadius).

Definition 2: (reference) Given a point p, a distance dRadius and a threshold t, if Density(p,dRadius)$\geq$t, p is called a reference, and t is called the density threshold.

References are not real points in input data, but virtual points.

Definition 3: (representing region) Each reference p represents a circular region, where p is the center and dRadius is the radius. The region is called p's representing region.

Definition 4: (neighboring references) Points p and q are references based on distance dRadius and density threshold t, if Dist(p,q)$\leq$2dRadius, which represents the distance between p and q is equal to or less than 2 times of dRadius, p and q are called neighboring references.

In fact if the representing circular regions of the two references are tangent, intersectant or equal to each other, the two references are neighboring references.

### 2.2 Clustering Algorithm

Now we describe the details of our clustering algorithm. CURD first finds the references which can correctly represents the shape and extent of input data; then it establishes the mapping between points and corresponding references; the references are then classified, and the references in the same class contains the basic information of a cluster; points are mapped to the corresponding clusters at last. Fig. 1. gives an overview of CURD algorithm.

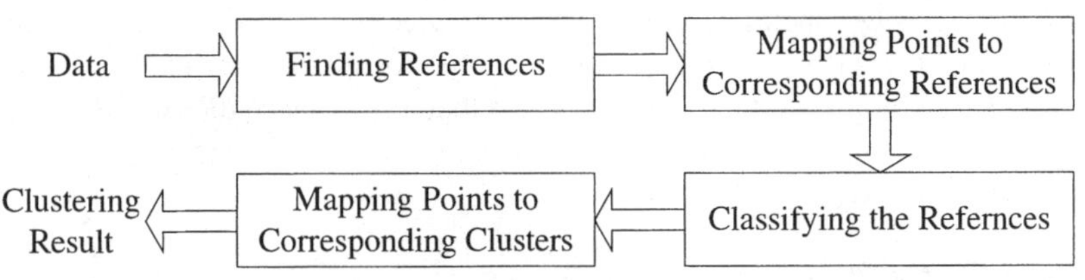


**Fig. 1.** Overview of CURD

### 2.2.1 Data Structure

For the importance of references, we first describe the data structure of references. Each reference record contains four kinds of data: $X_m$ and $Y_m$, which is the reference's X coordinate and Y coordinate; $X_s$ and $Y_s$, which is the sum of X coordinate and Y coordinate of all the points within the reference's representing region; $N_s$, which is the density of the reference or the number of points in the reference's representing region; the point set $P_s$, which is the set of all the points within the reference's representing region.

### 2.2.2 Finding References Procedure

Finding references procedure is divided into two steps: candidate references are found in the first step; the candidate references whose density is lower than the density threshold are filtered in the second step, and the remaining candidate references are real references. Filtering candidate references is very simple, so we mainly describe the procedure of finding candidate references (Prog. 1.). The Prog. 1. shows us that Finding_Candidate_References procedure iteratively calls Single_Scan procedure and Regenerate_Candidate_References procedure, thus we will describe them firstly.

**Prog. 1.** Program of Finding_Candidate_References Procedure

```
Finding_Candidate_References(PointSet,dRadius,Iterate)
 {Input:data set:PointSet,distance:dRadius,number of
 iterative times:Iterate;
 Output:candidate reference set:CandidateReferenceSet};
 begin
   CandidateReferenceSet := ∅; I := 0;
   repeat
     I :=I + 1;
     Single_Scan(PointSet,dRadius,CandidateReference-
     Set);
     Regenerate_Candidate_References(CandidateRefere-
     nceSet);
   until I = Iterate;
   Single_Scan(PointSet,dRadius,CandidateReferenceSet);
end.
```

Each call of Single_Scan procedure produces new candidate reference set, and its main operation is adding point p's information to the corresponding candidate reference. If the distances between p and all candidate references are larger than the distance dRadius, a new candidate reference is generated and added into the candidate references set; otherwise p's information is added to all the candidate references, whose distances with p are either equal to or less than the distance dRadius (Prog. 2.).

**Prog. 2.** Program of Single_Scan Procedure

```
Single_Scan(PointSet,dRadius,CandidateReferenceSet)
 {Input: data set: PointSet, distance: dRadius,
 candidate reference set: CandidateReferenceSet;
 OutPut:candidate reference set:CandidateReferenceSet};
 begin
   I := 0;
   repeat
     I := I + 1;
     For each candidate referenct R, whose distance
     with Pi is equal to or less than dRadius
     {Adding Pi's information to every candidate re-
     ference R}
       R.Xs := R.Xs + Pi.X;
       R.Ys := R.Ys + Pi.Y; R.Ns := R.Ns + 1;
     If the distances between Pi and all candidate
     references are larger than dRadius then
       begin
         Generated a new candidate reference R;
         R.Xm := Pi.X; R.Ym := Pi.Y;
         R.Xs := Pi.X; R.Ys := Pi.Y; R.Ns := 1;
         CandidateReferenceSet := CandidateReference-
         Set + {R};
       end;
   until I = PointSet.Size;
   Single_Scan(PointSet,dRadius,CandidateReferenceSet);
end.
```

Each call of Regenerate_Candidate_References procedure produces new candidate references. The mean of all the points in the representing region of a candidate reference replaces the candidate reference itself. Since the sum of X coordinate and Y coordinate of all the points in the references' representing region and the number of points in the references' representing region have been computed and stored in the Single_Scan procedure, the computation of the new candidate reference R′ of each candidate R is very simple, where $R'.X_m=R.X_s/R.N_s$, $R'.Y_m=R.Y_s/R.N_s$, $R'.X_s=0$, $R'.Y_s=0$, $R'.N_s=0$.

Finding_Candidate_References procedure iteratively calls Single_Scan procedure and Regenerate_ Candidate_References procedure, and each call of them is prone to generate candidate references that can better represent the shape and extent of input data. Through a series of optimization the final candidate references can coarsely represent the spatial geometric feature of input data. The candidate references are then filtered, and the candidate references whose densities are lower than the density threshold are removed. By this way the effect of noise data can be effectively eliminated, thus the references can quite correctly represent the spatial geometric feature of input data.

### 2.2.3 Mapping Points to Corresponging References

**Lemma 1.** In CURD, mapping point p to which reference has no effect on the final clustering result, only if the distance between p and the reference is equal to or less than dRadius.

**Proof:** Suppose there exist two references R1 and R2, and the distances between p and them are either equal to or less than dRadius. From the famous theorem of triangles: one side's length is less than the sum of the other two sides' length, it is easy to know that the distance between R1 and R2 is less than 2 times of dRadius, so R1 and R2 are neighboring references (left part of Fig. 2.). In high dimensional space, any three points that are not in the same line form a plane, so the theorem of triangles still works. In the special case, point p, references R1 and R2 are in the same line (right part of Fig. 2.), it is easy to known that the distance between R1 and R2 is equal to or less than two times of dRadius, so R1 and R2 are still neighboring references. In CURD algorithm, neighboring references contain the basic information of a cluster, and data belonging to the neighboring references are in the same cluster, thus either mapping p to R1 or R2, p belongs to the same cluster.

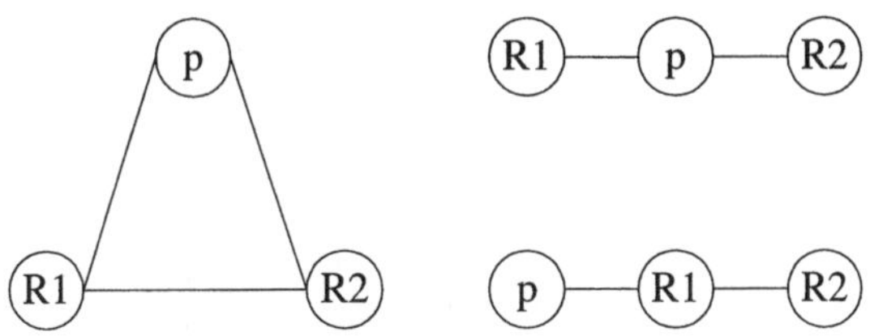


**Fig. 2.** Relative positions of p and R1, R2

Mapping_References_and_Points procedure establishes the mapping between references and the points within their corresponding representing regions. Theoretically, mapping point p to the reference that is closest to it is more reasonable. From Lemma 1, we know that mapping point p to which reference has no effect on the final clustering result, only if the distance between p and the reference is equal to or less than dRadius. Mapping_References_and_Points procedure orderly computes the distances between point p and the references, and if there exists a reference whose distance with p is equal to or less than dRadius, the mapping between p and the reference is established. After that, Mapping_References_and_Points procedure continues to process the next point. By that way, the algorithm's efficiency is improved (Prog. 3.).

**Prog. 3.** Program of Mapping_References_and_Points Procedure

```
Mapping_References_and_Points(PointSet,ReferenceSet,t,
dRadius)
```

```
{Input: data set: PointSet, reference set: Reference-
Set, density threshold: t, distance: dRadius;
OutPut: reference set: ReferenceSet};
begin
  For each reference R in ReferenceSet
  R.Ps := Ø;
  I := 0;
  repeat
    I :=I + 1;
    If the distance between Pi and some reference R
    is equal to or less than dRadius then
      R.Ps := R.Ps + {Pi};
    else if the distances between Pi and all the ref-
    erences are larger than dRadius then
      Pi is considered as noise and is discarded
  until I = PointSet.Size;
end.
```

### 2.2.4 Classifying the References

Given a reference set based on distance dRadius and threshold t, and if the distance between reference $R_1$ and $R_2$ is equal to or less than 2 times of dRadius, $R_1$ and $R_2$ are neighboring references. We can describe the reference set with an undirected graph, where the reference is vertex, and any two neighboring references form an edge. The references that are in the same connected sub-graph form a class.

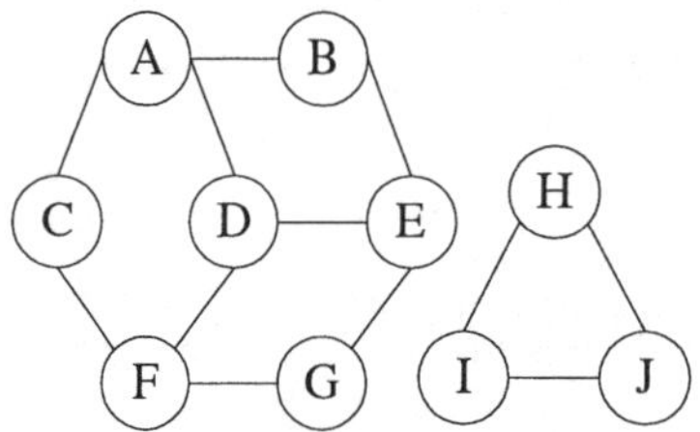


**Fig. 3.** Graph G

For example, {A, B, C, D, E, F, G} are the vertexes in the same connected sub-graph of graph G, so they form a class $C_1$={A, B, C, D, E, F, G}; {H, I, J} are also the vertexes in the same connected sub graph, so they form another class $C_2$={H, I, J} (Fig. 3.). It is easy to find the vertexes that are in the same connected subgraph through the graph's broad first search algorithm (BFS), so we do not describe the details of classifying the references. The references in a class contain the basic information of a cluster, and they correctly represent the spatial geometric feature of the clusters.

### 2.2.5 Mapping Points to Corresponding Clusters

The mapping $f_{points2references}$ between the points and the references has been established, and the procedure of classifying the references has established the mapping $f_{references2classes}$ between the references and the classes. The data belonging to the references, which are in the same class, form a cluster, so the mapping $f_{\text{points2clusters}}$ between the points and the clusters is very simple: $f_{\text{points2clusters}} = f_{\text{points2references}} \cdot f_{\text{references2classes}}$.

### 2.2.6 Time and Space Complexity

Suppose the number of input data is *n*, the maximum number of candidate references in the procedure of finding candidate references is *k*, the iterative number is *i*, the number of references is *m* and the number of clusters is *c*.

It is easy to know that the time complexity of Single_Scan procedure is O(*kn*) and the complexity of Regenerate_Candidate_References procedure is O(*k*), so the time complexity of Finding_Candidate _References procedure is O(*ikn+(i-1)k*); Filtering candidate references need O(*k*) time. Thus the time complexity of finding references procedure is O(*ikn+(i-1)k*)+O(*k*). Every point could find its corresponding references in time O(*m*), so mapping points to corresponging references procedure needs O(*mn*) time. The classification of references needs $O(m^2)$ time using graph's breadth first search algorithm (BFS). In fact the mapping between data and corresponding clusters has been established after the classification of references. From the above analysis, we know the time complexity of CURD algorithm is $O(ikn+(i-1)k)+O(k)+O(mn)+O(m^2)$, Normally $k,i,m << n$, so the time complexity approximately equals to O(*ikn+mn*), which has almost the same time complexity as K-MEANS.

The space complexity of CURD is O(*n*)+O(*k*)+O(*c*).

## 3 Performance Analysis

In this section, we evaluate the performance of CURD. We experimented three data sets containing points in 2 dimensions (Fig. 4.). DS1 comes from the Data set 1 of CURE; DS2 comes from database 3 of DBSCAN; we use the DBSCAN program that Dr. Jörg Sander provides to generate DS3, which is similar to the database 2 of DBSCAN. The data sizes are respectively 100000, 203 and 306.

All experiments are run on IBM Netfinity 5500: two X86 Family 6 Model 10 Stepping 1 GenuineIntel~700Mhz CPU, 512M main memory and 20G hard disk; the operation system is Microsoft Windows 2000 Server.

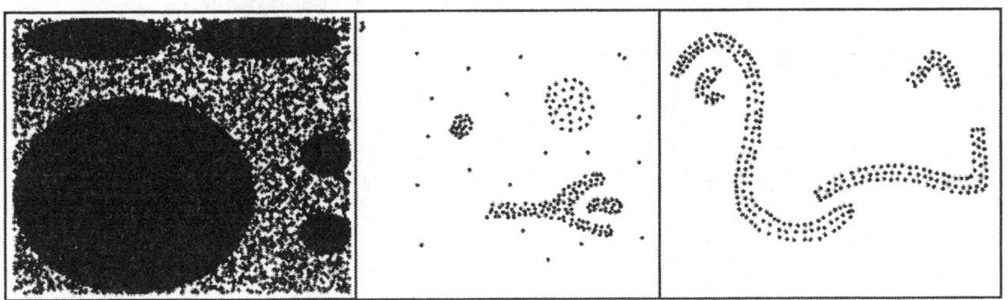

**Fig. 4.** Data sets

### 3.1 Comparison of Clustering Quality

Both CURD and DBSCAN are density based clustering algorithms; in the meanwhile the input parameters dRadius and t of CURD are similar to the input parameters of Eps and MinPts of DBSCAN, so we choose DBSCAN to compare the clustering quality with CURD.

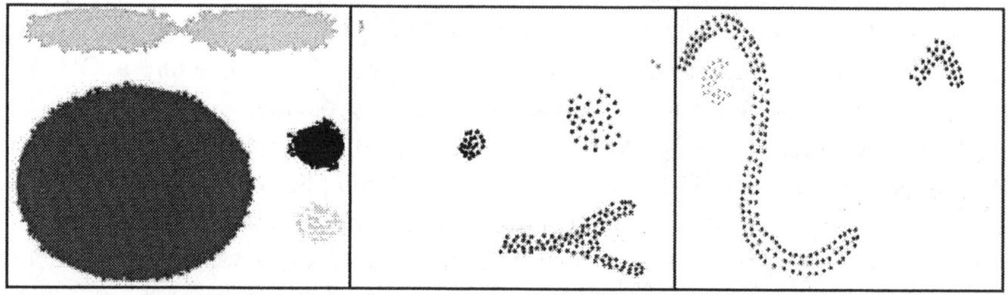

**Fig. 5.** Clustering results of DBSCAN, with the corresponding parameter Eps and MinPts are (0.5,6), (2,2), and (2,2) respectively

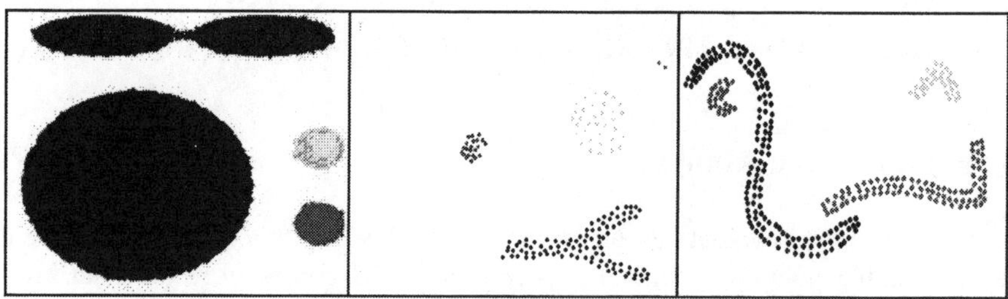

**Fig. 6.** Clustering results of CURD, with the corresponding parameter Radius and t are (0.5,60), (2,2), and (2,2) respectively

Fig. 6. shows the clustering results of CURD, from which we can see that CURD can effectively process clusters with arbitrary shape and is insensitive to noise data. Fig. 5. shows the clustering results of DBSCAN, from which we can see that the clustering results of DBSCAN and CURD are very similar to each other.

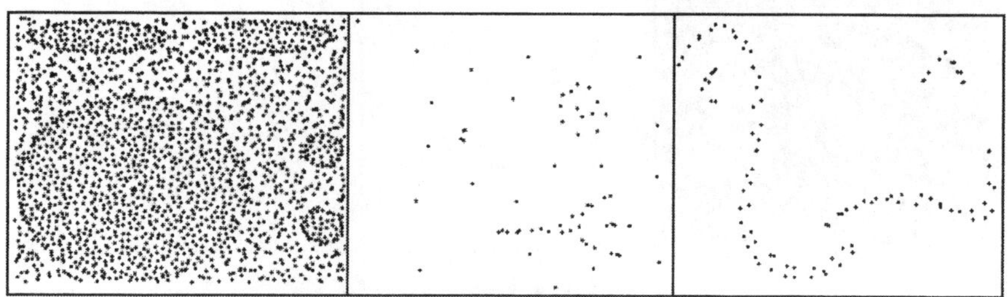

**Fig. 7.** Candidate references

### 3.2 Candidate References and References

Fig. 7. and Fig. 8. show the candidate references and references of DS1, DS2 and DS3. Fig. 7. shows that candidate references coarsely represent the spatial geometric feature of data set, but it is affected by the noise. In Fig. 8., the references correctly represent the spatial geometric feature of data set by filtering interferential candidate references whose density is lower than the density threshold.

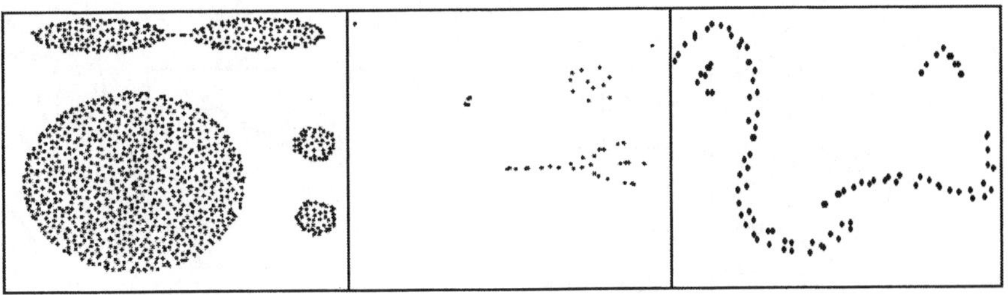

**Fig. 8.** References

### 3.3 Sensitive to Parameters

CURD has three main parameters: distance dRadius, density threshold t, and iterative times of Iterate. The values of the three parameters have effects on the clustering result and executing efficiency of CURD. In our experiments, we found that the CURD's clustering results are similar to DBSCAN's if the values of dRadius and t are the same as the values of Eps and MinPts respectively. In DBSCAN it is hard to determine the values of Eps and MinPts, but in CURD, we can set the values of dRadius and t easily. CURD generates better results if the value of dRadius equals to 1/50~1/100 of the whole data space. For example, DS1 is a 30X30 two dimensional data space, so the value of dRadius is set to 0.5; DS2 and DS3 are 100X100 two dimensional data space, so the value of dRadius is set to 2. The density threshold t can be set to the mean value of all candidate references' density, which can be computed automatically. As to the parameter Iterate, we should point out that all our experimental results are generated with the value of Iterate equal to 4. The bigger the values of Iterate, the better the clustering results, but longer the executing time.

### 3.4 Comparison of Executing Time with DBSCAN

There are mainly three reasons why we choose traditional R*-tree based DBSCAN algorithm to compare with CURD, which are as follows:

The two algorithms are both density based clustering algorithms;

Their key input parameters are similar to each other;

The time complexity of R*-tree based DBSCAN algorithm is O(*nlogn*), so it is already a very fast clustering algorithms.

Fig. 9. shows that the CURD's executing efficiency is much higher than DBSCAN's, so CURD is a very efficient clustering algorithm. In addition, R*-tree based DBSCAN algorithm need the support of R*-tree index, which needs much time to be established, so if the time of establishing index is considered, CURD is much more efficient than DBSCAN.

Fig. 10. shows that the executing details of CURD. Finding reference and mapping points to the corresponding references take most part of the executing time, especially finding references. Once mapping points to their corresponding references has been finished, CURD only takes little time to process the rest work.

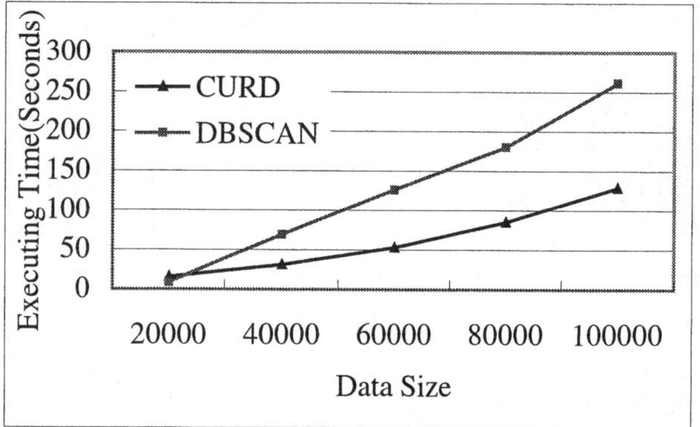


**Fig. 9.** Comparison of executing time

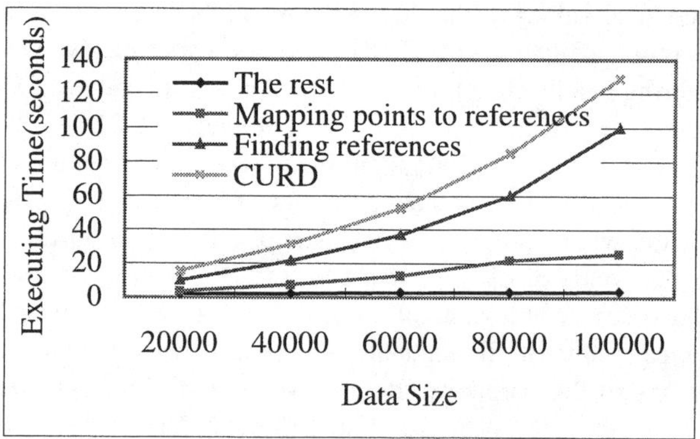


**Fig. 10.** Executing time details

## 4 Discussion and Future Work

In this paper, we propose a new method (using references) to represent the spatial geometric feature of data space, and we present a new fast clustering algorithm based on references and density. CURD not only preserves the advantages of density based clustering algorithms, which can discover clusters with arbitrary shape and is insensitive to noise data, but also it can reach high efficiency because of its approximately linear time complexity, which is nearly the same as K-MEANS'. Both our theoretic analysis and experimental results confirm the above conclusions.

High dimensional data can be transformed into one single dimension space based on distance [13,14], so CURD can process high dimensional data from this point. One of our future work is to experiment its performance in high dimensional space.

Last but not least, our algorithm finds references that can correctly represent the spatial geometric feature of data space, so we are thinking of sampling methods using this technology.

## References


1. Jiawei Han, Micheline Kambr. Data mining concepts and techniques, Morgan Kaufmann Publisher (2000) 145–176.
2. Anderberg, M. R. Cluster analysis for applications, Academic Press (1973).
3. M. Ester, H. P. Kriegel, J. Sander, and X. Xu. A density based algorithm for discovering clusters in large spatial databases with noise. Proceedings of International Conference on Knowledge Discovery and Data Mining (1996).
4. T. Zhang, R. Ramakrishnan, and M. Livny. BIRCH: An efficient data clustering method for very large databases. Proceedings of ACM SIGMOD International Conference on Management of Data, Montreal, Canada (1996) 103–114.
5. S. Guha, R. Rastogi and K. Shim. CURE: An efficient clustering algorithm for large databases. Proceedings of ACM SIGMOD International Conference on Management of Data, New York (1998) 73–84.
6. R. Aggrawal, J. Gehrke, D. Gunopulos, P. Raghavan. Automatic Subspace Clustering of High Dimensional Data for Data Mining Applications, Proceedings of ACM SIGMOD International Conference on Management of Data, Seattle, Washington (1998) 94–105.
7. Goil, Saniay, Harasha Nagesh and Alok Choundhary. MAFIA: Efficient and scalable Subspace Clustering for Very Large Data Sets. Technical Report Number CPDC-TR-9906-019, Center for Parallel and Distributed Computing, Northwestern University (1999).
8. Hinneburg, Alexander and Daniel A.Keim. Optimal Grid-Clustering: Towards Breaking the Curse of Dimensionality in High-Dimensional Clustering. Proceedings of the 25th VLDB Conference, Edinburgh, Scotland (1999).
9. Guha, S., Rastogi. R. and Shim K. Rock: A Robust Clustering Algorithm for Categorical Attributes, Proceedings of the International Conference on Data Engineering, Sydney, Australia (1999) 512–521.
10. Karypis George, Eui-Hong Han, and Vipin Kumar. CHAMELEON: A Hierarchical Clustering Algorithm Using Dynamic Modeling. IEEE Computer (1999) 68–75.
11. Estivill-Castro,Vladimir and Ickjai Lee. AMOEBA: Hierarchical Clustering Based on Spatial Proximity Using Delaunay Diagram. Proceedings of the 9th International Symposium on Spatial Data Handling. Beijing, China (2000).
12. Alexandros Nanopoulos, Yannis Theodoridis,Yannis Manolopoulos. C2P: Clustering based on Closest Pairs. Proceedings of the 27th VLDB Conference, Roma, Italy (2001).
13. S. Berchtold, C. Bohm, and H-P. Kriegel. The pyramid-technique: Towards breaking the curse of dimensionality. Proceedings of ACM SIGMOD International Conference on Management of Data (1998) 142–53.
14. C. Yu, B. C. Ooi, K.-L. Tan, and H. V. Jagadish. Indexing the Distance: An Efficient Method to KNN Processing. Proceedings of 27th VLDB Conference, Roma, Italy (2001).

# Classification Using Constrained Emerging Patterns

James Bailey, Thomas Manoukian, and Kotagiri Ramamohanarao

Department of Computer Science & Software Engineering
The University of Melbourne, Australia
{jbailey,tcm,rao}@cs.mu.oz.au

**Abstract.** Emerging Patterns are itemsets whose supports change significantly from one dataset to another. They are useful as a means of discovering distinctions inherently present amongst a collection of datasets and have been shown to be a powerful method for constructing accurate classifiers. In this paper, we present two techniques for significantly improving emerging pattern classifying power. The first strategy involves mining patterns which have a more targeted description of their relative supports in each dataset. The second technique is to employ a pairwise classification strategy for situations where more than two classes are present. Novel mining algorithms are also presented which emphasise dataset partitioning as a crucial mechanism in reducing the complexity of the task. We provide experimental results demonstrating the value of these techniques and show that in general, the resulting classifier performs demonstrably better than other preeminent methods, while mining time is considerably improved on earlier methods.

## 1 Introduction

Discovery of powerful distinguishable features between datasets is an important objective in data mining. Addressing this problem, work presented in [3] introduced the concept of *emerging patterns* or EPs. These are itemsets whose support changes significantly from one dataset to another. Because of sharp changes in support, emerging patterns have strong discriminating power and are very useful for describing the contrasts that exist between classes of data. They have been successfully applied for discovering patterns in gene expression data [13]. Work in [11,4,12] has shown how to use them as the basis for constructing competitive data classifiers.

Previous strategies for using emerging patterns in classification have, however, suffered from a number of limitations: i) An inability to identify patterns satisfying specified support constraints in each of the datasets (i.e. at least three occurrences in dataset A and less than two occurrences in dataset B). This can mean that powerful patterns may be excluded from the classification process. ii) Poorer classification performance in general for multi class scenarios. Challenges also exist in the mining of emerging patterns. Two well known obstacles are: i) the apriori property no longer holds for EPs ii) a large number of EPs may exist.

G. Dong et al. (Eds.): WAIM 2003, LNCS 2762, pp. 226–237, 2003.

In this paper, we tackle these problems, with the aim of improving the overall accuracy of emerging patterns for classification. Our main contributions are:

- We identify a useful new class of emerging pattern that we call a *constrained emerging pattern* (CEP), having known frequency bounds within each of the opposing datasets. We demonstrate its improved classification power in comparison to previous types of emerging patterns.
- We introduce algorithms for efficiently mining CEPs which achieve a 26-165 speedup on currently known techniques.
- We next show how classification accuracy for CEPs can be significantly improved for multi class problems by the use of pairwise classification.
- Finally, we compare the performance of CEPs with several other classifiers - CBA, Naive Bayes and C5.0 and show that CEPs generally have superior accuracy.

An outline of the remainder of this paper is as follows. In section 2 we give some necessary background and terminology. Section 3 motivates the use of CEPs for classification. Section 4 provides a detailed description of the algorithms used to mine CEPs and provides some experimental analysis of their performance. Section 5 compares the accuracy of the CEP based classifier against other emerging pattern methods and other state-of-the-art systems. Section 6 then discusses the use of pairwise classification for CEPs and extends the comparison with techniques seen in section 5. In section 7 we discuss related work. Finally, in section 8 we provide a summary and outline directions for future research.

## 2 Background and Terminology

Let the support of an itemset $i$ in a dataset $D$ be the count of the number transactions within $D$ containing $i$, denoted $supportD(i)$. Assume two data sets $D_p$ (positive dataset) and $D_n$ (negative dataset), the growth rate of an itemset $i$ in favour of $D_p$ is defined as $\rho = \frac{supportD_p(i)}{supportD_n(i)}$ ($\frac{0}{0}$ implies the pattern exists in neither dataset). An *emerging pattern* (EP) is an itemset whose support in one set of data differs from its support in another. The growth rate is thus either finite or infinite. Should it be infinite, we say the pattern is a *jumping emerging pattern* (JEP) (i.e. it is present in one and absent in the other).

Classification using emerging patterns is described in [11]. Initially all emerging patterns for each of the two classes are computed. Then, given some test instance, a score is calculated for each class. This score is equal to the sum of the contributions made by each individual emerging pattern contained within the test. The contribution of an individual EP to the overall score is equal to its support. The test instance is deemed to match the class with the highest overall score.

## 3 Constrained Emerging Patterns

We begin by discussing the two kinds of emerging patterns that have previously been used for classification. An EP is a pattern that has some specified growth rate $\rho$. A JEP is special kind of EP with $\rho = \infty$. The advantage of JEPs is that they represent very sharp contrasts between $D_p$ and $D_n$. Their disadvantage is that 'low quality' datasets may contain an abundance of low support JEPs and few high support JEPs. Thus the requirement that a JEP never occur within $D_n$ is often too strict and strong inherent features of $D_p$ may be overlooked.

Unlike JEPs, EPs may occur within $D_n$, provided the growth rate threshold $\rho$ is satisfied. Hence they are potentially more stable and resistant to noise. The disadvantage though, is that the contrasts may no longer be as 'sharp' (e.g. setting $\rho = 5$ is a common choice [17]) so the ability to mine an emerging pattern $i$ based on desired input values of $supportD_p(i), supportD_n(i)$ (from which $\rho$ can be derived) is likely to be valuable. This forms the basis of a new class of emerging pattern that we term a *constrained EP* (CEP). A CEP satisfies the following definition:

Given thresholds $\alpha$ and $\beta$, a CEP is an itemset $i$ satisfying the following two conditions: i) $supportD_p(i) \geq \alpha$ , ii) $supportD_n(i) \leq \beta$ . Clearly, by setting $\beta = 0$, CEPs reduce to JEPs. By varying the value of $\beta$, greater robustness to noise can be achieved.

Consider the following database defined on six attributes: (with all possible attribute values given in parentheses) Attr1 $(a, b, c)$, Attr2 $(d, e, f)$, Attr3 $(g, h, i)$, Attr4 $(j, k, l)$, Attr5 $(m, n, o)$ and Attr6 $(p, q, r)$.

**Table 1.** Sample Database

| Class 1 Instances | Class 2 Instances |
|---|---|
| $\{a, d, i, l, o, p\}$ | $\{c, d, i, l, o, r\}$ |
| $\{b, d, g, l, o, r\}$ | $\{a, f, g, k, n, q\}$ |
| $\{c, d, h, l, o, r\}$ | $\{b, d, h, j, m, p\}$ |

By observation we see that JEPs for class 1 include $\{a, i\}$, $\{o, p\}$, and $\{b, g\}$. JEPs for class 2 include $\{f\}$, $\{k\}$, and $\{n\}$. Class 1 also contains an EP, $\{o, r\}$ ($\rho = 2$) and a CEP, $\{d, l, o\}$ ($\alpha = 3$ and $\beta = 1$).

## 4 CEP Mining Issues and Objectives

The first work [3] introducing the mining of emerging patterns showed that the process is two stage.

- Represent both the positive and negative datasets being mined in terms of their border descriptions.
- Mine the emerging patterns by operating on the relevant borders.

The first stage of the procedure constructs two borders. One will represent the positive dataset such that only those itemsets with support $\geq \alpha$ are present and the other will represent the negative dataset where members have support $\geq \beta$.

The second stage implies taking these borders and applying a border-difference [3] operator, thus gaining the desired patterns. This operator extracts all minimal itemsets that occur in the positive border and are absent from the negative one.

Our work in [1] focused on JEP mining and provided an improved method of completing stage ii) of the mining process mentioned above. There $\alpha = 1$ and $\beta = 0$ so the border descriptions are simply the dataset transactions. CEP mining presents a much greater challenge, in this work we choose $\alpha = 3$ and $\beta = 1$, hence the borders are no longer trivially the original datasets themselves. We show that we can significantly improve completion of stage ii) by employing a more sophisticated scheme of data partitioning. We construct partitions with two primary aims:

**Property 1** To minimise the number of itemsets present in each partition

**Property 2** To minimise the cardinality of itemsets contained in large partitions

### 4.1 General Principles

The principal objective of the mining algorithm is to form partitions, containing both instances from the positive and negative border, in line with the properties listed above. On forming such a partition, we then apply the border-difference operator to each. This procedure equates to generating and solving many small problems rather than a single (possibly very large) one.

The primary data structure we use is a prefix-tree based upon the FP-Tree [9]. Such a tree can be viewed as containing many root nodes, one for each distinct prefix item. The sub-tree headed by all such root items are termed component trees. The basis of our algorithm is to:

- traverse branches such that each item visited acts as a partitioning item.

Given that all branches within any component tree share the root item this can be seen as a first partition, by selecting any other item (item $x$ for example) we can:

- accumulate all branches (itemsets) that share the root item and $x$ thus achieving a second partition of the database.

Once all relevant branches have been found, we can:

- invoke the border-difference operator on the itemsets.

To ensure that each component tree consists of all the branches which contain the root item we relocate all branches. This process involves the removal of the highest ordered item in the branch and re-inserting into the tree.

### 4.2 Item Ordering and Quality of Partitioning

Choice of item ordering is crucial for mining EPs, since it is the order of items which dictates the size and dimensionality of the itemsets within a partition.

**Root-Level Ordering.** An ordering of items will result in some particular component tree structure. Trees will exist that contain many branches and others not so many, these branches may be long (relocated few times) or short (relocated many times).

Choosing a frequent ordering (items are ordered in descending order of frequency with reference the set of transactions constituting both the positive and negative border) implies that the component tree headed by the most common item will contain all relevant branches at their maximum original size (remembering that relocating a branch reduces its size by 1). In this scenario the first few component trees contain many long branches. To address this we note that:

- the two-item partition will attract many branches.
- their lengths in many cases will be large.

both are contradictions of **Property 1** and **Property 2**. Irrespective of ordering, the branches that lie under any component tree will be identical in the sense that all information pertinent to that tree will be present. Therefore it is favourable to:

- minimise the length of the branches under the larger component trees.

An obvious solution is to use an infrequent ordering. Such a choice implies that:

- any branch containing a high frequency item will be short.

The actual length is dependent upon the number of relocations the branch has experienced. Before being relocated to some component tree headed by a high frequency each item (item $y$ for example), the branch would have been relocated (shortened in length by 1) $n$ times, where $n$ is the number of items present in the branch that reside higher than $y$ in the item order. In the case of the most frequent item, all branches will be of length 1.

**Internal Component-Tree Ordering.** An infrequent ordering on its own will not guarantee either of our two stated properties. A key contribution in this paper is to demonstrate how the application of a further internal level of ordering within component trees greatly improves the efficiency of CEP mining.

Given a top root-level ordering, we need to calculate a new ordering specific to the branches (itemsets) contained under each component tree. This ordering is based on the frequency of items present in all branches containing the root item of the component tree. For each component tree the process involves:

- finding which itemsets reside under the component tree.
- acquiring a frequency table for all items within the relevant itemsets.
- inserting itemsets using this internal order.

Work to this stage promotes a frequent ordering within each component tree as a useful general approach. The two-level ordering can be seen to tackle both of our mining objectives.

- The root-level ordering ensures that the ratio of branch length to component tree size (number of nodes) is minimised.
- average cardinality of itemsets within component trees headed by high frequency items is small.

These points are a direct consequence of the number of relocations individual branches undergo. The second-level ordering ensures:

- that the number of branches within any one component tree is minimised.
- any two-item partition attracts the smallest possible number of branches.

A frequent item order means that longer prefixes exist within component trees. As a result, component trees contain a minimal number of branches. Figure 1 shows a probable structure of component trees. Trees headed by high frequency items have branches of short length, component trees with long branches in turn have very few of them.

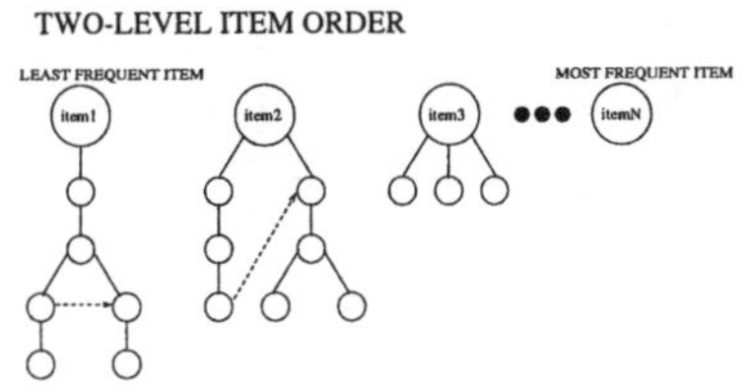


**Fig. 1.** Component Tree structure

**Implementation.** We now discuss some additional details concerning our algorithm. Maximal Frequent Itemsets (MFIs) were generated using the GenMax [8] algorithm. We present two approaches to mining CEPs that arise from questioning whether we should:

- find the positive border initially (eager approach) *or*
- find all EPs satisfying the negative support constraint and then prune away those not satisfying the minimum positive threshold (lazy approach).

The intention of the lazy approach is to avoid circumstances where the borders generated may be much larger than the initial datasets. By transferring the pruning away from the MFI generation stage, we may avoid dealing with a considerably sized positive border, pruning is then required as a post-processing step. Algorithm 1 provides pseudo-code for the entire mining process.

**Algorithm 1** CEP Mining

```
C = {Class_1, Class_2, ..., Class_n}
EPs = ∅
for all c ∈ C do
  pos_border = find_MFI(positive_dataset, α)
  neg_border = find_MFI(negative_dataset, β)
  root_level_order = find_infrequent_order(pos_border, neg_border)
  assign_all_branches_to_relevent_component_trees(pos_border, neg_border)
  for component_tree = 0 to num_component_trees do
    component_tree_level_order = find_frequent_order()
    insert_branches()
    for all branches b ∈ component_tree do
      for all items i ∈ b do
        relevant_branches = gather_all_branches()
        EPs = EPs ∪ border_difference(relevant_branches)
      end for
    end for
  end for
end for
```

We conducted experiments on three datasets from the UCI Machine Learning Repository [2] and compared the original method proposed in [3], in which no tree structures are used and the borders produced in stage i) are operated upon directly, the single-level ordering of [1], the method proposed here and its lazy variant. All experiments were performed on a Dell PowerEdge 2600 2.4GHz with 3GB memory running Solaris 8 /x86 with all times being user times. The 3rd column of the table shows the number of attributes and total number of distinct attribute values (items) present in each problem following discretisation.

**Table 2.** CEP Mining

| Dataset | #classes | #attr:items | #instances | original | single-level | CEP-Lazy | CEP-Eager | Speedup |
|---|---|---|---|---|---|---|---|---|
| census | 2 | 14:154 | 32561 | 5327.01 | 226.83 | 44.47 | **32.24** | 165.22 |
| chess | 2 | 36:73 | 3196 | 2050.85 | 206.90 | 153.94 | **78.30** | 26.19 |
| mushroom | 2 | 22:125 | 8124 | 519.58 | 14.09 | **4.50** | 6.16 | 115.46 |

The results of Table 2 indicate the superiority of the algorithms presented in this work for the mining of CEPs. In all cases, considerable speedups exist between these methods and those previously developed. In comparison to the method presented in [3] we see improvements between 26 and 165 times. In contrast to the single-level ordering of [1] the improvement ranges from 2 to 7 times faster. The performance of the lazy algorithm is dependent upon the ratio of EPs generated prior to pruning and those that remain following it. The fact that the lazy approach is outperformed by the eager method suggests that this ratio is high.

## 5 Classification Using CEPs

We have implemented a system for mining CEPs setting $\alpha = 3$ and $\beta = 1$ (values shown through experimentation to provide strong overall classification behaviour) We also use the heuristic that $\beta = 0$ if $|D_n| < 100$ - meaning that for situations where the negative dataset is sufficiently small, JEPs are mined instead.

A ten-fold cross-validation methodology was employed, with the same folds being used in all classifiers. The JEP classifier is implemented as described in [1]. The EP classifier is implemented as described in [4,17]. For each of the emerging pattern methods, the entropy technique in [6] was used for discretising continuous attributes.

**Table 3.** Classification Results: Two Class Problems

| Dataset | # classes | CEP | EP | JEP | CBA[14] | C5.0[16] | NB |
|---|---|---|---|---|---|---|---|
| australian | 2 | 85.36 | **85.80** | 84.64 | 84.10 | 84.78 | 76.96 |
| breast-w | 2 | 96.85 | **97.28** | 96.71 | 95.80 | 94.28 | 96.43 |
| cleve | 2 | **82.84** | 79.86 | 80.19 | 76.80 | 74.88 | 81.52 |
| heart | 2 | 82.22 | - | 81.48 | 80.00 | 76.30 | **83.70** |
| crx | 2 | **86.23** | 86.09 | 85.36 | 84.00 | 86.09 | 77.54 |
| tic-tac-toe | 2 | 92.07 | 89.66 | 97.28 | **100** | 86.43 | 69.63 |
| hepatitis | 2 | 84.50 | 84.46 | **85.17** | 81.30 | 74.21 | 83.21 |
| diabetes | 2 | 75.26 | 73.83 | 72.40 | 74.10 | 72.92 | **76.83** |
| horse-colic | 2 | 83.72 | 82.03 | 83.44 | 82.40 | **87.81** | 79.08 |
| house-votes-84 | 2 | 92.64 | 91.49 | 94.25 | 96.00 | **97.24** | 89.66 |
| labor-neg | 2 | 89.67 | 89.67 | 89.67 | 85.00 | 82.67 | **93.33** |
| hypothyroid | 2 | 98.74 | 96.43 | 98.61 | 98.20 | **99.21** | 97.72 |
| Two Class Ave | | **87.50** | 86.96 | 87.43 | 86.47 | 84.73 | 83.80 |

Observing the results for the two class datasets (Table 3), we see that the three emerging pattern classifiers all perform very strongly. Within the three, CEP has the best average accuracy and also has the most number of top accuracies.

Classification with multi class problems traditionally involved $n$ mining operations where mining for any particular class sees it act as the positive dataset and the remaining $n-1$ classes aggregated to form the negative dataset. The performance of the emerging pattern methods is far less competitive with respect to the non emerging pattern methods (see Table 4). This represents an important deficiency and addressing this problem is the subject of the next section.

## 6 Pairwise Classification for Multi Class Datasets

The results for multi-class problems are not so impressive. The crucial observation lies in our belief that all EP-based classifiers are inherently designed for

**Table 4.** Classification Results: Multi Class Problems

| Dataset | # classes | CEP | EP | JEP | CBA | C5.0 | NB |
|---|---|---|---|---|---|---|---|
| shuttle-small | 4 | 99.76 | 98.24 | **99.81** | 99.70 | 99.79 | 90.91 |
| iris | 3 | 94.67 | 92.00 | 94.67 | 93.60 | 94.67 | **96.67** |
| glass | 6 | 64.00 | 63.05 | 63.51 | **67.10** | 66.80 | 43.40 |
| yeast | 10 | 41.79 | 53.64 | 38.28 | 56.50 | 54.05 | **57.95** |
| lymphography | 4 | 81.10 | 81.76 | 78.38 | 80.40 | 79.05 | **83.76** |
| vehicle | 4 | 69.15 | 64.30 | 71.04 | 70.50 | **72.22** | 47.17 |
| flare | 6 | 61.62 | 69.33 | 65.73 | **73.80** | 72.78 | 71.20 |
| anneal | 5 | 93.09 | 94.32 | 93.76 | **96.10** | 92.53 | 81.41 |
| automobile | 6 | 75.14 | 68.81 | 77.57 | 71.70 | **82.45** | 52.21 |
| soybean-small | 4 | 95.50 | **100** | 95.50 | 97.50 | 95.50 | 98.00 |
| wine | 3 | 89.41 | 97.19 | 93.86 | 94.10 | 95.56 | **97.78** |
| nursery | 5 | 96.98 | 84.71 | **98.85** | 92.50 | 97.13 | 90.30 |
| zoo | 7 | 94.09 | 92.09 | **94.18** | 93.40 | 90.18 | 92.18 |
| Multi Class Ave | | 81.25 | 81.49 | 81.93 | 83.60 | **84.05** | 77.14 |

dealing with two-classes given the traditional approach mentioned in the last section. It is this procedure that we will alter so that this inherent feature is fully exploited.

Suppose there are $n$ different classes. Our mechanism sees an $n(n-1)/2$ number of mining operations (one for each pair) replacing the $n$ number traditionally performed. Following this process each class has a tally of votes in its favour. The class with the highest number of votes is assigned to the test case. Discretisation is performed for each pair of classes, rather than once at the beginning, a choice which we found greatly improves classification accuracy.

Table 5 shows the effect of performing binarisation on those multi-class problems examined previously. We only show the effect of pairwise classification for CEP, since it earlier outperformed both EPs and JEPs on two class problems (see Table 3, CEP had 6 top accuracies, EP had 2 and JEP had 3. CEP also had the best two class average.).

We also performed binarisation for C5.0 and NB, the overall effect was negligible in terms of average accuracy (C5.0 -0.36%, NB -0.67%) and top accuracies. We also conducted the experiment using JEPs with average accuracy rising to 83.86%. The results are clear in indicating the substantial increase in CEPs' performance with regard the multi-class problems. Noticeable improvement was found with *yeast* (14.07%), *glass* (7.49%), *wine* (5%) and *flare* (9.58%). The average accuracy increase (2.95%) over all multi-class datasets is also meaningful.

The most significant result is that CEP is now globally competitive when compared to the non emerging pattern classifiers. Our explanation of why this process is successful, centers around the underlying method of mining EPs.

– success of each class in generating patterns is related to the negative dataset.
– if these sets are similar a small number of patterns will result.

**Table 5.** CEP using Pair-Wise Algorithm

| Dataset | # classes | CEP | CBA | C5.0 | NB |
|---|---|---|---|---|---|
| shuttle-small | 4 | **99.81** | 99.70 | 99.79 | 90.91 |
| iris | 3 | 94.00 | 93.60 | 94.67 | **96.67** |
| glass | 6 | **71.49** | 67.10 | 66.80 | 43.40 |
| yeast | 10 | 55.86 | 56.50 | 54.05 | **57.95** |
| lymphography | 4 | 79.81 | 80.40 | 79.05 | **83.76** |
| vehicle | 4 | 65.96 | 70.50 | **72.22** | 47.17 |
| flare | 6 | 71.20 | **73.80** | 72.78 | 71.20 |
| anneal | 5 | 94.54 | **96.10** | 92.53 | 81.41 |
| automobile | 6 | 74.67 | 71.70 | **82.45** | 52.21 |
| soybean-small | 4 | **100** | 97.50 | 95.50 | 98.00 |
| wine | 3 | 94.41 | 94.10 | 95.56 | **97.78** |
| nursery | 5 | **97.77** | 92.50 | 97.13 | 90.30 |
| zoo | 7 | **95.09** | 93.40 | 90.18 | 92.18 |
| Multi Class Ave | | **84.20** | 83.60 | 84.05 | 77.14 |

– if the negative set size far exceeds the positive set size few patterns will be generated.

Our research indicated that these scenarios are more likely when the earlier method of handling of multi-class problems is used. In the case of *yeast*, each class is essentially paired against nine others and in the worst case (for the smallest class) over 99% of the entire dataset. In such circumstances the likelihood that such a class will produce any number of significant patterns (and thus be a viable alternative during classification) is remote. By reducing the size of the negative set that any one class competes against during mining, the chances that they will produce patterns increases. The gains made can be attributed to the outcome of this reasoning.

Looking at all the results in Table 5, using CEPs with pair-wise mining is extremely successful. In comparison to results obtained without its use, the CEP classifier, on multi-class problems, has improved by almost 3% on average accuracy. When contrasting against other popular classifiers we see that CEP achieves a higher overall average accuracy (+0.15% on nearest rival C5.0) and 5/13 top accuracies (C5.0 2, CBA 2, and NB 4). Coupled with the fact that it outperforms these three classifiers on two classes, a greater average accuracy of 1.03%, and 5/12 overall top accuracies (C5.0 3, CBA 1, NB 3), CEP is shown to be a very powerful alternative to those systems currently available.

## 7 Related Work

Emerging patterns first appeared in [3], which also introduced the notion of the border for concisely representing emerging patterns. Constrained emerging patterns were also defined in [10,3], where they were termed extended emerging patterns. However, no study was made of their efficient mining nor of their effectiveness in classification.

Jumping emerging patterns (JEPs) are similar to version spaces [15]. Given a set of positive and a set of negative training instances, a version space is the set of all generalisations that each match (or are contained in) every positive instance and no negative instance in the training set. In contrast, a jumping emerging pattern space is the set of all item patterns that each match (or are contained in) one or more (not necessarily every) positive instance and no negative instance in the set.

Work in [5] uses trees for mining of emerging patterns. The methodology is different, however, since the algorithm is not complete (i.e. it does not discover all emerging patterns that may exist within a dataset).

Our work in this paper examines the use of emerging patterns for eager classification. Work in [12] developed a lazy emerging pattern classifier. In a similar way, we could also adapt our results to the lazy context.

The CBA classifier [14] uses association rules for classification that can be interpreted as being a kind an emerging pattern. Rules must satisfy a minimum threshold (typically 1% relative support) and a minimum confidence (typically 50%). Translated into our framework, this would mean mining all emerging patterns having minimum relative support in $D_p$ of 1% and maximum relative support of $\beta$ in $D_n$, where $\beta \leq \alpha$. This constraint on the $\beta$ value is much more permissive than our CEP classifier, which uses the low value of $\beta = 1$.

Pairwise classification was discussed in [7], where it was applied to a number of classifiers and was seen to result in increased accuracies on some datasets. It was also observed that the gains achieved were roughly proportional to the number of classes. This is in line with our reported results in section 6.

## 8 Summary and Future Work

In this paper we have developed techniques for improving classification by emerging patterns. We identified a new class of pattern known as a constrained emerging pattern. This pattern allowed targeted specification of supports within each dataset. We then showed how pairwise classification dramatically improves the power of such patterns on multi class problems. The resulting classifier is superior to state of the art methods on a large number of datasets. Our algorithms for mining CEPs were also shown to be highly efficient in comparison to other applicable techniques. As part of future work, we plan to investigate

- Techniques for choosing the most interesting patterns within a collection of CEPs, based on their actual supports within $D_p$ and $D_n$.
- Improving the sophistication of the scoring function used to determine the overall winner.

**Acknowledgements.** This work was supported in part by an Expertise Grant from the Victorian Partnership for Advanced Computing.

## References

1. J. Bailey, T. Manoukian, and K. Ramamohanarao. Fast Algorithms For Mining Emerging Patterns. In *Proceedings of the Sixth European Conference on Principles of Data Mining and Knowledge Discovery*, pages 39–50, 2002.
2. C. L. Blake and P. M. Murphy. UCI Repository of Machine Learning Databases. www.ics.uci.edu/~mlearn/MLRepository.html.
3. G. Dong and J. Li. Efficient Mining of Emerging Patterns: Discovering Trends and Differences. In *Proceedings of the Fifth International Conference on Knowledge Discovery and Data Mining*, pages 43–52, 1999.
4. G. Dong, X. Zhang, L. Wong, and J. Li. CAEP: Classification by Aggregating Emerging Patterns. In *Proceedings of the Second International Conference on Discovery Science*, pages 30–42, 1999.
5. H. Fan and K. Ramamohanarao. An Efficient Single-Scan Algorithm for Mining Essential Jumping Emerging Patterns. In *Proceedings of the Sixth Pacific Asia Conference on Knowledge Discovery in Databases*, pages 456–462, 2002.
6. U. M. Fayyad and K. B. Irani. Multi-Interval Discretization of Continuous-Valued Attributes for Classification Learning. In *Proceedings of the Thirteenth International Joint Conference on Artificial Intelligence*, pages 1022–1027, 1993.
7. J. Furnkranz. Pairwise Classification as an Ensemble Technique. In *Proceedings of the Thirteenth European Conference on Machine Learning*, pages 97–110, 2002.
8. K. Gouda and M. J. Zaki. Efficiently Mining Maximal Frequent Itemsets. In *Proceedings of the First International Conference on Data Mining*, pages 163–170, 2001.
9. J. Han, J. Pei, and Y. Yin. Mining Frequent Patterns Without Candidate Generation. In *Proceedings of the International Conference on Management of Data*, pages 1–12, 2000.
10. J. Li. *Mining Emerging Patterns to Construct Accurate and Efficient Classifiers.* PhD thesis, University of Melbourne, 2001.
11. J. Li, G. Dong, and K. Ramamohanarao. Making use of the most Expressive Jumping Emerging Patterns for Classification. In *Proceedings of the Fourth Pacific Asia Conference on Knowledge Discovery in Databases*, pages 220–232, 2000.
12. J. Li, G.Dong, and K. Ramamohanarao. DeEPs: Instance-Based Classification by Emerging Patterns. In *Proceedings of the Fourth European Conference on Principles of Data Mining and Knowledge Discovery*, pages 191–200, 2000.
13. J. Li and L. Wong. Emerging Patterns and Gene Expression Data. In *Proceedings of the Twelfth Workshop on Genome Informatics*, pages 3–13, 2001.
14. B. Liu, W.Hsu, and Y. Ma. Integrating Classification and Association Rule Mining. In *Proceedings of the Fourth International Conference on Knowledge Discovery and Data Mining*, pages 80–86, 1998.
15. T. M. Mitchell. Generalization as Search. *Artificial Intelligence*, 18(2):203–226, 1982.
16. J. R. Quinlan. *C4.5 Programs for Machine Learning.* Morgan Kaufmann, 1993.
17. X. Zhang, G.Dong, and K. Ramamohanarao. Eploring Constraints to Efficiently Mine Emerging Patterns from Large High-Dimensional Datasets. In *Proceedings of the Sixth International Conference on Knowledge Discovery and Data Mining*, pages 310–314, 2000.

# A New Multivariate Decision Tree Construction Algorithm Based on Variable Precision Rough Set

Liang Zhang, Yun-Ming Ye, Shui Yu, and Fan-Yuan Ma

Department of Computer Science & Engineering, Shanghai Jiao Tong University
Shanghai , 200030 China
zhangliang@cs.sjtu.edu.cn

**Abstract.** In this paper we extend previous research and present a novel approach to construct multivariate decision tree, which has to some extent the ability of fault tolerance, by employing a development of RST, namely the variable precision rough sets (VPRS) model. Based on variable precision rough set theory, a new concept of generalization of one equivalence relation with respect to another one with precision $\beta$ is introduced and used for construction of multivariate decision tree. The experimentation result shows its fitness to create multivariate decision tree retrieved from noisy data.

## 1 Introduction

Rough Set Theory (RST) originated by Pawlak has been described as a new mathematical tool to deal with vagueness and uncertainty[1][2][3][5] and applied in the areas of machine learning, knowledge acquisition, decision analysis, knowledge discovery from databases, expert systems, decision support systems inductive reasoning and pattern recognition and so on[4][5][6]. RST incorporates the use of indiscernibility (equivalence) relations to approximate sets of objects by upper and lower set approximations[1][2]. D.Q. Miao[12] applied RST in the construction of multivariate decision tree and proposed an algorithm, however, it works only for the data sets in which there is no noise. Nevertheless, in general noisy is inevitable. Therefore, an algorithm constructing decision tree with the ability of fault tolerance is needed.

Variable precision rough sets (VPRS) model developed by Ziarko[5] [13][14] incorporates probabilistic decision rules. This is an important extension, since in real world decision making, uncertainty may appear due to lack of features, which makes two originally dissimilar points neighbors. Due to the incomplete knowledge describing the data, generally the input representation is not perfect. As a result, $<x_i,y_i>$and its neighbors appear similar in decision attribute, although they may not be similar when the magnitudes are augmented. It makes the input-output relationship one-to-many, and the uncertainty and inconsistence appears.

Relative to the traditional rough set approach, VPRS has the additional desirable property of allowing for partial classification compared to the complete classification required by RST. More specifically, when an object is classified using RST it is assumed that there is complete certainty that it is a correct classification. In contrast, VPRS facilitates a degree of confidence in classification, invoking a more informed

G. Dong et al. (Eds.): WAIM 2003, LNCS 2762, pp. 238–246, 2003.

analysis of the data, which is achieved through the use of a majority inclusion relation [5][7] [14].

It is obvious that the application of VPRS in the decision tree construction may increase the algorithm's ability of fault-tolerance. In this paper, we extend previous work and introduce a novel method to construct a multivariate decision tree for a decision table by using VPRS. The remainder of the paper is organized as follows: The basic notions of rough sets theory are reviewed and redefined in Section 2. We present a algorithm to construct multivariate decision trees of a decision table in Section 3. In Section 4, we illustrate our algorithm. Section 5 concludes with the concluding discussions.

## 2 Variable Precision Rough Sets Theory

Assume we are given a set of examples with a class label to indicate the class to which each example belongs to. We call the class label the decision attribute, and rest of the attributes the condition attributes in this paper. Attributes are either numeric, coming from an ordered domain, or symbolic, coming from an unordered domain. We don't consider numerical attributes in the paper because discretization of numerical attributes is considered as a preprocessing step in this research and there are a lot of discretization algorithms[15][16][17] which can convert the numeric attributes into discretized ones, the numeric attributes are treated as symbolic attributes after discretization.

**Definition 1.** If $S=(U,A\cup\{d\})$ is a decision table , where $A$ is the set of condition attributes and $\{d\}$ decision attribute, then we define a function

$$\delta_A(u)=\{i: there \text{ exists } u'ind(A)u \text{ and } d(u)=i\}$$

A decision table $S$ is called *consistent* if $card(\delta_A(u))=1$ for any $u\in U$ , otherwise, $S$ is *inconsistent*. Similarly, we define:

$$\gamma_A(u,i)=\{u'\in U: u'ind(A)u \text{ and } d(u')=i\}, \text{ where } u\in U \text{ and } i\in\delta_A(u)$$

$$\lambda_A(u,i)=\frac{card(\gamma_A(u,i))}{\sum_{j\in\delta_A(u)} card(\gamma_A(u,j))}, \text{ where } u\in U \text{ and } i\in\delta_A(u).$$

$\sigma_A(u)=\{i:\lambda_A(u,i)\geq\beta\}$, where $u\in U$ .

A decision table $S$ is called *consistent with precision* $\beta$ if $card(\sigma_A(u))=1$ for any $u\in U$ , otherwise $S$ is *inconsistent with precision* $\beta$ .

**Definition 2.** $Y \overset{\beta}{\supseteq} X \Leftrightarrow X \overset{\beta}{\subseteq} Y \Leftrightarrow \Pr(Y \mid X) \geq \beta$ We say that $X$ is contained with precision $\beta$ in $Y$ or $Y$ contains $X$ with precision $\beta$. (where $0 \leq \beta \leq 1$)

**Definition 3.** Let $(U, R)$ be an approximation space, where $U$ is a universe (i.e. a non-empty set of objects) and $R$ is a family of equivalence relation on $U$, $U / R = \{E_1, E_2, ..., E_n\}$ is equivalence classes of $R$, for any subset $X \subseteq U$, *lower and upper approximations with precision* $\beta$ are defined by

$$\underset{-\beta}{R} X = POS_R^\beta(X) = \cup\{E \in U / R \mid X \overset{\beta}{\supseteq} E\} = \bigcup_{\Pr(X \mid E_i) \geq \beta} \{E_i \in X\}$$

$$\bar{R}_\beta X = NONNEG_R^\beta(X) = \cup\{E \in U / R \mid X \overset{1-\beta}{\supseteq} E\} = \bigcup_{\Pr(X \mid E_i) \geq 1-\beta} \{E_i \in X\}$$

And the set $BN_R^\beta(X) = \bar{R}_\beta X - \underset{-\beta}{R} X$, will be called the boundary with the precision $\beta$ of $X$.

The set $\underset{-\beta}{R} X$ is the set of all elements of $U$ which can be with probability $\beta$ classified as elements of $X$, given the knowledge represented by attributes from $R$, $\bar{R}_\beta X$ is the set of elements of $U$ which can be with probability $1-\beta$ classified as elements of $X$, employing the knowledge represented by attributes from $R$, and $BN_R^\beta(X)$ is the set of elements which can be classified neither $X$ or $-X$ given knowledge $R$. The parameter $\beta$ controls how much we loosen our new definitions. Obviously, $\beta$ must be restricted to a range of 0.5, since below this limit one cannot reasonably speak of a majority, up to 1 where the new definitions converge to the original definitions. It approximates a given concept with precision $\beta$ from below and from above, using lower and upper approximations with precision $\beta$. Fig. 1 provides a schematic diagram of a various precision rough set.

**Definition 4.** A subset $B$ of the set $A$ of attributes of a consistent with precision $\beta$ decision table $S = (U, A \cup \{d\})$ is a relative reduct of $S$ with precision $\beta$ if and only if $B$ is a minimal set with the following property: $\sigma_A(u) = \sigma_B(u)$ for any $u$. The set of all relative reducts with precision $\beta$ in $S$ is denoted by

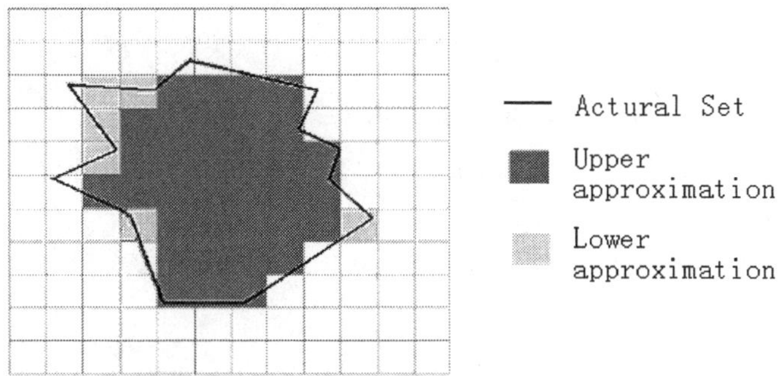


**Fig. 1.** Lower and upper approximation with precision $\beta$ (where $\beta$ =0.6 )

$RED_{\beta}(S, A \cup \{d\})$ and we define *the core of* $S$ *with precision* $\beta$ as follows:

$$CORE_{\beta}(S, A \cup \{d\}) = \cap \ RED_{\beta}(S, A \cup \{d\})$$

**Definition 5.** The importance factor of an attribute Cj in C is defined as

$$\text{importance-factor}=1-\frac{Card(C+d-C_i)}{Card(C+d)}$$

**Definition 6.** Let $P$ and $Q$ be two families of equivalence relations on the Universe set of U,

$$U/IND(P) = \{X_1, X_2, ..., X_n\} \quad U/IND(Q) = \{Y_1, Y_2, ..., Y_m\}$$

$$\text{Set } H_i = \bigcup_{x_j \in U/IND(P)} \{Xj \mid Xj \overset{\beta}{\subseteq} Yi\} \quad i = 1, 2, \ldots, m.$$

$$H_{m+1} = \bigcup_{x_j \in U/IND(P)} \{Xj \mid Xj \overset{\beta}{\not\subset} Yi\} \quad \forall i.$$

then $\{H_1, H_2, ...H_{m+1}\}$ is called *the generalization of P with precision* $\beta$ *with respect to Q*, denoted by $GENQ_{\beta}(P)$. (where $0.5 < \beta \le 1$)

**Theorem** $\{H_1, H_2, ...H_{m+1}\}$ *above is a partition of the universe set of U.*

**Proof:** According to the definition of partition , we must show the following two properties.

(a)every element of $U$ belongs to some set $H_i$, $i = 1, 2, ..., m+1$

(b) if $i \neq j, i, j = 1, 2, ..., m+1$ ,then $H_i \cap H_j \neq \varnothing$

Now property (a) is obviously true, since $\bigcup_{i=1}^{m+1} H_i = \bigcup_{i=1}^{n} X_i = U$.

Besides, definition 5 tells us that $H_i \cap H_j = \varnothing,\ i = 1,2,...m,\ j = m+1$

Next we show by contradiction the property (b) on the condition of $i \neq j,\ \ i, j = 1,2,...,m$.

If $H_i \cap H_j \neq \varnothing, i \neq j, i, j = 1,2,...,m$, then there is at least an element $x \in U$ such that $x \in H_i \cap H_j,\ \ i, j = 1,2,...,m$

We assume $x \in X_a$, according to the definition

$$H_i = \bigcup_{x_j \in U/IND(P)} \{Xj \mid Xj \overset{\beta}{\subseteq} Yi\} \quad i = 1,2,...,m.$$

$$\Rightarrow Xa \overset{\beta}{\subseteq} Yi \text{ and } Xa \overset{\beta}{\subseteq} Yj$$

Nevertheless, we know $Y_i \cap Y_j \neq \varnothing, i \neq j, i, j = 1,2,...,m$

$$\Rightarrow Xa \overset{\beta}{\not\subset} Yj \text{ and } Xa \overset{\beta}{\not\subset} Yi$$

that is, $Xa \overset{\beta}{\subseteq} Yi$ and $Xa \overset{\beta}{\not\subset} Yi$ are satisfied at the same time, so $\beta$ must be less than 0.5. This contradicts the value of $\beta$ of the definition 6, so we are done.

## 3 The Proposed Algorithm: VPRBMDTA

**Input:** The decision table $S = (U, A \cup \{d\}), \beta$
**Output:** a multivariable decision tree T.
**Method:**

*Initialize the tree variable T with the empty tree. Label the root by the set of all objects U and the current condition attributes set ( CCAS ) A, and fix the status of the root to be unready,*

```
While there is a leaf marked by unready do
  begin
    for any unready leave N of the tree T
    begin
    If there exists an object u labeling N σ_A(u) = ∅ then
        begin
            Printf("the decision table is
                  inconsistent with precision β ");
            Return;
        end
```

```
If for any object labeling N σ_A(u) is the same then
   begin
    Replace the object set at N by its common σ_A(u);
    Change the status of N to ready;
   end
   else
   begin
     compute P=CORE_β(N,CCAS ∪ {d});
     if P=∅ | P=CCAS then
        begin
           select attribute from the set CCAS
            with highest importance factor as P ;
        end
     compute GEND_β(P);
     CCAS = CCAS \ P;
     replace label of N by P and mark it as ready;
     create m+1 new nodes N_1,N_2,...,N_{m+1} with status
        unready as the child sub-trees of N, where
        N_i = H_i  i=1,2,...,m+1 and label them with
        CCAS;
     end
  end
end
return T
```

## 4 Experiment

In this section we will illustrate the algorithm VPRBMDTA. Given Table 1, we construct the multivariate decision tree of table 1 by the proposed algorithm ( where $\beta$ =0.6).

We note that the decision table is inconsistence, for there exists $u_9 ind(C) u_{10}$ and $d(u_9) \neq d(u_{10})$. Nevertheless it is consistence *consistent with precision* $\beta$.

U/ IND(C)
= {{1}, {2,4,18,21,22}, {3,7,9,10,14}, {5}, {6}, {8}, {11}, {12}, {13}, {15}, {16}, {17}, {19}, {20}}

U/ IND(D)={{1,2,3,4,7,9,12,14,18,20},{5,6,8,10,11,13,15,16,17,19,21,22}}

At first we got $\text{P=CORE}_\beta(N, CCAS \cup \{d\}) = \{C_1, C_4\}$

U/P={{1,12,13},{2,4,16,18,21,22},{3,7,9,10,14,20},{5,19},{6,8,15},{11,17}}.

Next according to definition 6 we compute $\mathrm{GEND}_{\beta}(\mathrm{P})$, we get:

H1={3,7,9,10,14,20},
H2={5, 6,8, 11,15,17,19,},
H3={1, 2,4,12,13,16,18,21,22},

and classified the universe of U into H1, H2,H3.
Similarly, we may get a multivariable decision tree (see Fig. 2.)
The rules given by the algorithm are showed as follows:

RULE 1: (C1=middle) $\rightarrow$ F

RULE 2: (C1=low or less than zero) $\wedge$ (C4=normal) $\rightarrow$ F)

RULE 3: (C1=low or less than zero) $\wedge$ (C4=good) $\rightarrow$ (H)

RULE 4: (C1=high) $\wedge$ ( C3=high) $\rightarrow$ H

RULE 5: (C1=high) $\wedge$ (C3=normal) $\rightarrow$ F

**Table 1.** Example of a decision table

| U | Condition Attributes | | | | Decision Attribute |
|---|---|---|---|---|---|
| | C1 | C2 | C3 | C4 | Class(D) |
| 1 | high | high | high | normal | H |
| 2 | high | high | high | good | H |
| 3 | low or less than zero | low | normal | good | H |
| 4 | high | high | high | good | H |
| 5 | middle | high | high | normal | F |
| 6 | low or less than zero | middle | high | normal | F |
| 7 | low or less than zero | low | normal | good | H |
| 8 | low or less than zero | low | normal | normal | F |
| 9 | low or less than zero | low | normal | good | H |
| 10 | low or less than zero | low | normal | good | F |
| 11 | middle | low | normal | good | F |
| 12 | high | middle | high | normal | H |
| 13 | high | low | normal | normal | F |
| 14 | low or less than zero | low | normal | good | H |
| 15 | low or less than zero | middle | normal | normal | F |
| 16 | high | middle | normal | good | F |
| 17 | middle | middle | high | good | F |
| 18 | high | high | high | good | H |
| 19 | middle | high | normal | normal | F |
| 20 | low or less than zero | middle | high | good | H |
| 21 | high | high | high | good | F |
| 22 | high | high | high | good | F |

From the Fig. 2 and the rule 3 we may know that the objects $u_9$ and $u_{10}$ belong to the class H although there exists $u_9 ind(C) u_{10}$ and $d(u_9) \neq d(u_{10})$. It show that although there exists noise in the decision table our algorithm still may outputs a multivariable decision tree with less nodes and better rules.

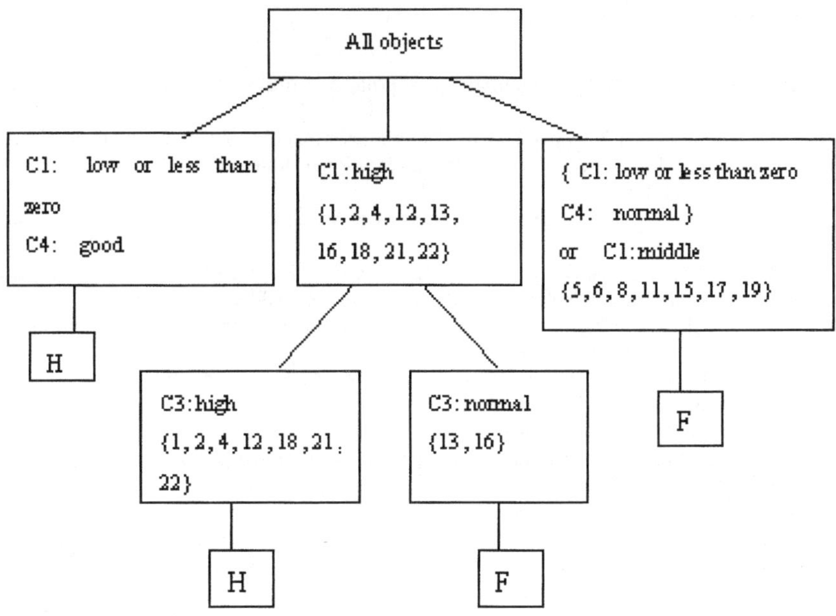


**Fig. 2.** The multivariable decision tree constructed by VPRBMDTA

## 5 Conclusions and Future Work

Considering that the decision tree construction method based on traditional Rough Sets Theory works only for consistence decision tables, we proposed a novel algorithm based on Various Precise Rough Sets Model, which has to some extent the ability of fault-tolerance, that is, even though there exists inconsistent data in the decision table, the algorithm may give a relatively satisfying result. Compared to the ID3 algorithm, our algorithm outputs a decision tree with less nodes and better rules. We have shown experimentally that this algorithm is valid and workable. This paper extends the application horizon of the VPRST. There remains some future work to be done. One is to select a proper precise value Beta to a problem. The goal is to automatically or adaptively determine a suitable model of precise value Beta that can reduce the effect of noises and outliers for a class of problems. Another is how to understand and interpreted the decision by an generalization.

**Acknowledgments.** Research described in this paper was supported by Science & Technology Committee of Shanghai Municipality Key Project Grant 02DJ14045.

## References

1. Pawlak Z.: Rough sets. In: International Journal of Information and Computer Sciences 1982;11(5):341–56.
2. Pawlak Z, Slowinski K, Slowinski R.: Rough classification of patients after highly selective vagotomy for duodenal ulcer. In: International Journal of Man–Machine Studies 1986;24:413–33.itor
3. Z. Pawlak, Rough Sets, Theoretical Aspects of Reasoning about Data. Dordrecht, Kluwer, 1991.
4. T. Mollestad and A. Skowron: A rough set framework for data mining of propositional default rules. In: Lecture Notes Comput. Sci., 1996, vol. 1079, pp. 448–457.
5. Ziarko, W. (1991). : Variable Precision Rough Set Model. In: Journal of Computer and System Sciences, 46, 39–59. 18
6. L. Polkowski and A. Skowron: Rough Sets in Knowledge Discovery 1 and 2. In: Heidelberg, Germany: Physica-Verlag, 1998.
7. Beynon, Malcolm J, Peel, Michael J: Variable precision rough set theory and data discretisation: an application to corporate failure prediction. In: Omega Volume: 29, Issue: 6, December, 2001, pp. 561–576
8. Beynon, Malcolm: Reducts within the variable precision rough sets model: A further investigation. In: European Journal of Operational Research Volume: 134, Issue: 3, November 1, 2001, pp. 592–605
9. Quinlan J.R.: Induction of decision trees. In: Machine Learning, ,1 986,1 (1 ):81~ 1 0 6
10. G. Lambert-Torres et al.: Power System Security Analysis based on Rough Classification. In: Rough-Fuzzy Hybridization: New Trend in Decision Making, por S.K. Pal & A. Skowron, Springer-Verlag Co., ISBN 981-4021-00-8, pp. 263–274, 1999.
11. Sushmita Mitra: Data Mining in Soft Computing Framework: A Survey. In: IEEE TRANSACTIONS ON NEURAL NETWORKS, VOL. 13, NO. 1, JANUARY 2002
12. D.Q. Miao,Yu Wang: Rough Sets Based Approach For Multivariate Decision Tree Construction. In: Journal of Software .1 997,8(6);425–431
13. Maria Zamfir Bleyberg and Arulkumar Elumalai: Using rough sets to construct sense type decision trees for text categorization. http://www.cis.ksu.edu/~maria/research.html
14. Ziarko W.: A variable precision rough set model. In: Journal of Computer and System Sciences 1993;46:39–59.
15. Fayyad U, Irani K.: Multi-interval discretization of continuous-valued attributes for classification learning. In: Proceedings of the 13th International Joint Conference on Arti9cial Intelligence. Chambery, France: Kaufmann, 1993.p. 1022–7.
16. Kerber R. ChiMerge: discretization of numeric attributes. In: Proceedings of the Ninth International Conference onArti9cial Intelligence (AAAI). Cambridge, MA: AAAI Press=The MITS Press, 1992. p. 123–8.
17. LiuH, Setiono R.: Feature selection via discretization. In: IEEE Transactions on Knowledge and Data Engineering 1997;9(4):642–5.
18. Zhang L., Yu S., Ye Y.M: SLMBSVMs: A structural-loss-minimization-based support vector machines approach. In: IEEE The First International Conference on Machine Learning and Cybernetics , 2002

# A New Heuristic Reduct Algorithm Base on Rough Sets Theory

Jing Zhang[1], Jianmin Wang[2], Deyi Li[2], Huacan He[1], and Jiaguang Sun[2]

[1] Department of Computer Science and Engineering, Northwestern Polytechnical University, 710072, Xi'an, P.R.China
jane_zhang@263.net

[2] School of Software, Tsinghua University, 100084, Beijing, P.R.China
jimwang@tsinghua.edu.cn

**Abstract.** Real world data sets usually have many features, which increases the complexity of data mining task. Feature selection, as a preprocessing step to the data mining, has been shown very effective in reducing dimensionality, removing irrelevant data, increasing learning accuracy, and improving comprehensibility. To find the optimal feature subsets is the aim of feature selection. Rough sets theory provides a mathematical approach to find optimal feature subset, but this approach is time consuming. In this paper, we propose a novel heuristic algorithm based on rough sets theory to find out the feature subset. This algorithm employs appearing frequency of attribute as heuristic information. Experiment results show in most times our algorithm can find out optimal feature subset quickly and efficiently.

## 1 Introduction

Real world data sets usually have many features; some of them are irrelevant or redundant. The exist of such feature will increase the complexity of data mining task, add noise to the data, and make the result of data mining difficult to understand. For data mining, a successful choice of features can improve the accuracy, save the computation time and memory space, and simplify its results. Feature selection is a process that chooses an optimal feature subset according to a certain criterion.[1] It will reduce the dimensionality of the data and may allow data mining to operate faster and more effectively. In some cases, accuracy on data mining results can be improved; in others, the result is a more compact, easily interpreted representation of the target concept. [2]

Reduct is an important concept introduced by rough sets theory. Finding reduct is similar to feature subset selection, and minimal reduct is equal to optimal feature subset, so rough sets theory provides a mathematical approach to find optimal feature subset. In rough sets theory, reduct can be calculated by discernibility function, but it is a NP-hard problem. In this paper, we propose a new heuristic algorithm of feature selection that is based on rough sets theory. In our approach, the features are evaluated by its frequencies appear in the

G. Dong et al. (Eds.): WAIM 2003, LNCS 2762, pp. 247–253, 2003.

discernibility matrix. Our algorithm can take out all redundant features from feature set effectively, and in most times the optimal result can be obtained.

The paper is organized as follows: the next section is about rough sets concept related to feature selection approach and a brief overview of related work based on rough sets theory. Section 3 introduces our heuristic approach of feature selection. Section 4 shows experimental results and compares our approach with a related method. Finally, Section 5 gives concluding remarks.

## 2 Rough Sets Theory

Rough sets theory was introduced by Pawlak [3] in the early 1980s as a mathematical tool to deal with uncertainty. Reduct is an important concept in rough sets theory. Reduct is those minimal attribute sets of information system, which keep the same classify capability with original attribute set. The aim of feature subset selection is to find out a minimum set of relevant attributes that describe the dataset as well as the original all attributes do. So finding reduct is similar to feature selection. Rough sets theory provides an approach to find out all reduct (all possible feature subsets). In this section, we introduce the principal concepts of rough sets theory related to our feature selection approach. The detail of the theory can be found in [4].

Reduct is those minimal attribute sets of information system, which keep the same classify capability with original attribute set. The aim of feature subset selection is to finding out a minimum set of relevant attributes that describe the dataset as well as the original all attributes do. So finding reduct is similar to feature selection.

**Information System:** In rough sets theory, an information system S is denoted as S={U,A,V,f}, where U is a finite set of instances, U={ $x_1$ , $x_2$ ,. . . , $x_n$ }, A is a finite set of attributes(features). The attributes in A is further classified into two disjoint subsets, condition attribute set C and decision attribute set D, A=C $\bigcup$ D and $C \bigcap D = \phi$ . $V = \bigcup_{p \in A} V_p$ and $V_p$ is a domain of attribute p. $f : U \times A \rightarrow V$ is a function that $f(x_i, q) \in V_p$ for every $q \in A, x_i \in U$ .

**Indiscernibility Relation:** Let $P \subseteq A$ , $x_i, x_j \in U$ . A binary relation IND called indiscernibility relation is defined as follow:

$$IND(P) = \{(x_i, x_j) | (x_i, x_j) \in U \times U, a \in P, f(x_i, a) = f(x_j, a)\} \quad (1)$$

Let $U/IND(P)$ denote the family of all equivalence classes of the relation IND(P) (the simplify notation is $U/P$ ).

**Lower Approximation:** Let $R \subseteq C$ and $X \subseteq U$ . The lower approximation of X with respect to R is defined as follow:

$$\underline{RX} = \bigcup \{Y \in U/R : Y \subseteq X\} \quad (2)$$

$\underline{RX}$ is the set of all elements of U which can be with certain classified as elements of X, according to knowledge R.

**Positive Region:** The positive region of decision attribute set D with respect to R is the set of all objects from universe U that can be classified with certainty to classes of U/D employing attributes from R. It can be presented formally as

$$POS_R(D) = \bigcup_{X \in U/D} \underline{RX} \tag{3}$$

**Indispensable Attribute:** Attribute $c \in R$ is dispensable feature in attributes subset $R \subseteq C$, if $POS_{(R-\{c\})}(D) = POS_R(D)$, otherwise attribute c is dispensable attribute.

**Reduct:** Let $R' \subseteq R$. R' is a reduct of R, if $POS_{R'}(D) = POS_R(D)$, and every attribute $c : c \in R'$ is indispensable respect to R'. So the reduct is the minimal attribute subset of information system, which classify capability is equal to original attribute (feature) set of information system. It is obviously that there may be several reducts of an information system.

**Core:** Core of information system S is the intersection of all reducts of S, i.e.

$$CORE(S) = \bigcap RED(S) \tag{4}$$

where RED(S) is the reduct of information system S.

**Discernibiliy Matrix and Discernibility Function:** The discernibility matrix M(S) of an information system $S = \{U, C \bigcup D, V, f\}$ is a $|U| \times |U|$ matrix of S, with entry defined as

$$m_{ij} = \{c | (c \in C, f(x_i, C) \neq f(x_j, c)) \wedge (d \in D, f(x_i, d) \neq f(x_j, d))\} \tag{5}$$

for $i, j = 1, 2, \cdots, n$

So $m_{ij}$ is the set of all attributes that can distinguish the instance $x_i$ and $x_j$ into different decision classes in U/IND(D). All reduct of information system can be obtained by discernibility function. A discernibility function F(M) for an information system S can be denoted as

$$F(M) = \wedge_{1 \leq j \leq i \leq n} \{\vee m_{ij}\} \tag{6}$$

where $\wedge$ and $\vee$ are Boolean conjunction and disjunction, $\vee m_{ij}$ means the disjunction of all attributes in discernibility matrix entry $m_{ij}$. The set of all prime implicants of F(M) determines all reducts of information system S. [5]

We can find out all reduct by constructing discernibility function. Unfortunately, finding out minimal or all reduct of information system are also NP-hard in rough sets theory. Hence the heuristic algorithm is a better choice. There some heuristic algorithms based on rough sets theory.

Keyun Hu proposed a heuristic algorithm using discernibility matrix. [6] Hu's approach provides a weighting mechanism to rank attributes.

In [7], Ning Zhong presents a wrapper approach using rough sets theory with greedy heuristics for feature selection. His algorithm employs the number of consistent instances as heuristics.

Although many reduct algorithms have been proposed, there is no accredited best heuristic reduct algorithm. So far, it's still an open research area in rough sets theory.

## 3 A New Heuristic Reduct Algorithm

As we mentioned in section 2, every entry in discernibility matrix is a set of attributes that can be distinguished by the attributes. The more frequent an attribute appears in entries of discernibility matrix, the more instance pairs can be distinguished by this attribute. So appearing frequency represents the distinguish ability of the attribute. In other words, appearing frequency implies relevance between attribute and class label. Thus attributes' frequency can be used as heuristic. We can sort attributes into ascending order by its frequency, and add first attribute (which one with highest appearing frequency) to reduct. Then we examine reduct by number of instance pairs that can be distinguished by this reduct. If threshold cannot be satisfied, next attribute is added to reduct. Do it recursively until stop criteria are satisfied.

In an optimal feature subset, feature should have high relevance with class label, and have low relevance with other features in the subset. This approach can take out irrelevant attributes, but how about redundant attributes? For example: Attribute a has highest appearing frequency in discernibility matrix. Attribute b is completely dependents with a, and b's appearing frequency only lower than attribute a. If there is attribute c with appearing frequency lower than attribute b, but attribute c is irrelevant with attribute attribute a. According this approach a should be added in reduct firstly, and then b is added. Attribute c is added to reduct after attribute b. But in fact, it is obviously attribute b cannot provide any additional distinguish ability to the feature subset, and it should be take out from reduct. So the above approach can not guarantee that attributes in subset have low relevance with each other. In order to solve this problem, we propose a simple but efficient method to avoid adding redundant attributes to reduct. After an attribute $a_i$ added to reduct, we remove all entries containing $a_i$ from discernibility matrix, recount attributes' appearing frequency in remained entries. Then attribute with highest new appearing frequency should be added to reduct. In fact, the remained entries represent the instances in boundary region with respect to attribute subset. According to attribute subsets, those instances cannot be distinctly classified into positive region or negative region. Thus the less boundary region attributes means the more powerful classify capacity.

On the other hand, length of entry means how many attributes can distinguish corresponding instance pair. Shorter entry implies only few attributes can distinguish corresponding instance pair. The shorter the entry is, the more important attributes in this entry are. Extremely, if entry length is 1, the only attribute contained in this entry is a member of core. So the length of entry also can be used as another heuristic information.

In our algorithm, every attribute has two properties: appearing frequency in discernibility matrix and shortest entry length. Attribute's appearing frequency is updated after a new attribute added to reduct; attribute's length is the length of shortest entry containing this attribute and it is calculated when discernibility matrix is computed. We select attribute according these two properties. The attribute with highest frequency is selected to reduct. If several attributes have same frequency, the shortest one will take precedence.

### 3.1 The Algorithm

We list our algorithm as follows:

```
Input:
  Information system: I; Condition attribute set: A;
  Decision attribute set: D; Threshold.
Output:
  A reduct of information system I: Reduct.
Initial State:
  Reduct = Null, k = 1.

Step 1:
  Generate discernibility matrix M, calculate frequency(ai) and
  length(ai).
  CardM = Card(M)
Step 2:
  Reduct = Core
  F = A - Core
Step 3:
  M = M - {m}, where intersection of entry m and Reduct is not
  empty.
  Recount frequency(ai) and length(ai)
Step 4:
  k = Card(M)/CardM
  if K <= Threshold, Stop.
Step 5:
  Choose highest appearing frequency attribute f form F.
  If there are several attributes with same appearing frequency,
  choose the shortest one as f.
  Reduct = reduct + {f},
  F = F - {f}
Step 6:
  Go to Step 3.
```

### 3.2 Implement and Time Complexity

In order to save space, attribute sets are implemented as bit vector. Length of bit vector is equal to number of attributes. A bit of bit vector is set to 1 if corresponding attribute is contained by attribute subset, 0 otherwise. For example, in an information system I with four attributes $\{a_1, a_2, a_3, a_4\}$ , a bit vector of attribute subset $\{a_1, a_4\}$ is represented as 1001.

Since discernibility matrix is a symmetrical matrix, there are $|U|(|U|-1)/2$ entries in matrix. To generate each entry, every attribute value of corresponding instance pair should be compared. So in step 1, the cost for generating discernibility matrix is $O(|A||U|^2)$ . But in fact, there are much less entries in discernibility matrix, since entry corresponding to same class instance pair is empty. Cost for finding out highest appearing frequency attribute is $O(|A|)$ , and cost for finding out shortest attribute is also $O(|A|)$ . In the worst case, supposing that there are no redundant and irrelevant attribute in information system, in order to generate reduct it would recur $|A|-1$ times. So the cost to calculate reduct is $(|A|^2|U|^2)$ .

In conclusion, the total cost of our algorithm is $O(|A||U|^2+2|A|+|A|^2|U|^2)$ . so the time complexity is $O(|A|^2|U|^2)$ . It is less than time complexity of Hu's alogrithm ( $O(|A|^3|U|^2)$ ).

## 4 Experiment

In order to evaluate the performance of our algorithm, we have tested it on UCI repository of machine learning database.[8] The continuous attributes are discretized by Entropy/MDL algorithm of Rossetta. [9] We also use RSES Exhaustive reducer of Rosetta to generate all reducts of data set, and compare all reducts with our result. The experiment results are list at table 1.

**Table 1.** Experiment Result

| Data set | Attributes | Instances | Selected Attributes | Reduct ? | Optimal ? |
|---|---|---|---|---|---|
| Breast Cancer | 11 | 699 | 4 | Reduct | Yes |
| Bridges | 13 | 108 | 2 | Reduct | Yes |
| Car | 7 | 1728 | 6 | Reduct | Yes |
| Glass | 11 | 214 | 6 | Reduct | Yes |
| Iris | 5 | 150 | 3 | Reduct | Yes |
| Monk1 | 7 | 124 | 3 | Reduct | Yes |
| Monk3 | 7 | 122 | 4 | Reduct | Yes |
| Pima | 9 | 768 | 4 | Reduct | No |
| Tic-tac-toe | 10 | 958 | 8 | Reduct | Yes |
| House-votes | 17 | 435 | 9 | Reduct | Yes |
| Zoo | 17 | 101 | 5 | Reduct | Yes |

In table 1, first column is the name of data set, and second one is attribute number, the third is instance number. Numbers of attributes selected by our algorithm are list in the fourth column. Reduct in fifth column means result of our algorithm is one of the data set's reducts. In sixth column, yes means result is the shortest reduct of data set.

For example,there are 17 attributes and 435 instances in data set house-votes. The result of our algorithm is {0,1,2,3,8,10,14,15} (number in bracket is attribute index). All reducts generated by Rosetta [9] are: {0,1,2,3,4,5,8,10,12,13,15}, {0,1,2,3,8,10,12,14,15} and {0,1,2,5,6,8,9,10,11,12,13,14,15}. The second one is the minimal reduct of house-votes. So our result is the optimal feature subset.

As the experiment result show, our algorithm can find out shortest reduct in most times. Even shortest reduct cannot be found; our algorithm can generate a shorter reduct without irrelevant and redundant attributes. According complexity analysis in section 4, our algorithm is faster than algorithms of [6] and [10]

## 5 Conclusion

In this paper we present a new heuristic algorithm to generate the optimal reduct. This algorithm employs appearing frequency of attribute as heuristic information to speed selection process, and proposes a simple but effective approach to eliminate redundant attributes from attributes subset. Its time complexity is $O(|A|^2|U|^2)$ . Experiments show in most times it can find minimal reduct. Sometimes even minimal reduct can not be found, our algorithm always can give a reduct without any redundant attributes.

No single algorithm is superior to all others. Our further research will focus on combination our algorithm with other approaches to improve performance of feature subset selection.

**Acknowledgements.** This research is supported by 2002CB312000 program of National 973 Fundamental Research Program.

## References

1. Huan Liu, Hiroshi Motoda.: Feature Selcection for Knowledge discovery and Data Mining. Kluwer Academic Publishers (1998)
2. Hall, M.A.: Correlation-based Feature Selection for Machine Learning. PHD thesis. Department of Computer Science, University of Waikato, Hamilton (1999)
3. Pawlak, Z.: Rough Sets, Int. J. Compute Inf. Sci. 11 (1982) 341–356
4. Pawlak, Z.: Rough Sets: Theoretical Aspects of Reasoning about Data. Kluwer Academic Publishers. (1991)
5. Skowron, A., rauszer, C.: The Discernibility matrices and Functions in Inforamtion Systems, in Intelligent Decision Support – Handbook of Applications and Advances of the Rough Sets Theory. (1992) 331–362
6. Keyun Hu, lili Diao and Chunyi Shi: A Heuristic Optimal Reduct algorithm. 22nd Intl. Sym. on Intelligent Data Engineering and Automated Learning (IDEAL2000), Hong Kong, (2002)
7. Ning Zhong, Junzhen Dong.: Using Rough Sets with Heuristics for Feature Selection, Journal of Intelligent Information Systems, 16 (2001) 199–214
8. Blake, C. L. and Merz, C. J.: UCI Repository of Machine Learning Databases. http://www.ics.uci.edu/ mlearn/MLRepositყory.html
9. Aleksander Øhrn: Inst. of Mathematics, University of Warsaw, Poland. http://www.idi.ntun.no/ aleks/rosetta/
10. Guan, J. W. and Bell, D. A.: Rough Computational methods for Information Systems, Artificial Intelligence, 1998.

# Using Rules to Analyse Bio-medical Data: A Comparison between C4.5 and PCL

Jinyan Li and Limsoon Wong

Institute for Infocomm Research,
21 Heng Mui Keng Terrace, Singapore, 119613
{jinyan, limsoon}@i2r.a-star.edu.sg

**Abstract.** For easy comprehensibility, rules are preferrable to non-linear kernel functions in the analysis of bio-medical data. In this paper, we describe two rule induction approaches—C4.5 and our PCL classifier—for discovering rules from both traditional clinical data and recent gene expression or proteomic profiling data. C4.5 is a widely used method, but it has two weaknesses, the single coverage constraint and the fragmentation problem, that affect its accuracy. PCL is a new rule-based classifier that overcomes these two weaknesses of decision trees by using many significant rules. We present a thorough comparison to show that our PCL method is much more accurate than C4.5, and it is also superior to Bagging and Boosting in general.

## 1 Introduction

In the analysis of bio-medical data, rule-based classifiers such as decision trees derived by C4.5 [16] or CART [2] have an advantage over non-linear kernel function based classifiers (e.g., support vector machines or neural networks). The advantage is that rules have easier comprehensibility than non-linear functions. Also, rules can capture interactions or causal relationships among features explicitly. However, the widely used C4.5 rule induction method is less accurate than other methods. Two factors are attributed to this inferior accuracy: the single coverage constraint and the fragmentation problem [14,7,13].

The single coverage constraint originates from the heuristic nature of the C4.5 method. The construction of C4.5 trees is a recursive process. The process first selects a feature which is most discriminatory with regard to the entire training data. Then the process goes to use this feature to split the data into non-overlapping sub-groups so that each sub-group contains as many samples of the same class as possible. Then the process is applied to each of these sub-groups of the training data, and iteratively applied to the resulting sub-groups until all sub-groups contain pure or almost pure class of samples.

Each sub-group of training data corresponds to a rule with which all samples in this sub-group satisfy. Because no training data is repeated in these sub-groups, no training samples can satisfy more than one rule's conditions. So, every training sample has one and only one rule in the tree to be satisfied. We call this the single coverage constraint or mutual exclusivity. Due to this constraint, decision tree methods do not encourage

G. Dong et al. (Eds.): WAIM 2003, LNCS 2762, pp. 254–265, 2003.

many significant rules to be generated, though there exist lots of significant rules in bio-medical data particularly for high-dimensional gene expression profiling data [8,18, 17,9]. The small number of significant rules can lead to biased predictions.

The fragmentation problem is that as less and less training data are used to search for root nodes of sub-trees (sub-groups), a series of many locally important but globally unimportant rules may be generated. These minor rules can in turn mis-guide the resulting system, decreasing the accuracy of the trees.

Recently, the Bagging [3] and Boosting [6] have been proposed to help improve C4.5 classifier. However the use of bootstrapped training data can cause other problems. For example, rules are not always true. As some samples are duplicated and some are removed during training, rules induced from bootstrapped training data may not be correct when applied to the original data. This is a critical concern in bio-medical applications such as the understanding and diagnosis of a disease. Although the approach may help to improve the resulting classifiers' accuracy, the rules should be interpreted cautiously.

How to discover many significant and true rules for a classifier so that the classifier can reach a high accuracy? This is the main motivation for us to propose the PCL classifier [10]. As shown later on a wide range of bio-medical data sets, PCL is more accurate than C4.5, Bagging, and Boosting. Its performance is sometimes better than SVM and $k$-nearest neighbour.

We make three main contributions in this paper:

- We found that the two weaknesses of decision trees mentioned earlier quite often exist in the analysis of high-dimensional bio-medical data.
- To solve the problem, we use multiple significant rules for classification, as adapted in our PCL classifier.
- To demonstrate the effectiveness of our idea, we conduct extensive experiments to show that our PCL classifier is more accurate than the C4.5 family of algorithms.

The core knowledge patterns used in PCL are called emerging patterns (or EPs for short) [4]. By definition, an emerging pattern is an itemset whose frequency changes significantly from one class to another class. If we interpret an item as a condition—the pair of a feature and its value, then an EP can be defined as a set of conditions. The following is an example of EP, as discovered from a gene expression profiling of the prostate disease [17],

$$\{\text{gene(37720\_at)} > 215, \text{gene(38028\_at)} <= 12\}$$

This EP can be interpreted as a conjunctive set of conditions: The expression of gene 37720_at is larger than 215 and the expression of gene 38028_at is not larger than 12. This condition is satisfied by about 73% of prostate disease cells, but is not satisfied by any normal cell. Thus, this EP jumps from its 0% frequency in the normal class to a high frequency of 73% in the tumor class. This paper focuses on this type of EPs. This EP also indicates a rule that if the expression of gene 37720_at is larger than 215 and the expression of gene 38028_at is not larger than 12, then this cell is a tumor cell. So an EP is also a rule; its significance is measured by its frequency change.

Every significant EP sharply differentiates two classes of data. Our PCL classifier can discover many significant EPs using an efficient global search method, and PCL can compactly integrate the discriminating power of multiple significant EPs. In contrast, C4.5 uses a minimum number of significant rules and also uses some minor rules for classification. This is the main reason for the high accuracy of our PCL classifier.

The rest of the paper is organized as follows. In Section 2, we present examples to show decision trees having thin structures—small number of features are contained in a tree, and the tree has almost perfect training accuracy. The thin structure is directly caused by the single coverage constraint. Such thin structures often occur in high dimensional bio-medical data sets, for example, gene expression profiling data or proteomic profiling data. Usually, the thin structure cannot provide high accuracy and reliability when real test data are encountered. To overcome this problem, we break the single coverage constraint, and allow every training data to be described by multiple rules. In Section 3, we describe steps for the discovery of emerging patterns from data. In Section 4, we briefly review our PCL classifier and give an example to show how to use this classifier. In Section 5, we describe two groups of data sets for comparing C4.5 and PCL and for evaluating our ideas. One group of data sets include the widely used bio-medical data sets stored at the UCI machine learning repository. The other include recently published high-dimensional medical profiling data. These high-dimensional data sets are usually described by more than 10000 features. In Section 6, we report our experimental results on the considered data sets, and compare the performance of C4.5 and PCL. Section 7 concludes this paper with a summary.

## 2 Thin Structure of Decision Trees

An ideal decision-tree based classifier should be a structure that contains a small number of features and that has perfect accuracy on both training and test data. By a thin structure, we mean that a decision tree that contains a small number of features and has perfect training accuracy, but its performance does not well support independent unknown test data.

Decision trees having a thin structure are often found in trees induced from high-dimensional bio-medical data such as gene expression profiles. We show some examples later. With these examples, we aim to explain the following three facts:

- A very tiny portion of features can establish a decision tree, and the tree can explain the training data very well.
- There are a lot of decision trees that can explain the training data similarly.
- The use of combined trees can reduce errors in classifying test samples.

These facts strongly support our idea of the PCL classifier that uses multiple significant rules for excellent classification.

We first use C4.5 [16] to discover a decision tree from a gene expression profiling data. The data consists of 215 training samples (14 MLL plus 201 others) and 112 test samples (6 MLL plus 106 others) for differentiating the MLL subtype from the other subtypes of childhood leukemia disease [18]. The data are described by 12558 features. Here each feature is a gene, having continuous expression values.

This decision tree has a structure as depicted in Figure 1. We note that this tree has only 4 non-leave nodes. That is only 4 features are used to clearly differentiate the training samples. Compared to the total 12558 number of features describing the data, the 4 features used in the tree is a very tiny fraction. We also note that this tree has perfect 100% accuracy on the 215 training samples, but it made 4 mistakes on the 112 test samples; about one third of the MLL class were wrongly classified. So, the tree did not maintain its high performance on the unseen test data.

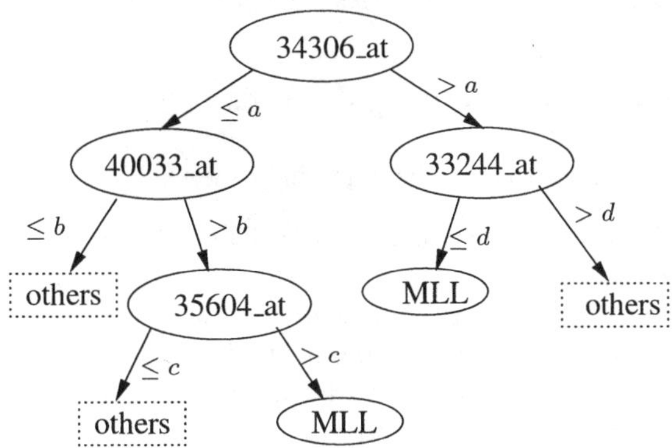


**Fig. 1.** A decision tree induced by C4.5 from the training data of the MLL-others data set for differentiating the subtype MLL against other subtypes of childhood leukemia [18]. Here $a = 13683.6, b = 3691.4, c = 986.9, d = 846.6$.

In fact, we discovered many different decision trees from this data set that have similar performance as the tree discovered by the C4.5 method. Our method for discovering decision trees is as follows: We force one of top-ranked features as root nodes sequentially to discover many decision trees. For example, to discover 10 decision trees, we use 10 of top-ranked features each as the root node of a tree. Table 1 summarizes the training and test performance, and the number of features used in our 10 trees that are discovered from the MLL-others data set. It can be seen that the 10 trees made similar numbers of errors on the training and test data in general. An interesting thing here is that the 5th, 8th, and 9th trees made smaller number of errors than the first tree made.

**Table 1.** The training and test errors of our 10 decision trees on the MLL-others data set that consist of 215 training and 112 test samples. The numbers of features in the 10 trees are also listed.

| Tree No. | 1 | 2 | 3 | 4 | 5 | 6 | 7 | 8 | 9 | 10 |
|---|---|---|---|---|---|---|---|---|---|---|
| Training errors | 0 | 0 | 0 | 0 | 0 | 0 | 1 | 0 | 0 | 0 |
| Test errors | 4 | 3 | 2 | 3 | 2 | 6 | 7 | 2 | 1 | 6 |
| # of features | 4 | 4 | 4 | 4 | 4 | 4 | 4 | 4 | 4 | 6 |

We also examined the performance of combined trees. If combining the first 4 trees, namely using 4 times more number of significant rules than the first tree, the committee did not made any errors on the 112 test samples, eliminating the 4 mistakes made by the first tree. Adding more trees till the 10th tree, the committee still maintains the perfect test accuracy. So, the use of multiple significant rules can reduce errors and therefore can overcome the thin structure problem of decision trees. This motivates us to discover many significant rules, for example using global search methods, from data and use them compactly for classification. In the next section, we use the concept of emerging patterns as a global search method to discover rules from data.

## 3 Real Examples of Emerging Patterns

We use the following steps to discover emerging patterns [4].

1. Using the entropy method [5], rank individually the features in terms of their power to distinguish two classes.
2. Select and discretize the top-ranked features. Usually, we select the 20 top features in the analysis of high-dimensional bio-medical data.
3. Discover significant emerging patterns from the discretized data by a naive method [10] or border-based algorithms [12,4,11].

Next we present important emerging patterns discovered from the training data of the MLL-others data set (mentioned earlier). The importance of emerging patterns is measured by their frequency in their home class. Table 2 shows 10 important EPs, and their counts and their frequency change between the two classes.

**Table 2.** A partial list of top-ranked EPs discovered from the MLL-others data set. The reference numbers contained in the patterns each represent an item (a condition). For example, the reference number 3 in the first EP stands for the condition "the expression of gene 36777_$at$ $<$ 5294.35", and similarly for other numbers.

| EPs | Counts (Frequency) in MLL class | Counts (Frequency) in others class |
|---|---|---|
| $\{1,3\}$ | 0 | 193 (96.02%) |
| $\{1,5,7\}$ | 0 | 192 (95.52%) |
| $\{1,7,36\}$ | 0 | 191 (95.02%) |
| $\{1,26\}$ | 0 | 190 (94.53%) |
| $\{11,36\}$ | 0 | 187 (93.03%) |
| $\{13,15,21,24,39\}$ | 14(100.00%) | 0 |
| $\{13,15,21,22,24\}$ | 14(100.00%) | 0 |
| $\{13,15,24,33,39\}$ | 14(100.00%) | 0 |
| $\{13,15,22,24,33\}$ | 14(100.00%) | 0 |
| $\{9,13,15,24,33\}$ | 14(100.00%) | 0 |

As already shown, the interpretation of EPs into rules is easy. Again for example, the first EP $\{1,3\}$ of Table 2 is translated into the following rule. If the expression of gene 34306_$at$ is less than 13630.3 and the expression of gene 36777_$at$ is less than 5294.35, then this leukemia cell is from others class but not from MLL. The two conditions are represented by the reference number 1 and 3 respectively. This is a strong rule because about 96.02% samples from the others class satisfy this rule. Another example is the last EP—$\{9, 13, 15, 24, 33\}$—of Table 2. It is interpreted as the following rule. If the five conditions (represented by the five items $9, 13, 15, 24, 33$) are satisfied, then this cell is from the MLL class, otherwise it is from the others class.

Observe that some training samples in this MLL-others data set can be explained by different significant rules. In classifying a test sample, even when one or two significant rules are missed, the other significant rules can still help to make accurate decision. In contrast, in C4.5, if a test sample misses a significant rule, then those minor rules may sometime mis-guide the classification. Our PCL classifier [10] makes use of multiple significant rules so that some possibly biased predictions could be avoided. Next we briefly review this algorithm.

## 4 PCL: Prediction by Collective Likelihood from Emerging Patterns

Given two training datasets $\mathcal{D}^P$ and $\mathcal{D}^N$ and a testing sample $T$, the first phase of the PCL classifier is to discover EPs from $\mathcal{D}^P$ and $\mathcal{D}^N$. Denote the ranked EPs of $\mathcal{D}^P$ as, $EP_1^P, EP_2^P, \cdots, EP_i^P$, in descending order of their frequency. Similarly, denote the ranked EPs of $\mathcal{D}^N$ as $EP_1^N, EP_2^N, \cdots, EP_j^N$ also in descending order of their frequency.

Suppose the test sample $T$ contains the following EPs of $\mathcal{D}^P$: $EP_{i_1}^P, EP_{i_2}^P, \cdots, EP_{i_x}^P$, where $i_1 < i_2 < \cdots < i_x \leq i$, and the following EPs of $\mathcal{D}^N$: $EP_{j_1}^N, EP_{j_2}^N, \cdots, EP_{j_y}^N$, where $j_1 < j_2 < \cdots < j_y \leq j$.

The next step is to calculate two scores for predicting the class label of $T$. Suppose we use $k$ ($k \ll i$ and $k \ll j$) top-ranked EPs of $\mathcal{D}^P$ and $\mathcal{D}^N$. Then we define the score of $T$ in the $\mathcal{D}^P$ class as $score(T, \mathcal{D}^P) = \sum_{m=1}^{k} \frac{frequency(EP_{i_m}^P)}{frequency(EP_m^P)}/k$, and similarly the score in the $\mathcal{D}^N$ class as $score(T, \mathcal{D}^N) = \sum_{m=1}^{k} \frac{frequency(EP_{j_m}^N)}{frequency(EP_m^N)}/k$. If $score(T, \mathcal{D}^P) > score(T, \mathcal{D}^N)$, then $T$ is predicted as the class of $\mathcal{D}^P$. Otherwise, it is predicted as the class of $\mathcal{D}^N$.

Next we demonstrate how the classification scores are computed. Suppose $k = 5$, and the frequencies of the 5 top-ranked EPs of the positive class are sorted as 90% ($EP_1^P$), 85% ($EP_2^P$), 80% ($EP_3^P$), 75% ($EP_4^P$), and 70% ($EP_5^P$). Assume the test sample $T$ contains $EP_1^P$ (90%), $EP_3^P$ (80%), $EP_5^P$ (70%), $EP_7^P$ (40%), and $EP_9^P$ (35%). Then $score(T, \mathcal{D}^P) = (\frac{90}{90} + \frac{80}{85} + \frac{70}{80} + \frac{40}{75} + \frac{35}{70})/5 = 0.75$.

Note that $0 \leq score(T, \mathcal{D}^P), score(T, \mathcal{D}^N) \leq 1$. So, the scores appear to be like likelihood. Let's explain when $score(T, \mathcal{D}^P) = 1$ and when $score(T, \mathcal{D}^N)$ is 0. The score $score(T, \mathcal{D}^P) = 1$ if and only if the test sample $T$ satisfies all $k$ top-ranked positive EPs: $EP_1^P, EP_2^P, \cdots, EP_k^P$. The other score $score(T, \mathcal{D}^N) = 0$ if and only if the test sample does not satisfy anyone of the $k$ top-ranked negative EPs. When such scores occur, the prediction is highly confident. If the two scores are close to each other, then the prediction should be taken carefully. But the tie-score cases rarely occurred in our analyses.

## 5 Data Sets Description

We use two groups of bio-medical data sets to compare the performance of C4.5 (single, Bagging and Boosting) and our PCL classifier. One group includes traditional clinical data sets stored at the widely used UCI machine learning repository [1]. The other group includes recently published high-dimensional profiling data sets such as gene expression profiles and proteomic mass/charge profiles.

We use Table 3 to summarize the background information of 10 bio-medical data sets from the UCI machine learning repository.

**Table 3.** Ten classical bio-medical data sets from the UCI machine learning repository. The total number of samples in a data set and the number of samples in each class are shown in the fourth column; while the third column can be used to match the data volume in a specific class.

| Data sets | # of features | Class names | # of samples |
|---|---|---|---|
| Breast-w | 9 | 2, 4 | $699(= 458 + 241)$ |
| Cleve | 13 | 1, 2 | $303(= 165 + 148)$ |
| Heart | 13 | 1, 2 | $270(= 150 + 120)$ |
| Hepatitis | 19 | 1, 2 | $155(= 32 + 123)$ |
| HIV | 8 | 0, 1 | $362(= 248 + 114)$ |
| Hypothyroid | 29 | h, n | $3163(= 151 + 3012)$ |
| Lymph | 18 | 2, 3 | $142(= 81 + 61)$ |
| Promoter | 60 | +, - | $106(= 53 + 53)$ |
| Sick | 29 | sick, negative | $3772(= 231 + 3541)$ |
| Splice | 60 | EI, IE, N | $3175(= 762 + 765 + 1648)$ |

The second group of data sets include 3 high-dimensional data sets for cancer diagnosis using gene expression or proteomic profiling data. Gene expression profiling has been widely used in post-genome cancer research studies [8,18,17,9], while mass spectrometry is also increasingly being used in the cancer research field for measuring the mass-charge ratios of molecular proteins in tumor tissues [15]. These technologies are breakthroughs in molecular biology because they can simultaneously measure values of thousands of features like genes' expression level or proteomic mass. The resulting data are very helpful in the subtype classification of a disease, in the classification of tumor or normal cells, in the prognosis of patients, and in the stage determination of a disease. Basically, all of these application are classical supervised learning problems. For example, in the childhood leukemia data set [18], the goal is to correctly classify subtypes of this heterogeneous disease; in the ovarian tumor data set [15], it is aimed to classify tumor and normal cells for diagnostic purpose; while in the lung cancer data set [9], it is aimed to differentiate two types of disease.

We use Table 4 to summarize the background information of 6 data sets for the subtype classification of the childhood leukemia disease. All these data are available at our Kent Ridge Bio-medical Data Sets Repository, whose URL is at `http://sdmc.lit.org.sg/GEDatasets/Datasets.html`.

**Table 4.** Data sets for the subtype classification of the childhood leukemia disease. The class names listed in the third column can be used to match the number of training or test samples in a specific class.

| Data sets | # of features | Class names | Training size | Test size |
|---|---|---|---|---|
| BCR-ABL | 12558 | BCR-ABL, others | $9 + 206$ | $6 + 106$ |
| E2A-PBX1 | 12558 | E2A-PBX1, others | $18 + 197$ | $9 + 103$ |
| HyperL50 | 12558 | HyperL50, others | $42 + 173$ | $22 + 90$ |
| MLL | 12558 | MLL, others | $14 + 201$ | $6 + 106$ |
| T-ALL | 12558 | T-ALL, others | $28 + 187$ | $15 + 97$ |
| TEL-AML1 | 12558 | TEL-AML1, others | $52 + 163$ | $27 + 85$ |

The background information of the ovarian disease and the lung cancer disease data sets are summarized in Table 5. The two data sets are also available at our website mentioned above.

**Table 5.** Basic information of the ovarian disease data set and the lung cancer data set. The "—" sign represents no independent test data are available.

| Data sets | # of features | Class names | Training size | Test size |
|---|---|---|---|---|
| Ovarian disease | 15154 | Cancer, Normal | $162 + 91$ | — |
| Lung cancer | 12533 | MPM, ADCA | $16 + 16$ | $15 + 134$ |

# 6 Comparison between C4.5 and PCL Using Experimental Results

We report the accuracy and error rates of the learning algorithms on the considered bio-medical data sets. The accuracy of a classifier is defined as the *percentage* of samples in a data set that are correctly classified by a classifier in a stratified 10-fold cross validation or in a validation on independent test data. The error rate of a classifier is defined as the *number* of samples in a data set that are wrongly classified by a classifier in a stratified 10-fold cross validation or in a validation on independent test data. The latter is specially called *test* error rates, which is widely used in the bio-medical field. When the error rates are represented in the format $z(x : y)$, it means that $x$ number of samples from the first class and $y$ number of samples from the second class are misclassified, and that a total $z(= x + y)$ number samples are wrongly classified.

Our computer is a PC of DELL dimension 4100 running RedHat Linux 7.1 with a CPU speed of 886MHz and with a 512KB Ram. The main software package used in the experiments is *Weka* version 3.2, its Java-written open source are available at `http://www.cs.waikato.ac.nz/~ml/weka/` under the GNU General Public License. Our in-house softwares like PCL are coded by C++. The C4.5 (single tree, Bagging and Boosting), SVM and $k$-NN programs were run under all default settings in the Weka package except that "the number of nearest neighbors to use in prediction" was reset as 3 of $k$-NN (the default is 1). For our PCL classifier, we set $k$ as 5 when applied to the UCI data sets, and set $k$ as 20 when applied to the high-dimensional bio-medical data sets.

Table 6 summarizes the performance of the classifiers on the 10 UCI bio-medical data sets. For a simple comparison, we give the following statistics numbers:

- Comparing PCL, C4.5, Bagging and Boosting, PCL won the best accuracy on 5 data sets (i.e., breast-w, cleve, heart, HIV, and promoter); Bagging won on 1 data set (hypothyroid); and Boosting won the best accuracy on 4 data sets (i.e., hepatitis, lymph, sick and splice).
- Comparing between PCL and C4.5, PCL won on 8 data sets, while C4.5 won on the rest 2 data sets.
- Comparing between PCL and Bagging, PCL won on 6 data sets, while Bagging won on 4 data sets.
- Comparing between PCL and Boosting, PCL won on 6 data sets, while Boosting won on 4 data sets.

**Table 6.** The performance of PCL and the C4.5 family algorithms on the 10 UCI bio-medical data sets. The accuracy is used for measuring the quality of both the learning algorithm and the data; while the error rate is used to show exact number of mistakes made in total and in each class on a data set by a learning algorithm.

| Data sets | Accuracy (%) | | | | Error rates | | | |
|---|---|---|---|---|---|---|---|---|
| | PCL | C4.5 | Bagging | Boost | PCL | C4.5 | Bagging | Boosting |
| Breast-w | 96.6 | 94.8 | 96.3 | 96.0 | 24(15:9) | 36(24:12) | 26(14:12) | 28(18:10) |
| Cleve | 81.8 | 76.8 | 79.8 | 78.5 | 55(31:24) | 70(32:38) | 61(28:33) | 65(33:32) |
| Heart | 83.3 | 81.0 | 79.3 | 80.0 | 45(25:20) | 50(21:29) | 56(33:23) | 54(25:29) |
| Hepatitis | 80.0 | 78.7 | 80.6 | 83.8 | 31(7:24) | 33(20:13) | 30(19:11) | 25(14:11) |
| HIV | 91.1 | 85.9 | 85.1 | 89.5 | 32(14:18) | 51(28:23) | 54(30:24) | 38(17:21) |
| Hypo | 98.9 | 99.2 | 99.2 | 98.8 | 38(13:25) | 25(14:11) | 24(13:11) | 39(17:22) |
| Lymph | 83.0 | 77.5 | 81.7 | 85.2 | 24(13:11) | 32(13:19) | 26(8:18) | 21(7:14) |
| Promoter | 91.5 | 79.2 | 82.1 | 89.6 | 9(4:5) | 22(10:12) | 19(11:8) | 11(1:10) |
| Sick | 98.4 | 98.6 | 98.9 | 99.2 | 62(32:30) | 52(30:22) | 42(31:11) | 30(20:10) |
| Splice | 94.4 | 94.3 | 94.5 | 94.7 | 179 (44:42:93) | 182 (23:61:98) | 174 (26:54:94) | 167 (27:55:85) |

On a closer examination, we found that: (1) on the lymph and splice data sets where Boosting got the best accuracy, PCL had a very comparable accuracy with Boosting; (2) on the hypothyroid data set where Bagging got the best accuracy, PCL was better than Boosting. So, generally speaking, our PCL classifier is more accurate than the traditional decision-tree based single classifier like C4.5 or committee classifiers like Bagging and Boosting. We also found that the accuracy provided by the committee classifiers are all better than C4.5. So, once again, these results confirm that the use of multiple significant rules is an effective way to improve the accuracy of C4.5.

We next report experimental results on the 8 high-mensional profiling data sets. The results are summarized in Table 7 and Table 8. We can see that PCL was consistently (with only one exception on the TEL-AML1 data set) better than or equal to the performance of the C4.5 family of algorithms.

**Table 7.** The error rates of 7 classification algorithms on the data sets for the subtype classification of childhood leukemia.

| Datasets | Error Rates for Test Data | | | | | |
|---|---|---|---|---|---|---|
| | PCL | C4.5 | Bagging | Boosting | SVM | 3-NN |
| BCR-ABL | 1:0 | 1:4 | 2:0 | 1:4 | 1:1 | 1:0 |
| E2A-PBX1 | 0:0 | 0:0 | 0:0 | 0:0 | 0:0 | 0:0 |
| HyperL50 | 2:2 | 4:5 | 4:2 | 1:4 | 0:3 | 1:4 |
| MLL | 0:0 | 1:1 | 0:0 | 1:1 | 0:0 | 0:0 |
| T-ALL | 0:0 | 0:1 | 0:1 | 0:1 | 0:0 | 0:0 |
| TEL-AML1 | 2:0 | 3:1 | 1:0 | 1:0 | 1:1 | 2:0 |
| Total errors | 7 | 21 | 10 | 14 | 7 | 8 |

**Table 8.** The error rates of 7 classification algorithms on the ovarian disease data set and the lung cancer data set.

| Datasets | Error Rates for Test Data | | | | | |
|---|---|---|---|---|---|---|
| | PCL | C4.5 | Bagging | Boosting | SVM | 3-NN |
| Ovarian | 4(3:1) | 10(5:5) | 8(4:4) | 5(3:2) | 5(2:3) | 5(2:3) |
| Lung Cancer | 3(1:2) | 27(4:23) | 18(2:16) | 27(4:23) | 1(1:0) | 1(1:0) |

Let's explain a bit more about the results on the lung cancer data set. The training part of this data set is small, having only 32 samples, but the test data consists about 4 times more samples than the training size. The C4.5 tree derived from this training data was very simple. It used only one feature to 100% accurately classify the 32 samples. However, this thin-structure tree made 27 mistakes on the test data. The Boosting algorithm made the same number of mistakes as C4.5 made. This is because the Boosting committee was a singleton— only one tree contained, unable to take a real committee power. This indicates that C4.5 has well learned only one aspect of the training data, and ignored many other significant rules. So, the possibility of making mistakes increases.

However, PCL discovered a total of 39 significant rules, and it used them as a committee. So, it is not a surprise to see that PCL was much better than C4.5 on this data set.

Compared to the non-linear classifiers such as SVM and nearest-neighbour, the performance of PCL is comparable and sometime is better. (See Tables 7 and 8.) As discussed previously, our advantage over SVM and nearest neighbour is that PCL can provide easily understandable rules.

We also conducted experiments to see the speed differences between PCL and C4.5. C4.5 was faster than PCL. This is because C4.5 is a heuristic search method, while PCL is a global search method. In theoretical worst cases, the candidate patterns searched by PCL is exponential to the number of features in a data set. This is a reason why PCL needs to select top-ranked features when handling high-dimensional medical data. However, on all the data sets presented in this paper, PCL completed each of the experiments within a couple of minutes, spending seconds on small data sets and longer time on other data sets. Such time are not that long for diagnostic purposes.

## 7 Conclusion

This paper has presented a comparison study on the performance between PCL and C4.5. Both PCL and C4.5 are rule-based classifiers. In their learning phase, explicit rules or interactions among relevant features are induced. Such a learning method differs from non-linear classifiers such as support vector machines or neural networks where the learning phase is to determine the parameters of the non-linear kernel functions. This advantage of rule-based classifiers is increasingly used in the analysis of bio-medical data.

We have compared the performance using two groups of bio-medical data sets. One group are benchmark data sets from the widely used UCI machine learning repository; the other are recently published high-dimensional profiling data for cancer diagnosis. Our experimental results have shown that PCL is more accurate than the C4.5 family of algorithms. These results indicate that the use of multiple significant rules can solve the thin structure problem of decision trees successfully.

As future work, we are planning to expand our research on the selection of top-ranked features, on the efficient discovery of emerging patterns, and on the integration methods for summarizing multiple rules.

**Acknowledgement.** We thank Huiqing Liu for providing some data and results.

## References

1. C.L. Blake and P.M. Murphy. The UCI machine learning repository. [`http://www.cs.uci.edu/~mlearn/MLRepository.html`]. In *Irvine, CA: University of California, Department of Information and Computer Science*, 1998.
2. L. Breiman, J. Friedman, R. Olshen, and C. Stone. *Classification and Regression Trees.* Wadsworth International Group, Belmont, CA, 1984.
3. Leo Breiman. Bagging predictors. *Machine Learning*, 24:123–140, 1996.
4. Guozhu Dong and Jinyan Li. Efficient mining of emerging patterns: Discovering trends and differences. In Surajit Chaudhuri and David Madigan, editors, *Proceedings of the Fifth ACM SIGKDD International Conference on Knowledge Discovery and Data Mining*, pages 43–52, San Diego, CA, 1999. ACM Press.
5. U.M. Fayyad and K.B. Irani. Multi-interval discretization of continuous-valued attributes for classification learning. In Ruzena Bajcsy, editor, *Proceedings of the Thirteenth International Joint Conference on Artificial Intelligence*, pages 1022–1029. Morgan Kaufmann, 1993.

6. Yoav Freund and Robert E. Schapire. Experiments with a new boosting algorithm. In Lorenza Saitta, editor, *Machine Learning: Proceedings of the Thirteenth International Conference*, pages 148–156, Bari, Italy, July 1996. Morgan Kaufmann.
7. Jerome H. Friedman, Ron Kohavi, and Yeogirl Yun. Lazy decision trees. In *Proceedings of the Thirteenth National Conference on Artificial Intelligence, AAAI 96*, pages 717–724, Portland, Oregon, August 1996. AAAI Press.
8. T. R. Golub, D. K. Slonim, P. Tamayo, C. Huard, M. Gaasenbeek, J. P. Mesirov, H. Coller, M. L. Loh, J.R. Downing, M. A. Caligiuri, C. D. Bloomfield, and E. S. Lander. Molecular classification of cancer: Class discovery and class prediction by gene expression monitoring. *Science*, 286:531–537, October 1999.
9. Gavin J. Gordon, Roderick V. Jensen, Li-Li Hsiao, Steven R. Gullans, Joshua E. Blumenstock, Sridhar Ramaswamy, William G. Richards, David J. Sugarbaker, and Raphael Bueno. Translation of microarray data into clinically relevant cancer diagnostic tests using gene expression ratios in lung cancer and mesothelioma. *Cancer Research*, 62:4963–4967, 2002.
10. Jinyan Li, Huiqing Liu, James R. Downing, Allen Eng-Juh Yeoh, and Limsoon Wong. Simple rules underlying gene expression profiles of more than six subtypes of acute lymphoblastic leukemia (ALL) patients. *Bioinformatics*, 19:71 –78, 2003.
11. Jinyan Li, Kotagiri Ramamohanarao, and Guozhu Dong. The space of jumping emerging patterns and its incremental maintenance algorithms. In *Proceedings of the Seventeenth International Conference on Machine Learning, Stanford, CA, USA*, pages 551–558, San Francisco, June 2000. Morgan Kaufmann.
12. Jinyan Li and Limsoon Wong. Identifying good diagnostic gene groups from gene expression profiles using the concept of emerging patterns. *Bioinformatics*, 18:725–734, 2002.
13. Jinyan Li and Limsoon Wong. Solving the fragmentation problem of decision trees by discovering boundary emerging patterns. In *Proceedings of 2002 IEEE International Conference on Data Mining (ICDM 2002)*, pages 653 – 656, Maebashi City, Japan, 2002. IEEE Computer Society.
14. Giulia Pagallo and David Haussler. Boolean feature discovery in empirical learning. *Machine Learning*, 5:71–99, 1990.
15. Emanuel F Petricoin, Ali M Ardekani, Ben A Hitt, Peter J Levine, Vincent A Fusaro, Seth M Steinberg, Gordon B Mills, Charles Simone, David A Fishman, Elise C Kohn, and Lance A Liotta. Use of proteomic patterns in serum to identify ovarian cancer. *Lancet*, 359:572–577, 2002.
16. J. R. Quinlan. *C4.5: Programs for Machine Learning*. Morgan Kaufmann, San Mateo, CA, 1993.
17. Dinesh Singh, Phillip G. Febbo1, Kenneth Ross, Donald G. Jackson, Judith Manola, Christine Ladd, Pablo Tamayo, Andrew A. Renshaw, Anthony V. D'Amico, Jerome P. Richie, Eric S. Lander, Massimo Loda, Philip W. Kantoff, Todd R. Golub, and William R. Sellers. Gene expression correlates of clinical prostate cancer behavior. *Cancer Cell*, 1:203–209, March 2002.
18. Eng-Juh Yeoh, Mary E. Ross, Sheila A. Shurtleff, W. Kent Williams, Divyen Patel, Rami Mahfouz, Fred G. Behm, Susana C. Raimondi, Mary V. Relling, Anami Patel, Cheng Cheng, Dario Campana, Dawn Wilkins, Xiaodong Zhou, Jinyan Li, Huiqing Liu, Ching-Hon Pui, William E. Evans, Clayton Naeve, Limsoon Wong, and James R. Downing. Classification, subtype discovery, and prediction of outcome in pediatric acute lymphoblastic leukemia by gene expression profiling. *Cancer Cell*, 1:133–143, 2002.

# A Protein Secondary Structure Prediction Framework Based on the Support Vector Machine

Xiaochun Yang[1], Bin Wang[2], Yiu-Kai Ng[1], Ge Yu[2], and Guoren Wang[2]

[1] Computer Science Department, Brigham Young University, Provo UT 84602, USA, {xiaochuny,ng}@cs.byu.edu,

[2] Department of Computer Science and Engineering, Northeastern University, Shenyang 110004, P.R.China

**Abstract.** Our framework for predicting protein secondary structures differs from existing prediction methods since we consider physio-chemical information and context information of secondary structure segments. We have employed Support Vector Machine (SVM) for training the CB513 and RS126 data sets, which are collections of protein secondary structure sequences, through sevenfold cross validation to uncover the structural differences of protein secondary structures. We apply the sliding window technique to test a set of protein sequences based on the group classification learned from the training data set. Our prediction approach achieves 77.8% segment overlap accuracy (SOV) and 75.2% three-state overall per-residue accuracy ($Q_3$) on CB513 set, which outperform existing protein secondary structure prediction methods.

## 1 Introduction

Understanding the function and the physiological role of proteins is a fundamental requirement for the discovery of novel medicines and protein-based products with medical and industrial applications. To enhance their understanding, many biologists focus on the functional analysis of genome these days. This functional analysis is a difficult problem, and the determination of protein three-dimensional structures is essential in the analysis of genome functions since a protein three-dimensional structure can help understand its function. Unfortunately, it happens that three-dimensional protein structures cannot be accurately predicted from protein sequences (i.e. amino acid sequences). An intermediate, but useful and fundamental, alternative step is to predict protein secondary structures since a protein three-dimensional structure results partially from its secondary structure. At present, we focus on predicting protein secondary structures to help provide valuable information for further analysis of their full three-dimensional structures.

In previous work on predicting protein secondary structures, researchers focused on classifying these states into three consolidated classes: helix, strand and coil classes, and among these classes the helix and strand classes are the major repetitive secondary structures [1]. It has also brought to our attention that

G. Dong et al. (Eds.): WAIM 2003, LNCS 2762, pp. 266–277, 2003.

these days the number of known protein sequences has far exceeded the number of known protein secondary structures, which have been obtained through chemical and biological methods such as the crystallography and NMR methods [2], and the rapid pace of the discovery of genomic sequences has further widened the gap. Thus, computational tools for predicting protein secondary structures from protein sequences are needed and they are essential in narrowing the widening gap [2]. However, after four decades of research work, the prediction of protein secondary structures has not attained the satisfying accuracy rate.

The secondary structure prediction methods developed in the past [3,4,5] use local information of a single sequence, but they exhibit major drawbacks. For example, the accuracy measures (Q3) on these methods are relatively low (57% for the 1st generation and 63% for the 2nd generation). The neural network approach may be an effective classifier; however, it is hard to explain why a given pattern is classified as a helix rather than a strand, and thus it is difficult to derive a conclusion on the merit of the approach. Hua et al. [6] introduce a prediction approach based on the Support Vector Machine (SVM) [7], which separates input data, i.e., protein secondary structure segments, into two classes to uncover the protein secondary structural classes. Most of the existing works, however, do not consider the roles of physio-chemical properties of each amino acid residue, and to the best of our knowledge, none of the existing approaches consider the roles of contexts of helices, strands, or coils in protein sequences, which might explain why their accuracy prediction ratios are low. Our prediction framework, called $SVM_{SSP}$ (SVM for Secondary Structure Prediction), weaves the properties of different chemical groups into secondary structure segments. We consider not only segments of interest (e.g. helices and strands), but also the contexts of the segments.

We employ SVM to train samples (segments) in two data sets CB513 [8] and RS126 [9], which contain 513 and 126 sequences of protein secondary structures, respectively. These protein sequences have been discovered by using different chemical and biological experiments. After obtaining the training data, we define our prediction framework to compare each predicted segments with known protein classes. $SVM_{SSP}$ yields encouraging experimental results according to various accuracy measures.

## 2 Pre-processing

In the pre-processing phase, a set of protein segments with the same size are extracted from each protein sequence in the training set, and each extracted segment is represented as an input vector for further training and prediction. Steps involved in this phase are shown in Fig. 1. We use the *n-gram segment extraction* approach to determine the appropriate length of protein segments and construct an encoding schema to encode protein segments into input vectors, which includes (i) *residue vectors* for representing protein segments, (ii) *cardinal vectors* for storing similar physio-chemical properties of amino acid residues, and

(iii) probability of different residues that captures the tendency of the location of a helix (strand or coil) in a protein segment.

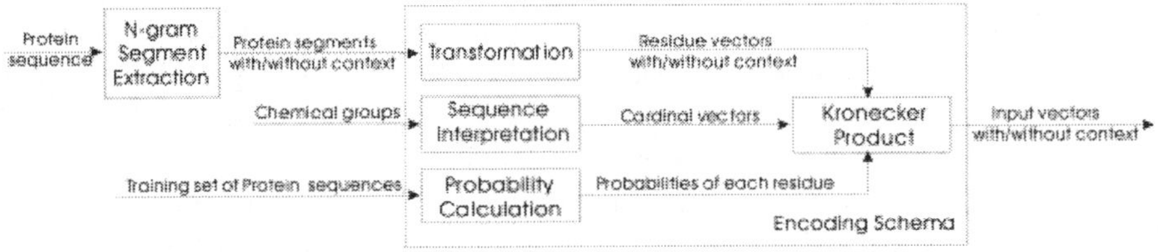


**Fig. 1.** The pre-processing steps for predicting protein secondary structures

## 2.1 *N*-Gram Segment Extraction

It has been well accepted that the order of amino acids in an amino acid sequence plays the most important role in determining its secondary structure [1]. We use the $n$-gram model, in which segments are of length $n$, where $n$ is the number of amino acid residues, to extract segments from amino acid sequences. The choice of $n$ is determined by the average length of different structure segments (helix or strand). Based on our study, in most helices (strands) the amino acid length is between five and 17 (five and 11). Thus, we choose $n$ to be between five and 17, and beginning with a small size, we gradually increase the size to determine the "best" size of protein segments for helix/non-helix (or strand/non-strand) prediction. We extract $m-n+1$ $n$-gram subsequences from each structure segment sequentially, where $m$ is the number of residues in the segment. We realize that simply extracting structure segments without retaining the contexts of the segments causes valuable information loss, because non-structural segments may have significant different properties from structural segments. For this reason, we consider the context subsequences of structure segments in $SVM_{SSP}$.

**Definition 1.** *$N$-gram context subsequences of structure segments. Given a protein sequence $s$ and a secondary structure segment $s_s$ of size $m$ that begins at position $i$ in $s$, the left $n$-gram context of $s_s$ is a subsequence of size $n$ that begins at position $i$ - $\lfloor \frac{n}{2} \rfloor$ in $s$, and the right $n$-gram context of $s_s$ is a subsequence of size $n$ that begins at position $i + m$ - $\lceil \frac{n}{2} \rceil$ in $s$.*

## 2.2 Encoding Schema

The transformation from $n$-gram subsequences into input vectors is an *encoding* process. In [10], which adopts the neural network approach in secondary structure prediction, the classical encoding schema is chosen in predicting protein secondary structures, in which each residue in a segment is encoded as an orthogonal binary vector $[1, 0, \ldots, 0]$, ..., or $[0, 0, \ldots, 1]$, and '1' in a vector indicates the relative position of the corresponding residue in the segment. This type of vectors is 21-dimensional, and each one of the first twenty coefficients of these vectors denotes a distinct amino acid in the segment and the last unit is used for specifying whether the corresponding residue is the "head" or the "tail" of the sequence [10]. However, since the "head" and the "tail" of a segment can not be accurately determined [2], we use only the first 20 units of each 21-dimensional vector to represent a residue, which is called 20-dimensional *residue vectors.*

**Table 1.** Five groups of biological information organized according to the physio-chemical properties of amino acid residues.

| R-group classification | 5-dimensional (5D) cardinal vectors | Amino acid residues |
|---|---|---|
| Nonpolar, aliphatic | [1, 0, 0, 0, 0] | A,V,L,I,M |
| Aromatic | [0, 1, 0, 0, 0] | F,Y,W |
| Polar, uncharged | [0, 0, 1, 0, 0] | G,S,P,T,C,N,Q |
| Positively charged | [0, 0, 0, 1, 0] | K,H,R |
| Negatively charged | [0, 0, 0, 0, 1] | D,E |

We define *cardinal vector* to incorporate different biological group information [1] of amino acid residues into a secondary structure sequence. Listed in Table 1 are twenty different amino acid residues that have been classified into five different *R-groups*, which are constructed by using Hydropathy index, molecular weights $M_r$, and $pI$ value together.

**Definition 2.** *Cardinal vector. Given an m-class biological group of amino acid residues, its m-dimensional (mD) cardinal vector is a binary vector* $\hat{vc}_m = [a_{c_1}, a_{c_2}, \ldots, a_{c_m}]$, *where* $a_{c_i} \in [0,1]$ $(1 \leq i \leq m)$ *and* $\sum_{i=1}^{m} a_{c_i}^2 = 1$.

**Definition 3.** *Probability of an m-class group with helix (strand or coil) structure in a training set. Given a training set s and an m-class group* $C=\{c_1, \ldots, c_m\}$ *of amino acid residues, the probability of a residue i in* $c_j$ $(1 \leq i \leq m)$ *has helical structure is*

$$p^H_{i,c_j} = \frac{1}{N_H} \sum_{i \in c_j} N_{H_i} \tag{1}$$

*where* $p^H_{i,c_j}$ $(1 \leq i \leq 20)$ *is the probability that residue i belongs to group* $c_j$ *and is a helix in s,* $N_H$ *is the total number of residues that have the conformations of helical structures in the training set, and* $N_{H_i}$ *is the number of residues in which residue i belongs to* $c_j$ *and residue i is a helix in s. (*$p^E_{i,c_j}$ *for strand and* $p^C_{i,c_j}$ *for coil structures are computed accordingly.)*

We use the Kronecker product [11] of residue vectors, cardinal vectors, and the frequency of appearances of residues in the training set to encode a residue, and we concatenate vectors of $n$ consecutive residues to encode an amino acid subsequence with $n$ residues. Residue vectors distinguish a residue from others, and cardinal vectors encapsulate the similar physio-chemical properties of residues, whereas the frequency of a residue captures the tendency of the residue that locates in which particular structure, and the concatenation of vectors exhibits the order of residues in a protein subsequence.

**Definition 4.** *Encoding schema of protein segments. Given a training set s and an m-class biological group* $C=\{c_1, \ldots, c_m\}$*, the encoded vector of a residue i w.r.t. a* $c_j$ $(1\leq i \leq m)$ *is*

$$\begin{aligned} v_{i,c_j} &= p^H_{i,c_j} \times v_{r_i} \otimes \hat{vc}_{m_{c_j}} = p^H_{i,c_j} \times [\ a_1 \times \hat{vc}_{m_{c_j}}, \ldots, \ a_{20} \times \hat{vc}_{m_{c_j}}\ ] \\ &= [\ p^H_{i,c_j} \times a_1 \times a_{c_1}, \ldots, p^H_{i,c_j} \times a_{20} \times a_{c_1}, \ldots, \\ &\quad p^H_{i,c_j} \times a_1 \times a_{c_m}, \ldots, p^H_{i,c_j} \times a_{20} \times a_{c_m}\ ] \end{aligned} \tag{2}$$

*where* $v_{r_i}$ $(= [a_1, a_2, \ldots, a_{20}])$ *is the residue vector of residue i,* $\hat{vc}_{m_{c_j}}$ $(= [a_{c_1}, a_{c_2}, \ldots, a_{c_m}])$ *is the cardinal vector of the m-class group to which i belongs, and* $p^H_{i,c_j}$ *is the probability that residue i is a helix in s and is belonged to group* $c_j$*. For each subsequence* $s_s$ *in s, the encoded schema of* $s_s$ *is the concatenation of vectors of the consecutive residues in* $s_s$*. Hence, the size of an encoded vector of a residue is* $20 \times m$*, and the size of an encoded vector of subsequence with n residues is* $20 \times m \times n$*.*

## 3 SVM-Based Training, Test, and Prediction

In SVM, a classifier with minimal error is represented by a *decision function* $f(\mathbf{x}) = sign(\sum_{i=1}^{m} y_i \alpha_i K(\mathbf{x}, \mathbf{x}_i))$, which is induced from vectors in a training set, where $m$ is the number of vectors $\mathbf{x}_i$ $(1 \leq i \leq m)$ in the training/test set, $y_i$ is either $+1$ or $-1$, vector $\mathbf{x}$ is one of the vectors in the test set, and $\alpha_i$ is a coefficient in the range between 0 and an upper bound value $C$. Using kernel function $K(\mathbf{x}, \mathbf{x}_i)$, $y_i \alpha_i \cdot K(\mathbf{x}, \mathbf{x}_i)$ calculates the distance between $\mathbf{x}$ and $\mathbf{x}_i$ with label $y_i$. Hence, $f(\mathbf{x})$ computes the distances between the sample vectors in each of the two classes (e.g., helix and non-helix) and $\mathbf{x}$. If $f(\mathbf{x}) = +1$, then $\mathbf{x}$ belongs to the positive class; otherwise, it belongs to the negative class.

The secondary structure prediction problem can be treated as a typical 3-classification problem, where the secondary structure of a given amino acid sequence is predicted into either a helix, strand, or coil class based on the alignment of residues in the sequence. The 3-classification problem can be restricted to the binary-categorization problem. That is if there are $m$ sample data items (sequences) in a training set, where each sample data item is transformed into an $n$-dimensional input vector $\mathbf{x}$ and the training set is regarded as an $n$-dimensional (where $n = 20 \times$ *window_size*) input space $\Re^n$, then for each $\mathbf{x}_i$ $(i = 1, 2, \ldots, m)$ $\in \Re^n$, there is a classification identifier $y_i \in \{+1, -1\}$ that indicates to which class, helix or non-helix, strand or non-strand, or coil, $\mathbf{x}_i$ belongs.

The SVM-based training and test phases are as shown in Fig. 2(a). Using a number of protein sequences in a training set, their encoded input vectors are fed into the *SVM classifier* to derive different decision functions. In the test phase, $SVM_{SSP}$ predicts secondary structures of protein sequences in a test set and evaluates the predicted results using a set of existing accuracy measurements. Since different sizes of $n$-gram and various parameter values considered in SVM training can derive different prediction results, $SVM_{SSP}$ selects the optimal parameters that yield the best accuracy for further prediction. In the prediction phase (see Fig. 2(b)), $SVM_{SSP}$ uses selected decision functions with the optimal parameters to predict any protein sequence with unknown structures.

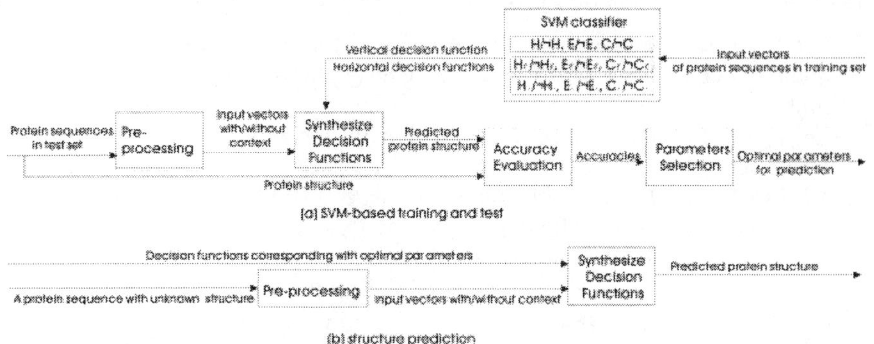


(a) SVM-based training and test

(b) structure prediction

**Fig. 2.** The architecture of $SVM_{SSP}$

### 3.1 Training Phase

Protein secondary structure prediction is a typical three-class classification problem. A simple strategy to handle the three-class classification problem is to cast it to a set of binary categorizations. For an $n$-class classification, $n-1$ classes are used to construct training sets. The $i$th class will be trained with all of the samples in the $i$th class assigned with "y = +1" labels and all other example data assigned with "y = −1" labels.

If input vectors are transformed from helix (strand or coil) segments, then the learned decision function is called *vertical decision function*, denoted $f_v$. However, if input vectors are transformed from context subsequences, then their learned decision function is called *horizontal decision function*, which can further be classified into *left horizontal decision function*, which is derived from left context subsequences, denoted $f_{h_l}$, and *right horizontal decision function*, which is derived from right context subsequences, denoted $f_{h_r}$. $SVM_{SSP}$ synthesizes $f_v$ and $f_{h_l}$ (or $f_{h_r}$), which will be discussed in details in Section 3.2.

### 3.2 Test Phase

We adopt the sliding window method to move the window over a test protein sequence. A window, which is a one-dimensional frame of slots, can be adopted for overlaiding on and moving over a test protein sequence to examine different segments of its amino acids. A sliding window extracts a protein segment of length $L$ ($L \geq 1$) to match a potential structure class using the derived decision function generated from the training phase. Note that the size of the sliding window should be the same size of $n$-grams so that test vectors can be fed into the same input space of the training vectors. We have developed a heuristic algorithm to synthesize the deduced decision function for prediction.

*Algorithm 1.* Prediction of a protein sequence $s$ with a sliding window of size $n$.

1. Let the sliding window size be $n$ and starting at position $i = 0$ in the sequence. Let (a flag) $Mark = L$ to identify the left context should be used first.
2. Let $s_s$ be the subsequence of size $n$ that begins at position $i$;
3. REPEAT
   - 3.1 Let $S_{l_i} = (f_{h_{l_i}}, f_{v_i}]$ be the left state of $s_s$ and $S_{r_i} = [f_{v_i}, f_{h_{r_i}})$ be the right state of $s_s$, where $f_{h_{l_i}}$, $f_{v_i}$, and $f_{h_{r_i}}$ are the derived vertical left horizontal decision function, decision function, and the right horizontal decision function, respectively, of $s_s$ beginning at position $i$;
   - 3.2. If $Mark ==$ L, then
     - 3.2.1. If $S_{l_i}$ == (-1, -1], then prediction $P_i$ of $s_s$ is "No," and the next position of the sliding window, i.e. $i = i + n$, is considered;
     - 3.2.2. Else if $S_{l_i}$ == (-1, 1], then
       - 3.2.2.1. If $i == 0$, then $P_i$ = "Yes" and $i = i + n$
       - 3.2.2.2. Else assign $P_i$ with the same prediction of the previous segment of $s_s$, $P_{i_{pre}}$, and set $i = i + n$. If $P_{i_{pre}}$ == "Yes", then $Mark = R$, else $Mark = L$
     - 3.2.3. Else if $S_{l_i}$ == (1, -1], then $P_i$ = "No," $i = i + \lfloor \frac{n}{2} \rfloor$, $Mark = R$
     - 3.2.4. Else if $S_{l_i}$ == (1, 1], then $P_i$ = "Yes" and $i = i + 1$
   - 3.3. Else
     - 3.3.1. If $S_{r_i}$ == [-1, -1), then $P_i$ = "No" and $i = i + n$;
     - 3.3.2. Else if $S_{r_i}$ == [-1, 1), then $P_i$ = "Yes" and $i = i + 1$
     - 3.3.3. Else if $S_{l_i}$ == [1, -1), then $P_i = P_{i_{pre}}$ and $i = i + n$. If $P_{i_{pre}}$ == "Yes", then $Mark = L$, else $Mark = R$
     - 3.3.4. Else if $S_{r_i}$ == [1, 1), then $P_i$ = "Yes" and $i = i + \lfloor \frac{n}{2} \rfloor$

   UNTIL all the residues in $s$ have been evaluated, i.e. until $i \geq |s|$.

For a helix/non-helix (strand/non-strand, coil/non-coil) classifier, we select the best accuracy value, the corresponding decision function $f(\mathbf{x})$, and $n$-gram for the prediction phase. Thus, given an unknown sequence $s$, we first use the sliding window with window size set to $n$ and different biological groups (cardinal vectors) to transform subsequences of $s$ into different sets of input vectors. Hereafter, for each set of vectors, we apply the derived decision functions to classify each subsequence into either the helix or non-helix (strand or non-strand, and coil or non-coil) class.

# 4 Experimental Data

Our experiments are carried out on the CB513 set [8] and RS126 set [9] with 513 and 126 non-redundant protein amino acid sequences, respectively.

We choose the DSSP [12] assignment so that we can compare $SVM_{SSP}$ with other prediction approaches. The DSSP assignment classifies eight states secondary structure, a-helix (H), $3_{10}$ helix (G), pi helix (I), isolated $\beta$-bridge (B), extended $\beta$-strand (E), hydrogen bonded turn (T), bend (S), and random coil (-) [13], into three classes *helix*(H), *strand*(E), and *coil*(C). Here, we use methods in [4,6] that treat H, G, and I as *helix*(H), E as *strand*(E), and other states as *coil*(C). This assignment is slightly different from other assignments reported in the literatures. For example, in the CASP competition [14], H contains DSSP classes H and G, while E contains DSSP classes E and B.

We use multiple cross-validation trials to minimize variation in the results caused by a particular chosen training or test sets. An $n$-fold cross validation is used on CB513 and RS126, where CB513 (RS126) is divided into $n$ subsets randomly, and each subset has similar size. Among these $n$ subsets, data in $n-1$ subsets are selected as training data and data in the remaining subset is selected as test data. We (i) use LIBSVM [15], an SVM software, to evaluate $SVM_{SSP}$ according to the selection of kernel function, parameter $C$, and window size, (ii) compare with other prediction methods, and (iii) justify the effectiveness of our encoding schema and the prediction framework.

For the evaluation of the effectiveness of $SVM_{SSP}$, we give the following metrics. The prediction accuracy using SVM is calculated as $AC_{SVM} = \frac{N_{c_i}}{N_i} \times 100\%$, where $i$ is a test set, $N_{c_i}$ is the number of residues correctly predicted in $i$, and $N_i$ is the number of residues in $i$. We employed several standard performance measures to assess prediction accuracy. Three-state overall per-residue accuracy ($Q_3$) [4], segment overlap accuracy $SOV$ [4], and the per-residue accuracy for each type of secondary structure ($Q_H, Q_E, Q_C$, $Q_H^{pre}, Q_E^{pre}, Q_C^{pre}$) [6] were calculated to evaluate accuracy.

## 4.1 Determination of Kernel Functions and Parameters in SVM

Given a data set, a proper kernel function and its parameters must be chosen to construct an SVM classifier. Different kernel functions and paraments can construct different SVM classifiers. We select an optimal kernel function and its parameters which achieve high testing accuracy $AC_{SVM}$. However, there does not exist any theoretically sounded methods in determining the optimal kernel function and its parameters. In [6], the author has proved that the gaussian radial basis function $\exp(-\gamma|\mathbf{x}_i - \mathbf{x}_j|^2)$ can provide superior performance in the generalization ability and converge speed. Therefore, we select different parameters and upper bound values $C$ on $\exp(-\gamma|\mathbf{x}_i - \mathbf{x}_j|^2)$ to compare $AC_{SVM}$ on helix/non-helix (H/$\neg$H) test. Since the average of helix in CB513 is eight, we use 8-gram to select the kernel function and parameter $C$ for H/$\neg$H.

As shown in Table 2, for each $C$, we choose $\gamma$ between 0.001 and 50, where 0.001 is the ratio of 1 to the number of dimensions 800 ($20 \times 5 \times 8$) in the training set. We found that the best accuracy ($accuracy_{SVM} = 84.72\%$) can be achieved by using gaussian radial basis function with $\gamma$ set to 0.2 and $C$ set to 1.5. Table 2 shows that for each $\gamma$ between 0.001 and 50, when $C$ increases, the accuracy on the test set first increases, and then decreases. Based on this observation, we conclude that if the value of $C$ is small, it yields poor accuracy, whereas if the value of $C$ is too large, it leads to overfitting. We choose a proper value of $C$ to achieve a good balance. In the protein sequence prediction domain, we found that $C = 1.5$ is appropriate, not just for H/¬H, but also for other classifiers. Hence, we choose $C = 1.5$ and $\gamma = 0.2$ to construct different SVM classifiers.

**Table 2.** Accuracies $AC_{SVM}$ of different parameters $\gamma$ and upper bounds $C$ for H/¬H using 8-gram on CB513 set, where * marks the best accuracy for each $C$

| C | $\gamma$ | | | | | | | |
|---|---|---|---|---|---|---|---|---|
| | 0.001 | 0.01 | 0.2 | 0.3 | 0.5 | 1 | 5 | 50 |
| 0.01 | 50.00% | 50.00% | 51.39% | 65.83% | 80.83% | *83.89% | 50.00% | 50.00% |
| 0.1 | 50.00% | 50.00% | 83.89% | 83.89% | 83.61% | *84.44% | 83.61% | 51.11% |
| 1.5 | 51.39% | 82.50% | *84.74% | 81.94% | 82.50% | 80.28% | 53.89% | 53.89% |
| 5 | 79.72% | 79.72% | 80.83% | *81.94% | 81.39% | 81.67% | 53.89% | 53.89% |
| 50 | 78.61% | 81.28% | *81.67% | 81.11% | 81.67% | 82.78% | 78.06% | 53.89% |

## 4.2 Choices of Window Size

There is a trade off between the number of residues used and the level of "noise" in deciding the size of the window. If the window size is too large, the prediction may be misled by the noise, whereas if the window size is too small, then the number of residues used may be insufficient.

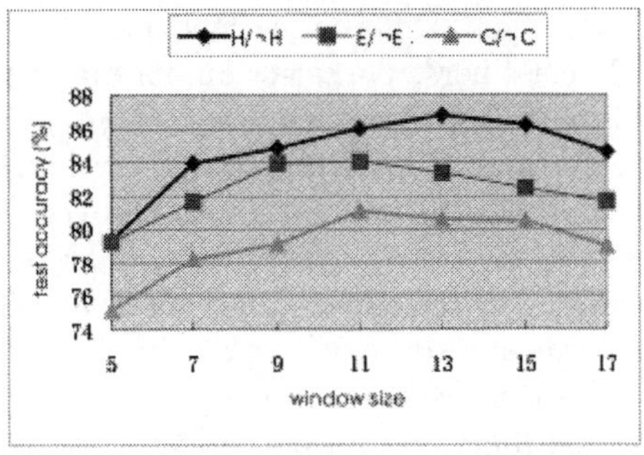


**Fig. 3.** Accuracies $AC_{SVM}$ of different window sizes for each binary classifier on CB513

We construct three different binary classifiers, i.e. H/¬H, E/¬E, and C/¬C. The optimal window size, for each binary classifier was determined by using the protein sequences in CB513. The results as shown in Fig. 3, indicate that the optimal window size is related to the average length of the secondary structure segments. In general, longer mean segments require larger optimal window sizes. (The average length of helix, strand, and coil in CB513 are 8, 5, and 5, respectively.) In addition, the results show that the testing accuracy of each binary classifier is not too sensitive to the window length. In fact, using window lengths in the interval [$n$-1, $n$+1], the variation of the testing accuracy is quite small, which is less than 1.0%. It is interesting to know that the optimal window size based on $SVM_{SSP}$ is similar in size used by other neural networks approaches [4,10], e.g. the optimal window sizes for H/¬H are both 13.

### 4.3 Effectiveness of Our Prediction Approach

We now turn our attention to evaluate the effectiveness of $SVM_{SSP}$. We first compare $SVM_{SSP}$ with PHD [4] and a SVM-based method [6]. PHD is one of the most accurate and reliable secondary structure prediction methods based on neural networks, whereas the SVM-based method is a newly proposed method that can outperform PHD. Our comparison is based on the same test data sets (CB513 and RS126), the same secondary structure definitions, and the same accuracy assessments. To simplify our discussion, we call the SVM-based method $SVM_{01}$. The comparison results among PHD, $SVM_{01}$, and $SVM_{SSP}$ are shown in Table 3, where '-' denotes that the results cannot be obtained.

**Table 3.** Comparison with results of other systems

| | | $Q_3$ | $Q_H$ | $Q_E$ | $Q_C$ | $Q_H^{pre}$ | $Q_E^{pre}$ | $Q_C^{pre}$ | $Sov$ |
|---|---|---|---|---|---|---|---|---|---|
| CB513 | $SVM_{01}$ | 73.5% | 75.0% | 60.0% | 79.0% | 79.0% | 67.0% | 70.0% | 76.2% |
| | $SVM_{SSP}$ | 75.2% | 77.5% | 64.8% | 79.9% | 82.1% | 70.5% | 70.6% | 77.8% |
| RS126 | PHD | 70.8% | 72.0% | 66.0% | 72.0% | 73.0% | 60.0% | - | 73.5% |
| | $SVM_{01}$ | 71.2% | 73.0% | 58.0% | 75.0% | 77.0% | 66.0% | 69.0% | 74.6% |
| | $SVM_{SSP}$ | 73.8% | 75.1% | 61.2% | 81.2% | 80.9% | 69.7% | 70.1% | 76.4% |

Using the CB513 set, the accuracy measure of $Q_3$ on $SVM_{SSP}$ is 75.2%, which is 1.7% higher than $SVM_{01}$, and the SOV of $SVM_{SSP}$ achieves 77.8%, which is 1.6% higher than $SVM_{01}$. The $Q_3$ and SOV scores of $SVM_{SSP}$ on the RS126 set are improved by 3.0% and 2.9%, respectively, compared with the PHD results. The comparison results between PHD and the two SVM-based methods indicate that the prediction methods based on SVM outperformed PHD, because the SVM-based method can successfully avoid many problems which other machine learning approaches often encounter. For example, structures of neural networks (especially the size of the hidden layer) are difficult to determine and gradient-based training algorithms only guarantee finding local minima. In addition, there are too many model parameters to be optimized, and overfitting problems are hard to avoid. The comparison results between $SVM_{01}$ and $SVM_{SSP}$ further show that the encoding schema of $SVM_{SSP}$ and the two dimensional prediction framework play significant roles on accurately predicting protein secondary structures.

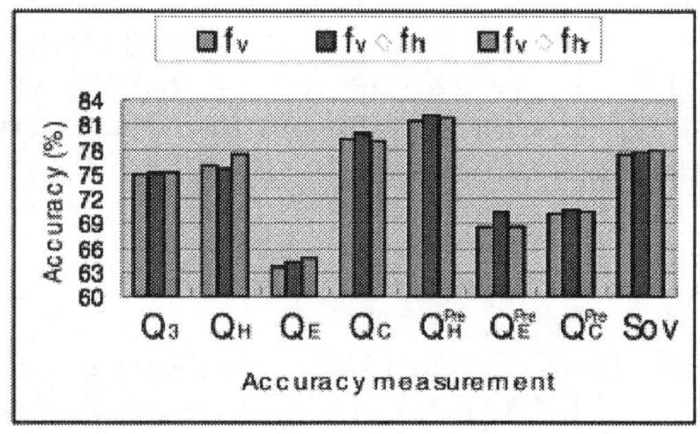


**Fig. 4.** Effectiveness of decision functions

### 4.4 Effectiveness of Synthesizing Different Decision Functions

We consider not only the secondary structure segments but also their context information to enhance the performance of $SVM_{SSP}$. Fig. 4 indicates that our two-dimensional predict framework improves the prediction accuracy, where $f_v$, $f_{h_l}$, and $f_{h_r}$ are the vertical decision function, the left horizontal decision function, and the right horizontal decision function, respectively, and we use '$\diamond$' to denote the synthesis operations between two different decision functions. It turns out that left contexts of protein segments help improve $Q_I^{pre}$, while right contexts of protein segments help improve the $Q_3$ values. This is because left contexts help filter out some incorrectly predicted residues and right contexts help identify more residues as helix (strand or coil) class.

## 5 Conclusions

We propose a framework, $SVM_{SSP}$, for predicting protein secondary structures using SVM. $SVM_{SSP}$ simply takes structural segments and contexts of structural segments extracted from a given protein sequence and matches it against the structural classification results computed by SVM. We incorporate the biological classifications of amino acid residues and statistical information into an encoding schema, consider not only structured segments but also their contexts, and choose the most ideal kernel function, parameters, and size of the window for the prediction of different protein structure classes. The experimental results show that $SVM_{SSP}$ outperforms existing prediction methods.

**Acknowledgments.** The authors would like to thank Jianyin Shao of the Chemistry and Biochemistry department at Brigham Young University for his helpful discussions and suggestions. Special thanks are also given to Chih-Chung Chang and Chih-Jen Lin for providing LIBSVM. Guoren Wang's research is partially supported by National Natural Science Foundation of China under grant No. 60273079.

## References

1. Nelson, D. L., Cox, M. M.: Lehninger Principles of Biochemistry Amino. Worth Publishers (2000)
2. Rashidi, H. H., Buehler, K. L.: Bioinformatics Basics Applications in Biological Science and Medicine. CRC Press (2000)
3. Garnier,J., Osguthorpe, D. J., Robson, B.: Analysis of the Accuracy and Implications of Simple Methods for Predicting the Secondary Structure of Globular Proteins. J. Mol Biol, Vol. 120 (1978) 97–120
4. Rost, B., Sander, C., Schneider, R.: Redefining the Goals of Protein Secondary Structure Prediction. J. Mol Biol, Vol. 235 (1994) 13–26
5. Zvelebil, M. J., Barton, G. J., Taylor, W. R., et al: Prediction of Protein Secondary Structure and Active Sites Using the Alignment of Homologous Sequences. J. Mol Biol, Vol. 195 (1987) 957–961
6. Hua, S., Sun, Z.: A Novel Method of Protein Secondary Structure Prediction with High Segment Overlap Measure: Support Vector Machine Approach. Bioinformatics, Vol. 308 (2001) 397–407
7. Vapnik, V.: The Nature of Statistical Learning Theory. Springer-Verlag, New York (1995)
8. Cuff, J. A., Barton, G. J.: Evaluation and Improvement of Multiple Sequence Methods for Protein Secondary Structure Prediction. Proteins: Struct. Funct. Genet., Vol. 34 (1999) 508–519
9. Rost, B., Sander, C.: Prediction of Protein Secondary Structure at Better Than 70% Accuracy. J. Mol. Biol, Vol. 232 (1993) 584–599
10. Qian, N., Sejnowski, T. J.: Predicting the Secondary Structure of Globular Proteins Using Neural Network Models. J. Mol. Biol, Vol. 202. (1988) 865–884
11. Zwillinger, D., Krantz, S. G., Rosen, K. H.: Standard Mathematical Tables and Formulae (30th edition). CRC Press (1996)
12. Kabsch, W., Sander, C.: A Dictionary of Protein Secondary Structure. Biopolymers, Vol. 22 (1983) 2577–2637
13. Protein Data Bank: http://www.rcsb.org/pdb/ (2002)
14. Moult. J., Hubbard, T., Fidelis, K., Pedersen, J.: Critical Assessment of Methods of Protein Structure Prediction (CASP): Round III. PROTEINS:Structure, Function, Genetics, Vol. 37, Suppl. 3 (1999) 2–6
15. Chang, C.-C., Lin, C.-J.: LIBSVM: a Library for Support Vector Machines. Software available at http://www.csie.ntu.edu.tw/~cjlin/libsvm (2001)

# Efficient Semantic Search in Peer-to-Peer Systems*

Aoying Zhou[1], Bo Ling[1], Zhiguo Lu[1], Weesiong Ng[2], Yanfeng Shu[2], and Kian-Lee Tan[2]

[1] Department of Computer Science and Engineering, Fudan University, China
{ayzhou, lingbo, luzhiguo}@fudan.edu.cn
[2] School of Computing, National University of Singapore, Singapore
{ngws, shuyanfe, tankl}@comp.nus.edu.sg

**Abstract.** While many P2P-based data sharing applications have been deployed, most of them just support semantics-free and coarse granularity (file level) sharing. Moreover, they are not efficient, either from user's view on service quality or in terms of resources utilization in the systems. In this paper, we present our solutions to support efficient semantic-based search in unstructured P2P systems. We propose a scheme to categorize and manage data in a peer based on the vector-space model. We also propose a scheme that allows peers with similar content to be clustered together. Finally, we examine an adaptive scheme to route queries. We conduct an extensive experimental study to evaluate the effectiveness of our solutions and obtain promising results.

## 1 Introduction

Peer-to-peer (P2P) technology is an emerging paradigm that is now regarded as a promising technology to re-construct distributed architectures (e.g., the Internet). In a P2P system, a large number of peers (e.g., PCs connected to the Internet) can potentially be pooled together to share their resources, information and services. Participating nodes that can consume as well as provide data and/or services, may join and leave the P2P network at any time, resulting in a truly dynamic and ad-hoc environment. These desirable features provide exciting opportunities for various applications, such as instant message (IM) [6], collaborative tool [5], CPU cycle sharing [12] and data sharing [2,3,7,9]. While most of the applications are established to share data, the current mechanisms are largely restricted to file level sharing by requesting file identifiers. The inability to share data based on their *semantics* results in information overload (as many irrelevant answers may be retrieved), and greatly hinders the deployment of other practical applications.

Moreover, current unstructured P2P systems are inefficient – from the user's view, the service quality is low (long response time and low recall); from the system's view, resources (e.g., bandwidth and cpu cycle) are not well utilized. For

* Suported by the Fok Ying Tung Education Foundation

G. Dong et al. (Eds.): WAIM 2003, LNCS 2762, pp. 278–289, 2003.

example, when searching for a desired file, Gnutella blindly floods the network with query messages and all queried peers in turn search their local repositories (even if they do not contain answer), resulting in huge wastage of bandwidth and computing resources.

In this paper, we propose our solution to facilitate semantic-based search in unstructured P2P systems. In particular, our contributions are as follows:

- We propose comprehensive metrics to evaluate the efficiency of P2P systems, including *response time* and *recall* (service quality for users), and *bandwidth* and *computing resource consumption* (utilization of system resource).
- We identify key issues that determine efficient semantic search in P2P systems, including local data management, data placement of systems, and the routing strategy. We also present their solutions.
- Finally, we have conducted extensive experiments, and the results show the effectiveness of our solutions.

The rest of the paper is organized as follows. Section 2 reviews some related work. Section 3 states the problems. Section 4 details optimization mechanisms. We evaluate our solutions in section 5, and conclude in section 6.

## 2 Related Work

Generally, P2P-based data sharing systems can be roughly divided into three types: hybrid, structured and unstructured systems. Some functionalities of hybrid systems are still centralized, so they are vulnerable to a single of failure and litigation. Recently, several structured systems have been developed, e.g., Past [2]. Supported by the overlays with distributed hash table functions (e.g., Pastry[10]), queries are guaranteed to be routed to their answer locations within a certain (bounded) number of hops. Therefore, they are very efficient in utilizing bandwidth and computing resources. However, they suffer from two major limitations. First, they cannot deal with non-exact queries. Second, data placement are tightly controlled, which implies that the cost to maintain the structured topology is high especially in a dynamic environment. Thus, we just focus on unstructured systems which we believe are more practical and scalable.

To improve the efficiency of unstructured P2P network, Garcia-Molina et al. have made contributions from two aspects. First, in [14], Yang and Garcia-Molina proposed three techniques that facilitate directed search : (i) In Iterative Deepening, multiple search cycles are initiated with successively larger depth, until either the query is satisfied or the maximal depth $d$ is arrived. (ii) In Directed BFT, queries are propagated only to a beneficial subset of the neighbors of each node. (iii) In Local Indices, each node maintains an index over the data of all peers within $r$ hops to itself, allowing each search to terminate after $(d-r)$ hops. Second, in [1] Crespo and Garcia-Molina introduced the technique of Routing Index (RI), a data structure that, given a query, returns a list of neighbors ranked based on the number of possibly available answers. Specifically, they proposed three routing indices: (i) Compound RI (*CRI*). A CRI contains the number of documents along each path and the number of each topic of interest (similar to our "favorite"). Its limitation is without considering the difference of "hops" necessary to reach a document. (ii) Hop-count RI. A hop-count RI has associated the aggregated RIs for each "hop" up to a maximal number of hops. It overcomes the ineffectiveness of CRI at a higher storage and transmission cost. (iii) A Exponential RI stores the result of applying the regular-tree cost formula to a hop-count RI. It overcomes the shortcomings of hop-count RI at the cost of some *potential* loss in accuracy. Both collections of techniques are orthogonal to ours and can be employed to our framework.

To achieve high performance, Triantafillou et al. in [13] also proposed architecture of peer clusters and document groups based on their semantics. However, our work is different in several ways. First, their peer clusters are predefined while ours *naturally* form. Second, their strategy to achieve performance is through "fair" workload balance (their foundation, the *popularity* of document, is hardly convincible), while ours is through three optimization mechanisms.

## 3 Problem Statement

### 3.1 Definitions and Concepts

First we define what a query and its answers look like. Without losing generality, we assume the objects to be shared in the P2P system are of text format. In such a context, a query takes the form $q = \langle k_1, \cdots, k_t,\ q_{id} \rangle$. Here, $\langle k_1, \cdots, k_t \rangle$ is a set of keywords submitted by a user to describe what he/she desires; while $q_{id}$ is a system-wide unique identifier of $q$ generated by its initiator. The answers to $q$ is a collection of files (along with their metadata e.g., index term, semantics category), whose semantics relatedness to $q$ is no less than a predefined *threshold*. We will discuss the semantics relatedness in section 4.1.

Second, although peers in a P2P network are of equal status, the relationship among them are different. The two important types are defined as follows:

*Definition 1.* Neighborhood: two peers are neighbors if they can directly connect with each other; Acquaintance: if a pair of peers interact with each other via one or several other peers, then one is defined as an acquaintance of another.

For example, in the figure 1, peer $C$ is a neighbor of peer $B$, while peer $D$ and $E$ are two acquaintances of peer $B$.

*Definition.2* Favorite of a peer (its user) is the distribution of semantics category of the files that the peer maintains, which reflects its user's interests.

### 3.2 Efficiency Metrics

Efficiency usually indicates how quickly a transaction is completed. However, in P2P-based data sharing systems, it should be enriched with more connotation. First, from the angle of service quality for user, it is defined as how efficient the

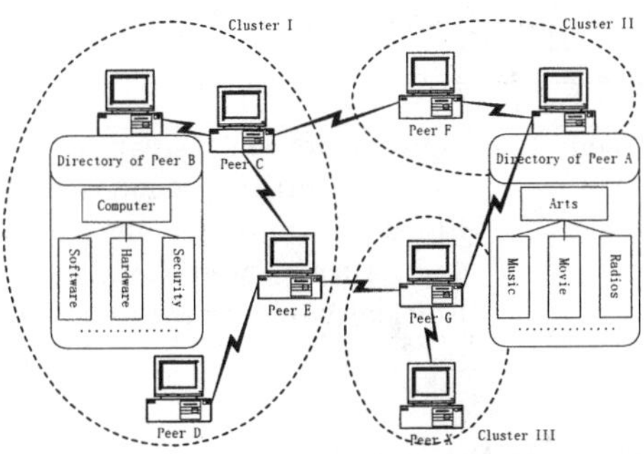


**Fig. 1.** Architecture of P2P System

P2P system satisfies their demands, which can be depicted with two dimensions. (I) Response rate, it is indicated by how long it takes to receive the answers after query submission. Although the physical status of the network and peers' processing power greatly affect response rate, to achieve deeper insight into P2P, we focus on processing algorithms and P2P protocol, the *soft* aspects. (II) Recall. It indicates whether a P2P system can obtain all or most of the currently available qualified answers to a given query, calculated by :

$$Recall = \frac{\sum_{Retrieved} Answer}{\sum_{System\ Available} Answer} \tag{1}$$

where $\sum_{Retrieved} Answer$ is the number of qualified answers retrieved during a predefined processing period; and $\sum_{SystemAvailable} Answer$ is the number of currently available qualified answers to the query in the system in the period.

Moreover, the efficiency should be measured by how efficiently the resources in a P2P system are utilized, including bandwidth and computing resources. For a given query, under the constraint of equal number of qualified answers, the less bandwidth is consumed, the more efficient the system is. The utilization of computing resources should also be measured in the same way. In summary, the efficiency metrics should include *Response Time, Recall, Bandwidth and Computing Resource consuming.*

### 3.3 Key Issues of Efficient Semantic Search

The efficiency of semantic search is decided by the following factors:

- How to efficiently identify the peers that can contribute semantic qualified answers to a given query?;
- How to efficiently route the query to its answer contributors and return the qualified answers to its initiator?; and
- When the contributors receive the query, how to efficiently identify and retrieve the qualified objects?

The mechanisms to address the issues are summarized in the table 1.

**Table 1.** Mechanism and Objective

| Mechanism | Objectives |
|---|---|
| Local Data Management | Support efficient semantic local processing; efficiently identifying answer contributors. |
| System Data Placement | Efficiently routing a query to answer contributors and return answers to the query initiator. |
| Routing Strategy | Efficiently routing a query to answer contributors. |

# 4 Optimization Mechanisms

## 4.1 Local Data Management

To support efficient semantic retrieval of text files, we propose a scheme of local data management having two merits. First, for a given query, it facilitates the currently queried peer to efficiently identify whether it probably has semantically related files and retrieve qualified ones if it does. Second, it facilitates peers to capture high level characteristics(e.g., favorites) of each other.

Our scheme employs techniques of information retrieval, including preprocessing and indexing, representation and classification. First, when a text file is first introduced into the system, it is preprocessed and its feature terms are obtained, which are used to index the file (in the form of inverted file) and reused to determine the semantic category of the file. Due to its advantages, the *kNN* [15] classifiers are recommended.

To support semantic retrieving, the preprocessed files are represented with the vector space model [11]. For the vector model, a pair $\langle k_i, d_j \rangle$ is associated with a weight $w_{i,j}$, where $k_i$ and $d_j$ are the $i$th index term (feature term) and $j$th file respectively. These keywords in $q$ are also weighted. Let $w_{i,q}$ be the weight associated pair $\langle k_i, q \rangle$ where $w_{i,q} \geqq 0$ . Then the *query vector* $\boldsymbol{q}$ is defined as $\boldsymbol{q} = (w_{1,q}, w_{2,q}, ..., w_{t,q})$ where $t$ is the total number of feature terms of such category files. Similarly, the *vector* for file $d_j$ is represented by: $\boldsymbol{d}_j = (w_{1,j}, w_{2,j}, ..., w_{t,j})$. Thus, the semantic relatedness between query $q$ and file $d_j$ is determined by:

$$SR(d_j, q) = \frac{\boldsymbol{d}_j \bullet \boldsymbol{q}}{|\boldsymbol{d}_j| \times |\boldsymbol{q}|} = \frac{\sum_{i=1}^{t} w_{i,j} \times w_{i,q}}{\sqrt{\sum_{i=1}^{t} w_{i,j}^2} \times \sqrt{\sum_{i=1}^{t} w_{i,q}^2}}. \qquad (2)$$

Above, $SR(d_j, q)$ is the semantic relatedness between query $q$ and file $d_j$; while $|\boldsymbol{d}_j|$ and $|\boldsymbol{q}|$ are the norms of $\boldsymbol{d}_j$ and $\boldsymbol{q}$ respectively. Based on the mechanism, for given a query $q$ and a file $d_j$ in the peer, if $SR(d_j, q) \geq threshold$, then the file is regarded as semantically qualified to $q$.

According to their semantic categories, the files in a peer can be organized into hierarchy, which has two merits. (i) Receiving a query, a peer can immediately decide whether the query can be answered locally with the help of metadata of its local files and if so, it can directly locate the specific semantic subset files relevant to the query, rather than scanning the whole repository, resulting in huge efficiency gain. (ii) It facilitates peers to capture their high level characteristics and maintain neighbors (acquaintances) and route their queries more intelligently.

## 4.2 Data Placement

Some researchers are already aware that data placement is one of the key issues deciding the performance of P2P systems, e.g., S. Gribblle et al. in [4] pointed out: "data must be placed in strategic locations and then used to improve query performance". However, they did not address how to identify such strategic locations. Indeed, since the peers in the network are not only of equal status but also dynamic and ad-hoc, it is hard to identify such locations, not even to say to put data in such peers. The more reasonable solution is to design intelligent protocol to guarantee peers that potentially benefit each other be clustered together to help them obtain what they demand in a small scope.

Since most of the files that peers maintain come from their searching, based on characteristics of the files they maintain, what kind of files they will search can be predicted with high probability. Therefore, for each category of its favorite files, a node should select and maintain several peers as its neighbors or acquaintances, whose semantics of such category files are very similar to that of its own's. By employing high level characteristics of each other, peers can determine the semantic similarity between their favorites by the following formula:

$$SimSem_C(P_i, P_j) = \frac{\boldsymbol{C_{P_i}} \bullet \boldsymbol{C_{P_j}}}{|\boldsymbol{C_{P_i}}| \times |\boldsymbol{C_{P_j}}|} \tag{3}$$

Here, $SimSem_C(P_i, P_j)$ indicates the *semantic similarity* of favorite of category $C$ between peer $P_i$ and peer $P_j$; $\boldsymbol{C_{P_i}}$ and $\boldsymbol{C_{P_j}}$ are the vectors of category C files of the two peers, while $|\boldsymbol{C_{P_i}}|$and $|\boldsymbol{C_{P_j}}|$ are their norms respectively.

Armed with intelligent protocol, such as reconfiguration of PeerDB [9], peers can intelligently select neighbors (acquaintances) when they first bootstrap or reconfigure their neighbors (acquaintances) during lifetime, so that they can manage to maintain those with whom it shares highest semantic similarity for each favorite category. Such a P2P system automatically evolves into a mesh of peer clusters in terms of favorites, i.e., peers in different clusters have different favorites while in the same cluster, the nearer two peers are, the higher the semantic similarity between them is. If a peer has several favorites, it logically belongs to several clusters at the same time; if peers change their favorites, they automatically join the appropriate clusters with the accumulation of files.

## 4.3 Self-Adaptive Routing Strategy

Most of unstructured P2P systems adopt the broadcast routing strategy. To avoid flooding the whole network with exponential query messages, each query is terminated based on the Time-to-Live $TTL$. However, this naive strategy is confronted with a dilemma: if the $TTL$ is set too small, search is confined within a small scope and results in poor recall, especially when the neighborhood is randomly defined; on the other hand, if it is set too large, the traffic over the peer network will be very heavy. How to achieve high recall while avoiding flooding the network is really a challenge. To address this issue, supported by the above optimization mechanisms, we propose a self-adaptive routing strategy, whose procedures are as follows:

- When a query is initiated by a peer, it is first parsed locally and its semantics category is decided. From the metadata of its own files and its neighbors' (acquaintances'), the peer can determine whether the query has located the desired semantics cluster or not, and take following steps respectively;
- If unfortunately, the peer finds out that its query has not locate such a cluster, guided by their high level information, it forwards the query to some of its neighbors or acquaintances who can lead the query to the target peer cluster with highest probabilities (if unfortunately, none of them can indicate the direction, it just forwards its query out of the scope of its acquaintances); the message receiver will in turn perform such processing and decision making. This kind of routing procedure will be terminated when the messages arrive at the destination, or its TTL arrives at *zero*;
- When the query has located the semantics cluster, if the queried peers provide files whose semantics relatedness is less than the pre-defined *threshold*, it will try to route the query to peers which may contain files of higher similarity to the query. After the query has been transmitted to peers contributing the most related answers, it will be terminated at those peers that begin to provide unqualified answers.

## 5 Evaluation

### 5.1 Experiment Setup

The experiments are conducted with 66 PCs in a LAN, all of which are equipped with an Intel Pentium 1.7 GHz processor and 128M RAM, running Windows 2000 operating system. We implemented the three optimization mechanisms on the top of *BestPeer*[8]. Thus, each PC is a peer of an autonomous information retrieval system and all of them form a P2P network. We generated a collection of files belonging to four semantic categories, and each file is about 10KB. We distribute 1,000 files of two categories to each peer. Specifically, 80% belongs to one category while another 20% to another. Based on the semantic categories of files each peer maintains, the network consists of 4 peer clusters whose numbers are 10, 22, 18, 16 respectively, while each peer belongs to two clusters at the same time. For comparison, we use these peers to build up a *Gnutella* network, where peers are not clustered and data are uniformly distributed.

### 5.2 Evaluation Methodology

Like the Internet search engines, the answers to a query in the real P2P network depend on the queried peers, which may not include every peer in the networks.

In addition, a query may involve different peers in different time, since peers are dynamic and ad-hoc. For purpose of evaluation, a controlled environment is necessary. Therefore, different scenarios should be evaluated based on a fixed set of nodes. To verify the effectiveness of our solutions, we propose three basic scenarios: (i) Searching favorite files, denoted by *Favorite*. This is the case where a peer searches for files belonging to the 80% semantic category; (ii)*Non-Favorite*. peers search files of semantic categories differ from those of its own's. (iii) Searching by Gnutella, denoted by *Gnutella*. For fairness, the queries in these three scenarios are identical, i.e., the ones used in *Favorite*. When carrying out scenario (ii), the query initiators are peers in another semantics cluster different from those of the initiators that (i) belong to; and the initiators in (iii) and (i) are the same. The experiments are conducted when the machines and the network are fully dedicated. The results presented are of the average of at least 10 different trials.

### 5.3 Response Rate

To evaluate the metric of *response rate*, we first generate a query $q$ to search the favorite files of a randomly selected peer, and the query is conducted 10 times ( *Favorite*). Second, we select another peer who is definitely out of the semantic clusters to initiate $q$ 10 times (*Non-Favorite*). Finally, the same query is submitted 10 times via the initiator of *Favorite* in the Gnutella network (*Gnutella*). To eliminate variance resulting from different initiators, all processing are repeated in three different initiators and the average results are plotted in figure 2.

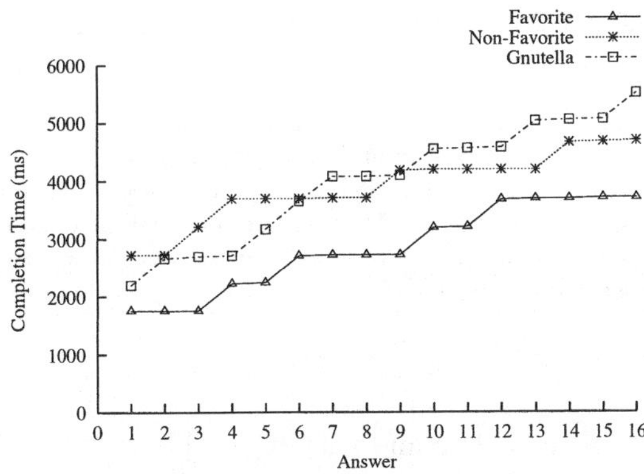


**Fig. 2.** Response Rate

From figure 2, we can see that the *Favorite* outperforms the other two in all circumstances. However, *Gnutella* is better than *Non-Favorite* in its first $\frac{1}{4}$ stage while worse than *Non-Favorite* in the rest of the stages. The reasons are as follows. First, based on the mechanism of *data placement*, the *Favorite* can obtain its answers in the same cluster, where all answer contributors are very near to the query initiator (the *Non-Favorite* is contrary), so that the delay in network transfer is much less than the other two. Because of the different *local data management* schemes, answer contributors of *Favorite* just need to search a subset of their local files while queried peers in *Gnutella* must traverse their whole repositories. Therefore, *Favorite* can retrieve the first few answers much quicker than *Gnutella*, even if both of their answers are from initiators themselves. Second, the first $\frac{1}{4}$ stage of *Gnutella*'s response rate is better than that of *Non-Favorite*, because the former can get the first answers nearer to the query initiator (even the initiator itself) than the later. However, since the answers of *Non-Favorite* are located in the same cluster, their distance to the initiator is very similar, while those of *Gnutella*' are uniformly (randomly in reality) distributed over the whole network. In addition, with the more intelligent local data managing, *Non-Favorite* performs better than *Gnutella* in the rest of the stages.

## 5.4 Recall

Although it is hard to measure the *recall* of real P2P systems, it is a metric that users are very concerned, since it decides whether users can obtain what they are looking for. To achieve a deep insight into what decides the recall of P2P systems, in this study, the *Adaptive Routing Strategy* is turned on in some cases while shut down in others. Therefore, two new scenarios are derived. The specification of five scenarios is shown in table 2.

**Table 2.** Evaluation Scenarios and Specification

| Abbreviation | Specification |
|---|---|
| AdF | Searching favorite files and adopting adaptive routing strategy. |
| NAdF | Searching favorite files and query messages are terminated by TTL. |
| AdNF | Searching non-favorite files and adopting adaptive routing strategy. |
| NAdNF | Searching non-favorite files and query messages are terminated by TTL. |
| Gnutella | semantic peer clustering and query messages are terminated by TTL. |

For each scenarios in table 2 and when the TTL is set to {3, 4, 5, 6, 7}, the query $q$ are performed similarly to that when we evaluate response rate, and the average results are plotted in figure 3.

We list the underlying reasons of the scenarios. (1)*AdF*, it can retrieve all its answers no matter what values of TTL, since when searching favorite objects, the query is initiated in the same cluster and it is terminated based on semantic relatedness but not TTL. However, in (2)*NAdF*, since the *Adaptive Routing Strategy* is turned off, the lifetime of a query is decided by TTL. As a consequence, it can just retrieve within the scope of TTL hops away from the initiator, when the TTL is set too small it cannot get all answers. It is why its *recall* is just about 60% when TTL is set to 3. When searching non-favorite

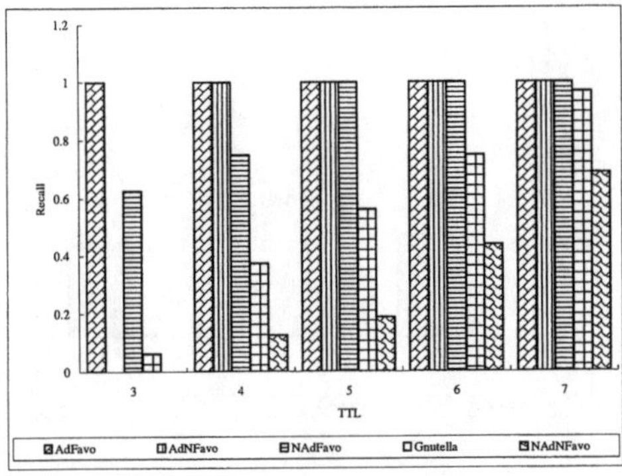


**Fig. 3.** Underlying reasons of Recall

files, the situation is similar except when the TTL is set too small. (3)When the TTL is set to 3, *AdNF* can obtain no answer, since before the messages of the query arrives at the cluster, it has expired before the *Adaptive Routing Strategy* works. (4) *NAdNF* can get more answers with larger TTL, since the query can access more peers; while its *recall* is still the worst because its answers are far away from the initiator. Finally, (5) *Gnutella* outperforms *NAdNF*, because its answers are uniformly distributed, and some answers are nearer to the query initiator than those of *NAdNF*. Based on the above analysis, we can draw the following conclusions:

- When searching favorite files, our schemes can get higher *recall* than the current P2P system, and can even obtain all currently available answers;
- Armed with *Adaptive Routing Strategy*, after some trial and error, user can obtain high *recall* and can efficiently use the system's resources;
- Since users commonly search their favorites, our schemes are more efficient than the current solutions.

### 5.5 Bandwidth Consumption

From now on, we begin to re-adopt the three scenarios defined in subsection 5.2. The bandwidth consumed by searching is measured by the number of query messages during processing. When evaluating *response rate*, the volume of query messages have been recorded and the average results are shown in figure 4.

Based on the *Aver.* in figure 4, we can confirm that the bandwidth is more efficiently utilized in our solution than in *Gnutella*. When searching favorites, our bandwidth is less than 50% that of *Gnutella*; when finding non-favorite file, our bandwidth cost is less than 70% that of the *Gnutella*'s. The other two attributes in figure 4 show that the workload is more balanced in our strategies.

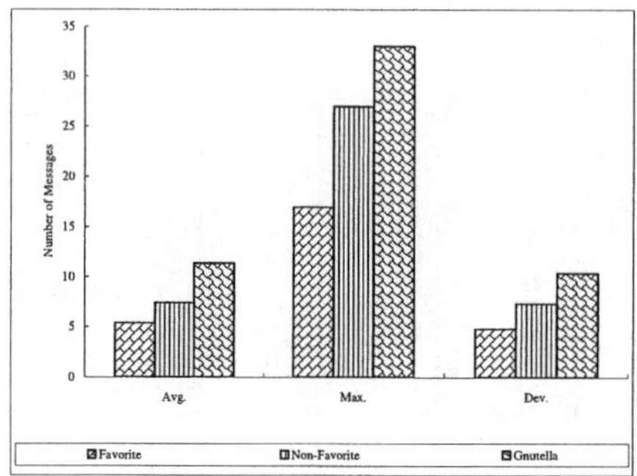


**Fig. 4.** Bandwidth Consuming Statistics

### 5.6 Utilization of Computating Resources

Computing resources consist of CPU cycles, memory and storage. Due to the space constraint, we just report the distribution of *CPU time* consumed during query processing, which are shown in figure 5.

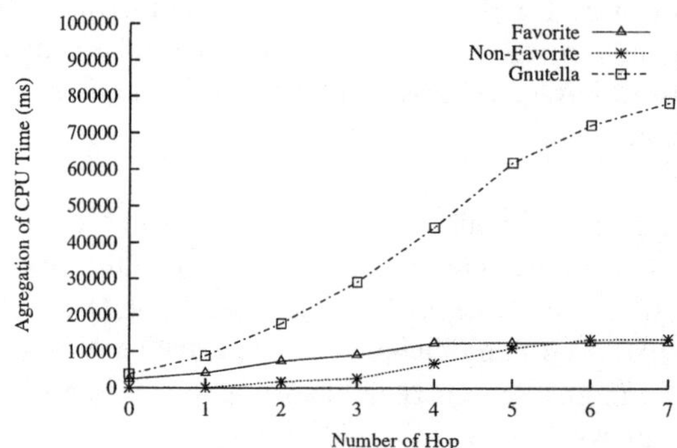


**Fig. 5.** CPU Consuming Distribution

In figure 5, the accumulated CPU time of *Gnutella* is much larger than those of our schemes. The first part of *Gnutella*'s curve is exponential due to its blind routing strategy, almost resulting in exponential processing sites. After 5 $\sim$ 6 hops, *Gnutella*'s *CPU time* increases much slower, since there are only 66 peers in our network, and after that horizon peers just deal with the repeated messages due to the link loops among peers, consuming tiny CPU cycle. Further, *Gnutella* is worsen by its naive local data management scheme. In the figure, the curve of *Favorite* is not only more even but much lower than that of *Gnutella*, since (i)the query just is routed to the neighbor of high semantics relatedness so that the number of processing peers is fewer; (ii) each processing peer just searches part of its repository, so each processing peer consumes less *CPU time*; (iii) the accumulated *CPU time* almost keeps the same just after hop 6, because there is no related enough peers farther than that horizon. *Non-Favorite*'s first part (before hop 3) is almost near *zero*, because there is no related peers within that scope, where peers just need forward messages, resulting in tiny CPU overload. However, from hops 4 onward, the query has located the semantics related cluster, the situation is the same as that of *Favorite*, so the two curves are very similar.

## 6 Conclusion

Research in P2P computing is still at its infancy, and current research mostly focus on data sharing. Existing systems support only semantic-free sharing, and are inefficient. In this paper, we have defined the metrics of P2P system efficiency and identify their deciding issues. Second, we proposed solutions to address each of them. Finally, we conducted extensive experiments to verify the effectiveness of our solutions. However, there are many other issues that need to be addressed, such as security and collaboration in the non-trusted environments. We plan to address some of these in the near future.

## References

1. A. Crespo and H. Garcia-Molina. Routing indices for peer-to-peer systems. In *ICDCS*, 2002.
2. P. Druschel. and A. Rowstron. Past: Persistent and anonymous storage in a peer-to-peer networking environment. In *Proceedings of the 8th IEEE Workshop on HotOS*, pages 65–70, 2001.
3. Gnutella Development Home Page. *http://gnutella.wego.com/.*
4. S. Gribble, A. Halevy, Z. Ives, M. Rodrig, and D. Suciu. What can databases do for peer-to-peer. In *WebDB*, 2001.
5. Groove Home Page. *http://www.groove.net.*
6. ICQ Home Page. *http://www.icq.com/.*
7. Napster Home Page. *http://www.napster.com/.*
8. W. S. Ng, B. C. Ooi, and K. L. Tan. Bestpeer: A self-configurable peer-to-peer system. In *Proceedings of ICDE.*, San Jose, CA, April 2002 (Poster Paper).
9. W. S. Ng, B. C. Ooi, K. L. Tan, and A. Zhou. Peerdb: A p2p-based system for distributed data sharing. In *Proceedings of ICDE.*, 2003.
10. A. Rowstron and P. Druschel. Pastry: Scalable, distributed object location and routing for large-scale peer-to-peer systems. In *Proceedings of the International Conference on Distributed Systems Platforms (Middleware)*, Germany, 2001.
11. G. Salton and M.E.Lesk. Computer evaluation of indexing and text processing. In *Journal of the ACM.*, Jan., 1968.
12. SETI@home Home Page. *http://setiathome.ssl.berkely.edu/.*
13. P. Triantafillou and C. X. et al. Towards high performance peer-to-peer content and resource sharing systems. In *Proceedings of CIDR.*
14. B. Yang and H. Garcia-Molina. Efficient search in peer-to-peer networks. In *ICDCS*, 2002.
15. Y. Yang and X. Liu. A re-examination of text categorization methods. In *Proceedings of ACM SIGIR.*, 1999.

# Enacting Business Processes in a Decentralised Environment with p2p-Based Workflow Support

Jun Yan[1], Yun Yang[1], and Gitesh K. Raikundalia[1,2]

[1] CICEC - Centre for Internet Computing and E-Commerce
School of Information Technology
Swinburne University of Technology
P.O. Box 218, Hawthorn, Melbourne, Australia 3122
{jyan,yyang}@it.swin.edu.au
[2] School of Computer Science and Mathematics
Victoria University
P.O. Box 14428, Melbourne City, MC 8001, Australia
Gitesh.Raikundalia@vu.edu.au

**Abstract.** Traditionally, workflow adopts a centralised client/server architecture to enact processes, which has exhibited many weaknesses. This paper combines concepts from workflow technology and peer-to-peer computing and presents an innovative approach to support decentralised process enactment. With this approach, both process instantiation and instance execution are carried out in a genuinely decentralised fashion, which reflects applications' increasingly distributed nature better. In general, the process instance is created with relevant participants creating various task instances at different locations. In addition, instance execution is coordinated through direct communication among relevant workflow participants.

## 1 Introduction

The run-time operation of a workflow management system provides enactment support for business processes, which includes process instantiation and instance execution [10]. Past efforts on workflow research and development normally use a dominating client/server architecture with process instances being created and managed by centralised workflow engines [6]. However, centralised workflow support has faced many challenges and left some problems unsolved, such as heavy-weight, poor scalability and human restrictions [8]. Thus, it is believed that the next generation of workflow will adopt a decentralised architecture and provide decentralised enactment support [13]. Consequently, both process instance creation and instance execution are expected to be carried out in a decentralised manner. Unfortunately, only little work has so far been done on this issue.

To address the above problems, this paper proposes an innovative approach to enable the enactment of a process instance in a peer-to-peer (p2p) based decentralised environment. The rest of this paper is organized as follows. In the next section, some previous work of the authors is described. The approach of decentralised process enactment is then illustrated in section 3, followed by an example in section 4. Some

G. Dong et al. (Eds.): WAIM 2003, LNCS 2762, pp. 290–297, 2003.

major related work is introduced in section 5. Finally, section 6 concludes the paper and outlines the authors' future work.

## 2 Background

Given the nature of the application environment and the technology involved, workflow applications are inherently distributed [2, 13]. This feature makes centralised workflow support relatively unsuitable. To reflect the increasingly distributed nature of workflow applications better, a decentralised process support environment is needed. On the other hand, p2p, which can be defined simply as the sharing of computer resources and services by direct communication, has attracted researchers' attention. Compared with the client/server model, p2p enables better scalability, eliminates the risk of single–source bottleneck, and provides load balancing. Thus, p2p is driving a major shift in the area of genuinely distributed computing [1].

Combining concepts of workflow and p2p, the authors have presented an innovative p2p-based decentralised workflow architecture known as SwinDew [12], which has neither a centralised data repository nor a centralised control engine. In this approach, a workflow system is designed as a p2p system. Each peer is a node, which is denoted as software residing on a physical machine to enable direct communication with other nodes to carry out workflow while, in most cases, a node is associated with a human being. Each node is involved in one or more virtual communities according to the associated human capabilities and knows the other nodes in the same communities. In addition, a node-discovery service is designed to allow a node to locate other nodes in different communities. By these means, each node functions independently and coordinates with other nodes by direct communication to fulfil key workflow functions in a decentralised manner.

To support business processes with the absence of a centralised data repository, the issues of distributed data storage have been further investigated and an innovative mechanism has been presented [11]. In essence, this mechanism proposes a policy called "*know what you should know*". After a process is defined, the process is converted into a number of intrinsically related partitions appropriately. Each partition, which represents a task and its position inside a process, is denoted as a six-tuple *T (process-id; task-id;* $C_{pre}$*;* $C_{post}$*; capability; resource-set)*. Then the individual partitions are distributed to relevant nodes which have the matched capabilities and will perform the instances of these tasks later.

## 3 Decentralised Process Enactment Support

Based on the previous work, this paper further investigates the issues of process enactment with the above p2p-based workflow architecture, which includes process instantiation and instance execution.

### 3.1 Process Instantiation

A process instance represents one individual enactment of the process. This is a network of task instances, which should be assigned to various nodes. In a decentralised workflow environment, a process instance cannot and should not be created at a single site. The approach proposed in this paper creates a process instance by instantiating relevant tasks one by one on various nodes. The node that creates a task instance actually performs the work represented by this task instance. The procedure of process instantiation can be described as follows.

(1) A starting task instance is created by a node under the guidance of management or as a response to a coming event, for example, receiving an application in an application processing workflow system. This node is known as the current instantiation node.
(2) The current instantiation node looks for other nodes to instantiate the direct succeeding tasks with the mechanism proposed in this paper.
(3) If the succeeding tasks have their own succeeding tasks, the selected nodes act the current instantiation node and repeat step (2) one by one.
(4) If the termination task is reached, process instantiation is completed.

Gradually, all the required task instances are created from the starting task to the termination task, on different nodes. A process instance becomes a network of relevant nodes on behalf of relevant performers performing various tasks.

#### 3.1.1 Task Instantiation Procedures

Once an instance of task $T_i$ is created by node $N_i$, it is $N_i$'s responsibility to find the performers of $T_i$'s direct succeeding tasks. The instantiation of $T_i$ is considered complete only after either all its direct succeeding task instances are created or it has no succeeding tasks at all. There are three main types of relationships between tasks, i.e., *sequence*, *branching* and *joining*. Correspondingly, there are different instantiation procedures for different relations as follows.

- *Sequence*: In a sequence relationship, a task only has one direct succeeding task. Assume an instance of task $T_i$ with definition *T* ($P_i$; $T_i$; $C_{pre}$; $T_j$; *capability; resource-set)* is created by node $N_i$. $N_i$ then activates a node-discovery service to search for a node that can perform task $T_j$. Suppose node $N_k$ is returned to $N_i$ as the result of the node-discovery service. Then $N_i$ sends to $N_k$ an *instantiation request* (*IR*). $N_k$ spreads the request in the corresponding virtual community to let other available nodes know this work. It relies on the nodes in this virtual community to negotiate automatically who will carry out this task instance eventually. Finally, $N_j$, the node selected to accept $T_j$, creates an instance of $T_j$, sends a response to $N_i$, and restarts the instantiation process to find successors of itself.
- *Branching:* In this case, task $T_i$ ($P_i$; $T_i$; $C_{pre}$; $C_{post}$; *capability; resource-set)* has more than one succeeding task. During the instantiation stage, each succeeding task should be instantiated. If node $N_i$ has created an instance of $T_i$, it executes algorithm (1) to instantiate $C_{post}$:

*for each* $T_k$ *in* $C_{post}$
*instantiate* $T_k$ *with the sequence mechanism described above* (1)

- *Joining:* In this case, task $T_i$ *($P_i$; $T_i$; $C_{pre}$; $C_{post}$; capability; resource-set)* has more than one direct preceding task. Each of $T_i$'s direct preceding task requests the instantiation of $T_i$ independently. If an *IR* is the first request from $C_{pre}$, i.e., an instance of $T_i$ has not been created, node $N_i$ then instantiates $T_i$ with the sequence mechanism described above. Otherwise, $N_i$ sends a confirmation to the request initiator indicating that an instance of $T_i$ has been created on node $N_i$.

### 3.1.2 Selection Policies

Regarding task instance allocation, it is possible that more than one available node in the capability community can accept. Therefore, relevant nodes can negotiate automatically to determine the allocation of the task instance. The main goal of dynamic allocation is to optimise system performance. This paper uses workload as a measurement of system performance and tries to balance workload to yield performance advantages.

To optimise the system locally, firstly, all the available nodes are identified. Then the workload of each available node *i* in a time period such as one day is calculated by formula $w_i = \sum t_k$, where $t_k$ is the workload of task instance *k* that has been assigned to node *i* in this time period. The task instance is eventually assigned to the node with minimum *w*. The objective of this algorithm is to bring the workload into proportion among the available nodes on the basis of the current condition. The coexistence of idle nodes with overwrought nodes could be avoided on a local scale.

However, it often happens that some key tasks require some high-level skills that only belong to a small number of participants such as managers. These important people usually have other lower-level capabilities to perform some routine tasks as well. If the selection policy is based on individual workload balance only, these people may be busy performing tasks requiring more common skills. In this case, when a key task arises, it could be the case that no node associated with these performers can accept it because all of them are engaged. Thus, the whole process instance is blocked and global performance is degraded. To optimise system performance globally, the performance bottleneck of the whole system should be identified and relieved. Given a workflow system with *n* virtual communities, the task instances are assigned to different communities according to the capability attributes, and are taken by various members involved in the communities. Thus, the overall system performance is determined by the community with the heaviest workload. To a particular community *i* with $m_i$ members, the mean workload of this community in the current time period is $\overline{w_i} = \sum_{k=1}^{m_i} w_k \Big/ m_i$, where $w_k$ is the workload of member *k* in the community. Therefore, the community with the heaviest workload becomes the bottleneck of the system performance, i.e., in a workflow system with *n* communities, the global performance is determined by $max(\overline{w_i}, i \in (1,n))$.

Based on the above analysis, algorithm (2) is designed considering the philosophy that for a node involved in more than one community, the assignment of a task adds workload to all the communities in which the node is involved.

*for each available node j*

$$w_j = max(\frac{\overline{w}_i \times m_i + w}{m_i}),\ i \in \{communities\ where\ j\ is\ involved\} \quad (2)$$

*assign the task instance to k with minimum* $w_k$

where $m_i$ is the number of nodes in community *i*, $\overline{w}_i$ is the current mean workload of community *i*. Obviously, every time when a new task instance needs to be created, this algorithm seeks a node to accept the instance, which pursues the lowest $max(\overline{w}_i, i \in (1,n))$, i.e., the best performance of the whole system.

Besides the performance optimisation, negotiation among available nodes allows the vast numbers of users who are not in management to be involved in task assignment, which is normally done by management. This involvement enables the users to play more active roles and helps to satisfy humans.

### 3.2 Instance Execution

Process instantiation and instance execution can be done in parallel. A task instance can be enacted immediately after it is instantiated without waiting for the complete creation of the whole process instance. To schedule the execution of various task instances in proper order without the assistance of a centralised workflow engine, there are two kinds of coordination: *data coordination* and *control coordination*. Correspondingly, there are two types of messages flowing among the nodes, i.e., *data messages* and *control messages*. A data message transfers real data related to the process instance to coordinate data dependency between tasks. A control message delivers information to coordinate control dependency, which is emphasised here. In general, three kinds of control messages perform different functions:

- Request and report: This message is transmitted to indicate the current status of a process instance. A node in charge of a task instance can report the status of this task instance, which could be one of *unacted*, *enacting* and *enacted*, to other nodes and query the statuses of other task instances from other nodes. By these means, a node can generate the whole picture of the process instance enactment.
- Instruction: This command-like control message instructs nodes to take actions. For example, a node may be directed to start enacting a task instance by instruction messages from its preceding nodes.
- Exception and erroneous situation: An exception message reports any exception occurred during the instance execution such as resource unavailability and execution errors. Mechanism supporting exceptions handling would be addressed in the future.

Put simply, instance execution is coordinated by direct communication among the nodes performing relevant task instances, which is light-weight and at a relatively low cost. A node performing a task receives instructions directly from its predecessors before it starts working. After the task is completed, this node also notifies the successors directly, according to the process definition and particular instance condition, and passes the corresponding data as predefined. The successors repeat the same procedure until the completion of the whole process.

## 4 An Example

To better illustrate how the process enactment works in the decentralised environment, this section applies the above approach to a very simplified home loan application. The process is depicted in Figure 1(a). At the same time, four nodes representing four users are involved in this workflow and form five virtual communities as depicted in Figure 1(b). During build-time, the task partitions are distributed to relevant nodes. For example, the definition of task *Application examination* is distributed to nodes for Tim, John and Lisa.

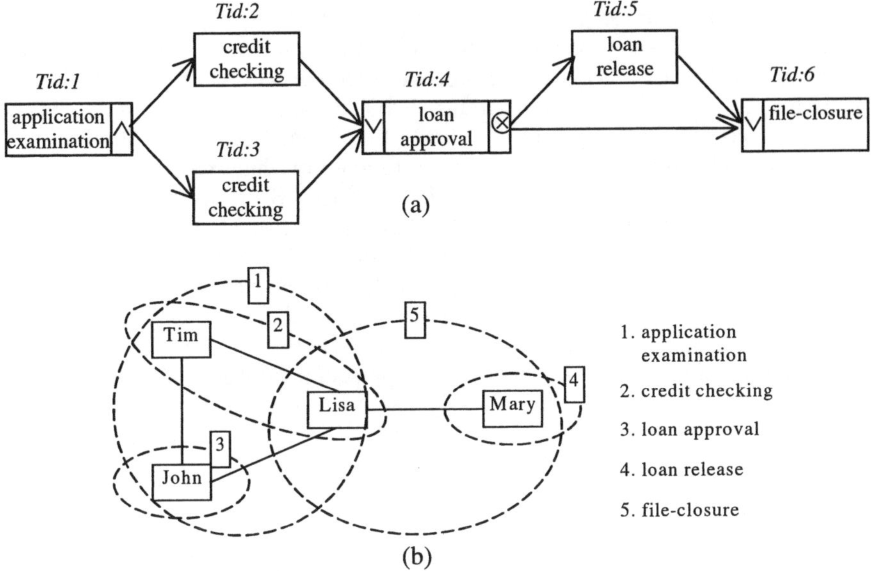


**Fig. 1.** A home loan application process and virtual communities of users

When a loan application arrives, a new process instance is created to handle it. Firstly, the instance of *application examination* is generated by a node from community one, for instance, the node for John. Then John starts enacting task 1 and looks for two other nodes to take *credit checking* at the same time. It is up to the automatic negotiation between the node for Tim and the node for Lisa to decide who performs task 2 and who performs task 3. The selection is based on either local or global optimisation. After that, since John is the only person who can approve the loan application, task 4 is assigned to John. Similarly, Mary is assigned task 5 and Lisa is assigned task 6. Finally, this process instance turns into a network connecting the nodes which create and fulfil various task instances. To coordinate instance execution, John advises Tim and Lisa directly through instruction messages immediately after the completion of *application examination* and receives the instruction messages directly from Tim and Lisa later to conduct *loan approval*. Similarly, the task instances are executed one by one until the loan file is closed. During this period, each node can grasp the overall status through the exchange of request and report messages. Exceptions can be reported via exception messages. A prototype implemented with the support of JXTA (http://www.jxta.com) demonstrates that the approach proposed works satisfactorily.

## 5 Related Work

As mentioned above, most of the current workflow systems depend on a dedicated server to provide run-time functions such as process navigation. Various task instances required are created on the server side and presented to the users via a work list. The execution of processes is controlled solely by the centralised workflow engine. Examples include Regatta [9], Action Workflow [7] and Spade [3].

Due to the unsolved problem associated with centralised process enactment support, in recent years, decentralised process execution has caught the attention of researchers. To name a few contributions, EXOTICA/FMQM [2] uses duplicated servers and persistent messages to coordinate the process execution. DartFlow [4] uses transportable agents as the backbone to control the execution of process instances. And METUFlow [5] assigns workflow to CORBA objects, with computed guards controlling distributed execution. All these approaches are appreciated as they add some distribution to workflow systems by different means. However, systems developed with these approaches are normally expensive, which make them unaffordable for small and medium enterprises (SMEs). In addition, most of these approaches still retain some centralised services like centralised process instantiation, which make them relatively inflexible in some application domains.

## 6 Conclusions and Future Work

This paper utilises p2p (peer-to-peer) computing and presents a truly decentralised process enactment approach aiming at providing a more flexible workflow environment at a relatively low cost, which is more suitable for SMEs (small and medium enterprises). All nodes in the system negotiate automatically to instantiate process instances and coordinate the execution of various task instances in a decentralised manner. The major contributions of this approach are summarised as follows:

1. This approach fully utilises the advantages of p2p computing to achieve the genuine decentralisation and provide light-weight coordination;
2. Process instantiation and task allocation happen on-the-fly in order to achieve enhanced flexibility and performance optimisation;
3. The workflow participants have more control over data and work, which helps to meet human satisfactions.

Currently, this approach mainly addresses the enactment of completely defined and distributed transactional processes, while incomplete process support is now under investigation. In the future, further research on decentralised workflow support will be conducted. Exceptions handling and human intervention during run-time will be explored. Issues such as adaptation and process evolution will be further investigated.

**Acknowledgement.** This work is partly supported by Swinburne Vice Chancellor's Strategic Research Initiative Grant 2002-2004. The authors are grateful for L. Setiawan's prototyping work.

## References

1. K. Aberer and M. Hauswirth, Peer-to-peer information systems: concepts and models, state-of-the-art, and future systems, Proc. 8th Euro. Soft. Eng. Conf. (ESEC) and 9th SIGSOFT Symposium on the Foundations of Soft. Eng. (FSE-9), 326–327, Vienna, Austria, Sept. 2001
2. G. Alonso, C. Mohan, R. Gűnthőr, D. Agrawal, A. El Abbadi and M.Kamath. Exotica/FMQM: A persistent message-based architecture for distributed workflow management, Proc. IFIP Working Conf. on Info. Sys. for Decentralised Organisations, Trondheim, Aug. 1995
3. S. Bandinelli, E. DiNitto, and A. Fuggetta, Supporting cooperation in the SPADE-1 environment, IEEE Trans. Soft. Eng., 22(12), 841–865, Dec. 1996
4. T. Cai, P. A. Gloor and S. Nog. DartFlow: A workflow management system on the Web using transportable agents, Technical Report PCS-TR96-283, Dartmouth College, 1996
5. E. Gokkoca, M. Altinel, R. Cingil, E. N. Tatbul, P. Koksal and A. Dogac. Design and implementation of a distributed workflow enactment service, Proc. 2nd IFCIS Conf. on Cooperative Info. Sys., 89–98, June 1997, IEEE Computer Soc. Press.
6. J. Grundy, M. Apperley, J. Hosking, and W. Mugridge, A decentralised architecture for software process modeling and enactment, IEEE Internet Computing, 2(5): 53–62, Sept/Oct. 1998
7. R. Medina-Mora, T. Winograd, R. Flores, F. Flores, The action workflow approach to workflow management technology, Proc. CSCW'92, ACM Press, 281–288, New York, 1992
8. C. Mohan, Workflow management in the Internet age, Advances in Databases and Information Systems, LNCS Vol 1475, 26–34, Springer Verlag. Sept. 1998
9. K. Swenson, R. Maxwell, T. Matsumoto, B. Saghari and K. Irwin, A business process environment supporting collaborative planning, J. Collaborative Computing, 1(1), 15–34, Jan. 1994, Chapman-Hall, London
10. Workflow Management Coalition, http://www.wfmc.org
11. J. Yan, Y. Yang and G. K. Raikundalia, A data storage mechanism for p2p-based decentralised workflow systems, Proc. 15th Int. Conf. on Soft. Eng. and Knowledge Eng. (SEKE2003), San Francisco, USA, July 2003, to appear
12. J. Yan, Y. Yang and G. K. Raikundalia, A decentralised architecture for workflow support, Proc. 7th Int. Symposium on Future Soft. Technology (ISFST02), CD ISBN: 4-916227-14-X, Wuhan, China, Oct. 2002.
13. Y. Yang, An architecture and the related mechanisms for Web-based global cooperative teamwork support, Int. Journal of Computing and Informatics, 24(1), 13–19, 2000

# Peer-Serv: A Framework of Web Services in Peer-to-Peer Environment*

Qing Wang[1], Yang Yuan[1], Junmei Zhou[2], and Aoying Zhou[1]

[1] Department of Computer Science and Engineering, Fudan University, 220 Handan Rd., Shanghai, China
{qingwang, yyuan, ayzhou}@fudan.edu.cn
http://www.cs.fudan.edu.cn/indexen.jsp

[2] Shanghai R&D Institute of ZTE Corporation, 396 Guilin Rd., Shanghai, China
zhou.junmei@zte.com.cn
http://www.zte.com.cn/english/

**Abstract.** Typically, Web services are published on a centralized registry, which may lead to many drawbacks. And Peer-to-Peer systems bring more availability, scalability, and extensibility. Considering the features of Web services and P2P technology, we provide the decentralized infrastructure Peer-Serv, which is composed of numerous service brokers, service provides and service requestors, to support sharing Web services in P2P environment. In order to process service queries efficiently, we also present some optimization mechanisms. Preliminary experimental results verify the effectiveness of those optimization techniques.

## 1 Introduction

With the development of Web Services, more and more applications based on Web services are emerging on the Web, especially in e-business community [8]. The typical workflow of Web services is: first, service providers publish their services in the service broker, then a service query is submitted to the service broker for finding the service provider, finally the service requestor binds its service request to the service provider and waits for the response from the provider. However, the centralized service broker leads to many drawbacks, such as bottleneck and overload of the service broker when a large number of service queries are executed on it, lack of mechanisms for both dealing with the single-point failure of the broker and providing the scalability of the providers. The current solution is that there exist few registry sites (e.g. Microsoft, IBM, HP, and SAP), and their data is exchanged and backuped among them periodically. However, it also results in some other drawbacks, such as the expensive data replication, unnecessary global service querying when local providers can satisfy the demands.

In this paper, we provide a framework of Web services in Peer-to-Peer (P2P) environment, called Peer-Serv (see Fig. 1). In Peer-Serv, there are three roles:

* This work is supported by the National High Technology Development 863 Program of China under Grant No.2002AA116020.

G. Dong et al. (Eds.): WAIM 2003, LNCS 2762, pp. 298–305, 2003.

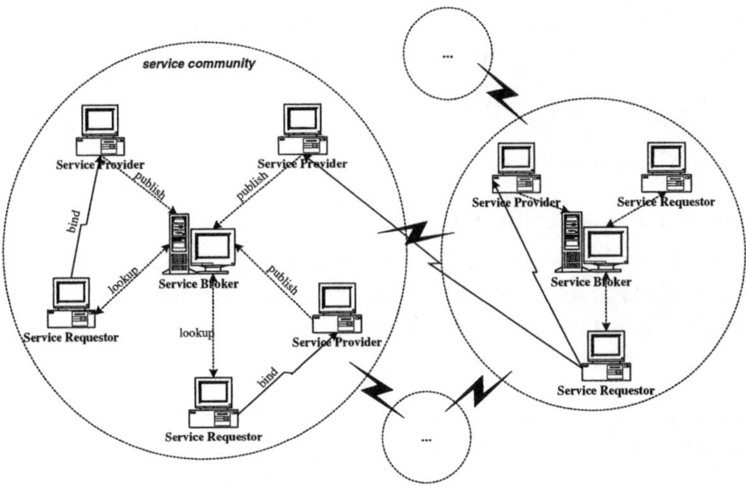


**Fig. 1.** An overview of Peer-Serv

*service providers* provide others with services, *service consumers* ask for services and *service brokers* are responsible for maintaining the status of peers (e.g. online or offline, IP address, etc.) and the information of services (e.g. usable or unusable, location, etc.).

To simplify the discussion, we permit only one role on a peer. In the following sections, a service provider or a service requestor is called a *normal peer*, distinguished from the service broker.

A service broker maintains some normal peers, which forms a *service community*. Service brokers make up a *broker federation* and different service communities can communicate with one another via their service brokers.

By adopting distributed approaches to implement service brokers, Peer-Serv reduces the bottleneck of the service brokers, and moreover, it improves the utilization of the network resource by partitioning it into numerous communities self-adaptively. That is, if the problem can be solved locally, it is unnecessary to visit other communities. Employing P2P technology, Peer-Serv is more reliable and flexible than those common Web service applications. Additionally, unlike those Web service applications adopting the P2P model, such as AXML [1] and Self-Serv [3,6], Peer-Serv uses P2P technology for not only service execution but service publishing and service querying. In order to process services queries efficiently, Peer-Serv adopts some optimization mechanisms, including the policy for normal peers to join, the strategy for service brokers to reconfigure neighbors, the strategy for service requestors to evolve the caching. This makes Peer-Serv give more probability to find out the providers than pure P2P systems, given a service query. Finally we have conducted a series of experiments. Our experimental results demonstrate that the optimization mechanisms can work well.

The remainder of this paper is organized as follows: Section 2 introduces the basic conceptions we used, and then Section 3 introduces the protocols and the optimization mechanisms. Section 4 shows some preliminary experimental results. Finally, section 5 summaries the entire paper and addresses the future work.

## 2 Basic Conceptions

### 2.1 Keyword-Based Similarity

**Definition 1.** *For a service provider $P$, the set $K(P)$ of keywords for publishing services is used to describe the functions of those services it providers. Likewise, for a service requestor $P'$, the set $K(P')$ of keywords for requesting services is used to describe its requests.*

**Definition 2.** *For a service broker $B$, the set of keywords for publishing services, denoted by $K_p(B)$, and the set of keywords for requesting services, denoted by $K_r(B)$, are used to describe the services provided and the services requested respectively in the service community maintained by $B$. They are given by*

$$K_p(B) = \bigcup_{i=1}^{p} K(P_i), \qquad K_r(B) = \bigcup_{i=1}^{r} K(P_i'),$$

*where the service providers $P_1, ..., P_p$ and the service requestors $P_1', ..., P_r'$ are in the service community.*

Next we present how to compute the degree of similarity between a service provider $P$ and a service broker $B$ by adopting an Information Retrieval (IR) [2] based approach. For the degree of similarity between a service requestor and a service broker, the way to compute the value is similar.

**Definition 3.** *Given a service provider $P$ and a service broker $B$, the degree of similarity between $P$ and $B$ is given by*

$$sim(P, B) = \frac{\mid K(P) \cap K_r(B) \mid}{\sqrt{\mid K(P) \mid} \times \sqrt{\mid K_r(B) \mid}},$$

*where $\mid A \mid$ refers to the cardinality of the set $A$.*

Intuitively, the similarity $sim(P, B)$ reflects how relevant the new coming service provider $P$ and those service requestors in the service community maintained by $B$ are: if it happens that $P$ provides those services which those service requestors wants, $sim(P, B)$ is high. Otherwise, it becomes low.

Likewise, the similarity from a service broker $B_i$ to another service broker $B_j$ can be quantified by

$$sim(B_i, B_j) = \frac{\mid K_r(B_i) \cap K_p(B_j) \mid}{\sqrt{\mid K_r(B_i) \mid} \times \sqrt{\mid K_p(B_j) \mid}}.$$

It reflects how possible it is that $B_j$ can satisfy the demands of $B_i$.

From Definition 3 we can specify $sim(B, P) = sim(P, B)$, where $P$ is a service provider and $B$ is a service broker. However, for two service brokers $B_i$ and $B_j$, we have the property $sim(B_i, B_j) \neq sim(B_j, B_i)$.

| PID | Authentication | Maintained By |
|---|---|---|
| 1 | 43220-3EA0-98FF | SELF |
| 2 | 5599C-BAEF-9873 | NULL |
| 3 | 8822E-FFAA-1129 | 10.11.3.1 |
| ... | ... | ... |

(a) Registry table on a service broker

| SB Address | PID | IP Address | Role |
|---|---|---|---|
| SELF | 1 | 10.100.11.232 | P |
| SELF | 3 | 10.11.1.45 | R |
| 10.11.2.1 | 1 | 10.11.2.5 | P |
| ... | ... | ... | ... |

(b) Active table on a service broker

| Neighbor | Sim |
|---|---|
| 10.11.2.1 | 0.78 |
| 10.11.3.1 | 0.6 |
| 10.11.4.1 | 0.55 |
| ... | ... |

(c) Neighbor table on a service broker

| SB Address | PID | WSDL | Prob |
|---|---|---|---|
| SELF | 1 | music.wsdl | 0.9 |
| SELF | 2 | Jazz.wsdl | 0.9 |
| 10.11.3.1 | 1 | movie.wsdl | 0.8 |
| ... | ... | ... | ... |

(d) Caching table on a service requestor

**Fig. 2.** Tables in Peer-Serv

### 2.2 Time Series-Based Probability

A service requestor $P'$ may send many requests to ask for services. For $P'$, at any time $t$ any service $s$ is in either of three states: sent and completed (i.e. the answer is returned to $P'$), sent and uncompleted (i.e. the answer is not returned yet), unsent (i.e. the request is not sent at all). We define the clock as follows: if the current time is $t-1$ and there exists one service completed, the system puts the clocks forward to $t$ and we say the service is completed at $t$. Or else, the current time is not changed.

**Definition 4.** *For a service requestor $P'$, a service $s$ provided by $P$ is completed at the time $t$, then the completeness degree of $s$ at $t$, denoted by $comp(s,t)$, is assigned to 1, and the completeness degree of $s'$ at $t$ is assigned to 0, where $s'$ is another uncompleted or unsent service.*

**Definition 5.** *For a service requestor $P'$, the probability of requesting the service $s$ at time $t+1$, denoted by $prob(s,t+1)$, is given by*

$$prob(s,t+1) = \alpha \times comp(s,t) + (1-\alpha) \times prob(s,t),$$

*where $\alpha$ ($\alpha \in [0,1]$) is a weight set by $P'$ and for any service $s$, $prob(s,1) = 0$ initially.*

The value $prob(s,t+1)$ reflects the probability for $P'$ to request $s$ at the next time $t+1$. From the above formula, we can see that if $s$ has been invoked recently, the value $prob(s,t+1)$ may be large; if $s$ has not been invoked for a long time, the weight $1-\alpha$ will make the value smaller and smaller at an exponential speed.

## 3 Protocols in Peer-Serv

### 3.1 Policy for Joining

For a fresh normal peer $P$, the process of registering is as follows: $P$ broadcasts a message for discovering service brokers. Those service brokers, which receive this message and can offer room for $P$'s registration, make responses to it. Note that the size of the registry tables on service brokers is limited, in order to avoid the overload and balance the traffic. After $P$ collects all service brokers $B_1, ..., B_n$ responding in a certain period, it computes $sim(P, B_i)$ $(1 \leq i \leq n)$ and selects the one with the highest value as its *initial service broker* $B$. Next $P$ sends its IP address to $B$ and then $B$ issues $P$ with a PID, and an authentication in the registry table on $B$ (see Fig. 2 (a)). Note that the IP address of $B$ and the PID are the globally unique ID of $P$, considering that the IP address of $P$ may change after reconnection later. Receiving the acknowledgement from $B$, $P$ records the IP address of $B$. Without loss of generality we now suppose $P$ is a service provider. $P$ logins to $B$ immediately iff $cur_{pro}^{B} < max_{pro}^{B}$, where $cur_{pro}^{B}$ is the current number of active (online) service providers in $B$'s community and $max_{pro}^{B}$ is used to limit the maximum number of active service providers which $B$ can maintain. Or else, it selects another broker by using the method below.

If $P$ has registered long time before, the process of logining after reconnection is as follows: $P$ gets a list of service brokers from its initial service broker $B$. They are $B$, the neighbors of $B$, the neighbors of those neighbors, and so on. The depth of neighborhood is a system parameter set by $P$. Note that for a service broker, its neighbors are other service brokers which it can communicate directly and they are all stored in its neighbor table (see Fig. 2 (c)). After filtering those brokers whose active tables are full (i.e. $cur_{pro} = max_{pro}$), $P$ computes the similarity between $P$ and the brokers left, selects one as its current service broker $B'$ with the highest value, and then sends the IP address of $B$, its PID, its own IP address and its authentication information to $B'$.

If $B'$ is $B$, the attribute `Maintained By` of $P$ in the registry table is updated with "SELF" after authenticating $P$'s identity. Otherwise, $B'$ forwards $P$'s authentication information to $B$. If the authentication is passed, $B$ records the IP address of $B'$ in the attribute `Maintained By`. A record containing $B$'s IP address, $P$'s PID, $P$'s IP address, and the role "P" is appended to the active table on $B'$ (see Fig. 2 (b)). Then $cur_{pro}^{B'}$ is increased by 1 and $K_p(B')$ is updated.

Note that all functions in Peer-Serv are also treated as Web services. For instance, for the process of registering above, the service providers are "those service brokers", the service requestor is "the normal peer", and messages transmitted in the process are all SOAP [7] messages.

### 3.2 Strategy for Reconfiguring Neighbor Tables

A service requestor $P'$ may look up services in the service broker $B$ which it logins to and then bind its request to the service provider $P$. For $B$, it needs to search appropriate services for $P'$. If the service query submitted by $P'$ cannot be hit on $B$, $B$ will consult the neighbor table and deliver the query message to its neighbors for help, where the query message contains not only the information about the query but the IP address of $P'$. Finally, when the service provider $P$ which provides the right services is found, the globally unique ID of $P$, as well as its IP address, is returned to $P'$ directly without going through the service brokers along the query path. Suppose that $P$ is in range of the service broker

$B'$ currently. The similarity from $B$ to $B'$ is computed at the same time and the neighbor table in $B$, which is built randomly and manually first, is updated by sorting in the decreasing order of the similarity and keeping $max_{neigh}^{B}$ neighbors with the highest values, where $max_{neigh}^{B}$ is a system parameter set by $B$.

In order to reduce the traffic over the whole network, a parameter like TTL (Time To Live) is initialized and 1 is subtracted from the value when the service query message is forwarded to next neighbor. As such, the search process is limited to a certain scope.

### 3.3 Strategy for Evolving Caching Tables

Now we assume that a service consumed recently is likely to be useful for future service requests. For a service requestor $P'$, it maintains a caching table which is empty at first (see Fig. 2 (d)). After a service $s$ completed, all probabilities of the services in the caching table, as well as that of $s$, are computed and the $max_{cache}^{P'}$ services with the highest values are retained in the caching table, where $max_{cache}^{P'}$ is also a system parameter set by $P'$. Later after a request is created, $P'$ consults its caching table first, and binds the request to $P$ directly if the service provider $P$ is found. If the provider cannot be found in the caching table, $P'$ searches for the provider by sending the service query to the service broker.

### 3.4 Address Resolution and Failure Detection

Now, consider the problem on how to map a globally unique ID into an IP address, for example, in the caching table. Suppose that a service requestor $P'$ knows the ID $B.n$ of a service provider $P$, where $B$ is the initial service broker of $P$ and $n$ is the PID on $B$. The process of address resolution is as follows: $P'$ sends a message to $B$ to obtain the IP address of the service broker (say $B'$) which $P$ logins to from the registry table on $B$. After receiving the IP address of $B'$, $P'$ can obtain $P$'s IP address from $B'$ by searching the active table on $B'$.

If $P'$ learns that $P$ does not provide the service which it wants any more, $P'$ will inform $B'$ to update the information of the services provided by $P$. Even worse, if $P'$ finds that $P$ has disconnected from the network, $P'$ will inform $B'$ that all services provided by $P$ are not available. At this time, $B'$ can update the information of the services, the status of $P$ in the active table and $cur_{pro}^{B'}$ after verifying the authenticity, and then send a message to notify $B$ to set the attribute `Maintained By` of the corresponding entry in the registry table from $B'$ to "NULL". For $P'$, it follows the above steps to look for replacers to fulfill its needs. As opposed to [4,5], adopting this approach instead of checking the validity periodically saves the bandwidth utilization. However, as far as service requestors are concerned, the broker needs to check the validity periodically.

## 4 Experiments

Our experiments were conducted on a large virtual network, which is simulated by running a software implementation on 3 733MHz Pentium III machines with

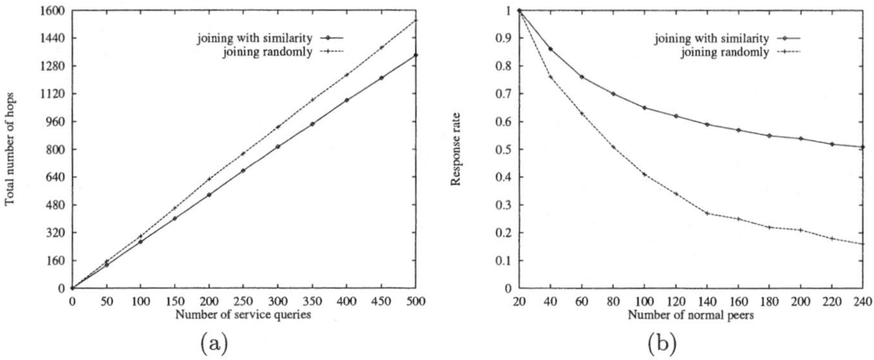


(a) (b)

**Fig. 3.** Benefits of joining policy

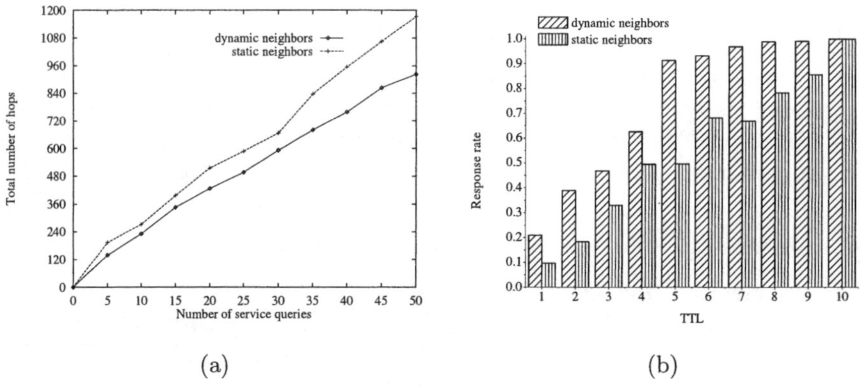


(a) (b)

**Fig. 4.** Benefits of neighbor strategy

256M of main memory. All machines connect together through the LAN of our campus.

Fig. 3 (a) depicts the impact of joining policy as a function of the number of queries. The total number of hops measures how many hops are taken when a certain number of service queries are created randomly and sent out, where TTL is set to 4. The experimental results indicate that joining policy can reduce the hops of the search process by a factor of up to 1.2.

Fig. 3 (b) depicts the impact of joining policy from another aspect as a function of the number of normal peers. In this case, we range the scale of the network. The response rate reflects the percentage of queries that can be hit to all queries sent. The experimental results demonstrate that joining policy can increase the response rate by a factor of up to 3.2. That is, more queries can be hit in a small scope than those without joining policy because Peer-Serv clusters "similar" peers together.

The next experiments demonstrate the benefits of neighbor strategy. The total number of hops measures how many hops a certain number of service queries, which are sent by a requestor repeatedly, cost for searching services within the network, where TTL is equivalent to 3. The experimental results, shown in Fig. 4 (a), tell us that the bandwidth is saved in that each broker treats those "useful" brokers as its neighbors dynamically according to its requests.

In Fig. 4 (b), we range the value of TTL to evaluate the response rate, which measures the rate of service queries hit within the search radius to all service queries sent. As the TTL decreases gradually, the benefit is more evident as the neighbors of the broker maintaining the requestor are adapted at run time. Due to space constraints, the experimental results on the caching table are omitted.

## 5 Conclusion and Future Work

In this paper, a framework Peer-Serv is proposed for efficient Web service applications by adopting P2P technology. In Peer-Serv, all entities work like peers in P2P systems, which brings more availability and scalability. Moreover, service brokers are implemented by using distributed approaches, which brings more benefits than the centralized registry. In addition, keeping the role of service brokers increases more opportunities for a service requestor to find a service provider than flooding queries in pure P2P systems. In order to process service queries efficiently, we also present some optimization mechanisms. Preliminary performance study shows they are effective. This paper also arouses some other interesting issues, e.g., how to adjust the parameters in practice to obtain the best performance, how to avoid that some communities are isolated from others when reconfiguring neighbor tables, and whether the number of overlapping keywords can be considered when we define similarity, and so forth.

## References

1. S. Abiteboul, O. Benjelloun, I. Manolescu, T. Milo, and R. Weber. Active XML: Peer-to-peer data and web services integration. In *Proc. of Int'l Conf. on Very Large Databases (VLDB)*, 2002.
2. R. A. Baeza-Yates and B. A. Ribeiro-Neto. *Modern Information Retrieval.* ACM Press/Addison-Wesley, 1999.
3. B. Benatallah, M. Dumas, Q. Z. Sheng, and A. H. Ngu. Declarative composition and peer-to-peer provisioning of dynamic web services. In *Proc. of IEEE Int'l Conf. on Data Engineering (ICDE)*, 2002.
4. W. S. Ng, B. C. Ooi, and K.-L. Tan. A self-configurable peer-to-peer system. In *Proc. of IEEE Int'l Conf. on Data Engineering (ICDE)*, 2002.
5. W. S. Ng, B. C. Ooi, K.-L. Tan, and A. Zhou. PeerDB: A P2P-based system for distributed data sharing. In *Proc. of IEEE Int'l Conf. on Data Engineering (ICDE)*, 2003.
6. Q. Z. Sheng, B. Benatallah, M. Dumas, and E. O.-Y. Mak. SELF-SERV: A platform for rapid composition of web services in a peer-to-peer environment. In *Proc. of Int'l Conf. on Very Large Databases (VLDB)*, 2002.
7. Simple Object Access Protocol (SOAP) 1.1. `http://www.w3.org/TR/SOAP`.
8. S. Tsur. Are web services the next revolution in e-commerce? In *Proc. of Int'l Conf. on Very Large Databases (VLDB)*, 2001.

# Dynamic Clustering-Based Query Answering in Peer-to-Peer Systems*

Weining Qian[1]**, Shuigeng Zhou[1], Yi Ren[1], Aoying Zhou[1], Beng Chin Ooi[2], and Kian-Lee Tan[2]

[1] Department of Computer Science and Engineering, Fudan University
[2] Department of Computer Science, National University of Singapore
{wnqian,sgzhou,ayzhou}@fudan.edu.cn, {ooibc, tankl}@comp.nus.edu.sg

**Abstract.** In this paper, we propose a new query answering model for P2P applications, which is termed as *clustering-based query answering* (CBQA). CBQA will retrieve the data objects that are in the same cluster of the query from the global dataset distributed over peers of a P2P system.

We first present a framework that support clustering based query answering. Then we give three concrete algorithms for different clustering criteria, namely $k$-nearest-neighbor, distance-based, and density-based clustering, along with detailed analyses. Finally, implementation issues, especially dynamic neighbors selection to enable the scalability are addressed. Theoretical analysis shows that our method can guarantee to find desirable objects in the interested cluster with modest overhead.

## 1 Introduction

Peer-to-peer (P2P) has become a new wave of innovative Internet-based computing technologies. It is well-known that current P2P systems support only or mainly key-based exact matching and keyword-based searching for files discovery and location, which is not enough to meet the requirements of more advanced applications. A natural advancement of key-based exact matching and keyword-based searching is similarity-based query. The number of returned query answers relies on the similarity threshold value: the larger the similarity threshold value is set, the more query answers can be obtained. Considering the decentralization nature of P2P environment, it is inefficient to conduct similarity query in P2P systems. Generally, data distribution implies a certain cluster structure. The clustering task is to expose the underlying structure by using different algorithms. And data objects in the same cluster inherently share more similarity that these in different clusters. With these in mind, in this paper we propose a new query model for P2P application. We term the new query model *Clustering-Based Query Answering* (CBQA). Given a query, we define CBQA as to retrieve the data objects that are in the same cluster of the query from the global dataset distributed over peers of a P2P system.

* This work is suported by the Fok Ying Tung Education Foundation.
** The author is partially supported by Microsoft Research Fellowship.

G. Dong et al. (Eds.): WAIM 2003, LNCS 2762, pp. 306–313, 2003.

In this paper, we propose the clustering based query answering model and give concrete solution to implement this model in P2P environments. Following aspects distinguish our work from other research on file sharing and information retrieval in P2P systems. 1) A new query model, i.e., *clustering-based query* is proposed. 2) A framework for implementing clustering-based query in P2P environments is provided. The proposed framework is independent from concrete clustering criteria, so that variety of clustering algorithms can be employed in it. 3) Three concrete algorithms for different clustering criteria, namely k-nearest-neighbor, distance-based, and density-based clustering, are developed, based on the framework mentioned above. The properties of the algorithms are discussed. 4) Dynamic neighbor selection, is discussed. With the help of it, our method can be scaled up to large-scale P2P applications. The techniques introduced in this paper may become the foundation of high-level P2P applications, such as information search and retrieval, data management, data mining, and so on.

## 2 Motivation and Problem Statement

Clustering-based query answering problem exists in many real-life applications which need to find *all* similar objects with respect to a query object in the same cluster. Many potential applications share the common characteristics in that, 1) Data are distributed on different peers, while the whole dataset is large; 2) *All* data similar to a query object should be retrieved, which means the data objects in the same cluster with the query object are interested; 3) The clustering could not be processed in advance, because of the absence of in-advance clustering condition or the frequently changing dataset. Such applications include health-care data management, personal digital collection sharing and genome database mining, etc. There are many other applications satisfied with these conditions, such as data caching, digital library, etc. They are all potential applications of clustering-based query. For formal definition of the answer with respect to a query of CBQA, we should define the *global clustering* result as the baseline. Global clustering can be viewed as the *virtual* process executes on the whole dataset, that is the intention of the user. It can adopt some widely accepted clustering criteria, which are introduced in the next section.

**Definition 1 (Global Clustering and Clustering-based Query)** *Given a dataset $DB$, and a clustering condition $c$, the* **global clustering result w.r.t. c** *is a set of sets $C_i$, for $i = 1, ..., n$, denoted by $\{C_i\}_c$, satisfied that $\bigcup_i C_i = DB$, and $C_i \cap C_j = \emptyset$ for $i \neq j$. Then, given a query object $o$, the* **o-based clustering result w.r.t. c** *is a set $C^o$, satisfied that $C^o \in \{C_i\}_c$, and $o \in C^o$.*

Since we usually cannot obtain the result of global clustering in P2P systems, only the clustering-based query result $C'^o$ w.r.t certain clustering condition $c'$ can be found. If $C'^o = C^o$, we call that clustering condition $c$ and $c'$ are **consistent on o**. Thus, the clustering-based query for $o$ is *to find $C'^o$ that is consistent to pre-defined clustering condition on $o$.*

## 3 Framework for CBQA in P2P Environments

The procedures for CBQA are shown in Algorithm 1 and 2. The main procedure obtains the cluster in which query object falls in. The *Query*() procedure tries to search the local database for data objects potentially belong to the final cluster.

The *mainCBQA*() procedure initializes the cluster $C$ that contains $o$ (line 1). The data objects already collected, that do not belong to the cluster, are stored in $D$. All data objects that have been collected are stored in $T$, while $E$ is used to store the new clustering result after the communication with neighbors, which are stored in $P$. If the new clustering result is not the same with the old one (line 6), the procedure retrieves new data objects from its neighbors based on *QueryFunction*() (loop from line 7 to 9). *Clustering*() procedure is executed on the new local dataset $T$, so that the clustering result is updated (line 11). Only peers with all answers in the cluster are queried further (line 15). But, if such peer does not exist, the peer cannot judge whether its neighbors have returned all related objects. Therefore, it needs to query all its neighbors (line 18). When a peer receives a query from another peer, it looks up its local database for those data objects that have not been returned before (line 1 of *Query*()). *QueryFunction*(), which is sent with the query, is evaluated on those data objects. The data objects satisfied the condition are returned to the query peer (line 6), and labelled *'has_been_sent'* in local site (line 4).

**Algorithm 1** *mainCBQA*

```
Input: query object o, peer p  Output: cluster C^o
 1: C ← {o}; {data in cluster}
 2: D ← ∅; {data not in cluster}
 3: E ← ∅; {new clustering result}
 4: T ← LDB; {all data collected on peer p}
 5: P ← {all p's neighbors}; {all neighbors of peer p}
 6: while C ≠ E do
 7:   for each q ∈ P do
 8:     T ← T ∪ q.Query(QueryFunction()); {query the neighbors}
 9:   end for
10:   C ← E;
11:   E ← Clustering(o,T); {get the new cluster based on the new T}
12:   D ← T − E;
13:   P ← ∅; {empty the neighbor list}
14:   if (D − LDB) ≠ ∅ then
15:     P ← {peer r|r only has answers in E}; {need more data objects from them}
16:   end if
17:   if P = ∅ then
18:     P ← {all p's neighbors}; {each neighbor sends objects for one more time}
19:   end if
20: end while
21: return C;
```

We call the procedure *Query*() is *order-consistent* if the data belong to the final cluster are returned before other data objects are returned. For the procedure *Clustering*(), if $(C^o \cap T_1) \subset (C^o \cap T_2)$ implies that $Clustering(o, T_1) \subseteq$

**Algorithm 2** *Query* procedure on peers

**Input**: *QueryFunction*() **Output**: result set $R$

$DB \leftarrow \{a | a \in LDB, a$ has not been sent$\}$;
$R \leftarrow QueryFunction(DB)$; {search the local database by using received function}
**for** each object $a \in R$ **do**
  $Label(a, 'has\_been\_sent')$; {each data object should be sent at most once}
**end for**
**return** $R$;

$Clustering(o, T_2)$, we say that it satisfies *monotone*. It means that, the more data a peer collects, the larger the cluster would be. If $T_1 \subset T_2$ implies that, $(T_1 - Clustering(o, T_1)) \subseteq (T_2 - Clustering(o, T_2))$, we say that it satisfies *anti-monotone*. It means that, if an object is not in the cluster in $T$, it would not be put back to the cluster after more data objects are collected. For *Clustering*() procedure, we call it is *locality-preservable* if it satisfies that $C^o \subseteq Clustering(o, T)$ and $C^o \subseteq T$ implies $Clustering(o, T) = C^o$.

**Lemma 1.** *If procedure Query() is order-consistent, while Clustering() is monotone or anti-monotone, and is locality-preservable, Algorithm 1 returns* $C^o$.

**Lemma 2.** *If Query() is order-consistent, while Clustering() is locality-preservable, then the total network transfer is less than* $\|C^o\| + \|P\| \times \|R\|$ *objects, where* $\|C^o\|$ *is the number of objects in* $C^o$, $\|P\|$ *is the number of peers that are involved in the clustering, and* $\|R\|$ *is* $\max\{$*objects returned by one peer once*$\}$; *the loop from line 6 to 20 in Algorithm 1 is executed at most* $\frac{\|C^o\|}{\|R\|} + 1$ *times.*

# 4 Clustering for Different Criteria

## 4.1 *K*-Nearest-Neighbor Search

$K$-NN is the process to find the $k$ nearest data objects to the query object. We apply the functions in Algorithm 3 and 4 to the framework introduced above. Here, $\alpha$ is a parameter whose domain is $[0, 1]$, which denotes the percentage of $k$ that should be retrieved from each neighbor. *QueryFunction*() searches in the local database for $\alpha k$ nearest data objects to $o$, while *Clustering*() finds in the collected data set $DB$ for the $k$ nearest neighbors. The result is the cluster.

**Algorithm 3** *QueryFunction* for $k$-NN clustering

**Input**: query object $o$, $k$, $\alpha$, $DB$ **Output**: result set $R$

$R \leftarrow \{$the closest $\alpha k$ objects in $DB$ to $o\}$;
**return** $R$;

It is obvious that by applying *QueryFunction*() of Algorithm 3, The *Query*() is order-consistent. The *Clustering*() in Algorithm 4 is anti-monotone

**Algorithm 4** *Clustering* for $k$-NN clustering

**Input**: query object $o$, $k$, $DB$ **Output**: cluster $C$

```
C ← {the closest k objects in DB to o};
return C;
```

and locality-preservable. The $k$-NN algorithm returns all and exact $k$-nearest-neighbors. By applying Lemma 2, the network transfer cost is $k+\alpha km$, in which $\alpha$ is introduced before, $m$ is the number of peers that returns result. The times for communication is $1+\frac{1}{\alpha}$. And the computation complexity is $O(mk\log k)$.

### 4.2 Distance-Based Clustering

Distance-based clustering is widely used in data mining. The clustering condition is defined as follows: 1) $o \in C^o$; 2) If $\min\{distance(p,q)|q \in C^o\} \leq d$, then $p \in C'$; 3) If $p \in C'$, then $p \in C^o$; 4) If $distance(o,p) \leq \max\{distance(o,q)|q \in C'\}$, then $p \in C^o$. The procedures in Algorithm 5 and 6 are applied in the framework. As in $k$-NN clustering, *QueryFunction*() looks in local database for several nearest objects to the query object, except that the number of objects is defined by parameter $k$, which is determined by users. *Clustering*() searches in the set of objects collected based on the second and third clustering condition (loop from line 6 to 11), and the fourth (loop from line 15 to 19).

**Algorithm 5** *QueryFunction* for distance-based clustering

**Input**: query object $o$, $k$, $DB$ **Output**: result set $R$

```
R ← {the closest k objects in DB to o};
return R;
```

By applying *QueryFunction*() of Algorithm 5, *Query*() is order-consistent. *Clustering*() in Algorithm 6 is monotone and locality-preservable. Hence, the distance-based clustering algorithm introduced above returns all and exact data objects in $C^o$ with respect to distance-based clustering criteria. By applying Lemma 2, the network transfer cost is $N + km$, in which $N$ is the size of $C^o$, $k$ is the number of objects returned each time, and $m$ is the number of peers who return result. The times for communication is $1 + \frac{N}{k}$, and the computation complexity is $O(N)$.

### 4.3 Density-Based Clustering

As long as distance-based clustering, density-based clustering is a kind of popular clustering criteria. The cell-based criteria, which is one of the density-based criteria [6], is adopted in our clustering-based query. The clustering condition is as follows: 1) All data objects fall in $o$'s cell belong to $C^o$; 2) If cell $c$'s density is larger than a threshold $d$, and $c$ is the neighbor of a cell whose objects all falls in $C^o$, then all data objects in $c$ belong to $C^o$.

**Algorithm 6** *Clustering* for distance-based clustering

**Input**: query object $o$, threshold $d$, $DB$ **Output**: cluster $C$

1: $C \leftarrow \{o\}$;<br>
2: $F \leftarrow \{o\}$;<br>
3: $T \leftarrow DB$; {all data objects}<br>
4: **while** $F \neq \emptyset$ **do**<br>
5:   $F \leftarrow \emptyset$;<br>
6:   **for** each object $t \in T$ **do**<br>
7:     **if** $distance(t, C) < d$ **then**<br>
8:       $F \leftarrow F \cup \{t\}$; {$t$ should be added into the cluster}<br>
9:       $T \leftarrow T - \{t\}$;<br>
10:     **end if**<br>
11:   **end for**<br>
12:   $C \leftarrow C \cup F$; {the cluster grows in batch}<br>
13: **end while**<br>
14: $max\_dis \leftarrow \max\{distance(o, s) | s \in C\}$;<br>
15: **for** each object $t \in T$ **do**<br>
16:   **if** $distance(o, t) \leq max\_dis$ **then**<br>
17:     $C \leftarrow C \cup \{t\}$; {add $t$ into the cluster since it satisfies the fourth condition}<br>
18:   **end if**<br>
19: **end for**<br>
20: **return** $C$;

Different with $k$-NN or distance-based clustering, it is hard to construct $QueryFunction()$ and $Clustering()$ directly from the clustering condition that satisfies the order-consistent, monotone/anti-monotone and locality-preservable respectively. We adopt another approach that employs the framework to solve the problem of density-based clustering. First, the clustering condition similar to distance-based CBQA, that is easy to be implemented under the framework, is defined: 1) $c_o \in C'^o$, in which $c_o$ is the cell $o$ falls in; 2) If $\min\{distance(c, q) | q \in C'^o$ and $density(c) > d\}$, then $c \in C'$; 3) If $c \in C'$, then $c \in C'^o$; 4) If $distance(c_o, p) \leq \max\{distance(c_o, q) | q \in C'\}$, then $p \in C'^o$. Here, a cell $c \in C$ means all data objects fall in $c$ belong to cluster $C$. The distance between two cells means the distance of the vectors for coordinates of two cells. It is obvious that distance-based clustering algorithm can be applied to solve the clustering problem defined by above condition. Thus, the density-based clustering algorithm is shown in Algorithm 7. The cells are clustered by using the new clustering condition in line 2, by using distance-based clustering criteria, while line 7 in Algorithm 6 is replaced by:

**if** $distance(t, C) \leq 1$ and $density(t) > d$ **then**

After the data objects that may fall in the cluster are collected, $DensityClustering()$ clusters them based on density-based clustering criteria. This is the centralized process. We omit the details here.

It is obvious that Algorithm 7 returns all and exact data objects in $C^o$ with respect to density-based clustering criteria. From the analysis to distance-based clustering, the network transfer and times for communication of density-based clustering is linear to the size of the final cluster.

**Algorithm 7** *DensityClustering* procedure

**Input**: query object $o$, $DB$ **Output**: cluster $C$

$c_o \leftarrow$ the cell contains $o$;
$C_c \leftarrow mainClustering(c_o, this)$; {clustering using the new condition over P2P system}
$C \leftarrow LocalDensityClustering(o, C_c)$; {clustering using the old condition in local}
**return** $C$;

## 5 Implementation Issues

The algorithms introduced in previous sections assume that the peer, who initiates the query, can maintain all peers, which may contain the result objects, as neighbors. However this is hardly true in most applications, since the system may involve more than thousands of peers. Keeping the connection to all the possible neighbors costs a lot of resource of a peer.

For handling the real-life applications, we adopt a *dynamic neighbor suggestion* mechanism. In line 15 of Algorithm 1, for each neighbor who did not return any answer belonging to the cluster in the last few iterations, it must be swapped out after suggesting one of its neighbors. The suggestion is based on following strategies: 1) Each peer sends the mean of the objects in its local database to its neighbor, when they are establishing connection; 2) The peer suggests the neighbor whose mean is the nearest one to the query object. Note that the request peer does not drop the data objects returned by the swapped-out neighbors. Therefore, the swapped-out peer still has chance to be chosen back (line 15 of Algorithm 1). Furthermore, it is usually impossible to wait until all peers are traversed, especially in a wide-area-network or Internet environment. The peer, who issues the query, sets up a time-out threshold, so that the query can be answered within an acceptable time.

## 6 Related Work

Researchers with different backgrounds study the P2P systems from different perspective. The routing and resource location problems has been studied in networking community, as they are reported in [8,9,7], etc. Although some issues of data mining in P2P systems have been mentioned in [3], to the best of our knowledge, clustering in P2P systems has not been researched before.

BestPeer [5] is a general purpose framework designed for advanced P2P-based applications, and is employed in implementation of our method. However, our method can be applied on any P2P platform supporting computing ability sharing on peers. Furthermore, the analysis and conclusions in this paper is BestPeer independent.

Clustering is one of the basic techniques in data mining [4] and pattern recognition [1]. Much work has been done on centralized site, from different perspective, e.g. effectiveness, efficiency, robustness, and applications, as they are surveyed in [4,2,6].

## 7 Conclusion

A novel query model, namely, *clustering-based query answering*, is studied intensively in this paper. The research is driven by the applictions, e.g. file sharing and information retrieval, in peer-to-peer environments. CBQA meets the requests of these applications in that, 1) the model generalizes several traditional clustering criteria, so that it can be used to solve more analysis problems than tranditional similarity queries. 2) Only a small portion of dataset need to be transferred over network under certain conditions, while the query result is proved to be consistent with the global clustering. In other words, the query result is guaranteed, while the cost is low. 3) The query model can be supported by current P2P platforms easily. The algorithm framework for CBQA is introduced and the properties are studied. Furthermore, we discussed the application of the model on three different, but widely employed, clustering criteria, i.e. $k$-NN, distance-based, and density-based clustering, in details. The theoretical analysis shows the effectiveness and efficiency of the algorithms. Furthermore, the implementaion details are discussed. These techniques enable our method to be applied in real-life P2P systems.

**Acknowledgement.** The authors would like to thank Wee Siong Ng, for providing the source code of BestPeer.

## References

1. R. O. Duda, P. E. Hart, and D. G. Stork. *Pattern Classification.* Wiley-Interscience, 2nd edition, 2000.
2. D. P. Fasulo. An analysis of recent work on clustering algorithms. Technical report, Department of Computer Science and Engineering, University of Washington, 1999.
3. F. Kaashoek and A. Powstron, editors. *Electronic Proceedings for the 1st International Workshop on Peer-to-Peer Systems (IPTPS'2002).* Available at: http://www.cs.rice.edu/Conferences/IPTPSO2/, 2002.
4. L. Kaufman and P. Rousseeuw. *Finding Groups in Data: An Introduction to Cluster Analysis.* John Wiley & Sons, 1990.
5. W. S. Ng, B. C. Ooi, and K.-L. Tan. Bestpeer: A self-configurable peer-to-peer system. In *Proceedings of IEEE Conference on Data Engineering (ICDE '2001).* IEEE Press, 2002.
6. W. Qian and A. Zhou. Analyzing popular clustering algorithms from different viewpoints. *Journal of Software*, 13(8), 2002.
7. S. Ratnasamy, P. Francis, K. Handley, R. Karp, and S. Shenker. A scalable content-addressable network. In *Proceedings of ACM SIGCOMM 2001*, 2001.
8. A. Rowstron and P. Druschel. Pastry: Scalable, distributed object location and routing for large-scale peer-to-peer systems. In *Proceedings of IFIP/ACM International Conference on Distributed Systems Platforms (Middleware)*, 2001.
9. I. Stoica, R. Morris, D. Karger, M. F. Kaashoek, and H. Balakrishnan. Chord: a scalable peer-to-peer lookup service for internet applications. In *Proceedings of ACM SIGCOMM 2001*, 2001.

# The RBAC Based Privilege Management for Authorization of Wireless Networks*

Dong-Gue Park and You-Ri Lee

Department of Information and Technology Engineering, College of Engineering,
SoonChunHyang University,
San 53-1, Eupnae-ri, Shinchang-myun Asan-si Choongnam, Korea
{dgpark,thisglass}@sch.ac.kr

**Abstract.** M-commerce have grown rapidly, it is very important to determine whether an identity is permitted to access a resource in mobile environments. In this paper we propose RBAC based Wireless Privilege Management Infrastructure(WPMI) model and Wireless Attribute Certificate(WAC) for authorization in mobile communication. All access control decisions are driven by an authorization policy, which is itself stored in an WAC. Authorization policies are written in XML according to a DTD that has been published at XML.org. Finally we show the effectiveness of the proposed RBAC by applying it to an example of M-commerce service.

## 1 Introduction

With the rapid development of wireless internet technology and offer of the application service such as mobile banking and wireless payment service, it is very important to determine whether an identity is permitted to access a resource in mobile environments.

Digital certificates are used to support integrity services by conforming that the information in a certificate has not been altered by unauthorized methods and belongs to the proper subject. Currently, there are two kinds of information which are supported by certificates: identity and attributes. While identity certificate is used for authentication service to verify the subjects of the certificates, an attribute certificate contains the subject's attribute information such as a role, access identity, group, or clearance and is used for authorization in order to determine whether an identity is permitted to access a resource.[10] A PKI supports the issuing and management of public-key certificates which identify and authenticate authorized users. A PMI provides attribute certificates particularly suitable for authorization purposes. With today's revolutionary innovations in mobile computing, we are encountering a series of security and privacy issues in wireless environments.[18]

* This work is supported by the Ministry of Information & Communication of Korea and by the sabbatical leave of the SoonChunHyang University.

G. Dong et al. (Eds.): WAIM 2003, LNCS 2762, pp. 314–326, 2003.

WPKI has become one of the most outstanding proposals referring to authentication in wireless environments, and several applications have been based on WPKI certificates in order to provide authentication services to well-known scenarios in mobile systems. But WPKI certificates do not support for authorization service to determine whether authorized users have the rights to access a resource in wireless environments, although they support for authentication of authorized users in wireless environments.[6] WPMI model and WAC structure were proposed in order to support authorization service for authorized users in wireless environments.[18]

Role-Based Access Control(RBAC) has recently received considerable attention as a promising alternative to traditional discretionary and mandatory access controls. RBAC ensures that only authorized users are given access to protected data or resources. A successful marriage of Web and RBAC technology can support effective security in large scale enterprise-wide systems.[16]

In this paper we propose RBAC based WPMI model and WAC for authorization in mobile communication. All access control decisions are driven by an authorization policy, which is itself stored in an WAC. Authorization policies are written in XML according to a DTD that has been published at XML.org. In an WPMI, the access rights are held within the privilege attributes of the WAC issued to users. Each privilege attribute within an WAC will describe one or more of the user's access rights. A target resource will then read a user's WAC to see if he or she is allowed to perform the action that is being requested. WPMI can support simple RBAC by defining role-specification ACs that hold the permissions granted to each role, and role-assignment ACs that assign various roles to the users. In the former case, the AC holder is the role, and the privilege attributes are permissions granted to the role. In the latter case, the AC holder is the user, and the privilege attributes are the roles assigned to the user. WPMI can support hierarchical RBAC by allowing both roles and privileges to be inserted as attributes in a role-specification AC so that the latter role inherits the privileges of the encapsulated roles.[17] And WPMI can support constraint RBAC by allowing roles for separation of duty(SOD) to be inserted as attributes in a role-specification AC.

The rest of this paper is organized as follows. Next, in Section 2, we describe the technologies related in our approach. In Section 3, we propose the RBAC policy. In Section 4, we provide an example about using RBAC based WPMI for mobile application. This is followed by our conclusion in Section 5.

## 2 Related Technologies

### 2.1 Public Key Infrastructure

PKI is the fundamental structure of public key management and offers five basic security services such as privacy, access control, integrity, certification and non-repudiation.[1][2] The basic structure of PKI consists of certification authority, registration authority, directory and user. Certification Authority(CA) is the pivot subject of the basic structure of public key, which can produce or nullify certificate according to the certification policy and make own coupled keys and user's key selectively. Registration Authority(RA) can certify user's identification and utilize application based on the basic structure of public key. Directory is the cache of logs including relevant information and is allowed to be searched.[3][4] User is the person within basic structure and takes advantage of the system. Moreover, user should be able to produce own secret key/public key.[5] Being asked for registration by user, RA saves user information to database and requests for registration to the CA. CA sends the result of registration and provides reference number and permission code and Relative Distinguished Name(RDN) for user certificate. Registration authority shows these informations to user. In the meantime, user makes a key pairs and requests for issuing a identity certificate to a CA. CA sends certificate and Certification Revocation List(CRL) to the directory sever. CA issues Public Key Certificate(PKC) to user.

### 2.2 Wireless Public Key Infrastructure

WPKI was proposed for authentication service in wireless environments. WPKI has become one of the most outstanding proposals referring to authentication in wireless environments, and several applications have been based on WPKI certificates in order to provide authentication services to well-known scenarios in mobile systems.[6]

WPKI is composed of CA, RA, wireless handset and mobile contents provider. CA provides certificate to mobile contents provider, who provides wireless internet service, and user owning wireless handset. RA confirms identity of user, which is located between CA and applications using PKI. CA and RA in WPKI have the same functions as them in PKI. Wireless handset provides on-line wireless public key certificate issuance service from CA and electronic signature and encryption service based on certificate in wireless internet. Also contents provider should support electronic signature and encryption service based on its own wireless public key certificate.

A major difference between PKI and WPKI is to verify certificates. Verifying certificates in wireless is very difficult according to the limit of computing power and memory in wireless environments and consuming cost and time occurred by downloading CRL periodically. To solve these problems, Online Certificate Status Protocol(OCSP) is used or certificate having short lived format is used. The certificate having short lived format has 48 hours as validity duration. And ECDSA algorithm having 160bit is used instead of RSA by limited performance of wireless handset.[7]

### 2.3 Privilege Management Infrastructure

Every legitimate task is performed under the approval of some authority that has ultimate responsibility for that part of the business process. In many cases there is a requirement that the entities performing a task must have the appropriate approval, or privilege to do so. An attribute-certificate based PMI is a mechanism that can be used to support enterprise authority structures. PMI is the infrastructure for issuing, storing and managing AC. PMI comprises SOA(Source of Authority), Attribute Authority(AA), Privilege Holder and Privilege Verifier.[8]

There are two distinct mechanisms for binding a privilege attribute to a holder. The binding for a privilege to an entity is provided by an authority through a digitally signed data structure called an AC or through a PKC containing an extension defined explicitly for this purpose. PKC can provide an authorization service directly. But in the more general case, entity privileges have lifetimes that do not match the validity period for a PKC. The CA who issue the PKC are not usually responsible for this authorization information. As a result, in most cases it is better to keep the attribute information separate from PKC.

An AC is a separate structure from a PKC. A user may have multiple AC associated with each of its PKC. While the PKC is issued by CA, the AC is issued by AA. The use of AC, issued by an AA, provides a flexible PMI which can be established and managed independently from a PKI. At the same time, there is a relationship between the two whereby the PKI is used to authenticate identities of issuers and holders in AC. IETF announced AC Profile at RFC3281 standard document, and ITU-T announced X.509v4 as standard document. The format of AC includes an extensibility mechanism and a set of specific certificate extensions.[9]

### 2.4 Wireless Privilege Management Infrastructure

As m-commerce have grown rapidly, it is very important to determine whether an identity is permitted to access a resource in mobile environments. But using previous AC structures based on PMI for authorization in wireless environment is almost impossible, because computing power, memory and communication bandwidth are limited in wireless environments. To solve these problems, a WAC Structure is proposed by modifying previous AC structures in order to use it efficiently in wireless environment. The format of WAC includes the base fields, Attribute Type, privilege revocation extensions, roles extensions and delegation extensions. Role attribute type and roles extensions in the proposed WAC structure are used for roles model and delegation extensions are used for delegation model.[18]

Revocation of AC may or may not be needed. An AC does not contain authentication information such as public key. Therefore Attributes must be coupled with the corresponding identities. There should be a mechanism to link attributes to proper identities. [12][14] Since the autonomic signature supports higher reusability of PKC than do tightly coupled mechanism, the autonomic signature is used to support individual CAs or different lifetimes for identity and attributes in WPMI model.[18]

WPMI is the infrastructure for issuing, storing and managing WAC and can be used to support authorization service for authorized users in wireless environments. A user at first requests WPKC to CA in WPKI for authentication, and then requests a WAC to AA for authorization by a gateway. When the user wants to access a resource in web server by wireless internet, it is verified with his WAC by web server that he has the right to access a resource. [18]

Verifying certificates in WPMI is very difficult according to the limit of computing power and memory in wireless environments like as WPKI. To solve these problems, Online Certificate Status Protocol(OCSP) may be used or certificate having short validity duration may be used. And cryptographic algorithms used in WPMI should be selected by considering limited performance of wireless handset and wireless environments.

## 3 The Policy of RBAC Based Wireless Privilege Management Infrastructure

The authorization policy specifies who has what type of access to which targets, and under what conditions. The separate access control lists configured into each target, is hard to manage and duplicates the effort of the administrators, since the task has to be repeated for each target. Policy based authorization on the other hand allows the domain administrator (the SOA) to specify the authorization policy for the whole domain, and all targets will then be controlled by the same set of rules. Domain wide policy authorization is far more preferable than having separate access control lists configured into each target.[15]

RBAC can support effective authorization in wireless environments by ensuring that only authorized users are given access to protected data or resources. We have specified an RBAC policy specifically designed for use with an wireless attribute certificate based WPMI. The RBAC policy based WPMI is composed of a number of sub-policies. The domain of the RBAC policy is the union of all the domains of the sub-policies. Each policy is given a unique object identifier (OID) that globally unambiguously identifies it. This OID is used in order to guarantee that the correct policy will be used in all the subsequent access control decisions made by the implementation. The permission role assignment policy specifies which roles have permission to perform which actions on which targets, and under which conditions. And the role hierarchy policy specifies the different roles and their hierarchical relationships to each other. The user role assignment policy specifies which roles may be allocated to which subjects by which SOAs. The SOD policy specifies separation of duty in RBAC.

All access control decisions are driven by an authorization policy, which is itself stored in an WAC. Authorization policies are written in XML according to a DTD that has been published at XML.org.

Table 1 and 2 show an example of the role and administrative role definitions and permissions in M-commerce system. Figure 1 shows the role hierarchy for access control of M-commerce system. Following Table 3 is an example of permission role assignment policy for M-commerce system. The permission role assignment policy comprises actions (privileges) assigned to each role.

The role hierarchy policy defines the role hierarchies that are supported by this RBAC policy. Table 4 is an example of role hierarchy policy for M-commerce

**Table 1.** Role Definitions and Permissions in M-commerce system

| role name | role definition | permission |
|---|---|---|
| Supervisor | Supervising Shopping Mall | Supervise Items and Sales |
| Item Provider | Gathering or Providering Items | Register Items and Manage Items |
| Item Manager | Managing Items | Manage Items |
| Sale Manager | Managing Sales | Managing Sales |
| Employee | Employee of Shopping Mall | Retrieve Items |
| Member | Customer of Shopping Mall | Request Items |
| Guest | Guest of Shopping Mall | Reading Items |

**Table 2.** Administrative Role Definitions and Permissions in M-commerce system

| role name | role definition | permission |
|---|---|---|
| Senior Security Officer | Administrate Roles | Administrate Roles |
| Shopping Mall Security Officer | Administrate Shopping Mall Roles | Administrate Item Provider Role, Item Manager role, Sale Manager Role, Employee Role |
| Member Security officer | Administrate Member Roles | Administrate Member Role, Guest Role |

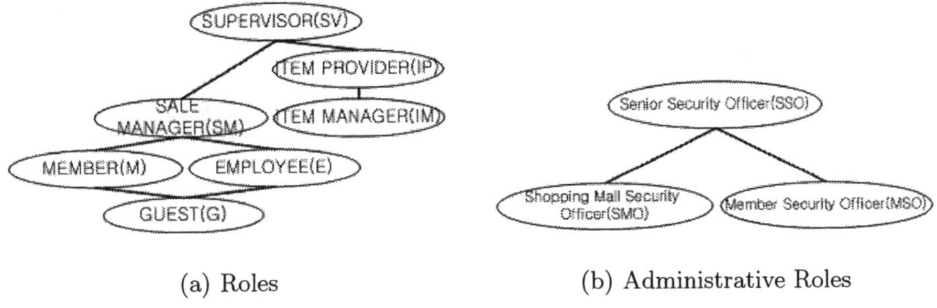


(a) Roles (b) Administrative Roles

**Fig. 1.** The Role Hierarchy and Administrative Role Hierarchy for M-commerce Systems

system Each role hierarchy (RoleSpec in the DTD) supports multiple superior roles inheriting the privileges of a common subordinate role.

The separation of duty(SOD) policy defines SOD in role-based system. Constrained RBAC is supported by this RBAC policy. Table 5 is an example of SOD policy for M-commerce system. The SOD is a time honored technique for reducing the possibility of fraud and accidental damage. Many different SOD requirements have been identified in the literature. These include static SOD(based on user-role assignment) and dynamic SOD(based on role activation).

The user role assignment policy specifies which roles can be assigned to which subjects by which SOAs. For each role assignment, it is specified in this policy

**Table 3.** An Example of Permission Role Assignment Policy

```
<PermissionroleassignPolicy>
        <Role name="Supervisor">
                <Definition_Value="Supervising Shopping Mall"/>
                <Permission Value="Supervise Item and Sales"/>
        </Role>
        <Role name="Item_ provider">
                <Definition Value="Gathering or Providering Items"/>
                <Permission Value="Register Items and Manage Items"/>
        </Role>
        <Role name="Item_ manager">
                <Definition Value="Managing Items"/>
                <Permission Value="Manage Items"/>
        </Role>
        <Role name="Sale_ manager">
                <Definition Value="Managing Sales"/>
                <Permission Value="Manage Sales"/>
        </Role>
        <Role name="Employee">
                <Definition Value="Employee of Shopping Mall"/>
                <Permission Value="Retrieve Items"/>
        </Role>
        <Role name="Member">
                <Definition Value="Customer of Shopping Mall"/>
                <Permission Value="Request Items"/>
        </Role>
        <Role name="Guest">
                <Definition Value="Guest of Shopping Mall"/>
                <Permission Value="Reading Items"/>
        </Role>
</PermissionroleassignPolicy>
```

whether the assigned roles can be delegated or not (see above), and whether there are any time constraints on the assignment. Table 6 is an example of user role assignment policy for M-commerce system.

## 4 The Example of RBAC Based Wireless Privilege Management Infrastructure

Figure 2 shows an example of M-commerce system. WPKI and WPMI are used for authentication and authorization of M-commerce system. Mobile user visits bank by off-line and receives ID/Password from the bank. The bank provides user information to Korea Financial Telecommunications and Clearings Institute(KFTC). Mobile user requests a WPKC to the KFTC by a gateway of the mobile company. KFTC verifies the identity of the mobile user and issues the WPKC for user and deposits it to directory server and transmits it to the mobile

**Table 4.** An Example of Role Hierarchy Policy

```
<RoleHierarchyPolicy>
        <RoleSpec Type="shoppingRole" OID="1.2.826.0.1.3344810.1.1.14">
            <SupRole Value="Supervisor">
                <SubRole1 Value="Item_provider">
                    <SubRole2 Value="Item_manager"/>
                </SubRole1>
                <SubRole1 Value="Sale_manager">
                    <SubRole2 Value="Member">
                        <SubRole3 Value="Guest"/>
                    </SubRole2>
                    <SubRole2 Value="Employee">
                        <SubRole3 Value="Guest"/>
                    </SubRole2>
                </SubRole1>
            </SupRole>
        </RoleSpec>
</RoleHierarchyPolicy>
```

**Table 5.** An Example of Separation of Duty Policy

```
<SeparationofDutyPolicy>
        <SodRoleList Type="SSD">
            <Role Type="shoppingRole" Value="Item_provider"/>
            <Role Type="shoppingRole" Value="Sale_manager"/>
        </SodRoleList>
        <SodRoleList Type="DSD">
            <Role Type="shoppingRole" Value="Member"/>
            <Role Type="shoppingRole" Value="Employee"/>
        </SodRoleList>
</SeparationofDutyPolicy>
```

**Table 6.** An Example of User Role Assignment Policy

```
<ConstrainRoleAssignmentPolicy>
        <ConstrainRoleAssignment>
            <SubjectDomain ID="Alice"/>
            <Role Type="shoppingRole" Value="Sale_Manager"/>
            <Delegate Depth="0"/>
            <SOA ID="PolicyOwner"/>
            <Validity>
                <Absolute Start="2003-2-21T12:00:00"/>
            </Validity>
        </ConstrainRoleAssignment>
<//ConstrainRoleAssignmentPolicy>
```

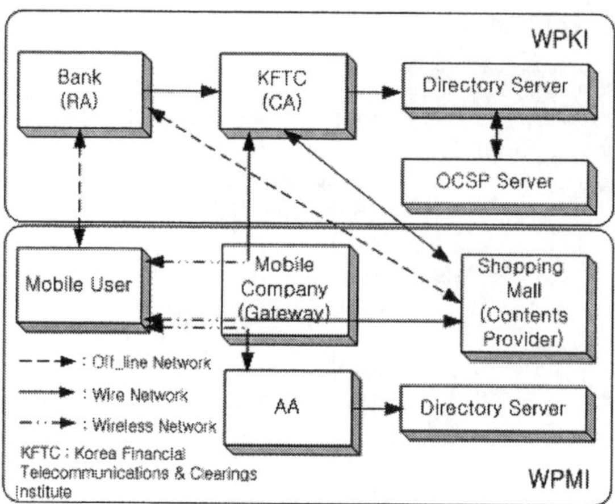


**Fig. 2.** An Example of M-Commerce System

user. Also, shopping mall receives it's own WPKC through these processes like the mobile user. As a result, a secure channel between the mobile user and shopping mall is established based on WPKI. When the mobile user wants to buy a item on M-commerce system, he must be authorized by the system whether he has a membership of it. Accordingly, he requests a WAC to AA with his WPKC. AA authenticates him with its own WPKC and assigns him to a member role like Figure 3 and issues WAC to him. And then, if the mobile user wants to buy a member-only item at the shopping mall, he sends his own WAC to the shopping mall and can be verified the his privilege about the membership by the shopping mall.

If the member role and item_provider in Figure 1 are dynamic separation of duty(DSD) and sale_manager and item_provider are static separation of duty(SSD) in SOD policy, SSD constraints between roles can be controlled by AA, which assigns user to at most one role in a mutually exclusive roles set and DSD constraints can be controlled by shopping mall in M-commerce system, which does not assign the mobile user to the member role and item_provider simultaneously. Even though there are SOD constraints between roles in M-commerce system, they can be effectively controlled by proposed RBAC based WPMI.

Figure 3 shows an example of hybrid model, which is mixed roles model and delegation model, based on WAC in order to assign member role to the mobile user. It is assumed in the Figure 3 that the diagram has been simplified and certificates associated with this are not shown. The delegation of authority to individuals is made by issuing role assignment certificates(RAC). The modelling of the actual role hierarchy in an organization for role-based model is made by issuing role specification certificates(RSC). The SOA delegates authority for administration of roles to the Senior Security Officer. The Senior Security Officer delegates authority for administration of shopping mall roles to Shopping Mall

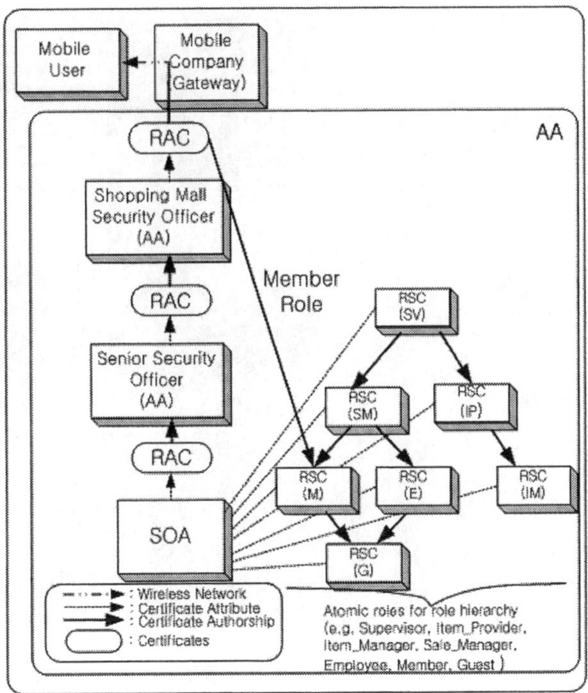


**Fig. 3.** An Example of User Role Assignment in AA

Security Officer. The Shopping Mall Security Officer assigns member role to the user. The validation of delegation chain ensures that the privilege is being exercised through an authorized role, and that the chain of commander assigning that role to the user has the right to delegate the privilege to individuals. When an end entity tries to access a controlled object, the privilege verifier protecting the object can ensure that the end entity possesses the privilege/security attribute required to access by ensuring that the chain of trust is not broken between the SOA and the end entity of the attribute. Even though the complexity of delegation chains results from attempting to mirror the distribution of privilege within a real organization, the complexity due to processing paths and retrieving certificates may be mitigated through the use of a cache within the verifier components and the flexibility of being able to model the actual privilege delegation paths in an organization is an advantage of this role-based model.[13]

Figure 4 shows the example of sequence illustrating service, which uses WPKI and WPMI for access control in M-commerce system. When Alice wants to access M-commerce system through gateway by handheld device, she must enter username and password in the phone and her WPKC and WAC must be verified by M-commerce system. When M-commerce system can verify her WPKC and WAC, it provides service corresponding to her role. M-commerce system recog-

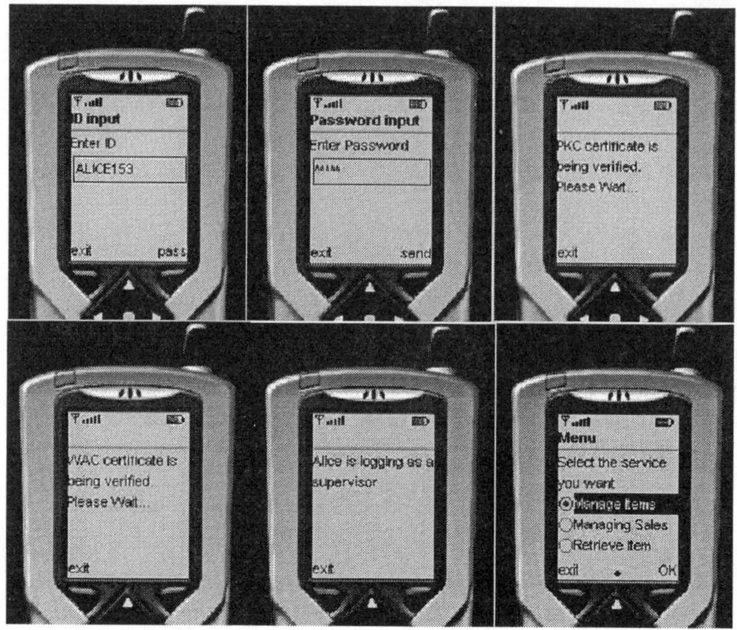


**Fig. 4.** Example of Access as a Supervisor Role in M-commerce system

nized Alice as a supervisor by her WPKC and WAC, and provided service menu suitable to the role in Figure 4.

Figure 5 shows the implementation of the RBAC in the WPMI. The WAA was implemented to create WAC in the Windows 2000 environment. AA administration module controls AA functions. It authenticates user by user's WPKC and accepts user's request and allocates privileges to users by authorization policy. Policy module creates policy ACs according to XML policy created by SOA and is used by AA administration module to allocate privileges to users. Policy administrator stores XML policy to XML Store. Policy module extracts the attributes used in the Policy AC from XML stores by java server extension method. And policy module creates Policy AC by issuing WAA's digital signature and stores the Policy AC to directory server. Cryptographic module operates the cryptographic functions relating with the creation and verification of certificate and WAC generation module creates user's WAC. Certificate administration module saves WAC in database and issues WAC to Gateway and processes WAC revocation and verification. Our implementation was developed by J2ME, MIDP, EJB components to provide effectively RBAC for wireless environments. The EJB components were implemented by using JBuilder8, Inprise Application Server 4.5. And the RBAC databases were implemented by using Oracle9i.

Through an example of M-commerce system, we show that RBAC based WPMI provides the benefit of fine-grained access control based on user authorizations or attributes in mobile environment.

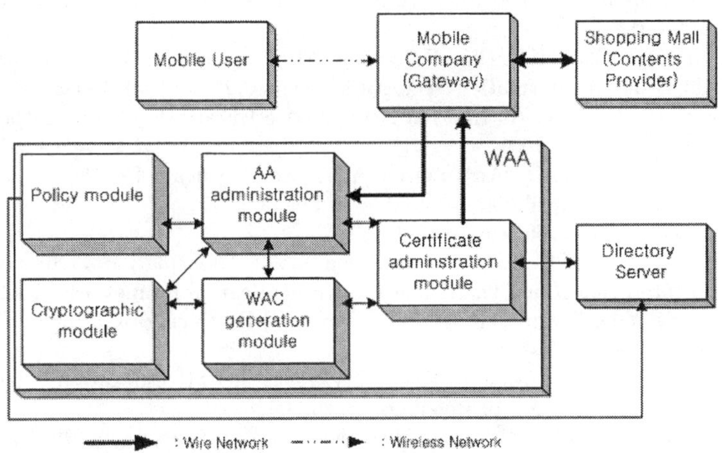


**Fig. 5.** Implementation of the RBAC in the WPMI

## 5 Conclusion

In this paper we proposed RBAC based WPMI model in order to support authorization service for authorized users in wireless environments. All access control decisions are driven by an authorization policy, which is itself stored in an WAC. Authorization policies are written in XML according to a DTD that has been published at XML.org. Finally we showed the effectiveness of the proposed RBAC by applying it to an example of M-commerce service. In the future we would like to investigate an efficient authorization method in ubiquitous environments.

## References

1. Alfred Arsenault, S. Turner: Internet X.509 Public Key Infrastructure PKIX Roadmap Work in Progress. Internet-draft 05, March 2000 <http://www.ietf.org/internet-drafts/ draft-ietf-pkix-roadmap-05.txt>
2. Adams, C and Lloyd, S.: Understanding Public-Key Infrastructure: Concepts, Standards, and Deployment Considerations. Macmillan Technical Publishing 1999
3. ITU-T Rec.: X.509 2000 |ISO/IEC 9594-8 The Directory: Authentication Framework
4. Russell Housley, Warwick Ford, Tim Polk, David Solo: Internet X.509 Public Key Infrastructure Certificate and CRL Profile. RFC 2459, IETF PKIX Working Group, January 1999 <http://www.ietf.org/rfc/rfc2459.txt>

5. A. Aresenault, S. Tuner: Internet X.509 Public Key Infrastructure, Internet Draft, November 2000
6. J.I.Lee, J.H.Park, J.S.Song: Domestic PKI model for WAP, Institute of Information Security & Cryptology Journal, October 2000
7. Wireless Application Protocol Wireless Transport Layer Security, WAP Forum 6th of April 2001
8. S.H. Jin, D.S. Choi, Y.S. Cho, E.J. Yoon: Attribute Authentication technology & PMI, Institute of Information Security & Cryptology Journal, December 2000
9. S. Farrell, R. Housley: An Internet Attribute Certificate Profile for Authorization, Internet Draft, June 2001
10. S. Farrell, R. Housley: "An Internet Attribute Certificate Profile for Authorization", RFC 3281, April 2002. available on line at http://www.ietf.org/rfc/rfc3281.txt
11. ISO/IEC 9594-8/ITU-T Recommendation X.509, "Information Technology-Open System Interconnection: The Directory: Authentication Framework" 2002
12. D.G. Park, Y.D. Hwang: "RBAC in Distributed Retrieving Systems by Attribute Certificates", IC2001.
13. Scott Knight, Chris Grandy: "Scalability Issues in PMI Delegation", 1st Annual PKI Research Workshop-proceedings, April 2002
14. J. S. Park, R. Sandhu: "Binding Identities and Attributes Using Digitally Signed Certificates" ACSAC 2000.
15. D.W.Chadwick, O.Otenko: "The PERMIS X.509 Role based Privilege Management Infrastructure" SACMAT2002.
16. D.W. Chadwick, A. Otenko: "RBAC Polices in XML for X.509 based Privilege Management" Sec 2000.
17. D.W. Chadwick: "Privilege Management Infrastructure" Business Briefing: Global Security Systems Reference Section.
18. D.G. Park, Y.R. Lee: "The PMI model for the wireless environment" KOCIES Conference 2002
19. Toni Nykanen: "Attribute Certificate in X.509" HUT TML 2000, Tik-110.501 Seminar on Network Security.

# Data Securing through Rule-Driven Mobile Agents and IPsec

Kun Yang[1,2], Xin Guo[1], Shaochun Zhong[3], Dongdai Zhou[3], and Wenyong Wang[3]

[1] University College London, Department of Electronic and Electrical Engineering, Torrington Place, London WC1E 7JE, United Kingdom
{kyang, xguo}@ee.ucl.ac.uk
[2] University of Essex, Department of Electronic Systems Engineering, Wivenhoe Park, Colchester Essex, CO4 3SQ, UK
[3] Northeast Normal University, School of Software, Changchun, China
sczhong@yahoo.com, ddzhou@public.cc.jl.cn, wenyongw@yeah.net

**Abstract.** While IP Virtual Private Network (VPN), especially its branch IPsec (IP Security), turns out to be a practical solution for secure data exchange through the Internet, it is suffering from the tedious deployment procedure due to the shortage of centralized network management capabilities, and this can easily causes safety outages. This paper proposes to use mobile agents to automate this deployment procedure so as to reach the final goal of real-time data securing across the Internet. The intelligence of mobile agents comes from rules guiding the management of IPsec as proposed by IETF Policy-based Network Management method. An object-oriented policy information model for IPsec is presented. A case study of inter-domain IPsec provisioning, a typical mechanism coping with data security across multiple domains, demonstrates the design and implementation of this data securing mechanism.

## 1 Background and Rationale

The wide existence of the Internet has practically proven itself a powerful means for information exchange. It is easily accessible, cost-effective and easy to use. However, it is lack of security mechanisms from the original design stage which partially contributed its wide success but at the same time exposes itself to plenty of malicious practices such as data tempering, eavesdropping and theft. Data security is getting more imperative with more increasingly growing requirement and practice of changing the Internet into a computing platform (typically driven by Web services), rather than a medium in which users primarily just view and download content. There are lots of researches ongoing on this issue, varying from one very specific field like creation/upgrading of new cryptography up to the security system architecture design such as virtual private network (VPN) [1]. The focus of this paper is to engineer the underlying networks that transport data so as to make sure that safety-sensitive data get the safety they need. And this should be done without disturbing the applications or the users who send data. This safety guarantee is achieved via various security mechanisms and the automation of the processing.

G. Dong et al. (Eds.): WAIM 2003, LNCS 2762, pp. 327–334, 2003.

As to the underlying network security mechanism, VPN turns out to be a very effective and flexible means for an organization to interconnect its distributed sites over a public network [1]. A good candidate to solve security problems that arises during provisioning of a VPN service via public networks is IPsec (Internet Protocol Security) [2]. It is applied on the network layer and provides a set of security services that cover data confidentiality, integrity, authentication, key management, and tunneling. But even though IPsec has proved to be cost-effective solutions, the lack of centralized network management capabilities of current IPsec deployment makes the management of growing networks error-prone and unsafe. In order to achieve the real-time data securing, a flexible and automated deployment/management of IPsec is a necessity. The emerging *policy-based network management* (PBNM) paradigm claims to be a solution to this flexibility requirement whereas *mobile agent technology* (MAT) can largely promote the automation.

Mobile agent paradigm intends to bring an increased performance and flexibility to distributed systems by promoting "autonomous code migration" (mobile code moving between places) instead of traditional RPC (remote procedure call) [3]. It turns out that more attention has been given to the mobility of mobile agent whereas the intelligence of mobile agent is seldom talked about in the mobile agent research community. Mobile agent technology is very successfully used in the network-related applications, especially network management where its mobility feature is largely explored [4]. But these mobile agents are usually lack of intelligence. This paper explores the potential use of mobile agent to manage/configure IPsec in a more intelligent and automated way. For this purpose, mobile agents should contain certain extent of intelligence to reasonably respond to the possible change in destination elements and perform negotiation. This kind of intelligence should reflect the management strategy of administrator. A straightforward way for network administrator to give network management command or guide is to produce high-level rules such as *if sourceHost is within finance then useSecureTunnel*. Then mobile agent can take this rule and enforce it automatically. By using rules to give network management command or strategy, a unique method of managing network can be guaranteed. The use of rule to management network is exactly what PBNM is about since policies usually appear as rules for network management.

Policies are seen as a way to guide the behavior of a network or distributed system through high-level declarative directives. In comparison with previous traditional network management approaches, such as TMN (Telecom Management Network) or TINA-C, PBNM offers a more flexible, customizable management solution that allows controlled elements to be configured or scheduled on the fly [5]. The integration of PBNM with mobile agents is engineered in this paper towards an automated IPsec provisioning for data securing.

Obviously, the introduction of mobile agents also results in new security threat to the system. As such mobile agent security facilities need to be taken into consideration. And this has been carried out in author's another paper [3], which tackles the potential security threats to mobile agents based on the lifecycle analysis of mobile agents. Therefore, this paper just focuses on the integration of mobile agents and PBNM without explicitly considering the mobile agent security strategies.

This paper is organized as follows. Firstly, a rule-driven MA-based IPsec management system architecture with emphasis on the functional components of IPsec is proposed; then a detailed explanation with respect to policy specification language and IPsec policy information model is presented. Finally, before the conclusions, a case study for inter-domain IPsec configuration is demonstrated, aiming to exemplify implementation of this management system for data securing on the Internet.

## 2 A Rule-Driven MA-Based IPsec Management Architecture

### 2.1 Architecture Overview

A rule-driven MA-based IPsec management system architecture and its main components are depicted in Fig. 1, which is organized based on the PBNM concept as suggested by IETF Policy Working Group [6]. IETF work on policy is adopted as the baseline for the PBNM system used in this paper due to its wide popularity. *Grasshopper* [7] is explored as mobile agent platform.

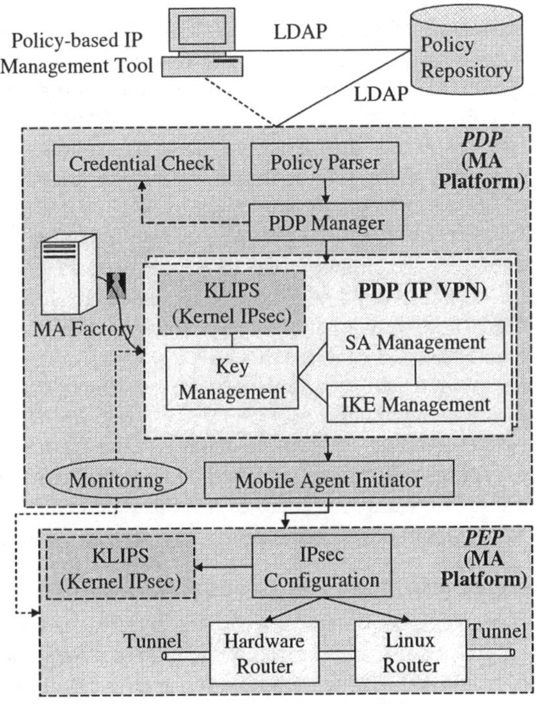


**Fig. 1.** Policy-driven MA-based IPsec Management Architecture

The PBNM system mainly includes four components: policy management tool, policy repository, Policy Decision Point (PDP) and Policy Enforcement Point (PEP). Policy management tool serves as a policy creation environment for the administrator to define/edit/view IPsec policies in a high-level declarative language. After validation, new or updated policies are translated into a kind of object oriented representation and stored in the policy repository, which is used for the storage of policies in the form of LDAP (Lightweight Directory Access Protocol) directory. Once the new or updated policy is stored, signaling information is sent to the corresponding PDP, which then retrieves the policy and enforces it on PEPs. In IPsec management environment, PEPs can locate in IP routers, Wireless LAN access points, or firewalls. If these resources don't easily support the installation of PEPs, a Linux box can be installed next to them to maintain the PEPs and provide proper communication mechanisms between PEP and these resources using, e.g., more popular SNMP.

Decision-making part of IPsec like IKE management as depicted in Fig. 1 can be regarded as a type of PDP since it performs a subnet of policy management functionality. For easy demonstration in Fig. 1, all the VPN functional components are placed into one single PDP box. In actual implementation, they are separated into different PDPs and are coordinated by IP VPN PDP manager.

## 2.2 IP VPN Components

Our IPsec implementation is based on FreeS/WAN IPsec [8], which is a Linux implementation of the IPsec (IP security) protocols. Since IPsec is built up via the Internet which is a shared public network with open transmission protocols, IPsec must include measures for packet encapsulation (tunneling), encryption and authentication so as to avoid the sensitive data from being tampered by any unauthorized third parties during data transit. Three protocols are used for this purpose: AH (Authentication Header) provides a packet-level authentication service; ESP (Encapsulating Security Payload) provides encryption plus authentication; and finally, IKE (Internet Key Exchange) negotiates connection parameters, including keys, for the other two [9]. Kernel of FreeS/WAN IPsec, KLIPS (kernel IPsec), has implemented AH, ESP, and packet handling [8]. Since KLIPS is working beyond the management plane and based on the result of IKE, more discussion is given to key management issues which are closely related to the policies delivered by administrator via policy management tool.

*Key Management Component:* Encryption usually is the starting point of any VPN solution. These encryption algorithms are well known and widely exist in lots of cryptographic libraries. The following features need to be taken into consideration for key management component: key generation, key length, key lifetime, and key exchange mechanism.

*IKE Management:* IKE protocol was developed to manage these key exchanges. Using IPSec with the IKE, a system can set up security associations (SAs) that include information on the algorithms for authenticating and encrypting data, the lifetime of the keys employed, the key lengths, etc; and these information are usually extracted from rule-based policies. Each pair of communicating computers will use a specific set of SAs to set up a VPN tunnel. The core of the IKE management is an IKE daemon that sits on the node to which SAs need to be negotiated. IKE daemon is distributed on each node that is to be an endpoint of an IKE-negotiated SA. IKE protocol sets up IPsec connections after negotiating appropriate parameters. This is done by exchanging packets on UDP port 500 between two gateways.

*SA Management:* Given any significant number of hosts communicating over an IPsec, the number of SAs that need to be negotiated for an IPsec session can be enormous. While the negotiation of cryptographic and other security parameters for

IPSec Security Associations is supported by key management protocols, the mechanism for the management of SAs themselves doesn't exist in IPsec key management layer. Basically, the *(destination address, SPI, protocol identifier)* combination is used for identify a SA. In our IPsec implementation, *ipsec spi* provided by IPsec FreeS/WAN are used to create and delete IPsec SAs [8]. A GUI, embedded inside the IPsec management GUI, can be brought up to view the current SAs and their features. The "Delete" button for deleting a selected SA is also very useful for experienced administrator to shut down a dead IPsec tunnel, while there is no general mechanism to do this is in the current IPsec protocols.

The ability of cohesively *monitoring* all VPN devices is vitally important. It is essential to ensure that policies are being satisfied by determining the level of performance and knowing what in the network is not working properly if there are. The monitoring component drawn in PDP box is actually a monitoring client for enquiring status of VPN devices or links. The real monitoring daemons are located next to the monitored elements and are implemented using different technologies depending on the features of monitored elements.

*Tunneling* component takes the real action for encapsulation and encryption of entire transmitted packets based on the decision from PDP; therefore it is the primary part of PEP. Cryptography library provides the necessary implementation for encryption or authentication algorithms as selected. The implementation of this tunneling work is mainly done by FreeS/WAN kernel, KLIPS, as mentioned before.

## 3 Policy Language and Information Model for IPsec Deployment

In order to provide an IPsec link between remote user and resource of data, apart from understanding the operational technologies for IPsec at the data plane and control plane, management plane functionality also needs to be identified so as to promote the automation of IPsec deployment. Based on the policy-based IPsec system architecture presented in the previous section, this section details the design and implementation of this policy framework in terms of two critical PBNM concerns, i.e., policy specification language and policy information model. This object-oriented policy information model also makes the real integration of rule-based policies and mobile agents a reality.

### 3.1 Policy Specification Language

A high level policy specification language has been designed and implemented to provide the administrator with the ability of adding and changing policies in the policy repository. Policy takes the following rule-based format:

```
IF {condition(s)} THEN {action(s)}
```

It means *action* is taken if the *condition* is true. Policy condition can be in both disjunctive normal form (DNF, an ORed set of AND conditions) or conjunctive normal form (CNF, and ANDed set of OR conditions).

An example of policy is given below, which forces the SA to specify which packets are to be discarded.

```
IF (sourceHost == skyfire) and (EncryptionAlgorithm ==
DES) THEN IPsecDiscard
```

An example of data securing can be simply expressed by the following policy, which means that IPsec tunnel needs to be set up between two ends of communication if the destination host of the communication is within user's enterprise network (this is predefined by user when user applied for this data-securing service).

```
IF (destHost within EnterpriseNet) and (userID within
subscriberList) THEN useTunnel
```

This piece of policy also implies that other traffic would not be protected by IPsec tunnel. By this means, any policies related to the data securing can be defined. The execution of these policies eventually trigger the IPsec deployment based on policy-driven mobile agents without affecting the policy information model.

### 3.2 Policy Information Model

An object oriented information model has been designed to represent the IPsec deployment policies, based on the IETF PCIM (Policy Core Information Model) [10] and its extension [11]. The major objective of such information models is to bridge the gap between the human policy administrator who enters the policies and the actual enforcement commands executed at the network elements. IETF has described an IPsec Configuration Policy Model [12] representing IPsec policies that result in configuring network elements to enforce the policies. Our information model extends the IETF IPsec policy model by adding more functionalities residing at a higher level (network management level).

Fig. 2 depicts part of the inheritance hierarchy of our information model representing the IPsec policies. It also indicates its relationships to IETF PCIM. Note that some of the actions are not directly modeled due to the space limitation.

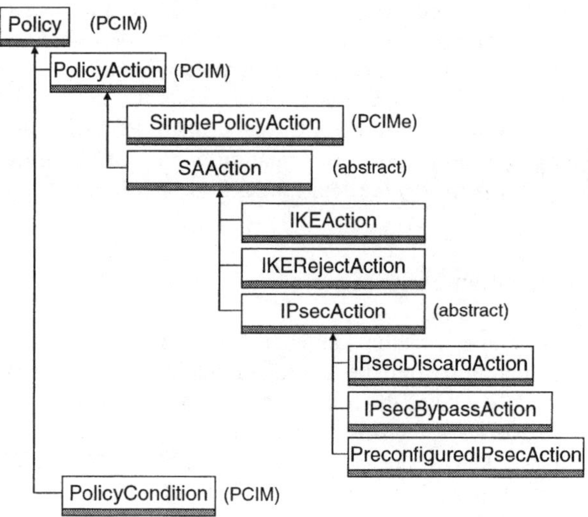


**Fig. 2.** Class Inheritance Hierarchy of IPsec Policy Information Model

Security policies define acceptable access privileges, which may depend upon combinations of factors including job titles, special projects, need-to-know, and level of trust. In addition, policies should be granular enough to allow differentiation by organization, server, group, and even user levels.

# 4 Case Study: IPsec for Inter-domain Data Securing

The automation of data securing across public network is vitally important to business information exchange like e-commerce. This paper provides, as a case study, a means to promote this process by introducing inter-domain IPsec provisioning based on rule-based mobile agents. Mobile agents play a very important role since the most essential components in PBNM, such as PDP and PEP, are in the form of mobile agents. Other non-movable components in PBNM architecture, such as policy receiving module, are in the form of stationary agents waiting for the communication with coming mobile agents.

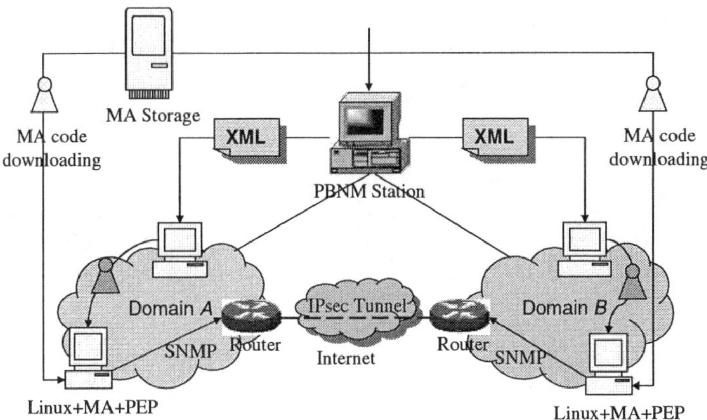


**Fig. 3.** Inter-domain IPsec Provisioning based on Rule-driven Mobile Agents

The entire scenario is depicted in Fig. 3. Network administrator uses PBNM Station to manage the underlying network environment (including two domains with one physical router and one Linux machine next to physical router at each domain) by giving policies. Policies are further translated into XML files and transported to the VPN PDPs on each relevant sub-domain policy-based management stations. Let's take Domain *A* as an example. Based on these policies which define security rules for IPsec such as the authentication algorithms for certain site etc, the PDP manager in domain *A* can download the proper PDP if it is not currently available, which is in the form of mobile agent, to make the policy decision. VPN PDP can also require the availability of PEP code, e.g., for new IPsec tunnel configuring, according to the requirement given in policies. If not available, the PEP, also in the form of mobile agent, moves itself to the Linux machine next to the physical router that may not be policy-sensitive (to simulate a more generic case). Then the selected or/and generated policies (VPN PDP can generate domain specific sub-policies if needed) are handed to PEP. The PEP firstly instantiates the code for new IPsec tunnel configuring with the SA parameters resulted from the IKE negotiation, then it uses SNMP (Simple Network Management Protocol) to configure the physical router so as to set up one end of IP VPN tunnel. Same process happens at the other domain, Domain *B*, to bring up the other end of IPsec tunnel.

# 5 Conclusions and Future Work

As shown in the above case study, after administrator provided the input requirements, the entire configuration procedure processed automatically. Administrator didn't need to know or analyse the specific sub-domain information thanks to the mobility and intelligence of mobile agents. This data securing mechanism also in some extent frees the network administrator from the tedious configuration of VPN deployments.

Defining a full range of policies/rules regarding IPsec management and the study of how they can coexist together towards further integration with other data processing mechanisms are the future work. The refinement of the IPsec policy information model is also needed. Policy conflict check and resolution mechanisms will also require more work as the number of policies dramatically increases.

# References

1. E. Herscovitz. "Secure virtual private networks: the future of data communications". *International Journal of Network Management,* 9(4): 213–220, August 1999.
2. IETF IP Security Protocol (IPsec) Workgroup. http://www.ietf.org/html.charters/ipsec-charter.html
3. K. Yang, A. Galis, T. Mota, and A. Michalas. "Mobile Agent Security Facility for Safe Configuration of IP Networks". *Proc. of 2nd Int. Workshop on Security of Mobile Multi-agent Systems*: 72–77, Italy, July 2002.
4. S. Papavassiliou, A. Puliafito, O. Tomarchio, J. Ye. "Mobile agent-based approach for efficient network management and resource allocation: framework and applications". *IEEE Journal on Selected Areas in Communications*, 20(4): 858–872, May 2002.
5. M. Sloman. "Policy Driven Management For Distributed Systems". *Journal of Network and System Management*, 2(4): 333–60, Dec. 1994.
6. IETF Policy workgroup group web page: http://www.ietf.org/html.charters/policy-charter.html
7. Grasshopper website: http://www.grasshopper.de
8. FreeS/WAN website: http://www.freeswan.org/
9. S. Kent. "Security Architecture for the Internet Protocol", IETF RFC 2401, Nov., 1998. Available at: http://www.ietf.org/rfc/rfc2401.txt
10. J. Strassner, E. Ellesson, and B. Moore. "Policy Framework Core Information Model". Internet Draft, May, 1999. Available at: http://search.ietf.org/internet-drafts/draft-ietf-policycore-schema-03.txt.
11. B. Moore. "Policy Core Information Model Extensions". IETF-Draft, IETF Policy Framework Working Group. 2002. Available at: http://www.ietf.org/internet-drafts/draft-ietf-policy-pcim-ext-08.txt.
12. Jamie Jason. IPsec Configuration Policy Model. IETF draft, August, 2002. Available at: http://www.ietf.org/internet-drafts/draft-ietf-ipsp-config-policy-model-06.txt

# Site-Role Based GreedyDual-Size Replacement Algorithm[1]

Xingjun Zhang[1], Depei Qian[1], Dajun Wu[2], Yi Liu[1], and Tao Liu[1]

[1]Computer Department of Xi'an Jiaotong University, Xi'an, 710049, China
[2]Institute for Infocomm Research, Singapore, 119613
xjzhang@xjtu.edu.cn

**Abstract.** Web caching is an effective Web performance enhancement technique that has been used widely. Web caching aims at reducing network traffic, server load, and user-perceived retrieval delays by replicating popular content on proxy caches that are strategically placed within the network. The replacement algorithm is the key to Web caching. This paper introduces a novel cache replacement algorithm, Site-Role Based GreedyDual-Size (termed SRB-GDS), which is a generalization of GreedyDual-Size. We argue that each website has different roles on different proxies. The proxy residing at the network edge has special characteristic that reflects the common interests of the community behind the proxy. According to its business, a community has its own interests, thus having its own favorite websites. However, this information is seldom incorporated in cache replacement algorithm policies. In addition to the consideration of the recently passed time, the size and the access cost of the document, the site role on proxy is also taken into account in SRB-GDS. Our trace-driven simulation experiment results have shown the superior performance of SRB-GDS when compared to other Web cache replacement policies proposed in the literature.

## 1 Introduction

The World Wide Web is one of the most popular applications currently running on the Internet. Its size is growing in exponential order and the Web information overload reduces the usability of the Web, resulting in network congestion and server overloading. Web caching has been recognized as one of the effective schemes to alleviate the service bottleneck and reduce the network traffic, thereby minimizing the user access latency.

The document replacement algorithm is the key to the effectiveness of proxy caches. Previous studies [1, 9] indicate that a better algorithm that increases hit ratios by only several percentage points would be equivalent to a several fold increase in

[1] This work was supported by the National Key Basic Research Plan project (973) under the grant No. G1999032710.

G. Dong et al. (Eds.): WAIM 2003, LNCS 2762, pp. 335–343, 2003.

cache size. The main factors concerned by the existing document replacement algorithms are inter-access time, the number of previous accesses, besides the size and access latency of the document. We argue that each website has different roles on different proxies. The proxy that resides at the network edge has special characteristic that reflects the common interests of the community behind the proxy. According to its business, a community has its own interests, therefore having its own favorite websites. This information is seldom incorporated in cache replacement algorithm policies.

In this paper, we propose a novel cache replacement algorithm, Site-Role Based GreedyDual-Size, which is a generalization of GreedyDual-Size. In addition to the consideration of the recently passed time, the size; and the access cost of the document, the site role on proxy is also taken into account. Our trace-driven simulation experiments show the superior performance of SRB-GDS when compared to other Web cache replacement policies proposed in the literature.

The remainder of this paper is organized as follows. We first review earlier work on Web caching replacement algorithms. Next, we present our novel SRB-GDS algorithm. Then we evaluate the performance of the proposed algorithm by comparing it to existing main replacement algorithms. Finally, the conclusion is made in the summary.

## 2 Related Work

Cache replacement algorithm is always the keystone study. Below we describe five main of them, which attempt to minimize various cost metrics, such as miss ratio, byte miss ratio, and average latency. It is convenient to view each request for a document as being satisfied in the following way: the algorithm brings the newly requested document into the cache and then evicts documents until the capacity of the cache is no longer exceeded. Algorithms are then distinguished by how they choose which documents to evict.

1. Least-Recently-Used (LRU): evicts the document that was requested the least recently.
2. Size[2] evicts the largest document.
3. Hybrid[6] aims at reducing the total latency. A function is computed for each document that is designed to capture the utility of retaining a give document in the cache. The document with the smallest function value is then evicted. The detail definition of this function can be found in the literature [6].
4. Lowest Relative Value (LRV) [7] includes the cost and size of a document in the calculation of a value that estimates the utility of keeping a document in the cache. The algorithm evicts the document with the lowest value. The calculation of the value is based on extensive empirical analysis of trace data.
5. GreedyDual-Size (GDS)[1] enables a cache replacement strategy to be sensitive to both the variability in document sizes and retrieval cost. When a document $p$ is requested, GDS algorithm computes its key value $K(p)$ as formula (1), where $C(p)$ is the cost to bring document $p$ into the cache; $S(p)$ is the document size; $L$ is an aging

factor that starts at 0 and is updated to the key value of the last replaced document. Among all documents, GDS evicts the one with lowest key value. GDS algorithm has several variations of cost function. When the cost function (*C(p)*) for each document is set to 1, the algorithm is called GDS(1). To achieve a balance between hit ratio ant byte hit ratio, GDS(packets) sets cost function for each document to 2+*S(p)*/536 [1].

$$K(p) = L + C(p) / S(p) \tag{1}$$

GDS combines locality, cost and size considerations in a unified way without using any weighting function or parameter. It outperforms above replacement algorithms LRU, Size, Hybrid and LRV in the performance aspects of hit ratios, byte hit ratios and latency reduction.

# 3 Site-Role Based GDS Algorithm

## 3.1 Characterizing Site's Role on a Proxy

Cache replacement algorithm studies have always using huge Web access log data. In our research we used three types proxy trace files: NLANR proxy traces [10], Boeing proxy traces [11], and the proxy traces that produced from May 2002 to Dec 2002 in our ActLab laboratory Squid proxy, which located in Beihang University. In order to analyze Web access properties conveniently, the format of these proxy traces has been changed. For example, a trace record's format is: *1035189610.054 2 211.71.7.190 TCP_IMS_HIT/304 207 GET http://image2.sina.com.cn/c.gif - NONE/- image/gif*. After processed, the format become: *31210.054 2 207 1 1 1 1 2 304 1*. The items of server name, URL address, protocol, method, and data type have been digitized. We analyzed the traces to understand the access patterns of Web requests seen by the proxies. We found:

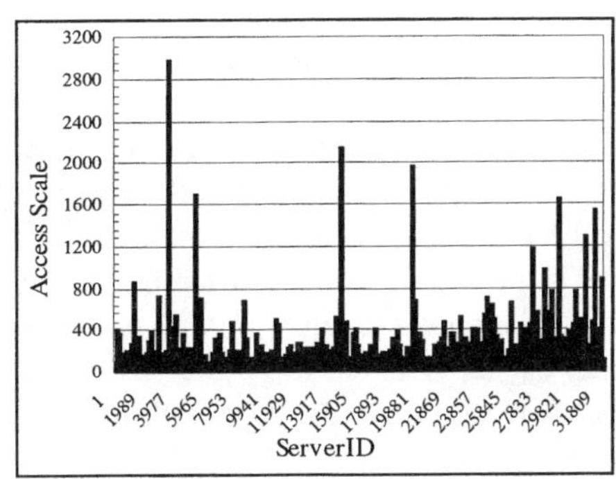


**Fig. 1.** Sites access scale distribution

- It is not balance to access sites, the 10 percent sites service 80 percent Web access. This result is same as the results of literature [13]. For example, the Figure 1 is the results of analyzing Boeing trace.
- The same site has different Web access scale in different web proxies.
- In a Web proxy; the sites, which have same Web access scale, have different unique access scale.

The analysis results indicate that each website has different importance on different proxies. We use Site-Role to characterize those properties, which can be calculated using following formula:

$$SR_p = D_s / U_s * \frac{1}{\lambda} \tag{2}$$

where $SR_p$ is the role value on proxy of the site which the document $p$ belong to; $D_s$ is total access scale of a server $s$, in which the document $p$ reside; $U_s$ is the no repeated access scale to server $s$; $\lambda$ is the constant factor that balance the $SR_p$.

The site role information is seldom taken into account by the existing replacement algorithms, which treat the cached documents that come from different sites using a same manner. Given two documents $D_a$ and $D_b$, which have same size. The document $D_a$ comes from the users favorite and always access site $S_a$. The $D_b$ comes from the user seldom access site $S_b$. With existing replacement algorithms, suppose the two documents have same replacement algorithm weight $H$ after a period of times. When the proxy cache capacity is not enough and the replacement algorithm wants to select the document with replacement weight value $H$ to evict, the document $D_a$ should be kept in cache. For example, the results of analyzing our ActLab laboratory trace data show that the Sina news site's access scale always locates in top 10 sites. Suppose the cached document $D_a$, which is requested by a student, be a news document that published by Sina. The access scale of the site, in which the document $D_b$ resides, is far lower than that of Sina. Then, the probability that the document $D_a$ will be requested again is far higher than that of the document $D_b$. Therefore, the document which should be evicted first is the $D_b$ rather than the document $D_a$, when $D_a$ and $D_b$ have the same replacement weight. The previous replacement algorithms cannot do like this.

### 3.2 From GDS to SRB-GDS

The original GreedyDual algorithm is proposed for memory paging. It is actually a range of algorithms; the GDS is based on one particular version that is a generalization of LRU. This version algorithm is concerned with the case when pages in a cache have the same size, but incur different costs to fetch from a secondary storage. The algorithm associates a value, $H$, with each cached page $p$. Initially, when a page is brought into cache; $H$ is set to be the cost of bringing into the cache. When a replacement needs to be made, the page with the lowest $H$ value, *minH*, is replaced, and then all pages reduce their $H$ values by *minH*. If a page is accessed, its $H$ value is restored to the cost of bringing it into the cache. Thus, the $H$ values of recently accessed pages retain a larger portion of the original cost than those of pages that have not been accessed for a long time. By reducing the $H$ values as time goes on and restoring them upon access, the algorithm integrates the locality and cost concerns in a seamless fashion [1]. Web caching is variable-size caching, and the GDS extend the GreedyDual algorithm by incorporating the different sizes of the document. The GDS set $H$ to *cost/size* upon an access to a document, where *cost* is the cost of binging the document, and *size* is the size of the document in bytes. The definition of *cost* depends on the goal of the replacement algorithm: *cost* is set to 1 if the goal is to maximize hit ratio, it is set to the network cost if the goal is to minimize the total cost. The GDS outperforms those of replacement algorithm LRU, Size, Hybrid and LRV in many performance aspects, including hit ratio, latency reduction, and network cost reduction.

One of the weaknesses of GDS is its without concerning the information of site role on a proxy. SRB-GDS generalizes GDS by taking into consideration this information in its replacement weight calculation.

### 3.3 Web Caching Replacement Scheme

The topic of Web caching replacement algorithms has been studied widely. The common tread in this area is the fact that cache objects have arbitrary sizes. Since the cache space in any practical system is limited, a replacement algorithm must be employed in determining which object(s) should be replaced when a new object is received. An important question is finding the best replacement algorithm assuming a certain request pattern and cost model [8]. The process that the Web object(s) is replaced can be formalized as an optimal problem tackling.

For a given finite universe of Web objects $WO=\{wo_i|i=1,2,...n\}$. Associated with each object $wo_i$ is a positive size $s_i$ and a replacement weight $h_i$ (when the object is cached). Let $B$ denotes the set of the objects cached by proxy, and then $B_j$ is the set of the objects that are cached in proxy at time $j$. The capacity of the cache is $C$. Let $S(\beta)$ denotes the size of object set $\beta$, and then $S(B_i)$ denotes the size of $B$ at time $i$. A Web request sequence shows as $R=\{r_j|j=1,2,...m\}$, let $r_k = i$ denotes that the Web object $wo_i$ is requested at time $k$, $r_i<r_j$ imply that $r_i$ is earlier than $r_j$. The state of $B$ will be changed with the change of the request sequence $R$. The cache replacement process is for all requests $r_i, i=1,2,...,m$, to find a $B_i$, which satisfying the conditions (3) and make the value of $\sum_{k=1}^{m} h_{r_k}$ is biggest.

$$B_i = \begin{cases} B_{i-1} & if \;\; wq \in B_{i-1} \\ B_{i-1} \cup \{wo_i\} & if \;\; wq \notin B_{i-1} \;\; and \;\; S(B_{i-1})+s_i <= C \\ \{B_{i-1}-\lambda\} \cup \{wo_i\} & if \;\; wq \notin B_{i-1} \;\; and \;\; S(B_{i-1})+s_i > C \;\; and \;\; S(B_{i-1})-S(\lambda)+s_i <= C \end{cases} , \quad \lambda \subset B_{i-1} \qquad (3)$$

The differences of the replacement algorithms rest with the differences of the method that calculate the replacement weight $h_i$. There are many factors that affect the calculation of $h_i$. Those factors include object size, miss penalty, temporary locality, and access frequency. The replacement algorithm can only concern one factor or incorporate several factors. In any case, it is a tenet to improve the algorithm performance to the best of its abilities.

It is a NP-complete problem to find above optimal replacement algorithm [8]. With the growth of the object set *WO*, the calculation scale will grow in exponential order. The following implementation of the SRB-GDS is a near solution of this problem.

### 3.4 Implement of the SRB-GDS

The implementation of SRB-GDS maintains a priority queue with key *H(p)*. The value *H(p)* for a document *p* is defined as following:

$$H(p) = L + C_p * SR_p / S_p \tag{4}$$

where $C_p$ is the retrieval cost of *p*, $S_p$ is its size, *L* is an inflation value [1], and $SR_p$ is the site role value. The general steps are described as the pseudo code of SRB-GDS (Figure 2).

It has the same overhead as GreedyDual-Size, handling either a hit or a replacement requires *O*(*logn*) time. The method of setting $C_p$ is same as the method of GDS: $C_p$ is set to 1 if the goal is to maximize hit ratio, it is set to 2+size/536, which is the estimated number of network packets sent and received if a miss to the document happens, if the goal is to minimize the network traffic resulting from the cache misses. The $SR_p$ value is computed according to formula (2), its complexity is same as that of calculation of document access frequency.

```
Algorithm SRB-GDS:
Initialize L = 0;
Process each request document in turn:
The current request is for document p:
if p is already in memory
    H(p) = L + Cp*SRp/Sp;
if p is not in memory {
    while there is not enough room in memory for p {
            L = min_{q∈M} H(q);
            Evict q such that H(q) = L;
    }
    Bring p into memory;
    H(p) = L + Cp*SRp/Sp;
}
```

**Fig. 2.** Pseudo code of SRB-GDS Algorithm

## 4 Performance Evaluation

In this section, we present the results of extensive trace-driven simulation that have been conducted to evaluate the performance of SRB-GDS.

### 4.1 Traces Used

In our trace-driven simulation we used traces from NLANR [10] and Boeing [11]. We only use the results obtained from Jan 1 1999 to Jan 6 1999 of the NLANR trace and from Mar 1 1999 to Mar 2 1999 of the Boeing trace. Our preprocessing of the traces followed the same procedures described in [1]. In particular, we excluded the records which size is 0. Some of the characteristics of these traces are shown in Table 1.

**Table 1.** Trace Files

| Trace | Time Duration | Number of Request | The Size of Trace Files |
|---|---|---|---|
| NLANR | Fri Jan 1 16:00:14 1999 ~ Wed Jan 6 16:00:01 1999 | 3,093,868 | 431,866KB |
| Boeing | Mon Mar 1 15:59:50 1999 ~ Tues Mar 2 15:59:04 1999 | 4,231,700 | 589,028KB |

### 4.2 Experimental Setup and Metrics

Performance measures of interest in the Web caching realm can be defined according to the goal of caching. The three popular performance measures used in Web caching, that is, the hit rate, the byte hit rate, and the delay-savings ratio, denoted as HR, BHR, and DSR, respectively, can be described as follows:

$$HR = \sum h_i / \sum r_i \ , \ BHR = \sum (s_i * h_i) / \sum (s_i * r_i) \ , \ DSR = \sum (d_i * h_i) / \sum (d_i * r_i) \ .$$

where

$h_i$: number of hit references to document i,

$r_i$ : total number of references to document i (number of hits + number of misses),

$s_i$: size of document i,

$d_i$: delay time to fetch document i from the original server to the cache.

HR represents the number of hit references over the total number of references. BHR represents the number of bytes saved from retransmission by using the cache over the total amount of bytes referenced. BHR considers the size of the Web document, but does not consider the difference in retrieval costs. DSR represents the reduced latency by virtue of a cache hit over the total latency incurred when assuming caches are not used. One may also define other new performance measures that reflect the focus of interest one wants to measure [12].

In general, having a good HR is the goal that most proxies pursue. It can allow most user requests be responded from proxy caches, and then reduce the mean user request delay, which is the most interested for Web users. On the other hand, one of the most important differences between traditional caching and Web caching is the high variability of the size of Web objects. Thus, in our experiments, we consider two main performance metrics: HR and BHR.

Our simulating host is a dual-processor Langchao server NP320 with 1.13 GHz Pentium III CPUs, a Gigabytes memory, and running Redhat 7.2. The simulator is based on Cao's simulator [1], and added SRB-GDS implementation into it. It uses a priority queue processing to simulate cache replacement process. The cache sizes investigated in the simulation were chosen by taking a fixed percentage of the total sizes of all distinct documents requested in the sequence. The percentages are 0.05%, 0.5%, 5%, 10%, and 20%. We compare SRB-GDS with LRU, Size, Hybrid, LRV, and GDS. SRB-GDS is based on GDS. Like GDS, we adopt two models, constant cost model and packet cost model, to run simulator. In constant cost model, we assume that objects have the same retrieval cost. The resulting algorithm is termed SRB-GDS(1). Under the packet cost model, we assume that document retrieval costs are *2+size/536*. The resulting algorithm is termed SRB-GDS(packets). The former tries to minimize miss hit, and the last tries to minimize the network traffic resulting from the misses.

### 4.3 Performance under Constant Cost

Figure 3 and Figure 4 show the hit ratios for the different traces (Figure 3 is for NLANR trace; Figure 4 is for Boeing trace). In each plot, the x-axis re presents the cache size and the y-axis represents the HR. The results show that SRB-GDS(1)

achieves the best HR among other algorithms across traces and cache sizes. The shew of SRB-GDS(1) looks like that of GDS very much. The SRB-GDS HR approaches the maximal achievable hit ratio very fast, being able to achieve over 95% of the maximal hit ratio when the cache size is only 5% of the total data set size. It illuminates that SRB-GDS(1) performs particularly well for small caches, suggesting that it would be a good replacement algorithm for main memory caching of web pages.

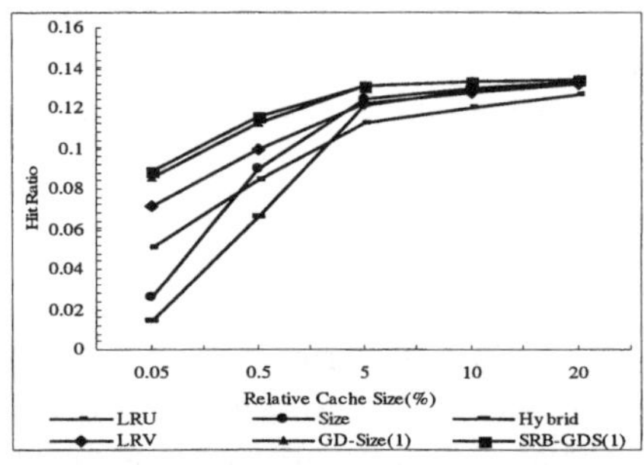


Fig. 3. HR vs. cache size(NLANR trace)

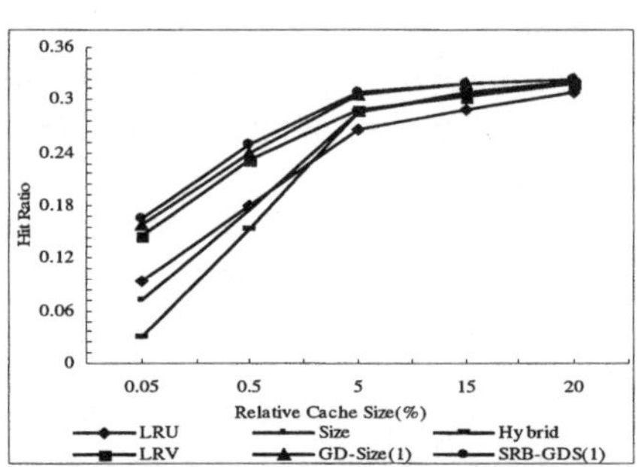


Fig. 4. HR vs. cache size (Boeing trace)

### 4.4 Performance under Packet Cost Assumption

We knew from literature [1] that GDS(packets) achieves the overall highest BHR than those algorithms of LRU, Size, LRV, and Hybrid. To highlight the differences between the SRB-GDS(packets) and GDS(packets), Figure 5 and Figure 6 only show the BHR for the two trace groups under the two algorithms.

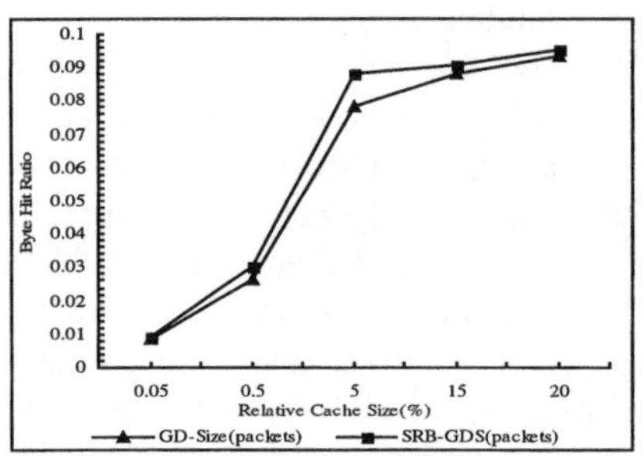


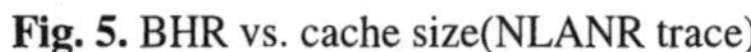

Fig. 5. BHR vs. cache size(NLANR trace)

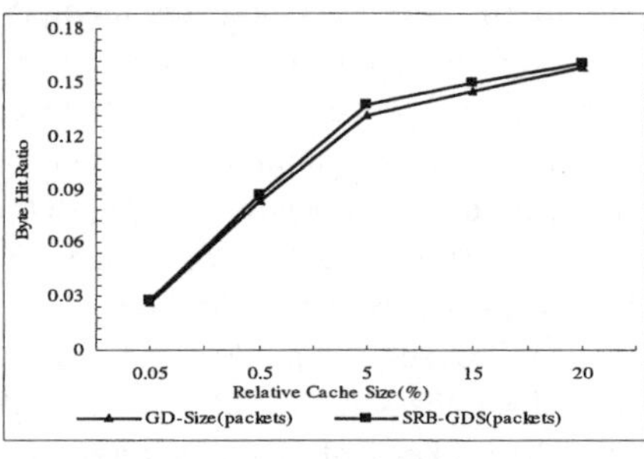


Fig. 6. BHR vs. cache size (Boeing trace)

The results show the SRB-GDS BHR is higher than GDS BHR across traces and cache sizes.

In summary, for proxy designers that seek to maximize hit ratio, SRB-GDS(1) is the appropriate algorithm. If byte hit ratio is desired, SRB-GDS(packets) is the appropriate algorithm. From the algorithm plots trends we can see, when the cache sizes are infinite, the performances of all the algorithms are identical.

## 5 Summary

This paper introduces a novel web cache replacement algorithm: Site-Role Based GreedyDual Size. The algorithm generalizes GreedyDual-Size by incorporating site role on proxy. Our evaluation using trace-driven simulation show that it outperforms replacement algorithms, which is proposed in the literature, in many performance aspects, including hit ratios and byte hit ratios, and so on. However, SRB-GDS algorithm has several aspects to be completed and improved. One of our future works is to look into how to adjust the algorithm when the goal is to optimize more than one performance measures at a time. Meanwhile, we will incorporate the semantic contents of the Web documents into the calculation of $SR_p$.

## References

1. Cao, P., Irani, S. Cost-Aware www proxy caching algorithms. In: Proceedings of the 1997 USENIX Symposium on Internet Technology and Systems. 1997. 193–206
2. S. Williams, M. Abrams, C.R. Standbridge, G.Abdulla and E.A. Fox. Removal Policies in Network Caches For World-Wide Web Documents. In Proceedings of the ACM Sigcomm96, August 1996, Standford University
3. C. Aggarwal, J. L.Wolf, and P. S. Yu. Caching on the World Wide Web. IEEE Transactions on Knowledge and Data Engineering, 11(1):94–106, January/February 1999
4. M. F. Arlitt, L. Cherkasova, J. Dilley, R. Friedrich, and T. Jin. Evaluating Content Management Techniques forWeb Proxy Caches. In Second Workshop on Internet Server Performance – WISP'99, Atlanta, Georgia, 1999. In conjunction with ACM Sigmetrics'99
5. M. F. Arlitt, R. Friedrich, and T. Jin. Performance Evaluation of Web Proxy Cache Replacement Policies. Erformance Evaluation, 40(4):149–164, 2000
6. R.Wooster and M. Abrams. Proxy Caching the Estimates Pages Load Delays. In the 6th International World Wide Web Conference, April 7–11, 1997, Santa Clara, CA
7. Cristina Duarte Murta, and Virgilio Almeida. Using Performance Maps to Understand the Behavior of Web Caching Policies, the 2nd IEEE Workshop on Internet Applications, July 23–24 ,2001, San Jose, CA
8. Saied Hosseini-Khayat. On Optimal Replacement of Nonuniform Cache Objects. IEEE Transactions on Computers 49(8): 769–778 (2000)
9. Shudong Jin and Azer Bestavros. Popularity-aware GreedyDual-Size Web proxy caching algorithms. In Proceedings of IEEE ICDCS 2000
10. ftp://researchsmp2.cc.vt.edu/pub/nlanr1999/
11. ftp://researchsmp2.cc.vt.edu/pub/boeing/
12. Hyokyung Bahn, Sam H. Noh, Sang Lyul Min and Kern Koh, Using Full Reference History for Efficient Document Replacement in Web Caches. In proceedings of USITS'99, Boulder, Colorado, 1999
13. Danny Dolev, Osnat Mokryn, Yuval Shavitt, Innocenty Sukhov. An Integrated Architecture for The Scalable Delivery of Semi-Dynamic Web Content. Proceedings of the IEEE Symposium on Computers and Communications, Italy, July 2002. IEEE

# A Study on the Two Window-Based Marking Algorithm in Differentiated Services Network

Sungkeun Lee[1] and Byeongkyu Cho[2]

[1] Dept. of Multimedia Engineering,
Sunchon National University, Sunchon-si, Chonnam, 540-742, Korea
sklee@sunchon.ac.kr
[2] GPRS group,
ALTO Telecom, 895-3 Dongcheon-Dong Buk-Gu Daegu, 702-250,Korea
bkcho@altotelecom.com

**Abstract.** One of the essential functions to realize the differentiated services network is the traffic conditioning mechanisms to support the required services. In this paper, we propose TS2W3C (time sliding two window three color) marking algorithm based on TSW. The feature of the mechanism is that it utilizes two windows, one is used to measure the rate transition in a short period while the other is exploited for measurement of rate change in a relatively long period. We experiment with the proposed marking algorithm using ns-2 simulator. The simulation results indicate that our proposed marking scheme do fulfill better throughput assurance and fairness, under the case that AS flows require different target rate and co-exist with non-responsive UDP flows.

## 1 Introduction

The Differentiated Services Network (DiffServ) is currently a popular research topic to provide Quality of Service (QoS) to the different applications in the Internet. This approach proposes a scalable means to deliver IP QoS based on handling of traffic aggregates[1,2]. Two per-hop behaviors(PHBs) are being standardized at the IETF to allow development of end-to-end differentiated services. Expedited Forwarding (EF) PHB provides low loss, low latency, low jitter and assured bandwidth[3]. Assured Forwarding (AF) PHB allows a service provider to support different levels of forwarding assurance according to the customer's profile[4]. In this paper, we focus on the bandwidth fair share on assured service in DiffServ. Figure 1 shows the typical DiffServ architecture[5]. In the DiffServ architecture, a source specifies a service profile. It indicates the amount of traffic that the sender negotiates to send in the specified class. The traffic conditioner of the edge router monitors packets of flow and marks them properly. The packets of a flow that conform the service profile are marked as IN and the packets that are beyond the service profile are marked as OUT. The core routers give preference to IN packets while dropping OUT packets disproportionately at the time of congestion. In the current DiffServ architecture, the time sliding window (TSW) are the most widely used traffic conditioner, and RED with IN and OUT

G. Dong et al. (Eds.): WAIM 2003, LNCS 2762, pp. 344–351, 2003.

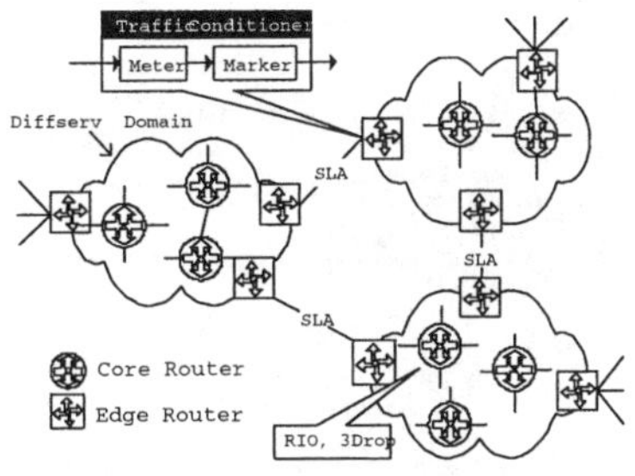


**Fig. 1.** A typical DiffServ architecture.

(RIO) has received the most attention among all the router mechanism[5]. Issues related to bandwidth assurance in DiffServ have been investigated in recent studies[6][7][8]. Some of the factors that can bias bandwidth assurance are Round Trip Time, different target rates and UDP/TCP interaction[9][12]. In this paper, we propose TS2W3C (time sliding two window three color) marking algorithm based on TSW marking algorithm. The simulation results indicate that TS2W3C marking scheme do fulfill better throughput assurance and fairness, under the case that AS flows require different target rate and co-exist with non-responsive UDP flows. The rest of the paper is organized as follows. Section 2 gives a brief introduction to TSW commonly used traffic markers. Section 3 presents our proposed TS2W3C marking scheme. In section 4, we present simulation results comparing fairness of previous marking scheme with our new scheme. Section 6 concludes this paper.

## 2 Time Sliding Window Marking Algorithm

TSW marking algorithm is one of the traffic conditioning methods in assured service based on the evaluation of average rate[5]. It decides drop precedence by the fact that if any flow exceeds the contract target rate on service profile in edge router and marks a packet as IN or OUT. Fundamentally, TSW marking algorithm has the two independent components, a rate estimator which estimates the achieved rate over a certain period of time, and a tagger which marks a packet as IN or OUT based on the estimated rate by the rate estimator. TSW estimates the transmission rate upon each packet arrival and decays the past history over time. TSW maintains three local state variables : *Win_length, Avg_rate and T_front.* As described in [5], it calculates an average rate by adding the previous rate to the current one so that it smoothens the TCP burstness. If the estimated rate R becomes less than the reserved rate R$t$, the tagger will mark a packet as IN. Otherwise, it will mark a packet as OUT with probability. In TSW marker, the rate information can be understood differently according to the *Win_length* value. When the *Win_length* value is relatively small, it can reflect the information from the short term traffic well, but the information from the long term

```
Estimate sending rate LR and SR

if LR <= LIR
     calculate DR = SR * Pdrop
     if SR <= LIR  .................. (1)
          mark packet as Green
     else if SR > LIR and SR < SIR .. (2)
          if DR > LIR ............... (a)
               mark packet as Yellow
          else
               mark packet as Green
     else if SR > SIR ............... (3)
          if DR > SIR   ............. (b)
               mark packet as Red
          else
               mark packet as Yellow
else
     calculate DR = LR * Pdrop
     if SR <= LIR           ............. (4)
          if DR > LIR   ............ (c)
               mark packet as Yellow
          else
               mark packet as Green
     else if SR > LIR and SR < SIR ... (5)
          if DR > LIR   ............ (d)
               mark packet as Red
          else
               mark packet as Yellow
     else if SR > SIR   ............. (6)
          mark packet as Red

 Pdrop : drop probability.
 DR    : calculated downgrade rate.
```

**Fig. 2.** Enhanced marking algorithm.

TCP traffic is estimated relatively inappropriately[6]. And when the *Win_length* value is relatively large, it will do vice versa. This fact leads to inaccurate traffic information on incoming flows. It was observed that TSW couldn't achieve the throughput assurance and fairness requirements under certain cases[5][6].

## 3 Enhanced Marking Algorithm

In the existing TSW marking algorithm[5], the estimated average rate can be measured differently according to value of the *Win_length*. As in the TSW algorithm, the proposed algorithm consists of a rate estimator and a marker for measurement of data transmission rate and for marking packet priority, respectively. However, the proposed algorithm utilizes an additional window. In the rate estimator, one window is used to measure the rate transition in a short period while the other is exploited for measurement of rate change in a relatively long period, so that it can estimate the average rate in a constant period. With this approach, the rate estimator can measure an abrupt traffic change in a short term as well as the average transmission rate for the longer period of time, and it is able to provide them to the marker in the edge router. The marker will therefore have more accurate information and mark packets more precisely. As in the TSW algorithm, the marker marks (or tags) packets based on the estimated rate. The proposed algorithm is depicted in Figure 2.

The proposed algorithm checks whether LIR (long-term committed information rate) and SIR (short-term committed information rate) exceed their target rate based on the estimated LR (long-term average rate) and SR (short- term average rate). According to the relationship between LR and SR, there are six incoming traffic conditions as follows:

In case 1 (when both LR and SR are less than or equal to LIR), TCP is generating initial traffic where incoming flows are relatively small or the network has enough resources to receive TCP traffic. In case 2 (when LR is less than LIR and SR is greater than LIR), the long-term rate is low and the short-term rate is somewhat high, and therefore, the incoming traffic is increasing. Case 3 is similar to Case 2, but the instant incoming traffic dramatically increases in case 3. Case 4 (when LR is greater than LIR and SR is less than LIR) represents the condition that the incoming traffic is suddenly decreasing, and thus TCP is in recovery state after experiencing congestion. In case 5, the incoming traffic is consistently high, and in case 6, the network is in congestion state. In summary, we can use the more precise flow states to mark packets with the six conditions explained above. When the long-term rate LR is less than LIR, the incoming rate is very low. In this case, the proposed algorithm leads packets to be marked with the low dropping precedence as in (a) and (b). Also, when LR is greater than LIR, packets are marked with high dropping precedence as in (c) and (d). Hence, the proposed algorithm can proactively control the incoming traffic even when a router is in congestion.

# 4 Simulation Result and Analysis

## 4.1 Simulation Setup

In order to validate the throughput assurance and fairness of TS2W3C, we perform simulations using the modification of the ns-2.1b8[10]. Figure 3 describes the simulation topology in which bottleneck link capacity with a delay of 5ms is determined to be traffic sources' total bandwidth (30Mbps) plus excess bandwidth (3Mbps) shared to all flows. Source nodes(1-10) transmit TCP traffics to destination nodes(11-20) via router A and B. Each source node and destination node is connected to A and B with 10Mbps link whose delay is 5ms

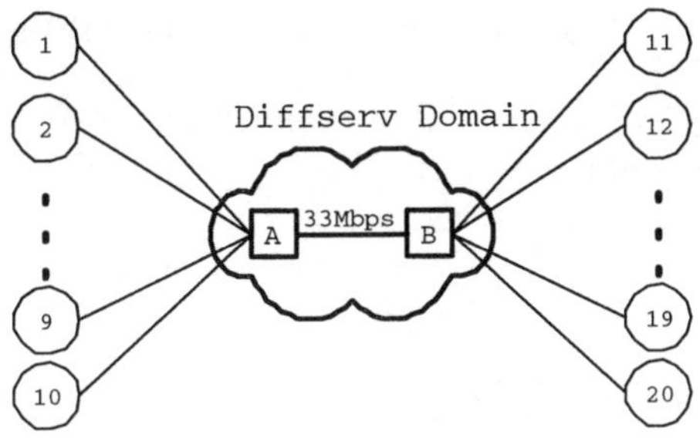


**Fig. 3.** Simulation topology.

**Table 1.** Throughput comparison of TS2W3C and TSW (Mbps).

| flow id | Reserved rate | Target rate | TS2W3C | TSW |
|---|---|---|---|---|
| 1 | 1 | 1.3 | 1.40000 | 1.73088 |
| 2 | 1 | 1.3 | 1.25248 | 1.63552 |
| 3 | 2 | 2.3 | 2.24000 | 2.13152 |
| 4 | 2 | 2.3 | 2.04960 | 2.34496 |
| 5 | 3 | 3.3 | 2.95072 | 3.05472 |
| 6 | 3 | 3.3 | 3.13504 | 3.24096 |
| 7 | 4 | 4.3 | 4.19520 | 4.15968 |
| 8 | 4 | 4.3 | 4.19616 | 3.94848 |
| 9 | 5 | 5.3 | 5.37536 | 4.90848 |
| 10 | 5 | 5.3 | 5.49248 | 5.11712 |
| tatal | 30 | 33.0 | 32.25824 | 32.27232 |

respectively. Each source node sends one TCP flow, which conveys a bulk-data transfer through FTP. TCP segment size is 1000 bytes and simulation time is 30sec. We compare TS2W3C with both target rate and TSW marker. The target rate represents the idealized service level that adds equal share of the excess network bandwidth to the reserved rate. Assuming that R$i$ stands for the reserved bandwidth of flow $i$, backbone link capacity is C and the number of flows which use backbone link is n, we can formulate the target rate R$t$ of flow $i$ as equation 1.

$$(Rt = Ri + 1/n \times (C - \sum_{i=1}^{n} Ri)) \tag{1}$$

The total target rate is 30Mbps and thus this network is over-provisioned by 3Mbps. TS2W3C consists of two window-based TSW and three color marking policy. It is implemented on the input interface of the router A. The two thresholds and the dropping probability used for IN and OUT packets in RIO are 10/40/0.02 and 40/70/0.02, respectively. We also use three drop RIO parameters 64/128/0.02 for green, 48/96/0.13 for yellow and 32/64/0.2 for red.

### 4.2 Performance of TS2W3C for Flows with Different Target Rates

To compare TS2W3C with TSW, *Win_length* value in TSW is set to 1 sec and short-term *Win_length* and long-term *Win_length* in TS2W3C are set to 0.3 sec and 1.2 sec respectively. SIR in this proposed algorithm is setup by multiplying a constant value to reserved bandwidth for each flow, as in equation 2. In this paper, the constant value is configured as 2.0.

$$(SIR = LIR(Rt) \times SIRFactor) \tag{2}$$

We simulated this topology for 30sec and calculated throughput from 5 to 25 sec after entering the steady state of TCP. The results of the simulation are shown

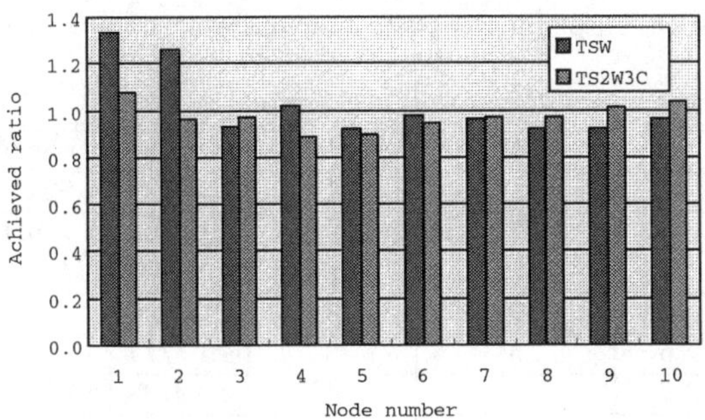


**Fig. 4.** Comparison for achieved ratio of TS2W3C and TSW.

in Table 2. In TSW and TS2W3C, most of the flows achieved their reserved rates. In TSW, the flows with smaller target rates exceed their targets rates and the flow with the higher target rates can't reach their target rates. But TS2w3C realizes rates fairly close to target rates. The bias on throughput per target rate in TSW are high, compared to that of our proposed algorithm. It means that our algorithm positively affected to the fairness for the bandwidth share. In Figure 4, we present the achieved ratio per throughput and target rate for each flow. The standard deviation on throughput per target rate for our TS2W3C algorithm is 0.0583 and for TSW algorithm is 0.148. It shows that our algorithm improves the fairness of excess bandwidth sharing by alleviating the throughput bias.

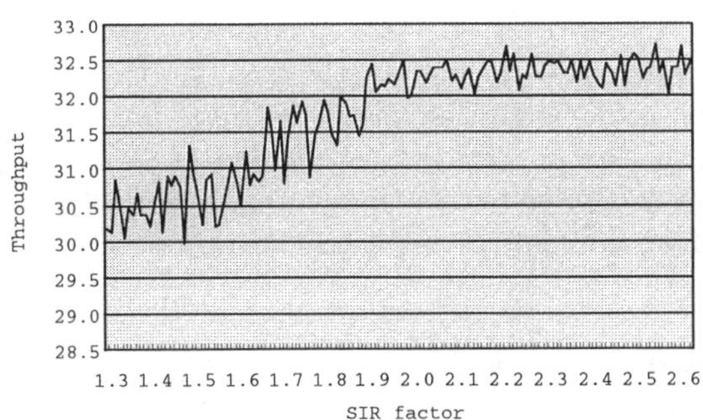


**Fig. 5.** Throughput by SIR factor.

Figure 5 show the standard deviation of achieved ratio for each flow with SIR factor ranging from 1.33 to 2.66 for searching the optimum SIR factor value. We could see that the standard deviation of achieved ratio becomes relatively stable states after SIR factor is over 1.9.

**Table 2.** Throughput per flow including UDP source(Mbps).

| flow id | Reserved rate | Target rate | TS2W3C | TSW |
|---|---|---|---|---|
| 1 | 1 | 1 | 0.80480 | 0.85536 |
| 2 | 1 | 1 | 0.74336 | 1.02496 |
| 3 | 2 | 2 | 1.69760 | 1.79616 |
| 4 | 2 | 2 | 1.82304 | 1.56704 |
| 5 | 3 | 3 | 2.59520 | 2.48416 |
| 6 | 3 | 3 | 2.67744 | 2.18016 |
| 7 | 4 | 4 | 3.19168 | 3.30336 |
| 8 | 4 | 4 | 3.52288 | 3.13248 |
| 9 | 5 | 5 | 5.05696 | 4.09984 |
| 10 | 5 | 5 | 4.39136 | 4.03040 |
| 11 | 3 | 3 | 6.49408 | 8.48320 |
| tatal | 33 | 33.0 | 32.9984 | 32.95712 |

### 4.3 Dealing with Non-responsive Connection

Non-responsive flow doesn't follow TCP's congestion mechanism. So when a packet drop happens, it doesn't reduce its transmission rate. Therefore, non-responsive flow often makes network congestion and is the main reason to make bias for the fair share of bandwidth[11]. We performed another simulation for the effect of non-responsive flow. This simulation environment is the same with the above one but includes UDP source which generates its traffic with 10Mbps. Reserve rate for UDP source is 3Mbps which is the average reserved rate from TCP sources. In Table 3, we show the simulation result and we got achieved ratio per target rate for each flow. In this simulation, we acquired the better total throughput on our algorithm by 26.5Mbps than on TSW by 24.4Mbps. The standard deviation of achieved ratio is better on our algorithm by 0.072 than on TSW by 0.080. It means that our proposed algorithm improves the fairness for per flow throughput and total throughput.

## 5 Conclusion

In the existing TSW marking algorithm, the estimated average rate can be measured differently according to value of the window length. The proposed algorithm consists of a rate estimator and a marker for measurement of data transmission rate and for marking packet priority, respectively. However, the proposed algorithm utilizes an additional window. In the rate estimator, one window is used to measure the rate transition in a short period while the other is exploited for measurement of rate change in a relatively long period, so that it can estimate the average rate in a constant period. With this approach, the rate estimator can measure an abrupt traffic change in a short term as well as the average transmission rate for the longer period of time, and it is able to provide them to the marker in the edge router. The marker will therefore have more accurate information and mark packets more precisely.

Using ns-2, we simulated the two markers, TSW and our proposed algorithm TS2W3CM. The simulation results indicated that TS2W3C marking scheme did fulfill better throughput assurance and fairness, under the case that AS flows require different target rate and co-exist with non-responsive UDP flows. For the next research, we need the study of SIR factor definition based on network load state and we find the proper window size by analyzing the different performance results with applying different window sizes. Also, we need the performance analysis for various network topologies and traffic sources.

**Acknowledgement.** University fundamental Research Program supported by Ministry of Information & Communication in republic of Korea.

## References

1. K. Nichols, S. Blake, F. Baker and D. L. Black, "Definition of the Differentiated Service Field (DS Field) in the Ipv4 and Ipv6 Headers", RFC2474, Network Working Group, Dec., 1998.
2. S. Blake, D. Black, M. Carlson, E. Davies, Z. Wang and W. Weiss, "An Architecture for Differentiated Services", RFC2475, Network Working Group, Dec., 1998.
3. V. Jacobson, K. Nichols and K. Poduri, "An Expedited Forwarding PHB Group", RFC2598, Network Working Group, June, 1998.
4. J. Heinanen, F. Baker, W. Weiss and J. Wroclawski, "Assured Forwarding PHB Group", RFC2597, Network Working Group, June, 1998.
5. D. Clark and W. Fang, "Explicit allocation of best effort packet delivery service", IEEE/ACM Transaction on Networking, vol. 6, no. 4, pp. 362–373, Aug., 1998.
6. W. Lin, R. Zheng and J. Hou, "How to Make Assures Services More Assured", In Proceedings of ICNP, Toronto, Canada, Oct., 1999.
7. I. Yeom and N. Reddy, "Realizing throughput guarantees in a Differentiated Services network", In Proceedings of ICMCS, Florence, Italy, June, 1999.
8. N. Seddigh, B. Nandy and P. Pieda, "Bandwidth Assurance Issues for TCP flows in a Differentiated Services network", In Proceedings of Globecom '99, Rio De Janeiro, Dec., 1999.
9. B. Nandy, N. Seddigh, P. Pieda and J. Ethridge, "Intelligent Traffic Conditioners for Assured Forwarding Based Differentiated Services Networks", In Proceedings of IFIP High Performance Networking, Paris, France, June, 2000.
10. Network simulator(Ns), University of California at Berkeley, CA, 1997. Available via http://www-nrg.ee.lbl.gov/ns/.
11. S. Floyd, K. Fall, "Promoting the Use of End-to-End Congestion control in the Internet," IEEE/ACM Transactions on Networking, May, 1999.
12. I. Yeom and N. Reddy, "Impact of marking strategy on aggregated flows in a DiffServ network", IEEE ICMCS '99, Dec., 1999.

# A Mobility-Aware Location Update Protocol to Track Mobile Users in Location-Based Services

MoonBae Song, JeHyok Ryu, and Chong-Sun Hwang

Department of Computer Science and Engineering, Korea University
5-1, Anam-dong, Seongbuk-Ku, Seoul 136-701, Korea
{mbsong, jhryu, hwang}@disys.korea.ac.kr

**Abstract.** In mobile computing environments, mobility plays an important role in data management issues inherently. In most existing works, however, the mobility issue has been disregarded and too simplified as linear function of time. In this paper, we propose a new dynamic state transition model, namely *state-based mobility model* (SMM) to provide more generalized framework for both describing the mobility and updating location information of mobile objects. We also introduce the *state-based location update protocol* (SLUP), which has mobility-awareness property by applying several update policies and choose the optimal update policy dynamically. We show that our proposal can greatly reduce the number of update messages, as the temporal locality of movement patterns increases.

## 1 Introduction

In mobile computing environments, the mobility of mobile terminal (MT) is emerging in many forms and applications such as database, network and so on. And MTs, like cellular phones, PDAs, and mobile PCs, can dynamically change their locations over time. The objects which continuously change their location and extent are called *moving objects*. Thus, what is important in mobile computing environment is how to model the location and movement of moving objects efficiently. Therefore, a software infrastructure for providing location-based services, called *moving objects database* (MOD), is significantly needed.

Recently, there is a lot of work on the representation and management of moving objects [8,5]. Wolfson *et al.* present the well-known data model called *Moving Object Spatio-Temporal* (MOST) for representing moving objects [8]. In the MOST model, the location of moving objects is simply given as a linear function of time, which is specified by two parameters: the position and velocity vector for an object. Thus, the location server can compute the location of a moving object at given time $t$ without frequent update message. The update message is only issued when the parameter of linear function changed. In general, we say that this update approach is *dead-reckoning*. This approach can provide a great performance benefit in linear mobility patterns. But the performance is decreased when the randomness of mobility pattern increases. So this approach may be suffered great performance degradation in non-linear mobility patterns.

G. Dong et al. (Eds.): WAIM 2003, LNCS 2762, pp. 352–359, 2003.

Another major drawback is the inaccuracy of the predicted location by linear interpolation.

In this paper, we look at the mobility model for MOD and an appropriate location update protocol. The purpose of our scheme is to model the overall movement patterns in probabilistic manner. Depending on the temporal locality of mobility patterns, the proposed scheme can greatly reduce the number of update messages.

## 2 Motivation

A great diversity of mobility patterns of real-life objects is quite natural. But, there's some specific repeated patterns in the movements. For example, in the *linear* mobility patterns, the trajectory of an object is almost a line in $d$-dimensional space. Otherwise, if we can't find the implicit knowledge of a specific pattern, let us identify this portion of trajectory as a *random walk*. In this work, we will classify the whole trajectory of a user into 'pause', 'linear movement', and 'random movement' in the rough. And, of course, we have to consider the temporal pattern of movements as Markovian process. Our approach to the problem of mobility modeling is primarily motivated by the following observations [2,6,9].

- A mobile subscriber will mainly switch between two states: *stop* and *move*. A traveling salesman has a tendency to remain in the same state rather than switching states [9].
- The majority of objects in the real world do not move according to statistical parameters but, rather, move intentionally [6,9].
- Most moving objects use a fast path to their destination [2,9].
- Moving objects belong to a class. This class restricts the maximum speed of the object. Different groups of moving objects exhibit different kinds of behavior [2,6].

The above properties are digested from dozens of papers in the location management of PCS and the spatiotemporal database. Despite all these observations, the most of existing works have been disregarded and too simplified as linear function of time. Mobility models and its applications are widely studied in location management of PCS environments. Many existing location management proposals use some version of a random mobility model [3]. Modeling the random-walk as a mathematical formula is a simple process without difficulty. However, such mobility patterns no longer reflect reality. On the contrary, most of previous works in spatiotemporal database assumed that the movement pattern of a user closely approximated a line. For example, the MOST data model assumed that the movement pattern of real-life objects is very close to 1 dimension.

As we mentioned above, both MOD and the location management in PCS environments aim to study the movement patterns of real-life objects. Yet there is a difference in their assumption, approach, and environments. Therefore, more flexible and realistic model for the consideration of real-life mobility patterns is highly demanded.

## 3 State-Based Mobility Model (SMM)

A mobility model, in the context of location management, is an understanding of daily movements of a user [3] and the description of this understanding. Motivated by this aim, various mobility models have been developed in mobile computing environments [3,9]. The mobility modeling in MOD is tricker than that in PCS because of the higher location granularity. Moreover, a matter of concerns in MOD is not a symbolic location, like *cell-id*, but the very geographical location of MT obtained by a location-sensing device such as GPS. Thus, a mobility model in MOD is essentially needed to consider a "compositive" movement containing both a random and a linear movement patterns.

From this understanding, we propose the *state-based mobility model* (SMM) considering a compositive mobility pattern as a set of simple movement components using a finite state Markov chain based on the classification discussed in Section 2.

**Definition 1.** *A movement state $s_i$ is a 3-tuple $(v_{min}, v_{max}, \phi)$, where $v_{min}$ and $v_{max}$ are the minimum and maximum speed of a moving object respectively. $\phi$ is a function of movement which is either probabilistic or non-probabilistic function. $S$ is a finite set of movement states.*

**Definition 2.** *The state-based mobility model (SMM) describes a user mobility patterns using a finite state Markov Chain $\{state_n\}$, where $state_n$ denotes the movement state at step $n$, $state_n \in S$. And, the chain can be described completely by its* transition probability *as $p_{ij} \equiv Pr\{state_{n+1} = s_j | state_n = s_i\}$* for all *$i, j \in S$. These probabilities can be grouped together into a* transition matrix *as $\mathbf{P} \equiv (p_{ij})_{i,j \in S}$.*

In this paper, we assume only that the whole mobility patterns are divided into three basic movement states such as *pause*, *linear*, and *random*. Each state has the self-transition probability $p_{ii}$, generally called *temporal locality*. In our model, we assume that the temporal locality of each state is likely to be very close to 1.0 for most of real-life applications.

**Definition 3.** *The self-transition probability vector (STPV) $\tilde{\pi}$ of a transition probability matrix is defined as $\tilde{\pi} = (p_{ii})_{i \in S}$. Also, the temporal locality (or simply locality) $\tau$ is defined as $\tau = \left(\prod_{i \in S} p_{ii}\right)^{1/|S|}$.*

As an example of SMM model, we describe a practical instance of the proposed model based on the three states described above, $S_0 = \{P \equiv pause, L \equiv linear, R \equiv random\}$. Fig. 1 shows a state transition diagram for this instance. Let us define two measurements that estimate how much each state has an influence on the whole movement patterns in this simplified model.

**Definition 4.** ***Linearity** $\ell$ is defined as $\ell = \frac{\sum_{i \in S} p_{iL}}{\sum_{i,j \in S, j \neq L} p_{ij}}$. Also **randomness** $\gamma$ is defined as $\gamma = \frac{\sum_{i \in S} p_{iR}}{\sum_{i,j \in S, j \neq R} p_{ij}}$.*

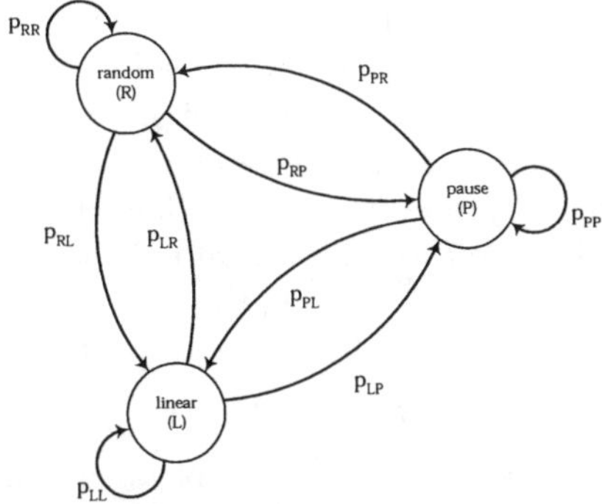


**Fig. 1.** An instance of SMM Model: $S_0 = \{P \equiv pause, L \equiv linear, R \equiv random\}$

# 4 State-Based Location Update Protocols (SLUP)

## 4.1 The Basic Idea

Suppose that there are a huge number of moving objects in $d$-dimensional space $\mathbb{R}^d = [0,1]^d$. For any time $t$, the position of the $i$th object is given by $o_i(t)$, which is a point in a $d$-dimensional space. Then, the *movement history* of the object is described as a trajectory in $(d+1)$-dimensional space, which consists of $\langle o_i(0), o_i(1), ..., o_i(now)\rangle$. For location-dependent query processing, the location server (LS) should track the trajectory of network-registered moving objects. Thus, an efficient protocol which updates their location information in the LS is highly needed. The goal of a location update protocol is to provide more accurate location information with fewer update messages to LS. Clearly, this issue has a tradeoff between accuracy and efficiency.

Location update protocols are classified into four major classes in terms of when the update message is transmitted: time-based, movement-based, distance-based, and dead-reckoning [1,5]. Each update protocol has its own characteristics and different performance depending on underlying mobility model. We introduce a new criterion to compare the efficiency of update protocols using a simple formula by measuring the update cost and the imprecision cost for a certain amount of time. This criterion is called $UITR$ (update-and-imprecision to time ratio) (see Eq. 1).

$$C_{UITR} = \frac{\sum_{k=1}^{wndsize} (w_{\mathcal{U}} \mathcal{U}_k + w_\epsilon \epsilon_k)}{wndsize} \tag{1}$$

To compute the value of $UITR$ efficiently, we employ the update window ($UWin$) and the imprecision window ($IWin$) in the form of a circular queue. Each update flag ($\mathcal{U}_k$) in $UWin$ is true if an update message is transmitted, or false if it does not. Each item $\epsilon_k$ of $IWin$ is the Euclidean distance between the actual location and the database location. We only assume $d$-dimensional space $[0,1]^d$. This is the reason why $\sum_{k=1}^{wndsize} \mathcal{U}_k \gg \sum_{k=1}^{wndsize} \epsilon_k$. To cope with this inequality, we have to consider a suitable weight such as $w_{\mathcal{U}}$ and $w_\epsilon$.

Exhibiting complementarity with respect to mobility patterns, different (*mutually complement*) update policies can be applied to the aforementioned states. In the *linear* state, the dead-reckoning approach has a great performance benefit especially in a constant speed [8]. In the *random* state, the movement patterns of an object have a special property of spatial locality. In this case, we employ the distance-based update protocol. Two comprehensive surveys of the subject are [1,5]

### 4.2 Overview of the SLUP Protocol

During the life of a connection, the SLUP protocol running in each moving object makes transitions through various states. The state of a moving object is modeled as a state-transition diagram (Fig. 2). Exploiting temporal locality of mobility patterns, the update policy phase is decomposed into small fractions of update state such as UP_PAUSE, UP_LINEAR, and UP_RANDOM. Each update state consists of an update policy that is how the location information of an object is reflected in the location databases, the state-transition function determining the next states of the object, and information relative to the state. Due to lack of space, we omit the details of other states.

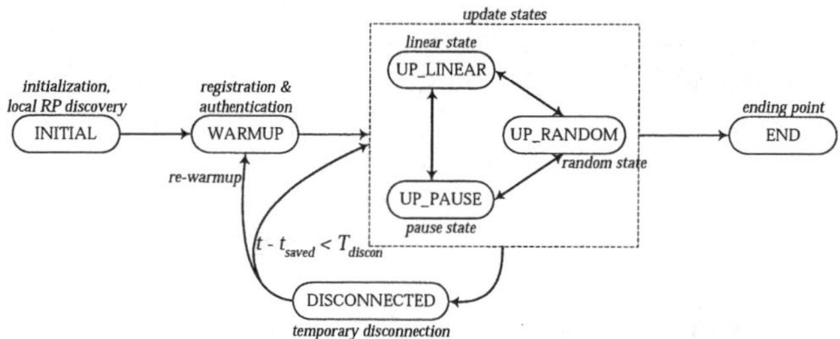


**Fig. 2.** The state transition diagram for the SLUP protocol

As mentioned previously, each moving object performs not only the current update policy but also the others. Then the optimal update policy with the minimum UITR can be decided without any difficulty. The additional cost, a few memory and a small number of operation, are acceptable owing to its reflective effectiveness in the location update cost and the development of hardware technology. We provide a detailed algorithm in Fig. 3.

**Definition 5.** *The SLUP Protocol is based on the SMM model we proposed, and is represented by a finite set of update policy called* update policy list $\mathcal{UPL} = \{\mu_1, \mu_2, \cdots, \mu_N\}$ *and the optimal update policy index* opt.

**Definition 6.** *An update policy $\mu$ is a 6-tuple $(\hat{l}, f, C, UWin, IWin, \delta)$ consisting of the estimated location $\hat{l}$ by $f$, a location estimation function $f$, the cost function $C$, the update window $UWin$, the imprecision window $IWin$, and a predefined location uncertainty $\delta$.*

**Algorithm** *State-based Location Update Protocol*
**Input:** A set of update policies $\mathcal{UPL} = \{\mu_P, \mu_L, \mu_R\}$

**repeat**
  **do for** each state $\mu_i \in \mathcal{UPL}$
    **do** $\hat{l}_i \leftarrow f_i(t)$
      **if** $d(\hat{l}_i, l_{now}) > \delta_i$
        **then** $UWin_i[t \textbf{ mod } uwnd_i] \leftarrow$ **true**
          $\hat{l}_i \leftarrow l_{now}$  // pseudo-update
        **else** $UWin_i[t \textbf{ mod } uwnd_i] \leftarrow$ **false**
      $IWin_i[t \textbf{ mod } iwnd_i] \leftarrow d(\hat{l}_i, l_{now})$
      $C_i \leftarrow computeCost(UWin_i, IWin_i)$
  $opt \leftarrow \arg\min_{i \in S} C_i$
  **if** $\mu_{opt}$ is pseudo-updated
    **then** $SendUpdateMsg(opt, \hat{l}_{opt}, f_{opt}, \delta_{opt}, t)$ to LocationServer.
  $t \leftarrow t + 1$
**until** satisfy termination condition

**Fig. 3.** Algorithm for SLUP Protocol

## 5 Performance Evaluation

Since the real datasets in spatio-temporal database are very hard to achieve, the method of synthesizing data is widely used in the literature [2,6,7]. Based on the instance $S_0$ of SMM Model in Section 3, we employ the following state transition matrices $\mathbf{L}(\ell)$ and $\mathbf{T}(\tau)$ by omitting state $P$.

$$\mathbf{L}(\ell) = \begin{matrix} & L & R \\ L & \frac{\ell}{\ell+1} & \frac{1}{\ell+1} \\ R & \frac{\ell}{\ell+1} & \frac{1}{\ell+1} \end{matrix}, \quad \textit{where } 0 \leq \ell \leq \infty \text{ and } \tau = \sqrt{\ell/(\ell+1)^2}. \tag{2}$$

$$\mathbf{T}(\tau) = \begin{matrix} & L & R \\ L & \tau & 1-\tau \\ R & 1-\tau & \tau \end{matrix}, \quad \textit{where } \ell = 1 \text{ and } 0 \leq \tau \leq 1. \tag{3}$$

The first mobility pattern is the pure *random-walk* situation, $\mathbf{L}(0)$. If the moving objects exist in the dimension $\mathbb{R}^d$, it means that the probability of movement to all directions is the same. The movement vector extracted from uniform distribution in the range of $[-v_{max}, +v_{max}]$ in each dimension. On the other hand, we may consider a linear mobility pattern for all moving objects, $\mathbf{L}(\infty)$. In this situation, the trajectory of movements is almost straight line. We assume the constant speed in this situation and the movement vector is generated by the same way with random state. But the mobility patterns are more realistic if the two characteristics of movements, random-walk and linear mobility, are mixed appropriately because the mobility patterns for the real world may be both of all. Therefore, these mobility patterns are required for an approximate pattern to real world. We can generate the workloads by changing the linearity and locality.

Firstly, we discuss the impact of varying *linearity* $\ell$. The experiment is performed on the transition matrix $\mathbf{L}(0) \sim \mathbf{L}(\infty)$ with 1,000 moving objects during 1,000 generations. And the maximum speed $v_{max}$ of all objects is 0.005. Fig. 4 shows the average number of update messages and the average imprecision for an object with varying *linearity* $\ell$ and $\delta$ parameters. In the distance-based approach, increasing the linearity gave rise to increasing the number of update messages. This is because the displacement of L state is comparatively larger than that of R state in the same amount of time. The average update count of distance-based approach to linear movement patterns is approximately $\frac{\sqrt{2}}{2}\frac{v_{max}}{\delta}$. On the other hand, the linear functional approach performs very well in the case of increasing linearity. Above all, the performance has increased considerably when the parameter *linearity* bigger than 1.0. The proposed approach has outperformed than the MOST approach in the every case of varying linearity.

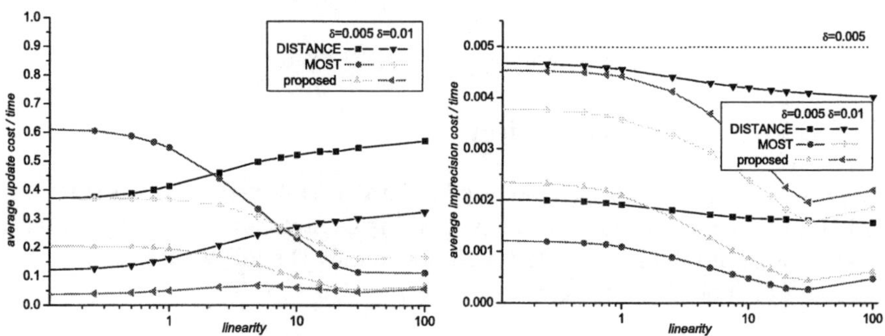


**Fig. 4.** The average update cost and imprecision cost with varying *linearity*

Secondly, we discuss the impact of varying *locality*. The experiment is performed on the transition matrix $\mathbf{T}(0) \sim \mathbf{T}(1)$ with 1,000 moving objects during 1,000 generations. And the maximum speed $v_{max}$ of all objects is 0.005. The matrix $\mathbf{T}(\tau)$ can be defined as a state-transition matrix with fixed *linearity* 1.0 and varying *locality* $\tau$. In respect of the matrix, the quantity of random movements is identical with that of linear movements, for the linearity is fixed to 1.0. However, a transition matrix with larger locality is likely to have more linear movements than the opposite one. The linear functional approach, therefore, will be advantageous for a larger locality under the same linearity. Fig. 5 shows the average number of update messages and the average imprecision for an object with varying *locality* $\tau$ and $\delta$ parameters. In the distance-based approach, increasing the locality gave rise to increasing the number of update messages. Since the linearity is fixed to 1.0, such performance degradation in the previous section can be avoided. Like the previous results, moreover, the performance of proposed approach is likely to have the same curve as that of MOST approach. The proposed approach has outperformed than the MOST in the every case of varying linearity.

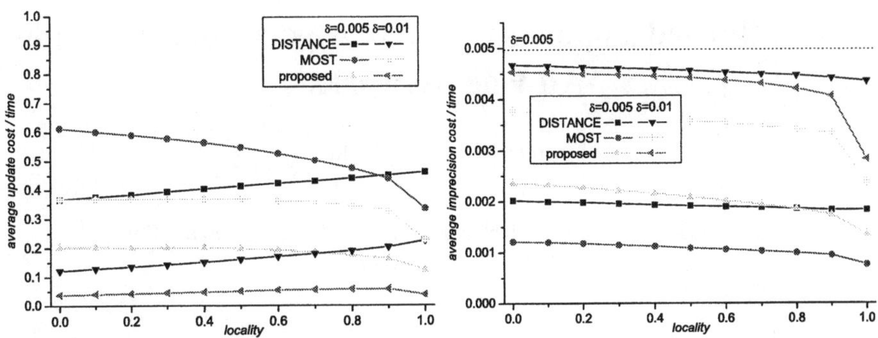


**Fig. 5.** The average update cost and imprecision cost with varying *locality*

# 6 Conclusions

We conclude that a generalized mobility model for moving objects database is crucial for location-based services and mobile computing environments. Few studies have been done in the literature. In order to provide efficient location update strategy, we have proposed a new mobility model called SMM to describe movement patterns of real-life objects in probabilistic manners. As we assumed, this approach outperforms in the mixed situation with linear movements and random movements. Moreover, in every case, the proposed approach outperforms the dead-reckoning approach (MOST).

# References

1. A. Bhattacharya ans S. K. Das. "LeZi-Update: An Information-Theoretic Approach to Track Mobile Users in PCS Networks," *Proc. ACM/IEEE Int. Conf. on Mobile Computing and Networking*, 1999.
2. T. Brinkhoff. "Generating Network-Based Moving Objects," *Proc. Int'l Conf. Scientific and Statistical Database Management*, 2000.
3. T. Kunz, Atif A. Siddiqi, and John Scourias. "The Peril of Evaluating Location Management Proposals," *Wireless Networks*, 2001.
4. D.L. Minh. *Applied Probability Models*, Brooks/Cole Pub., 2001.
5. E. Pitoura and G. Samaras. "Locating Objects in Mobile Computing," *IEEE Trans. on Knowledge and Data Engineering*, 2001.
6. D. Pfoser and Y. Theodoridis. "Generating Semantics-Based Trajectories of Moving Objects," *Workshop on Emerging Technologies for Geo-Based App.*, 2000.
7. J.-M Saglio and J. Moreira. "Oporto: A Realistic Scenario Generator for Moving Objects," *DEXA Workshop on Spatio-Temporal Data Models and Languages*, 1999.
8. O. Wolfson, A. P. Sistla, S. Chamberlain, and Y. Yesha. "Updating and Querying Databases that Track Mobile Units," *Distributed and Parallel Databases*, 1999.
9. M.-H. Yang, L.-W. Chen, Y.-C. Tseng, and J.-P. Sheu. "A Traveling Salesman Mobility Model and Its Location Tracking in PCS Networks," *ICDCS*, 2001.

# An Optimized Topology Control Algorithm for Mobile Ad Hoc Networks[1]

Daohua Yuan and Zhishu Li

Department of Computer, Sichuan University, 610064, Chengdu, China
ydhct@scu.edu.cn

**Abstract.** Ad hoc wireless networks have received significant attention in recent years. An ad hoc wireless network is an infrastructureless network composed of mobile nodes. Each node acts as a router and moves in an arbitrary manner. The primary concerns in ad hoc networks are resource limitations (such as operational energy, bandwidth, etc.) and unpredictable topology changes. Considerable research has been done on routing in ad hoc networks, but the research on topology control has received little attention. This paper proposes a distributed topology control algorithm for mobile ad hoc networks. It maintains the connected topology using minimum power through finding the closest node pairs between different partitions of the network. The algorithm combines with some routing protocol (such as link-state protocol), so there is hardly additional control overhead to the topology control mechanism. The performance of multihop mobile wireless networks and the network lifetime can be substantially increased with topology control.

**Keywords.** Ad hoc mobile wireless network, Topology control, Network partition, Connectivity maintenance, Power optimisation.

## 1 Introduction

Wireless communications among mobile users is becoming more and more popular than ever before. There are two distinct approaches for enabling wireless mobile computers to communicate with each other. The first is to utilize the existing cellular network infrastructure originally developed for voice communications using cellular phones. The other approach is to let users who wish to communicate with each other form an ad hoc network and collaborate amongst themselves to deliver data packets from a source to its destination possibly via one or more intermediate nodes.

An ad-hoc network is a collection of wireless mobile nodes, which form a temporary network without relaying on the existing network infrastructure or centralized administration[9]. Mobile nodes communicate with each other using multihop wireless links. Each mobile node in the network also acts as a router, forwarding data packets for other nodes. Ad hoc wireless networks have received significant attention in recent years due to their potential applications in conferences, natural disasters, battlefields, emergency and relief scenarios. In ad hoc networks,

[1] Supported by the Natural Science Foundation of China No.60073046 and Doctoral Foundation of China No.20020610007.

G. Dong et al. (Eds.): WAIM 2003, LNCS 2762, pp. 360–368, 2003.

since mobile nodes move randomly, disconnections occur frequently, and this causes frequent network topology changes even network partitions. Therefore maintaining strong connectivity is an important requirement of ad hoc network. Additionally, the lifetime of a wireless mobile network that is operating on battery power is limited by the capacity of its energy source. Minimizing power consumption in ad hoc network has been one of the major design goals.

Topology control in ad hoc networks is intended to create and maintain desired topology (such as connected network) by adjusting and optimizing the use of transmission power of each node. The improper topology can considerably reduce the capacity and performance, increase the end-to-end packet delay, decrease the robustness to node failures, and shorten network lifetime. In a multihop wireless network, each node is expected to potentially send and receive messages from many nodes. After the network partitions, mobile nodes in the different partitions can not communicate with each other. So we need to control the topology of ad hoc networks to maintain the efficient communications between nodes. Topology control is usually done by changing the transmit and receive powers of nodes in an ad hoc network. In this paper, we propose a distributed topology control algorithm for mobile ad hoc networks. It maintains the connected topology using minimum power through finding the closest node pairs between different partitions. Consequently, an energy efficient link (with minimized power consumption) is set up between two different partitions. Energy efficient routes directly impact (extend) the network lifetime.

## 2 Related Works

Although the problem domain is fairly clear, there has been only a limited amount of work in the general area of topology control and network design, especially for mobile ad hoc network. Hu [1] describes a distributed, Delaunay triangulation-based algorithm for choosing logical links and as a consequence carrying out topology control. In choosing these links he follows a few heuristic guidelines such as not exceeding an upper bound on the degree of each node and choosing links that create a regular and uniform graph structure. He does not take advantage of adaptive transmission power control. Ramanathan and Rosales-Hain [2] describe two centralized optimum algorithms for creating connected and bi-connected static networks with the objective of minimizing the maximum transmission power for each node. Additionally, they describe two distributed heuristic algorithms for mobile networks, that adjust node transmit powers in response to topological changes and attempt to maintain a connected topology using minimum power. Their reasoning and algorithms are based on simple heuristics and consequently do not guarantee network connectivity in all cases. Rodoplu and Meng [3] propose an ingenious distributed topology control algorithm that guarantees connectivity of the entire network. Their algorithm relies on a simple radio propagation model for transmit power roll-off as $1/d^n$, $n \geq 2$. Using this they achieve the minimum power topology, which contains the minimum-power paths from each node to a designated master-site node. Wattenhofer and LiLi etc [4] propose a novel distributed cone-based topology control algorithm, that increases network lifetime by determining the minimal operational power requirement for each node while guarantying the same maximum connected node set as when all nodes are transmitting with maximum power. They prove that the algorithm is correct (results in a connected graph) and the routes that can be found in the graph are power efficient while cone with angle $\alpha \leq 2\pi/3$ and $\alpha \leq \pi/2$ respectively.

The current studies in topology control mainly limit to static ad hoc networks. Few papers address topology control in mobile ad hoc networks, and there are not good solutions to this problem. [2] presents two distributed heuristic algorithms for mobile networks, LINT and LILT. LINT uses locally available neighbor information collected by a routing protocol, and attempts to keep the degree(number of neighbors) of each node bounded, consequently desired transmit power. In order to keep desired degree, the node needs to increase or decrease its operational power. Let $d_c$ and $p_c$ denote, respectively, the current degree and current transmit power, and $d_d$ and $p_d$ denote, respectively, the desired degree and targeted transmit power of a node. The following equation (1) can be used to calculate the new power periodically. The value of $\varepsilon$ is usually between 2 and 5, depending on the environment.

$$p_d = p_c - 5 \cdot \varepsilon \cdot \log(d_d / d_c) \quad (1)$$

In LINT, the power optimization is done in an indirect manner by limiting the number of neighbors, and is at best a poor approximation to an optimal solution. A significant shortcoming of LINT is its incognizance of network connectivity and the consequent danger of a network partition. LILT also uses the freely available neighbor information, but additionally exploits the global topology information that is available with some routing protocols such as link-state protocols[2]. There are two main parts to LILT – the neighbor reduction protocol (NRP) and the neighbor addition protocol (NAP). The NRP is essentially the LINT mechanism. The NAP is triggered whenever an event driven or periodic link-state update arrives. Its purpose is to override the high threshold bounds on the node degree and increase the power if the topology change indicated by the routing update results in undesirable connectivity.

A node receiving a routing update first determines which of three states the updated topology is in – disconnected, connected but not biconnected, or biconnected. If it is biconnected, no action is taken. If it is disconnected, the node increases its transmit power to the maximum possible value. If it is connected, but not biconnected, the node first finds its distance from the closest articulation point. An articulation point is a node whose removal will partition the network. The node then sets a timer for a value *t* that is randomized around an exponential function of the distance from the articulation point. If after time *t* the network is still not biconnected, the node increases its power to the maximum possible.

In LILT, the NRP reduces the powers to an appropriate level in time.

## 3 Algorithm Description

The transmit power adjustment in LILT described in section II is not optimized in that it is possible that the network over-reacts by having multiple nodes maximize their power for fixing the connectivity. What is not optimized is embodied on two aspects:

• Which nodes should increase their transmit powers to fix the connectivity?

• What levels should these nodes increase their powers to? (Not necessarily maximum)

Additionally, above algorithms do not guarantee network connectivity in all cases. In LILT, when a node maximizes its transmit power, the other side node may not increase its power correspondingly. This results in that formed link is unidirectional.

In this paper, we want to discuss topology control for mobile ad hoc networks. Our algorithm is an optimization and improvement of algorithms proposed in [2], and guarantees network connectivity in all cases. It also exploits the global topology information provided by link-state routing protocol, that is available locally at every node. Such global connectivity information is used to recognize and repair network partitions. So our algorithm is a distributed, global topology information based, topology control algorithm. Its objective is fixing network connectivity using minimum power when the network partitions in mobile ad hoc networks.

The Optimized Link State Routing(OLSR) protocol, as a working document of the Internet Engineering Task Force (IETF), is available for mobile ad hoc networks [7]. OLSR is an optimization over the pure(normal) link state protocol, tailored for mobile ad hoc networks. Firstly, it reduces the size of the control messages: rather than declaring all links, a node declares only a subset of links with its neighbors, namely the links to those nodes which are its MPR (Multipoint Relay) selectors. Secondly, OLSR minimizes the flooding overhead of control traffic by using only selected nodes, called MPRs, to forward the broadcast packets. This technique significantly reduces the number of retransmissions in a flooding or broadcast procedure. MPRs enable a better scalability in the distribution of topology information.

Our algorithm is based on the following assumptions:

• It is position-based, assuming each node equipped with a global positioning unit (GPS).

• It exploits periodical routing updates and maintains the network connectivity, assuming that we select the periodical time interval that makes only one node move during each period.

• Each node in the network maintains topological information about the network, using the adjacency list.

This algorithm is applicable to the ad hoc network that its size is not very large, so that the link-state updates can be efficiently propagated within the related partitions, and the network mobility is not high.

### 3.1 General Idea of Our Algorithm

Ad hoc network topology is highly dynamic due to frequent node migration, and this causes frequent network division. Mobile nodes in the different partitions can not communicate and access data with each other. Therefore, maintaining the connectivity is significant for mobile ad hoc networks. We expect to recover the network connectivity using minimum power through finding the closest node pairs between different partitions. Assume that network topology is divided into following three partitions (connected components) due to node's movement, as in Figure 1:

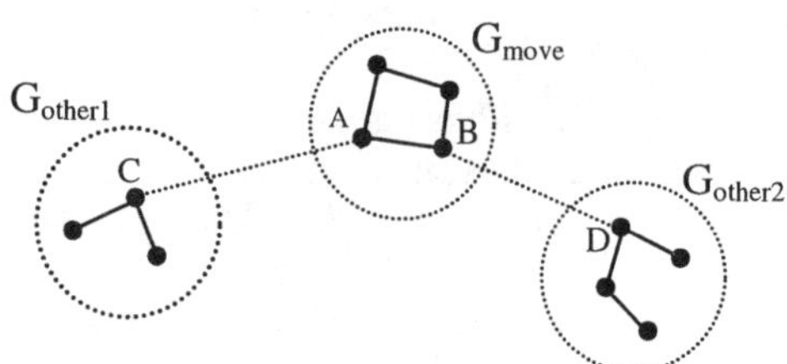


**Fig. 1.** Network partitions due to node's movement

$G_{move}$ is the partition where the moving node is, determined by the position information in the received link-state update packet. For fixing the network connectivity, we need to connect together these components. Our algorithm centers on component $G_{move,}$ because those nodes in $G_{move}$ have the full knowledge about the global network topology after the network partitions.

• Each node in $G_{move}$ calculates and finds the closest node pairs between $G_{move}$ and every other component in order to connect them. In above diagram, the closest node pairs between $G_{move}$ and $G_{other1}$ are (A, C), and the closest node pairs between $G_{move}$ and $G_{other2}$ are (B, D).

• If the node belongs to some selected node pairs, it (here, A and B) increases its transmit power, according to the distance of the node pairs, so that a link can be set up between the node pairs. Moreover, it sends a *link-setup* message to the other node of the node pairs.

• When the other node in other component receives the *link-setup* message, it increases its transmit power correspondingly to set up a symmetric link between the node pairs. Consequently, the two components the node pairs are in are connected.

The *link-setup* message carries updated global topology information.

### 3.2 Detail Description of Our Algorithm

In ad hoc networks, the node movement and adjustment of transmit power may cause link up/downs. In many routing protocols, this causes routing updates. Our algorithm uses periodical link-state routing update protocol in order to propagate changing network topology information in time. In our approach, the link-state update packet exchanged between nodes has following format:

| Sender | Position | Sequence number | Adjacent link-state updates (or Neighbors information) |
|---|---|---|---|

*Sender* is the source node sending out the link-state update packet. *Position* denotes current location of the sender. *Adjacent link-state updates* are a set of link-state updates(LSUs), where each LSU contains two endpoints of a link and a flag of up/down.

Each node detects adjacent link connectivity changes (i.e. link up/downs) using different measures, and periodically constructs and distributes the link-state update packet to other nodes if its position or adjacent link connectivity changes.

When a node receives the routing updates (link-state updates) from other nodes, it updates current network topology and determine whether or not the updated topology is connected. If it is connected, no action is taken. If the updated topology is not connected, the node attempts to participate in fixing this disconnected network topology. First it identifies various connected components in the topology. Some standard graph-traversal methods can be used to identify the network connectivity and connected components [6]. In Section 5, we give a depth-first search algorithm for it. Then those nodes, in the component where the moving node is (denoted by $G_{move}$), calculate and find the closest node pairs between their component and other components, that links are needed between these node pairs in order to repair the connectivity. The closest node pair (x, y) between component $G_{move}$ and other component $G_{other\,i}$ is defined as:

$$\underset{(x,\,y)}{\text{MIN}}\ \text{distance}(l_x, l_y) \mid x \in G_{move} \wedge y \in G_{other\,i} \tag{2}$$

where $l_x$ and $l_y$ are the locations of nodes x and y respectively. If some node itself in $G_{move}$ belongs to the selected node pairs, it increases its transmit power to the value at that it is able to just reach the other node, in other component, of the node pairs. According to the well-known radio propagation model[5], the power required to support a link between two nodes separated by distance r is $r^{\alpha}$, where $\alpha$ typically takes on a value between 2 and 4 depending on the environment.

For setting up a bidirectional or symmetric link, after a node in component $G_{move}$ increases its transmit power, it send a *link-setup* message to other node of the node pairs. The *link-setup* message carries the current position of moving node and overall link-state updates(reflecting the currently entire network topology), that have not been propagated to other components due to the network partition. When other node of the node pairs receives the *link-setup* message, it increases its transmit power correspondingly (according to the distance of node pairs) for setting up a link between the node pairs and propagates the received overall link-state updates in its component. Consequently, the network connectivity is fixed and the newly global topology information is flooded to all nodes in the network.

Periodically, our algorithm propagates updates and maintains the network connectivity. So the global network topology information is known to every node before next update period. Based on the known network topology and currently received link-state updates, a node can construct new topology and identify the connectivity of the network. After the network partitions, those nodes in a connected component have the same network topology, and all nodes in component $G_{move}$ know the currently complete network topology, including the positions of all nodes in the network. Therefore these nodes can calculate exactly the distances of all node pairs between component $G_{move}$ and other components. Consequently, they can figure out the closest node pairs between different components for fixing the network connectivity.

In our algorithm, when the degree (number of neighbors) of a node is greater than a threshold value, the node reduces its operational power.

## 4 Instance Analysis

The Figure 2 (a) and (b) are the network topologies before node E moves and after E moves respectively. The links (B, E) and (E, F) are broken due to node E's movement, consequently the topology is divided into three connected components G1, G2 and G3.

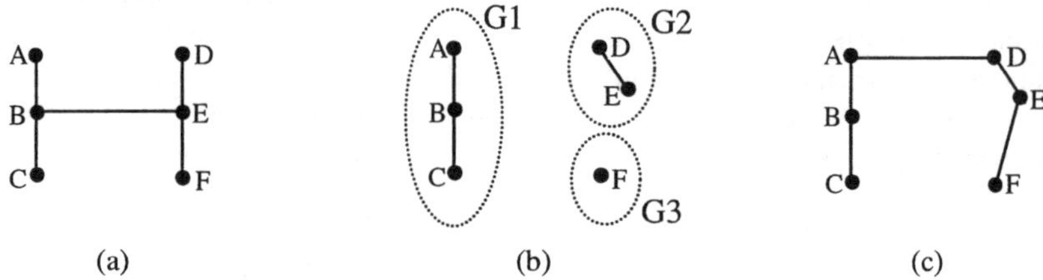


**Fig. 2.** (a) Topology before E moves (b) topology after E moves (c) topology after fixing the connectivity

Node B only detects link (B, E) failure and propagates the link-state update to all nodes in G1. Node E detects link (B, E) and (E, F) failures and propagates the link-state updates to all nodes in G2. Node F only detects link (E, F) failure and propagates the link-state update to all nodes in G3. The nodes in G1 identify the updated topology as two components G1 and G2+G3+link(E,F), not complete network topology. The nodes in G3 identify the updated topology as two components G3 and G1+G2+link(B,E), also not complete topology. The nodes in G2, the component where moving node E is, identify the updated topology as three components G1, G2 and G3, the complete network topology. Further the nodes in G2 find the closest node pairs between G2 and G1 are (D, A), and the closest node pairs between G2 and G3 are (E, F). In G2, node D increases its transmit power to be able to just reach A, according to the distance between node D and A, and sends a *link-setup* message to A. The current power level of node E is high enough to reach F, so node E does not increase its transmit power anymore, but it still sends a *link-setup* message to F. In G1, when A receives the *link-setup* message from D, it increases its transmit power to be able to just reach D and propagates the complete topology information carried by *link-setup* message in component G1. In G3, when F receives the *link-setup* message from E, it increases its transmit power to be able to just reach E and propagates the complete topology information carried by *link-setup* message in component G3. The Figure 2 (c) is the network topology after fixing the connectivity.

## 5 A Depth-First Search Algorithm for Identifying the Network Connectivity and Connected Components

We use adjacency-structure to represent the network topology graph within the computer. In the adjacency-structure, each node has an adjacency list (linked list), listing all its neighboring nodes. All nodes in the graph are numbered between 1 and *V*, where *V* is the number of nodes. An array *adj* indexed by node number, array[*1..maxV*] of *link*, points to the adjacency lists of every node. The type *link* is defined as:

type *link* = ↑*node*; *node* = record *v*: integer; *next*: *link* end;

where *v* indicates node number. The following is a depth-first search program based on the topology representation with adjacency lists.

```
procedure listdfs;
   var id,k: integer;
       val: array[1..maxV] of integer;
   procedure visit(k: integer);
      var t: link;
      begin
        id:=id+1; val[k]:=id;
        t:=adj[k];
        while t <> nil do
          begin
            if val[t↑.v]=0 then visit(t↑.v);
            t:=t↑.next
          end
      end;
   begin
     id:=0;
     for k:=1 to V do val[k]:=0;
     for k:=1 to V do
       if val[k]=0 then visit(k)
   end;
```

This program fills in an array *val*[*1..V*] as it visits every node of a topology graph. The array is initially set to all zeros, so *val*[*k*]=0 indicates that node *k* has not yet been visited. The goal is to systematically visit all the nodes of the graph, setting the *val* entry for the *id*th node visited to *id*, for *id=1, 2, …, V*. The program uses a recursive procedure *visit* that visits all the nodes in the same connected component as the node given in the argument. When ***visit(1)*** is called in last **for** statement, if all nodes in the network are visited, then the topology is connected, else partitioned. The times of nonrecursive calls to ***visit*** indicate the number of connected components that network topology is partitioned.

## 6 Conclusion

Ad hoc wireless networks have received significant attention in recent years due to their typical applications in military maneuver, emergency and disaster recovery, and so on. Considerable research has been done on routing in ad hoc networks, but the research on topology control has received little attention. This paper proposes a distributed topology control algorithm for mobile ad hoc networks. It maintains the connected topology using minimum power through finding the closest node pairs between different partitions of the network. The algorithm combines with some routing protocol (such as link-state protocol), and exploits the global topology information that is available with this routing protocol. So, there is no additional overhead to the topology control mechanism, except locally sent few *link-setup* messages. Simulation analysis demonstrates that the throughput of multihop mobile wireless networks and the network lifetime can be substantially increased with the topology control algorithm. In future research, we shall study the optimized topology control under arbitrary network mobility.

## References

1. L.Hu: Topology control for multihop packet radio networks. IEEE Trans. on Communications, vol.41, no.10, October 1993.
2. R.Ramanathan and R.Rosales-Hain: Topology control of multihop wireless networks using transmit power adjustment. in Proc. IEEE Infocom 2000, March 2000.
3. V.Rodoplu and T.H.Meng: Minimum energy mobile wireless networks. IEEE J. Selected Areas in Communications, vol.17, no.8, August 1999.
4. R.Wattenhofer and L.Li et al.: Distributed Topology Control for Power Efficient Operation in Multihop Wireless Ad Hoc Networks. in Proc. IEEE Infocom 2001, vol.3, 2001.
5. T.S.Rappaport: Wireless communications: principles and practice. Prentice Hall, 1996.
6. R.Sedgewick: Algorithms. Addison-Wesley, 1988.
7. P.Jacquet and P.Muhlethaler et al.: Optimized Link State Routing Protocol. Internet-Draft, draft-ietf-manet-olsr-04.txt, March 2001.
8. J.-H.Chang and L.Tassiulas: Energy Conserving Routing in Wireless Ad-hoc Networks. IEEE INFOCOM 2000.
9. D.B.Johnson and D.A.Maltz: Dynamic source routing in ad-hoc wireless networks. Mobile Computing, chapter 5, Kluwer Academic Publishers, 1996.

# Efficient Evaluation of Composite Correlations for Streaming Time Series

Min Wang[1] and X. Sean Wang[2]

[1] Data Management Dept., IBM T. J. Watson Research Ctr., Hawthorne, NY 10532
min@us.ibm.com

[2] ISE Department, George Mason University, Fairfax, Virginia 22030
xywang@gmu.edu

**Abstract.** In applications ranging from stock trading to space mission operations, it is important to monitor the correlations among multiple streaming time series efficiently in order to make timely decisions. The challenge is that both the number of streaming time series and the number of interested correlations can be large. The straightforward way of performing the evaluation by computing the correlation value for each relevant stream pair at each time position is not efficient enough in many situations.

In this paper, we introduce an efficient method for the case where we need to monitor composite correlations, i.e., conjunctions of high correlations among multiple pairs of streaming time series. We use a simple mechanism to predict the correlation values of relevant stream pairs at the next time position and rank the stream pairs carefully so that the pairs that are likely to have low correlation values are evaluated first. We show, through experiments, that the method significantly reduces the total number of pairs for which we need to compute the correlation values due to the conjunctive nature of the composites.

## 1 Introduction

Many applications have a need to deal with multiple streaming time series. Examples of such applications include financial applications, network monitoring, security, telecommunications data management, and sensor network. In these applications, we are usually interested in monitoring the occurrences of strong correlations among pairs of streams efficiently in order to make timely decisions. The challenge is that both the number of streaming time series and the number of interested correlations can be large. The straightforward way of performing the evaluation by computing the correlation value for each relevant stream pair at each time position is not efficient enough in many situations.

In [16], Zhu and Shasha propose efficient methods for monitoring high correlations among all pairs of streams. Their methods are based on Discrete Fourier Transform (DFT) and a three-level time interval hierarchy and can monitor the pairwise correlation of thousands of data streams in real time. For example, one can use their methods for the following application:

G. Dong et al. (Eds.): WAIM 2003, LNCS 2762, pp. 369–380, 2003.

*Example 1.* There are 5,000 stocks trading in a stock market. Report which pairs of stocks were correlated with a correlation value of over 0.95 for the last hour.

In this paper, we target at a different application scenario. Instead of monitoring high correlations among *all* pairs of streams, we assume we have knowledge of the interesting correlation patterns and need to monitor the occurrences of those interested patterns only. Such knowledge may be obtained from data mining tools on historical data. We consider the general case where the interested patterns are in the form of composite correlations, i.e., conjunctions of high correlations among multiple pairs of streaming time series. For example, our method can be used for the following application:

*Example 2.* There are 5,000 stocks, denoted as $\{s^1, s^2, \ldots, s^{5000}\}$, trading in a stock market. Give an alert, together with the corresponding pattern identifier, when any of the given patterns occurs. Two example patterns are as follows.

$p_1$ For the last hour, stocks $s^1$ and $s^2$ were correlated with a correlation value above 0.85 *and* stocks $s^1$ and $s^3$ were correlated with a correlation value above 0.75.

$p_2$ For the last hour, stocks $s^4$ and $s^5$ were correlated with a correlation value above 0.8 *and* stocks $s^6$ and $s^7$ were correlated with a correlation value above 0.7 *and* stocks $s^8$ and $s^9$ were correlated with a correlation value above 0.85.

In the above example, we want to monitor the occurrence of any pre-defined interested pattern. In practice, the number of interested patterns are usually very large while the likelihood of a pattern to be false is usually much higher than that of a pattern to be true. That is, at any time position, the number of alerts is usually very small comparing to the total number of interested patterns. In other words, we are usually monitoring *rare events.*

In this paper, we use a simple mechanism to predict the correlation values of relevant stream pairs at the next time position and rank the stream pairs carefully so that the pairs that are likely to have low correlation values are evaluated first. We show, through experiments, that the method significantly reduces the total number of pairs for which we need to compute the correlation values due to the conjunctive nature of the composites.

Correlation on time series is related to similarity-based queries on time series and streaming time series. These have attracted attention recently. For example, [4] uses an FFT (Fast Fourier Transform) and prediction-based approach to optimize queries involving streaming time series. The same authors also considered a pre-fetching algorithm when the data volume is huge [5]. However, they only discuss the operation of finding the nearest neighbor of a streaming series in isolation. Also, streaming data in general has attracted a lot of attention recently. For example, [14,2,11,1,9,3]. In terms of continuous queries, this paper deals with a special case where correlation patterns need to be monitored.

The rest of the paper is organized as follows. In the next section, we introduce some basic notation and formulate the problem. Section 3 describes our predication-based method of evaluating composite correlations for streaming time series. We present our experimental results in Section 4 and draw conclusions in Section 5.

## 2 Problem Formulation

We first define time series and streaming time series used in applications. A *time series* is a finite sequence of real numbers. A *streaming time series* is an infinite sequence of real numbers. At each time position $t$, however, the streaming time series takes the form of a finite sequence, assuming the last real number is the one that arrived at the time position $t$.

We adopt the notations in [16]. Data entries in a streaming time series are in the triple form of (*streamID*, *timePosition*, *value*). Each stream consists of all those triples having the same *streamID*. (In the above examples, a *streamID* corresponds to a stock.) The streams are synchronized.

Each stream has a new value available at every unit time interval, e.g., every second. We call the interval value index the *timePosition*. For example, if the unit time interval is second and the current time position is $i$, after one second, all the streams will have a new value with *timePosition* $i+1$.

Let $s_i$ or $s[i]$ denote the value of stream $s$ at *timePosition* $i$ and $s[i \ldots j]$ denotes the subsequence of stream $s$ from *timePosition* $i$ through $j$ inclusive. Let $s^i$ denote the stream with *streamID* $i$. We use $t$ to denote the latest *timePosition*, i.e., now.

**Definition 1.** *Consider two streams, $s$ and $r$. The* correlation value *of them are defined over a* sliding window. *Given $w$, the length of a sliding window, and $t$, the current timePosition, the current correlation value of $s$ and $r$ is computed as follow:*

$$corr(s,r) = \frac{\sum_{i=1}^{w} s_i r_i - w\overline{s}\,\overline{r}}{\sqrt{\sum_{i=1}^{w} s_i^2 - w\overline{s}^2}\sqrt{\sum_{i=1}^{w} r_i^2 - w\overline{r}^2}},$$

*where $\overline{s}$ ($\overline{r}$) is the average value of stream $s$ ($r$) over the sliding window.*

**Definition 2.** *A correlation condition is defined on a pair of streams, $s$ and $r$, and a given threshold value range $c_r = [c_l, c_h]$ ( $-1 \leq c_l \leq c_h \leq 1$). We say $s$ and $r$ are correlated with respect to $c_r$ if and only if $c_l \leq corr(s,r) \leq c_h$. We call $c_l \leq corr(s,r) \leq c_h$* a correlation term.

The correlation value[1] of any steam pair is always in the range of [-1, 1]. In most applications, we are interested in correlation condition with a high threshold value range, i.e., we are interested in the occurrence of high correlation value. By high correlation value, we mean the magnitude (absolute value) of the correlation value is large. High correlation values thus correspond to values that are close to -1 (for high negative correlations) and 1 (for high positive correlations).

[1] We use the term "correlation value" and "correlation" interchangeably.

**Definition 3.** *A composite correlation pattern is in the form of* $t_1 \wedge t_2 \wedge \ldots \wedge t_n$*, where* $t_i$ $(1 \leq i \leq n)$ *is a correlation term.*

A composite correlation pattern can be evaluated at any *timePosition* and is evaluated to be either *true* or *false* at any given *timePosition*. Different applications may have different requirements on how often a correlation pattern needs to be evaluated. Similar to [16], we subdivide the sliding windows equally into shorter windows, which we call *basic window*. The size of basic window models the time granularity of the evaluation.

Using the above definitions, the problem we address in this paper can be stated formally as follows. Given a set of streams $S = \{s^1, s^2, \ldots, s^m\}$ and a set of composite correlation patterns $P = \{p_1, p_2, \ldots, p_k\}$ defined over the streams in $S$, at each *timePosition* that corresponds to the last *timePosition* of a basic window, we want to report all the patterns in $P$ that are evaluated to be true.

## 3 Prediction-Based Evaluation of Composite Correlations

To evaluate the composite correlation patterns, a straightforward algorithm, which we call the *naive* algorithm, is to evaluate all the correlation terms for each correlation pattern at the end of each basic window. If a correlation term turns out to be false, then the pattern itself is false and we can skip evaluating the rest of the correlation terms in this pattern.

From the above naive algorithm, we see that the order of evaluation of the correlation terms in a pattern may be important. Indeed, if the a pattern is eventually evaluated false, at least one of the terms is false and an obvious strategy is to evaluate that particular term before other terms. As mentioned in the introduction, the likelihood of a pattern to be false is usually high and this strategy should help a lot in reducing computation cost.

Another observation is that when correlation terms in multiple patterns involve the same pair of streams, the computation of the correlation value on the pair of streams can be shared. Furthermore, since our intention is to look for high (positive or negative) correlations, if a pair of streams have low correlation (both positive and negative), then it is most likely that all the patterns involving this pair of streams will be false due to the false value of the term with this stream pair.

Our optimized algorithm is based on the above observations. The question remains as how we decide the order of evaluation of correlation terms. In this paper, we use a simple prediction model. Specifically, we postulate that *if a pair of streams has low correlation at the end of one basic window, it likely remains so at the end of the next basic window.* We use this simple prediction model to decide the order of the correlation evaluation of pairs of streams and quickly "falsify" patterns. The expected overall effect is reduced number of correlation calculations. We call this algorithm the *optimized algorithm*, and Figure 1 shows an outline of it.

A number of issues need consideration in the algorithm of Figure 1. The first is *how exactly the pairs are ranked* in Step 1. If there are prediction models for

<table>
<tr><td>Input:</td><td>1. A set of streaming time series.<br>2. A set of correlation patterns.<br>3. $w$, the length of the sliding window.<br>4. $b$, the length of the basic window.</td></tr>
<tr><td>Output:</td><td>At the end of each basic window, report all the correlation patterns that are evaluated true.</td></tr>
<tr><td>Method:</td><td>Let $\mathcal{SP}$ be the set of stream pairs that appear in the given correlation patterns. For each stream pair in $\mathcal{SP}$, associate it with the number of the correlation patterns it appears in. For each pair $(s, r)$, denote this as $\#P(s, r)$.<br>At the end of each basic window, restore $\#P(s, r)$ to their original value for all pairs $(s, r)$. Then do<br><br>Step 1. Rank all the pairs of streams in $\mathcal{SP}$.<br>Step 2. Evaluate the correlation of each pair $(s, r)$ of streams in the order given by Step 1. Only need to evaluate the pairs $(s, r)$ such that $\#P(s, r) > 0$.<br>1. For each correlation pattern that involves the evaluated pair, decide if it is falsified.<br>2. For each falsified pattern, go over each of stream pair $(s, r)$ in it, and reduce $\#P(s, r)$ by 1.</td></tr>
</table>

**Fig. 1.** Optimized algorithm.

time series in the application domain we are dealing with, we may use them. As mentioned earlier, we use a simple prediction model by looking at how many patterns a pair of streams falsified (Step 2.1), denoted $rej$, and in which basic window, denoted $win$, this happened (since the correlations of pairs are not calculated at every basic window). We want to "reward" the pairs with greater $rej$ value while at the same time reduce the "reward" if it happened too far in the past. Therefore, if $win$ is taken as the last *timePosition* of the basic window (hence the bigger the value, the more recent the basic window is), we use the formula

$$(win)^2 * rej$$

to give the weight to a pair. We rank all the pairs in the decreasing order of their weights. If the correlation of a pair has never been calculated, we set $win$ and $rej$ to be 0.

Another issue is the *prediction frequency*. Indeed, although in our algorithm we use a simple method, it still costs time to rank and sort. There is a tradeoff between the overhead of this cost and the gain in terms of the reduction of calculation. When done too frequently, prediction step will out-weight the gain of saving, while too infrequently, the saving in the prediction cost may not justify the loss of savings obtained from prediction. Obviously, where is the point of "best return" depends on the situation we are dealing with. In this paper, we use experiments to determine this point of best return.

## 4 Experimental Results

In this section, we describe the experiments used to evaluate the performance of our method and compare it with that of the naive method.

Through our experiments, we answer four important questions about the effectiveness of our predication-based optimization method:

1. Does the optimized algorithm significantly reduce the total number of pairs for which we need to evaluate the correlation values compared to the naive algorithm?
2. Does the optimized algorithm significant reduce the CPU time per basic window compared to the naive method?
3. Is the superiority of optimized algorithm stable with respect to the types of pattern sets?
4. Does the optimized algorithm scale well with respect to the number of streams and the number of patterns?

We implement two methods in C/C++ as our methods of comparison: the naive method and our predication-based optimization method. For our experiments, we use WinXP on an Intel Pentium 4 processor of 1.8GHZ with 256 MB of main memory.

**Data Generation.** We generate the streaming data sets using the random walk model. For stream $s$,

$$s_i = u_0 + \sum_{j=1}^{i} u_j, \qquad i = 1, 2, \ldots, L$$

where all $u_j$ ($j \geq 0$) are uniformly distributed, independent variables. Variable $u_0$ gives an integer value in $[-50, 50]$ and each $u_j$, $j > 0$, gives an integer value in [-5, 5].

A data set is modeled by two parameters: *numStream*, the number of streams in the data set, and *lenStream*, the length of each stream.

**Pattern Set Generation.** We use our own pattern generator to generate a set of interested composite correlation patterns for a given streaming data set.

To generate a pattern set, the first step is to generate the composite correlation patterns without considering the threshold value range for each correlation term. The second step is to generate the corresponding threshold range for each correlation term.

The first step is modeled by four parameters: *numPattern*, the number of composite correlation patterns in the set, *zPair*, the Zipf parameter for the frequency distribution of stream pairs, *minTerm*, the minimum number of correlation terms in a composite correlation pattern, and *maxTerm*, the maximum number of correlation terms in a composite correlation pattern.

The *zPair* parameter is not as straightforward as other parameters and needs a little more explanation. For a given stream pair $(s^i, s^j)$ and a pattern set $P$, we call the number of occurrences of term $c_l \le corr(s^i, s^j) \le c_h$ in $P$ the *occurrence frequency* of pair $(s^i, s^j)$ in $P$.

For example, suppose $P = \{p_1, p_2, p_3\}$, where

$$p_1 = \left(0.8 \le (corr(s^1, s^2) \le 0.9\right) \bigwedge \left(0.85 \le corr(s^1, s^3) \le 0.95\right),$$

$$p_2 = \left(0.6 \le corr(s^1, s^2) \le 0.7\right) \bigwedge \left(0.75 \le corr(s^2, s^3) \le 0.85\right),$$

$$p_3 = \left(0.5 \le corr(s^1, s^2) \le 0.8\right) \bigwedge \left(0.45 \le corr(s^3, s^4) \le 0.75\right),$$

then the occurrence frequencies of stream pairs $(s^1, s^2)$, $(s^1, s^3)$, $(s^2, s^3)$, and $(s^3, s^4)$ are 3, 1, 1, and 1, respectively. It is easy to understand that in most applications, the distribution of the occurrence frequency for stream pairs is usually skewed, i.e., some pairs occur more frequently than other pairs in the pattern set. As in a lot of previous work (e.g., [10,13]), we use Zipf distribution to model the skewed distribution of occurrence frequency for stream pairs [17]. A higher *zPair* value corresponds to fewer very high frequencies, i.e., a few stream pairs appear in most of the patterns while other stream pairs rarely appear.

In the second step, we generate the corresponding threshold range for each correlation term. Since we are usually interested in high correlation value, we pick the threshold range from the high ends.[2] Note that the effectiveness of our predication-based optimization method does not depend on any specific choice of the threshold range. To figure out what is the "reasonable" threshold range for a given stream pair $(s^i, s^j)$, we compute the minimum negative correlation value (*minNegCorr*), the maximum negative correlation value (*maxNegCorr*), the minimum positive correlation value (*minPosCorr*), and the maximum positive correlation value (*maxPosCorr*) for the pair. For positive correlation, we always set $c_h = maxPosCorr$ and $c_l = c_h - \alpha(maxPosCorr - minPosCorr)$, where $\alpha$ is a uniformly distributed random variable in $[minRangeSize, maxRangeSize]$.[3] Similarly, for negative correlation, we always set $c_l = minNegCorr$ and $c_h = c_l + \alpha(maxNegCorr - minNegCorr)$.

**Parameter Setting.** We show our experimental results on several representative data sets and pattern sets in Figure 2–6. Unless otherwise specified, the default values for the parameters used in the experiments are as listed in Table 1.

In the setting given by Table 1, the number of patterns that are evaluated true is around 30 at each basic window among the given 10,000 patterns. This is consistent with our assumption that the monitored events should be rare events. The CPU time that the algorithms spent for each basic window is around 30ms and 15ms for the naive algorithm and the optimized algorithm, respectively. Since the basic window has 10 data values, it is generally true that the algorithm

---

[2] By high correlation value, we mean the magnitude (absolute value) of the correlation value is large. High ends thus correspond to the correlation values that are close to -1 (for high negative correlations) and 1 (for high positive correlations).

[3] Parameters *minRangeSize* and *maxRangeSize* are specified by the user and $0 \le minRangeSize \le maxRangeSize \le 1$.

**Table 1.** Parameter setting for experiments

| *Parameter* | *Meaning* | *Default Value* |
|---|---|---|
| *numStream* | number of streams in the data set | 2,000 |
| *lenStream* | length of each stream | 10,000 |
| *w* | length of sliding window | 100 |
| *b* | length of basic window | 10 |
| *numPattern* | number of patterns in pattern set | 10,000 |
| *minTerm* | minimum number of correlation terms in a pattern | 2 |
| *maxTerm* | maximum number of correlation terms in a pattern | 5 |
| *zPair* | Zipf parameter for the frequency distribution of stream pairs | 1.3 |
| *minRangeSize* | minimum range size factor | 0.2 |
| *maxRangeSize* | maximum range size factor | 0.4 |
| *predFreq* | prediction frequency | 400 |

can handle (with the optimized algorithm) a stream rate of roughly up to 700 values per second for each stream under the default setting (with 2000 streams, among other parameters).

**Experimental Results.** In accordance with the goal of the experiments, we performed five groups of tests. In each group of tests, we pick one of the parameters shown in Table 1 and vary it in different ways while keeping the other parameters fixed to these shown in Table 1. We then measure two metrics. The first is the CPU time comparison of the naive algorithm and the optimized algorithm, and the second is the comparison of the number of correlation calculations by these two algorithms. We randomly generate data and queries as described earlier and for each combination of parameters, we perform five runs and use the average value of the five runs as the value reported in the figures.

Figure 2 reports the result of a set of tests where we only change the number of correlation patterns we deal with. In Figure 2(a), the CPU time is measured for each case. In Figure 2(b), the two algorithms are compared in terms of the number of correlation calculations. The value in the figure is the result of the formula $(n-o)/n$, where $n$ ($o$, respectively) is the number of correlation calculations performed in the naive algorithm (optimized algorithm, respectively).

From the figure, for the savings in terms of number of correlation calculations, the optimized algorithm only perform around 20-30% of the calculations that the naive algorithm does. In terms of CPU time, however, the savings is not as much due to the overhead of ranking process of the stream pairs (Step 1 in Figure 1). Also observe that the savings tend to become smaller when the number of patterns goes up, although the CPU time goes up slower for the optimized algorithm than the naive algorithm. It is due to the fact that when the number of correlation patterns increases while the number of streams stay constant, there is a tendency that the correlation patterns have fewer shared correlation terms. Thus, the effect of Step 2.2 of Figure 1 decreases. The savings will mostly be achieved in terms of the evaluation order of the correlation terms in a pattern.

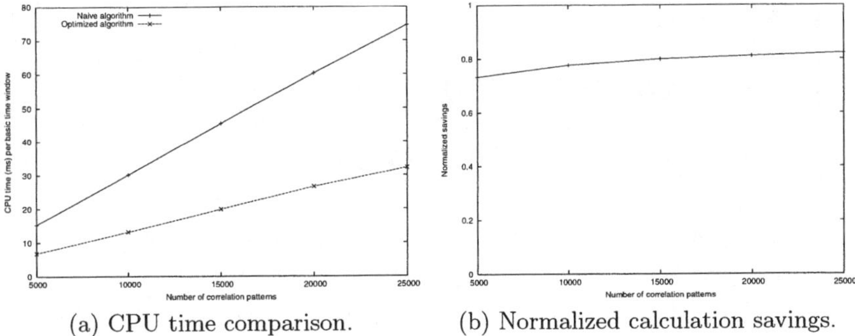


(a) CPU time comparison. (b) Normalized calculation savings.

**Fig. 2.** Scalability with number of correlation patterns.

Since the number of terms is not large (on average each pattern has 3.5 terms in the default setting), the naive algorithm will eventually perform similarly as the optimized algorithm when the number of patterns continue to go up.

Figure 3 gives the test results when the number streams is varied. Both the CPU time and the number of correlation calculations do not go up with the increase of the number of the streams. This is true for both the naive algorithm and the optimized algorithm. This is due to the fact that when the number of streams increases while the number of patterns stays the same, the number of pairs of streams that appear in patterns do not change much (due to the skewness of the selection of stream pairs). Hence, the overall performance of the algorithms is not too sensitive to the number of streams.

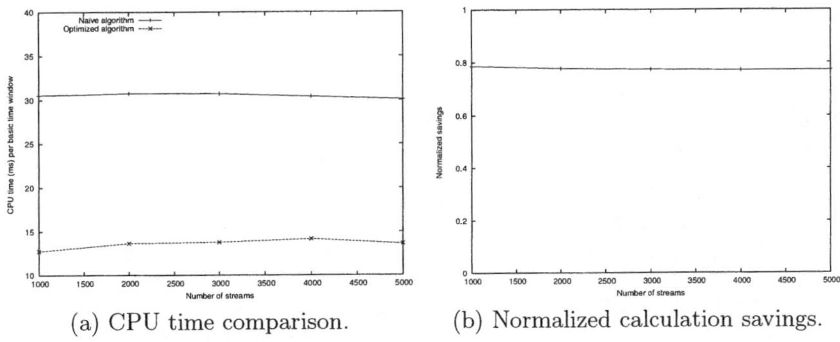


(a) CPU time comparison. (b) Normalized calculation savings.

**Fig. 3.** Scalability with number of streams.

In Figure 4, we give the test results when we change the average number of correlation terms in a pattern. The results are as expected that the savings decrease as the number of terms in a pattern goes up. Indeed, in this case, since other parameters are fixed, the number of stream pairs will increase and the effect of Step 2.2 will decrease.

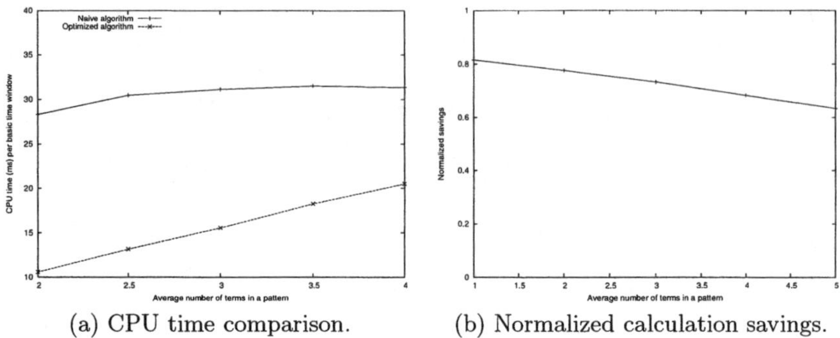


(a) CPU time comparison. (b) Normalized calculation savings.

**Fig. 4.** Scalability with number of terms in patterns.

The skewness of our patterns also has an effect on the performance of our algorithms. With less skewed pattern set, the overhead will overcome the savings, while more skewed pattern set is, the more saving we have. Experiment result in Figure 5 confirms this general trend. Note that when the Zipf value is 1.0, the naive algorithm outperforms the optimized algorithm in terms of the CPU time, while in terms of the number of calculated correlations, the optimized algorithm still wins. The reason is that the overhead of the optimized algorithm in this case cannot be compensated by the savings in the number of correlation calculations. We believe, in practice, the skew level of the pattern set is usually high.

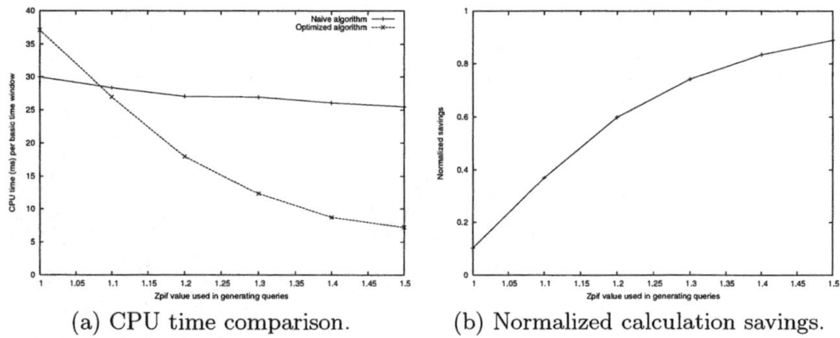


(a) CPU time comparison. (b) Normalized calculation savings.

**Fig. 5.** Effect of skewness of patterns.

As the last experiment result, we show in Figure 6 the effect of the frequency of prediction step (Step 1 of Figure 1). The general trend of the savings is consistent with our observations, namely, too frequent and too infrequent prediction step are both counterproductive. In this figure, the trend is not as clear cut as other figures and we use a fitting line in Figure 6(a) to highlight the trend. In Figure 6(b), the trend is a little clearer, i.e., in general, the more frequent (smaller step) the prediction is performed, the more saving we obtain. However, the savings may not compensate the overhead incurred. Therefore, there is usually a point of the "best return".

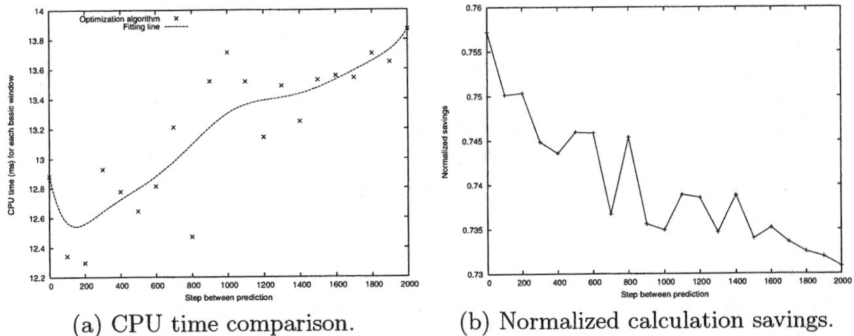


(a) CPU time comparison. (b) Normalized calculation savings.

**Fig. 6.** Effect of prediction frequency.

# 5 Conclusions

In this paper, we present a prediction-based method that can efficiently evaluate composite correlations for multiple streaming time series. We show, through experiments, that our method significantly improves the performance of the evaluation process comparing to the naive method.

While we have focused on monitoring patterns in conjunctive form, our method can easily be extended to deal with disjunctions. As a result, our method can be used to evaluate patterns in general composite forms.

There are two basic building blocks for our method: (1) an efficient algorithm for computing the correlation value for a given pair of streaming time series, and (2) an accurate and effective prediction mechanism for predicting the future correlation value of a given stream pair. We did not discuss (1) in this paper and used a very simple prediction method for (2). To improve the performance of our method, we can certainly plug in any advanced algorithm for (1), e.g., the approximation algorithm proposed in [16]. The prediction mechanism is more domain specific and we refer the interested readers to [7,8,12,6,15] for more insights.

An interesting research problem is how to handle the tradeoff between the overhead and computational saving introduced by applying the predication and ranking step in a better way. While we used a fixed predication frequency in our experiments, a better approach should be adjusting the predication frequency adaptively: the predication and ranking step should be applied when the performance drops to certain level due to inaccurate predication.

## References


1. S. Babu and J. Widom. Continuous queries over data streams. *SIGMOD Record*, 30(3):109–120, 2001.
2. J. Chen, D. J. DeWitt, F. Tian, and Y. Wang. NiagaraCQ: a scalable continuous query system for Internet databases. In *SIGMOD Conference*, pages 379–390, 2000.
3. Y. Chen, G. Dong, J. Han, B. W. Wah, and J. Wang. Multi-dimensional regression analysis of time-series data streams. In *VLDB Conference*, pages 323–334, 2002.
4. L. Gao and X. S. Wang. Continually evaluating similarity-based pattern queries on a streaming time series. In *SIGMOD Conference*, pages 370–381, 2002.
5. L. Gao and X. S. Wang. Improving the performance of continuous queries on fast data streams: Time series case. In *Workshop on Research Issues in Data Mining and Knowledge Discovery (DMKD)*, 2002.
6. T. V. Gestel, J. Suykens, D.-E. Baestaens, A. Lambrechts, G. Lanckriet, B. Vandaele, D. B. Moor, and J. Vandewalle. Financial time series prediction using least squares support vector machines within the evidence framework. *IEEE Transactions on Neural Networks*, 12(4):809–821, 2001.
7. L. Gyorfi, G. Lugosi, and G. Morvai. A simple randomized algorithm for sequential prediction of ergodic time series. *IEEE Transactions on Information Theory*, 45(7):2642–2650, 1999.
8. I. Kim and S.-R. Lee. A fuzzy time series prediction method based on consecutive values. In *Fuzzy Systems Conference Proceedings, 1999. FUZZ-IEEE '99.*, volume 2, pages 703–707, 1999.
9. S. Madden and M. J. Franklin. Fjording the stream: An architecture for queries over streaming sensor data. In *ICDE Conference*, 2002.
10. Y. Matias, J. S. Vitter, and M. Wang. Wavelet-based histograms for selectivity estimation. In *Proceedings of the 1998 ACM SIGMOD International Conference on Management of Data*, pages 448–459, Seattle, WA, June 1998.
11. B. Plale and K. Schwan. Optimizations enabled by a relational data model view to querying data streams. In *Proc. of 15th International Parallel and Distributed Processing Symposium*, page 20, 2001.
12. S. Policker and A. Geva. A new algorithm for time series prediction by temporal fuzzy clustering. In *Proceedings. 15th International Conference on Pattern Recognition*, volume 2, pages 728–731, 2000.
13. V. Poosala, Y. E. Ioannidis, P. J. Haas, and E. Shekita. Improved histograms for selectivity estimation of range predicates. In *Proceedings of the 1996 ACM SIGMOD International Conference on Management of Data*, Montreal, Canada, May 1996.
14. D. Terry, D. Goldberg, D. Nichols, and B. Oki. Continuous queries over append-only databases. In *SIGMOD Conference*, pages 321–330, 1992.
15. L. Wang, K. K. Teo, and Z. Lin. Predicting time series with wavelet packet neural networks. *Proc. International Joint Conference on Neural Networks*, 3:1593–1597, 2001.
16. D. S. Yunyue Zhu. Statstream: Statistical monitoring of thousands of data streams in real time. In *Proceedings of the 28th International Conference on Very Large Data Bases*, pages 358–369, 2002.
17. G. K. Zipf. *Human Behaviour and the Principle of Least Effort.* Addison-Wesley, Reading, MA, 1949.

# An Efficient Computational Method for Measuring Similarity between Two Conceptual Entities

Miyoung Cho[1], Junho Choi[1], and Pankoo Kim[2*]

[1] Dept. of Computer Science,
Chosun University, Gwangju 501-759 Korea
{irune80, spica}@mina.chosun.ac.kr
[2] Dept. of CSE,
Chosun University, Gwangju 501-759 Korea
pkkim@chosun.ac.kr

**Abstract.** Previous definitions of semantic similarity can be classified into two approaches. The node(information content)-based approach uses an entropy measure that is computed on the basis of child node population. The edge-based approach involves the use of the number of edges between two concepts within a hierarchical conceptual structure. The edge-based distance method is more intuitive, while the node-based information content approach is more theoretically sound. We consider a combined model that is derived from the edge-based notion with the addition of the information content. In this paper, we propose a method for computerized conceptual similarity calculation in WordNet space. The proposed method provides a degree of conceptual dissimilarity between two concepts. It gives a higher correlation value with a criterion based on human similarity judgment.

## 1 Introduction

The problem of similarity measurement has been studied in philosophy, psychology and artificial intelligence, and many different approaches to this problem have been suggested. Recent research on this topic in the area of computational linguistics has focused on the notion of semantic similarity between two concepts in a lexical resource, or its inverse, semantic distance[10]. Also, measuring the conceptual similarity is important for dealing with the uncertainty on conceptual graphs when there is only partial matching between them.

A natural way to evaluate semantic similarity in WordNet is to evaluate the distance between the nodes corresponding to the items being compared– i.e. the shorter the path from one node to another, the more similarity they have. However, one problem with this approach is that it doesn't consider the other factors (e.g. link type, link density, etc.) included in WordNet. There are many potential types of relations that can be considered: hierarchical(e.g. IS-A, HAS_PART, etc.), associative(e.g. cause-effect), equivalence(synonymy), etc.

In this paper, we propose a method for computerized conceptual similarity calculation in WordNet space. The proposed similarity model considers edge, depth, link type and

* Corresponding author

G. Dong et al. (Eds.): WAIM 2003, LNCS 2762, pp. 381–388, 2003.

link density, as well as the existence of common ancestors. Therefore, the proposed method provides a means of measuring the degree of conceptual dissimilarity between two concepts. Among these, the hierarchical relation represents the major and most important type, and has been widely studied and applied as it maps well to the Nyman cognitive view of classification.

This paper is organized as follows. Section 2 discusses related works. Section 3 describes semantic similarity measurement between concepts in WordNet. Section 4 presents a performance evaluation of similarity measurement in comparison with human similarity judgment, using the simple edge-based method and node-based method. This paper concludes with section 5.

## 2 Related Works

The node(information content)-based approach uses an entropy measure that is computed on the basis of child node population. Even though this method is derived from solid theory, it does not use the conceptual structure provided by ontology. Moreover, its similarity measure is too coarse. The edge-based conceptual distance measurement makes use of a more perceptually natural approach. A semantic distance, in this approach, is defined by the number of edges between two concepts within a hierarchical conceptual structure.

However, due to the composition of the hierarchical structure of the ontology, the depth-scaling factor does not adjust the overall similarity computation. We found, in our experiments, that most unexpected similarity calculations are caused by the following factors:

① Ambiguity in the concept classification hierarchy on the top-level ontology
② No consideration of connection strength between concepts.
③ Similarity measurement is too coarse.

The first problem arises due to the fact that most lexicographical ontologies, such as WordNet, are not developed with formal concept analysis. The second is related to the similarity calculation function itself. However, in certain cases the depth factor and edge type factor are not able to discriminate between two semantic distances correctly, even though the two conceptual entities originate from two distinct conceptual entities. The integration of information content with the edge-based approach proposed by [6] simply adds two supplementary factors to the similarity calculation. In addition, it requires ad-hoc assignments of the depth factor and density factor.

## 3 Semantic Similarity Measurement between Concepts

Two widely accepted approaches for measuring the semantic similarity between two conceptual entities in a given ontology are the node-based approach and the edge-based approach.

### 3.1 Node-Based (Information Content) Approach

The information content of a conceptual entity, $H(c)$ is measured by using the number of words that are subsumed by $c$.

$$H(c) = -\log P(c) \tag{1}$$

where $P(c)$ is the probability of encountering an instance of the concept $c$. As the node's probability increases, its information content decreases. If there is a unique top node in the hierarchy, then its probability is 1, hence its information content is 0.

Resnik[3] proposed the following similarity measure between conceptual entities using information content.

$$sim(c_1, c_2) = \max_{c \in S(c_1, c_2)} [-\log p(c)] \tag{2}$$

where, $S(c_1, c_2)$is the set of concepts that subsume both $c_1$ and $c_2$. To maximize the representative, the similarity value is set to the information content value of the node, whose H(c) value is the largest among these super classes. From Figure 1, we find that the similarity between car and bicycle is the information content value of vehicle, which has the maximum value among all the classes that subsume both of the two concepts, i.e. *sim*(car,bicycle)=**H**(vehicle). In contrast, *sim*(car, fork)=**H**(artifact). These results conform to our perception that car and fork are less similar than car and bicycle.

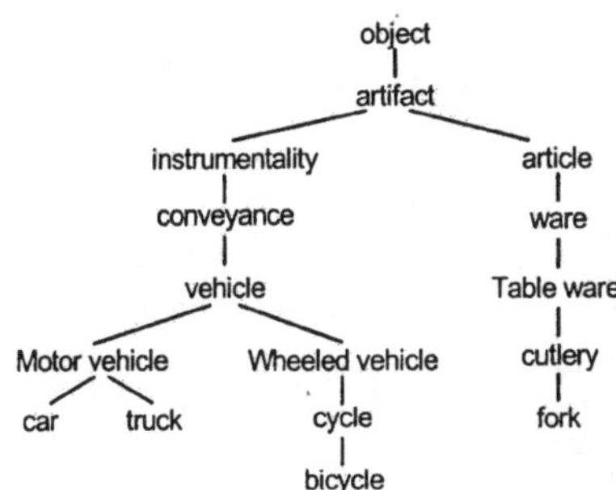


**Fig. 1.** Similarity between car, bicycle and fork

### 3.2 Edge-Based (Distance) Approach

The edge based approach is a more natural and direct way of evaluating semantic similarity in WordNet. It estimates the distance(e.g. edge length) between nodes. Sussna[2] defined the similarity distance between two conceptual entities as a weighted path length.

A weight between two conceptual entities is defined as follows:

$$w(c_x \rightarrow_r c_y) = \max_r - \frac{\max_r - \min_r}{n_r(x)} \tag{3}$$

$$w(c_i, c_j) = \frac{w(c_i \rightarrow_r c_j) + w(c_j \rightarrow_{r'} c_i)}{2d} \tag{4}$$

The symbols ,$\rightarrow_r$ and $\rightarrow_{r'}$, represent a relation type $r$ and its reverse. $max_r$ and $min_r$ are the maximum and minimum weights possible for a specific relation type, $r$, respectively. $n_r(x)$ is the number of relations of type r leaving a conceptual entity, $x$. Therefore, the $w(c_i \rightarrow_r c_j)$ measurement considers both the density of the connections and the connection type. Finally, the similarity distance,$d$, between two concepts is defined as the minimum path length.

### 3.3 Proposed Similarity Measurement

We propose a combined model that is derived from the edge-based notion with the addition of the information content. With careful investigation of ontological structures such as WordNet, we considered the following facts:

(1) There is a correlation between conceptual similarity and the number of shared parent concepts in the conceptual hierarchy.
(2) A link type indicates a semantic relation between two conceptual entities such as IS_A, HAS_PART, and so on. Therefore, the link type should be taken into consideration in the conceptual closeness calculation.
(3) From the top to the bottom, any conceptual closeness between a node and its adjacent child node may not be equal.
(4) As depth increases, the conceptual closeness between a given node and its adjacent child node decreases(Classification Resolution Factor).
(5) Information content is based on the population of nodes. However, population is not uniform over the entire ontological structure. Certain nodes may have hundreds of children.

Our method of measuring the similarity between two concepts is based on the above observations. First of all, let us assume that the semantic distance between two adjacent nodes(one of them is a parent) is represented by the following equation :

$$S_{ADJ}(c_i^l, c_j^{l-1}) = d(c_{j \rightarrow i}^l) \cdot f(d) \tag{5}$$

where, $f(d)$ is a function that returns a depth factor. Depth is its topological location in a conceptual space(WordNet). In the above equation, $c^l$, refers to the concept at the topological location, $l$. As the depth level increases, the classification is based on finer and finer criteria. So the depth of a node containing a concept is deeper, and so $f(d)$ returns a larger value. $d(c_{j \rightarrow i}^l)$ indicates the density function. Since the overall semantic mass is of a certain amount for a given node, the density effect would suggest that the greater the density, the closer the distance between the nodes[4]. To explain this, as can be seen in Figure 2, it can be argued that the parent node, *Life_form,* is more strongly connected with the child nodes, *Animal*, *Plant* and *Person*, than with the nodes, *Aerobe* and *plankton*. In order to incorporate this factor into our calculations, we used the reciprocal of the difference between the parent node and the child node.

We will expand $S_{ADJ}(c_i^l, c_j^{l-1})$ to handle the case where more than one edge is included in the shortest path between two concepts. Suppose we have the shortest path, $p$,

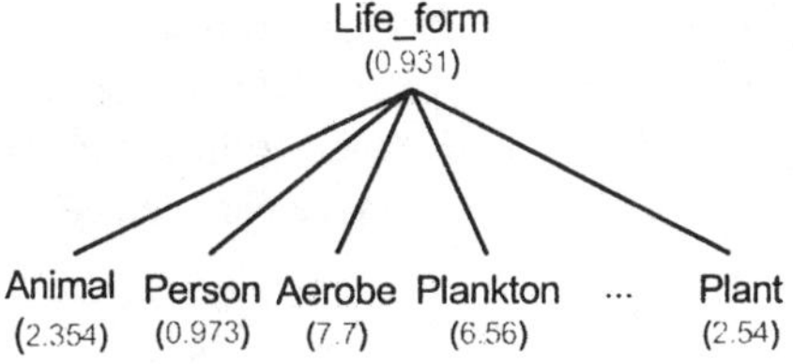


**Fig. 2.** Tree between Life_form and its child nodes

from two concepts, $c_i$ and $c_j$, such that $p = \{(t_0, c_0, c_1), (t_1, c_1, c_2)...(t_{n-1}, c_{n-1}, c_n\}$. The shortest path $p$ is the sum of the adjacent nodes. Therefore, the distance measure between $c_i$ and $c_j$ is as follows:

$$S_{edge}(c_i, c_j) = D(L_{j \to i}) \cdot \sum_{k=0}^{n} W(t_k) \cdot S_{ADJ}(c_k, c_{k+1}) \tag{6}$$

where, $D(L_{j \to i})$is a function that returns a distance factor between $c_i$ and $c_j$. The shorter the path from one node to the other, the more similar they are. So, the distance between two nodes, $c_i$ and $c_j$, is in inverse proportion to their similarity. $W(t_k)$ indicates the weight function that decides the weight value based on the link type. The simplest form of the weight function is the step function. If the edge type is IS_A, then $W(t)$ returns 1 and otherwise returns a certain number that is more than 1 or less than 1. If the weight function is well-defined, it may return a negative value when the two concepts involved are associated by an antonym relation. However, the similarity between two concepts cannot be represented by a negative value. So we assume that the value of the antonym relation is the lowest positive value.

Equation 6 only considers the link types and the number of edges. What is missing in equation 6 is a means of taking into account shared concepts(as the number of shared concepts increases, the similarity also increases). To incorporate this into our similarity measurement, we propose the following equation.

$$S(c_i, c_j) = S_{edge} \cdot max[H(c)] \tag{7}$$

where, $H(c)$is the information content of the concept that subsumes both $c_i$ and $c_j$. The above equation tells us that the total amount of similarity is proportional to the amount of shared information.

### 3.4 Example of Similarity Calculation

In the similarity comparison (see Figure 3), the semantic distance calculated using the distance and relation between the nodes, $S^d(automobile\sharp boot, footware\sharp boot)$ is (9×1.5×1+9×2+9×3+9×4+9×5+9×6)+(9×6+9×5+9×4) = 328.5. In figure 3, $level$ means depth and $w$is the weight of each relation type(note, the weight of HAS_PART is 1.5).

Let us consider three conceptual entities, “covering”, “transport”, and “automobile”. Conceptually, automobile is much closer to transport than covering. The number of links from covering to transport, and from automobile to transport is the same (they are both 3). With our calculation, 9×6+9×6+9×5 = 153 is the distance from covering to transport. However, 9×2+9×3+9×4 = 81 is the distance from automobile to transport. So far, we have demonstrated how the semantic distance between conceptual entities appear as nouns in a conceptual hierarchy.

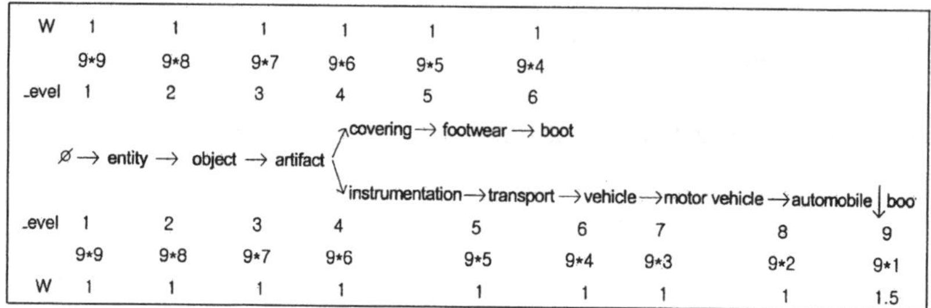


**Fig. 3.** Conceptual similarity calculations

## 4 Analysis of Similarity Measurement

It would be reasonable to evaluate the performance of similarity measurements between concepts by comparing them with human ratings. The simplest way to implement this is to set up an experiment to rate the similarity of a set of word pairs. Also, we can present the correlation between human judgment and machine calculations using the correlation coefficient.

We used the noun portion of the latest version 1.6 of WordNet. It contains about 60,000 noun nodes (synsets). To make our experimental results comparable to those of other previous methods, we decided to use the same sample of 30 noun pairs. The M&C means are the average ratings for each pair, as determined by Miller and Charles[1]. This list includes only 30 noun pairs and is usually used for experiments involving similarity measurement. The replication means are taken from the special web site for word similarity
(http://www.cs.technion.ac.il/~gabr/resources/data/wordsim353/wordsim353.html). Table 1 lists the complete results of each similarity rating measure for each word pair, as determined by various methods, such as the node-based and edge based methods, as well as our proposed method.

To evaluate the similarity measurement of the proposed method, we use correlation values. For consistency in comparison, we will use semantic similarity measures rather than semantic distance measures.

Note that this conversion does not affect the result of the evaluation, since a linear transformation of each datum will not change the magnitude of the resulting correlation coefficient, although its sign may change from positive to negative. The correlation values between the similarity ratings and the mean ratings reported by Millers and Charles are

**Table 1.** Word pair semantic similarity measurement

| Word pair | | M&C means | Replication means | Sim. means by node based | Sim. means by edge based | Sim. means by our system |
|---|---|---|---|---|---|---|
| Car | automobile | 3.92 | 8.94 | 7.45 | 32 | 11.95 |
| Gem | Jewel | 3.84 | 8.96 | 12.54 | 32 | 14.7 |
| journey | Voyage | 3.84 | 9.29 | 6.87 | 31 | 11.18 |
| boy | Lad | 3.76 | 8.83 | 7.44 | 31 | 10.86 |
| coast | Shore | 3.7 | 9.1 | 8.67 | 31 | 11.74 |
| asylum | Madhouse | 3.61 | 8.87 | 10.93 | 31 | 13.78 |
| magician | Wizard | 3.5 | 9.02 | 9.5 | 32 | 13.34 |
| midday | Noon | 3.42 | 9.29 | 10.24 | 32 | 13.82 |
| furnace | Stove | 3.11 | 8.79 | 2.4 | 25 | 5.83 |
| food | Fruit | 3.08 | 7.52 | 1.61 | 26 | 5.29 |
| bird | Cock | 3.05 | 7.1 | 5.64 | 31 | 10.29 |
| bird | Crane | 2.97 | 7.38 | 5.64 | 29 | 8.88 |
| tool | Implement | 2.95 | 6.46 | 5.76 | 31 | 10.39 |
| brother | Monk | 2.82 | 6.27 | 10.24 | 27 | 11.57 |
| crane | Implement | 1.68 | 2.69 | 3.31 | 28 | 7.48 |
| lad | Brother | 1.66 | 4.46 | 2.33 | 28 | 6.55 |
| journey | Car | 1.16 | 5.85 | 0 | 0 | 1 |
| monk | Oracle | 1.1 | 5 | 2.33 | 25 | 5.74 |
| cemetery | Woodland | 0.95 | 2.08 | 1.62 | 25 | 5.1 |
| food | Rooster | 0.89 | 4.42 | 0.79 | 20 | 2.83 |
| coast | Hill | 0.87 | 4.38 | 6.2 | 28 | 9.46 |
| forest | Graveyard | 0.84 | 1.85 | 1.62 | 25 | 5.1 |
| shore | Woodland | 0.63 | 3.08 | 1.62 | 27 | 5.56 |
| monk | Slave | 0.55 | 0.92 | 2.33 | 28 | 6.55 |
| coast | Forest | 0.42 | 3.15 | 1.61 | 26 | 5.3 |
| lad | Wizard | 0.42 | 0.92 | 2.33 | 28 | 6.55 |
| chord | Smile | 0.13 | 0.54 | 2.88 | 22 | 5.2 |
| glass | Magician | 0.11 | 2.08 | 0.79 | 24 | 2.45 |
| noon | String | 0.08 | 0.54 | 0 | 0 | 1 |
| rooster | Voyage | 0.08 | 0.62 | 0 | 0 | 1 |

**Table 2.** Word pair semantic similarity measurement

| Similarity Method | Correlation |
|---|---|
| Human Judgment | 0.9494 |
| Node Based | 0.8011 |
| Edge Based | 0.5789 |
| Proposed Method | 0.8262 |

listed in Table 2. In particular, Table 2 shows that the result of our method is relatively close to the value accorded to human judgment.

## 5 Conclusion

In conclusion, we propose a combined model that is derived from the edge-based notion with the addition of the information content. We consider the edge, depth, link type and density, as well as the existence of common ancestors. In particular, our proposed method provides a method of determining the link strength of an edge that links a parent node to a child node. The link strength is comprised of (1) the density (the number of child links that span out from a parent node) and (2) their topological location in WordNet space. The proposed method is verified by experiment. The proposed method also helps users to conceptually navigate in ontologies.

Finally, future directions include the use of a larger number of word pairs and the development of a specific ontology, which allows for more efficient classification and retrieval of information.

## References


1. George A. Miller "Introduction to WordNet: An On-line Lexical Database", International Journal of Lexicography, 1990.
2. Sussna "WordSense Disambiguation for Free-text Indexing Using a Massive Semantic Network" Proceedings of the Second International Conference on Information and Knowledge Management, CIKM'93.
3. Philip Resnik "Using Information Content to Evaluate Semantic Similarity in a Taxonomy" Proceedings of the 14th International Joint Conference on Artificial Intelligence, 1995.
4. R.Richardson, A.F. Smeaton "Using WordNet as a Knowledge-Base for Measuring Semantic Similarity between Words", Working paper, CA-1294, School of Computer Applications, Dublin City University, Ireland, 1995
5. Eneko Agirre and German Rigau. "Word sense disambiguation using conceptual density" In Proceedings of the 16th International Conference on Computational Linguistics, pp. 16–22, Copenhagen, 1996.
6. Jay J Jiang, David W. Conrath "Semantic Similarity Based Corpus Statistics and Lexical Taxonomy", Proc. Of International Conference Research on Computational Linguistics, 1997.
7. Y.C. Park, F. Golshani, S. Panchanathan, "Conceptualization and Ontology: Tools for Efficient Storage and Retrieval of Semantic Visual Information", Internet Multimedia Management Systems Conference, 2000.
8. http://www.cogsci.princeton.edu/∼wn/
9. Guarino, N. and Welty, C. "Supporting Ontological Analysis of Taxonomic Relationships." Data and Knowledge Engineering (in press), 2001.
10. Budanitsky, A., and G. Hirst, "Semantic Distance in WordNet: An Experimental, Application-oriented Evaluation of Five Measures", Workshop on WordNet and Other Lexical Resources, in the North American Chapter of the Association for Computational Linguistics (NAACL-2000), Pittsburgh, PA, June 2001.

# Ontology-Based Access to Distributed Statistical Databases

Yaxin Bi[1], David Bell[1], Joanne Lamb[2], and Kieran Greer[3]

[1]School of Computer Science, The Queen's University of Belfast, Belfast BT7 1NN, UK
{y.bi, da.bell}@qub.ac.uk
[2]CES, University of Edinburgh, St John's Land, Holyrood Road, Edinburgh, EH8 8AQ, UK
J.M.Lamb@ed.ac.uk
[3]Faculty of Informatics, University of Ulster, Newtownabbey, Co. Antrim, BT37 0QB, UK
krc.greer@ulster.ac.uk

**Abstract.** In this paper we describe some commonly-required functionality for constructing, visualizing and manipulating ontologies. These make extensive use of XML and DOM technologies. The functions developed are based on practical applications needing access to distributed statistical databases and intelligent content management. They fulfill the needs identified as new features for next generation ontology development and application. These system features have been implemented in Java and JAXP.

## 1 Introduction

In scenarios involving interoperability between distributed database systems, semantic heterogeneity is a significant problem and it will continue to be so in the future [1]. A variety of solutions to this problem have been proposed in the past decade, including the mediation approach, schema matching, and ontology-based approaches [2]. Ontologies are useful because they form a basis for integrating separate databases through the identification of semantic connections or constraints between the data or pieces of information. This paper addresses the issues of ontology structure, construction and manipulation.

The concept of "ontology" is well-known in knowledge engineering and it was originally developed for knowledge-based systems. The recognition of its usefulness has led to its applications to data integration [3], an intelligent content management [4], and the Semantic Web [5]. A solution to the problem of semantic heterogeneity is to formally specify the meaning of the terminology of each system and to define a correspondence between system terminologies, in which the terminologies will be specified using *ontologies* and the correspondence between them will be defined by *ontology mappings* [1]. Ontologies can therefore take different forms with different purposes and can be used in different phases of different applications. For example, we may have *source* and *receiver ontologies*, which define the terminology used by specific data sources and receivers, respectively. The latter makes use of *query ontologies*, which define the terminology for a range of users. Another type is *shared ontologies*, which are used as the reference terminology among different systems.

Considerable research exists in developing ontologies and their application. As described in [5], the building of ontologies was done in an *ad hoc* fashion in the past,

G. Dong et al. (Eds.): WAIM 2003, LNCS 2762, pp. 389–396, 2003.

but more recently there have been some proposals for guiding the ontology development process. For instance, [6] gives formal guidelines for constructing a consistent and reusable ontology and a few Web-based initiatives are aimed at addressing the scale and scope of development of ontologies for the Semantic Web[7].

In contrast to these methodologies, which mostly confine their attention to the ontology itself, in our work we focus on the application-driven development and exploitation of ontologies, in particular focusing on the official statistics domain and on intelligent content management. These involve various technical aspects of ontology construction, visualization, mapping, exploitation in a query scenario. We describe our practical experiences obtained from the MISSION [3] and ICONS [4] projects. The work reported here is related to our other work: user interaction styles with distributed database systems [8] and a visual querying paradigm [9].

## 2 Ontologies

An ontology is defined as a shared formal conceptualization of a particular domain [10]. It can be used to specify what concepts represent and how they are related. Practically, ontologies are characterised into two types of *simple* ontologies and *sophisticated* ontologies. We concentrate on simple ontologies. A *simple* ontology should hold mandatory properties such as [11]:

- Finite controlled (extensible) terms (values)
- Unambiguous interpretation of concepts and term relationships
- Explicit hierarchical sub-concept relationships between concepts

Currently, some simple ontologies are available in many forms – some exist as freeware on the web, such as UN Classifications Registry a classification scheme for universal products and services [12]. A hierarchical structure may contain many levels in order to precisely represent the relationships between concepts, i.e. a concept may be broken down into a group of sub-concepts, each of which in turn may be divided into smaller ones, and so on. Notice that such a decomposition process is recursive, and for convenience of discussion, we assume an ontology is composed of three levels as shown in Fig. 1 (a). i.e. Ontology → Concept → Value. Such a hierarchical structure provides a natural way to visualize an ontology as a tree, illustrated in Fig. 1 (b).

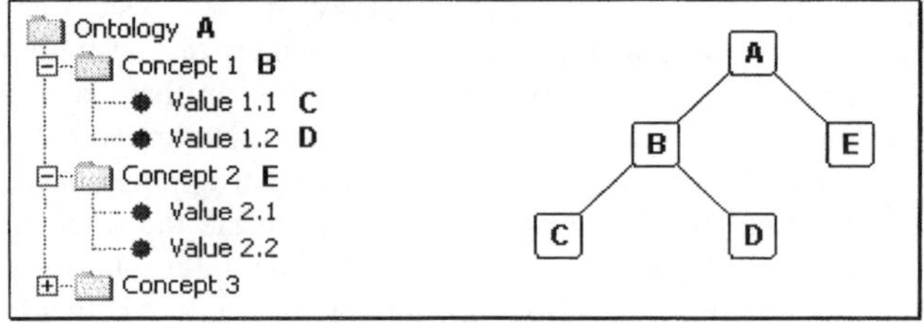


**Fig. 1.** An abstract structure for ontologies (left: a, right: b)

Ontologies can be represented in various ways, such as description logic and RDF [7]. To address issues in the content representation of databases, ontology construction and visualization, we employ XML to represent ontologies, because it deals well with hierarchies, and covers various types of data. In particular, it is well suited to the generation of hierarchies as required by different kinds of operations involved in data integration and the Semantic Web services.

Our ontologies are simple and each consists of a set of variables (concepts or nomenclatures). These can have hierarchical structure, and each variable may comprise a set of category values.

## 3 Developing Ontologies

The problem of developing ontologies has been well studied. A comparative analysis of relevant methodologies can be found in [5]. One of the major conclusions of that study was that the best approach to take in developing an ontology should be determined by the eventual purpose of the application.

In our work, we develop a *content-driven* approach for developing ontologies. This approach defines a template with XML syntax, being composed of two major parts: keywords and hierarchical structures. The template plays a vital role in mapping data with a flat structure into a hierarchical structure. To store metadata, we make use of the flexibility of a 3-ary relational schema (for data dictionary). The advantage of such a schema and its application in e-commerce has been described in [13]. We describe how to use a template to construct an ontology below.

### 3.1 Metadata and Data Dictionary

It is frequently the case in scientific data archives, for example, that raw (micro) data is of value encoded form, which are accompanied with a considerable amount of metadata for interpretation (see Table 1). The metadata can be regarded as a content interpretation of databases. For example, the attribute *Land* – physical name – occurring in a relation has a logical name *Country* and its domain consists of a set of values {Scotland, France, Sweden, Netherlands, Ireland}. All of the attributes and values constitute granularities of ontologies.

**Table 1.** A piece of metadata

| Attribute | Logical name | Type | Label |
|---|---|---|---|
| Land | Country | Categorical (geographical) | {Scotland, France, Sweden, Netherlands, Ireland} |
| Sex | Gender | Categorical | {male, female, Not answered} |

To store metadata, we develop a 3-ary schema, consisting of attributes *Role*, *Attr* and *Ext*. In general, *Attr* and *Ext* represent mnemonic and logical names of attributes and domain values, respectively, and *Role* represents equivalence relations of *Attr* and *Ext* in terms of keywords. Fig. 2 shows a piece of metadata held in a 3-ary relation (table), called a data dictionary. The domain of attribute *Role* comprise *frame*, *geo* and *map*, *label* (*categorical* is treated as a constant value), representing different relations between pairs of *Attr* and *Ext*. For example, *map* means that *Land* and

*Country* are semantically equivalent. To extract content from a data dictionary, we specify the content of the data dictionary by using the keywords and structure to be imposed on the content in a template (see Section 3.2).

| Role | Info | Ext |
|---|---|---|
| frame | Catewe | * |
| geo | Ireland | Country |
| map | Land | Country |
| categorical | 0 | * |
| label | Scotland | Country |
| label | France | Country |
| ... | | |

**Fig. 2.** A fragment of data dictionary

## 3.2 Ontology Construction Using Content-Driven Extraction

Given a hierarchical structure of ontologies and a data dictionary, the idea of content-driven extraction is to retrieve data from a data dictionary using keywords specified in a template and fill them into the structure defined in the template. This structure strictly complies with the structure of a given ontology. A template is defined with two elements of *element* and *attribute*, and it conforms to XML syntax.

In a template, *element* is used to define tag names via its attribute, and *attribute* is for defining attributes of elements with either the keywords or constant values. If a keyword is used with the parameter *column*, that means that attribute values of elements and values of attributes will be extracted from the corresponding column in a data dictionary, otherwise these values are constant values, such as *Catewe* and *categorical* at line 2 and 4 in Fig. 3.

The nested relation between *element* and *attribute* defines hierarchical relations, which reflect ontology structures to be formed, i.e. the *attribute* of an element is always nested at one level lower than that element. Fig. 3 illustrates a fragment of a template. Three tag names Ontology, CONCEPT and VALUE are specified by *element* in line 1, 3 and 7, respectively, and the nested relations between tags are restricted by *attributes*, and the resulting hierarchical structure is the same as one described in Fig. 1(a).

```
1. <element name="Ontology">
2.   <attribute name="name">Catewe</attribute>
3.   <element name="CONCEPT">
4.       <attribute name="vartype">categorical</attribute>
5.       <attribute phname="mnemonic" column="2">map</attribute>
6.       <attribute lgname="name" column="3">map</attribute>
7.       <element name="VALUE">
8.           <attribute name="value" column="2">label</attribute >
...
```

**Fig. 3.** A fragment of template

With the template and data dictionary, we now briefly look at how ontologies can be constructed. The construction algorithm has been implemented in MISSION as a functional module called XML Extractor to extract partial information from a data dictionary to generate ontology as shown in Fig. 4 (a). The key idea of XMLExtractor is to take as input a template, remotely connect to a data dictionary, and retrieve a data dictionary using the keywords specified in the template, and then recursively generate XML fragments based on the structure specified in the template. A fragment of the ontology generated from the data dictionary in Fig. 2 is shown in Fig. 5.

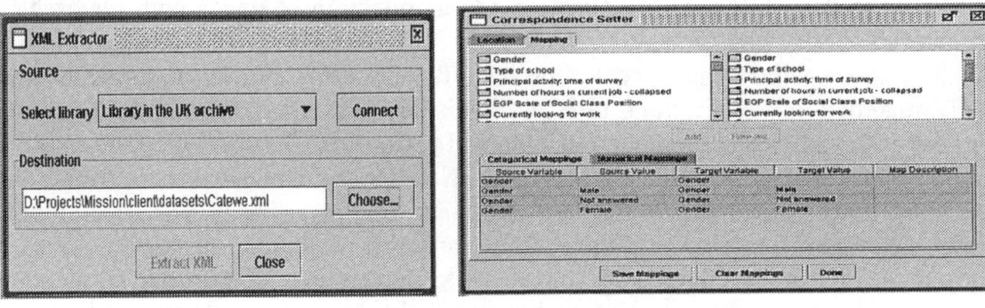


**Fig. 4.** Ontology construction (left: a) and mapping (right: b)

```
<Ontology name="Catewe">
<CONCEPT datatype = "" vartype = "geographical" mnemonic = "LAND" name = "Country">
        <VALUE value="Ireland"/>
        <VALUE value="Netherlands"/>
        ...
```

**Fig. 5.** A XML fragment of the ontology Catewe

The advantage of this approach is twofold: 1) it provides a means of converting from data with a flat structure to a hierarchical structure and 2) it has a generic character which is capable of coping with different structures defined in the templates, without having to change the extraction algorithm. Our approach is different from most methods which are built on the mapping between database schemas and XML documents [14]. The underlying difference lies in that our approach does not utilize the structure of database schema in generating XML documents. Instead, it is based on the content reflected in the database and structure reflected in ontologies, as defined in the templates.

## 4 Ontology Visualization

As mentioned previously, ontologies can be used for different purposes. To use an ontology as a user interface component, the visualization of ontologies is important. In an ontology-based query scenario, a *query ontology* can be treated as a view of data sources – a content representation. As indicated in [15], one of the difficult problems related to such a query model is how to visualize the ontologies as query views in terms of their structure and content. The issue associated with ontology visualization is also pointed in [6], i.e. in the future, ontology visualization will be seen as an important facility in applying ontologies.

In this work, we describe an approach to visualizing ontologies by means of the DOM (Document Object Model) [16]. DOM is a platform- and language-neutral application programming interface. It allows programs to dynamically access and manipulate the content and structure of XML documents. DOM is used to define the tree-like structure of documents and provide a standard set of objects for representing XML documents, along with a standard interface for accessing and manipulating them. Therefore the use of DOM is an ideal way for managing and visualizing XML documents.

A DOM instance can be defined as a tree model and implemented as a tree. According to the DOM, a XML document is a collection of nodes with hierarchical structure. Nodes are of 12 types, but there are only three types that are important to our discussion: element node, text node and attribute node. Fig. 6 (a) shows how an XML fragement of the ontology in Fig. 4 is displayed using DOM. In the figure the element nodes may have element, attribute and text nodes. For example Ontology has the element node CONCEPT, attribute node ATTRS and #text, but the attribute and text nodes only carry texts, which are terminals. It is possible to visualize element nodes as proper tree nodes, acting as an accurate depiction of the contents of distributed data, rather than being an accurate description of the data structure as represented by the DOM., as illustrated in Fig. 6 (b). Instead of filtering attribute and text nodes out, there is a need to encapsulate element, attribute and text nodes into objects since they are important constraints to respective elements. We have developed an algorithm to meet this requirement.

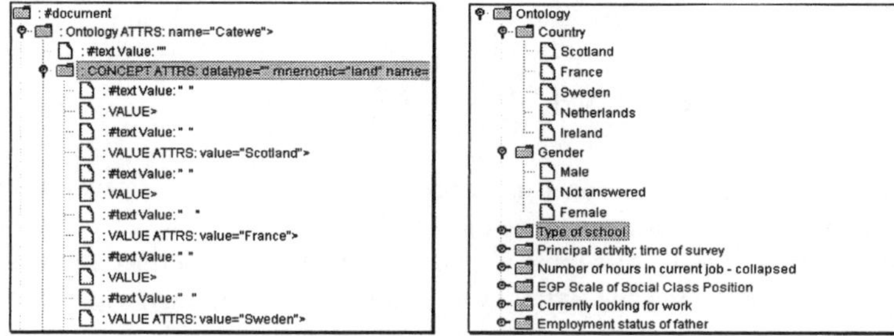


**Fig. 6.** Visualizing ontologies (left (a): a DOM tree; right (b): an ontology tree)

# 5 Mappings between Schemas and Ontologies

In a relational database system, a schema defines a relational table. An ontology, on the other hand, defines the meanings of the terms used in the schema, and hierarchical relationships between them as described in Fig. 1. It is not always feasible to directly map an ontology to a schema because of this hierarchical structure. We confine our attention to the simple case where a schema corresponds only to an ontology, i.e. one-to-one mapping. For example, we define a schema and construct an ontology based on Table 1. It is straightforward to establish the mapping between the schema and the ontology through mapping the attributes in the schema to the meanings of the corresponding attributes within the ontology, e.g. *Land* mapping *Country*.

Defining mappings between ontologies is another aspect in the integration of diverse data sources. An ontology normally includes more semantics than a schema, the existence of such semantics provides an effective means for coping with semantic heterogeneity reflected in data sources and makes it possible to implement an automated approach to creating mappings between ontologies. In the MISSION project, we have implemented an ontology mapping function, called *Correspondence*

*Setter* for data providers in order to define mapping rules between source ontologies. A screenshot of this function module is shown in Fig. 4(b).

In this work, we propose two ways to define mappings to indicate how terms in one ontology correspond to terms in another [17].

- *peer to peer mapping* – mapping rules are defined for each pair of ontologies which directly map from one ontology into another.
- *Mapping via a standard reference classification* (*taxonomy*) – mapping rules are defined for each source ontology into a shared reference classification to be derived from public classification repositories as described in [12].

Both mapping rules can be defined manually using the function of the *Correspondence Setter* as illustrated in Fig. 4 (b). For example, peer-to-peer mappings are possible of the corresponding terms in the source ontologies Catewe Ireland and Catewe Scotland via this function. Notice that mappings occur at the levels of both variables such as *Gender* ↔ *Gender* and the value set such as Male ↔ Male. Resulting mappings will be stored in relations called *correspondence tables* for use in query processing. In addition to this, we have implemented a function to allow ontologies to be merged together into a master ontology based on the amount of semantic overlap between ontologies. In fact, mappings can occur at multi-levels, such as ontology, variable, classification and value, etc. The support for complicated and dynamical mappings between ontologies is currently under development.

## 6 Queries against Ontologies

Queries are composed using the terms defined in the ontologies, and posed against the ontologies, instead of schemas or views, as in an alternative to schema and the views-based systems. To answer them, a relationship is defined between the ontology and the schema. Processing these efficiently converts a query expression derived from the ontology into the internal schema-based expression of the query.

Any query composed of the terms defined in the ontology must be converted to an equivalent executable query against the schema. In a system, queries are visually specified over query ontologies and expressed in a high-level query language. These high-level user queries are translated into queries over the definitions at the ontology mapping layer, and ontology terms are replaced by schema attributes. More detail is described in our internal paper [9].

## 7 Summary

Ontologies play a key role in coping with semantic heterogeneity occurring in a variety of applications. Some development environments exist for building ontologies, such as Ontolingua [6] and OntoEdit [7], and there exist some repositories of simple ontologies as well, but application-oriented methods and techniques in relation to specific applications are still under development.

Experience with the ontology development and exploitation in connection with official statistics and general intelligent content management, and an exhaustive analysis of current ontology research, have led us to develop functionality such as content-driven construction, visualization based on DOM, and ontology mappings, all of which are regarded as essential features of next-generation ontology construction and applications. Although these have been developed specifically for statistical databases in the MISSION project, an attempt is being made to tailor these features to general applications, such as those using the ICONS.

**Acknowledgement.** The work is partially supported by the MISSION project (IST 1999-10655) and partially supported by the ICONS project (IST-2001-32429), which are funded by the European Framework V.

## References

1. Zhan, C., Jones, D., and O'Brien, P. Semantic B2B integration: issues in ontology-based approaches. ACM SIGMOD Record, Vol.31 (1), (2002) 43–48.
2. Mena, E., Illarramendi, A., Kashyap, P., Sheth, A. P.: OBSERVER: An Approach for Query Processing in Global Information Systems Based on Interoperation Across Pre-Existing Ontologies. Distributed and Parallel Databases 8(2): (2000) 223–271.
3. Specification of the MISSION system (Multi-Agent Integration Of Shared Statistical Information Over The (Inter)Net) (Deliverable 6), 2001.
4. Bell, D, Bi, Y., *el at.* Analysis and selection of the ICONS (Intelligent Content Management System) project research base (Deliverable 6), June 2002.
5. Staab, S. Methodology for Development and Employment of Ontology based Knowledge Management Applications in Semantic Web, Database Management and Information Systems: Overview of the Special Issue, SIGMOD Record, No.4, December 2002.
6. Fikes, R., Farquhar, A. Large-Scale Repositories of Highly Expressive Reusable Knowledge; IEEE Intelligent Systems, Vol. 14, No. 2, March/April 1999.
7. D. Fensel. On-To-Knowledge: Semantic Web Enabled Knowledge Management, IEEE Computer, 35(11), 2002.
8. Bi,Y., Bell, D. and Lamb, J. Aggregate Table-driven Querying Via Navigation Ontologies in Distributed Statistical Databases (to appear in BNCOD 2003).
9. Bi,Y., Bell, D. and Lamb, J., Greer, K. Visual Query with Ontologies for Distributed Databases (internal paper).
10. Gruber,T.: A translation Approach to Portable Ontology Specifications. Knowledge Acquisition. Vol. **5**(2), (1993)199–220.
11. McGuinness, D., L. Ontologies Come of Age. In Fensel, D., Hendler, J., Lieberman, H. and Wahlster, W., (eds). Spinning the Semantic Web: Bringing the World Wide Web to Its Full Potential. MIT Press, 2003.
12. UN Classifications Registry, esa.un.org/unsd/cr/registry, (April 2002).
13. Rakesh Agrawal, Amit Somani, Yirong Xu: "Storage and Querying of E-Commerce data", 27th Int'l Conference on Very Large Data Bases Rome, September 2001.
14. Shanmugasundaram, J., Shekita, E., Barr, R., Carey, M., Lindsay, B., Pirahesh, H. and Reinwald, B. Efficiently publishing relational data as XML documents. VLDB Journal: Very Large Data Bases, vol (10) 2-3, (2001)133–154.
15. Wache, H. Vogele, T. Visser, U. Stuckenschmidt, H. Schuster, G. Neumann, H., Hubner, S.: Ontology-based integration of information – a survey of existing approaches. In Stuckenschmidt, H. (ed.): IJCAI-01 Workshop: Ontologies and Information Sharing, (2001) 108–117.
16. Document Object Model, http://www.w3.org/DOM/ (October 2002).
17. McClean, S., Páircéir, R., Scotney, B., Greer, K. A Negotiation Agent for Distributed Heterogeneous Statistical Databases in SSDBM (2002) 207–217.

# A Filter Index for Complex Queries on Semi-structured Data

Wang Lian, Nikos Mamoulis, and David W. Cheung

Department of Computer Science and Information Systems,
The University of Hong Kong, Pokfulam, Hong Kong.
{wlian, nikos, dcheung}@csis.hku.hk

**Abstract.** Answering a query on XML data usually involves breaking it into a number of small components (e.g., edges, paths, twigs, etc.), evaluating them and joining the results. In this paper we propose an alternative technique that uses these components to filter a large part of the database that does not qualify them, before validating the query on the actual data. Our methodology uses a signature index to search fast and prune effectively the search space. The efficiency of the proposed technique is demonstrated by comparison with an existing index, on real data.

## 1 Introduction

With XML becoming a standard for information exchange, there has been an increasing volume of information in semi-structure format which need to be queried and analyzed efficiently. Conventional query evaluation techniques are not readily applicable due to the loosely defined schema of semi-structured data. As a result, a number of specialized techniques have been developed, for processing queries that conform to XML languages, like XPath [12] and XQuery [13].

XML documents can be modeled as (directed) graphs having as nodes elements or values and as edges the parent/child relationships between them. Typical queries on XML data ask for documents (or parts of them) that contain a *path* or *subgraph* (e.g., twig) expression. An example of such a query is $article/[author = \text{'}John\ \ Smith\text{'}\ \ AND\ \ year = \text{'2000'}]$, which asks for all articles of 'John Smith' which were published in year 2000.

The diverse nature of structures and queries renders query evaluation hard. A common solution [11] is to decompose the structural part of the documents into a number of relational tables that capture the relative position of the various *elements* (e.g., journal, author, etc.) into the graph structures. Pattern queries are processed by joining these tables, in order to bring back parent/child relationships. Join processing can become very expensive, especially if the queries involve relative path expressions. This problem was alleviated with the introduction of special encoding schemes for XML graphs [6,9]. The encoding can be utilized by merge-join like algorithms [1,2], for structural queries. However these schemes are defined only for the case where the documents are *tree* structures. It

G. Dong et al. (Eds.): WAIM 2003, LNCS 2762, pp. 397–408, 2003.

is not clear how to apply similar encodings on arbitrary graph structures. Using summarized graphs [4,10] to evaluate queries usually involves breaking it into small pieces, e.g., paths, evaluating the most selective one(s), and then verifying the remaining query constraints on the candidate results [6]. This process may require traversing parts of a large number of candidate documents, or performing a large number of joins. As a result, for many applications, where the XML data are arbitrary graphs, evaluating queries either on simple relational tables [11] or on exact/summarized graphs [4,10] can be rather expensive.

We follow a different approach to handle complex queries based on the rationale that we need to utilize as much as possible the selectivity of a query to reduce the search effort. Our methodology is based on breaking the query into a number of small components and use them to filter documents that do not qualify these components. Given an XML database consisting of many documents (i.e., XML graphs), we generate a signature bitmap for each document, indicating the components which are present in the document. These signatures are organized in a hierarchical structure named **SG-tree** which is similar to the R–tree [5]. Each query is also transformed to a signature bitmap indicating the components it contains. After traversing the SG-tree, we can efficiently filter out most of the documents, which do not satisfy the query. Finally, all nonfiltered documents are validated to give the exact answer. The advantages of the proposed SG-tree can be summarized as follows:

- It is simple to implement and its construction/maintenance cost is low, compared to sophisticated graph-based indexes [4,10,7]. Moreover, it is a disk-based structure, which can be implemented in limited memory conditions, as opposed to graph-based indexes which do not fit in memory if the data volume is large.
- We propose a technique that encodes value ranges in the indexed components. In this way, the index is useful in filtering queries not only based on structure, but also based on value selections.
- Our techniques can be used to index arbitrary graph structures as opposed to methods restricted to only tree-structured documents [6,9,1,2].

Experiments comparing the SG-tree with the A(k)-index [7] on real data show that the SG-tree is a powerful filter index for high selective queries.

The rest of the paper is organized as follows. Section 2 provides background and reviews previous work on XML query processing. Section 3 describes the proposed indexing techniques and Section 4 the query decomposition method. In Section 5, we evaluate the filter effectiveness and time efficiency of the proposed techniques by real data. Finally, Section 6 concludes with a discussion and directions for future work.

## 2 Background and Related Work

In our data model we assume a database of XML documents. Each document is represented by a directed, node-labeled graph $G = (V_G, E_G)$, where each (non-terminal) node $v \in V_G$ has a unique *oid* and a label (which corresponds to an

XML element). Nodes with no outcoming edges (terminal nodes) contain values. $E_G$ contains the edges of the graph, which are either parent-child relationships or $IDREF$ links between elements. For simplicity, attributes and elements are represented by a single construct (i.e., non-terminal node). Figure 1 shows an example of two XML documents represented by node-labeled graphs. The document on the left is an item of a bibliography database. The graph in this case, is a tree, i.e., there are no links between elements. The document on the right contains information about a part (i.e., mechanical component). A nut can be paired with a bolt, so there are links between elements, represented by dashed lines.

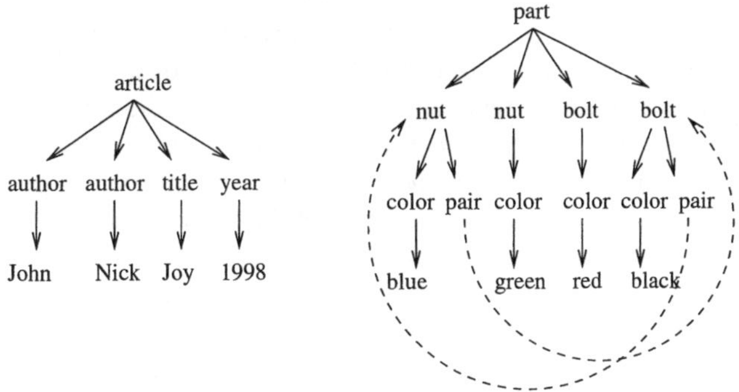


**Fig. 1.** XML documents represented as directed graphs

Queries are defined by paths/structural patterns between XML elements potentially enriched by selection predicates on attribute values. Following an XQuery-like notation, we use '/' to denote direct parent/child relationships, '//' to denote descendant/ancestor relationships and '$/ * /$' to denote descendant/ancestor relationships interleaved by one node. The root is denoted by a label at the beginning of the query with a '/' before it. Branches are expressed using brackets '[]'. E.g., $/a/[b]/c$ denotes a twig having $a$ as root and $b$, $c$ as left and right son, respectively. Selection predicates on attributes are also enclosed by brackets. An example is '$article/[author =$ '$John'$ $AND$ $year =$ '$1998'$]', asking for all documents with $article$ as root label, having at least two attributes $author$ and $year$, with values 'John' and 1998, respectively. A query result is therefore a set of document subgraphs which match the query predicates (e.g., the left document of Figure 1).

## 2.1 Previous Work

Many XML database applications decompose the data and store them into relational tables that capture the structural relationships between them. A straightforward solution defines a database schema using the Document Type Definition

(DTD) of the documents [11]. This approach fragments the data into a small number of tables and expensive joins are required to bring back structural information. A more efficient solution is to encode [6,9] the relative positions of the nodes in the documents using a preorder traversal of the structure and store them into tables clustered by node label. Thus parent/child queries $a/b$ (or ancestor/descendant queries $a//b$, in general) can be evaluated by first selecting the nodes labeled $a$ and $b$ into two lists and then traverse the two lists in a sort-merge join fashion verifying the structural relationships between the elements [1]. A complex query containing path or twig expressions can be evaluated by decomposing it into a set of binary joins and then merging the partial results. Recently [2], stack-based algorithms were proposed to avoid this multi-step process by evaluating synchronously all structural components of the query. Nevertheless these approaches can operate only on tree structures, whereas in general XML documents are graph-structured. Some researchers have proposed the use of graph summaries that capture most of the characteristics of the original graph, serving thus as a structural abstraction of them [4,10]. Path queries are evaluated on these summaries rather on the original documents. There are several limitations of these indexes. First, they are usually very large (with size comparable to the size of the original documents) and therefore accessing them is costly. This problem is alleviated in [7], where a family of progressively more refined summaries is introduced and one that achieves a good space-time trade-off is chosen. Second, queries are usually evaluated by first finding the nodes with the same label as the first element of the query and then traversing the graph until a path condition fails, or the final element is found (together with a result). This process is rather expensive for relative path queries, since large part of the graph may need to be accessed before the qualifying paths are found. Finally, they are appropriate only for simple path queries and cannot be used directly to evaluate complex ones that contain conjunctions of simple paths.

Summarizing, evaluating generic queries on XML graph structures is still a hard problem. In the next section, we propose a methodology that aims to reduce the size of the problem using indexes that filter fast documents which do not qualify complex queries involving multiple structural components.

## 3 Methodology

Since evaluating complex queries directly on the documents (or on decomposed data) can be expensive, it is a good idea to minimize the number of documents that need to be searched for a specific query. Our aim is to develop methods which (i) are lightweight, (ii) have low construction and maintenance costs, (iii) prune efficiently the search space, and (iv) apply for arbitrary (i.e., not only path) queries. On the other hand, we are not interested to create an index that provides exact answers, but one that filters out as many documents as possible.

Our methodology is based on indexing structural components that appear frequently in query patterns. These components can be edges, paths, twigs, relative path expressions, etc. Given a query workload, a data mining algorithm

[3] can be employed to extract a set of frequent structural components. Then an index that finds fast which documents contain these components is built. Queries are preprocessed to extract the components contained in them and the index is used to locate fast the documents that contain these components and filter-out the ones that do not. Finally, the candidate documents are searched using some well-established XML query processing technique to verify the rest of the query predicates and to retrieve the query results.

Most queries involve selections on attribute values in a document. Furthermore, value range selections are expected to be much more selective than edges between elements. For instance, the query *article/author* is not very selective. On the other hand, the query $//[author = `Zebra']$ is possibly very selective.

Therefore, it is a good idea to index also frequent query components containing values. There are two limitations here. First, the number of potential values for an attribute is very large and index all of them is too expensive. Second, queries on attribute values not only differ in nature and selectivity, but also show diverse distributions on the attribute domains.

Based on the nature and distribution of the queries and the size of the domains, we split them into classes and use the class values as new tags. For example, consider the year/value pair in the bibliography database, and assume that items published from 1995 to 2002 are queried more frequently than ones before 1995. We can define 10 query ranges: one for each year from 1995 to 2002, one for the range 1990-1994 and one for the years before 1990.

### 3.1 Indexing Document Signatures

If a large number of components appear in the query, scanning and merging all the relevant lists or bitmaps could be expensive. We consider an alternative approach that models each document with a bitmap indicating which components are present in the document. We call this bitmap the *signature* of the document.

The query is also transformed to a signature, based on the existence of components in it and compared to the document signatures using bitwise operators. The index is motivated by the following observation: if the signature of a query does not match with a document signature, then the document does not contain an answer to the query, thus it can be safely filtered from consideration. In Section 3.1, we will describe an index that organizes hierarchically the signatures and can accelerate query processing.

Before we show in detail how queries are filtered against signature representations we need to define some operations on bitmaps.

**Definition 1.** *Let $s$ be a binary signature. The* **length** *of $s$, denoted by $Len(s)$, is defined by the number of bits in $s$. The* **area** *of $s$, denoted by $Area(s)$, is defined by the number of 1's in $s$.*

**Definition 2.** *Let $s_1, s_2$ be two binary signatures, such that $Len(s_1) = Len(s_2)$. Let $\wedge$, $\vee$, and $\otimes$ denote the bitwise operations AND, OR and XOR, respectively, on signatures of the same length. The* **overlap** *$Ovr(s_1, s_2)$ between $s_1$ and $s_2$*

*is defined by* $Area(s_1 \wedge s_2)$*. The* **distance** $Dist(s_1, s_2)$ *between* $s_1$ *and* $s_2$ *is defined by* $Area(s_1 \otimes s_2)$*. The* **difference** $Diff(s_1, s_2)$ *of* $s_1$ *from* $s_2$ *is defined by* $Area(s_1 \otimes (s_1 \wedge s_2))$*. Finally,* $s_1$ *is said to* **contain** *or* **cover** $s_2$ *iff* $s_1 \wedge s_2 = s_2$*.*

In other words, the overlap between two signatures is the number of common 1-bits in them, the (*hamming*) distance is the number of bits with different values in them, and the difference $Diff(s_1, s_2)$ (non-commutative) is the number of 1-bits in $s_1$ but not in $s_2$. Finally, $s_1$ contains (or covers) $s_2$ if all set bits in $s_2$ are also set in $s_1$. For example, $Area(10110) = 3$, $Ovr(10110, 00011) = 1$, $Dist(10110, 00011) = 3$, $Diff(10110, 00011) = 2$, and 10111 covers both 10110 and 00011.

**An example.** Consider the two XML documents (containing bibliography items) shown in Figure 2(a). Assume that the domain of attribute *author* is divided into two classes $J*$ and $N*$ representing author names starting with J and N, respectively. Similarly, the domain of *title* is divided into 2 classes ($J*$, $P*$), and the domains of *publisher* and *year* are considered as categorical with one class per category value.

Figure 2(b) shows the signatures of the two documents and also an *edge directory* (in general *component directory*) that encodes the potential edges of the database. It also shows graph-representations of the signatures (called *s-graphs*). Notice that there is a common edge between the s-graphs ($author/J*$). Also the number of encoded edges, i.e., the number of rows in the edge directory, is defined by the potential edges that can be found in a document. Invalid edges (e.g., ones which do not conform to the DTD), like *article/publisher*) are excluded to save space.

Given a query (e.g., $author/`Nick'$) if a signature (e.g., $sig(D_1)$) contains the corresponding edge (e.g., $author/N*$), the corresponding document (e.g., $D_1$) may qualify the query. Otherwise, (e.g., document $D_2$) it can be excluded from consideration.

**The signature tree (SG–tree).** The signatures of all documents can be stored as $\langle signature, document\_id \rangle$ tuples, sequentially in a *signature file*. Since scanning the whole file for a query can be expensive, we propose an alternative organization of the signatures in a hierarchical structure. So it is a good idea to cluster them based on their similarity. A nice property of the signatures is that we can use the *same* representation, i.e., a bitmap, for documents and document groups. Therefore, in the signature of a group of documents an edge is on iff this edge exists in at least one document of the group. We employ this property to define a simple, but efficient, hierarchical index for signatures.

The SG–tree (or *signature* tree) is a dynamic balanced tree similar to R–tree [5] for signature bitmaps. Each node of the tree corresponds to a disk page (using multipage nodes is a potential implementation) and contains entries of the form $\langle sig, ptr \rangle$. In a leaf node entry, *sig* is the signature of the document and *ptr* is a pointer to the file that contains the document (i.e., the *document_id*). The signature of a directory node entry is the logical OR of all signatures in the node pointed by it and *ptr* is a pointer to this node. In other words, the signature of each entry *covers* all signatures in the subtree pointed by it. All nodes contain

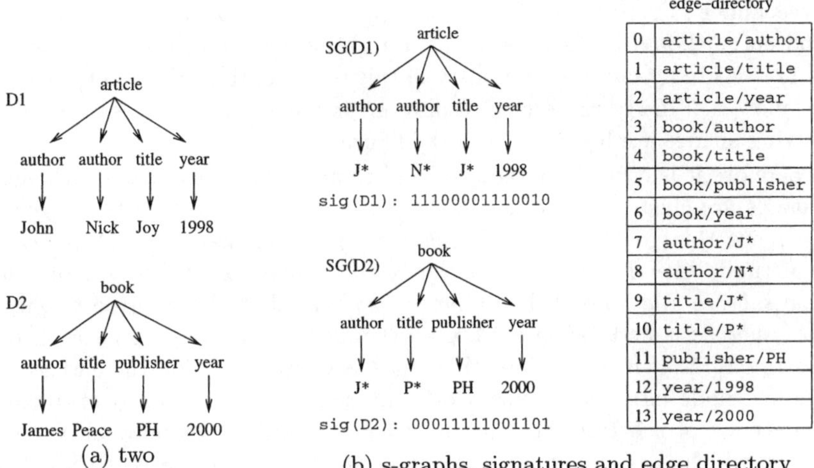


(a) two XML-documents

(b) s-graphs, signatures and edge directory

**Fig. 2.** Example of s-graphs and signature encoding

between $c$ and $C$ entries, where $C$ is the maximum capacity and $c \leq C/2$, except from the root which may contain fewer entries. Figure 3 shows an example of a signature tree. The leaf entries contain signatures of nine documents and pointers to them. In this graphical example the maximum node capacity $C$ is three and the length of the signatures six. in practice, $C$ is in the order of several tens and the length of the signatures in the order of several hundreds.

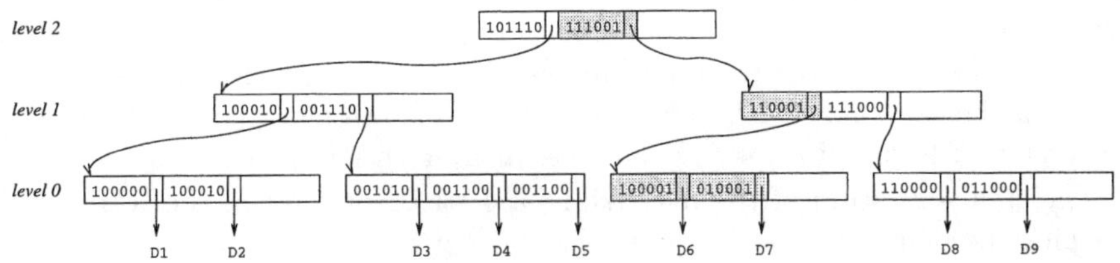


**Fig. 3.** Example of a signature tree

The tree is designed to answer fast *signature containment queries*, e.g., find all documents containing edges $a/b$ and $c/d$. The query is transformed to a signature $qs$ and the tree is traversed in a depth-first fashion, following entries whose signature contains $qs$; if the signature of an entry does not contain $qs$, no document indexed in the subtree below it can contain a query result. Consider for example the tree of Figure 3 and a query which contains a component encoded by the last (i.e., sixth) signature bit. Since the first entry of the root has 0 in the sixth position of its signature, we know that no document indexed in the subtree under it can participate in the query result. On the other hand, the second entry should be followed and the rightmost node of the next level (i.e., level 1) is visited. Only the first entry of this node contains the component, and it is followed. Finally the query results are found in the third leaf node. The qualifying entries are highlighted in the figure.

Therefore it is crucial for the tree performance that documents with similar signatures are clustered together in the leaf nodes. A good insertion algorithm can achieve this goal. A generic insertion algorithm used for hierarchical access methods like the B–tree and the R–tree usually contains two functions: *choose_subtree* and *split*. When a new entry $e$ needs to be inserted to the tree *choose_subtree* is first called to chooses the most appropriate node $n$, in order to insert $e$ in it. If $n$ is overflow, then *split* is called to divide the entries of an overflowed node into two groups. Both functions should be tuned to maximize the efficiency of the tree. For the SG–tree, we need to define quality criteria based on which these functions operate. A good tree minimizes the number of nodes that need to be accessed during a signature containment query. Therefore the directory node entries of a good tree should have (i) a small area[1] and (ii) small overlap between them, if they are at the same level.

The algorithm *choose_subtree* shown in Figure 4 distinguishes three cases. In the first case only one entry $e_i \in n$ contains the new entry $e$ and it is directly chosen. In the second case multiple entries contain $e$. The algorithm chooses the one with the minimum area, since this refines the structure (in analogy to choosing the smaller MBR among a number of ones that contain the new entry in R–trees). Finally, the third case applies when no $e_i \in n$ contains $e$. The algorithm in this case picks the one which requires the smallest area enlargement to index $e$ under it, or more formally the entry for which $Diff(e, e_i)$ is the minimum. Ties are broken by choosing the entry with the minimum length. We also implemented another version of *choose_subtree* that picks the entry which after extended causes the minimum increase in its overlap with the rest of the entries in the same node. Nevertheless, through experimentation we found that the version of Figure 4 gives as good trees at a much lower insertion cost.

The split algorithm of the SG–tree is also based on that of the R–tree. We first pick the pair of entries in the overflowed node with the maximum distance (i.e., with the maximum number of bits in their exclusive OR). We call these two entries *seeds* and assign them to two groups. The signatures of the groups is the logical OR of the members of the group (in accordance with the MBRs in an R–tree). The rest of the entries are assigned to the group that requires the minimum extension to include them. Ties are broken by (i) choosing the group with the minimum area and (ii) the group with the minimum number of entries. If at some point the cardinality of a group plus the number of remaining entries equals $c$, the remaining entries are assigned to the group to avoid underflow of the new node. Finally, deletions in the SG–tree are handled as in the R–tree; if a leaf node underflows, it is deleted and its entries are reinserted to the tree.

[1] For simplicity, we extend the function definitions of Section 3.1, to apply on SG-tree node entries, e.g., $Area(e) \equiv Area(e.sig)$.

**function** *choose_subtree*(Node $n$, Entry $e$): Node *son* {
  **if** $e$ is contained in exactly one entry $e_i \in n$ **then**
    **return** $e_i$;
  **else if** $e$ is contained in multiple entries $e_i \in n$ **then**
    **return** $e_i$ with the minimum $Area(e_i)$;
  **else** /* $e$ is contained in no entry $e_i \in n$ */
    pick the entry which requires the minimum area enlargement to contain $e$;
    break ties by choosing the entry with the minimum area;
}

**Fig. 4.** The *choose_subtree* algorithm

### 3.2 Which Components to Index?

In Figure 2, we used the edges as the indexed components of all documents, however other frequently queried components (e.g., relative edge, paths or twigs) can also be considered.

In general the number of distinct edges is small, while the number of pathes and twigs can be huge, it is impossible to index all of them. In this case, data-mining tools should be used to find out some valuable components for indexing. Our requirement of being a valuable component is intuitive : (a)small size (b)high selectivity. How to find interesting components is out of the range of this paper. Since there are lots of available methods for discovering patterns from trees or graphes, they can easily be adopted for our task.

In our experiments, the indexed components are relative edge denoted by $RE$. That is all pair of elements with ancestor and descendant relationship. For example, in path */article/author/address*, we can find three $RE$s: *article//author*, *article//address*, *author//address*.

## 4 Query Decomposition

Given a query and a set of valuable components, the query decomposition is to find out all valuable components that are contained in the query. Because the number of valuable components is rather small, we can use edge-based inverted index to organize them. This inverted index can remove all components that contain one or more edges which are missed in the query. Remaining components should be checked with the query by tree or graph matching to determine whether they are contained in the query. After finding all components in a query, a signature bitmap of this query is constructed and feed into SG-tree to dig out all documents that possibly satisfy the query.

## 5 Experiments

In order to evaluate the efficiency of SG-tree, we use the DBLP bibliography database [8] in our experiments. The indexed component unit in our tests is the

Relative Edge. The decomposition of all queries are based on all indexed *RE*s. To take care of the values, we used a equi-depth split algorithm to divide the domains of common values (e.g., names of authors) to a number of ranges with an equal number of documents in each range, and generated tag-aliases for them. The total number of *RE* that appear in the set of 200,000 DBLP documents is 371, i.e., the length of the signatures is about 47 bytes. This definition resulted in 182,224 distinct signatures. Because of the space limitation, we only show two sets of experiments: comparison of SG-tree with A(k)-index and the scalability of SG-tree.

### 5.1 Query Generation

In order to evaluate the efficiency of SG-tree we generate queries from documents. The queries were generated by randomly picking a document and removing some edges from it. The removed edges are randomly replaced either by // or by logical AND. The remaining edges along with their structural/logical relationships formulate the final query. For instance a document $a/[b/c]/d/e$, after removing edges $a/b$ and $d/e$ becomes query $a/d//e \wedge b/c$, which contains the (edge) components $b/c$ and $a/d$.

For each document set, we generate five groups of queries with 100 queries in each groups. The selectivity of all queries in group one is smaller than 0.1%; The selectivity of all queries in group two is from 0.1% to 0.5%; The selectivity of all queries in group three is from 0.5% to 1%; The selectivity of all queries in group four is from 1% to 5%; The selectivity of all queries in group five is from 5% to 10%;

Our generation process ensures the generated queries satisfy the selectivity requirement for each group.

### 5.2 SG-Tree vs. A(3)-Index

In this set of experiments we compare SG-tree with A(3)-index from two perspective, CPU time and I/O cost. The dataset contains about 25000 documents. Except the I/O cost, the CPU time for creating A(3)-index is about 12 hours, (It needs several days to create A(3)-index for a large dataset, so we only test it on a rather small dataset) while the SG-tree is created in 1 minute.

Figure 5 shows the average performance of the A(3)-index and the SG-tree varying the query selectivity. As expected, the performance of the SG-tree is much better than that of A(3)-index in both CPU and I/O cost, especially for high and medium selective queries(<5%) Just like R-tree, the performance of SG-tree degrades as the query selectivity decreases. On the other hand, the I/O cost and CPU cost of the A(3)-index decreases. The reason is: the lower the selectivity of a query, the higher probability that query contains less pathes, therefore the total number of disk access may be reduced for get the partial result for all pathes in a query. The fewer the paths in a query, the less the CPU time required to merge the results of different paths to answer a query. Hence, it may not be a good idea of using SG-tree for queries with low selectivity(>10%).

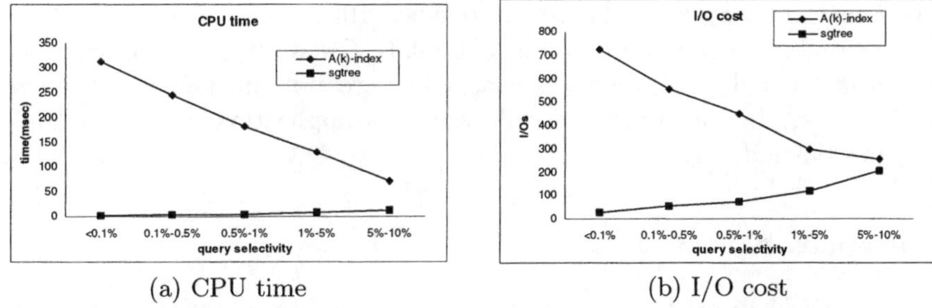


(a) CPU time (b) I/O cost

**Fig. 5.** Average query performance of A(3)-index and SG-tree

Figure 6 shows the performance of SG-tree as the number of documents increases. This experiment clearly shows that SG-tree performs well on large datasets. Generally, SG-tree is more efficiently for high selective queries on a large dataset, The R-tree like structure makes it easy to update and organise a large number of signatures. Highly selective queries traverse only few nodes of SG-tree and all operations are bitwise during the traversal, which leads to low CPU and I/O cost.

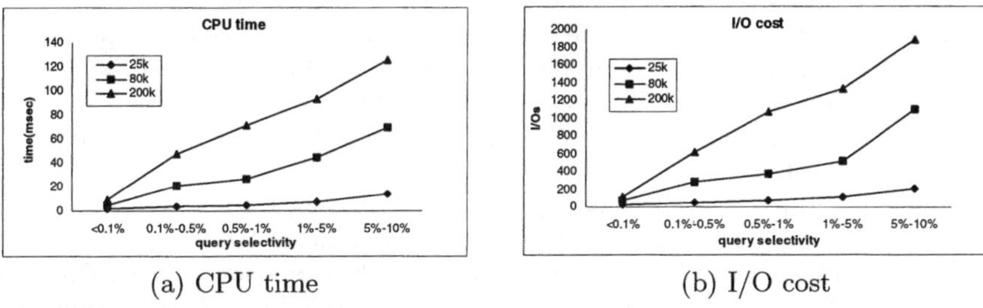


(a) CPU time (b) I/O cost

**Fig. 6.** Scalability of SG-tree

## 6 Conclusions

In this paper we attempt to support XML queries from a different angle. Our goal is to define a lightweight index that reduces the size of the problem by filtering from consideration documents which may not possibly contain the query. To do this, we extract some components from the XML documents, and create bit-string representations of the documents based on the extracted components. The signatures are indexed using the SG-tree, an R-tree like structure. The incoming query is also transformed into a bit-signature according to the extraced components, which is used as a key to travse the SG-tree to retrieve all document signatures that contain it. This process may filter out a large percentage of documents that do not satisfy the query. The query is finally evaluated on the candidates using techniques from previous work.

Our methodology is similar to the 1-index [10] and $A(k)$-index [7] in what we use structural summaries to index the data. However, our proposed index is much faster and it occupies less space. The creation and maintenance costs are also lower. In the future, we will study its application on more complex structures beyond edges.

## References


1. S. Al-Khalifa, H. V. Jagadish, N. Koudas, J. M. Patel, D. Srivastava, and Y. Wu. Structural joins: A primitive for efficient xml query pattern matching. In *International Conference on Data Engineering*. IEEE Computer Society, 2002.
2. N. Bruno, N. Koudas, and D. Srivastava. Holistic twig joins: Optimal xml pattern matching. In *SIGMOD Conference*. ACM Press, 2002.
3. C.-W. Chung, J.-K. Min, and K. Shim. Apex: An adaptive path index for xml data. In *SIGMOD Conference*. ACM Press, 2002.
4. R. Goldman and J. Widom. Dataguides: Enabling query formulation and optimization in semistructured databases. In *VLDB Conference*, pages 436–445. Morgan Kaufmann, 1997.
5. A. Guttman. R-trees: A dynamic index structure for spatial searching. In B. Yormark, editor, *SIGMOD Conference*, pages 47–57. ACM Press, 1984.
6. R. Kaushik, P. Bohannon, J. F. Naughton, and H. F. Korth. Covering indexes for branching path queries. In *SIGMOD Conference*. ACM Press, 2002.
7. R. Kaushik, P. Shenoy, P. Bohannon, and E. Gudes. Exploiting local similarity for efficient indexing of paths in graph structured data. In *International Conference on Data Engineering*. IEEE Computer Society, 2002.
8. M. Ley. Dblp computer science bibliography database. http://www.informatik.uni-trier.de/ ley/db/.
9. Q. Li and B. Moon. Indexing and querying xml data for regular path expressions. In *VLDB Conference*, pages 361–370. Morgan Kaufmann, 2001.
10. T. Milo and D. Suciu. Index structures for path expressions. In C. Beeri and P. Buneman, editors, *International Conference on Database Theory*, volume 1540 of *Lecture Notes in Computer Science*, pages 277–295. Springer, 1999.
11. J. Shanmugasundaram, K. Tufte, C. Zhang, G. He, D. J. DeWitt, and J. F. Naughton. Relational databases for querying xml documents: Limitations and opportunities. In *VLDB Conference*, pages 302–314, 1999.
12. W3C. Xml path language (xpath). http://www.w3.org/TR/xpath.
13. W3C. Xml query language (xquery). http://www.w3.org/TR/xquery.

# An Improved Framework for Online Adaptive Information Filtering[1]

Liang Ma, Qunxiu Chen, and Lianhong Cai

State Key Lab of Intelligent Technology and Systems, Department of Computer Science and Technology, Tsinghua University, Beijing 100084, China
maliang00@mails.tsinghua.edu.cn, cqx@s1000e.cs.tsinghua.edu.cn, clh-dcs@mail.tsinghua.edu.cn

**Abstract.** Adaptive information filtering is an emerging filtering technology that can learn the user interest/topic automatically during the filtering process and adjust its output accordingly. It provides a better performance and broader applicability than the traditional filtering technology, therefore is useful in Internet for managing sensitive information and presenting personalized content to Web user. In this paper we propose a new framework for online adaptive filtering, in which two different scoring/weighting and feedback mechanisms are implemented. Based on them, an incremental profile training method is introduced for locating user interest accurately, and a profile self-learning algorithm is also developed for adjusting user focus in test filtering. The experiments in the Reuters online news show our system performs better than the exist systems in the profile training and overall filtering results.

## 1 Introduction

The rapid growth of the Internet make it difficult for Web users to get their favorite information fast and freely. The information filtering, a technology in information retrieval(IR), is selected as an effective solution for this problem. It can be used in pushing relevant Web information to users actively according to their personal interest, and masking certain sensitive content (such as nation security, sex, violence, etc) from the users. While in traditional mechanism (batch filtering), a number of initial positive training documents are required (commonly impossible for various instant user interest in Web), and the filtering model for user interest/topic can not be adjusted in filtering. As an improved version, adaptive information filtering needs only a few initial training documents, and in filtering period it can do self-adjusting to refine the filtering model by run-time judgement, therefore further lift the overall performance. All these features make the adaptive filtering the best choice for Web filtering.

There are two steps in process of adaptive filtering: (1) profile training; (2) test filtering (include profile learning). In training process, we try to construct a basic topic

[1] The research work is supported by the National 863 High Technology Project (Project No: 2001AA114040).

G. Dong et al. (Eds.): WAIM 2003, LNCS 2762, pp. 409–420, 2003.

profile from the initial training documents and training corpus. Then from the basic profile, we do the test filtering in target document stream. All the documents in stream are processed by certain order(such as time sequence). The relevant documents (judged by user or profile) are taken as output of the filtering. In this period, the topic profile keep learning using the feedback from these documents newly retrieved.

In a general framework of filtering, user interest/topic model is typically defined by topic profile, which is typically composed with topic vector (including topic features and corresponding weights) and a threshold for selecting relevant documents. The accuracy of topic profile is the key to the overall filtering result. It is obvious that the profile can be refined by adaptive profile learning in test filtering. But it seems not enough. In training if there are much noise features (can not present original topic) are selected in basic topic profile, the profile in deed will be some different from the topic we really want(we called it a biased profile). Starting filtering from a biased profile, the profile learning mechanism will develop the profile in a deviated focus. Therefore the training for unbiased profile is also a fundamental factor for filtering performance.

In adaptive filtering system, the feature weighting/document scoring model is the backbone mechanism. Also the feedback algorithm used in profile learning is very important for improving the running performance of the profile. Complex profile learning mechanism based on specific feedback algorithm is now under hot pursuit.

In this paper, we present an improved framework for Web adaptive information filtering. After the analysis to current running frameworks for adaptive filtering, we introduce the new ideas and improved algorithms used in our framework. Then the experiment results are listed and the final conclusion is given out accordingly.

## 2 New Challenges in Web Online Filtering

In current framework for general purpose adaptive filtering, there are some different requirements when it is used for Web online filtering:

1. Due to the various focus in Web topics, for an instant topic to be filtered, usually only a few initial positive documents can be used for profile training.
2. There are enormous Web documents to be filtered, so the relevance judgement to documents which is done by user manually before, is done by the topic profile automatically. The system use profile vector to score the document, and decide whether the document is positive by profile threshold.
3. In profile learning, only positive documents are selected for feedback, for these negative documents usually are not kept by user in practical filtering.

For these new challenges in Web adaptive filtering, there are some problems emerging in current framework and need further improvements.

1. **Feature selection in feedback algorithm.** In profile learning, the feedback algorithm is used to select topic features from positive documents to improve the profile, thus the criteria for feature selection is important for unbiased profile. In current feedback methods, no matter Rocchio feedback[3] or other mechanisms[4], new features are often selected mainly according to its statistical score (such as TF or probability in document set). But the statistical score computed either from

newly retrieved positive documents(usually not much) or whole training set can not exactly show how much in degree the feature is relevant to the topic, thus many noise features are also added to the profile, which lead to a biased profile.

2. **Profile training.** In current research, profile training is much less concerned than profile learning in test filtering, for people believe that the improvement in profile learning can raise the system performance more. Since the positive documents (used for feedback in profile learning) now are chosen by the profile instead of user himself, the overall performance is much dependent on the basic profile derived from training. Unfortunately, the limited initial training documents for a topic make it not easy to construct a well-defined basic profile. Without an unbiased profile, even a perfect profile learning mechanism will also suffer the poor result.
3. **Weighting/scoring model.** In existing adaptive filtering systems, Vector Space Model(VSM) [1,5] and probability model[6] are two popular IR models used. They work well but there is no much space for improvement. In recent years, a new IR mechanism based on language model, is proved to be efficient in some Web IR applications. It seems also a promising model for Web adaptive filtering.

## 3 New Framework

Based on the analysis to the existing systems and new requirements in Web, we develop an improved framework for online adaptive filtering in Web. The related mechanisms and algorithms in the framework will be discussed in following section.

### 3.1 Scoring/Weighting/Feedback Models

Different from other systems, in our framework two different scoring/weighting models are implemented respectively, in order to provide higher flexibility for various Web environments. For each model, one specific feedback algorithm(used in training and profile learning) is also selected.

Vector Space Model(VSM) is the first choice used here because of its steady performance in traditional models. The document is presented as document vector, the features in vector are weighted by its TF*IDF score(we use Okapi TF Formula[6]) in the document set. Also we use improved Rocchio feedback algorithm that does feedback only using positive documents.

Language Model(LM) [7] is another IR model used. It provides a completely new mechanism for adaptive filtering. A version of LM mechanism, including SimpleKL scoring schema[8] and Mixture[9] feedback algorithm, is implemented here.

### 3.2 Two Phase in Filtering Process

The whole process of adaptive filtering is done in two steps. The first step is profile training, in which a basic profile is constructed using the initial positive documents and training corpus. In test filtering (the second step), there is much work to do.

Set $U_p$ as a set for positive documents already retrieved, and let $U_f$ as a set for documents already retrieved. The test filtering is done as following loop:

(1) Fetch a new document from test document stream(should be in certain order).
(2) Using the profile to score current document.
(3) If the score of document is higher than the profile threshold, the document is judged to be positive and added to $U_f$ and $U_p$. Otherwise, throw the document.
(4) When the number of positive documents in $U_p$ reach system setup, do profile learning using the documents in $U_p$. After that, set the $U_p$ empty.
(5) If there is no document in document stream, the filtering is finished. The documents in $U_f$ are the final output. Otherwise, return step(1) for next loop.

As we know, the kernel issue in test filtering is adaptive profile learning, by which the basic profile is refined. But only the positive documents recently retrieved(not all the documents retrieved) are used in learning, because usually the documents retrieved long time ago can not still be saved by user.

# 4 Improved Mechanisms in Framework

Based on the backbone IR model introduced in section 3, the details of the enhanced mechanisms and algorithms in new framework will be discussed in this section.

## 4.1 Feature Selection in Rocchio Feedback

As we mentioned, in training and learning, much noise features are added to profile because they are selected simply by their statistical score, which is not precise for defining its relevance to the topic when there are only a small amount of documents.

In such case, for a feature, its linguistic properties in the passage should be more accurate and meaningful than statistical score and thereby is helpful for removing the noise features. In natural language processing, there is not much knowledge[10] available. The syntax information can be an immediate tip. Using a syntax parser, each positive document is converted to a parsing tree, from which the features are extracted by specific syntactic properties. Then from these newly extracted features instead of all features in original document, we update the profile by specific feedback algorithm.

For all the syntactic properties, only Part Of Speech(POS) and syntactic function component(such as clause) are useful. A deep study to these properties tell us:

**Rule 1:** most of the profile features are noun, verb and adjective.
**Rule 2:** noun (including noun phrase and proper noun) act as big part of features.
**Rule 3:** adjective in subject and attribute clause is a potential feature.
**Rule 4:** verb (in predicate) maybe a useful feature.

Before feedback, all the candidate features are extracted using above rules and reconstruct a shrunk document. Set $D_t$ as the collection of newly shrunk documents.

For the feature t in $D_t$, its weight is assigned not as common statistical value (such as TF*IDF) in original document, because the weight is not exact after some word features are eliminated from document. Let $W_{avg}(P)$ be the average weight of all the features in profile P. Set Df(t) as document frequency(DF) in $D_t$. The weight of t is:

$$W(t) = W_{avg}(P) * \sqrt{Df(t)} \tag{1}$$

Here the DF score is more helpful than other criteria(TF or TF*IDF) in feature weighting because most of the noise is removed previously. A simple formula is applied for W(t), for there is no sign for that a complex one will be more precise.

After these work, the features can be selected under Rocchio feedback algorithm. Specifically, the centroid vector of the feedback document(shrunk document) vectors is computed and the feature terms are ranked by their centroid weight. The $K_m$ best-ranked features are selected. Let $N_p$ be the number of feedback documents, then $K_m$ is:

$$K_m = 5 + 5 * \log(N_p + 1) \tag{2}$$

The mechanism is designed only for Rocchio feedback using VSM model. It is not used for LM-based feedback because of the different weighting/scoring mechanism.

### 4.2 Incremental Profile Training

As one of the main processes of adaptive filtering, the task of profile training is to form a basic topic profile later used in test filtering.

In most cases, there are only a few initial positive training documents provided for training, these documents are not enough for an unbiased profile because of limited topic features can be extracted from them. A training corpus in this case is often used for expanding more topic features for profile.

A popular way for construct a basic topic profile now[11,12] is to select certain number (usually several dozen) of new documents(thought as pseudo positive) from whole train corpus(the documents in corpus are scored using initial profile which is constructed only by initial positive documents), then by these pseudo documents, expand the topic features in basic profile with certain relevance feedback algorithm (for example, Rocchio). After that a topic profile is ready for use. The training process is a one-pass feedback using many pseudo documents. But when many pseudo documents are selected, the precision of them fluctuate much on the limited features in initial profile, thus increase the risk to be biased profile after feedback.

In our training mechanism, topic profile is iteratively updated by relevance feedback more than once. In each feedback, only several (not many) pseudo documents most similar to the exist training documents are used. Then by improved profile we select new pseudo documents for next feedback. By this repeated way profile can be expanded by enough pseudo documents, at the same time it is a little far from being a biased profile because of pretty limited features added in each feedback.

Before start of the training, an initial topic profile is constructed by the collection of initial positive training documents. All the words in each positive document are pre-processed with stop-word removing and word stemming. The features selected here are stemmed words with high TF*IDF score in the collection. The score is also assigned to feature as its weight in profile. After that, define a set $U_t$ for positive documents, then add these initial positive training documents to it.

Starting from initial profile, the whole training is running as follow:

(1) Use profile to query the whole training corpus.
(2) Select new pseudo positive documents from scored training corpus.
(3) Parse the new pseudo documents and filter noise feature by syntax analysis.
(4) Update profile with these pseudo documents using certain feedback algorithm.
(5) Add these pseudo positive documents to $U_t$.
(6) If there is no new pseudo documents selected in step(2) or already do feedback for $T_n$ times, finish training. Otherwise repeat the process from step(1).

In step(2), the scored documents in training set are sorted by their score in descending order. For each document not in set $U_t$ yet, it will be pseudo positive document by either of criteria there:

**Fixed number m:** If its score is one of the top m score of all the scores.
**Adaptive Threshold $T_h$:** If its score are higher than $T_h$. $T_h$ is an adaptive threshold determined mainly by the scores of the documents already in $U_t$.

The m is set to a small number to keep unbiased feedback and $T_n$ is also setup for repeated times(m*$T_n$ is the number of the pseudo documents selected in training). By adaptive threshold, there is no fixed setup for selecting documents. We keep a strict threshold setup mechanism for limited documents in each feedback. If no document is selected or a max feedback times is reached, the training is finished.

In step (3), each new pseudo document is parsed and some candidate word features are extracted by specific syntactic properties. Then the document is re-constructed only by these features instead of all the words in original document. By this way, much noise features are removed. Then the document collection of these newly constructed documents is ready for feedback in next step.

The improved Rocchio algorithm used in step (4) is a little different from the classic Rocchio. The candidate features to be ranked are weighted by formula (1) and pre-filtered by syntactic properties (not statistical score).

Now the topic vector is filled with enough topic features. To do relevance judgement in test filtering, the profile threshold for the topic vector also needs initialization. A method used now is to set the initial threshold with the value that can result in the highest score of certain measures (such as Linear Utility or F-Beta) in training. We follow the idea, but the difference is all the documents in $U_t$ (not only the initial positive documents) are used as positive documents in calculating the measures.

### 4.3 Adaptive Profile Learning in Test Filtering

In test filtering, the profile does the relevance scoring to the documents and selects the positive documents by threshold. At the same time, the profile is continuously improved using adaptive learning for higher filtering precision in subsequent documents. Due to its immediate impact to the precision of final output, a good mechanism for adaptive profile learning become the research focus in test filtering.

In adaptive profile learning, each element in profile, including the profile vector and threshold, need to be self-adjusted by new positive documents retrieved.

In existing systems, a better way for adjust profile is to use an expectation model[13] based on the statistic to documents already retrieved. The assumption of this mechanism is the relative steady distribution for relevance document in whole stream. But it is not so for the Web document stream, where the various documents are delivered in highly random order.

#### 4.3.1 Adjust Profile Vector

In updating profile vector, the new profile features is primarily selected by feedback algorithm, while there are still two items left for consideration: how many positive documents used for one feedback and how many features are selected to profile.

In our framework, a fixed feedback interval is chosen. The profile vector is updated when $F_n$($F_n$ =5) new positive documents retrieved. As to the number of features added to profile, it is determined by ***Decay Rate***. In test filtering, profile is keeping refined by feedback. As the learning is going on, more effective features are in the profile and less features are needed. Add fixed number of features in each feedback is not wise.

We use decay rate d(n) to decrease the features selected as the increasing feedback times. Let P as the number of features added to profile in current feedback, and set its initial value as $P_0$. For n-th update, we have $P = P_0 * d(n)$. The d(n) is defined as:

$$d(n) = \alpha + (1.0 - \alpha) * e^{-n\beta} \qquad \alpha, \beta \in (0,1) \tag{3}$$

#### 4.3.2 Adjust Threshold

In filtering, the profile threshold will be adjusted when meet either conditions:

**Condition (1):** When profile vector is updated

**Condition (2):** When distribution density of retrieved positive documents since last profile update exceed the expectation value.

Now we set t as the sequence number of the document in the stream. Then:

n(t): the number of documents processed up to t;

$n_R(t)$: the number of positive documents judged by system up to t;

$n_N(t)$ the number of negative documents judged by system up to t;

T(t): profile threshold at t

W(t): weight sum of all features in profiles up to t

$S(t_k,t_{k+1})$: average relevance score of the documents filtered in $(t_k,t_{k+1})$ interval

$S_R(t_k,t_{k+1})$: average relevance score of positive documents retrieved in $(t_k,t_{k+1})$

$D_R(t_k,t_{k+1})$: distribution density of positive documents retrieved since last profile update. $D_R(t_k, t_{k+1}) = [n_R(t+1) - n_R(t)]/[n(t+1) - n(t)]$

For two conditions, we have different way for adjusting the threshold:

**For Condition (1):**

$$T(t+1) = T(t)e + T(t) * \frac{Ws(t+1) - Ws(t)}{Ws(t)} * e^{-\gamma} \tag{4}$$

Here $\gamma = S_R(t_k, t_{k+1})/S(t_k, t_{k+1})$

**For Condition (2):**

$$T(t+1) = T(t) * \theta(t+1) \tag{5}$$

The $\theta(t+1)$ is defined as follow:

If $D_R(t_k + t_{k+1}) < V_r * D_{exp}$ Then //decrease threshold

$\theta(t+1) = A + (1.0 - A) * S(t_k, t_{k+1})/T(t)$

Else

If $D_R(t_k + t_{k+1}) > (1.0 / V_r) * D_{exp}$ Then // increase threshold

$\theta(t+1) = 1.0 + B * S_R(t_k, t_{k+1})/T(t)$

$V_r$ is a rate controlling the varying scale of distribution density. $D_{exp}$ denote the expectation for distribution density of positive documents in training set. We use $D_{exp}$ in test set because we assume both set has the similar positive distribution density.

## 5 Experiments

There are comprehensive experiments for evaluation to our framework. First, we will estimate the each improved factors in our system, then the overall performance of the system, together with the adaptive profile learning mechanism, are tested.

All the experiments for new framework are tested using the official resource of TREC 2002 adaptive filtering track, in order to gain comparable evaluation to other systems. As one of the most important conference[14] in information retrieval, the TREC(Text REtrieval Conference) is working for promoting the retrieval on mass data such as Web. In adaptive filtering track[15] of 2002, an open, uniform platform is provided for estimating the performance of 21 adaptive filtering systems all over the world. The Reuters Corpus Volume 1, an online English document collection of Reuters news, is used for training and test filtering. The whole corpus is divided into training set(83650 documents) and test set (other 723141 news documents ordered by publish time). From the corpus, 100 topics in various news issues are selected for test, the first 50 topics(R101-R150) and the second 50 topics (R151-R200) are judged in different way. For each topic, 3 initial positive training documents(from training set), together with a short description to the topic, are provided for training.

### 5.1 Feature Selection Mechanism in Feedback

In our feedback algorithm, syntactic properties (especially the POS properties) are introduced for pre-filter the candidate features. MINIPAR is chosen for syntax analysis. It is an English parser[16] efficient in building a parsing tree and provide enough syntactic properties required in experiment. Different POSs properties are used separately, so as to evaluate their individual contribution in feature selection.

Due to the limited features added to profile in each feedback, to test the effect brought by improved feature selection mechanism, we have to do feedback for enough times. Thinking that the profile training in our framework is using an iterative feedback mechanism, our ideas for feature selection is tested using the same method as that in profile training (will be discussed in next section).

## 5.2 Profile Training

In our improved framework, an incremental profile training mechanism by iterative feedback is implemented. Its promotion to the topic profile is analyzed here.

Before training, the basic topic profile for each topic is constructed by the way defined in section 4.2. The difference is the TREC topic description is also included. All the runs start with the same basic profile.

The best way to evaluate profile training is to study the filtering result after test filtering by current profile, while it is not practical because of the impact from adaptive profile learning mechanism in test filtering. Since enough relevance documents is helpful for unbiased profile when they are used for feedback, we use the precision of the pseudo positive documents in profile training(after training is finished) as measure for profile training. Let $P_n$ be the total number of pseudo documents got in training. And set $P_r$ as the number of relevance documents in $P_n$ (here the initial positive documents should be excluded from $P_n$ and $P_r$), then $Precison = P_r/P_n$.

To test the performance of incremental training mechanism, we first do a training by old way which do one-pass feedback (Run-1) for initial profile, then we have two run (Run-2 and Run-3) by multi-pass mechanism, which select pseudo positive documents by fixed number m (set m=3) or threshold $T_h$ (set to the average score of all positive documents in $U_t$). The three runs all use classical Rocchio positive feedback method. In each run, we get the score for each topic, but only the mean score of all topics, together with the parameters of each run, are listed in table 1 (the $P_n$ and $P_r$ are float value because they are average score of all topics).

**Table 1.** One-pass and multi-pass mechanism in profile training

| Run | Num of Pass | Parameters | | Mean Score | | |
|---|---|---|---|---|---|---|
| | | | | $P_n$ | $P_r$ | Precision |
| 1 | One-Pass | $T_n$ =1 | m=15 | 15.0 | 4.5 | 32.73 % |
| 2 | Multi-Pass | $T_n$ =5 | m=3 | 15.0 | 4.9 | 34.67 % |
| 3 | | adaptive threshold $T_h$ | | 12.1 | 4.3 | 39.26 % |

The following experiment is for analyzing the idea that using syntactic properties aiding feature selection in feedback. All the POS properties (noun, adjective and verb) in syntactic Rule 1 are divided into two properties sets: Set A (noun+adjective) and Set B(verb only). The noun and adjective are included in one set because of their tight relation in syntax structure. The two sets are tested respectively in Run-4 and Run-5, then work together for overall contribution (Run-6). After this, we do one run again (Run-7) with all POS types by hand parsing(only for 20 topics because of the heavy duty in it). The average score of the same 20 topics in Run-6 and Run-2(no syntactic properties used) are also listed as Run-6A and Run-2A, in order to find out the impact by accuracy of parser. All the runs(listed in table 2) use the multi-pass feedback with fixed setting(m=3 ,$T_n$ =5, $P_n$ =15) same to Run-2.

**Table 2.** Syntactic properties used for feedback

| Run | Parser | POS Types Used | Mean Score | |
|---|---|---|---|---|
| | | | $P_r$ | Precision |
| 4 | MINIPAR | Set A (Noun+Adjective) | 4.5 | 32.35 % |
| 5 | MINIPAR | Set B (Adverb) | 4.3 | 29.23 % |
| 6 | MINIPAR | Set A + Set B | 4.3 | 30.32 % |
| 7 | Hand parsing | | 4.7 | 36.15 % |
| 6A | MINIPAR 20 topics | | 4.6 | 33.25 % |
| 2A | No parser 20 topics | No POSs used | 4.6 | 34.15 % |

## 5.3 Overall Performance

In adaptive filtering, the adaptive profile learning mechanism in test filtering usually is not evaluated individually. Instead it is often estimated in the estimation to overall system performance, for its output is the final result of system.

There are two measures, F-Beta and Linear Utility, widely used in estimating the adaptive filtering system. In TREC-2002, they are defined as T11F and T11SU. For a filtering topic, set $FD_t$ as filtering result(positive set), and let N=| $FD_t$|. Then:

R = total number of the relevance documents

$R_p$ = number of relevance document in $FD_t$

$N_p$= number of non-relevance document in $FD_t$. $N_p$=N - $R_p$

Then :

$$T11F = \begin{cases} 0 & \text{if } R_p = 0 \\ (1.25 * R_p)/(N + 0.25 * R) & \text{otherwise} \end{cases}$$

$$T11SU = \frac{\max(T11NU, MinNU) - MinNU}{1 - MinNU} \quad MinNU = 0.5 \quad T11NU = \frac{2 * R_p - N_p}{2 * N}$$

Under the requirement of TREC-2002 adaptive filtering track, we submit two runs and get the TREC official evaluation, so that our system can be compared to other system in clear way. The two runs are running based on two weighting/scoring models of our system respectively and all optimized by same criteria (T11F), therefore we can have more insight to the real power of two models.

For each run, the related mechanism and their TREC evaluation are shown in table 3(see the next page). The mean score of all TREC runs (submitted by all the participant systems) in this track are also listed. We mainly focus on the T11F score because our runs are all optimized by this measure. You will find that performance of our runs is much higher than the average level of current research.

The final TREC evaluation report[15] show that our system (Tsinghua University) is ranked as one of the best systems(evaluated by T11F score). The top-4 best participant systems and related scores (T11F means score) are given in table 4.

**Table 3.** Related mechanisms and TREC evaluation of the submitted runs

| Run | Mechanism used | | | Evaluation (mean score) | | | |
|---|---|---|---|---|---|---|---|
| | Scoring /Weighting | Adaptive Learning | | R101- R150 | | R151- R200 | |
| | | Feedback Algorithm | POSs | T11U | T11F | T11U | T11F |
| ThuT 11af2 | VSM BM25 TF*IDF | Rocchio | Used | 0.389 | 0.422 | 0.061 | 0.052 |
| ThuT 11af3 | Language Model SimpleKL | Mixture | No | 0.277 | 0.337 | 0.052 | 0.030 |
| Mean score of all TREC runs(39 runs) | | | | 0.381 | 0.306 | 0.257 | 0.020 |

**Table 4.** Average performance of top-4 participant systems (T11F)

| Assessor Topics（R101-R150） | | Intersection Topics（R151-R200） | |
|---|---|---|---|
| Participant Team | Score | Participant Team | Score |
| Chinese Academy of Sciences | 0.428 | Chinese Academy of Sciences | 0.062 |
| KerMIT Consortium | 0.426 | KerMIT Consortium | 0.056 |
| Carnegie Mellon University | 0.401 | Informatique de Toulouse | 0.054 |
| Tsinghua University | 0.422 | Tsinghua University | 0.052 |

## 6 Discussions and Conclusions

In table 1, compared to one-pass mechanism in Run-1, the precision is lightly lifted when multi-pass feedback used in Run-2 and Run-3, indicating that incremental training mechanism using iterative feedback is helpful for unbiased training. The Run-3 perform better than Run-2, revealing us that selecting pseudo documents by adaptive threshold is self-adaptive and in highly precision (partly due to the strict threshold setup used), and can be used for various training sets in different scale.

In table 2, only Run-4 in first three runs has a comparable result as traditional way, but this poor performance is partly because the parser provide a low accuracy (less than 65%) in parsing complex compound statements. In fact, the performance gap in Run-2A, Run-6A and Run-7 show us the real power of POS properties in feature selection. Also an accurate parser for specific syntactic purpose is proved necessary.

The score in table 3 and table 4 show our system is running in a good status, mainly because of the improvements in profile training and adaptive profile learning. Also its final rank in all the participant systems demonstrates its outstanding ability for Web-based online adaptive filtering. The only unsatisfied result is that the run (ThuT11af3) based on Language Model perform not well as we expect, possibly because of the little work in performance tuning.

In this paper, we present an improved framework for online adaptive filtering in Web. The comprehensive experiments on the TREC platform show the system based on this framework give a satisfied result and perform better than the other similar systems, indicating the new ideas used here is effective. But the Language Model IR mechanism does not show a satisfied result in adaptive filtering and need more experiments for evaluating it. Other future work also includes perfect mechanism for unbiased training and adaptive profile threshold setup.

## References

1. Ricardo Baeza-ates, Berthier Ribeiro-Neto. Modern Information Retrieval. Addison-Wesley, 1999
2. T. M. Cover and J. A. Thomas. Elements of Information Theory. Wiley, 1991
3. J.Rocchio. Relevance Feedback in Information Retrieval, In: Salton, Gerard (Editor), The SMART Retrieval System, Prentice-Hall, Englewood 1971
4. Robert E.Schapire, Yoram Singer Amit Singhal. Boosting and Rocchio Applied to Text Filtering. In 21th ACM SIGIR Conference on Research and Development in Information Retrieval. 1998
5. Chris Buckley et al. The Smart/Empire TIPSTER IR system. In Proceedings of TIPSTER Phase 3 Workshop, 1999
6. Stephen Roberson, S.Walker. Okapi/keenbow at TREC-8. In Proceedings of 8th Text Retrieval Conference (TREC-8). 1999
7. J. Lafferty, C. Zhai. Risk minimization and language modeling in information retrieval. In 24th ACM SIGIR Conference on Research and Development in Information Retrieval. 2001
8. Chengxiang Zhai, et,al. The Lemur Toolkit for Language Modeling and Information Retrieval. http://www-2.cs.cmu.edu/ ~lemur/
9. Chengxiang Zhai, John Lafferty. Model-based Feedback in the Language Modeling Approach to Information Retrieval. The 10th International Conference on Information and Knowledge Management (CIKM), 2001
10. Claire Cardie, Vincent Ng, David Pierce, and Chris Buckley. Examining the role of statistical and linguistic knowledge sources in a general knowledge question-answering system. In Proceedings of the 6th Applied Natural Language Processing Conference, 2000
11. Lide Wu, Xuanjing Huang, Junyu Niu, Yikun Guo, Yingju Xia, Zhe Feng: Filtering, QA, Web and Video Tasks. In Proceeding of Text Retrieval Conference (TREC-10). 2001
12. Chengxiang Zhai, Peter Jansen, Norbert Roma, Emilia Stoica, David A. Evans. Optimization in CLARIT TREC-8 Adaptive Filtering. In Proceeding of 8th Text Retrieval Conference (TREC-8). 1999
13. Unbiased S-D Threshold Optimization, Initial Query Degradation, Incrementality, for Adaptive Filtering. In Proceeding of 10th Text Retrieval Conference (TREC-10). 2001
14. E. M. Voorhees. Overview of the 11th Text REtrieval Conference. In Proceeding of 11th Text Retrieval Conference (TREC-11). 2002
15. Stephen Robertson, Ian Soboroff. The TREC 2002 Filtering Track Report. In Proceeding of 11th Text Retrieval Conference (TREC-11). 2002
16. Dekang Lin. Dependency-based Evaluation of MINIPAR. Workshop on the Evaluation of Parsing Systems, Granada, Spain, May, 1998

# An Image Retrieval Method Based on Information Filtering of User Relevance Feedback Records

Xiangdong Zhou, Qi Zhang, Li Liu, Ailin Deng, Liang Zhang, and Baile Shi

Department of Computing and Information Technology
Fudan University
Shanghai, China, 200433
xidzhou@etang.com

**Abstract.** This paper presents a composite image retrieval approach based on the analysis of the accumulated user relevance feedback records. To improve efficiency, semi-supervised fuzzy clustering is employed to classify the RF records, and the subsequent information filtering within the target cluster is performed to guide the refinement of query parameters. During information filtering, both the user's relevance evaluations and the corresponding query images of the records are used to predict the semantic correlation between the database images and the current retrieval. Experiment results show that our method outperforms the traditional ones in both efficiency and effectiveness.

## 1 Introduction

As a major application of multimedia database, the research on content-based image retrieval (CBIR) is of special significance. However, due to the limitation of the current computer vision techniques, exact mappings between semantic and visual features of image cannot be properly established. As a result, CBIR systems based on mere visual feature comparison can hardly meet the practical requirement effectively.

To remedy the problem, user's Relevance Feedback (RF) has been borrowed from textual Information Retrieval (IR). RF is an interactive and iterative process which improves the retrieval performance by adjusting query parameters based on user's relevance evaluation of the output result. Because of its effective power in bridging the Semantic-Visual Gap, relevance feedback has gained substantial popularity in recent years. Early work primarily falls into the kind of query parameter refinement according to various heuristic ideas [8],or optimal methods [4,9], some recent approaches incorporated some machine learning methods, such as SVM [10] etc, into the RF process to improve the retrieval precision.

Recently, employing long-term learning exploiting historical RF information is extracting growing attention. [5,3,11,12,1]. Generally, the accumulated feedback data consists of two kinds of information: the query image and the relevance

G. Dong et al. (Eds.): WAIM 2003, LNCS 2762, pp. 421–432, 2003.

evaluation toward the corresponding retrieval. Current approaches mainly focus on the exploiture of the user's evaluation data, with the basic idea of analyzing the semantic correlation through mining of the correlation between feedback records. However, for this kind of approach, the retrieval performance largely depends on the degree of the correlation between the user's evaluation records. In other words, when less correlation is found in the evaluation records, the system performance will subject to a considerable degradation. Furthermore, with the ever-increasing size of the record database, an effective analysis method is demanded to keep the problem manageable.

In this paper, we propose a retrieval method based on the fuzzy clustering of the query images included in the RF records. The fuzzy clustering is semi-supervised by the user's evaluation information of the RF records. Based on the clustering of the RF records, the retrieval process can be performed as follows: when a new round of retrieval starts, the nearest cluster centroid to the query image is first found out as the target cluster; then the information filtering is conducted on the RF records of the target cluster to obtain the correlated images; finally these images are analyzed to adjust the query parameters and improve the retrieval precision.

The rest of this paper is organized as follows. Section 2 provides background and related work. Section 3 introduces the RF method based on information filtering. In Section 4, the fuzzy clustering of user relevance feedback records is explained in detail. Algorithms are described in section 5. Experiment results are presented and analyzed in Section 6. Section 7 concludes the paper.

## 2 Previous Work

Relevance feedback is a powerful tool in CBIR. Much work has been carried out to employ RF to bridge the Semantic-Visual Gap. Generally, there are two kinds of relevance feedback: query point movement and re-weighting. Described by Rocchio's equation [7], the former technique is designed to move the query point toward positive points leading to a better result and away from negative ones. Rui [8] proposed a weight updating method focusing on feature component distribution of scored images along each vector dimension measured by their standard deviation. Besides, MinderReader [4] used the generalized Euclidean distance to measure the similarity among images. The optimization method was adopted to estimate the "optimal" weight matrices.

In the aspect of using long-term learning strategy to improve retrieval performance, Muller et al. [5] presented an image retrieval system based on the usage of a big set of features and the analysis of the user's relevance feedback log. Yang et al. [11] proposed a method to improve the retrieval effectiveness by using the user's relevant evaluation, which is recorded and can be extracted from the feedback log file. Their method is based on the classic tf/idf function in IR domain. The basic idea is to set up a semantic correlation index (called Peer Index) according to the coupling of user evaluation information. He et al. [3] set up a latent semantic sub-space by exploiting the user relevance feedback records. With the extracted latent semantic feature from the feedback data, on-line training was performed using a learned classifier.

As to the utilization of the image visual content of the feedback records, there is FeedbackBypass proposed by Bartolin et al. [1]. In their approach, mappings between the query sample and the "optimal" parameters are recorded into database. When a new round of retrieval starts, the "optimal" query parameters are first retrieved out by matching the low level features between the current query sample and the recorded query samples, then the initial retrieval round begins equipped with those "optimal" parameters.

## 3 Image Semantic Correlation Measurement

### 3.1 Vector Model of User Relevance Feedback Pattern

In the process of one retrieval session, several rounds of relevance feedback are often conducted by the user, during which feedback images are given to tune the system. When the session is concluded, we can get a series of image numbers (representing the positive samples given by the user). Actually, such a sequence reflects the user's evaluation regarding the current retrieval, so we store it into the log file as the Relevance Feedback record. By accumulating the records through user's retrievals overtime, the log file forms into a RF database. The vector model of user relevance feedback pattern is defined as follows:

**Definition 1.** User Relevance Feedback Pattern

Suppose $I$ denotes the set of all the images in the database (represented as unique numbers), where $|I| = n$, and $R$ denotes the RF database, where $r_i \in R$ represents the $i$th RF record, which consists of the corresponding query feature vector and the user evaluation data of the $i$th retrieval session. Let $Q$ denote the feature vector set of the submitted query samples, $W$ denote the relevance evaluation record set given by user. Suppose $w_i \in W$ is represented by an $n$-dimension vector $w_i = (w_{1,i}, w_{2,i}, \dots, w_{n,i})$, where $w_{k,i}$ is the weight of the relevance between the $k$th image and the $i$th RF record. Then the Relevance Feedback Pattern of $r_i$ is defined by a mapping $f : Q \leftrightarrow W$.

For example, the RF pattern of $r_i$ is $F(q_i) = (w_{1,i}, w_{2,i}, \dots, w_{n,i})$. Additionally, we use $r_i(q)$ to denote the feature vector of $q_i$, which is the query sample of $r_i$, and $r_i(w)$ to denote the corresponding user evaluation vector.

User RF log database can be illustrated in Fig. 1: the database consists of the data of 4 retrievals conducted on a 5-image mini image library. In the user relevance evaluation records, "1" represents relevance and "0" represents non-evaluation.

### 3.2 User Filtering Method and Related Problem

Fig. 1 shows that there is coupling information embedded in the user's relevance feedback data. For example, $a$ and $b$ are both retrievals about plane, so that in their corresponding evaluation records, image 2 and 3 get the same relevance

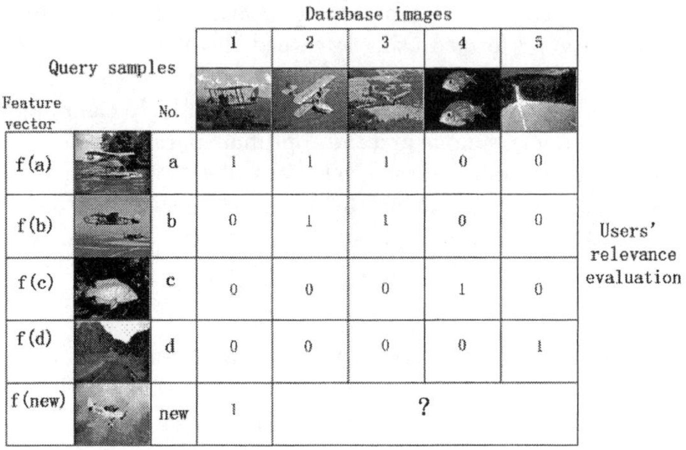

| Query samples: Feature vector | No. | Database images: 1 | 2 | 3 | 4 | 5 |
|---|---|---|---|---|---|---|
| f(a) | a | 1 | 1 | 1 | 0 | 0 |
| f(b) | b | 0 | 1 | 1 | 0 | 0 |
| f(c) | c | 0 | 0 | 0 | 1 | 0 |
| f(d) | d | 0 | 0 | 0 | 0 | 1 |
| f(new) | new | 1 | ? | | | |

Users' relevance evaluation

**Fig. 1.** Feedback log database

degree. Therefore, it is advantageous to make use of these coupling information by statistical analysis. As illustrated in Figure 1, user designates image 1 to be a relevant image with regard to the new retrieval. Also in record $a$, image 1 is denoted by 1 to show its relevance. Therefore, by this hint of semantic correlation of the new query and record $a$, we can infer that image 2, which is a relevant image in $a$, is probably relevant to the new retrieval as well. In this paper, such an analysis method of mining semantic correlation knowledge from user evaluation records is referred to as the "User Filtering" technique [3,11, 12]. It is very similar with the User Collaborative Filtering (CF), named by D. Goldberg [2]in a mail filtering system, which is a method for prediction of the preference or characteristics of unknown user (object) by using the information about the user group (related object group) already known. In light of CF, the user-filtering-based RF record analysis can be formulated as follows:

Let $d_i$ denote the set of images evaluated by user in retrieval $i$, thus $\hat{r}_i(w) = \frac{1}{|d_i|}\sum_{j \in I} r_i(w_j)$ is the average evaluation of images in retrieval $i$. Assume $a$ is the feedback vector of current retrieval, then the expectation value of relevance evaluation of image $j$ concerning the current retrieval can be described by the following equation:

$$P_{r_a(w),j} = \hat{r}_a(w) + \lambda \sum_{i=1}^{m} \{\phi(r_a(w), r_i(w))[r_i(w_j) - \hat{r}_i(w)]\}, \quad (1)$$

where $m$ is the number of feedback records in relevance feedback database, the weight $\phi(r_a(w), r_i(w))$ represents the similarity degree between $a$ and other feedback records and $\lambda$ is the normalization factor.

User filtering is an effective tool to exploit the RF data, however, there are some problems remaining to be solved. One of such imitations is that at the first round of a new retrieval (a new query image), when there is no evaluation information available, the system cannot use the user filtering method to improve the retrieval performance. Besides, when there is not enough evaluation given by the user in each retrieval is too little, i.e., only a few RF images are given by the user, the probability of coupling will decrease dramatically, which brings degradation to the system performance. For instance, from Fig.1 we can see that, the similar retrieval with the new retrieval are $a$ and $b$, but unlike $a$, record $b$ has no coupling user evaluation with the new retrieval, therefore in terms of user filtering, no useful information can be obtained from $b$ to benefit the current retrieval. In fact, the new query and the query sample in $b$ have high similarity in visual feature. If visual feature is utilized to judge the coupling of the RF records, $b$ will be determined as a correlated record to the new query and provide help for the prediction of semantic correlated images.

### 3.3 Image Semantic Correlation Measurement Based on Information Filtering

Inspired by the above idea, we incorporate the visual content information into the user filtering model and set up a more effective retrieval method based on image semantic correlation measurement. Since our method utilizes the image's visual feature and the user's evaluation data, it's actually an expansion to the user filtering and we name it Information Filtering (IF).

For any $r_i \in R$, let $r_i(w_j)$ denote the relevance value of image $j$ in record $i$. If the current RF pattern is denoted as $r_a$, then the relevance evaluation of image $j$ to the current retrieval is defined as follows

**Definition 2.** The similarity degree of image $j$ and RF record $r_a$ can be represented by $sim(r_a, j)$

$$sim(r_a, j) = \lambda_1 \left\{ \sum_{i=1}^{m} \left[ \alpha\phi(r_a(w), r_i(w)) + (1-\alpha)\lambda_2 L_\omega(r_a(q), r_i(q)) \right] \times r_i(w_j) \right\}, \tag{2}$$

where $m$ is the number of records in the RF database, $\lambda_1, \lambda_2$ are the normalization factors, $\alpha$ is the factor to adjust the ratio of the user filtering and content filtering, and $L_w$ is the weighted Euclidean distance. The $i$th feature weight $\omega_i$ can be computed according to [8]: $\omega_i \propto \frac{1}{\sum_{j=1}^{N} \pi_i (x_{ij} - \hat{x}_i)^2}$, here $\{x_1, x_2, \ldots, x_N\}$ denotes the feedback images appeared in $r_a$, $x_{nj}$ represents the feature vector of the $n$th feedback image on the $j$th visual feature, and $\pi = \{\pi_1, \pi_2, \ldots, \pi_N\}$ represents user relevance evaluation.

When $r_a(w)$ is empty for the first round of retrieval, the similarity degree of image $j$ and $r_a$ is measured by the similarity of the visual features of the corresponding images. The definition is as follows:

$$sim(r_a, j) = \lambda_1 \sum_{i=1}^{m} \left[ L_\omega(r_a(q), r_i(q)) \times r_i(w_j) \right]. \tag{3}$$

# 4 Fuzzy Clustering on Query Sample Images of RF Records

According to definition 1, there is a mapping between query feature vector and the corresponding user evaluation data in each RF record, so the records of the RF database can be grouped by performing clustering on the query feature vectors included in the RF records. Considering the diversity and ambiguity of the image semantic information, the Fuzzy C-Means clustering method is adopted to classify the records.

## 4.1 The Semantic Neighbor Set of RF Records

For any RF records $r_i, r_j \in R$, the similarity (distance) between $r_i(w)$ and $r_j(w)$ can be estimated by computing their vector cosine: $cos(r_i(w), r_j(w)) = \frac{\|r_i(w)\| \|r_j(w)\|}{r_i(w) r_j(w)}$. Through conducting K-NN search on the evaluation data of $R$, we can get the neighbor set $N_i$ of $r_i$ in the feedback records database, where $N_i = \{r_{i_j}\}$, $j = 1, 2, \ldots, l$, $N_i \subseteq R$. In this paper, we call $N_i$ the semantic neighbor set of $r_i$, because the evaluation given by user reflects the semantic relevance between images.

Due to the Semantic-Visual Gap of the image, mere visual feature comparison has many limitations and cannot ensure a satisfactory clustering result. Obviously, the query images in the neighbor set $N_i$ have a higher semantic correlation with the query image of $r_i$. Therefore it makes sense to employ the semantic neighbor set to improve the clustering of the query images of RF records. In the following, we present a method of making use of the semantic neighbor set to improve the fuzzy c means clustering of query images of RF records.

## 4.2 Semi-supervised Fuzzy C-Means Clustering

Using the known information to guide the clustering process is called the Semi-Supervision clustering. Pedrycz et al. [6] proposed a fuzzy clustering framework based on the utilization of part of the known classification information. Suppose $X = \{X_1, X_2, \ldots, X_n\}$ denotes the feature set of all the query images included in RF set $R$. Let $\mu_{ij}$ represent the membership degree of $X_j$ to sub-class $i$, and $V_i$ represent the centroid of the $i$th sub-class, where $i = 1, 2, \ldots, c$. The goal of the clustering process is to minimize the following object function:

$$J = \sum_{i=1}^{c} \sum_{j=1}^{n} u_{ij}^{m} |X_j - V_i|^2 + \beta \sum_{i=1}^{c} \sum_{j=1}^{n} (u_{ij} - b_j f_{ij})^m |X_j - V_i|^2, \tag{4}$$

while $m > 1$ is the fuzzy factor, then

$$V_i = \frac{\sum_{j=1}^{n} (\mu_{ij})^m X_j}{\sum_{j=1}^{n} (\mu_{ij})^m}, \tag{5}$$

$$u_{ij} = \frac{1}{1+\beta}\left[\frac{1+(1-b_j\sum_{i=1}^{c}f_{ij})}{\sum_{k=1}^{c}\left(\frac{d^2(X_j,V_i)}{d^2(X_j,V_k)}\right)^{1/(m-1)}} + \beta f_{ij}b_j\right], \tag{6}$$

where $b_j = \begin{cases} 1, & X_j\text{'s classification is known} \\ 0, & \text{otherwise} \end{cases}$, $f_{ij}$ is the known membership degree of $X_j$ to sub-class $i$ when $b_j = 1$.

Based on Pedryze's[6] framework, we propose a semi-supervised clustering method by using user's evaluation information to assist the inference of the actual membership of the query sample images. Our method is described as follows:

Since the query images in the neighbor set $N_i$ have a higher semantic correlation with the query image of $r_i$, we can deduce the membership degree of $r_i(q)$ from the $\{r_{i_j}(q)\}$ of $N_i$. Iterative optimization method is often adopted in fuzzy c means clustering, during which the membership of each element of $X$ changes iteratively. As a result, in the clustering procedure, a proper criterion should be set up to infer the membership degree of $r_i(q)$ by using the membership degrees of the elements in $\{r_{i_j}(q)\}$. A simple and feasible criterion can be: when all the elements in $\{r_{i_j}(q)\}$ have the consistent membership degree, we can deduce that $r_i(q)$ has the same membership degree. If the condition is relaxed a little, we have the following rule.

**Definition 3.** The membership degree determination function is represented as follows:

For each $r_{i_j} \in N_i$, let $u_{ki_j}$ denote its membership degree to sub-class $k$, the clustering consistency on $r_{i_j}$ can be determined by the variances on the membership degree of all the $r_{i_j}$ to sub-class $K$,$j = 1, 2, \ldots, l$.

$$e_i = \sum_{j=1}^{l}(u_{Ki_j} - \hat{u}_{Ki})^2, \tag{7}$$

where,

$$K = \left\{ k \,\middle|\, \max\left\{\sum_{j=1}^{l} u_{ki_j}\right\}, k = 1, 2, \ldots, c \right\}$$

is the sub-class with the maximal sum of membership degree, and $\hat{u}_{ki} = mean(u_{ki_j})$ is the mean of $u_{ki_j}$. Let $b_i$ denote the class tag of $r_i(q)$, if $e_i$ is lower than a certain threshold, then set $b_i = 1$, $f_{ki} = mean(u_{ki_j})$, and then the new membership degree of $r_i(q)$ can be computed according to Equ.6.

After the fuzzy clustering for the given $c$ sub-classes on the $m$ RF records, we use a 2-dimensional table $T_{c\times(m+1)}$ (classification table for RF records) to store the clustering result. In table $T$, each row represents a sub-class and each column represents a RF record. Therefore, $t_{ij} \in T$ represents the membership degree of record $r_j$ to the $i$th sub-class. Let $t_{i0}$ denote the centroid of the $i$th class (fuzzy means).

## 5 Algorithm for Generating Semantic Correlated Image Set

Initially, fuzzy clustering is conducted on RF records to generate the RF record classification table $T$. Then during a new round of retrieval, the algorithm first retrieves in $T$ to locate the nearest cluster centroid; then searches in the target cluster to form the neighbor RF record set; finally performs the statistical analysis on the neighbor set to get the semantic correlated image set. The detailed algorithm is described as follows:

Let $I = I_1, I_2, \ldots, I_n$ represent the database image set, the result of the fuzzy clustering analysis on RF set $R$ is represented as a $c \times (m+1)$ table $T$, where the designated image set in record $r_i$ is denoted by $d(r_i)$. The current RF vector is represented as $r_a$. The generation algorithm for semantic correlated image set is as follows:

**Algorithm 1.** Create correlation image set

Input:
  $\varepsilon_3$:threshold for semantic relevance, $r_a$:current RF record
Output:
  $result$ : correlation image number and relevance degree
$result$ = GetCorrelationSet( $r_a$, $\varepsilon_3$ )
$maxMembership = 0$
For each $t_{i0} \in T$, employ Equ.6 to compute the membership degree $u_{ai}$ of the current query sample $r_a(q)$ to $V_i(t_{i0})$.
  If $u_{ai}$ is bigger than $maxMembership$ then
    $maxMembership = u_{ai}$
    $k = i;$
  Endif
Endfor
$R_k = T_k$
$I' = \emptyset$
For each $r_i \in R_k$, $I' = I' \cup d(r_i)$ Endfor
For each image $p_j \in I'$
  If $r_a(w) == \emptyset$ then
    employ Equ.3 to compute $sim(r_a, p_j)$
  Else
    employ Equ.2 to compute $sim(r_a, p_j)$
  Endif
  $correlation(p_i) = sim(r_a, p_j)$
Endfor
For each image $p_i \in I'$, normalize $correlation(p_i)$
  If $correlation(p_i) > \varepsilon_3$
    $result \leftarrow result \cup (p_i, correlation(p_i))$
  Endif
Endfor

The proper value of threshold $\varepsilon_3$ can be determined by experiments, and in our experiment $\varepsilon_3 = 0.8$. The complexity of this algorithm in the worst case is $O(n \times m)$, where $n = |R_k|$, $m = \sum_{i=1}^{|R_k|} |r_i|$. In most cases, $m$ is a small number, the time complexity is determined by the number of the RF records. Therefore, we can easily control the computing time by adjusting the threshold to manage the number of the elements in each sub-class.

## 6 Experiment and Analysis

### 6.1 Experiment System

Our experimental system is based on the visual features of color and texture, being represented by color histogram and standard deviations of the wavelet coefficients of each sub-band. As to color feature, the following transformed color space is used: $u = \frac{R}{R+G+B}, v = \frac{G}{R+G+B}$. Both $u$ and $v$ are divided into 16 bins respectively, and thus a 32-dimension vector is formed. Meanwhile, we use the standard deviation of the 10 sub-band wavelet coefficients of each image to form a 10-dimension feature vector. The feedback model proposed by [9] is adopted to refine both the query and the weights. Based on the above, the retrieval method addressed in this paper is realized. For the purpose of comparison, the method previously cited [9] has been also implemented, which is referred to as the default method in the following part. The testing image set used in experiment consists of 11,000 various images[1]., from which we manually classified 10 classes each including 100 relevant images as the "truth". Additionally, for each class, we randomly select 50 images to form the training set, leaving the rest images as the testing set. All experiments of the paper were carried out by naive users who were instructed in the basic operations of the interface of our prototype system. In multimedia retrieval system, the commonly adopted metrics for performance evaluation are Recall and Precision. Given that each subject contains 100 relevant images, only the top 100 output images are counted for relevant ones serving as both recall and precision. Since they are numerically equal in this experiment, we refer to both as precision.

### 6.2 Experiment Result

**The Performance of the Information Filtering Retrieval Method Based on Fuzzy Clustering of RF records.** The first part of the experiment is to evaluate the retrieval performance of the information filtering retrieval method based on fuzzy clustering of RF records. The comparative methods are traditional CBIR, CFCM and CUFCM, where CFCM is the information filtering method based on the fuzzy clustering of using only the query sample's feature vector, and CUFCM represents the information filtering method based on semi-supervised fuzzy clustering. 400 retrievals about the testing set images of the

---

[1] Thanks for Dr. James WANG providing images test set http://jzw.standford.edu/IMAGE/download/corel1m.60k.tar

ten categories are performed to make up the RF records. In experiment, fuzzy clustering is conducted for both information filtering methods, the number of centroids is set to 40, also in CUFCM, we set $\epsilon_1 = 0.003$, $|N_i| = 3$. We randomly select 5 query samples from each of the 7 subjects (surf, train, plane, horse race, castle, dog and road), then totally 35 retrievals (9/4) are performed on the three methods. Fig.2 compares CUFCM and the traditional method (CBIR), it can be easily seen that CUFCM obtains an apparent precision improvement in the initial round of retrieval, and its performance after just 2 rounds has exceeds that of the traditional method after 9 rounds. Fig.3 shows the comparison between CFCM and CUFCM. Apparently, CUFCM reveals a better performance in both initial precision and maximum precision.

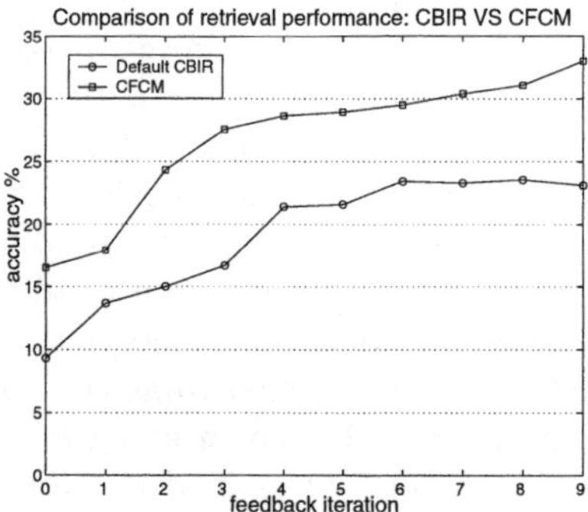


**Fig. 2.** Comparison between CBIR and CFCM

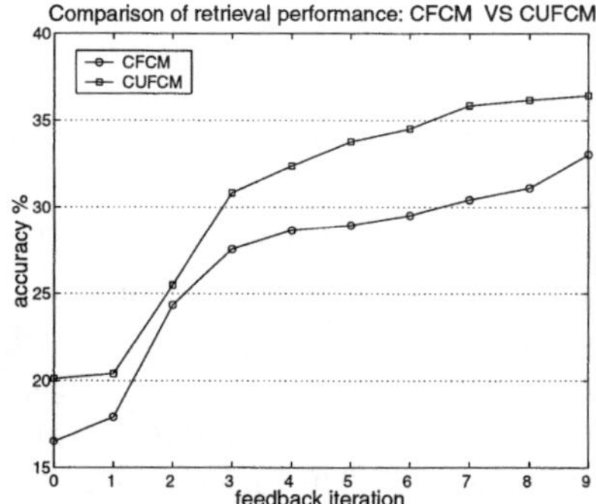


**Fig. 3.** Comparison between CFCM and CUFCM

**Comparison Between Information Filtering Based on Fuzzy Clustering and User filtering.** The second part of the experiment (experiment 3) is the comparison between CUFCM and the user filtering method. Two aspects are considered for comparison: the retrieval performance and the efficiency of the usage of RF records. The experiment is designed as follows. First we get two copy $T_1$,$T_2$ of the table $T$ from the clustering result in the former experiment. Let each sub-class in $T_1(T_2)$ contains the top 25(50) records with the maximum membership degree. Then for each of the seven image classes, 2 query images are randomly chosen from the corresponding class in the testing set. Comparative experiments were conducted regarding these 14 selected retrievals(9/4). The experimental result is shown in Fig.5. From the comparison of the two methods, CUFCM outperforms the User Filtering method at each feedback iteration. In order to compare the efficiency of the use of RF records, we define the usage efficiency as:$UsageEfficiency = \frac{RetrievalPrecision \times 100}{NumberOfRecords}$. Fig.6 shows the comparison in Usage Efficiency of the user filtering method, CUFCM method using T1 and CUFCM method using T2. Apparently, CUFCM performs better than the user filtering method. And CUFCM using T1 has the highest Usage Efficiency(for each round of RF, only the first 25 records are retrieved for similar records in each feedback iteration).

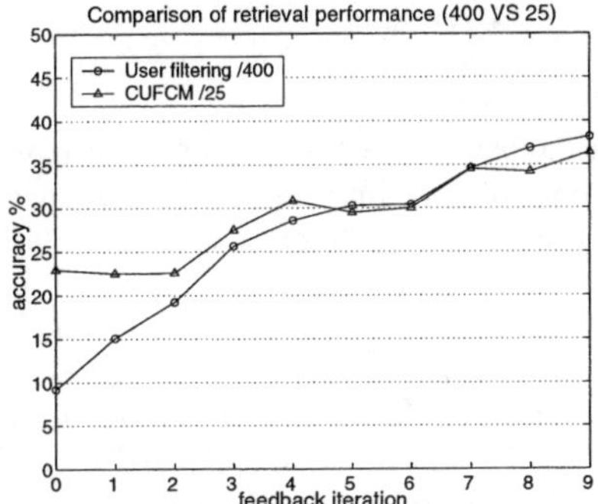


**Fig. 4.** Comparison in precision between User Filtering method and CUFCM when number of records in each sub-class is 25

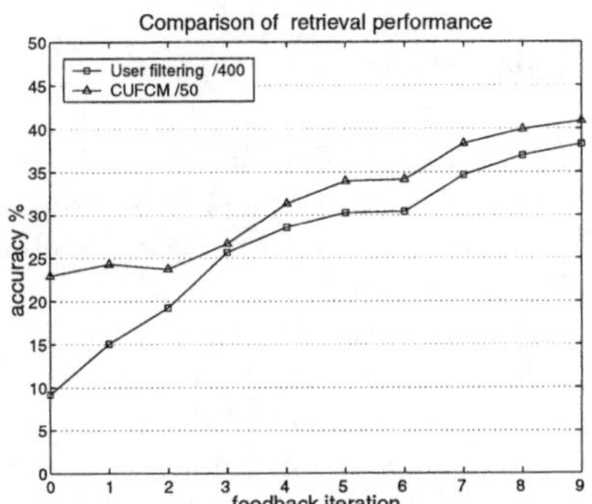


**Fig. 5.** Comparison in precision between User Filtering method and CUFCM when number of records in each sub-class is 50

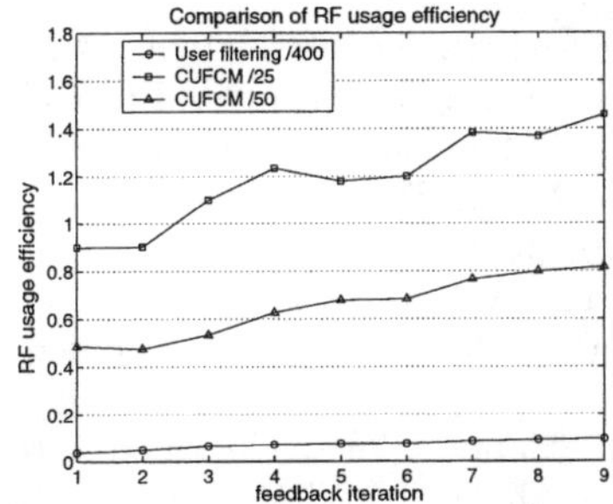


**Fig. 6.** Comparison of record usage efficiency between User Filtering and CUFCM

## 7 Conclusion

In this paper, we proposed a retrieval method using both the higher-level user relevance evaluation and the lower-level query sample's visual feature. By predicting the semantic correlation based on the analysis of the two-level features, retrieval effectiveness can be significantly improved. In addition, the initial query is also benefited although no RF is yet provided at the beginning of a new session. The efficiency of RF records usage is another problem discussed in this paper. By conducting semi-supervision fuzzy clustering, we can limit the K-NN search in a sub-class rather than the much larger global space in the information filtering, so that efficiency can be considerably improved. Experimental results show that our method outperforms the traditional method and the user-filtering-based method in both effectiveness and efficiency.

## References

1. Bartolini I., Ciaccia P. and Waas F. "FeedbackBypass:A New Approach to Interactive Similarity Query Processing". In Proceedings of 27th International Conference on Very Large Data Bases, September 2001, Roma, Italy. Morgan Kaufmann 2001 pp. 201–210.
2. D. Goldberg, D. Nichols, B. Oki, and D. Terry. "Using collaborative filtering to weave an information tapestry", Communications of the ACM, 351261-70, 1992
3. X. He, O.King, W.-Y. Ma, M. Li and H.-J. Zhang. "Learning and Inferring a Semantic Space from User's relevance feedback for image retrieval", In Proc. of the 10th ACM Int.'l Multimedia Conference, France. ACM Press, 2002
4. Y. Ishikawa, R. Subramanya,and C. Faloustos. MinderReader:Query database through multimple examples. In Proc. Of VLDB 1998
5. H. Muller, W. Muller and D. Squire. "Learning Feature Weights from User Behavior in Content-Based Image Retrieval". In Proceedings of the International Workshop on Multimedia Data Mining( MDM/KDD2000), USA. August 2000.
6. W. Pedrycz and J. Waletzky. "Fuzzy clustering with partial supervision" In Tran. on System, man and cybernetics – part B: Cybernetics, V.27 N.5 Octb. 1997 787–795
7. J. Rocchio. Relevance feedback in information retrieval. The SMART retrieval system – experiments in automatic Document Processing, p. 313–323, 1971
8. Rui Y., Huang T. S. and Mehrotra S. "Content-based Image Retrieval with Relevance Feedback in MARS". In Proceedings of IEEE International Conference on Image Processing , 1997. pp. II 815–818,
9. Y. Rui, and T.S. Huang. "A Novel Relevance Feedback Technique in Image Retrieval". In Proceedings of the 7th ACM Int'l conference on Multimedia. ACM press, 1999. pp. 67–70.
10. S. Tong and E. Chang. "Support Vector Machine Active Learning for Image Retrieval". In Proc. of the 9th ACM Int'l Multimedia Conference, Ottawa, Canada. ACM Press, 2001 pp. 107–119.
11. J. Yang, Q. Li, and Y. Zhuang, "Image retrieval and relevance feedback using peer index", In Proc. of 2002 IEEE Int'l Conf. on Multimedia and Expo, Lausanne, Switzerland, Aug, 2002.
12. X. Zhou, L. Zhang, Q. Zhang, L. Liu, B. Shi, "A relevance feedback method in image retrieval by analyzing feedback log file" In Proc. of IEEE Int'l Conf. on Machine Learning and Cybernetics, Beijing, Nov. 2002

# A New Similar Trajectory Retrieval Scheme Using k-Warping Distance Algorithm for Moving Objects

Choon-Bo Shim and Jae-Woo Chang

Dept. of Computer Engineering,
Research Center of Industrial Technology, Engineering Research Institute
Chonbuk National University, Chonju, Chonbuk 561-756, South Korea
{cbsim,jwchang}@dblab.chonbuk.ac.kr

**Abstract.** In this paper, we propose a new similar trajectory retrieval scheme for efficient retrieval on both a single trajectory of a moving object and multiple trajectories of two or more moving objects. Our similar trajectory retrieval scheme can support multiple properties including direction, distance, and time and can provide the approximate matching that is superior to the exact matching. For this, we propose a k-warping distance algorithm which enhances the existing time warping distance algorithm by permitting up to k replications for an arbitrary motion of a query trajectory so that we measure the similarity between two trajectories accurately. In addition, we show from our experiment that our similar trajectory retrieval scheme using the k-warping distance algorithm outperforms Li's (no-warping) and Shan's schemes (infinite-warping) in terms of precision and recall measures. Finally, we implement a content-based soccer video retrieval system in order to show the usefulness of applying our similar trajectory retrieval scheme to a real application.

## 1 Introduction

Due to the wide spreading of mobile communication facilities such as PCS, PDA, and CNS (Car Navigation System) as well as the rapid increment of sport video data such as soccer, it is necessary to deal with the various information of moving objects efficiently. Thus, a lot of researches have recently been done on the research topic in the field of video database and spatio-temporal databases [1, 2]. Meanwhile, the trajectory of moving objects can be represented as a spatio-temporal relationship combining its spatial and temporal property, which plays an important role in doing video analysis and retrieval in video databases [3, 4]. A typical trajectory-based user query on the spatio-temporal relationship is as follows: *"Finds all objects whose motion trajectory is similar to the trajectory shown in a user interface window"*. A moving object is defined as a salient object that is continuously changing at its spatial location over the time. The trajectory of a moving object is defined as a collection of successive motions, each being represented as a spatio-temporal relationship. The moving objects' trajectories are the subject of concern by a user in both video databases and spatio-temporal databases. Similar trajectory retrieval means searching for sub-trajectories in data trajectories which are similar to a given query trajectory.

G. Dong et al. (Eds.): WAIM 2003, LNCS 2762, pp. 433–444, 2003.

In this paper, we first propose a k-warping distance algorithm which calculates a k-warping distance between a given query trajectory and a data trajectory by permitting up to k replications for an arbitrary motion of a query trajectory to measure the similarity between two trajectories. Using our k-warping distance algorithm, we also propose a new similar trajectory retrieval scheme for efficient retrieval on moving objects' trajectories in both video databases and spatio-temporal databases. Our scheme can support multiple properties including direction, distance, and time, instead of supporting a single property of direction which is previously used for modeling moving objects' trajectories. In addition, our similar trajectory retrieval scheme can provide an approximate matching which is generally superior to an exact matching for calculating the similarity between two trajectories. In order to show the usefulness of applying our similar trajectory retrieval scheme to a real application, we implement a content-based soccer video retrieval system, called CSVR system.
This paper is organized as follows. In Section 2, we introduce related researches on similar trajectory retrieval. In Section 3, we propose both a k-warping distance algorithm and a new similar trajectory retrieval scheme using our k-warping distance algorithm. In Section 4, we do the performance analysis of our similar trajectory retrieval scheme. In Section 5, we implement a content-based soccer video retrieval system, called CSVR system, as its application. Finally, we draw our conclusions and suggest future work in Section 6.

## 2 Related Work

There have been two main researches on retrieval based on similar sub-trajectory by measuring the similarity between a given query trajectory and data trajectories, i.e., Li's scheme and Shan's scheme. First, Li et al. [3, 4] represented the trajectory of a moving object as eight directions, such as North(NT), Northwest(NW), Northeast(NE), West(WT), Southwest(SW), East(ET), Southeast(SE), and Southwest(SW). They represented as $(S_i, d_i, I_i)$ the trajectory of a moving object A over a given time interval $I_i$ where $S_i$ is the displacement of A and $d_i$ is a direction. For a set of time interval $<I_1, I_2, \cdots, I_n>$, the trajectories of A can be represented as a list of motions, like $<(S_1, d_1, I_1), (S_2, d_2, I_2), \ldots, (S_n, d_n, I_n)>$. Based on the representation for moving objects' trajectories, they present a similarity measures to computes the similarity of spatio-temporal relationships between two moving object.
Secondly, Shan and Lee [5] represented the trajectory of a moving object as a sequence of segments, each being expressed as the slope with real angle ranging from 0 to 360 degree for content-based retrieval. They also proposed two similarity measure algorithms, OCM (Optimal Consecutive Mapping) and OCMR (Optimal Consecutive Mapping with Replication), which can measure similarity between query trajectory $Q=(q_1, q_2, \ldots, q_M)$ and data trajectory $V=(v_1, v_2, \ldots, v_N)$. The OCM algorithm that supports exact matching measures the similarity for one-to-one segment mapping between query trajectory and data trajectory. The OCMR algorithm supports approximate matching. In order to measure the similarity, each motion of query trajectory can be permitted to map with more than one motions of data trajectory.
Meanwhile, Similar sub-sequence retrieval [6, 7, 8] is an operation that finds data sequences whose changing patterns are similar to that of a given query sequence. There are many application areas, such as sequence of stock price, money exchanges

rates, temperature data, and product sales data. The sequence database is a set of data sequence, each of which is an ordered list of elements. In a sequence S(=<s[1], s[2], ..., s[|S|]), |S| is the length of S and s[i] is its i-th element. s[i:j] and s[i:-] is a sub-sequence of S that includes the elements from i-th element to j-th element and from i-th element to the end, respectively. () denotes an empty sequence or null sequence. For efficient similar sub-sequence retrieval, time warping transformation is proposed. The time warping is a generalization of classical algorithms for comparing discrete sequences with sequences of continuous values and enables each element of a sequence to match one or more neighboring elements of the other sequence. It supports the approximate matching which guarantees a result to be retrieved based on the modification of a user query within some threshold for an inaccurate query. The time warping distance is defined as the smallest distance between two sequences transformed by time warping. Given two sequence S and Q, the time warping distance $D_{tw}$ is defined recursively as follows:

$D_{tw}((), ()) = 0$

$D_{tw}(S, ()) = D_{tw}((), Q) = \infty$

$D_{tw}(S, Q) = D_{base}(S[1], Q[1]) + \min(D_{tw}((S, Q[2:-], D_{tw}(S[2:-], Q), D_{tw}(S[2:-], Q[2:-]))$

$D_{base}(a, b) = |a-b|$

Here, $D_{base}$ can be any Lp function that returns a distance between two elements. We use a distance function appropriate to application areas. Time warping is a transformation that allows both data and query sequence elements to replicate itself infinitely as many times as needed.

## 3 A New Similar Trajectory Retrieval Scheme

Moving objects are salient objects that are continuously changing its locations over time in various application areas such as video database and spatio-temporal databases. Thus, in order to effectively deal with moving objects, it is necessary to consider both spatial and temporal relationships. Existing schemes, like Li's scheme and Shan's scheme, consider only direction information and spatial (topological) information for modeling the trajectory of moving objects. But, our spatio-temporal representation scheme which was already proposed in [9] takes into account moving distance information in addition.

### 3.1 Similarity Measure for Single Trajectory

We present three considerations for supporting efficient similar sub-trajectory retrieval on moving objects.

1. The time warping transformation used for a similar sub-sequence matching in sequence databases can allow the infinitive replication of a data sequence as well as a query sequence. However, for similar sub-trajectory retrieval in spatio-temporal databases, it is necessary to allow the replication of only a query trajectory.
2. The time warping transformation for a similar sub-sequence matching can allow the infinitive replication of an arbitrary motion. However, for the similar sub-

trajectory retrieval, it is necessary to support the replication of up to the fixed number (k) of motions, so called k-warping distance.
3. For modeling motions being composed of the trajectory of a moving object, it is necessary to support multiple properties including angle, distance, and time, instead of the single property of angle.

The consideration 1 is generally needed for supporting an approximation matching from similar sub-trajectory retrieval and the considerations 2 and 3 are needed for improving the effectiveness of the approximation matching. In addition, the considerations 2 and 3 are very sensitive, depending on application areas. The similar subsequence matching approach which is used for the existing time warping transformation does not satisfy all of the above three considerations. The reason is why the characteristic of data used in sequence database is different from that of trajectory data of moving objects in spatio-temporal databases. Generally, the sequence data has a detailed and elaborate feature and the number of elements consisting of a sequence reaches scores or hundreds. On the other hand, the trajectory data of moving objects in spatio-temporal databases are composed of motions over a time interval and the number of motions consisting of a trajectory is less than scores. Meanwhile, the Shan's OCMR scheme can satisfy the considerations 1, but it does not satisfy the considerations 2 and 3.
Therefore, we propose a new k-warping distance algorithm which can support an approximation matching and satisfy the above three considerations for similar sub-trajectory retrieval. In order to satisfy the consideration 3, we generally define the trajectory of moving objects as a collection of consecutive motions consisting of n-dimensional properties.
**[Definition 1.]** The trajectory of moving object S is defined as a set of consecutive motions, S= (s[1], s[2], ..., s[|S|]), where each motion s[i] is composed of n-dimensional properties as follows:

$$\mathbf{s[i] = (s[i, 1], s[i, 2], \cdots, s[i, n])}$$

For measuring a similarity between two trajectories, we define a k-warping distance as follows, which is newly made by applying the concept of time warping distance used for time-series databases to the trajectory data of moving objects in spatio-temporal databases.
**[Definition 2.]** Given two trajectory of moving objects S and Q, the k-warping distance $D_{kw}$ is defined recursively as follows:

$$\mathbf{D_{kw}(0, 0) = 0, D_{kw}(S, 0) = D_{kw}(0, Q) = \infty}$$
$$\mathbf{D_{kw}(S, Q) = D_{base}(S[1], Q[1]) + min(\{D_{kw}((S[2+i:-], Q), 0 \le i < k), D_{kw}(S[2:-], Q[2:-])\})}$$
$$\mathbf{D_{base}(a, b) = d_{df}(a, b)}$$

Figure 1 depicts an example of our k-warping distance algorithm which can calculate similarity between trajectory S and Q when k is 2. We can permit up to 2(=k) times replications for an arbitrary motion of only query trajectory Q. In the above example, we can obtain the minimum distance value, that is, the maximum similarity value, between S and Q when q[1] of trajectory Q is mapped to each s[1], s[2], and s[3] of trajectory S, instead of the exact matching, namely, one-to-one mapping between trajectory S and Q. Therefore, it is shown that the approximate matching is superior to the exact mating for calculating the similarity between trajectories in spatio-temporal databases.

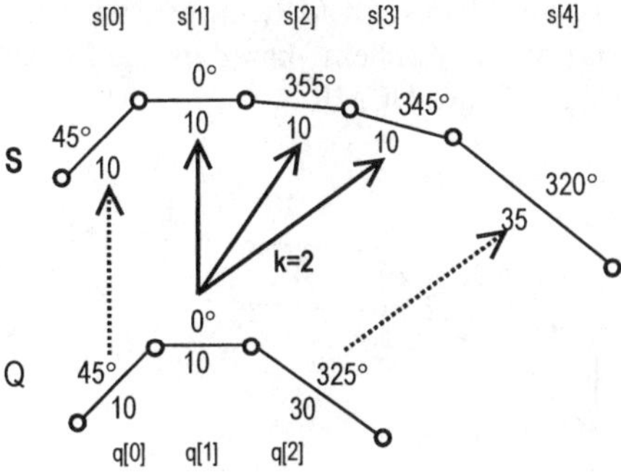


**Fig. 1.** Mapping of motions between S and Q when k=2

Based on our k-warping distance algorithm, we will define a similarity measure for a single trajectory. Since we measure a similarity between i-th motion in query trajectory Q and j-th motion in data trajectory S, we define a distance function between two motions, $d_{df}(q[i], s[j])$, as follows.

**[Definition 3.]** A distance function, $d_{df}(q[i], s[j])$, to measure the similarity between the arbitrary motion s[i] of a data trajectory S and the arbitrary motion q[j] of a query trajectory Q is defined as follows.

$$d_{dis}(s[i,2], q[j,2]) = | s[i, 2] - q[j, 2] |$$
$$\text{if } | s[i, 1] - q[j, 1] | > 180 \text{ then } d_{ang}(s[i, 1], q[j, 1]) = (360 - | s[i, 1] - q[j, 1] |)$$
$$\text{else } d_{ang}(s[i, 1], q[j, 1]) = | s[i, 1] - q[j, 1] |$$

$$\mathbf{d_{df}(s[i], q[j]) = ( ((d_{ang} / 180) * \alpha) + ((d_{dis}/100) * \beta) )}$$

Here, $d_{ang}$ is a distance function for the direction (angle) property for all the motions of a trajectory and $d_{dis}$ is a distance function for the distance property. s[i, 1] and s[i, 2] are the direction and the distance value of the i-th motion in a trajectory S, respectively. $\alpha$ and $\beta$ mean the weight of the direction and the distance, respectively, when $\alpha+\beta=1.0$.

For example, by using our k-warping distance algorithm, a similarity distance between a data trajectory S={(45,10), (0,10), (355,10), (345,10), (4,40), (325,45)} and a query trajectory Q={(45,10), (0,10), (325,10)} can be calculated in Figure 2. The value of the last column of the last row means the minimum distance 0.30 by permitting the infinitive replications of the query trajectory Q as shown in trajectory S1. In the case of k-warping distance, the motion of q[0] in the query trajectory Q corresponds to the s[0] in the data trajectory S, the motion of q[1] to the s[1], the motion of q[1] to the s[2], and the motion of q[2] to the s[3] respectively as shown in trajectory S2. Finally, we can find a path starting from the first column of the first row within the last column of the last row, thus obtaining the minimum distance by permitting up to k(=2) replications. We can summarize the differences of distance between each motion of the query and the data trajectory on the path, that is, |q[0]-s[0]|+|q[1]-s[1]|+|q[1]-s[2]|+|q[2]-s[3]|= 0.00 + 0.00 + 0.02 + 0.07 = 0.09. This is a minimum distance value between the two trajectories by using our k-warping distance algorithm. Thus, the similarity degree between S and Q is 91%(=1-0.09) while the similarity degree based on Shan's OCMR(infinite warping) is 70%(=1-0.30). In conclusion, our similarity measure scheme based on the k-warping distance algorithm provides a better result than Shan's OCMR.

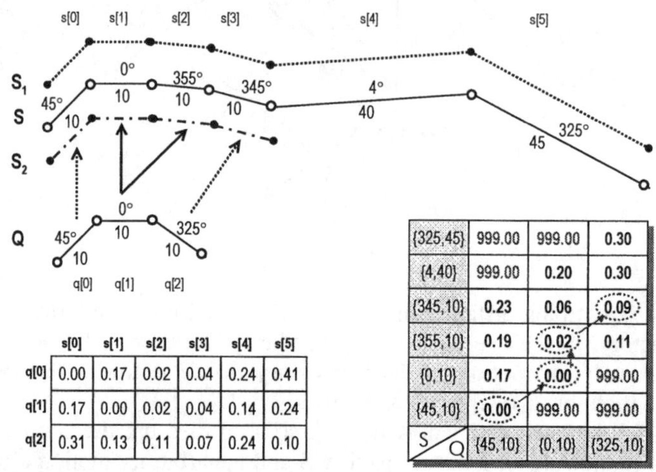


| | s[0] | s[1] | s[2] | s[3] | s[4] | s[5] |
|---|---|---|---|---|---|---|
| q[0] | 0.00 | 0.17 | 0.02 | 0.04 | 0.24 | 0.41 |
| q[1] | 0.17 | 0.00 | 0.02 | 0.04 | 0.14 | 0.24 |
| q[2] | 0.31 | 0.13 | 0.11 | 0.07 | 0.24 | 0.10 |

| {325,45} | 999.00 | 999.00 | 0.30 |
|---|---|---|---|
| {4,40} | 999.00 | 0.20 | 0.30 |
| {345,10} | 0.23 | 0.06 | 0.09 |
| {355,10} | 0.19 | 0.02 | 0.11 |
| {0,10} | 0.17 | 0.00 | 999.00 |
| {45,10} | 0.00 | 999.00 | 999.00 |
| S / Q | {45,10} | {0,10} | {325,10} |

**Fig. 2.** Example of similarity measure between S and Q (k=2)

### 3.2 Similarity Measure for Multiple Trajectories

We first define the similarity measure for a relationship trajectory between two trajectories. For this, we makes use of topological relationships between multiple moving objects as well as moving direction and moving distance, by using our k-warping distance algorithm. Hence, we define a distance function using three-dimensional properties as follows.

**[Definition 4.]** A distance function, $d_{df}(q[i], s[j])$, to measure the similarity between the arbitrary motion s[i] of a data trajectory S and the arbitrary motion q[j] of a query trajectory Q is defined as follows.

$$d_{top}(s[i,3], q[j,3]) = (top\_dist(s[i, 3], q[j, 3]))^2$$
$$d_{dis}(s[i,2], q[j,2]) = | s[i, 2] - q[j, 2] |$$
$$\text{if } | s[i, 1] - q[j, 1] | > 180 \text{ then } d_{ang}(s[i, 1], q[j, 1]) = (360 - | s[i, 1] - q[j, 1] | )$$
$$\text{else } d_{ang}(s[i, 1], q[j, 1]) = | s[i, 1] - q[j, 1] |$$

$$\mathbf{d_{df}(s[i], q[j]) = ( ((d_{ang} / 180) * \alpha) + ((d_{dis}/100) * \beta ) + ((d_{top}/25)*\gamma) )}$$

Here $d_{ang}$ is a distance function for the direction (angle) property for all the motions of a trajectory, $d_{dis}$ is a distance function for the distance property and $d_{top}$ is a distance function for the topology property. s[i, 1], s[i, 2] and s[i, 3] are the angle, the distance and the topology value of the i-th motion in a multiple trajectory S, respectively. $\alpha$, $\beta$ and $\gamma$ mean the weight of the angle, the distance and the topology, respectively, when $\alpha+\beta+\gamma=1.0$. Also, top_dist(a, b) means the similarity distance for topological relations between a and b, that is, FA(FarAway), DJ(DisJoint), ME(MEet), OL(OverLap), CL(is inCLuded by), IN(INclude), and SA(SAme)[10].

A list of multiple trajectories of at least two or more moving objects, MT($A_1$, $A_2$, ⋯, $A_n$), can be represented as a combination of single trajectory(ST) and relationship trajectories(RT).

**[Definition 5.]** Let us suppose that i and j is the number of moving objects and stationary objects, respectively (n=i+j). The similarity for multiple trajectories of objects $A_1$, $A_2$, ⋯, $A_n$, MT($A_1$, $A_2$, ⋯, $A_n$), is calculated as follows:

$$MT_{sim}(A_1, A_2, ..., A_n) = \frac{\sum_{p=1}^{i} ST_{sim}(A_p) + \sum_{q=1}^{k} RT_{sim}(A_q, A_{q+1})}{i+k} \quad , k={}_nC_2 - {}_jC_2$$

Here $ST_{sim}(A_i)$ is the similarity value of single trajectory of object $A_i$. $RT_{sim}(A_k, A_{k+1})$ is the similarity value of relationship trajectories between objects $A_k$ and $A_{k+1}$ where k is the number of relationship trajectories between two moving objects as well as between a moving object and a stationary object.

## 4 Performance Analysis

In order to verify the usefulness of our similar trajectory retrieval scheme for both the single trajectory and the multiple trajectories, we do the performance analysis by using real soccer video data. Since the soccer video data has many trajectories of soccer balls, i.e., salient objects, we extract the trajectories of moving objects from the soccer ball. Table 1 describes the experimental data used for our performance analysis. Most of video data (formatted as MPEG file) used in our experiment include a shot of 'getting a goal'. We extract the trajectories of a soccer ball by manually tracing the ball in a ground field. For our experiment, we make forty query trajectories consisting of twenty in 'the right field' and twenty in 'the left field' from the half line of the ground field.

**Table 1.** Experimental data for performance analysis

| Parameters | Data Set | |
|---|---|---|
| | Single Trajectory | Multiple Trajectories |
| Data domain | Soccer Video Data | |
| Salient moving object | Soccer Ball | Soccer Ball and Player |
| The number of data | 350 | 200 |
| The average motion number of data trajectory | 8.4 | 8.9 |
| The number of query | 40 | 10 |
| The average motion number of query trajectory | 3.8 | 3.1 |

For our performance analysis, we implemented our similar trajectory retrieval scheme using our k-warping distance algorithm by using C++ language. We compare our similar trajectory retrieval scheme using the k-warping distance with the Li's (no-warping) and Shan's ones (infinite-warping) in terms of retrieval effectiveness, that is, average precision and recall measures [11]. Let RD (Relevant data in Database) be the number of video data relevant to a given query which are selected from the database, RQ (Retrieved data by Query) be the total number of data retrieved by a given query, and RR (Relevant data that are Retrieved) be the number of relevant data retrieved by a given query. In order to obtain RD, we make a test panel which selects relevant data manually from the database. The test panel is composed of 20 graduate school students from the computer engineering department of Chonbuk National University, South Korea. The precision is defined as the proportion of retrieved data being relevant and the recall is defined as the proportion of relevant data being retrieved as follows.

$$\text{Precision} = \frac{RR}{RQ} \qquad \text{Recall} = \frac{RR}{RD}$$

For our performance comparison, we adopt the 11-point measure [11], which is most widely used for measuring the precision and recall. For a single trajectory, we consider the weight of angle ($W_a$) and the weight of distance ($W_d$) separately since we use both angle and distance for modeling the trajectory of moving objects. We also take into account the number of replications (k) since k is a very important parameter, depending on an application area. Here we do our experiment when k=0, 1, and 2 owing to the characteristics of the trajectory of the soccer ball in soccer video data. k=0 is exact matching and k=1 and 2 is approximate matching. We show from our experiment that there is no difference on retrieval effectiveness when k is greater than 2. Table 2 shows the retrieval effectiveness of our similar trajectory retrieval scheme, Li's scheme, and Shan's scheme. In case we do our performance analysis based on only the angle property ($W_a$=1.0 and $W_d$=0.0), it is shown that our scheme achieves about 10-15% higher precision than that of Li's and Shan's schemes while it holds about the same recall. In case we consider the weight of angle about two times greater than that of distance ($W_a$ =0.7 and $W_d$=0.3), it is shown that our scheme achieves about 15-20% higher precision than that of Li's and Shan's schemes while it holds about the same recall.

**Table 2.** Performance result for single trajectory

| | | **Avg. Precision** | | | **Avg. Recall** | | |
|---|---|---|---|---|---|---|---|
| | **# of warping** | **k = 0** | **k = 1** | **k = 2** | **k = 1** | **k = 1** | **k = 2** |
| **$W_a$:$W_d$= 1.0:0.0** | **Li's Scheme** | | **0.25** | | | **0.45** | |
| | **Shan's Scheme** | | **0.30** | | | **0.44** | |
| | **Our Scheme** | **0.34** | **0.38** | **0.40** | **0.51** | **0.48** | **0.47** |
| **$W_a$:$W_d$= 0.7:0.3** | **Li's Scheme** | | **0.25** | | | **0.45** | |
| | **Shan's Scheme** | | **0.30** | | | **0.44** | |
| | **Our Scheme** | **0.39** | **0.44** | **0.45** | **0.50** | **0.46** | **0.47** |

For multiple trajectories, we consider the weight of angle ($W_a$), the weight of distance ($W_d$) and the weight of topological relations ($W_t$) according to modeling the trajectory of multiple moving objects. When k is greater than 1, it is very difficult to obtain a relevant set for the multiple trajectories of a given query. Thus, we do our experiment for multiple trajectories when k=0 and 1. Table 3 depicts the performance results for multiple trajectories in our scheme, Li's scheme, and Shan's scheme. In case we consider the angle and the topological relation about two times more importantly than the distance ($W_a$ =0.4, $W_d$=0.2, and $W_t$=0.4), it is shown that our scheme achieves about 20% higher precision than that of Li's and Shan's schemes while it holds about the same recall.

**Table 3.** Performance result for multiple trajectories

| | | Avg. Precision | | Avg. Recall | |
|---|---|---|---|---|---|
| | **# of warping** | **k = 0** | **k = 1** | **k = 0** | **k=1** |
| **$W_a$:$W_d$:$W_t$ = 0.5:0.0:0.5** | **Li's Scheme** | **0.37** | | **0.49** | |
| | **Shan's Scheme** | **0.30** | | **0.41** | |
| | **Our Scheme** | **0.39** | **0.52** | **0.48** | **0.52** |
| **$W_a$:$W_d$:$W_t$ = 0.4:0.2:0.4** | **Li's Scheme** | **0.25** | | **0.49** | |
| | **Shan's Scheme** | **0.30** | | **0.41** | |
| | **Our Scheme** | **0.45** | **0.53** | **0.51** | **0.54** |

From our experiment, we finally show that our similar trajectory retrieval scheme using our k-warping distance algorithm achieves better performance on average precision than Li's and Shan's schemes while it holds about the same recall in the single trajectory and multiple trajectories. Particularly, in case of the single trajectory, the performance of our scheme is the best when the weight of angle is over two times than that of distance ($W_a$=0.7 and $W_d$=0.3). In case of the multiple trajectories, the performance of our scheme is the best when the weight of angle and topology is over two times than that of distance ($W_a$=0.4, $W_d$=0.2 and $W_t$=0.4). In terms of the number of replications (k), we show that the performance of our scheme when k=1 is better than the performance when k=0. Also, the performance when k=2 is better than the one when k=1. Thus, it is shown that the approximate matching is better on the performance of similar trajectory retrieval than the exact matching, i.e., k=0.

## 5 Implementation of Content-Based Soccer Video Retrieval System

To show the possibility of applying our similar trajectory retrieval scheme to real applications, we implement the Content-based Soccer Video Retrieval system, called CSVR. This is because soccer video data have many trajectories of salient objects, such as soccer ball, player, and referee. Additionally, the trajectory information plays an important role in indexing soccer video data and detecting the scene with 'goal in' in soccer video database. We implement the CSVR system which supports the indexing and searching on soccer video data, under Windows 2000 O.S with Pentium III-800 and 512 MB memory by using Microsoft Visual C++ 6.0 compiler. Figure 3 first shows a graphic user interface (GUI) for soccer video indexing which can help users to extract the trajectory information of soccer ball semi-automatically from soccer video data, e.g. moving direction, moving distance, # of frame, player name, and so on. We implement it so as to work well under Window platform. Our GUI for soccer video indexing is composed of two windows: main window and soccer ground window. The former is to browse raw soccer video data formatted as mpeg and to extract the trajectory information of soccer ball and main player. The latter is to transform the location of soccer ball in raw video data into an absolute location on the coordinate of soccer ground field. For this, we make use of so-called Affined Transformation algorithm which is mainly used in computer vision or image processing fields [12].

**Fig. 3.** GUI for soccer video indexing in CSVR system

Figure 4 depicts a GUI for soccer video retrieval which can help users to retrieve the results acquired in soccer video databases. We implement it by using a JAVA in order to work well independently without regard to a specific system platform. We can provide three types of user queries, that is, trajectory-based query, semantic-based query, and actor-based query as shown in the left part of Figure 4. The trajectory-based query is based on the trajectory of moving objects such as soccer ball and player as the following query: *"Finds all video shots whose trajectory is similar to the trajectory sketched by a user on soccer video retrieval interface"*. The semantic-based query is based on important semantics such as 'penalty kick', 'corner kick' and 'goal in' in soccer video databases: *"Finds all video shots including a scene 'goal in' "*. Finally, the actor-based query is based on the interested player name such as 'Ronaldo', 'Rivaldo' and 'Zidane' in soccer video databases: *"Finds all video shots including a scene 'goal in' by planer name 'Ronaldo' "*. The retrieved results on a user query are provided in the form of trajectory images with the similar trajectory as shown in the right part of Figure 4. We can browse them in the order of the degree of relevance to a user query. The real soccer video shot corresponding to the trajectory image retrieved can be shown by clicking its trajectory image with the mouse button.

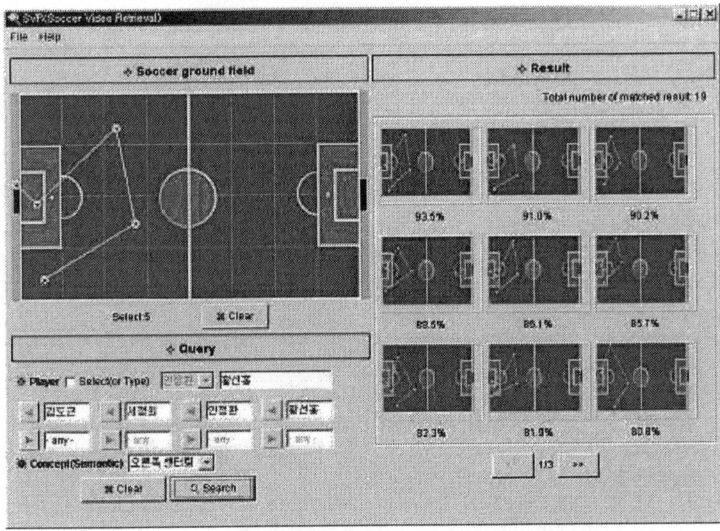


**Fig. 4.** GUI for soccer video retrieval in CSVR system

## 6 Conclusions and Future Work

For similarity measure between given two trajectories, we proposed a new k-warping distance algorithm which enhanced the existing time distance algorithm by permitting up to k replications for an arbitrary motion of a query trajectory. Based on our k-warping distance algorithm, we also propose a new similar trajectory retrieval scheme for efficient retrieval on both a single trajectory of a moving object and multiple trajectories of two or more moving objects. Our similar trajectory retrieval scheme can support multiple properties including direction, distance, and time and can provide the approximate matching that is superior to the exact matching. In addition, we showed from our experiment that our similar trajectory retrieval scheme using the k-warping distance outperformed Li's (no-warping) and Shan's schemes (infinite-warping) in terms of precision and recall measures. In the result of single trajectory, the performance of our scheme achieves about 15-20% performance improvement against Li's and Shan's scheme when the weight of angle is over two times greater than that of distance. In the result of multiple trajectories, the performance of our scheme achieves about 20% performance improvement when the weights of angle and topological relation are over two times greater than that of distance. Finally, we implemented a content-based soccer video retrieval system in order to show the usefulness of applying our similar trajectory retrieval scheme to a real application. As future work, it is required to study on indexing methods to support good retrieval efficiency when the amount of trajectory data of moving objects is very large.

**Acknowledgement.** This work was supported in part by the Research Center of Industrial Technology, Engineering Research Institute at Chonbuk National University (CNU), South Korea

## References

[1] L. Forlizzi, R. H. Guting, E. Nardelli, and M. Schneider, "A Data Model and Data Structures for Moving Objects Databases," Proc. of ACM SIGMOD Conf, pp. 319–330, 2000.

[2] R. H. Guting, et al., "A Foundation for Representing and Querying Moving Objects," ACM Transaction on Database Systems, Vol. 25, No. 1, pp. 1–42, 2000.

[3] J. Z. Li, M. T. Ozsu, and D. Szafron, "Modeling Video Temporal Relationships in an Object Database Management System," in Proceedings of Multimedia Computing and Networking(MMCN97), pp. 80–91, 1997.

[4] J. Z. Li, M. T. Ozsu, and D. Szafron, "Modeling of Video Spatial Relationships in an Objectbase Management System," in Proceedings of International Workshop on Multimedia DBMS, pp. 124–133, 1996.

[5] M. K. Shan and S. Y. Lee, "Content-based Video Retrieval via Motion Trajectories," in Proceedings of SPIE Electronic Imaging and Multimedia System II, Vol. 3561, pp. 52–61, 1998.

[6] B. K. Yi, H. V. Lagadish, and C. Faloutsos, "Efficient Retrieval of Similar Time Sequences Under Time Warping," In Proc. Int'l. Conf. on Data Engineering, IEEE, pp. 201–208, 1998.

[7] S. H. Park, et al., "Efficient Searches for Similar Subsequence of Difference Lengths in Sequence Databases," In Proc. Int'l. Conf. on Data Engineering. IEEE, pp. 23–32, 2000.

[8] S. W. Kim, S. H. Park, and W. W. Chu, "An Index-Based Approach for Similarity Search Supporting Time Warping in Large Sequence Databases," In Proc. Int'l. Conf. on Data Engineering. IEEE, pp. 607–614, 2001.

[9] C. B. Shim and J. W. Chang, "A Spatio-Temporal Representation Scheme for Content- and Semantic-Based Video Retrieval on Moving Objects' Trajectories," WAIM 2002, Lecture Notes in Computer Science (LNCS), Vol. 2419, pp. 52–63, 2002.

[10] J. W. Chang, Y. J. Kim, and K. J. Chang, "A Spatial Match Representation Scheme Indexing and Querying in Iconic Image Databases," ACM Int'l. Conf. on Information and Knowledge Management, pp. 169–176, 1997.

[11] G. Salton and M. McGill, An introduction to Modern Information Retrieval, McGraw-Hill, 1993.

[12] H. S. Yoon, J. Soh, B. W. Min, and Y. K. Yang, "Soccer image sequence mosaicing using reverse affine transform," In Proc. of Int'l Technical Conference on Circuits/Systems, Computers and Communications, pp. 877–800, 2000.

# TupleRank and Implicit Relationship Discovery in Relational Databases

Xiao (Andy) Huang[1], Qiang Xue[2], and Jun Yang[2]

[1] Systems Group, IBM,
3039 Cornwallis Road, Research Triangle Park, NC 27709, USA
{xhuang}@us.ibm.com

[2] Department of Computer Science, Duke University,
Durham, NC 27708, USA
{xue, junyang}@cs.duke.edu

**Abstract.** Google's successful PageRank brings to the Web an order that well reflects the relative importance of Web pages. Inspired by PageRank, we propose a similar scheme called TupleRank for ranking tuples in a relational database. Database tuples naturally relate to each other through referential integrity constraints declared in the schema. However, such constraints cannot capture more general relationships such as similarity. Furthermore, relationships determined statically from the database schema do not reflect actual query patterns that arise at runtime. To address these deficiencies of static TupleRank, we introduce the notion of query-driven TupleRank. We develop techniques to compute query-driven TupleRank accurately and efficiently with low space requirement. We further augment query-driven TupleRank so that it can better utilize the access frequency information collected from the workload. Preliminary experiment results demonstrate that TupleRank is both informative and intuitive, and they confirm the advantages of query-driven TupleRank over static TupleRank.

## 1 Introduction

The Google search engine [3] has brought to the enormous Web an order that well reflects the relative "importance" of Web pages. The ranking is called *PageRank* [12], which is based on a simple yet elegant idea: A Web page is "important" if many "important" Web pages link to it. PageRank can be computed efficiently over the link structure of the Web using an iterative procedure. The success of Google is the best testimony to the effectiveness of PageRank.

Inspired by PageRank, we propose to bring to relational databases a similar order, called *TupleRank*, which measures the relative importance of database tuples. In a relational database, there naturally exists a link structure induced by the referential integrity relationships between tuples. Based on this link structure, we can define TupleRank in the same way as PageRank. Intuitively, a tuple will have a high TupleRank value if it is referenced by many tuples with high TupleRank values. We call this definition of TupleRank *static* because it is based on the referential integrity constraints declared as part of the database schema.

G. Dong et al. (Eds.): WAIM 2003, LNCS 2762, pp. 445–457, 2003.

However, explicitly declared database constraints often fail to capture all interesting relationships among database tuples. First, not all constraints can be conveniently declared in SQL. For example, referential integrity constraints are only a special case of inclusion dependencies. Inclusion dependencies indicate more general links between tuples that share values for some attributes. However, there is no direct way in SQL to declare general inclusion dependencies.

Secondly, database tuples could relate to each other in ways that are not reflected at all by constraints. For example, a tuple with an image attribute containing a picture of the Great Wall should be considered related to another tuple with a text attribute containing the string "`Great Wall`." In general, tuples may be related by any join condition that is meaningful to the application, which can be based on exact equality or fuzzy measures of similarity.

Finally, database constraints are static, and do not capture the dynamics of a real workload. Intuitively, tuples (or links between tuples) that are accessed (or traversed) frequently in a workload should be considered as more "important" than those that are not.

Therefore, we argue that the link structure of a database should be discovered dynamically from a query workload, rather than determined statically from the database schema. Specifically, tuples are considered to be related if they are joined together by a query in the workload. We can then compute TupleRank over this dynamically discovered link structure. We call this definition of TupleRank *query-driven* because the link structure is derived from a query workload. In contrast to static TupleRank, query-driven TupleRank can capture relationships that are not explicitly declared as database constraints. Furthermore, query-driven TupleRank reflects the tuple access pattern of the workload. This feature raises the interesting possibility of defining, for each user community of the database, a "customized" TupleRank computed according to the community's typical query workload.

The major challenge in implementing query-driven TupleRank is how to keep track of the joins of database tuples generated by a large workload. A possible solution is to model query result tuples explicitly in the link structure and have them connect to joining database tuples, a trick reminiscent of the use of *connecting entity sets* in E/R design [8]. However, this simple solution is not scalable because the size of the link structure grows with the number of result tuples generated by the workload. To overcome this problem, we generalize the link structure to a *weighted TupleLink graph*, and develop a series of graph compaction techniques to reduce the size of the graph to $O(m^2)$, where $m$ is the number of database tuples, without affecting the accuracy of TupleRank. In practice, we find the size of the graph to be much smaller, typically $\Theta(m)$.

In summary, the main contributions of our work are:

- The extension of PageRank to TupleRank for relational databases.
- The idea of inferring the link structure of a database dynamically from a query workload (rather than statically from the database schema), allowing the capture of the implicit relationships and access frequency information in the workload.

- Techniques for compacting the link structure, allowing it to be constructed incrementally from a workload using at most $O(m^2)$ space, and enabling efficient and accurate computation of query-driven TupleRank.

*Related work.* The idea of querying a relational database as a graph is proposed by Goldman et al. [9]. In their work on proximity search in databases, nodes of the graph represent tuples and attributes, and undirected weighted edges connect nodes having relationships between them. The relationships, however, are all based on static database constraints.

There is a flurry of recent work on supporting keyword-style searches in relational databases. Most of them are based on constraints declared in the database schema. Goldman et al. [9] propose the idea of proximity searches by locating a database subgraph whose nodes are within a certain distance to a query node. Bhalotia et al. [2] further incorporate in their BANKS search engine the concept of node prestige. However, their node prestige only depends on the in-degree of a node, and all edges in their database graph are derived from referential integrity constraints (they also mention inclusion dependency). Similar systems include DataSpot [6], which also uses edges based on the static database schema and user-defined associations, and DISCOVER [10], which uses the database schema graph to generate joins to answer keyword search queries.

## 2 Static TupleRank

PageRank views the Web as a directed graph, whose nodes represent Web pages and edges represent hyperlinks between Web pages. The PageRank of a page $p$, denoted $\text{PageRank}(p)$, is defined by:

$$\text{PageRank}(p) = \sum_{q \in B(p)} \frac{\text{PageRank}(q)}{N(q)}, \tag{1}$$

where $B(p)$ is the set of pages that point to $p$, and $N(q)$ is the number of hyperlinks on page $q$. PageRank can be computed through a simple iterative algorithm, whose convergence is guaranteed by introducing a damping factor $d \in (0,1)$. Let $\text{PageRank}^{(k)}(p)$ denote the PageRank of $p$ at iteration $k$. We have

$$\text{PageRank}^{(k+1)}(p) = d \cdot \sum_{q \in B(p)} \frac{\text{PageRank}^{(k)}(q)}{N(q)} + (1-d). \tag{2}$$

Intuitively, $\text{PageRank}(p)$ corresponds to the probability that $p$ is visited by a surfer in the *random surfer model* [12]. Damping factor $d$ is the probability that a surfer follows one of the hyperlinks on the current page (instead of jumping directly to some random page).

Similarly, we define a *static TupleLink graph* based on the referential integrity relationships between tuples in a database. A static TupleLink graph is a directed graph whose nodes represent database tuples. There is a directed edge from tuple

$t_i$ to tuple $t_j$ (and from $t_j$ to $t_i$) if $t_i$'s foreign key references $t_j$'s primary key. We define the *static TupleRank* of a tuple $t$, denoted TupleRank($t$), as follows:

$$\text{TupleRank}(t) = \sum_{t' \in B(t)} \frac{\text{TupleRank}(t')}{N(t')}, \tag{3}$$

where $B(t)$ is the set of tuples with outgoing edges to $t$ in the TupleLink graph, and $N(t')$ is the number of outgoing edges from tuple $t'$. The TupleLink graph and TupleRank defined above are static, because the relationships between tuples are derived from static schema information.

Let $m$ be the total number of tuples in the database. Let $\mathbf{r}$ be a vector of size $m$, where $\mathbf{r}_i = \text{TupleRank}(t_i)$. Let $\mathbf{A}$ be an $m \times m$ matrix, where $\mathbf{A}_{ij} = 1/N(t_j)$ if there is an edge from $t_j$ to $t_i$ in the TupleLink graph, or 0 otherwise. Then, TupleRank can be computed by a simple iterative procedure using a damping factor $d$, just like PageRank:

$$\mathbf{r}^{(k+1)} = d\mathbf{A}\mathbf{r}^{(k)} + (1-d). \tag{4}$$

*Experiments.* We have computed static TupleRank for a relationship-rich geographical database, Mondial [1]. The database contains about ten thousand tuples storing information about countries, cities, rivers, seas, and other geographical entities. The schema of Mondial (with all referential integrity constraints) can be found on the Mondial [1] Web site.

To compute static TupleRank, we use a straightforward implementation based on the sparse matrix library `sparselib++` [7], using $d = 0.85$. The results are stored in a new database table *TupleRanks*(*TupleId*, *TupleRank*). Here, the *TupleId* of a database tuple consists of its table name and primary key value (which makes *TupleId* unique within the database).

Users of our system have found TupleRank to be quite interesting and informative. For example, the three top-ranking `Organization` tuples are the Universal Postal Union, World Health Organization, and United Nations. The two top-ranking `City` tuples in United States are New York City and Washington,DC. In general, most rankings are consistent with users' intuitive understanding of the relative importance of tuples in the geographical sense.

## 3 Query-Driven TupleRank

The main idea behind query-driven TupleRank is quite intuitive: Each query result tuple $q$ obtained by joining database tuples $t_1, \ldots, t_n$ should be considered as an "evidence" that $t_1, \ldots, t_n$ are "related." To capture this idea in a TupleLink graph, we can treat the result tuple $q$ as node that is connected to $t_1, \ldots, t_n$ (Figure 1). Formally, we define a *query-driven TupleLink graph* as a triple $(T, Q, E)$, where

- $T$ is a set of nodes that correspond to database tuples.
- $Q$ is a set of nodes that correspond to query result tuples.

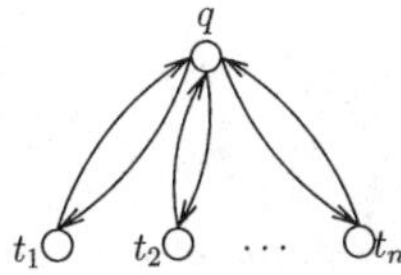


**Fig. 1.** Example of a TupleLink graph capturing an $n$-way join relationship.

- $E$ is a set of directed edges connecting nodes in $T \cup Q$.

A naive algorithm for constructing a query-driven TupleLink graph from a query workload works as follows:

- For each database tuple, create a node in $T$.
- For each query in the workload, and for each result tuple $q$ of the query:
  - ◇ Create a node in $Q$.
  - ◇ Suppose $q$ is obtained by joining database tuples $t_1, \ldots, t_n$. Create a directed edge in $E$ from $q$ to each $t_i$ ($1 \leq i \leq n$), and from each $t_i$ to $q$.

We can capture referential integrity relationships by manually adding to the workload queries that join foreign keys with corresponding primary keys. In practice, however, we expect such queries to arise naturally in a workload, so there is no need to deal with referential integrity relationships explicitly.

For now, we assume that the workload contains only simple select-project-join (SPJ) queries with no duplicate elimination. These queries usually constitute the bulk of common workloads. For these queries, it is clear that a result tuple is derived from joining database tuples. For other types of queries, such as those that use `EXCEPT`, it is less obvious which database tuples contribute to a result tuple. We plan to address other types of queries as future work. Work on lineage tracing [5] may provide a good starting point.

Given a query-driven TupleLink graph $(T, Q, E)$, we can define the *query-driven TupleRank* of a tuple $t$ in either $T$ or $Q$ as follows:

$$\text{TupleRank}(t) = \sum_{t' \in B(t)} \frac{\text{TupleRank}(t')}{N(t')}, \tag{5}$$

where $B(t)$ and $N(t')$ have the same definitions as in static TupleRank.

Although the query-driven TupleLink graph and TupleRank have very intuitive definitions, they pose serious implementation problems. As more queries enter the workload, more result tuples are generated, and $|Q|$ and $|E|$ can grow without any bound. In Section 3.1, we propose a series of techniques for compacting the TupleLink graph. In Section 3.2, we describe an algorithm for computing query-driven TupleRank by building a compact TupleLink graph that requires only $O(|T|^2)$ space, independent of the size of the workload. In Section 3.2, we also introduce a further enhancement of query-driven TupleRank which does a better job utilizing the access frequency information collected from the workload. Preliminary experiment results are presented in Section 3.3.

**Fig. 2.** Example of edge merging.

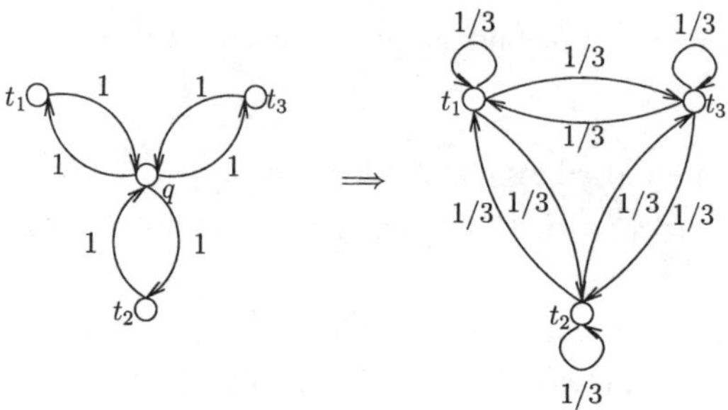


**Fig. 3.** Example of node removal.

### 3.1 Weighted TupleLink Graph and Graph Compaction Techniques

The first step towards compacting the TupleLink graph is generalizing it to a *weighted TupleLink graph*. The basic idea is to associate a positive weight with each edge. The static TupleLink graph can be seen as a special case where all weights are 1. Formally, we define a weighted TupleLink graph as a quadruple $(T, Q, E, w)$, where $T$, $Q$, $E$ have the same definitions as before, and $w : E \to (0, \infty)$ is a function that assigns a positive weight to each edge in $E$. Furthermore, we allow nodes to connect to themselves via self-loop edges, and a pair of nodes to be connected by multiple edges. For convenience, we define $w(t)$, the weight of a node $t \in T \cup Q$, as the sum of weights on the edges coming out of $t$.

We now define TupleRank on a weighted TupleLink graph $(T, Q, E, w)$:

$$\text{TupleRank}(t) = \sum_{e \in \mathit{into}(t)} \frac{w(e) \cdot \text{TupleRank}(\mathit{from}(e))}{w(\mathit{from}(e))}, \tag{6}$$

where $\mathit{into}(t)$ is the set of edges coming into $t$ in the weighted TupleRank graph, and $\mathit{from}(e)$ is the source node of edge $e$. Intuitively, the TupleRank of a node is distributed to all nodes that it points to, weighted by the edge and scaled by the total weight of outgoing edges.

*Edge merging.* Intuitively, if two edges share the same source and destination nodes, we can replace these two edges by one whose weight is the sum of the weights of the original edges. The result TupleLink graph after edge merging should produce identical TupleRank values for all nodes as the original graph. An example is shown in Figure 2. Formally, we have the following lemma.

**Lemma 1.** *Consider a weighted TupleLink graph $G(T, Q, E, w)$. Suppose that $e_1, e_2 \in E$ both go from $t_1$ to $t_2$, where $t_1, t_2 \in T \cup Q$. Define a second graph $G'(T, Q, E', w')$, where*

- *$E' = E - \{e_1, e_2\} \cup \{e_3\}$, where $e_3$ is a new edge that goes from $t_1$ to $t_2$.*
- *$\forall e \in E - \{e_1, e_2\} : w'(e) = w(e)$.*
- *$w'(e_3) = w(e_1) + w(e_2)$.*

*Then, $G$ and $G'$ produce identical TupleRank values (as defined by Equation 6) for all nodes in $T \cup Q$.*

Note that this lemma still holds when $t_1 = t_2$, i.e., both $e_1$ and $e_2$ are self-loops.

Lemma 1 alone is not enough to compact a TupleRank graph since Lemma 1 does not reduce the number of nodes in the graph. Next, we propose a technique for removing nodes in the graph.

*Node removal.* Recall that a TupleLink graph is defined in terms of two sets of nodes: those that correspond to database tuples ($T$) and those that correspond to query result tuples ($Q$). The goal of node removal is to eliminate all nodes from $Q$ without affecting the TupleRank values of nodes in $T$.

To motivate the next lemma, we use a very simple example of a query result tuple $q$ that joins three database tuples $t_1$, $t_2$, and $t_3$, as shown on the left in Figure 3. Let $R_1$ denote the contribution to TupleRank($t_1$) from edges that are not incident to/from $q$ (not shown in the figure). $R_2$ and $R_3$ are defined similarly for $t_2$ and $t_3$. According to Equation 6,

$$\text{TupleRank}(t_1) = R_1 + \frac{1 \cdot \text{TupleRank}(q)}{3}; \tag{7}$$

$$\text{TupleRank}(t_2) = R_2 + \frac{1 \cdot \text{TupleRank}(q)}{3}; \tag{8}$$

$$\text{TupleRank}(t_3) = R_3 + \frac{1 \cdot \text{TupleRank}(q)}{3}; \tag{9}$$

$$\text{TupleRank}(q) = \frac{1 \cdot \text{TupleRank}(t_1)}{w(t_1)} + \frac{1 \cdot \text{TupleRank}(t_2)}{w(t_2)} + \frac{1 \cdot \text{TupleRank}(t_3)}{w(t_3)}. \tag{10}$$

Consider the graph on the right, where $q$ and its incident edges are removed, and new edges between $t_1$, $t_2$, and $t_3$ and self-loops on them are added, all with weight 1/3. Note that in this graph, $w(t_1)$, $w(t_2)$, and $w(t_3)$ remain the same as before, because for each node, the weights on three outgoing edges add up to 1. According to Equation 6,

$$\text{TupleRank}(t_1) = R_1 + \Big(\frac{\frac{1}{3} \cdot \text{TupleRank}(t_1)}{w(t_1)} + \frac{\frac{1}{3} \cdot \text{TupleRank}(t_2)}{w(t_2)} + \frac{\frac{1}{3} \cdot \text{TupleRank}(t_3)}{w(t_3)}\Big);$$

$$\text{TupleRank}(t_2) = R_2 + \Big(\frac{\frac{1}{3} \cdot \text{TupleRank}(t_1)}{w(t_1)} + \frac{\frac{1}{3} \cdot \text{TupleRank}(t_2)}{w(t_2)} + \frac{\frac{1}{3} \cdot \text{TupleRank}(t_3)}{w(t_3)}\Big);$$

$$\text{TupleRank}(t_3) = R_3 + \Big(\frac{\frac{1}{3} \cdot \text{TupleRank}(t_1)}{w(t_1)} + \frac{\frac{1}{3} \cdot \text{TupleRank}(t_2)}{w(t_2)} + \frac{\frac{1}{3} \cdot \text{TupleRank}(t_3)}{w(t_3)}\Big).$$

It is easy to see that the above three equations are equivalent to Equations 7–9, if we simply substitute the definition of TupleRank($q$) in Equation 10 into Equations 7–9. For any other node $t$ in the graph (not shown in the figure),

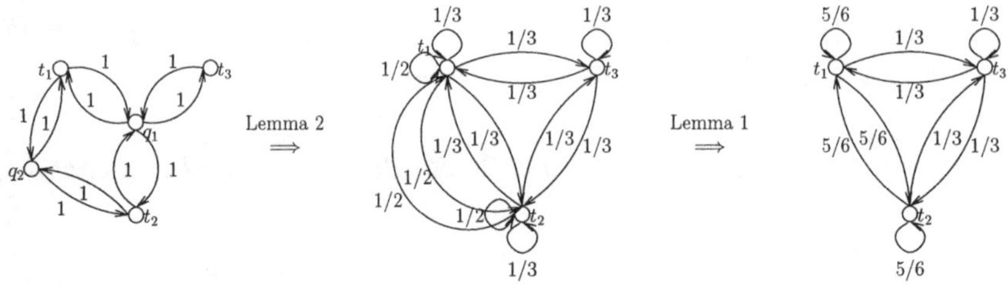


**Fig. 4.** Example of graph compaction.

TupleRank($t$) and $w(t)$ should have identical definitions as before, since the set of edges incident to/from $t$ has not changed. Therefore, the definitions of $R_1$, $R_2$, and $R_3$ also remain the same as before.

In general, we can remove a $n$-way join result tuple $q$ by adding edges between all pairs of database tuples that $q$ connects to, as well as edges from each such tuple to itself. All new edges should have weight $1/n$. Formally, we have the following lemma, which has been generalized for the case where edges do not necessarily have unit weights.

**Lemma 2.** *Consider a weighted TupleLink graph $G(T, Q, E, w)$. Suppose that $q \in Q$ has $n$ outgoing edges to tuples $t_1, \ldots, t_n$ with weights $w_1, \ldots, w_n$, respectively, and $n$ incoming edges from $t_1, \ldots, t_n$ with same weights $w_1, \ldots, w_n$, respectively. Define a second graph $G'(T, Q', E', w')$, where*

- $Q' = Q - \{q\}$.
- $\nabla E = \{(q, t_i) \mid 1 \le i \le n\} \cup \{(t_i, q) \mid 1 \le i \le n\}$.
- $\Delta E = \{(t_i, t_j) \mid 1 \le i \le n, 1 \le j \le n\}$.
- $E' = E - \nabla E \cup \Delta E$.
- $\forall e \in E - \nabla E : w'(e) = w(e)$.
- $\forall e(t_i, t_j) \in \Delta E : w'(e) = (w_i \cdot w_j)/(\sum_{1 \le k \le n} w_k)$.

*Then, $G$ and $G'$ produce identical TupleRank values (as defined by Equation 6) for all nodes in $T \cup Q'$.*

Note that the lemma holds in the case of self-joins, i.e., $t_i = t_j$ for some $i$ and $j$.

Starting with any weighted TupleLink graph $G(T, Q, E, w)$, we can apply Lemma 2 repeatedly to remove all nodes from $Q$, one at a time, while adding more edges to $E$ between nodes in $T$. Then, we can apply Lemma 1 repeatedly to merge edges in $E$ until only one edge remains for each pair of nodes in $T$. In the result graph, $Q = \varnothing$ and $|E| \le |T|^2$. A very simple example of this process (starting with a graph with $|Q| = 2$) is illustrated in Figure 4.

### 3.2 Compact TupleLink Graph Construction and TupleRank Computation

We now present an algorithm for computing query-driven TupleRank by incrementally building a compact TupleLink graph from a query workload. Suppose the database contains $m$ tuples $t_1, \ldots, t_m$. The weighted TupleLink graph can be encoded by an $m \times m$ matrix $\mathbf{A}$. We also maintain the access frequency of each tuple in a frequency vector $\mathbf{f}$ of size $m$, which can be used to enhance TupleRank computation, as we shall discuss later in this section.

- Initially, set all entries of $\mathbf{A}$ and $\mathbf{f}$ to 0.
- For each query in the workload, and for each result tuple $q$ of the query:
  - ◇ Suppose that $q$ is obtained by joining $n$ database tuples $t_{i_1}, \ldots, t_{i_n}$.
  - ◇ For each integer $u \in [1, n]$, and for each integer $v \in [1, n]$, update $\mathbf{A}$ as follows: $\mathbf{A}_{i_u,i_v} \leftarrow \mathbf{A}_{i_u,i_v} + 1/n$, and $\mathbf{A}_{i_v,i_u} \leftarrow \mathbf{A}_{i_v,i_u} + 1/n$.
  - ◇ For each integer $u \in [1, n]$, increment $\mathbf{f}_{i_u}$ by 1.
- Finally, we scale $\mathbf{A}$ to ensure that entries in each column sum up to 1 (unless the column consists entirely of 0's): $\mathbf{A}_{i,j} \leftarrow \mathbf{A}_{i,j} / \sum_{1 \leq k \leq m} \mathbf{A}_{i,k}$ (provided that $\sum_{1 \leq k \leq m} \mathbf{A}_{i,k} \neq 0$).
- We also scale $\mathbf{f}$ to ensure that all entries sum up to 1: $\mathbf{f}_i \leftarrow \mathbf{f}_i / \sum_{1 \leq k \leq m} \mathbf{f}_k$.

Let $\mathbf{r}$ be a vector of size $m$, where $\mathbf{r}_i = \text{TupleRank}(t_i)$. We then have the following equivalent formulation of query-driven TupleRank:

$$\mathbf{r} = \mathbf{A}\mathbf{r}. \tag{11}$$

From Lemmas 1 and 2, the following theorem follows naturally:

**Theorem 1.** *Given a database and a query workload, construct a query-driven TupleLink graph $(T, Q, E)$ using the naive algorithm discussed at the beginning of Section 3, and construct a matrix $\mathbf{A}$ using the algorithm discussed in Section 3.2. Then, the TupleRank definition in Equation 5 based on $(T, Q, E)$ is equivalent to the TupleRank definition in Equation 11 based on $\mathbf{A}$.*

Again, TupleRank can be computed by a simple iterative procedure with a damping factor $d$, starting from $\mathbf{r}^{(0)} = (1, 1, \ldots)$:

$$\mathbf{r}^{(k+1)} = d\mathbf{A}\mathbf{r}^{(k)} + (1 - d). \tag{12}$$

We introduce another enhancement of TupleRank which makes better use of the access frequency information stored in $\mathbf{f}$. Recall that we can regard the damping factor $d$ as the probability that a database user chooses to follow a link from the current tuple. With probability $1 - d$, the user chooses a random tuple to revisit next. Equation 12 above simply assumes that the next tuple is chosen uniformly at random (similar to PageRank). However, with the access frequency information from the workload, we may assume instead that the next tuple is chosen according to the frequency vector $\mathbf{f}$. Thus, starting with $\mathbf{r}^{(0)} = (1/m, 1/m, \ldots)$, we have

$$\mathbf{r}^{(k+1)} = d\mathbf{A}'\mathbf{r}^{(k)} + (1 - d)\mathbf{f}, \tag{13}$$

where $\mathbf{A}' = \mathbf{A} - \text{diag}(\mathbf{A})$, and further scaled to ensure that entries in each column sum up to 1.

The reason for zeroing out the diagonal entries is the following. From the construction algorithm, we can easily see that the diagonal entries of $\mathbf{A}$ also capture the tuple access frequency information as does $\mathbf{f}$. Since Equation 13 already makes explicit use of the frequency information through $\mathbf{f}$, it makes sense to remove this information in $\mathbf{A}'$ to avoid overuse. We find that TupleRank can make more effective use of the frequency information with $\mathbf{f}$ than with $\mathbf{A}$, because the diagonal entries of $\mathbf{A}$, representing the self-loops on nodes in the TupleLink graph, tend to increase the total weight of outgoing edges from a node, making it harder for the node to contribute its TupleRank to others. On the other hand, the contribution from $\mathbf{f}$ can be propagated to others more easily.

### 3.3 Implementation and Experiments

In implementing query-driven TupleRank, the first issue that must be addressed is how to determine which database tuples contribute to a query result tuple. As mentioned earlier in Section 3, for simple SPJ queries with no duplicate elimination, it is clear that a result tuple is derived from joining database tuples. Given one such query in the workload, we can rewrite its `SELECT` clause to return the *TupleId* values (as defined earlier in Section 2) for tables in the `FROM` clause. For queries involving subqueries, we often can flatten them into simple unnested select-project-join queries and then use the approach to identify the joining tuples. As mentioned earlier, we plan to address other types of queries as future work. In practice, the algorithm presented in Section 3.2 can be implemented using the following approaches:

1. *Using a copy of the production database.* We continuously ship queries and updates from the production database to a copy of it. Updates are applied verbatim on the copy. Queries are rewritten to return *TupleId* values (as described above) and then processed on the copy. The returned *TupleId* values allow us to update $\mathbf{A}$ and $\mathbf{f}$.
2. *Directly on top of the production database.* A layer can be implemented directly on top of the database API (e.g., JDBC) to intercept application queries. We augment these queries to return *TupleId* values before passing them to the database for evaluation. The returned *TupleId* values allow us to update $\mathbf{A}$ and $\mathbf{f}$. Before returning to the application, we must remove these extraneous *TupleId* values from the result.

The first series of experiments are conducted on Mondial, with the primary goal of evaluating the intuitiveness of query-driven TupleRank. Mondial is a large and complex database, so we focus on tracking TupleRank for a small number of tuples as we adjust the query workload. Specifically, we track six `Country` tuples that correspond to the six French-speaking countries (according to Mondial, which may not be complete): France, Switzerland, Belgium, Guinea, Haiti, and French Guiana. Static TupleRank for these `Country` tuples are shown in the second column of Table 1. Instead of showing their actual TupleRank values, we show their *ranks* among all `Country` tuples, which are more meaningful. For

**Table 1.** TupleRank of French-speaking countries in Mondial.

| Country | static | query-driven ($W_{\text{ref}}$) | query-driven ($W_2$) | query-driven ($W_3$) |
|---|---|---|---|---|
| France | 6 | 6 | 7 | 5 |
| Switzerland | 11 | 11 | 12 | 7 |
| Belgium | 28 | 28 | 29 | 14 |
| Guinea | 81 | 81 | 83 | 50 |
| Haiti | 137 | 137 | 1 | 37 |
| French Guiana | 192 | 192 | 192 | 184 |

**Table 2.** Result of experiments on TPC-W.

| Number of EB's/items | 10/100,000 | 30/100,000 | 10/1,000 | 30/1,000 |
|---|---|---|---|---|
| Number of Database tuples | 340,748 | 773,665 | 217,114 | 649,370 |
| Number of queries generated | 2,454 | 6,042 | 2,608 | 8,104 |
| Number of result tuples | 32,402 | 107,496 | 531,585 | 4,491,969 |
| Number of non-zero entries in **A** | 23,400 | 36,084 | 295,803 | 894,699 |
| Sparsity of **A** | 99.99998% | 99.99999% | 99.99994% | 99.99999% |
| TupleRank computation time (sec) | 2.1 | 3.1 | 11.2 | 38.6 |

example, France is ranked sixth among all countries, while French Guiana is ranked 192nd.

We start with a query workload $W_{\text{ref}}$ consisting of join queries along all referential integrity relationships declared in Mondial's schema. We compute the query-driven TupleRank for $W_{\text{ref}}$ and find the result ranking (shown in the third column of Table 1) to be identical to that of static TupleRank, as expected.

Next, we construct a second workload $W_2$ by adding a huge number (1000) of the following query to $W_{\text{ref}}$:

```
SELECT * FROM Language WHERE country = 'RH';
```

where `RH` is the country code representing Haiti. These queries drive up the access frequency of the selected `Language` tuple, but the access frequencies of all other database tuples remain unchanged as in $W_{\text{ref}}$. We show the query-driven TupleRank computed for $W_2$ in the fourth column of Table 1. Note that Haiti becomes the top-ranking `Country` tuple, even though its access frequency has not changed. The reason is that the selected `Language` tuple is related to the `Country` tuple for Haiti through a referential integrity constraint. Thus, Haiti receives a boost in TupleRank through the selected `Language`. This result clearly demonstrates that query-driven TupleRank is frequency-aware, yet it offers more than a simple ranking based on access frequency alone.

On the other hand, TupleRank values for other French-speaking countries remain practically unchanged. A closer look at Mondial's schema (available at [1] and in the full version of this paper [11]) reveals the problem: There is no link between two countries that speak the same language.

Fortunately, query-driven TupleRank comes to rescue. To capture the relationship between countries speaking the same language, we construct a third workload $W_3$ by adding the following query (once is enough) to $W_2$:

```
SELECT * FROM Language L1, Language L2 WHERE L1.name = L2.name;
```

The query-driven TupleRank values for $W_3$ are shown in the last column of Table 1. Note that the ranks of French-speaking countries all improve consistently. Compared with static TupleRank, Haiti still receives the most significant boost; after all, it is most closely related to the particular Language tuple being accessed 1000 times. On the other hand, the boost is not as much as in the case of $W_2$, because now the boost is also distributed to other French-speaking countries. The last two experiments together demonstrate the inadequacy of static TupleRank and the need for discovering relationships from query workloads.

We have also experimented with TPC-W[13], a benchmark designed to evaluate the performance of a complete Web e-commerce solution. We use a Java implementation of the TPC-W from University of Wisconsin [4] to generate the workload for query-driven TupleRank. Since TPC-W is a synthetic database, it is not meaningful to report TupleRank for randomly generated tuples. Therefore, the primary goal of our TPC-W experiments is to evaluate the efficiency of query-driven TupleRank. The results are shown in Table 2. All experiments use the TPC-W browsing mix since we are interested primarily in queries. We vary the number of EB's (emulated client browsers running concurrently) as well as the number of items for sale. A larger number of EB's means that more queries, and consequently more result tuples, will be generated. On the other hand, although a larger number of items implies a larger database, the number of result tuples is actually smaller. The reason is that the workload contains a number of queries that compute the join between orders and best-selling items. With fewer items, each item will have more orders, so the join result will be larger.

Computation of TupleRank is done on a Sun Blade 100 workstation with a 500MHz UltraSPARC-IIe processor and 256MB of RAM. Overall, we see that the matrix $\mathbf{A}$ is extremely sparse, because each database tuple usually joins with a constant number of tuples. Hence, in practice, the space requirement of our algorithm tends to be $\Theta(m)$, where $m$ is the number of database tuples. Size of the workload has no significant effect on either space or time required by TupleRank computation.

## 4 Conclusion and Future Work

To conclude, we have proposed a scheme called TupleRank for ranking tuples in a relational database. We have also introduced the notion of query-driven TupleRank, which is based on a link structure that is dynamically constructed from a workload. To the best of our knowledge, we are the first to propose using such a query-driven link structure for determining relationships among database tuples. As we have shown, query-driven TupleRank can capture the implicit relationships and access frequency information in a query workload, both of which are beyond the capabilities of traditional approaches based on static schema information. Finally, we have developed techniques to compute query-driven TupleRank accurately and efficiently. In the following, we briefly outline some future directions.

- We are currently investigating more applications of TupleRank, e.g., in designing cache replacement and replication policies. Intuitively, tuples with higher TupleRank values are more worthy of caching or replicating.
- Currently, we recompute TupleRank and reset **A** and **f** periodically. A better approach is to update **A** and **f** incrementally and gradually decrease the effect of past queries on them. A related problem is how to compute TupleRank incrementally given small perturbations to **A** and **f**.
- As mentioned in Section 3, we plan to investigate how to use non-SPJ queries to identify more relationships among tuples. We also plan to experiment with the second implementation approach discussed in Section 3.3.
- Our current graph compaction techniques still ensure the accuracy of TupleRank. The next natural question is whether we can trade the accuracy of TupleRank for further space and time reductions.

## References


1. Mondial. `http://user.informatik.uni-goettingen.de/~may/Mondial`.
2. G. Bhalotia, C. Nakhe, A. Hulgeri, S. Chakrabarti, and S. Sudarshan. Keyword searching and browsing in databases using BANKS. In *Proc. of the 2002 Intl. Conf. on Data Engineering*, San Jose, California, February 2002.
3. S. Brin and L. Page. The anatomy of a large-scale hypertextual Web search engine. In *Proc. of the 1998 Intl. World Wide Web Conf.*, Brisbane, Australia, April 1998.
4. H. W. Cain, R. Rajwar, M. Marden, and M. H. Lipasti. An architectural evaluation of Java TPC-W. In *Proc. of the 2001 Intl. Symp. on High-Performance Computer Architecture*, January 2001.
5. Y. Cui and J. Widom. Lineage tracing for general data warehouse transformations. In *Proc. of the 2001 Intl. Conf. on Very Large Data Bases*, pages 471–480, Roma, Italy, September 2001.
6. S. Dar, G. Entin, S. Geva, and E. Palmon. DTL's DataSpot: Database exploration using plain language. In *Proc. of the 1998 Intl. Conf. on Very Large Data Bases*, pages 645–649, New York City, New York, August 1998.
7. J. Dongarra, A. Lumsdaine, R. Pozo, and K. Remington. A sparse matrix library in C++ for high performance architectures. In *Proc. of the Second Object-Oriented Numerics Conference*, pages 214–218, 1994.
8. H. Garcia-Molina, J. D. Ullman, and J. Widom. *Database Systems: The Complete Book*. Prentice Hall, Upper Saddle River, New Jersey, 2002.
9. R. Goldman, N. Shivakumar, S. Venkatasubramanian, and H. Garcia-Molina. Proximity search in databases. In *Proc. of the 1998 Intl. Conf. on Very Large Data Bases*, pages 26–37, New York City, New York, August 1998.
10. V. Hristidis and Y. Papakonstantinou. DISCOVER: Keyword search in relational databases. In *Proc. of the 2002 Intl. Conf. on Very Large Data Bases*, pages 670–681, Hong Kong, China, August 2002.
11. X. Huang, Q. Xue, and J. Yang. TupleRank and implicit relationship discovery in relational databases. Technical report, Duke University, March 2003. `http://www.cs.duke.edu/~junyang/papers/hxy-tuplerank.ps`.
12. L. Page, S. Brin, R. Motwani, and T. Winograd. The PageRank citation ranking: Bringing order to the Web. Technical report, Stanford University, November 1999.
13. Transaction Processing Performance Council. TPC-W benchmark specification. `http://www.tpc.org/wspec.html`.

# Top-*N* Query: Query Language, Distance Function, and Processing Strategies

Yuxi Chen and Weiyi Meng

Department of Computer Science, State University of New York at Binghamton
Binghamton, NY 13902, USA, meng@cs.binghamton.edu

**Abstract.** The top-*N* query problem is to find the *N* results that satisfy the query condition the best but not necessarily completely. It is gaining importance in relational databases and in e-commerce where services and products are sold on the Internet. This paper addresses three important issues related to the top-*N* query problem in a relational database context. First, we propose a new query language to facilitate the specification of various top-N queries. This language adds new features to existing languages. Second, we make a case that the *sum* function is a more appropriate distance function for ranking tuples when attributes involved in a top-N query are incomparable. Third, based on the *sum* distance function, we discuss how to process top-*N* queries.

**Keywords:** Top-*N* query, query language, query processing, distance function.

## 1 Introduction

In recent years, there has been increasing interest in the top-*N* query problem in relational databases [3, 5, 9]. For a given query against a database table, the problem is how to efficiently find the *N* tuples that satisfy the query condition the best but not necessarily completely.

**Example 1.** Consider a table *Employees* (*Name*, *Age*, *Salary*). Suppose we want to find young employees who earn a good salary. The query cannot be directly specified using the standard SQL. If SQL must be used, a user may write a query as follows:

SELECT *Name* FROM *Employees* WHERE *Age* < *30* AND *Salary* > *50000*

Suppose there are four employees: *A* = *(Dave, 28, 70000)*, *B* = *(Nicky, 29, 60000)*, *C* = *(Randy, 31, 48000)* and *D* = *(Karen, 32, 47000)*. Obviously, both *A* and *B* satisfy the query condition but *A* could be interpreted as satisfying the condition better because *Dave* is younger and earns more money than *Nicky*. In addition, neither *C* nor *D* satisfies the query condition but *C* can be considered to satisfy the condition better than D. Therefore, for "finding young employees who earn a good salary", the tuples should be ordered by {*A*, *B*, *C*, *D*}. If top 1 or top 3 tuples are desired, then {*A*} or {*A*, *B*, *C*} should be selected respectively.

Many applications can benefit from the capability of top-*N* queries. For example, when searching for a used car or a house to buy, it is desirable to have the results ranked based on how well a car or a house matches with a user-provided specification and have only certain number of top results displayed.

G. Dong et al. (Eds.): WAIM 2003, LNCS 2762, pp. 458–470, 2003.

There are a number of research issues in the top-*N* query problem. (1) How to specify top-*N* queries? Appropriate extensions to SQL are needed to allow top-*N* queries to be expressed. (2) How to rank the results? If a condition involves only one attribute, this is trivial. When multiple attributes are involved, the problem becomes more complex. Suppose, for example, if the tuple *D* above is changed to (*Karen, 32, 49000*), it is less easy to rank *C* or *D*. (3) How to efficiently evaluate top-*N* queries?

In this paper, we report our research on the above three issues. Our contributions are summarized below. For issue (1), we propose significant extensions to SQL so that a variety of top-N queries can be specified. New operators and new concepts are introduced to better capture new semantics to top-*N* queries. For issue (2), we make a case for the *sum* function for ranking tuples for a given query. While several distance functions, such as Euclidean distance function and the *sum* functions [3, 7], have been used for top-N applications, there is little discussion on the appropriateness of a particular function. We argue that the *sum* function is appropriate when attributes involved in a query are not comparable. For issue (3), we provide a new strategy for the efficient processing of top-*N* queries when the *sum* scoring function is used. The objective is to minimize the size of the search space. This strategy is suitable when the data are approximately uniformly distributed.

### 1.1 Related Work

Here we briefly review some existing work related to the issues mentioned above.

1. *Syntax of Top-N Queries*: In [4], the ORDER BY clause was extended to allow a distance function to be specified for ranking tuples and a STOP AFTER clause was added to specify how many tuples are desired in the result. However, only tuples that satisfy the query conditions will be ranked. Thus, if *N* tuples are desired but fewer than *N* tuples satisfy the WHERE clause of a query, then less than N tuples will be returned. In [3], the ORDER BY clause was extended to allow both the desired number of tuples and the distance function to be specified (i.e., order *N* by score). However, only equality conditions are considered, i.e., no range condition is considered. We believe more general query conditions should be supported. In [7], general conditions are allowed and tuples satisfying the condition are always ranked ahead of tuples not satisfying the condition. Again, the ORDER BY clause was extended to allow a distance function to be specified. [7] also supports different priorities for different conditions in the same query to be specified. None of the existing extensions to SQL for top-*N* query specification has the flexibility and expressiveness of our proposed language.
2. *Distance Function*: The condition C of a top-*N* query may involve multiple attributes. For a given tuple and a given attribute involved in C, a distance measuring how well the tuple satisfying C can be obtained easily. The problem here is how to combine the distances on individual attributes into a combined distance so that all tuples can be ranked. Several distance functions for combining purpose have been mentioned and they include the *Euclidean* distance function [3,7], the *sum* (or *Manhattan*) distance function [3,7] and the *min* function [3,6]. Current proposals have two weaknesses. First, users are either given too much control or not enough flexibility. In several proposals, the user is

required to provide the distance function as part of a query [3,4,7]. In practice, most ordinary users don't know what distance function is appropriate to use. In other proposals, a pre-determined distance function is used and users do not have any choice [6]. A single function is unlikely to be suitable for different applications. Our approach is a middle of the road approach. We allow a user to provide his/her preferred distance function if he/she knows what function is appropriate for his/her application. However, a default distance function will be used by the system if a user does not provide his/her own function. Second, there is a lack of in-depth study on why a particular function should be used. In this paper, we argue that the *sum* function is reasonable when the involved attributes are not comparable.

3. Top-N Query Processing: There have been several proposals in the literature (e.g., [3,7]). Most of them are working on how to determine the search range by exploiting the statistics available to a relational DBMS, and the impact of the quality of these statistics on the retrieval efficiency of the resulting scheme. In this paper, we propose a simple approach that is suitable when the data are approximately uniformly distributed.

The remainder of this paper is organized as follows. In Section 2, we propose a new query language called topNSQL for specifying top-N queries. Only conjunct conditions are considered in this paper. In Section 3, we make a case that the *sum* distance function is more appropriate for top-N queries when attributes involved in the query condition are incomparable. In Section 4, we propose a new strategy for processing top-N queries based on the *sum* function. Section 5 concludes the paper.

## 2 Extending SQL

In this section, we discuss different possible semantics of top-*N* queries. Based on the discussion, we propose our extensions to the syntax of standard SQL so that all possible semantics can be represented.

*Regular operators and emphatic operators*

**Example 2.** Let *price* be an attribute of Books. In standard SQL, a simple condition 'price < 20' indicates that the user is interested in books that cost less than $20. Now consider how to interpret this condition in the context of top-N queries. There are two reasonable interpretations. (1) All books less than $20 are equally good. If N or more books satisfy the condition, arbitrarily select N of them to return to the user. If there are less than N such books, then select additional books whose prices are closest to $20 but higher. In this case, interval [0, 20) is used as a *reference space* to calculate the distance of a book with the query. Specifically, let *p* be the price of a book *b*. If $0 \leq p < 20$, then the distance of *b* is zero; if p >= 20, then the distance of b is p – 20. (2) Cheaper books are better, regardless of whether the price is less than $20 or not. Based on this interpretation, 0 is the *reference point* for calculating the distances of books.

Both interpretations discussed above are reasonable and can be useful in practice. Therefore, it is important to differentiate the two interpretations syntactically. We propose to use 'price < 20' for the first interpretation only, consistent with the standard SQL. For the second interpretation, we propose to use ‘price << 20’. In other words, the operator “<<” has the meaning of “the smaller, the better”. Similarly, “>>” can be used to represent “the larger, the better”. For easy discussion, the standard operators such as ‘<’ and ‘<=’ will be called *regular operators* while new operators ‘<<’, ‘<<=’, ‘>>’ and ‘>>=’ will be called *emphatic operators*. Another interesting observation that can be made from Example 2 is that the reference point for calculating the distances of tuples for ranking purposes is dependent on the interpretation.

*Condition Space and Reference Space*

For a given query Q, let the space defined by the condition of Q be called the *condition space* of Q. Furthermore, if a condition space is a point, the condition is called a *point condition.* For example, ‘weight = 120 and height = 170’ is a point condition as (120, 170) represents a point in the two-dimensional space of (weight, height). If a condition space is a rectangle, the condition is called a *rectangle condition.* An example of a rectangle condition is ‘weight < 120 and height >= 170’. For the purpose of defining the condition space of a query, regular operators and emphatic operators are not differentiated.

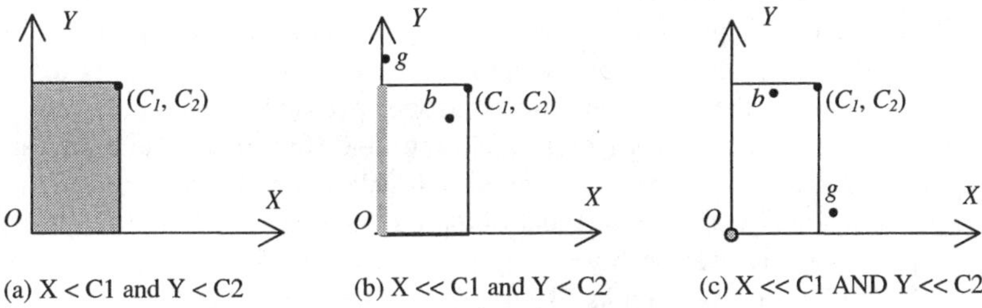


(a) X < C1 and Y < C2 (b) X << C1 and Y < C2 (c) X << C1 AND Y << C2

**Fig. 2.1.** Example Condition Spaces and Reference Spaces

For query Q, its *reference space* needs to be derived for ranking tuples. The distance of a tuple for Q is the distance between the point corresponding to the tuple and the reference space of Q. The reference space of Q is determined by the operators used in the condition specification and may be different from the condition space of Q. In Example 2, for ‘price < 20’, the condition space and the reference space are both [0, 20) (note that for any price p >= 20, the distance between p and [0, 20) is the same as that between p and 20). For ‘price << 20’, the condition space is still [0, 20) but the reference space becomes [0, 0]. In general, for a given query, when emphatic operators are not used, the condition space and the reference space are the same, and when emphatic operators are used, the condition space and the reference space are different. When one or more emphatic operators are involved, the reference space is derived as follows. Let each attribute represent one dimension in the condition space. Let min(X) and max(X) be the smallest and the largest possible values of attribute X. If ‘X << v’ or ‘X <<= v’ appears in the condition, where v is a constant, then the reference space is obtained by collapsing the condition space along the dimension of X to min(X) (i.e., the X-dimension becomes a point, min(X)); If ‘X >> v’ or ‘X >>= v’ appears in the condition, the reference space collapses along the X-dimension to max(X). In Figure 2.1, three condition spaces and three reference spaces for three different query conditions are drawn. For all three conditions, the condition space is the same rectangle (0<=X<C1, 0<=Y<C2), but the three reference spaces are different (see shaded areas).

*Distance Factor and Satisfaction Factor*

The above discussion can be summarized as follows. From a given query condition, a *condition space* and a *reference space* can be determined. Both types of spaces can affect the ranking of a tuple as discussed below.

1. *Distance factor*. Each tuple has a distance with respect to the reference space of the query. Tuples should be ranked in ascending distance values.
2. *Satisfaction factor*. Tuples satisfying the condition (i.e., falling into the condition space) should be ranked ahead of tuples not satisfying the condition. In this case, tuples satisfying and not satisfying the condition can be ordered separately by a distance function, and the tuples in the first group are placed ahead of those in the second group.

The following example illustrates that the above two factors are not always consistent when rectangle conditions are involved. It is possible that a tuple satisfying the query condition has a larger distance than a tuple not satisfying the condition.

**Example 3.** Consider a book search service that can find books for customers to buy from multiple sources. Suppose a user wants to find a book (of a given title) with the lowest total cost (cost of the book plus shipping fee), but the user is willing to pay up to $45 for the book. As the query condition must be specified based on the cost of the book and the shipping fee, the user breaks $45 into $40 (for cost of the book) and $5 (for shipping). As a result, the query condition involving the attributes *cost* and *shipping_fee* becomes 'cost <<= 40 and shipping_fee <<= 5'. For this query, the condition space is (0<=cost<=40, 0<=shipping_fee<=5) while the reference space is the point (0, 0). Consider two books, B1 and B2, of the same title from two sources. B1 sells for $39 with a $5 shipping fee and B2 sells for $41 with a $2 shipping fee. According to the satisfaction factor, B1 should be ranked ahead of B2. But according to the distance factor (obviously the appropriate distance function for this example should be *sum* and the distance should be with respect to (0, 0)), B2 should be ranked ahead of B1. Also in Figure 2.1 (b) and (c), point *b* satisfies the query condition while point *g* does not, but *g* has a smaller distance to the query than *b*.

In general, there are applications that prefer to rank tuples strictly by distances and there are also applications that would like to take the satisfaction factor into consideration. We believe that both types of applications should be supported. To the best of our knowledge, no existing research has pointed out the inconsistency between the satisfaction factor and the distance factor. Indeed, such an inconsistency does not exist when the query condition is a point condition. For the rest of this paper, top-N queries that rank tuples strictly by distances will be called *Type-1* queries and those that take the satisfaction factor into consideration are called *Type-2* queries.

*Importance Factor of a Condition*

Conditions of the same query may have different importance for ranking tuples.

**Example 4.** Suppose a user wants to purchase a used car worth no more than $10,000 with the mileage no more than 10,000. Using our notation, this query is expressed as "price <<= 10000 and mileage <<= 10000". The reference space of the query is (0, 0).

Consider two used cars C1 = ($11,000, 10,000 miles) and C2 = ($10,000, 11,000 miles). The distance between C1 and the reference space of the query for price is 11,000 and the distance between C2 and the reference space of the query for mileage is also 11,000. In practice, C2 should be ranked ahead of C1 because one-dollar difference is more significant than one-mile difference. To reflect the difference of different conditions in importance, appropriate *importance factors* can be associated to these conditions [7]. For example, if one-dollar difference is equivalent to ten-mile difference, we can multiply the distance for mileage by 10 and multiply the distance for price by 1, where 10 and 1 are the importance factors. (Note: Since smaller distance is better, a smaller importance factor indicates higher significance.)

In general, importance factors can be used to adjust scaling/unit differences of different attributes for ranking tuples in top-N queries.

*Strict-N and Loose-N*

Let us take a closer look at how many tuples should be returned for a top-*N* query. Obviously, if ≤ N tuples are in the database, then all tuples should be returned. Furthermore, if the distance of the (N+1)-th ranked tuple is larger than that of the N-th ranked tuple, then exactly N tuples should be returned. When the distances of the N-th and the (N+1)-th ranked tuples are identical, two possibilities exist:

- *Strict-N*: Exactly N tuples are returned. In this case, the returned set of tuples is not unique. This may cause non-deterministic result.
- *Loose-N*: All tuples that have the same distance as the N-th ranked tuple are returned. Clearly, this may cause more than N tuples to be returned to the user. However, the non-deterministic problem is avoided.

The proposed top-N query syntax supports the specification of a user's preference on Strict-N or Loose-N.

*TopNSQL Syntax*

Based on the discussion above, we propose the following syntax for top-*N* queries.

SELECT <expression> FROM <table_reference> WHERE **<query_condition>**
**ORDER BY** <sort specification> **STOP AFTER** [exact] <value expression>

Notes:

- The SELECT and FROM clauses are the same as in standard SQL.
- <query-condition> may contain both regular operators and emphatic operators. Furthermore, each condition is of the format "A op v (r)", where A is the name of an attribute, op is an operator, v is a constant and r is the importance factor of the condition. The default importance factor is 1. Namely, when (r) is absent, it is implied that r = 1.
- <sort specification> specifies how tuples should be ordered. <sort specification> has two components with the format 'order mode, distance function'. When "order mode = 1", tuples will be ordered solely based on their distances with the reference space of the query condition. In other words, the query is a Type-1 query. When "order mode = 2", tuples satisfying the query condition will be ranked ahead of tuples not satisfying the condition, namely the query is a Type-2 query. The second component, namely "distance function", can be provided by the user according to the semantics of the application. If the user does not provide the function, the system provides a default one.

- The STOP AFTER clause was introduced in [4] and we adopt it here in our query language and extend it with the "exact" option. If the "exact" is present, exactly N tuples will be returned if ≥ N tuples are in the database (i.e., the Strict-N is chosen); else, more than N tuples may be retrieved (i.e., the Loose-N option is chosen). <value expression> is any expression that evaluates to an integer *N*, the number of tuples desired.

**Example 3** (continued). Suppose a user wants to find the top 5 matches for a book titled "Advanced Database Query Processing" and no more than 5 results are needed. Based on the syntax for top-N queries introduced above, this query should be expressed as follows:

SELECT * FROM *BOOKS*
WHERE *title* = *'Advanced Database Query Processing'* AND *price<<=40* AND *shipping_fee<<=5*
ORDER BY 1, sum STOP AFTER exact *5*

## 3 Distance Functions

In this section, we discuss what distance function is appropriate for ranking tuples for top-N queries. We argue, through the theory of Raw Relation Sets [1], that the *sum* function is reasonable when the attributes referenced in a query condition are not semantically comparable.

In general, the right choice of the distance function for a given top-N query depends on the application. For example, in Example 3, when books are ranked in ascending order of the total cost (book cost and shipping_fee), *sum* is the only appropriate function to use. As another example, consider a geographical information system in which the locations of all cities are represented as coordinates in a 2-dimensional space. For a top-N query for finding the closest cities to a given city, the right function to use is the Euclidean function. It is precisely because there does not exist a single distance function that is suitable for all applications, all proposed query languages for top-N queries let users supply the distance function when specifying a query. We also adopt this approach. On the other hand, there are many applications for which it is not clear what is the appropriate distance function to use. In this case, it may not be reasonable to expect an ordinary user to supply the distance function. This situation usually occurs when the attributes involved in the query condition are not comparable. For instance, in Example 1, the two attributes in the query condition, namely *age* and *salary*, have different meanings, and it is not clear what is the appropriate function to combine the distances due to individual attributes. Currently, there is no serious study on how to combine distances due to individual attributes when the attributes have incomparable values.

In this section, we provide a theoretic justification for using the *sum* function to combine distances due to individual attributes when the attributes have incomparable values based on the Raw Relation Sets theory [1]. Such a justification makes *sum* a good candidate to serve as the default distance function.

For simplicity, we will generally focus on two-dimensional condition space involving attributes X and Y, but our discussion and conclusion can be extended to condition space of higher dimensions. Without loss of generality, we assume that the two attributes are of the same importance for ranking tuples in the sense that one unit of difference of two values in X is of the same significance as one unit of difference in Y (otherwise, we use adjusted units after appropriate importance factors are applied).

Raw Relation Sets [1,2] is a mathematical theory for solving the problem of generating an overall order from individual orders over the same set of objects. Each individual order is described by a set of binary relationships between every pair of objects in the set. Three types of relationships may exist between two objects p and q: *larger than* (denoted by (p, q); *smaller than* is not considered since "p is smaller than q" is the same as "q is larger than p"), *equal* (denoted by <=p, q=>) and *Unknown* (denoted by <p, q>) and exactly one relationship exists between each pair of objects. Each relationship is modeled as an object in the set of relationships (the next level of objects). The fact that "object p is larger than object q" to a larger extent than "object p is larger than object r" can be represented by (p, q) and (p, r) in the first level and ((p, q), (p, r)) in the second level (i.e., (p, q) is larger than (p, r) in the second level). Informally speaking, a *raw relation set* over a set of objects is a multi-level description of the relationships between a set of objects. The general problem the raw relation set theory attempts to solve can be stated as follows:

*There is a set of objects O and there is a set of voters V (e.g., a voter could be a judge in a competition or a criterion for ranking objects); each voter provides an order for the objects in O and the order is represented as a raw relation set; there is also an order for all voters (e.g., some judges/criteria are more important than others) and this order is also represented as a raw relation set. Based on the* |*V*| + *1 raw relation sets, obtain an overall order for the objects in O.*

Due to space limitation, details of raw relation sets will not be discussed in this paper. Instead, we are interested in only applying this theory to help finding a default distance function in the context of this paper. The problem at hand is a much simplified version of the general problem described above. Here, each dimension (i.e., an attribute referenced in a query condition) corresponds to a voter and for any two values v1 and v2 (objects) along this dimension, either v1 > v2, v2 > v1 or v1 = v2 is true (there is no *don't know* relationship). Moreover, all dimensions (voters) are considered to be of the same importance (i.e., only *equal* relationship exists between dimensions).

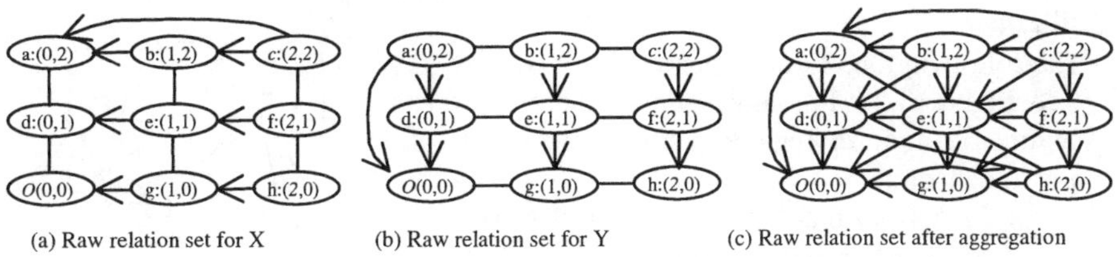


(a) Raw relation set for X (b) Raw relation set for Y (c) Raw relation set after aggregation

**Fig. 3.1.** A raw sets of 9 nodes (not all edges are shown).

We now use a small example to illustrate how the raw relation set theory works to produce an overall order from individual orders. Consider Figure 3.1. In this example, the origin O(0, 0) is the reference point. The arrows indicate the *larger than* relationships, that is, "p → q" means that p is larger than q. Arrows along dimension X indicate that for any given Y-value, X-values farther away from the origin are larger (see Figure 3.1(a)). Similarly, arrows along dimension Y indicate that for any given X-value, Y-values farther away from the origin are larger (see Figure 3.1(b)). Now the question is how to order all the 9 nodes in the figure when both dimensions are taken into consideration. Raw relation set theory uses the following two key steps to tackle this problem:

1. Establish a direct relationship between any two nodes (objects) after all dimensions are considered. Simple rules are used for this purpose. Consider two nodes p and q. Some of the rules are as follows. (1) If along both dimensions, p > q is true, then p > q overall. (2) If along one dimension, p > q, and along another dimension, p = q, then p > q overall. (3) If along one dimension, p > q, and along another dimension, q > p, then p = q overall. Based on the basic relationships as shown Figure 3.1(a)-(b), 36 direct relationships can be established between the nine nodes (see Figure 3.1(c); for simplicity, not all of the direct relationships are shown there) using these rules and some examples are e > O, h > g, e = h, d = h.
2. Use all the direct relationships established in Step 1 to produce a final order (not necessarily unique) among all nodes. Intuitively, the reason that the direct relationship between two nodes may be different from the final relationship of the two nodes is because other direct relationships may affect the outcome. This can probably be best explained by an analogy in some sports competition: the fact that team A beats team B does not necessarily mean that A will be ahead of team B in the final standing because the games between these two teams and other teams will be considered in determining the order of teams in the final standing. It can be shown (see below) that there is an *anti-symmetric relationship* among the nodes with respect to the diagonal line from the upper-left corner to the lower-right corner of the two-dimensional space. This relationship indicates that among the widely used distance functions, *sum* is the most appropriate.

Consider the nodes in a general m×m space (Figure 3.1 shows a 3×3 space). The following properties can be observed about these $m^2$ nodes (let $V$ denote the set of nodes) and the direct relationships among them.

1. There is a diagonal line $l$ from the upper-left corner to the lower-right corner of the two-dimensional space, which consists of nodes: (0, m), (1, m-1), … , (m, 0).
2. The direct relationships among the nodes on $l$ are all *Equal*.
3. The following one-to-one mapping $f$: $V \rightarrow V$ exists (see Figure 3.2). For any node $a$, there exists a symmetric node $a$' regarding line $l$, such that for any node $v$ on $l$:

   if $a$ is *Larger* than $v$ then $a$' is *Smaller* than $v$;
   if $a$ is *Smaller* than $v$ then $a$' is *Larger* than $v$;
   if $a$ is *Equal* to $v$ then $a$' is *Equal* $v$.

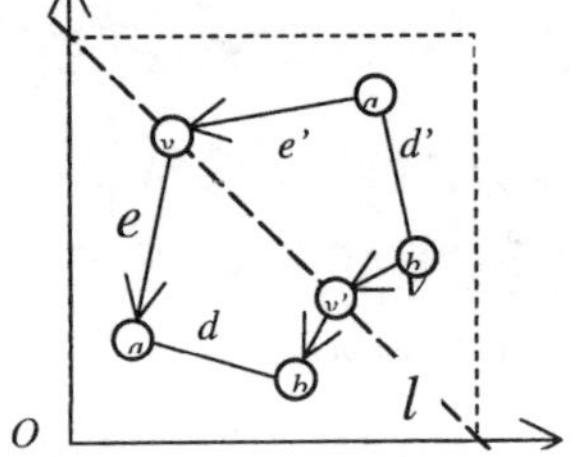

**Fig. 3.2.** Anti-Symmetry Relationship of Nodes

Furthermore, for any edge "$a$, $b$", the relationship between $a$ and $b$ is identical to the relationship between $b$' and $a$'. For example, for Figure 3.1(c), the mapping: f(O)=c; f(d)=b; f(g)=f; f(a)=a, f(e)=e; f(h)=h, satisfies all of the above properties.

A graph with the above properties is referred to as an *anti-symmetric* graph.

*Anti-symmetric rule*: If graph G is anti-symmetric, then the nodes on the line l should all have the Equal relationship and be all ranked in the middle of the final ordered list of all nodes.

It can be seen that among the three most widely used distance functions, namely, *min*, *Euclidean* and *sum*, only the *sum* function satisfies the anti-symmetric rule.

## 4 Top-*N* Query Processing

In this section, we present a simple method for evaluating top-N queries. We assume that the execution engine is a traditional relational database engine that supports single as well as possibly multi-attribute indexes. We consider only the *sum* distance function.

A naïve method to evaluate a top-N query is to compute the distance of every tuple with the query, rank all tuples as specified by the ORDER BY clause of the query and return the top N tuples to the user. This solution is inefficient in several aspects. First, it requires all tuples to be retrieved from the database, incurring high database retrieval cost. Second, it requires the distances of all tuples with respect to the query to be computed, incurring high computation cost. Finally, it requires the sort of all tuples, incurring high sorting cost. The problem of top-N query optimization is to find efficient ways to evaluate top-N queries. The idea is to convert a top-N query to a regular database query that minimizes the retrieval of useless tuples from the database. In this section, we provide a new method to minimize the retrieval of useless tuples from the database for a given top-N query.

We make several general assumptions to simplify our discussion. None of these assumptions fundamentally change the nature of the problem under consideration. The first assumption is that all query conditions are based on attributes of numeric type. Currently, only this type of conditions is used to rank tuples. Other types of conditions, e.g., conditions involving character strings, if exist, are assumed to be evaluated first. The second assumption is that each attribute takes values between 0 and 1. This can be achieved by normalizing the values of each attribute. The third assumption is that only two attributes are involved in the query condition. Let X and Y be the attributes involved. The problem of optimizing the query is to find four values x1, x2, y2 and y2 such that all top N tuples of the query are retrieved by condition "x1 ≤ X ≤ x2 and y1 ≤ Y ≤ y2" and the rectangle defined by [x1, x2] and [y1, y2] is as small as possible. The space [x1, x2] and [y1, y2] will be called the *search space*. The following notations will be used in this section: Q is the user submitted top-N query, Q* is the converted database query to be submitted to the underlying database system, and *n* is the number of tuples in the *universe space* $0 \leq X \leq 1, 0 \leq Y \leq 1$.

We now describe our method for evaluating top-N queries based on the assumption that tuples are uniformly distributed.

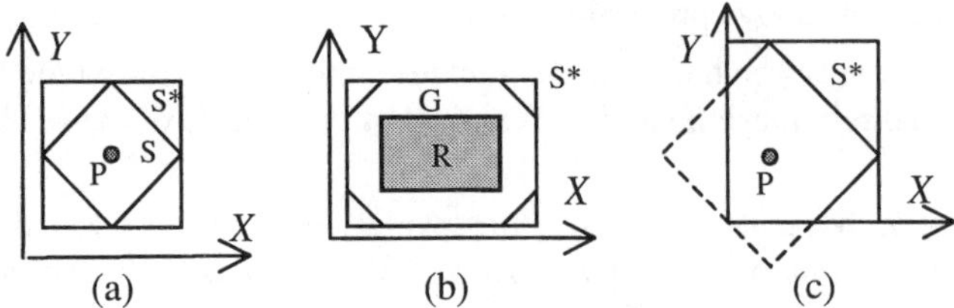


**Fig. 4.1.** Top-*N* search spaces.

We first assume that the top-N query Q has a point condition. In this case, there is no difference between Type-1 query and Type-2 query.

**Algorithm Basic:**

1. Obtain the reference space from the condition space of the query Q (see Section 2). It is assumed that the reference space is a point for now. Let P(x, y) denote the point, $0 \le x \le 1$, $0 \le y \le 1$.
2. Obtain a tentative search space S for Q*. Intuitively, S should satisfy two conditions. First, the size of S should be large enough to contain N tuples. Based on the uniform distribution of all tuples, the size of S can be estimated to be (N/n)*U, where U is the size of the universe space (U = 1). For now we assume that S is entirely contained in the universe space (this assumption will be removed later). Second, tuples inside S should be closer to P than tuples outside S. Based on the *sum* function, S is a square whose sides have 45° angle with the axes (see Figure 4.1(a)). It can be seen that all points on the edges of S have the same distance from P based on the *sum* distance function. Squares such as S will be called *rotated squares* in this paper.
3. Obtain the final search space. Current database systems are not capable of processing queries whose search space is of shape S. Therefore, another square S* that is the smallest to contain S with sides parallel to the axes is obtained as the final search space for Q* (see Figure 4.1(a)). It is easy to see that the size of S* is 2N/n.
4. From S*, the condition of query Q* is obtained as "$x - \sqrt{N/2n} \le X \le x + \sqrt{N/2n}$ and $y - \sqrt{N/2n} \le Y \le y + \sqrt{N/2n}$".

It is easy to see that the size of S* is exactly twice of that of the desired search space S. We now discuss how to remove ssome assumptions used by Algorithm Basic.

1. Algorithm Basic assumed that the reference space is a point. We now consider the case when the reference space is a rectangle R defined by $x1 \le X \le x2$ and $y1 \le Y \le y2$ (note that a line segment is a special case with either x1 = x2 or y1 = y2). All tuples in R have zero distance with the query. It is possible that R may contain N or more tuples (i.e., R is of the same size as or larger than S). In this case, if Loose-N is specified in the query, R will be searched directly and all retrieved tuples will be returned to the user; if Strict-N is specified, then search any rectangle that is contained in R and is of size S. In the following, we assume that R is smaller than S.

As we pointed out in Section 2, when the reference space is a rectangle, different results may be obtained depending on whether a query is of Type-1 or Type-2. For Type-1 query, the rotated square S* in Figure 4.1(a) needs to be extended to an octagon G in order to guarantee that all points on the edges of the octagon are the same distance away from the rectangle R (see Figure 4.1(b)). The size of G is the same as S. From G, the smallest rectangle containing G can be obtained and will be used as the search space for query Q*.

For Type-2 query, one method is to form two queries for the database system. The first query Q1 is obtained directly from Q after emphatic operators are replaced by corresponding regular operators and the ORDER BY and the STOP AFTER clauses are removed. This query retrieves all tuples that satisfy the query condition (i.e., tuples in the condition space C). The second query Q2 searches the space S* - C. That is, Q2 retrieves all tuples that are closest to the query condition but are not retrieved by Q1. The two sets of tuples are merged into one list by first listing the tuples retrieved by Q1 in ascending order of distance and then tuples retrieved by Q2 in ascending order of distance. The main drawback of this method is that two queries need to be processed by the database system. Even though no redundant tuples are retrieved by the two queries, two invocations to the database system from an application program can be costly. An alternative method for Type-2 query is as follows. Note that the reference space and the condition space may be different due to the possible existence of emphatic operators. As a result, it is possible that C is not contained in S*. The alternative method is to form one query whose search space (a rectangle) is the smallest to contain both C and S*. This may lead to a larger search space than the two-query approach but in requires just one invocation to the database system. Our preliminary experiments (not reported here due to space limitation) indicate that the one-query alternative is usually more cost effective than the two-query method.

2. Algorithm Basic assumed that the entire S* is contained in the universe space. When the reference point P is on or near the boundary of the universe space, the final search space may no longer be a square but a general rectangle. In this case, step 2 of the algorithm needs to be modified to obtain a rotated square such that the intersection area of the square and the universe space is the same as S and the distance between P and every point on the edges of the square is the same (see Figure 4.1(c) for an example). Generalization to cases where the reference space is rectangle is straightforward (in this case the rotated square will be an octagon).

Even though query Q* is expected to retrieve 2N tuples (S* is twice the size of S), there is no guarantee that Q* will retrieve at least *N* tuples from the database when the data are seriously skewed. If less than *N* tuples are retrieved, the search space needs to be expanded to retrieve additional tuples. Let Q** denote the new query based on the expanded space only (the search space of Q** does not include the search space of Q*) and $r$ is the number of additional tuples that need to be retrieved by Q**. The size of the search space of Q** can be computed by $R*r/t$ [2], where $R$ is the size of the unsearched space (universe space minus the search space of Q*) and $t$ is the total number of tuples in $R$. The ratio $r/t$ will be called the *expansion rate*. The expansion may be repeated until enough tuples are retrieved. It is shown in [2] that when the tuples are uniformly distributed, the expected number of expansions needed is 1.

## 5 Conclusions

In this paper, we explored the three important issues related to top-*N* queries in a relational database context:

1. Query language: We proposed an extension to the SQL query language to facilitate the specification of various top-N queries. New operators such as << and >> are introduced and difference ranking options (Type-1 versus Type-2) are incorporated to allow users to express their top-N queries more clearly.
2. Distance function: We made a case for the *sum* function arguing that it is a more appropriate for ranking tuples when attributes involved in a top-N query are incomparable.
3. Query processing: We proposed a simple method to process top-N queries based on the *sum* distance function and the uniform distribution assumption of data. This method is easy to implement and yields small search spaces.

## References

1. Y. Chen. Raw Sets. The Journal of Fuzzy Mathematics, Vol.8, No.3,2000, Los Angeles. pp. 607–617.
2. Y. Chen. Raw Relation Sets, Order Fusion And Top-*N* Query Problem. Ph.D. Dissertation, Department of Computer Science, Binghamton University, 2002.
3. S. Chaudhuri and L. Gravano. Evaluating Top-*k* Selection Queries. 25$^{th}$ VLDB Conference, Edinburgh, Scotland, 1999. pp.399–410.
4. M. J. Carey and D. Kossmann. On saying "Enough Already!" in SQL. ACM International Conf on Management of Data (SIGMOD'97), May 1997. p219–230.
5. D. Donjerkovic and R. Ramakrishnan. Probabilistic Optimization of Top N Queries. In Proc of the 25$^{th}$ VLDB Conf., Edinburgh, Scotland, 1999. p411–422.
6. R. Fagin. Combining Fuzzy Information from Multiple Systems. PODS'96, Montreal, Canada. pp.216–226.
7. C.Yu, P.Sharma, W. Meng, and Y, Qin. Database Selection for Processing k Nearest Neighbors Queries in Distributed Environments. First ACM/IEEE Joint Conference on Digital Libraries, Roanoke, VA, June 2001.

# Scalable Query Reformulation Using Views in the Presence of Functional Dependencies

Qingyuan Bai, Jun Hong, and Michael F. McTear

School of Computing and Mathematics, University of Ulster at Jordanstown
Newtownabbey, Co. Antrim, BT37 0QB, UK
{q.bai,j.hong,mf.mctear}@ulster.ac.uk

**Abstract.** The problem of answering queries using views in data integration has recently received considerable attention. A number of algorithms, such as the bucket algorithm, the SVB algorithm, the MiniCon algorithm, and the inverse rules algorithm, have been proposed. However, integrity constraints, such as functional dependencies, have not been considered in these algorithms. Some efforts have been made in some inverse rule-based algorithms in the presence of functional dependencies. In this paper, we extend the bucket-based algorithms to handle query rewritings using views in the presence of functional dependencies. We build relationships between views containing no subgoal of a given query and the query itself. We present an algorithm which is scalable compared to the inverse rule-based algorithms. The problem of missing query rewritings in the presence of functional dependencies that occurs in the previous bucket-based algorithms is avoided. We prove that the query rewritings generated by our algorithm are maximally-contained rewritings relative to functional dependencies.

## 1 Introduction

In data integration, user queries over a mediated schema need to be reformulated into queries over the schemas of data sources using source descriptions. There are two main approaches to query reformulation in data integration, i.e., Global As View (GAV for short) and Local As View (LAV for short). In the LAV approach, data sources are described by views that are defined over a mediated schema, and user queries are also posed in terms of the mediated schema. The LAV approach to query reformulation is closely related to the problem of answering queries using views, which has recently received considerable attention because of its relevance to a wide variety of data management problems: query optimization, maintenance of physical data independence, data integration, and data warehouse and web-site design [11]. Informally speaking, the problem is as follows. Suppose we are given a query Q over a database schema, and a set of view definitions $V_1,\dots,V_m$ over the same schema. Is it possible to answer query Q using only the answers to $V_1,\dots,V_m$, and if so, how?

In data integration, views describe a set of distributed, autonomous, and heterogeneous data sources. Thus, in this context we can usually find only maximally-contained rewritings that provide the best possible answers for a given query. Many

G. Dong et al. (Eds.): WAIM 2003, LNCS 2762, pp. 471–482, 2003.

algorithms including the bucket algorithm [12],[13], the inverse rules algorithm [16],[3], the Shared Variables Bucket (SVB for short) algorithm [14], and the MiniCon algorithm [15], have been proposed. These algorithms can generate all the maximally-contained query rewritings in the absence of functional dependencies. However, they have not considered the problem of answering query using views in the presence of functional dependencies in a mediated schema. As a result, they might sometimes miss query rewritings in this case.

**Example 1 [4].** Suppose that there are three relations in a mediated schema:

Conference(P, C), Year(P, Y), and Location(C, Y, L),

where, attributes P, C, Y, and L refer to Paper, Conference, Year, and Location respectively. A paper is only presented at a conference and published in a year. Also, in a given year a conference is held at a specific location. Therefore, we have the following functional dependencies:

Conference: P→C; Year: P→Y; Location: C, Y→L.

Suppose that there are two data sources (views):

$V_1$(P, C, Y):- Conference(P, C), Year(P, Y).

$V_2$(P, L):- Conference(P, C), Year(P, Y), Location(C, Y, L).

Assume that a query asks where PODS'89 was held:

Q(L):-Location ("PODS", "1989", L).

For the sake of simplicity, we change the query with constants into the following form:

Q(L):-Location (C, Y, L), C= "PODS", Y= "1989".

All the bucket-based algorithms would try to find the mappings between the subgoals of the query and those in views. Thus, $V_1$ would not appear in any query rewriting generated by these algorithms, because it does not contain the subgoal Location. Therefore all the previous bucket-based algorithms would fail to generate the following correct rewriting in the presence of functional dependencies:

Q'(L):- $V_1$(P, C, Y),$V_2$(P, L), C= "PODS", Y= "1989".

In [4], an algorithm based on use of inverse rules is proposed to solve this problem by using binary relations to describe functional dependencies. The papers [6],[7],[9] also consider query rewriting using views in the presence of functional dependencies. However, no bucket-based algorithm has so far been developed to address this issue. In this paper, we present a bucket-based algorithm to solve this problem. Our main contribution is the extension of the MiniCon algorithm in the presence of functional dependencies.

In Section 2, we have a brief look at the previous algorithms. In Section 3, the preliminaries are given. In Section 4, we first show how our algorithm works using an example and then present our algorithm to handle query rewritings using views in the presence of functional dependencies in a mediated schema. In Section 5, we prove the correctness and computational complexity of our algorithm. At the end of the paper, we conclude and discuss our future work.

## 2 Related Work

We divide all the algorithms for query rewriting into two categories. The algorithms of the first category are based on use of buckets while the ones of the second category are based on use of inverse rules.

### 2.1 The Algorithms Based on Use of Buckets

The bucket algorithm [12],[13] proceeds in two stages. Initially, a bucket is created for each subgoal of a query. A view is put in the bucket if it can be unified with a subgoal in the query. Next, candidate query plans are generated by picking one view from each bucket. These plans are then verified using containment tests.

A non-distinguished variable that appears in more than one subgoal of a query is called a shared variable. In the SVB algorithm [14], given a query Q, two types of buckets are created. The first type of buckets, the single-subgoal buckets are built in the same way as the bucket algorithm. The second type of buckets, the shared-variable buckets are created by checking the containment mapping from a set of subgoals in Q containing a shared variable to some subgoals in a view. Once all the buckets are created, the algorithm constructs rewritings by combining views from buckets which contain disjoint sets of subgoals of Q.

The MiniCon algorithm [15] proceeds in principle in the same way as the SVB algorithm. Both algorithms focus on the roles of distinguished variables and shared variables in a query. In the first phase of the MiniCon algorithm, a MiniCon Description (MCD for short) for a query Q over a view V is formed to contain a set of subgoals in Q and the mapping information. The MCDs and the minimum MCDs in the MiniCon algorithm correspond to the single-subgoal buckets and the shared-variable buckets in the SVB algorithm respectively. In the second phase, the MiniCon algorithm combines the MCDs to generate query rewritings. In [15], it is shown that the MiniCon algorithm significantly outperforms the bucket and the SVB algorithms and scales up to hundreds of views.

### 2.2 The Algorithm Based on Use of Inverse Rules

The key idea underlying the inverse rules algorithm [16],[3] is to first construct a set of rules called inverse rules that invert the view definitions, and then replace existential variables in the view definitions with Skolem functions in the heads of the inverse rules. The rewriting of a query Q using the set of views V is simply the composition of Q and the inverse rules for V by the transformation method in [3] or the unification-join method in [16].

A key advantage of the inverse rules algorithm is its conceptual simplicity. The inverse rules can be constructed in advance in polynomial time, independent of a particular query. However, even if the computational cost of constructing rewriting is polynomial, the rewriting contains rules that may cause accessing irrelevant views. The problem of eliminating irrelevant rules has exponential time complexity. Another drawback is that evaluating the inverse rules over the source extension may invert some useful computation done to produce the views. Hence, much of the computational advantage of exploiting the materialized view is lost due to recomputing the extensions of the database relations.

## 3 Preliminaries

**Queries and views.** We consider the problem of answering conjunctive queries using views. A conjunctive query has the form:

$$Q(\bar{X}):-R_1(\bar{X}_1),...,R_k(\bar{X}_k)$$

where $R_1(\bar{X}_1),...,R_k(\bar{X}_k)$ are the subgoals referred to database relations. $Q(\bar{X})$ is the head of the query. The tuples $\bar{X},\bar{X}_1,...,\bar{X}_k$ contain either variables or constants. We require that the query be safe, i.e., $\bar{X} \subseteq \bar{X}_1 \cup ... \cup \bar{X}_k$. The variables in $\bar{X}$ are the distinguished variables, and others are existential variables. We use Vars(Q), Q(D) to refer to all variables in Q and the evaluating result of Q over the database D respectively.

A view is a named query. If the query results are stored, we refer to them as a materialized view, and we refer to the result set as the extension of the view.

**Query containment and equivalence.** The concepts of query containment and equivalence enable us to compare between queries and rewritings. We say that a query $Q_1$ is contained in the $Q_2$, denoted by $Q_1 \subseteq Q_2$, if the answers to $Q_1$ are a subset of the answers to $Q_2$ for any database instance. Containment mappings provide a necessary and sufficient condition for testing query containment. A mapping φ from Vars($Q_2$) to Vars($Q_1$) is a containment mapping if

(1) φ maps every subgoal in the body of $Q_2$ to a subgoal in the body of $Q_1$, and
(2) φ maps the head of $Q_2$ to the head of $Q_1$.

The query $Q_2$ contains $Q_1$ if and only if there is a containment mapping from $Q_2$ to $Q_1$. The query $Q_1$ is equivalent to $Q_2$ if and only if $Q_1 \subseteq Q_2$ and $Q_2 \subseteq Q_1$.

**Answering queries using views.** Given a query Q and a set of view definitions $\mathcal{V}=V_1,...,V_m$, a rewriting of Q using the views is a query expression Q' whose body predicates are only from $V_1,...,V_m$.

Note that the views are not assumed to contain all the tuples in their definitions since the data sources are managed autonomously. Moreover, we cannot always find an equivalent rewriting of the query using the views because data sources may not contain all of the answers to the query. Instead, we consider the problem of finding maximally-contained rewritings as follows.

**Definition 1 (Maximally-contained rewriting [15]).** Q' is a maximally-contained rewriting of a query Q using the views $\mathcal{V}=V_1,...,V_m$ with respect to a query language $\mathcal{L}$ if

1. for any database D, and extensions $v_1,...,v_m$ of the views such that $v_i \subseteq V_i(D)$, for $1 \le i \le m$, then $Q'(v_1,...,v_m) \subseteq Q(D)$ for all i,

2. there is no other query $Q_1$ in the language L, such for every database D and extensions $v_1,...,v_m$ as above (1) $Q'(v_1,...,v_m) \subseteq Q_1(v_1,...,v_m)$ and (2) $Q_1(v_1,...,v_m) \subseteq Q(D)$, and there exists at least one database for which (1) is a strict subset.

**The MiniCon Algorithm [15].** Since our aim in this paper is to extend the MiniCon algorithm in the presence of functional dependencies, let us here have a detailed look at it.

In the MiniCon algorithm, a MCD plays an important role like a bucket in the bucket algorithm. It contains information about the unification and containment of subgoals between a given query and a view.

**Definition 2 (MiniCon Descriptions).** A MCD C for a query Q over a view V is a tuple of the form $(h_C, V(\bar{Y})_C, \varphi_C, G_C)$ where:

- $h_C$ is a head homomorphism on V,
- $V(\bar{Y})_C$ is the result of applying $h_C$ to V, i.e., $\bar{Y} = h_C(\bar{A})$, where $\bar{A}$ are the head variables of V,
- $\varphi_C$ is a partial mapping from Vars(Q) to $h_C$(Vars(V)),
- $G_C$ is a set of subgoals in Q which are covered by some subgoal in $h_C$(V) and $\varphi_C$.

A head homomorphism *h* on a view V is a mapping *h* from Vars(V) to Vars(V) that is the identity on the existential variables, but may equate distinguished variables.

The MiniCon algorithm proceeds in the following two steps.

**Step 1: Forming the minimum MCDs.** For each subgoal *R* of Q and each subgoal *R'* of view V, find a least restrictive head homomorphism *h* on V such that there exists a mapping $\varphi$ such that $\varphi(R)$=h(*R'*). If *h* and $\varphi$ exist, then extend the domain of $\varphi$ to variables in a minimum set G of subgoals of Q such that,

(a) G is mapped to a subgoal of *h*(V) by $\varphi$;
(b) each head variable in G is mapped to a head variable in *h*(V);
(c) if an existential variable *x* in G is mapped to an existential variable of *h*(V), then (i) each subgoal of Q involving *x* is in G; (ii) all variables in the comparisons B of Q that involve *x* are in the domain of $\varphi$ and comparisons of Q and *h*(V) are consistent.

**Step 2: Generating rewritings [17].** If there are minimum MCDs $(h_i, v_i(Y_i), \varphi_i, G_i)$, i=1,...,k, such that i≠j, $G_i \cap G_j = \emptyset$, and $G_1 \cup G_2 \cup ... \cup G_k$=subgoals(Q), then

(1) If $\varphi_i$ maps two or more variables $x_1,...,x_s$ in $G_i$ to the same argument, then choose one of the variable as a representative variable, denote the representative variable of $x_j$ by $EC_i(x_j)$. For each x in Q, if $EC_i(x) \neq EC_j(x)$ $(1 \le i,j \le k)$, then let EC(x) be one of them but consistently across all y for which $EC_i(y)=EC_i(x)$.
(2) For each $y \in Y_i$, if exists x such that $\varphi_i(x)=y$, then let $\psi_i(y)=x$, otherwise let $\psi(y)$ be a distinct new variable;
(3) Create the conjunctive rewriting: $Q'(EC(X))$:- $v_1(EC(\psi_1(Y_1)))$,..., $v_k(EC(\psi_k(Y_k)))$.

**Functional Dependencies.** An instance of a relation R satisfies the functional dependency $A_1,..., A_n \rightarrow B$ if for every two tuples t and u in R with $t.A_i=u.A_i$ for i=1,...,n, also t.B=u.B. If $A \rightarrow B$ and $B \rightarrow C$ hold, then $A \rightarrow C$ holds.

When the relations satisfy a set of functional dependencies $\Sigma$, we define our notion of query containment as query containment relative to $\Sigma$. Query $Q_1$ is contained in query $Q_2$ relative to $\Sigma$ , denoted $Q_1 \subseteq_\Sigma Q_2$, if for each database D satisfying the functional dependencies in $\Sigma$, $Q_1(D) \subseteq Q_2(D)$. Maximal query containment relative to $\Sigma$ can be defined accordingly.

## 4 Query Rewriting in the Presence of Functional Dependencies

Now we consider query rewriting in the presence of functional dependencies. In the context of databases, any database schema has some integrity constraints, such as functional dependencies, and/or inclusion dependencies. Thus, this issue has practical significance.

We note that the MiniCon algorithm fails to form a MCD for a given query Q over a view V if

(1) V contains no subgoal in Q, or

(2) there is a violation on containment mapping from Vars(Q) to Vars(V), for example, a distinguished variable of Q is mapped into an existential variable of V, or

(3) there is any inconsistency between comparison predicates in Q and ones in V.

In this paper, we address the above problem (1) by making use of functional dependencies. We first use an example to give a detail description about the idea underlying our algorithm, and we then present our algorithm.

Continue with Example 1. The following query rewriting is correct in the presence of functional dependencies:

Q'(L):- $V_1$(P,C,Y),$V_2$(P,L), C= "PODS",Y= "1989".

Informally, this query rewriting is generated as follows. It first finds some paper presented at PODS'89 using $V_1$, and then finds the location of the conference at which the paper was presented using $V_2$. This plan is correct only because every paper is presented at one conference and in one year. Note that $V_1$ is needed in the query rewriting even though $V_1$ does not contain any subgoal in Q. In the previous algorithms, only views that contain subgoals appearing in the query are considered. In this example, the MiniCon algorithm would not generate any query rewriting containing $V_1$. As a result, it would fail to find the above rewriting. In other words, all bucket-based algorithm encounters the problem of missing query rewritings in the presence of functional dependencies in a mediated schema.

In $V_1$, attributes P, C, and Y are distinguished variables and we have in *Conference*, P→C, in *Year*, P→Y. There are two constants to appear in the form of C= "PODS", Y= "1989" in the query Q. According to the definition of functional dependencies, there are some values (maybe single value) of P in *Conference* for C= "PODS", and some values of P in *Year* for Y= "1989". This indicates that $V_1$ containing Conference and Year might be useful for answering the query because it can provide information about attribute P, which is also a distinguished variable in other views given C= "PODS", Y= "1989".

We try to find out this kind of relationships between $V_1$ and Q in the presence of functional dependencies. We first identify views that contain no subgoal of the query and then check whether these views can provide any useful information for the query. Among the subgoals in an identified view there may exist a set of functional dependencies that have transitive relationships with the ones among the subgoals in the query. For example, $V_1$ contains no subgoal of Q, and there is a set of functional dependencies {P→C, P→Y} on its subgoals. In Q, there is a functional dependency {C,Y→L}. We find that there exists a relationship between $V_1$ and Q, i.e., implicit functional dependency.

In $V_2$, attributes P and L are distinguished variables, but attributes C and Y are shared variables. The MiniCon algorithm can unify the subgoal *Location* in Q with one in $V_2$ and create a MCD for *Location* over $V_2$ as follows (here, $\rightarrow_m$ means the mapping through this paper):

| V(Y) | *h* | $\phi$ | G |
|---|---|---|---|
| $V_2$(P,L) | P $\rightarrow_m$ P, L $\rightarrow_m$ L | P $\rightarrow_m$ P, C $\rightarrow_m$ C, Y $\rightarrow_m$ Y | Location |

However, attributes C and Y in $V_2$ are not distinguished variables. Therefore, $V_2$ can not answer Q alone given C="PODS", Y="1989". Note that attributes P and L are distinguished variables in $V_2$ and functional dependency {P→L} holds, which means if some values of P can be passed from $V_1$ to $V_2$, then the value of L can be determined using $V_2$. Thus, we can combine $V_1$ and $V_2$ to form a query rewriting of Q as follows:

Q'(L):- $V_1$(P,C,Y),$V_2$(P,L), C= "PODS",Y= "1989".

Assume that a mediated schema consists of a set of relations $R_1, R_2,..., R_m$. The data sources are described by views $V_1,...,V_n$ that are defined in the mediated schema. Without loss of generality, we assume that there exists at most one functional dependency, A→B in a relation R , where *B* is a single attribute in R, *A* may be a set of attributes in R. We denote a set of functional dependencies in a mediated schema as $\Sigma=\{A_i\rightarrow B_i, A_i, B_i \in R_i, 1\le i\le m\}$.

Given a conjunctive query Q over a mediated schema:

$$Q(\bar{X}):-R_1(\bar{X}_1),R_2(\bar{X}_2),...,R_k(\bar{X}_k)$$

Assume that there are $k_1$ ($1\le k_1\le k$) functional dependencies among $R_1,...,R_{k_1}$, i.e., $\Sigma_Q=\{A_i\rightarrow B_i, A_i, B_i \in R_i, 1\le i\le k_1\}$. Given views $V_1,...,V_n$, we divide them into two groups: $V^1=\{V_j^1, j=1,2,\ldots,n_1\}$ and $V^2=\{V_j^2, j=1,2,\ldots,n_2\}$, where each view in $V^1$ contains at least one subgoal of Q while each view in $V^2$ contains no subgoal of Q. We check each view $V_j^2$ ($1\le j\le n_2$) in $V^2$ to see whether it can make any contribution to answering Q in the presence of functional dependencies.

Assume that there is a set of functional dependencies: $\{C_j\rightarrow D_j, C_j, D_j \in$ subgoal R in the body of $V_j^2$, $1\le j\le n_2\}$. If

(1) there exists $\{R_i: A_i\rightarrow B_i\}\in\Sigma_Q$ such that $D_j$ is identical to $A_i$, and $A_i$ appears in $\Sigma_Q$,
(2) $C_j$ is a distinguished variable in $V_j^2$, and
(3) $A_i$ appears as a constant in Q,

then, $V_j^2$ might be used for answering Q. $V_j^2$ is put into a bucket as follows:

| V(Y) | FD | SQ(subgoal of Q) |
|---|---|---|
| $V^2_j$ | $C_j \rightarrow A_j$ | $R_i$ |

For each view $V_i^1$ in $V^1$, $1 \leq i \leq n_1$, the MCDs are formed using the MiniCon algorithm. The MCDs of the form $(h_C, V(\bar{Y})_C, \varphi_C, G_C)$ are divided into two sets as $C^1=\{C^1_j, 1 \leq j \leq m_1\}$ and $C^2=\{C^2_j, 1 \leq j \leq m_2\}$. A MCD is put in $C^1$ if its component $V(\bar{Y})$ contains the distinguished variables $C_j$ and $B_j$, where $C_j$ and $B_j$ are distinguished variables in some view, say $V^2_j$, in $V^2$ and in Q respectively, and satisfy:

(4) $C_j \rightarrow D_j$ holds in the body of $V_j^2$,

(5) $A_j \rightarrow B_j$ holds in the body of Q, and

(6) $D_j$ is identical to $A_j$.

Thus, such a view, say $V^1_i$, can participate in join operations on $C_j$ with $V^2_j$ to get the values of $B_j$. The rest of the MCDs is put in $C^2$.

Now we have a set of buckets for $V_j^2$ (j=1,2,...,), two sets of the MCDs, $C^1$ and $C^2$. The MCDs in $C^2$ can be used to generate query rewritings alone. The buckets for $V_j^2$ (j=1,2,...,) are combined with the MCDs in $C^1$ to generate other query rewritings.

**Algorithm.** Bucket-Based Query Rewriting in the Presence of Functional Dependencies

**Input:** A set of the relations in a mediated schema, $R_1, R_2, \ldots, R_m$ and a set of functional dependencies $\Sigma=\{A_i \rightarrow B_i,\ A_i,\ B_i \in R_i,\ 1 \leq i \leq m\}$; A set of the views $V=\{V_1, V_2, \ldots, V_n\}$; A conjunctive query in the form of $Q(\bar{X}) :- R_1(\bar{X}_1), R_2(\bar{X}_2), \ldots, R_k(\bar{X}_k)$; A set of functional dependencies in the body of Q: $\Sigma_Q=\{A_i \rightarrow B_i,\ A_i,\ B_i \in R_i,\ 1 \leq i \leq k\}$.

**Output:** Q's, the maximally-contained rewritings of Q relative to functional dependency $\Sigma$.

**Method:**

We divide all views into two groups $V^1$ and $V^2$ as described above.

**Step 1:** Check whether each view in $V^2$ satisfies the above conditions (1), (2), and (3). If so, the view is put into a bucket defined above.

**Step 2:** Form a MCD for each view in $V^1$ using the MiniCon algorithm [15]. The MCDs are divided into two sets $C^1$ and $C^2$.

**Step 3:** Generate all possible query rewritings Q's. Some query rewritings are generated in the same way as the MiniCon algorithm using the MCDs in $C^2$. The others are generated by combining the MCDs in $C^1$ with the obtained buckets for views in $V^2$ as follows.

- For every subset $\{C^1_j, 1 \leq j \leq m_1\}$ of $C^1$ such that:
  $G^1_1 \cup G^1_2 \cup \ldots \cup G^1_{m1}$=subgoals(Q) and for every $i \neq j$, $G^1_i \cap G^1_j = \varnothing$.

- For every subset of buckets for views in $V^2$ such that the union of a set of functional dependencies in these buckets and a set of functional dependencies in the MCDs in $C^1$ can imply the functional dependencies of Q.
- Combine the views in $C^1_j$, $1 \le j \le m_l$ with the views in buckets in the same way as in the MiniCon algorithm to generate query rewritings.

We end this section by the following example which shows the complete procedure of our algorithm.

**Example 2.** Suppose that there are three data sources:
$V_1$(P,C,Y):-Conference(P,C),Year(P,Y).
$V_2$(P,L):-Conference(P,C),Year(P,Y),Location(C,Y,L).
$V_3$(C,Y,L):-Location(C,Y,L).
Conference, Year, and Location as well as functional dependencies are the same as in Example 1. We also have the same query:
Q(L):-Location (C,Y,L),C= "PODS",Y= "1989".

We divide these views into $V^1$={$V_2$,$V_3$} and $V^2$ ={$V_1$}. By checking the above conditions (1)-(3), a bucket is built for $V_1$.
Using the MiniCon algorithm, we get the following MCDs over the views in $V^1$:

| V(Y) | $h$ | $\phi$ | G |
|---|---|---|---|
| $V_2$(P,L) | $P \to_m P$, $L \to_m L$ | $P \to_m P$, $C \to_m C$, $Y \to_m Y$ | Location |
| $V_3$(C,Y,L) | $C \to_m C$, $Y \to_m Y$, $L \to_m L$ | $C \to_m C$, $Y \to_m Y$, $L \to_m L$ | Location |

The first MCD belongs to $C^1$ and the second is in $C^2$, because in $V_2$ of the first MCD, P is a distinguished variable in a view in $V^2$ and L is a distinguished variable in Q, and functional dependency {P→L} holds. Hence, we get a query rewriting of Q from $C^2$ alone.
Q'(L):- $V_3$(C,Y,L), C= "PODS",Y= "1989".

Another rewriting is generated by combining $V_1$ with $V_2$.
Q''(L):- $V_1$(P,C,Y),$V_2$(P,L),C= "PODS",Y= "1989".

## 5 Computational Complexity and Correctness of Our Algorithm

In this section, we illustrate that our algorithm is a scalable extension of the MiniCon algorithm by taking into account functional dependencies in query reformulation and prove the correctness of our algorithm.

### 5.1 Computational Complexity of the Algorithm

In the MiniCon algorithm, any views in either $V^1$ or $V^2$ are considered for forming the MCDs. In Step 1 of our algorithm, the algorithm checks for each view in $V^2$ by testing above three conditions (1)-(3). In the worst case the complexity of this process is $n*|\Sigma_Q|*|\Sigma_{VQ}|$, where n is the number of the views in the second group, $|\Sigma_Q|$ and $|\Sigma_{VQ}|$ are the numbers of functional dependencies in the query and in each view in $V^2$ respectively. In Step 2 of our algorithm, the computation is the same as in the MiniCon algorithm when forming the MCDs for each view in $V^1$. The computation is increased when dividing the MCDs into two groups. In the worst case the complexity of this process is $n*|\Sigma_Q|*|\Sigma_{VQ}|$. In Step 3, the complexity of our algorithm is the same as the MiniCon algorithm when generating the query rewritings from the MCDs in $C^2$. Due to generating additional query rewritings by combining the MCDs in $C^1$ and the buckets for views in $V^2$ , the computation of this step is exponential in terms of $|V^2|*|C^1|$. However, in the worst case, the computation of the MiniCon algorithm is exponential in terms of the number of the views. In [15], it is shown that the MiniCon algorithm can scale up to hundreds of views. Our algorithm has the same scale-up.

## 5.2 Correctness of the Algorithm

**Theorem 1.** Given a conjunctive query Q, conjunctive views $V$, and a set of functional dependencies $\Sigma$ in a mediated schema, our algorithm produces the union of conjunctive queries that is the maximally-contained rewriting of Q using $V$ relative to $\Sigma$.

**Proof:** In our algorithm, some query rewritings are generated from the MCDs in $C^2$ along in the same way as the MiniCon algorithm. Therefore, these rewritings are maximally-contained rewritings. The others are generated by combining the MCDs in $C^1$ with the buckets of views in $V^2$. We show that these rewritings are also maximally-contained rewritings.

As shown above, the MCDs of $C^1$ are needed to answer the query if the other information is required. We claim that (1) the conditions (1)-(3) show the buckets of views in $V^2$ have useful information for answering the query, and (2) the conditions (4)-(6) guarantee the combination of the MCDs of $C^1$ with the buckets of $V^2$ in Step 3 of our algorithm can exactly provide the answers to the query. The claim (1) is valid for the following reasons: The conditions (1) and (3) mean that for evaluating attribute $A_i$ in a subgoal $R_i$ of a query, the value of another attribute $C_j$ in a subgoal $R_j$ of view V is needed even though V does not contain any subgoal of the query. The condition (2) guarantees that the required value of $C_j$ can be transferred to the query because $C_j$ is a distinguished variable. The claim (2) is valid because for the MCDs in $C^1$, their components $V(\bar{Y})$ contain the distinguished variables $C_j$, $B_j$, and the conditions (4)-(6) guarantee that the transitive property of functional dependencies holds among the query, the views in $C^1$ and the views in $V^2$. Therefore, the combination of the MCDs of $C^1$ with the buckets of $V^2$ in the same way as the MiniCon algorithm can provide the answers to the query in the presence of functional dependencies. According to the proofs given in [15], if there exist some query rewritings, then these rewritings are the maximally-contained rewritings.

## 6 Conclusion and Future Work

In this paper, we have considered the query rewriting problem in data integration by using the approach of answering query using views. The algorithms for this problem can be divided into two groups, bucket-based algorithms and inverse rules-based algorithms. The algorithms based on inverse rules have considered the problem of query rewriting in the presence of functional dependencies and inclusion dependencies in a mediated schema. However, there has been no bucket-based algorithm for this problem. We consider query rewriting in the presence of functional dependencies in a mediated schema. We give three conditions to check whether a view which does not contain any subgoal of a query is needed for answering the query when there are a set of functional dependencies in a mediated schema. We divide all the MCDs in the MiniCon algorithm into two groups. The MCDs in one of groups can not answer the query alone. We combine these MCDs with the buckets created for views identified by the above three conditions, and then generate the query rewritings which are missed by the previous bucket-based algorithms. The problem of missing query rewritings in the presence of functional dependencies that occurs in the previous bucket-based algorithms is avoided. Our algorithm is scalable compared to the inverse rule-based algorithms for query rewriting in the presence of functional dependencies.

In the future, we will study the problem of query rewriting in the presence of functional dependencies in the case of join lossless decomposition. Inclusion dependencies are another important type of integrity constraints in databases. There has been no bucket-based algorithm for query rewriting in the presence of inclusion dependencies. This would be another issue to be addressed in the future.

## References


1. S. Abiteboul, R. Hull, and V. Vianu. Foundations of Databases, Addison-Wesley Publishing Company, 1995.
2. A.V. Aho, Y. Sagiv, and J.D. Ullman. Equivalences among relational expressions, SIAM Journal on Computing, 8(3): 218–246, May 1979.
3. O.M. Duschka and M.R. Genesereth. Answering Recursive Queries Using Views, Proc. of 16th ACM Conference on Principles of Database Systems, PODS, Tucson, AZ, May 1997.
4. O.M. Duschka, M.R. Genesereth, and A.Y. Levy. Recursive Query Plans for Data Integration. Journal of Logic Programming, special issue on Logic Based Heterogeneous Information Systems,43(1),49–73, 2000.
5. P. Godfrey, J. Grant, J. Gryz, and J. Minker. Integrity Constraints: Semantics and Applications. Logics for Databases and Information Systems, J.Chomicki and G.Saake, Kluwer, 1998.
6. J. Grant and J. Minker. A logic-based approach to data integration, TLP 2(3):323–368, 2002.
7. Jarek Gryz. An Algorithm for Query Folding with Functional Dependencies. Intelligent Information Systems VII Proceedings of the Workshop, Malbork, Poland, June, 1998.
8. Jarek Gryz. Query Folding with Inclusion Dependencies. Proceedings of ICDE'98, Orlando, Florida, USA. IEEE Computer Society 1998, ISBN 0-8186-8289-2.
9. Jarek Gryz. Query rewriting using views in the presence of functional and inclusion dependencies. Information System, 1999, 24(7):597–612.

10. D.S. Johnson and A. Klug. Testing Containment of Conjunctive Queries under Functional and Inclusion Dependencies. Journal of Computer and system Sciences 28, 167-189, 1984.
11. A.Y. Levy. Answering Queries Using Views: A Survey. VLDB Journal,10(4),270–294, 2001.
12. A.Y. Levy, A. Rajaraman, and J.J. Ordille. Querying Heterogeneous Information Sources Using Source Descriptions. Proceedings of the 22nd VLDB Conference,1996.
13. A.Y.Levy, A. Rajaraman, and J.J. Ordille. Query-Answering Algorithms for Information Agents. Proceedings of the AAAI 1996 .
14. Prasenjit Mitra. An Algorithm for Answering Queries Efficiently Using Views. In Proceedings of the 12th Australian Database Conference, 2001.
15. Rachel Pottinger and Alon Y. Levy. A Scalable Algorithm for Answering Queries Using Views. Proc. of the 26th International Conference on Very Large Data Bases(VLDB), Cairo, Egypt, 2000.
16. X. Qian. Query folding. In Proceedings of the 12th IEEE International Conference on Data Engineering(ICDE'96),48–55,1999.
17. J. Wang, M. Maher, and R. Topor. Rewriting General Conjunctive Queries Using Views. Proceedings of 13th Australian Database Conference (ADC2002),2002.

# Multimedia Tampering Localization Based on the Perturbation in Reverse Processing

Xianfeng Zhao, Weinong Wang, and Kefei Chen

Department of Computer Science and Engineering, Shanghai Jiaotong University, Shanghai 200030, P. R. China
{zhao-xf, wnwang, kfchen}@sjtu.edu.cn

**Abstract.** A new fragile watermarking scheme, which exploits the perturbation in reverse processing, is proposed to enhance the tampering localizability of multimedia authentication. In verifying data integrity or authenticating signatures, the new method performs the reverse processing of watermark embedding. Typically, it solves an embedding equation or de-filters the distributed version instead of really extracting the watermark. If any tampering happened, the output of the method perturbs because the manipulated data, which can be regarded as the observation error, is drastically enlarged by such processing. The perturbed values indicate the degree of the tampering, and their positions directly draw the shapes of the manipulated areas. Compared with the mostly used block-based fragile watermarking, the new method localizes the tampering almost sample-wise other than block-wise. It also supports the adaptive embedding, which does not evenly scale the watermark, and avoids the vulnerabilities resulting from the block-based approaches.

## 1 Background

In cryptography, signing a hash-code is the mostly used method for verifying the integrity and origin of data. However, digital watermarking is more feasible for authenticating multimedia [1]. The cryptographic approach produces additional data, which must accompany the original data in accordance of some protocols. And it has difficulty locating the positions modified by unauthorized manipulations. In contrast, fragile watermarking embeds an imperceptible watermark into the original data, and is ready to detect and locate any tampering afterwards. The technology is widely researched and used for authenticating multimedia in recent years because human beings generally cannot tell such a slight distortion brought by watermarking these kinds of data [2]. Fragile watermarking is different to robust watermarking, which is orientated to protect copyright. This paper only studies the former.

The performance requirements of fragile watermarking often conflict with each other under current technologies [2,3]. The sensitivity requires detecting any slight alteration. The localizability requires localizing very fine manipulation. The imperceptibility demands that the embedding should not perceptually degrade the distributed version. The blindness presupposes that the verification cannot depend on the availability of original data. The security implies that the algorithms should be reliable and key-controlled. To implement the requirements, most current

G. Dong et al. (Eds.): WAIM 2003, LNCS 2762, pp. 483–494, 2003.

technologies partition the original data into small blocks and evenly embed a watermark [4-6]. The extracted watermark then can be examined either statistically or cryptographically. However, deciding the partition size is very knotty. Because the reliability of either statistical approaches or cryptographic approaches depends on data size, using small block to enhance the localizability could results in many security problems [3]. Furthermore, the block-based methods are intrinsically incompatible with the adaptive embedding [7,8], which keeps more perceptual quality. The main related issues will be discussed in Sect.2.

To enhance the performance, particularly the localizability, this paper is intended to exploit the perturbation phenomenon of reverse processing [9] in the design of a fragile watermarking scheme. It will be found that the reverse processing of embedding can be enabled to provoke the desired perturbation, which not only detects but also characterizes the probable unauthorized manipulation. The reason why the reverse processing is used is explained in Sect.2. Then Sect.3 investigates the properties of the perturbation and designs the watermarking scheme. Sect.4 gives the steps and the results of our experiments on images. Sect.5 draws the conclusions.

## 2 Existing Problems and Introduction of the Reverse Processing

Before making a comment on the existing implementation of the above requirements, this section now generalizes 2 mainstream schemes. One of them is based on statistics [4,5], and the other is based on cryptography [6]. Let $\boldsymbol{x}$ denote original data, $\boldsymbol{w}$ denote a watermark, and $\boldsymbol{k}$ denote a secret key or stream key. They can be each partitioned in spatial or temporal domain into $n_b$ blocks or segments, respectively denoted by $\boldsymbol{x}_i$, $\boldsymbol{w}_i$ and $\boldsymbol{k}_i$, $i = 0, 1, \cdots, n_b - 1$. The embedding and the extraction then work block-wise. The first scheme can be expressed by

$$\begin{cases} \text{embedding}: \boldsymbol{x}'_i = emb(\boldsymbol{x}_i, ciph(\boldsymbol{w}_i, \boldsymbol{k}_i)), \\ \text{extraction}\ : \boldsymbol{w}'_i = deciph(extr(\boldsymbol{x}'_i), \boldsymbol{k}_i). \end{cases} \tag{1}$$

Here, *ciph*(·,·) ciphers a watermark block; *deciph*(·,·) does the reverse work. *emb*(·,·) embeds a ciphered watermark block into an original block, changing certain statistical property; *extr*(·) extracts the embedded form of watermark block by examining the states of the property. Obviously, the authentication can then made its conclusion through the deciphered watermark $\boldsymbol{w}'$. In the second scheme, all least significant bits (LSB) within $\boldsymbol{x}_i$, denoted by $\boldsymbol{x}_i(lsb)$, carry the embedded block, which is the ciphered result of the exclusive OR between the hash-code of the non LSB area $\boldsymbol{x}_i(nolsb)$ and the watermark block $\boldsymbol{w}_i$. Thus the equivalent form of Eq.(1) is

$$\begin{cases} \boldsymbol{x}'_i = \begin{cases} \boldsymbol{x}'_i(lsb) = ciph(hash(\boldsymbol{x}_i(nolsb)) \oplus \boldsymbol{w}_i, \boldsymbol{k}), \\ \boldsymbol{x}'_i(nolsb) = \boldsymbol{x}_i(nolsb), \end{cases} \\ \boldsymbol{w}'_i = hash(\boldsymbol{x}'_i(nolsb)) \oplus deciph(\boldsymbol{x}'_i(lsb), \boldsymbol{k}), \end{cases} \tag{2}$$

where *hash*(•) represents a hash function, and $\oplus$ denotes exclusive OR.

Some knotty problems emerges from the above description:

**Block Size Conflict.** The localizability demands for small size [3,6]. However, the sensitivity and imperceptibility prefer large size because a larger block provides more watermark capacity. Moreover, small size is related to the collision problem that will be explained next.

**Block Value Collision.** Most existing schemes use small blocks to improve the localizability. Nevertheless, block size not large enough might result in the collision between a true original block and a fabricated one, that is, their distributed blocks are identical. In [6], the length of a hash-code to be embedded in a small block has to be cut to 64 bits that are significantly shorter than the required 128 bits [3,10]. In [4] and [5], an extracted bit, which is decided by the oddness or evenness of a quotient, might happen to be correct within a small area.

**Block Shift Problem.** Because the authentication is block-based, it can validate a block that was pasted from another place [3]. The attackers might use valid blocks to fabricate another distributed version, which is also valid. Making the thing worse, the smaller the block, the more flexible the fabrication.

**Intensity Distribution Problem.** Being evenly partitioned and embedded, the distributed version has meager watermark capacity and has difficulty maintaining the imperceptibility at low frequency areas [7]. And the existing schemes are not compatible with adaptive embedding because they cannot regenerate the scale factor under the requirement of blindness.

Adaptively embedding and not relying on partition, the new approach this paper will propose is based on the perturbation of reverse processing [9]. We briefly give the idea here. If $h(\bullet)$ represents a perceptually adaptive algorithm that computes the scale factor $\boldsymbol{a}$, a generalized adaptive embedding can be expressed by

$$\boldsymbol{x}' = \boldsymbol{x} + h(\boldsymbol{x}) \otimes ciph(\boldsymbol{w}, \boldsymbol{k}) = \boldsymbol{x} + \boldsymbol{a} \otimes \boldsymbol{c} = \boldsymbol{x} + \boldsymbol{s} \ , \tag{3}$$

Here, $\boldsymbol{c}$ denotes the ciphered watermark, and $\boldsymbol{s}$ denotes the scaled watermark. $\otimes$ represents direct multiplication of vectors. The original need not be partitioned into blocks. Although the method embeds watermark on every sample of an original, $h(\bullet)$ ensures the desired imperceptibility. In authentication, the embedded data need not be extracted. By the following 2 mathematical facts [11,12], solving Eq.(3), where $\boldsymbol{x}$ is supposed to be the only unknown variable, could directly detect and localize the tampering. First, the solution might be perturbed drastically if $\boldsymbol{x}'$ has been tampered with, for the modification can be viewed as the observation error introduced into Eq.(3). Second, the perturbed areas could just be the manipulated areas because a local error influences the local part of the solution more heavily. This paper calls equations like Eq.(3) the embedding equation. It will be found that the method will eliminate or temper the above problems because it is not block-based. It is worth mentioning that solving the embedding equation is only one of the methods of reverse processing [9]. Other methods, such as de-filtering and signal restoration that can provoke controllable perturbations [13], might be exploited here. We concentrate on solving embedding equations since it is typical and equivalent to many other methods.

## 3 Designing the Perturbation Based Fragile Watermarking

The method to be proposed adopts linear adaptive embedding for its ease of control, but the perturbation provoked by the reverse processing is nonlinear. The basic idea is applicable to nonlinear embedding as well.

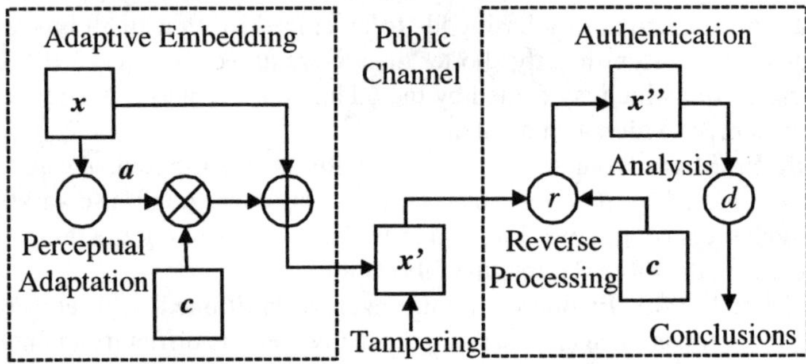


**Fig. 1.** The model of the perturbation based fragile watermarking (**x**: original, **x**′: distributed version, **x**″ : solved original, **c**: stream key or ciphered watermark, **a**: scale factor)

### 3.1 The Adaptive Embedding and the Reverse Processing

To facilitate the discussion, adaptive watermarking is here modeled as a linear system in matrix form [13]. Let us begin with 1-dimensional situation first. Suppose that the original is $x(n)$, $n = 0, 1, \cdots, l-1$, and the coefficients of a perceptually adaptive filter are $h(n)$, $n = 0, \pm 1, \cdots, \pm l_h$ (Fig.1). Then the scale factor $a(n)$, which is used for adjusting the embedding intensity, can be expressed by $a(n) = h(n) * x(n)$. Here, $*$ denotes the convolution operator. When zero-padding is used, the equivalent matrix form is

$$\boldsymbol{a}_{l\times 1} = H_{l\times l} \cdot \boldsymbol{x}_{l\times 1}\,, \tag{4}$$

where $\boldsymbol{a}_{l\times 1} = [a(0)\ a(1)\ \cdots\ a(l-1)]^T$, $\boldsymbol{x}_{l\times 1} = [x(0)\ x(1)\ \cdots\ x(l-1)]^T$, and

$$H_{l\times l} = \begin{bmatrix} h(0) & \cdots & h(-l_h) & & \\ \vdots & \ddots & & \ddots & \\ h(l_h) & & \ddots & & \ddots \\ & \ddots & & \ddots & h(-l_h) \\ & & \ddots & & \vdots \\ & & h(l_h) & \cdots & h(0) \end{bmatrix} \tag{5}$$

$$\triangleq toep[[h(0)\ \cdots\ h(-l_h)], [h(0)\ \cdots\ h(l_h)]^T]_{l\times l}\,.$$

Here, $H_{l\times l}$ is a Toeplitz matrix deduced from $h(n)$. $[\cdot]^T$ represents the transpose operation, and $\triangleq$ means 'denoted by'. When symmetrical extension is used, the filter coefficients outside of $H_{l\times l}$ can be reflected back and added to $H_{l\times l}$. If the vector form of a ciphered watermark or just stream key, $c(n)$, is $\boldsymbol{c}=[c(0)\,c(1)\cdots c(l-1)]$, its diagonal matrix form $\hat{C}_{l\times l}=diag(\boldsymbol{c})$, where $\hat{c}_{i,i}=c(i)$, and $\hat{c}_{i,j}=0$ wherever $i\neq j$, is used to replace direct multiplication in Eq.(3) with normal matrix multiplication. Let $E$ denote the identity matrix. Then the adaptive embedding equation can be expressed in matrix form by

$$\boldsymbol{x}'_{l\times 1}=\hat{C}_{l\times l}\cdot\boldsymbol{a}_{l\times 1}+\boldsymbol{x}_{l\times 1}=\hat{C}\cdot(H\cdot\boldsymbol{x})+\boldsymbol{x}=\boldsymbol{s}+\boldsymbol{x}=(\hat{C}\cdot H+E)\cdot\boldsymbol{x}\,, \tag{6}$$

whose computational cost is at the acceptable level of $O(l\cdot l_h)$. Because the coefficient matrix, $\ddot{C}\cdot H+E$, is often a diagonally dominant and narrow band matrix, it could be nonsingular from beginning or through easy design of $H$. Consequently, this paper assumes that its inverse, $(C\cdot H+E)^{-1}$, exists. Thus, when $\boldsymbol{x}$ is supposed to be the only unknown variable, the solution of the embedding equation can be expressed by

$$\boldsymbol{x}''=(\hat{C}\cdot H+E)^{-1}\cdot\boldsymbol{x}'\,, \tag{7}$$

where probably $\boldsymbol{x}'$ is tampered with, and $\boldsymbol{x}''$ is subject to drastic perturbation.

The above model will be extended to 2-dimensional situation before the further discussion. Suppose that the original is $x(m,n)$, $m=0,1,\cdots,u-1$, $n=0,1,\cdots,v-1$, and the coefficients of a 2-dimensional perceptually adaptive filter are $h(m,n)$, $m=0,\pm1,\cdots,\pm l_{hu}$, $n=0,\pm1,\cdots,\pm l_{hv}$. Eq.(4) can then be replaced with

$$\boldsymbol{a}_{uv\times 1}=H_{uv\times uv}\cdot\boldsymbol{x}_{uv\times 1}\,, \tag{8}$$

where

$$\boldsymbol{a}_{uv\times 1}=[\boldsymbol{a}_0^T\ \boldsymbol{a}_1^T\ \cdots\ \boldsymbol{a}_{u-1}^T]^T,\ \boldsymbol{a}_i=[a(i,0)\ a(i,1)\ \cdots\ a(i,v-1)]\,, \tag{9}$$

$$\boldsymbol{x}_{uv\times 1}=[\boldsymbol{x}_0^T\ \boldsymbol{x}_1^T\ \cdots\ \boldsymbol{x}_{u-1}^T]^T,\ \boldsymbol{x}_i=[x(i,0)\ x(i,1)\ \cdots\ x(i,v-1)]\,, \tag{10}$$

$$H_{uv\times uv}=toep[[H_0\ \cdots\ H_{-l_{hu}}],[H_0\ \cdots\ H_{l_{hv}}]^T]_{u\times u}\,, \tag{11}$$

$$H_i=toep[[h(i,0)\ \cdots\ h(i,-l_{hu})],[h(i,0)\ \cdots\ h(i,l_{hv})]^T]_{v\times v}\,.$$

Here, $H_i$ is constructed by the $i$th row of $h(m,n)$. Similarly, to participate in normal matrix multiplications, the ciphered watermark or stream key, $c(m,n)$, which has the matrix form of

$$C_{u\times v}=[\boldsymbol{c}_0\ \boldsymbol{c}_1\ \cdots\ \boldsymbol{c}_{u-1}]^T,\ \boldsymbol{c}_i=[c(i,0)\ c(i,1)\ \cdots\ c(i,v-1)]\,, \tag{12}$$

should also be changed into its diagonal matrix form:

$$\hat{C}_{uv\times uv} = diag(diag(\boldsymbol{c}_0)\ diag(\boldsymbol{c}_1)\ \cdots\ diag(\boldsymbol{c}_{u-1}))\,. \tag{13}$$

Finally, Eq.(6) and Eq.(7) can both have their 2-dimensional expressions.

### 3.2 Detecting and Localizing the Tampering

In principle of inverse problems [9], one might have great difficulty acquiring a reversed original $\boldsymbol{x}''$ that is perceptually acceptable by solving the embedding equation if the released version $\boldsymbol{x}'$ had been tampered with. As for the above model, the perturbation in solving linear equations [11,12] gives an approach for detecting and localizing the tampering.

The condition number of the coefficient matrix of the embedding equation helps to investigate the perturbations and estimate their levels. The condition number of a matrix $A$ is defined by $cond(A) = \| A^{-1} \| \cdot \| A \|$. In this paper, $\| \cdot \|$ represents the Euclidean norm of a matrix or vector [12]. Let $A$ denote $\ddot{C} \cdot H + E$ of Eq.(7). Suppose that $\boldsymbol{x}'$ in the embedding equation $A \cdot \boldsymbol{x} = \boldsymbol{x}'$ has been modified by $\delta\,\boldsymbol{x}'$, and the solution is perturbed by $\delta\,\boldsymbol{x}$ accordingly. Then we have

$$\left.\begin{array}{r} A\cdot\boldsymbol{x}'' = A\cdot(\boldsymbol{x}+\delta\,\boldsymbol{x}) = \boldsymbol{x}'+\delta\,\boldsymbol{x}' \\ A\cdot\boldsymbol{x} = \boldsymbol{x}' \end{array}\right\} \Rightarrow \delta\,\boldsymbol{x} = A^{-1}\cdot\delta\,\boldsymbol{x}'\,. \tag{14}$$

By the compatible property of matrix norm and vector norm, we also have

$$\|\boldsymbol{x}'\| \le \|A\|\cdot\|\boldsymbol{x}\|\,,\ \|\boldsymbol{x}''-\boldsymbol{x}\| = \|\delta\,\boldsymbol{x}\| \le \|A^{-1}\|\cdot\|\delta\,\boldsymbol{x}'\|\,. \tag{15}$$

Thus, the upper bound of the discrepancy between $\boldsymbol{x}''$ and $\boldsymbol{x}$ can be assessed by

$$\|\boldsymbol{x}''-\boldsymbol{x}\| \le \|\boldsymbol{x}\|\cdot(\|\delta\,\boldsymbol{x}'\|/\|\boldsymbol{x}'\|)\cdot cond(A)\,. \tag{16}$$

Eq.(16) indicates that the perturbation level increases with the level of tampering in scale of the condition number. When $cond(A)$ is large enough, $\boldsymbol{x}''$ can be far from $\boldsymbol{x}$. In actuality, even a human being can perceive the dissimilarity.

Notably, because the original data and the distributed data are very similar, there exist

$$\|\boldsymbol{x}\| \approx \|\boldsymbol{x}'\|\,,\ \|\boldsymbol{x}''-\boldsymbol{x}\| \approx \|\boldsymbol{x}''-\boldsymbol{x}'\|\,. \tag{17}$$

Thus, the solved original $\boldsymbol{x}''$ is also far from the distributed $\boldsymbol{x}'$ so that the latter can be used as a reference of the real original $\boldsymbol{x}$ when the perturbation is above a certain level. The blindness, which requires that an authentication not depend on the availability of the original, will be implemented by the observation.

When the embedding must round the watermarked samples into codewords, a comparatively slight perturbation occurs simultaneously. Let $\delta\boldsymbol{q}$ denote the rounding error. By the triangle inequality of norms, the range indicating the tampering in the overall perturbation can be expressed by

$$\begin{aligned} &\|\boldsymbol{x}\|\cdot(\|\delta\,\boldsymbol{q}\|/\|\boldsymbol{x}'\|)\cdot cond(A) \le \|\boldsymbol{x}''-\boldsymbol{x}\| \\ &\le \|\boldsymbol{x}\|\cdot(\|\delta\,\boldsymbol{q}\|/\|\boldsymbol{x}'\|+\|\delta\,\boldsymbol{x}'\|/\|\boldsymbol{x}'\|)\cdot cond(A). \end{aligned} \tag{18}$$

By applying Eq.(17), the above inequality can be replaced with

$$\|\delta \boldsymbol{q}\| \cdot cond(A) \le \| \boldsymbol{x}'' - \boldsymbol{x}' \| \le (\|\delta \boldsymbol{q}\| + \|\delta \boldsymbol{x}'\|) \cdot cond(A) . \tag{19}$$

Eq.(19) implies that the authentication could dispose of the original, achieving the desired blindness. Furthermore, it also shows that there is a large detection range between the upper bound of the accompanying perturbation and that of the combined one because $\delta \boldsymbol{x}'$ is significant larger than $\delta \boldsymbol{q}$. We name the property the layered bounds. Fig.2 illustrates the relations in a normed space.

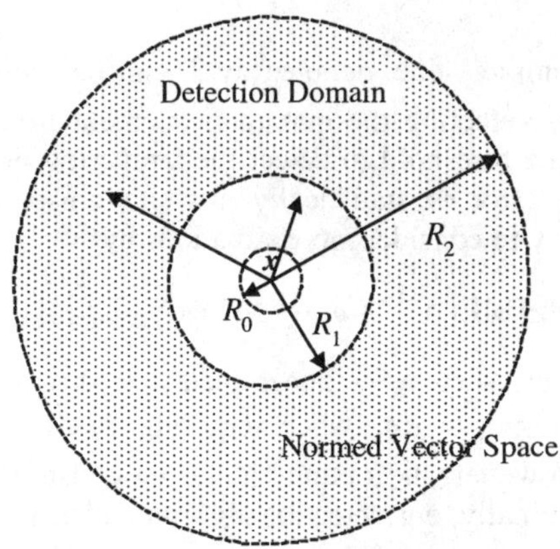


**Fig. 2.** Illustration of the perturbation in a normed space ($R_0$: upper bound of the distortion between the centered original $\boldsymbol{x}$, and the distributed version, $R_1$: upper bound of the perturbation in case of only rounding error, $R_2$: upper bound of the perturbation in case of tampering)

It is found that the positions where the solution perturbs are just the positions where tampering occurred. This paper calls the property the locally propagated perturbation. Since the ciphered watermark or stream key, $c(m,n)$, is coded in a 0/1 sequence, any element at the diagonal of the matrix $\ddot{C}$ only can be 0 or 1. Consequently, the matrix $A$, which denotes $\ddot{C} \cdot H + E$, is diagonally blocked, and its inverse,

$$A^{-1} = \begin{bmatrix} B_{n_1 \times n_1} & & & \\ & B_{n_2 \times n_2} & & \\ & & \ddots & \\ & & & B_{n_l \times n_l} \end{bmatrix}^{-1} = \begin{bmatrix} B^{-1}_{n_1 \times n_1} & & & \\ & B^{-1}_{n_2 \times n_2} & & \\ & & \ddots & \\ & & & B^{-1}_{n_l \times n_l} \end{bmatrix}, \tag{20}$$

is also diagonally blocked. Therefore, the locally propagated perturbation is supported by the fact that the $A^{-1}$ is also a narrow band matrix so that

$$\boldsymbol{x}'' = A^{-1} \cdot [\boldsymbol{x}'_{n_1} \; \boldsymbol{x}'_{n_2} \; \cdots \; \boldsymbol{x}'_{n_l}]^T = [B^{-1}_{n_1 \times n_1} \boldsymbol{x}'_{n_1} \; B^{-1}_{n_2 \times n_2} \boldsymbol{x}'_{n_2} \; \cdots \; B^{-1}_{n_l \times n_{l1}} \boldsymbol{x}'_{n_l}]^T . \tag{21}$$

Obviously, the influence of a local input and its possible modification on the output is also local.

By the properties of the locally propagated perturbation and the layered bounds, we could deduce that it is possible to detect and localize the tampering on one sample in its very near neighborhood. However, the accompanying perturbation should be distinguished to avoid any false alarm. We now give a reliable statistical method. When there are only rounding errors, Eq.(14) can be rewritten by

$$\left.\begin{array}{r} A\cdot \boldsymbol{x}'' = A\cdot(\boldsymbol{x}+\delta\,\boldsymbol{x}) = \boldsymbol{x}'+\delta\,\boldsymbol{q} \\ A\cdot\boldsymbol{x}=\boldsymbol{x}' \end{array}\right\} \Rightarrow \delta\,\boldsymbol{x} = A^{-1}\cdot\delta\,\boldsymbol{q}\,. \tag{22}$$

Then the maximum sample value, denoted by $T$, can be acquired by $\mathrm{ME}(A^{-1}\cdot\delta\,\boldsymbol{q})$, where 'ME' represents selecting the maximum element in a vector. Intuitively, we can directly use $T$ as the threshold to detect the tampering on one sample. However, because the rounding error is statistically a white noise, to get a more reliable threshold, it is necessary to consider more situations by

$$T = \mathrm{ME}[\mathrm{ME}(A^{-1}\cdot\delta\,\boldsymbol{q}_1)\cdots\mathrm{ME}(A^{-1}\cdot\delta\,\boldsymbol{q}_N)]^T\,. \tag{23}$$

Here, a noise generator, such as a linear feedback shift register, can be used to produce the $i$th rounding error $\delta\boldsymbol{q}_i$ when acquiring a sufficient number of rounding errors is infeasible. However, the output should be constrained so that they can be valid rounding errors. Finally, our detection algorithm alarms just when and where the difference between $x_i''$, an element of the reversed original, and $x_i'$, the element of the distributed version at the same position, is larger than $T$, although the threshold can be lowered to visualize the trace of tampering in more details.

Because the level of perturbation in case of only rounding errors is far below that in case of tampering, the possibility that $x_i''$ or one of its neighboring samples is not above the threshold is negligible. The experiments in next section will support the observation.

## 4 Image Experiments

This section verifies the above analysis through some experiments on images. The results are judged by human vision as well as objective measurements.

**Table 1.** Condition numbers and thresholds used in 10 experiments ($\gamma$: global intensity factor, $D$: $cond(\hat{C}\cdot H+E)$ where $H$ is deduced from $H(\gamma)$ according to Eq.(11), $T$: threshold)

| $\gamma$ | 0.25 | 0.275 | 0.30 | 0.325 | 0.35 | 0.375 | 0.40 | 0.425 | 0.45 | 0.475 |
|---|---|---|---|---|---|---|---|---|---|---|
| $D$ | 14.9 | 38.08 | 486 | 19456 | 22179 | 62311 | 38040 | 32194 | 29050 | 35548 |
| $T$ | 20.3 | 22.48 | 24.29 | 735.8 | 1179 | 532.3 | 1131 | 444.17 | 437.7 | 551.3 |

The perceptually adaptive filters are chosen according to both their generality and their contribution to condition numbers. The output of such a filter often reflects the degree of variation within a local part of the original [14]. The more variable the part is, the more heavily the location can be embedded. A chosen filter estimates the variation by the mean of the gray level difference between a processed sample and its neighbors. In 1-dimensional case, it can be expressed by

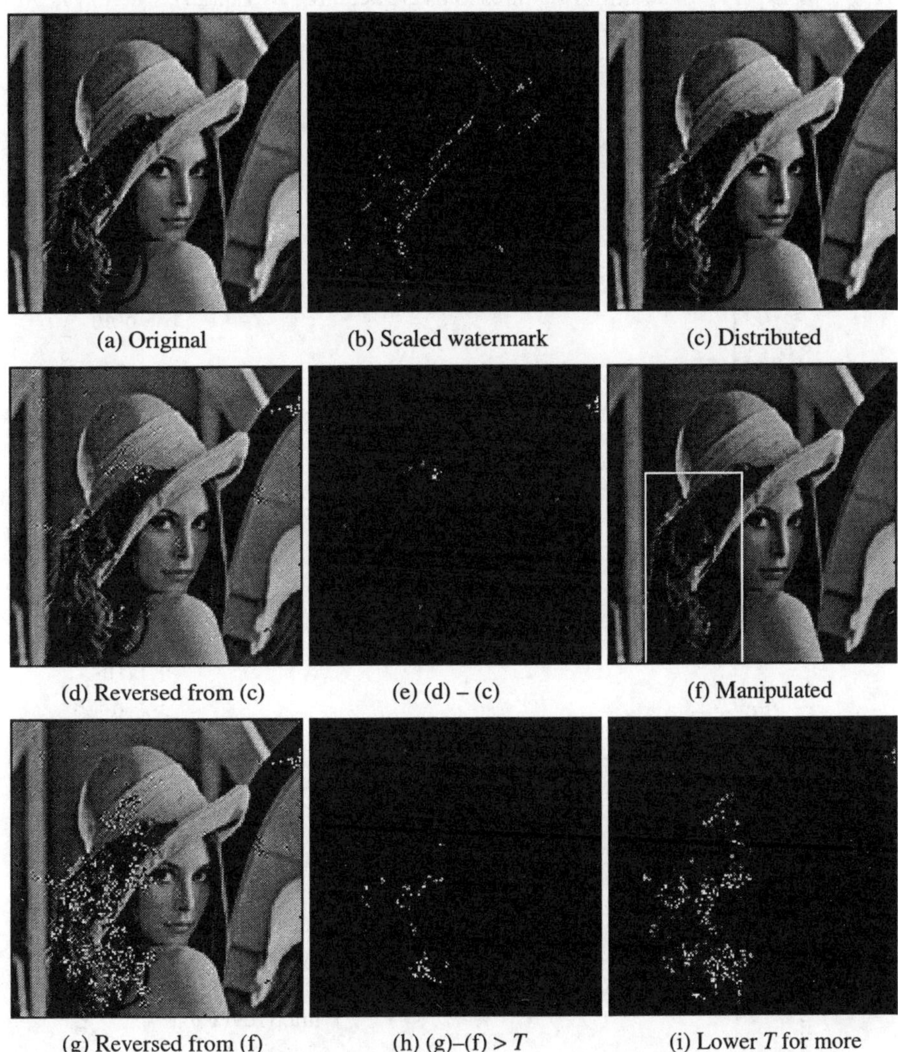

(a) Original (b) Scaled watermark (c) Distributed

(d) Reversed from (c) (e) (d) – (c) (f) Manipulated

(g) Reversed from (f) (h) (g)–(f) > $T$ (i) Lower $T$ for more

**Fig. 3.** A group of images generated in one of the experiments (grayscale=256,  = 0.45, $T$=437.7)

$$\pm[(x_n - x_{n-1}) + (x_n - x_{n+1})]/2 = \mp x_{n-1}/2 \pm x_n \mp x_{n+1}/2\,. \tag{24}$$

Thus the coefficients of the short-sized filter can be represented by $\boldsymbol{h} = [0.5\ \ -1\ \ 0.5]$ or $\boldsymbol{h} = [-0.5\ \ 1\ \ -0.5]$. However, the former is chosen because its lowpass effect is related to the perturbation in reverse processing [13] and the enlargement of the condition numbers. When the filter is applied along 2 directions, it is easy to construct a separable 2-dimensional filter, whose coefficients can be represented by $H(\gamma) = \gamma\, \boldsymbol{h}^t \cdot \boldsymbol{h}$, where $\gamma$ is a global scale factor. $H(\gamma)$ is then used to compute $H_{uv \times uv}$ by Eq.(11). In addition, the thresholds are acquired by Eq.(23), where $N$ is 50.

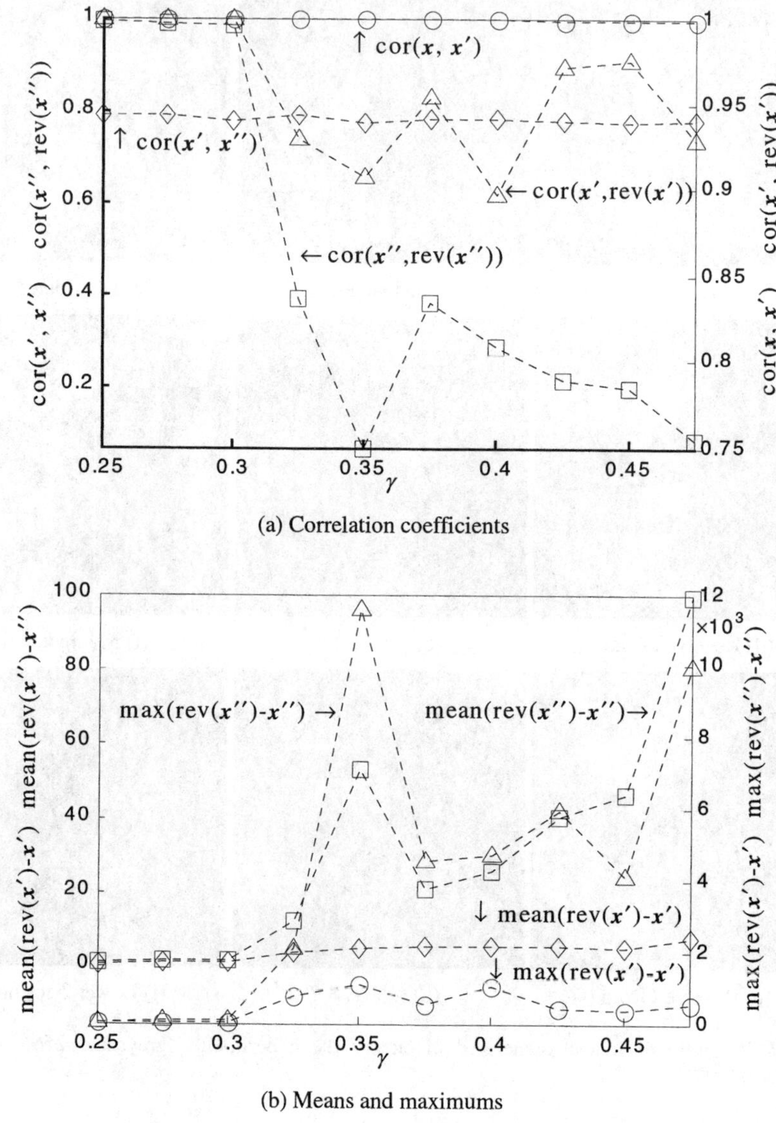


(a) Correlation coefficients

(b) Means and maximums

**Fig. 4.** The measured statistics in the 10 experiments ($\boldsymbol{x}$: the original, $\boldsymbol{x}'$: the distributed, $\boldsymbol{x}''$: the manipulated, $\gamma$: global scale factor, cor: correlation coefficient, rev: reverse processing, max: maximum value, mean: mean value)

The experiments will show that they are very reliable. Table 1 lists 10 condition numbers together with the related thresholds varying with $\gamma$.

Fig.3 not only displays a set of typical images from one of the experiments, but also gives the basic authentication steps. Fig.3(a)-Fig.3(c) indicate that embedding an adaptively scaled watermark keeps the visual quality of the distributed version well. Fig.3(d) and Fig.3(e) demonstrate the slight perturbation resulting from the rounding error. Fig.3(g) shows that even human eyes can catch the manipulated areas with the aid of the perturbation. Nevertheless, the perturbed values exceeding the threshold $T$ in Fig.3(h) are used to reliably detect and sketch the tampering. Finally, one can see more details of the manipulation, as what is shown in Fig.3(i), by lowering the threshold gradually after the tampering is detected.

Fig.4 shows some significant measurements in 10 experiments that have different condition numbers (Table 1). In Fig.4(a), that the correlations between the originals and their distributed versions are so near to 1 indicates again that the adaptive embedding ensures the imperceptibility. That the correlations between the intact distributed versions and their reversed ones are above 0.9 verifies that the accompanying perturbation is slight. The descending correlations between the manipulated versions and their reversed ones demonstrate that great discrepancies between them occur in case of large condition numbers. From another viewpoint, Fig.4(b) demonstrates that a large condition number can greatly enlarge the differences between the sample values before and after the reverse processing, making the tampering more perceptible. It also shows that the level of the differences resulting from only rounding errors is far below that of the combined modification, implying the reliability of the thresholds.

## 5 Conclusions

Having investigated the perturbation in reverse processing, we find that the phenomenon does help to design fragile watermarking and enhance the performance, especially the localizability. First, because the drastically perturbed samples indicate the positions where the manipulation occurred, the proposed method does not need to partition the original into blocks and authenticates the distributed version almost sample-wise. Consequently, the localizability is improved. Second, the vulnerabilities related to block-based approaches are avoided. Third, the method is fully compatible with the adaptive embedding that keeps the perceptual quality well. Fourth, the fact that no effective tampering can be slighter than the rounding error guarantees the correctness of the detection. Finally, instead of really extracting the watermark, just solving the embedding equation by the ciphered watermark or stream key does not need refer to the original so that the blindness is achieved.

However, 2 things must be considered before exploiting the phenomenon. One is that the perturbation should be above a certain level, which can be guaranteed by a large condition number of the coefficient matrix of the embedding equation. Another thing is that the accompanying perturbation resulting from rounding error should be distinguished. In our method, the maximal perturbed sample value in case of no tampering is used as the detection threshold to eliminate the interference.

Although we only experimented on images, the general conclusions of this paper are apparently applicable to other multimedia, e.g. audio and video, as well.

## References


1. Nahrstedt, K., Dittmann, J., Wohlmacher, P.: Approaches to multimedia and security. In: Proc. of IEEE Intern. Conf. on Multimedia and Expo, Vol.3, New York, NY, Aug. 2000, 1275–1278.
2. Lin, E. T., Delp, E. J.: A review of fragile image watermarks. In: Proc. of Multimedia and Security Workshop at ACM Multimedia, Orlando, Florida, Oct. 1999, 25–29.
3. Barreto, P. S., Kim, H. Y.: Pitfalls in public key watermarking. In: Proc. of 12th IEEE Brazilian Symposium on Computer Graphics and Image Processing, São Paulo, Brazil, Oct. 1999, 241–242.
4. Kundur, D., Hatzinakos, D.: Towards a telltale watermarking technique for tamper-proofing. In Proc. of IEEE Intern. Conf. on Image Processing, Vol.2, Chicago, Illinois, Oct. 1998, 409–413.
5. Lin, C. Y., Chang, S. F.: Semi-fragile watermarking for authenticating JPEG visual content. In SPIE Proc. of Security and Watermarking of Multimedia Contents II, Vol.3971, San Jose, California, Jan. 2000, 140–151.
6. Wong, P. W.: A public key watermarking for image verification and authentication. In Proc. of IEEE Intern. Conf. on Image Processing, Vol.1, Chicago, Illinois, Oct. 1998, 455–459.
7. Cox, I. J., Miller, M. I.: A review of watermarking and the importance of perceptual modeling. In SPIE Proc. of Human Vision and Electronic Imaging II, Vol.3016, San Jose, California, June 1997, 92–99.
8. Podilchuk, C. I., Zeng, W.: Image-adaptive watermarking using visual models. IEEE Journal on Selected Areas in Communications, 1998, 16(4): 525–539.
9. Kirsch, A.: An Introduction to the Mathematical Theory of Inverse Problems. Springer-Verlag, Berlin, Heidelberg, and New York, 1996.
10. Menezes, A. J., van Oorschot, P. C., Vanstone, S. A.: Handbook of Applied Cryptography. CRC Press, Boca Raton, Florida, 1997.
11. Lancaster, P., Tismenetsky, M.: The Theory of Matrix, 2nd ed. Academic Press, Orlando, Florida, 1985.
12. Burden, R. L., Faires, J. D.: Numerical Analysis, 7th ed. Thomson Learning, Stamford, Connecticut, 2001.
13. Castleman, K. R.: Digital Image Processing, 2nd ed. Prentice Hall, Englewood Cliffs, New Jersey, 1997.
14. Wu, D. C., Tsai, W. H.: Embedding of any type of data in images based on a human visual model and multiple-based number conversion. Pattern Recognition Letters, 1999, 20(14): 1511–1517.

# Discovering Image Semantics from Web Pages Using a Text Mining Approach

Hsin-Chang Yang[1] and Chung-Hong Lee[2]

[1] Department of Information Management, Chang Jung University, Tainan, Taiwan
hcyang@mail.cju.edu.tw

[2] Department of Electric Engineering, National Kaohsiung University of Applied Sciences, Kaohsiung, Taiwan
leechung@mail.ee.kuas.edu.tw

**Abstract.** Traditional content-based image retrieval (CBIR) systems often fail to fulfill a user's need due to the 'semantic gap' existed between the extracted features of the systems and the user's query. In this paper we propose a novel approach to bridge the semantic gap which is the major deficiency of CBIR systems. We conquer the deficiency by extracting semantics of an image from the environmental texts around it. We apply a text mining process, which adopts the self-organizing map (SOM) learning algorithm as a kernel, on the environmental texts of an image to extract the semantic information from this image. Some implicit semantic information of the images can be discovered after the text mining process. We also define a semantic relevance measure to achieve the semantic-based image retrieval task. We performed experiments on a set of images which are collected from web pages and obtained promising results.

## 1 Introduction

Recently the task of image retrieval has received lots of attention from the web community since there are so many images existed in web pages. Image retrieval is a branch of information retrieval which task is to retrieve some pieces of information (the *documents*) to fulfill a user's information need according to some (semantic) relevance measurements. Nowadays most information retrieval systems retrieve documents based on their 'contents'. That is, they measure the relevance between the query and a document according to their internal representations or derived features. Such representations or features will vary for different document styles and retrieval schemes. For text retrieval systems, the contents are often represented by a set of selected keywords that are intended to capture the semantics of the documents. Many works have devoted to representing the semantics of text documents and obtained successful results [1]. For image retrieval systems, the representation of image content generally contains a set of visual features extracted from the image that hopefully may well represent the image. Many schemes have been proposed to describe the image contents [2, 3,4]. However, the semantics of an image is hard to be revealed by these features.

G. Dong et al. (Eds.): WAIM 2003, LNCS 2762, pp. 495–502, 2003.

Thus we often retrieve irrelevant images even when they have similar features. For example, an image with 70% green color and 30% blue color could be a scenic view of a meadow or a book cover. Another example is a round object with a hold in it could be a wheel or a compact disc. These examples show that a user may obtain images that are totally irrelevant to his query through CBIR approaches. Such difference between the user's information need and the image representation is called the 'semantic gap' occurred in the CBIR systems. Thus CBIR systems only work in considerably small domains of data sets. To obtain more reasonable result, semantic-based image retrieval (SBIR) systems are devised to bridge the semantic gap.

Unlike CBIR systems which use 'contents' to retrieve images, SBIR) systems try to discover the real semantic meaning of an image and use it to retrieve relevant images. However, understanding and discovering the semantics of a piece of information are high-level cognitive tasks and thus hard to automate. Several attempts have been made to tackle this problem. Most of the methods inherit from the CBIR techniques such that primitive features are used to derive higher order image semantics. However, CBIR systems use no explicit knowledge about the image and limit their applications to fields such as fingerprint identification and trade mark retrieval, etc. To levitate the users' satisfaction about the query result, we must incorporate more semantics into the retrieval process. However, there are three major difficulties in such incorporation. The first is that we must have some kind of high-level description scheme for describing the semantics. The second, a semantics extraction scheme is necessary for mapping visual features to high-level semantics. Finally, we must develop a query processing and matching method for the retrieval process. Many works have been devised to remedy these difficulties, as we will discuss later. In this work we propose a novel approach to solve these difficulties using a simple framework. First we incorporate explicit knowledge into the framework by representing the images with their surrounding texts in the web pages. Such representation also solves the difficulty of semantics representation. The semantics extraction process is achieved in our framework by using a text mining process on these texts. We also design a semantic relevance measure for matching the user's query and images in the image collection. This solves the third difficulty. Our idea comes of the recognition that it is too hard to directly extract semantics from images. Thus we avoid direct access of the image contents which is generally time-consuming and imprecise. Instead, we try to obtain image semantics by their environmental texts which are generally contextually relevant to the images.

Most of SBIR systems extract semantics directly from the image contents; however, our method adopts an indirect approach. Direct extraction of semantics has the following advantages. Firstly, provided that there is a good extraction scheme, the extracted semantics could exactly reflect the real meaning of the image since it is derived from the image content. Secondly, there are a bunch of well-developed methods for extracting visual features from the image. This may simplify the interpretation of such features and make such interpretation more precise. However, interpretation of image content is a high-level cognitive process and is hard to automate. Thus there is still no satisfactory semantics extraction scheme up to now. On the other hand, extracting semantics from the accompanying text of an image seems to be inexact and require much efforts. However, it has the advantage that extracting semantics from texts is much easier than from images if we can correctly find the accompanying text of an image. The major contributions of our work are to devise a text extraction scheme to find the accompanying text of an image and a text mining scheme for interpreting the semantics of the image by the accompanying texts. We also devise a semantic measure to evaluate our method. In this way we achieve satisfactory result in the experiments.

## 2 Text Mining for Semantic Image Retrieval

In this section we will give a detailed description of the proposed method. We will start from the preprocessing and encoding of documents in Sec. 2.1. The encoded documents are then trained by self-organizing map algorithm in Sec. 2.2. A text mining process is applied to the training result to discover the relationships among images as well as the subjects of the images, which are considered as a kind of semantics of the images. Finally, we use the text mining result to retrieve images in Sec. 2.3.

### 2.1 Document Preprocessing

A document in our corpus is a typical web page which contains both texts and images. A web page generally exists in HTML format which uses a set of predefined tags to perform actions such as typesetting the page, inserting hyperlinks and multimedia objects, etc. In this article we interest in image retrieval so we should first extract images from the documents. We then extract environmental texts from the web pages corresponding to each extracted image. Note that we will discard a web page if it contains no qualified image or environmental texts.

**Extracting Images from Web Pages.** In HTML we use the `<img>` tag to add images to the web pages. Thus we can extract images from the web pages by examining the `<img>` tags. We will discard extremely small images because they often contain little amount of information. For example, many web pages contain small icons such as buttons and rulers that are used for alignment, segmentation, and marking, etc. The threshold of image size is determined experimentally. That is, we will collect all images and then determine a threshold that can discriminate such small images. A typical threshold value is a few kilobytes. Besides image size, there is nearly no limit on the image properties in our method since we do not directly extract features from the images. Notice that we treat duplicated images as separate ones to allow different interpretations of the same images.

**Extracting Environmental Texts.** The remaining part of the web page is further processed to extract necessary texts. These texts are called the environmental texts (ETs) of these images. There are several types of environmental texts related to an image. For example, we can identify nearby texts, captions, alternate texts, and filenames from a HTML-format web page. In this article, two types of ETs are extracted. The first type (denoted by ET-Normal) is the ordinary texts which locate outside any HTML tags. ET-Normal includes important texts such as titles, which is often enclosed by the `<title>` and `</title>` tags, and nearby texts which are in nearby paragraphs of the image. The second type (denoted by ET-Caption) includes alternate texts, captions, and filenames that are extracted from the `<img>` tag. For example, the HTML statement `<img src="myphoto.jpg" alt="My Picture">` contains a filename `myphoto.jpg` and an alternate text `My Picture`.

ET-Normal includes the nearby texts of an image. The nearby texts include texts that satisfy the following criteria:

1. texts in the same row or column of the image if the image occurs in a table environment
2. texts in the same paragraph of the image
3. texts with a small distance to the `<img>` tag

The first criterion can be justified by simply examining the `td` tags in the table environment. The second criterion is also easy to be justified since HTML uses `<p>` tags to separate paragraphs. The distance in the third criterion can be measured in characters or words. Unlike the first two criteria which use logical units to determine the ETs, the third one uses physical units which are hard to tune for satisfactory result. We need to perform some experiments to decide the best value of such distance. A plausible scheme is to set the distance being propositional to the total size of normal texts in the web page. For example, if a web page contains 1000 words and we let texts within fourth of the size of the web page be ETs. This will make the 250 words before and after the image location being the ETs respectively. Notice that the third criterion can be considered as a replacement of the second one for they differ only in the measurement of proximity. All above criteria are subject to change according to different proximity requirements. For example, we can expand the first criterion to include the texts in the same table. Likewise, we can expand the second criterion to include texts in preceded and succeeded paragraphs or even the whole page.

On the other hand, ET-Caption is easy to extract by examining the attributes of `img` tags. When both ET-Normal and ET-Caption associated with each image have been extracted, a word extractor is used to segment these ETs into a list of terms. We discard those terms in a standard stoplist to reduce the vocabulary size. We also discard terms that occur only once in the ETs. Stemming is also applied for further reduction. We use the resulting list of terms to represent the image. We call these terms the environmental keywords (EKs) of their associated image.

**Encoding Images.** We adopt a binary vector representation resembles to the vector space model to encode the images. All the ETs associated with an image are collectively transformed to a binary vector such that each component corresponds to an EK associated with this image. A component of the vector with value 1 and 0 indicates the presence and absence of an EK in its associated document respectively. We do not use any term weighting method such as *tf·idf* scheme. The reason is our text mining process take no advantage by using term weighting scheme, as we will discuss later.

### 2.2 Discovering Image Semantics by Text Mining

**Document Clustering Using Self-organizing Maps.** In this subsection we will describe how to organize images and EKs into clusters by their co-occurrence similarities. The images in the corpus are first encoded into a set of vectors as described in Sec. 2.1. We intend to organize these images into a set of clusters such that similar images will fall into the same cluster. Moreover, similar clusters should be 'close' in some manner. The unsupervised learning algorithm of SOM networks [5] fulfills our needs.

We define some denotations that will be used later here. Let $\mathbf{x}_i = \{x_{i_n} \in \{0,1\} | 1 \leq n \leq N\}, 1 \leq i \leq M$, be the encoded vector of the $i$th image in the corpus, where $N$ and $M$ are the total number of EKs and images in the corpus respectively. We use these vectors as the training inputs to the SOM network. The network consists of a regular grid of neurons which has $N$ synapses each. Let $\mathbf{w}_j = \{w_{j_n} | 1 \leq n \leq N\}, 1 \leq j \leq J$, be the synaptic weight vector of the $j$th neuron in the network, while $J$ is the number of neurons in the network. We train the network by the SOM algorithm that performs the clustering task. Applying the SOM algorithm to the image vectors, we actually perform a clustering process about the corpus. A neuron in the map can be considered as a cluster. Similar images will fall into the same or neighboring neurons (clusters). Besides, the similarity of two clusters can be measured by the geometrical distance between their corresponding neurons. To decide the cluster to which an image or an EK belongs, we apply a labeling process to the images and the EKs, respectively. After the labeling process, each image associates with a neuron in the map. We record such associations and form the image cluster map (ICM). In the same manner, we label each EK to the map and form the keyword cluster map (KCM). We then use these two maps for image semantics discovery. The clustering and labeling process were described in detail in our previous work [6].

### 2.3 Image Retrieval by Semantics

After obtaining the image clusters and keyword clusters, we may use them for semantic image retrieval. Two types of query methods are allowed in our scheme, namely the keyword-based queries and query by example. We will discuss them in the following subsections.

**Semantic Image Retrieval by Keywords.** When a user specifies some keywords as a query, the images that are semantically relevant to this query can be retrieved by using the KCM. Basically, the query is transformed to a query vector in the same way as the image vector. Let $\mathbf{q} = \{q_i \in \{0,1\} | 1 \leq i \leq N\}$ denote the query vector. We also transform each keyword cluster in KCM to a vector. Let $\mathbf{k}_j = \{k_{j_i} \in \{0,1\} | 1 \leq i \leq N\}$ be the encoded vector for the keyword cluster associated with neuron $j$. The similarity between the query vector and an image vector is calculated with an extension of the cosine measurement in the vector space model:

$$S_{\mathbf{q},\mathbf{x}} = A\frac{|\mathbf{q} \cdot \mathbf{k}_j|}{|\mathbf{q}||\mathbf{k}_j|} + \frac{|\mathbf{q} \cdot \mathbf{x}|}{|\mathbf{q}||\mathbf{x}|}. \tag{1}$$

We let $\mathbf{x}$ be the encoded vector of an image associated with neuron $j$. The first term of the right hand side of Eq. 1 measures the similarity between the query vector and the cluster vector. The second term measures the similarity between the query vector and an image vector associated with neuron $j$. $A$ is a scaling parameter that is big enough to differentiate the contributions from cluster and individual image. We let $A$ be big enough since the degree of match between keywords should be the major part of the similarity.

**Semantic Image Retrieval by Example Image.** When an image is used as a query, we should first find its environmental texts from its associated web page as described in Sec. 2.1. These texts are then transformed to a query vector as in Sec. 2.1. The similarity between the query image and an image in the corpus can then be measured by Eq. 1. We now discuss some alternate approaches. To speed up the matching process, we may divide the similarity computation into two stages. In the first stage, we may only compute the first terms in Eq. 1. Only those clusters that have the highest results will be used in the second stage. In the second stage, we may then order the images according to the second terms. This approach takes advantage of the fact that the number of neurons $J$ is generally much smaller than the number of images $M$. Thus in the first stage we only need to compute $J$ similarities instead of $M$. In the second stage we may need another dozens of computations of the second term. Since the user generally only interests in the top rank images, the two-stage scheme may achieve adequate result.

## 3 Experimental Result

We test the method with a set of manually collected web pages. The web pages were collected according to the Yahoo! web site directory. The reason for using Yahoo! directory hierarchy is that it has been a standard test bed for categorization and semantics development of web pages. Thus many works have used Yahoo! hierarchy in their experiments. There are 14 top-level category in the Yahoo! directory. We adopt the "Art & Humanity" category as our source of web pages. The Art category contains 26 sub-categories. We denote these sub-categories level-1 categories. Each level-1 category also contains several sub-categories. We denote them level-2 categories. A level-1 or level-2 category contains two parts of hyperlinks. The first part is denoted by 'Categories' and contains hyperlinks which link to lower level categories, i.e. level-($n$+1) category where $n$ is the current level. The second part is the 'Site Listings' and includes the instantiation hyperlinks which link to corresponding web pages. In this work we collect web pages which are linked by all instantiation hyperlinks in all level-1 and level-2 categories. There are total 7736 web pages in the corpus. All pages were preprocessed so that images are extracted and their ETs are also identified. We then transformed each image to a image vector. We extracted 44782 images from the 7736 pages and discarded 8932 unqualified images. Since the `alt` strings are often used to describe the semantics of the image and thus images without `alt` strings may be considered less important, we may further reduce the number of images to 27567 by discarding those images without `alt` strings. We adopted this approach and used these 27567 images as the training vectors.

To train the image vectors we constructed a self-organizing map which consists of 400 neurons in $20 \times 20$ grid format. The number of neurons is determined by a simple rule of thumb that the dimension of the map should be close the average number of items associated with a neuron. The initial gain is set to 0.4 and the maximum training time is set to 500 in the training process. Both parameters are determined experimentally to obtain a better result. After the training, we label each image to a neuron.

We may design an evaluation measure for our method as follows:

$$E = \sum_{1 \leq i \leq M} CSD(\mathbf{q}, \mathbf{x}_i), \tag{2}$$

where $CSD$ is a function which returns the categorical semantic distance (CSD) between its two arguments. We define the CSD according to the relationships between categories in the Yahoo! hierarchy. There are five types of relationships between two different categories. The first type is the equivalent relationship such that the two categories are identical. The second type is the parent-child relationship such that one category is the parent of the other category. The third type is the sibling relationship such that the two categories have the same parent. The fourth type is the cross-level relationship such that the two categories are in different levels and they do not have the parent-child relationship. The last type is the equi-level relationship such that the two categories are both in the level 2 but with different parents or they are both level-1 categories. The value for each type of relationship is determined according to the length of the optimal path between two categories with such relationship. For example, when two level-2 categories have the same parent, the length of the optimal path between these categories is 2. According to such definition, the CSDs for the five types of relationships are 0, 1, 2, 3, and 4 respectively.

To evaluate the method, we used every image in the corpus as queries. We then measure the evaluation measure for each query. Table 1 lists the statistics of all the evaluation measures.

**Table 1.** The statistics of the $E$ over all image queries

| Range for $E$ | Number of images in range |
|---|---|
| more than 10000 | 0 |
| 9000-9999 | 11 |
| 8000-8999 | 5 |
| 7000-7999 | 93 |
| 6000-6999 | 87 |
| 5000-5999 | 348 |
| 4000-4999 | 1365 |
| 3000-3999 | 1469 |
| 2000-2999 | 2876 |
| 1000-1999 | 5478 |
| less than 1000 | 15835 |

## 4 Conclusions

In this work we propose a novel approach for semantic-based image retrieval. The method applies a proposed text mining approach to discover the semantically related images. Unlike other semantic-based image retrieval approach, we avoid direct analysis of images and rely on their environmental texts to discover their semantics. The approach was applied on a set of web pages and obtained promising result. Our method can only apply on documents with both images and texts.

## References

1. Baeza-Yates, R., Ribeiro-Neto, B.: Modern Information Retrieval. 1 edn. ACM Press, New York (1999)
2. De Marsicoi, M., Cinque, L., Levialdi, S.: Indexing pictorial documents by their content: a survey of current techniques. Image and Vision Computing **15** (1997) 119–141
3. Doermann, D.: The indexing and retrieval of document images: A survey. Computer Vision and Image Understanding **70** (1998) 287–298
4. Gupta, A., Jain, R.: Visual information retrieval. Communications of the ACM **40** (1997) 71–79
5. Kohonen, T.: Self-Organizing Maps. Springer-Verlag, Berlin (1997)
6. Lee, C.H., Yang, H.C.: A web text mining approach based on self-organizing map. In: Proc. ACM CIKM'99 2nd Workshop on Web Information and Data Management, Kansas City, MI (1999) 59–62

# Creating Customized Metasearch Engines on Demand Using SE-LEGO
## (Extended Abstract)

Zonghuan Wu[1], Vijay Raghavan[1], Weiyi Meng[2], Hai He[2], Clement Yu[3], and Chun Du[1]

[1]University of Louisiana at Lafayette, Center for Advan. Computer Studies
Lafayette, LA 70504, {zwu,raghavan}@cacs.louisiana.edu
[2]Department of Computer Science, State University of New York at Binghamton
Binghamton, NY 13902, USA, meng@cs.binghamton.edu
[3]Dept. of Computer Science, University of Illinois at Chicago
Chicago, IL 60607, yu@cs.uic.edu

## 1 Introduction

Frequently, the documents needed by a user are available only via multiple search engines. For example, research papers about a particular subject may be found from the search engines of related digital libraries and journals. It is inconvenient for the user to search these search engines separately. An effective way to address this problem is to employ a metasearch engine, which is a system that provides unified access to multiple existing search systems. When a metasearch engine receives a user query, it passes the query to its underlying search engines. The results returned by the search engines, are then combined by the metasearch engine to form a single ranked list for presentation to the user [2].

Building customized metasearch engines is important to many people and organizations. For example, a researcher may use a particular set of search engines for finding papers on a particular subject. A customized metasearch engine based on these search engines will provide convenience and efficiency for this researcher. As another example, a company may have several competitors and it keeps track of these competitors using their search engines. In this case, a customized metasearch engine on top of the competitors' search engines can be very useful to the company. In both examples, the set of the search engines one wishes to use as well as the characteristics of the search engines themselves may change (e.g., a competitor's search engine may need to be added and a search engine changes its result format). Therefore, the metasearch engines need to change accordingly. Currently, building and maintaining a metasearch engine are expensive and labor-intensive tasks that need diverse expertise. As a result, it is difficult for an ordinary Web user to create and maintain a metasearch engine based on the search engines of the user's choice. Some metasearch engine companies (e.g., ProFusion) allow users to build customized metasearch engines, but only search engines in a pre-compiled list can be used because the capability to connect to these search engines needs to be established in advance.

G. Dong et al. (Eds.): WAIM 2003, LNCS 2762, pp. 503–505, 2003.

In this demonstration, we present an automatic metasearch engine construction tool, SE-LEGO. When the URLs of the desired search engines are provided, SE-LEGO creates a customized metasearch engine based on these search engines on demand.

SE-LEGO is also useful for building large-scale metasearch engines connecting to numerous search engines. It is estimated that there are hundreds of thousands of search engines on the Web, including both the Surface Web and the Deep Web [1]. At present, the largest metasearch engines such as ProFusion (www.profusion.com) connect to about 1,000 search engines. This means that only a small fraction of the information sources on the Web are connected. The goal of our WebScales project is to create a metasearch engine that connects to all useful search engines on the Web. Clearly, in the context of WebScales, it will be too costly to manually produce the connection program for every search engine. Furthermore, changes/upgrades of the connection format of a search engine may affect the connection program, causing a maintenance nightmare when a huge number of search engines are involved. The automatic connection capability of SE-LEGO is necessary for our WebScales project.

## 2 Components of SE-LEGO

SE-LEGO consists of the following components:

1. *Automatic Search Engine Connection*: This component automatically analyzes the source (HTML) file of the interface of any given search engine and generates a program that can pass queries to the search engine. Based on the analysis, important attributes for search engine connection such as the URL of the search engine service agent program, the HTTP communication method and other parameters in the search engine form are extracted. The extracted information is then used to automatically generate the connection program for the search engine.
2. *Automatic Search Result Extraction*: For any given search engine, this component automatically generates a program to extract the results (e.g., URLs) related to the retrieved pages from the result pages of the search engine. Typically, a search engine result page contains not only the URLs of retrieved documents but also URLs of advertisement/internal organization pages. The issue is how to differentiate useful URLs (those of retrieved pages) from useless URLs automatically. This component also extracts the number of hits and the next page pattern for retrieving more result URLs than shown in the initial result page.
3. *Query Dispatching and Result Merging*: This component dispatches queries to appropriate search engines and merges the results extracted from the returned pages into a single ranked list for presentation to the user. Different result merging algorithms are implemented. The basic algorithm ranks the results based on their local ranks in local search engines. Another algorithm ranks the retrieved documents based on a global match of the contents of each page with the query.

## 3 Demonstration

During the demonstration, we will show how to use SE-LEGO to build a metasearch engine on demand and then conduct metasearching. People in the audience are welcome to provide the URLs of Web search engines for the demonstration.

**Acknowledgements.** This work is supported in part by the following grants from NSF (IIS-0208574, IIS-0208434, EIA-9911099), Army Research Office (ARO-2-5-30267), and the IT Initiative of the State of Louisiana to Lafayette.

## References

1. M. Bergman. The Deep Web: Surfacing the Hidden Value. BrightPlanet White Paper (www.completeplanet.com/Tutorials/DeepWeb/index.asp), 2000.
2. W. Meng, C. Yu, K. Liu. Building Efficient and Effective Metasearch Engines. ACM Computing Surveys, 34(1), March 2002, pp.48–84.

# SQL-Relay: An Event-Driven Rule-Based Database Gateway

Qingsong Yao and Aijun An

Department of Computer Science, York University,Canada
{qingsong,ann}@cs.yorku.ca

## 1 Introduction

Database users often submit *similar queries* to retrieve certain information from the database. We use *user access event* to represent a set of *similar queries.* A user access event contains an SQL template and a set of parameters, where the value of a parameter can be a constant or a variable. For example, event *("select name from customer where id =%",101)* represents a single query which retrieves the name of customer *101*, while event *("select name from customer where id =%",g_cid)* represents a set of queries thats retrieve the name of given customer. The event execution orders are represented by using dependency graphs, which are called user access paths.

In this paper, we propose an event-driven rule-based database gateway, *SQL-Relay.* It makes use of user access patterns to improve query performance. The principle of our solution is as follows. For each frequent user access event (i.e., the frequency of the event is higher than a predefined threshold), we predefine a set of execution rules. When a query is submitted, we find the best matched event, and execute the predefined rules associated with it. There are three kinds of rules: global rewriting rules, local rewriting rules and prefetching rules. A global rewriting rule aims to rewrite the current event, e.g., make use of indices, materialized views, to get a better response time. A prefetching rule pre-fetches the answer of a query to be submitted according to the current request sequence. In some cases, semantic relationships exist between the queries of a user access path, and a local rewriting rule can make use of such semantic relationship to rewrite the current query to answer multiple queries. For example, if we know a user will submit a query whose answer *contains* that of the current query, we can submit it instead of the current query to the server, and use the query result to answer both queries.

## 2 Overview of SQL-Relay

The architecture of SQL-Relay is illustrated in Fig. 1. The SQL-Relay contains *client machine, state machine, event parser, event processor, event action table* and *cache manager.* Each *client machine* corresponds to one type of client application or a group of users who have the similar behavior. For each connected client or user, the SQL-Relay creates an instance of *client machine* to process

G. Dong et al. (Eds.): WAIM 2003, LNCS 2762, pp. 506–507, 2003.

the requests. It is called a *state machine.* The *state machine* contains a set of state variables, and maintains the user request sequence to help to find the best matched user access path and make prediction. The *event action table* contains a set of predefined rules for the events. The *event processor* contains a set of utilities, which can build a SQL query from an SQL template and the parameters, or retrieve the query answer from the caches.

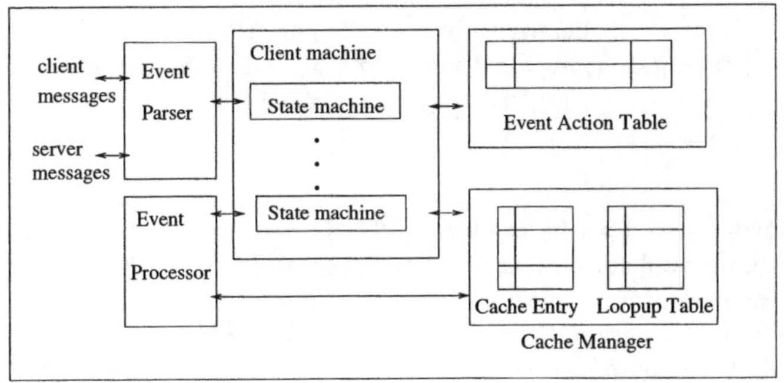


**Fig. 1.** The Architecture of SQL Replay

The cache manager manages two kinds of caches, the global cache and the local cache. A global cache is always available to answer queries and can not be replaced by other caches unless it is temporarily unavailable due to the updating of the base relations. A local cache may be replaced by other caches. All *client machines* share a global cache pool, and each of them has a local cache pool which changes dynamically as new data is cached. We use a hash-like *lookup table* to find if the answer of a query is in the caches.

Compared with other data caching techniques, our approach has several advantages. First, one client can use the cached query results of other clients. It has better performance than caching query answers at each client. Second, our approach caches the query answers instead of caching the whole tables [1,2]. It improves the cache performance since the submitted queries represent how a user retrieves the data. Compared with the query rewriting facilities provided by the query optimizer, the time to find a rule by the *SQL-Relay* is shorter than the time to rewrite a query by the optimizer.

## References

1. The TimesTen Team. Mid-Tire Caching: The TimersTen Appreach. In Procs. of ACM SIGMOD, 2002.
2. Oracle9iAS Database Cache. (`http://www.oracle.com`).

# CyberETL: Towards Visual Debugging Transformations in Data Integration

Youlin Fang, DongQing Yang, ShiWei Tang, Yunhai Tong, Weihua Zhang, Libo Yu, and Qiang Fu

School of Information Science and Technology,
Peking University, Beijing, China
{ylfang, dqyang, swtang, yhtong, zwh}@db.pku.edu.cn
{yulb, fuq}@cis.pku.edu.cn

**Abstract.** we describe the CyberETL system for visual designing and debugging transformations in data integration. CyberETL has some innovative features, such as visual designing of transformations, bi-direction translation between transformations and SQL queries, and lineage-based data comparison and debugging. This enables very robust and fast integration of data in ETL process without the bother and nail-biting of error-prone transformation designing.

## 1 Introduction and Motivation

Motivated by the requirements in data integration process[1][2] ,we have developed the CyberETL system for visual designing and debugging of transformations in data integration. The innovative features of CyberETL are highlighted as follows.

**Feature 1. CyberETL has a user-friendly visual interface to design data transformation.**

CyberETL has a user-friendly visual interface to design various transformations. CyberETL provide a number of transformation templates, each representing a special kind of SQL query. Users can visually set value of the property related with the template. For example, when a user want to define a select transformation, he cam set the condition value in the field of the "*select condition*" property. Users can define transformations as shared, and reuse them in the modeling process.

**Feature 2. CyberETL can translate SQL queries into data transformations and vice versa.**

CyberETL not only provide the ability of translating SQL queries into data transformations in order to let the experience expert directly write some SQL queries more conveniently , it also provide the ability of translating data transformations into SQL queries to let user know what the transformation mean in SQL.

Because there are many SQL queries serving as ETL scripts in legacy systems and there are also many SQL queries are very refined (such as TPC-H queries),

G. Dong et al. (Eds.): WAIM 2003, LNCS 2762, pp. 508–509, 2003.

with CyberETL it is rather more effective to reuse it directly than to translate them into shared transformations and then reuse them. And at the same time, it would be more straightway to provide a SQL view of the transformations so that it is more easily find out the problem and crux lying in the design.

**Feature 3. CyberETL supports fine-grained lineage tracing in data transformations.**

CyberETL supports two kinds of lineage tracing. One is to tracing the lineage of the data which really contribute to the data attributes, which is called as Where-provenance[1]. The other is to tracing the lineage of data which contribute to the data so it appears in the result, which is called as Why-provenance[1]. CyberETL illustrates both lineages in different colors in a hierarchical level.

With such an assistant, users can easily debugging transformations and effectively determine whether the transformations are appropriate. When we check whether the transformation is the right one that we need and whether it produce the correct result by lineage tracing, we would be more easily find the problem existing in the transformations.

**Feature 4. CyberETL provides data comparison mechanism in designing debugging.**

CyberETL provides data comparison mechanism in designing debugging. The data comparison function consist of three aspects. One is to compare the data set directly, that is, given two transformation tables, to find out the different part and the same one between them. CyberETL can also comparison the result of two transformation sequences. CyberETL also provides the ability of data lineage comparison through different transformation sequences. By such functions, CyberETL can implement designing version management and compare the difference among different version and realize undo actions.

## 2 Description of the Demo

We plan to demonstrate the latest version of CyberETL. The demonstration consists of five parts as follows.

Part 1. System Design of CyberETL and Performance Study
Part 2. Data Transformation Designing Visualization
Part 3. Data Transformation Reverse Engineering
Part 4. Data Lineage Tracing for Data Transformation
Part 5. Data Differentiation in Debugging Transformations

## References

1. Buneman, P., Khanna S., TAN, W.-C.: Why and Where: A Characterization of Data Provenance. In Proc. of 13th International Conference on Data Theory(ICDT'01)
2. McBrien, P., Poulovassilis, A.: Data Integration by Bi-Directional Schema Transformation Rules. In Proc. of 19th International Conference on Data Engineering (ICDE'03)

# Author Index


An, Aijun 506
Asai, Daisuke 181
Asano, Yasuhito 37

Bai, Qingyuan 471
Bailey, James 226
Bao, Yongguang 181
Bell, David 389
Bi, Yaxin 389
Bouras, Christos 25

Cai, Lianhong 409
Chang, Jae-Woo 433
Chen, Kefei 483
Chen, Qunxiu 409
Chen, Yuxi 458
Cheung, David W. 397
Cho, Byeongkyu 344
Cho, Miyoung 381
Choi, Junho 381

Deng, Ailin 421
Du, Chun 503
Du, Xiaoyong 181
Dunham, Margaret H. 47
Duong, Doan Dai 92

Fan, Hongjian 189
Fang, Youlin 508
Fu, Qiang 508
Fung, Gabriel Pui Cheong 148

Gao, Hong 104
Gao, Jun 214
Greer, Kieran 389
Guo, Xin 327

He, Hai 503
He, Huacan 247
He, Zhenying 104
Hong, Jun 471
Huang, Shang-teng 173
Huang, Xiao (Andy) 445
Hwang, Chong-Sun 352

Imai, Hiroshi 37
Ishii, Naohiro 181
Ito, Tsuyoshi 37

Jajodia, Sushil 1

Kim, Pankoo 381
Kitsuregawa, Masaru 37
Konidaris, Agisilaos 25
Kostoulas, Dionysios 25

Lamb, Joanne 389
Lau, Ho-Lam 128
Lee, Chung-Hong 495
Lee, Sungkeun 344
Lee, You-Ri 314
Li, Cunhua 202
Li, Deyi 247
Li, Jianzhong 104
Li, Jinyan 254
Li, Zhigang 47
Li, Zhishu 360
Lian, Wang 397
Liau, Chu Yee 2
Ling, Bo 278
Liu, Baoliang 161
Liu, Chengfei 55
Liu, Hong 173
Liu, Jixue 55
Liu, Li 421
Liu, Mengchi 80
Liu, Tao 335
Liu, Yi 335
Lu, Hongen 13
Lu, Hongjun 148
Lu, Zhiguo 278
Lv, Jianhua 116

Ma, Fan-Yuan 238
Ma, Liang 409
Ma, Shuai 214
Mamoulis, Nikos 397
Manoukian, Thomas 226
McTear, Michael F. 471
Meng, Weiyi 458, 503

Ng, Weesiong 278
Ng, Wilfred 128
Ng, Yiu-Kai 266

Ooi, Beng Chin 2, 306

Park, Dong-Gue 314

Qian, Depei 335
Qian, Weining 306

Raghavan, Vijay 503
Raikundalia, Gitesh K. 290
Ramamohanarao, Kotagiri 189, 226
Ren, Yi 306
Ryu, JeHyok 352

Shi, Baile 421
Shim, Choon-Bo 433
Shu, Yanfeng 278
Song, MoonBae 352
Song, Yuqing 202
Sun, Bing 116
Sun, Jiaguang 247
Sun, Ming-Tan 47
Sun, Zhihui 202

Tan, Kian-Lee 2, 278, 306
Tan, Shaohua 140
Tang, ShiWei 140, 214, 508
Tong, Yunhai 508
Toyoda, Masashi 37

Vincent, Millist W. 55

Wang, Bin 266
Wang, Guoren 80, 116, 266
Wang, Hongzhi 104
Wang, Jianmin 247
Wang, Min 369
Wang, Qing 68, 298
Wang, TengJiao 214
Wang, Weinong 483
Wang, Wenyong 327
Wang, X. Sean 369
Wong, Limsoon 254
Wu, Dajun 335
Wu, Hongwei 68
Wu, Zonghuan 503
Wuwongse, Vilas 92

Xiao, Yongqiao 47
Xue, Qiang 445

Yan, Jun 290
Yang, DongQing 140, 214, 508
Yang, Hsin-Chang 495
Yang, Jun 445
Yang, Kun 327
Yang, Xiaochun 266
Yang, Yan 161
Yang, Yun 290
Yao, Qingsong 506
Ye, Yun-Ming 238
Yu, Clement 503
Yu, Ge 116, 266
Yu, Jeffrey Xu 68, 148
Yu, Libo 508
Yu, Shui 238
Yuan, Daohua 360
Yuan, Yang 298

Zhang, Jing 247
Zhang, Liang 238, 421
Zhang, Qi 421
Zhang, Weihua 508
Zhang, Xingjun 335
Zhang, Zhaogong 161
Zhao, Wenbing 140
Zhao, Xianfeng 483
Zhong, Shaochun 327
Zhou, Aoying 68, 278, 298, 306
Zhou, Bo 116
Zhou, Dongdai 327
Zhou, Junmei 298
Zhou, Shuigeng 68, 306
Zhou, Xiangdong 421

# Lecture Notes in Computer Science

For information about Vols. 1–2665
please contact your bookseller or Springer-Verlag

Vol. 2666: C. Guerra, S. Istrail (Eds.), Mathematical Methods for Protein Structure Analysis and Design. Proceedings, 2000. XI, 157 pages. 2003. (Subseries LNBI).

Vol. 2667: V. Kumar, M.L. Gavrilova, C.J.K. Tan, P. L'Ecuyer (Eds.), Computational Science and Its Applications – ICCSA 2003. Proceedings, Part I. 2003. XXXIV, 1060 pages. 2003.

Vol. 2668: V. Kumar, M.L. Gavrilova, C.J.K. Tan, P. L'Ecuyer (Eds.), Computational Science and Its Applications – ICCSA 2003. Proceedings, Part II. 2003. XXXIV, 942 pages. 2003.

Vol. 2669: V. Kumar, M.L. Gavrilova, C.J.K. Tan, P. L'Ecuyer (Eds.), Computational Science and Its Applications – ICCSA 2003. Proceedings, Part III. 2003. XXXIV, 948 pages. 2003.

Vol. 2670: R. Peña, T. Arts (Eds.), Implementation of Functional Languages. Proceedings, 2002. X, 249 pages. 2003.

Vol. 2671: Y. Xiang, B. Chaib-draa (Eds.), Advances in Artificial Intelligence. Proceedings, 2003. XIV, 642 pages. 2003. (Subseries LNAI).

Vol. 2672: M. Endler, D. Schmidt (Eds.), Middleware 2003. Proceedings, 2003. XIII, 513 pages. 2003.

Vol. 2673: N. Ayache, H. Delingette (Eds.), Surgery Simulation and Soft Tissue Modeling. Proceedings, 2003. XII, 386 pages. 2003.

Vol. 2674: I.E. Magnin, J. Montagnat, P. Clarysse, J. Nenonen, T. Katila (Eds.), Functional Imaging and Modeling of the Heart. Proceedings, 2003. XI, 308 pages. 2003.

Vol. 2675: M. Marchesi, G. Succi (Eds.), Extreme Programming and Agile Processes in Software Engineering. Proceedings, 2003. XV, 464 pages. 2003.

Vol. 2676: R. Baeza-Yates, E. Chávez, M. Crochemore (Eds.), Combinatorial Pattern Matching. Proceedings, 2003. XI, 403 pages. 2003.

Vol. 2678: W. van der Aalst, A. ter Hofstede, M. Weske (Eds.), Business Process Management. Proceedings, 2003. XI, 391 pages. 2003.

Vol. 2679: W. van der Aalst, E. Best (Eds.), Applications and Theory of Petri Nets 2003. Proceedings, 2003. XI, 508 pages. 2003.

Vol. 2680: P. Blackburn, C. Ghidini, R.M. Turner, F. Giunchiglia (Eds.), Modeling and Using Context. Proceedings, 2003. XII, 525 pages. 2003. (Subseries LNAI).

Vol. 2681: J. Eder, M. Missikoff (Eds.), Advanced Information Systems Engineering. Proceedings, 2003. XV, 740 pages. 2003.

Vol. 2683: A. Rangarajan, M. Figueiredo, J. Zerubia (Eds.), Energy Minimization Methods in Computer Vision and Pattern Recognition. Proceedings, 2003. XI, 534 pages. 2003.

Vol. 2684: M.V. Butz, O. Sigaud, P. Gérard (Eds.), Anticipatory Behavior in Adaptive Learning Systems. X, 303 pages. 2003. (Subseries LNAI).

Vol. 2685: C. Freksa, W. Brauer, C. Habel, K.F. Wender (Eds.), Spatial Cognition III. X, 415 pages. 2003. (Subseries LNAI).

Vol. 2686: J. Mira, J.R. Álvarez (Eds.), Computational Methods in Neural Modeling. Proceedings, Part I. 2003. XXVII, 764 pages. 2003.

Vol. 2687: J. Mira, J.R. Álvarez (Eds.), Artificial Neural Nets Problem Solving Methods. Proceedings, Part II. 2003. XXVII, 820 pages. 2003.

Vol. 2688: J. Kittler, M.S. Nixon (Eds.), Audio- and Video-Based Biometric Person Authentication. Proceedings, 2003. XVII, 978 pages. 2003.

Vol. 2689: K.D. Ashley, D.G. Bridge (Eds.), Case-Based Reasoning Research and Development. Proceedings, 2003. XV, 734 pages. 2003. (Subseries LNAI).

Vol. 2690: J. Liu, Y. Cheung, H. Yin (Eds.), Intelligent Data Engineering and Automated Learning. Proceedings, 2003. XXI, 1141 pages. 2003.

Vol. 2691: V. Mařík, J. Müller, M. Pěchouček (Eds.), Multi-Agent Systems and Applications III. Proceedings, 2003. XIV, 660 pages. 2003. (Subseries LNAI).

Vol. 2692: P. Nixon, S. Terzis (Eds.), Trust Management. Proceedings, 2003. X, 349 pages. 2003.

Vol. 2693: A. Cechich, M. Piattini, A. Vallecillo (Eds.), Component-Based Software Quality. X, 403 pages. 2003.

Vol. 2694: R. Cousot (Ed.), Static Analysis. Proceedings, 2003. XIV, 505 pages. 2003.

Vol. 2695: L.D. Griffin, M. Lillholm (Eds.), Scale Space Methods in Computer Vision. Proceedings, 2003. XII, 816 pages. 2003.

Vol. 2696: J. Feigenbaum (Ed.), Digital Rights Management. Proceedings, 2002. X, 221 pages. 2003.

Vol. 2697: T. Warnow, B. Zhu (Eds.), Computing and Combinatorics. Proceedings, 2003. XIII, 560 pages. 2003.

Vol. 2698: W. Burakowski, B. Koch, A. Bęben (Eds.), Architectures for Quality of Service in the Internet. Proceedings, 2003. XI, 305 pages. 2003.

Vol. 2700: M.T. Pazienza (Ed.), Information Extraction in the Web Era. XIII, 163 pages. 2003. (Subseries LNAI).

Vol. 2701: M. Hofmann (Ed.), Typed Lambda Calculi and Applications. Proceedings, 2003. VIII, 317 pages. 2003.

Vol. 2702: P. Brusilovsky, A. Corbett, F. de Rosis (Eds.), User Modeling 2003. Proceedings, 2003. XIV, 436 pages. 2003. (Subseries LNAI).

Vol. 2704: S.-T. Huang, T. Herman (Eds.), Self-Stabilizing Systems. Proceedings, 2003. X, 215 pages. 2003.

Vol. 2706: R. Nieuwenhuis (Ed.), Rewriting Techniques and Applications. Proceedings, 2003. XI, 515 pages. 2003.

Vol. 2707: K. Jeffay, I. Stoica, K. Wehrle (Eds.), Quality of Service – IWQoS 2003. Proceedings, 2003. XI, 517 pages. 2003.

Vol. 2708: R. Reed, J. Reed (Eds.), SDL 2003: System Design. Proceedings, 2003. XI, 405 pages. 2003.

Vol. 2709: T. Windeatt, F. Roli (Eds.), Multiple Classifier Systems. Proceedings, 2003. X, 406 pages. 2003.

Vol. 2710: Z. Ésik, Z, Fülöp (Eds.), Developments in Language Theory. Proceedings, 2003. XI, 437 pages. 2003.

Vol. 2711: T.D. Nielsen, N.L. Zhang (Eds.), Symbolic and Quantitative Approaches to Reasoning with Uncertainty. Proceedings, 2003. XII, 608 pages. 2003. (Subseries LNAI).

Vol. 2712: A. James, B. Lings, M. Younas (Eds.), New Horizons in Information Management. Proceedings, 2003. XII, 281 pages. 2003.

Vol. 2713: C.-W. Chung, C.-K. Kim, W. Kim, T.-W. Ling, K.-H. Song (Eds.), Web and Communication Technologies and Internet-Related Social Issues – HSI 2003. Proceedings, 2003. XXII, 773 pages. 2003.

Vol. 2714: O. Kaynak, E. Alpaydin, E. Oja, L. Xu (Eds.), Artificial Neural Networks and Neural Information Processing – ICANN/ICONIP 2003. Proceedings, 2003. XXII, 1188 pages. 2003.

Vol. 2715: T. Bilgiç, B. De Baets, O. Kaynak (Eds.), Fuzzy Sets and Systems – IFSA 2003. Proceedings, 2003. XV, 735 pages. 2003. (Subseries LNAI).

Vol. 2716: M.J. Voss (Ed.), OpenMP Shared Memory Parallel Programming. Proceedings, 2003. VIII, 271 pages. 2003.

Vol. 2718: P. W. H. Chung, C. Hinde, M. Ali (Eds.), Developments in Applied Artificial Intelligence. Proceedings, 2003. XIV, 817 pages. 2003. (Subseries LNAI).

Vol. 2719: J.C.M. Baeten, J.K. Lenstra, J. Parrow, G.J. Woeginger (Eds.), Automata, Languages and Programming. Proceedings, 2003. XVIII, 1199 pages. 2003.

Vol. 2720: M. Marques Freire, P. Lorenz, M.M.-O. Lee (Eds.), High-Speed Networks and Multimedia Communications. Proceedings, 2003. XIII, 582 pages. 2003.

Vol. 2721: N.J. Mamede, J. Baptista, I. Trancoso, M. das Graças Volpe Nunes (Eds.), Computational Processing of the Portuguese Language. Proceedings, 2003. XIV, 268 pages. 2003. (Subseries LNAI).

Vol. 2722: J.M. Cueva Lovelle, B.M. González Rodríguez, L. Joyanes Aguilar, J.E. Labra Gayo, M. del Puerto Paule Ruiz (Eds.), Web Engineering. Proceedings, 2003. XIX, 554 pages. 2003.

Vol. 2723: E. Cantú-Paz, J.A. Foster, K. Deb, L.D. Davis, R. Roy, U.-M. O'Reilly, H.-G. Beyer, R. Standish, G. Kendall, S. Wilson, M. Harman, J. Wegener, D. Dasgupta, M.A. Potter, A.C. Schultz, K.A. Dowsland, N. Jonoska, J. Miller (Eds.), Genetic and Evolutionary Computation – GECCO 2003. Proceedings, Part I. 2003. XLVII, 1252 pages. 2003.

Vol. 2724: E. Cantú-Paz, J.A. Foster, K. Deb, L.D. Davis, R. Roy, U.-M. O'Reilly, H.-G. Beyer, R. Standish, G. Kendall, S. Wilson, M. Harman, J. Wegener, D. Dasgupta, M.A. Potter, A.C. Schultz, K.A. Dowsland, N. Jonoska, J. Miller (Eds.), Genetic and Evolutionary Computation – GECCO 2003. Proceedings, Part II. 2003. XLVII, 1274 pages. 2003.

Vol. 2725: W.A. Hunt, Jr., F. Somenzi (Eds.), Computer Aided Verification. Proceedings, 2003. XII, 462 pages. 2003.

Vol. 2726: E. Hancock, M. Vento (Eds.), Graph Based Representations in Pattern Recognition. Proceedings, 2003. VIII, 271 pages. 2003.

Vol. 2727: R. Safavi-Naini, J. Seberry (Eds.), Information Security and Privacy. Proceedings, 2003. XII, 534 pages. 2003.

Vol. 2728: E.M. Bakker, T.S. Huang, M.S. Lew, N. Sebe, X.S. Zhou (Eds.), Image and Video Retrieval. Proceedings, 2003. XIII, 512 pages. 2003.

Vol. 2729: D. Boneh (Ed.), Advances in Cryptology – CRYPTO 2003. Proceedings, 2003. XII, 631 pages. 2003.

Vol. 2731: C.S. Calude, M.J. Dinneen, V. Vajnovszki (Eds.), Discrete Mathematics and Theoretical Computer Science. Proceedings, 2003. VIII, 301 pages. 2003.

Vol. 2732: C. Taylor, J.A. Noble (Eds.), Information Processing in Medical Imaging. Proceedings, 2003. XVI, 698 pages. 2003.

Vol. 2733: A. Butz, A. Krüger, P. Olivier (Eds.), Smart Graphics. Proceedings, 2003. XI, 261 pages. 2003.

Vol. 2734: P. Perner, A. Rosenfeld (Eds.), Machine Learning and Data Mining in Pattern Recognition. Proceedings, 2003. XII, 440 pages. 2003. (Subseries LNAI).

Vol. 2741: F. Baader (Ed.), Automated Deduction – CADE-19. Proceedings, 2003. XII, 503 pages. 2003. (Subseries LNAI).

Vol. 2742: R. N. Wright (Ed.), Financial Cryptography. Proceedings, 2003. VIII, 321 pages. 2003.

Vol. 2743: L. Cardelli (Ed.), ECOOP 2003 – Object-Oriented Programming. Proceedings, 2003. X, 501 pages. 2003.

Vol. 2745: M. Guo, L.T. Yang (Eds.), Parallel and Distributed Processing and Applications. Proceedings, 2003. XII, 450 pages. 2003.

Vol. 2746: A. de Moor, W. Lex, B. Ganter (Eds.), Conceptual Structures for Knowledge Creation and Communication. Proceedings, 2003. XI, 405 pages. 2003. (Subseries LNAI).

Vol. 2748: F. Dehne, J.-R. Sack, M. Smid (Eds.), Algorithms and Data Structures. Proceedings, 2003. XII, 522 pages. 2003.

Vol. 2749: J. Bigun, T. Gustavsson (Eds.), Image Analysis. Proceedings, 2003. XXII, 1174 pages. 2003.

Vol. 2750: T. Hadzilacos, Y. Manolopoulos, J.F. Roddick, Y. Theodoridis (Eds.), Advances in Spatial and Temporal Databases. Proceedings, 2003. XIII, 525 pages. 2003.

Vol. 2751: A. Lingas, B.J. Nilsson (Eds.), Fundamentals of Computation Theory. Proceedings, 2003. XII, 433 pages. 2003.

Vol. 2752: G.A. Kaminka, P.U. Lima, R. Rojas (Eds.), RoboCup 2002: Robot Soccer World Cup VI. XVI, 498 pages. 2003. (Subseries LNAI).

Vol. 2753: F. Maurer, D. Wells (Eds.), Extreme Programming and Agile Methods – XP/Agile Universe 2003. Proceedings, 2003. XI, 215 pages. 2003.

Vol. 2758: D. Basin, B. Wolff (Eds.), Theorem Proving in Higher Order Logics. Proceedings, 2003. X, 367 pages. 2003.

Vol. 2759: O.H. Ibarra, Z. Dang (Eds.), Implementation and Application of Automata. Proceedings, 2003. XI, 312 pages. 2003.

Vol. 2762: G. Dong, C. Tang, W. Wang (Eds.), Advances in Web-Age Information Management. Proceedings, 2003. XIII, 512 pages. 2003.